Loving Music Till It Hurts

Loving Music Till It Hurts

WILLIAM CHENG

OXFORD

UNIVERSITY PRESS

OXFORD
UNIVERSITY PRESS

Oxford University Press is a department of the University of Oxford. It furthers
the University's objective of excellence in research, scholarship, and education
by publishing worldwide. Oxford is a registered trade mark of Oxford University
Press in the UK and certain other countries.

Published in the United States of America by Oxford University Press
198 Madison Avenue, New York, NY 10016, United States of America.

Library of Congress Cataloging-in-Publication Data
Names: Cheng, William, 1985– author.
Title: Loving music till it hurts / William Cheng.
Description: New York : Oxford University Press, [2019] |
Includes bibliographical references and index.
Identifiers: LCCN 2019021008 | ISBN 9780190620134 (hardback) |
ISBN 9780190620141 (updf) | ISBN 9780190620158 (epub) |
ISBN 9780190620165 (oso)
Subjects: LCSH: Music—Social aspects. | Music—Moral and ethical aspects.
Classification: LCC ML3916 .C49 2019 | DDC 781.1/1—dc23
LC record available at https://lccn.loc.gov/2019021008

1 3 5 7 9 8 6 4 2

Printed by Integrated Books International, United States of America

In memory of Ellen Wang—愛倫老師—my first piano teacher
(1970–2017)

Contents

Acknowledgments

Friends, family, and colleagues sustained the long labors of love poured into this project since its inception in 2013. Linda Shaver-Gleason, Marcus Pyle, Mark Katz, and two anonymous reviewers took time to provide vital feedback on the full manuscript. Editor Norm Hirschy at Oxford University Press offered keen guidance and advice. Book production and copy-editing benefited from the patience and expertise of Aishwarya Krishnamoorthy, Santhosh Kumar, and Leslie Safford. Among the friends who read and improved one or more chapters were Alexander Rehding, Andrea Moore, Andrew Dell'Antonio, Anna-Lise Santella, Brandi Neal, Braxton Shelley, Brianne Gallagher, Charles Hiroshi Garrett, Dale Chapman, Dana Gooley, Dana Gorzelany-Mostak, Diane Pecknold, Eric Smialek, Francesca Inglese, Frank Lehman, Fritz Trümpi, Ian Copeland, Jacqueline Warwick, Jessica Holmes, Katherine Meizel, Lily Hirsch, Loren Kajikawa, Melinda O'Neal, Michael Heller, Naomi André, Oliver Wang, Pamela Pilch, Paula Harper, Phil Ford, Richard Beaudoin, Sebastian Smallshaw, Ted Levin, Tom Wetmore, Wade Dean, Will Robin, William Osborne, and Yana Stainova. Other companions who variously enriched this book via conversations and morale boosts include Alisha Lola Jones, Amy Wlodarski, Anabel Maler, Anna Maria Busse Berger, Anne Shreffler, Annegret Fauser, Ashley Fure, Barbara Will, Berthold Hoeckner, Blake Howe, Byrd McDaniel, Carol Oja, Daniel Goldmark, Danielle Fosler-Lussier, Darrell Tong, Don Pease, Ellie Hisama, Eric Lubarsky, Erin Maher, Eva Kim, Felicia Miyakawa, Gabriel Solis, George Lewis, Gregory Barz, Gundula Kreuzer, Hannah Lewis, Heather Hadlock, Imani Mosley, Ingrid Monson, James Deaville, Jeannette DiBernardo Jones, Jennifer Iverson, Jen-yen Chen, Jeremy Denk, Joseph Auner, Joseph Straus, Karol Berger, Kay Kaufman Shelemay, Kiri Miller, Krystal Klingenberg, Kyounghwa Kim, Laurie Lee, Louis Epstein, Lucy McBath, Manish Mishra, Mary Francis, Mary Lou Aleskie, Michael Austin, Michael Beckerman, Michael Casey, Mitchell Morris, Nancy Shafman, Neil Lerner, Noah Feldman, Rachel Edens, Regina Bradley, Rena Roussin, Richard Leppert, Rob Walser, Roger Moseley, Rosemarie Garland-Thomson, Rowland Moseley, Ron Davis, Samantha Bassler, Sarah Coulter, Scott Burnham, Scott DeVeaux,

Stephan Pennington, Stephanie Jensen-Moulton, Stephen Hough, Steve Rings, Steve Swayne, Susan Brison, Susan McClary, Susan Thomas, Susana Kwon, Suzanne Cusick, Tom Grey, Tom Kelly, Trica Keaton, and William Bares. Any semblance of composure or organization in my research process owed largely to the staff of the Dartmouth Music Department and Music Library, notably Bevan Dunbar, Catherine LaTouche, Craig Pallett, David Bowden, Memory Apata, Patricia Fisken, and Samantha Candon, as well as Amrit Ahluwalia, Abigail Mihaly, Aditya Hans Prasad, Alexandria Chen, Amy Zhang, Anna Raley, Betty Kim, Chelsea Lim, Cheryl Chang, Christina Reagan, David Ramirez, Faith Rotich, Grant Cook, Hannah F. Hua, Hanting Guo, Isabel Hurley, Katie Wee, Laura Barthold, Lexington Foote, Marcus Gresham, Matthew Levine, Michael Ortiz, Sally Yi, Sophia Kinne, Sophie G. Huang, Tyné Freeman, and Zoe Yu. Without the loving support of Chris Schepici and my parents, this book wouldn't exist at all.

Excerpts of *Loving Music Till It Hurts* were presented at Bates College, Carleton University, Case Western Reserve University, Columbia University, CUNY Graduate Center, Dalhousie University, Dartmouth College, Florida State University, Hanyang University, Harvard University, Howard University, McGill University, National Taiwan University, Tufts University, UNC Asheville, UNC Chapel Hill, Universität für Musik und darstellende Kunst Wien, University of British Columbia, University of Chicago, University of Georgia, University of Illinois at Urbana-Champaign, University of Michigan, University of Tennessee, UT Austin, and Yale University.Earlier versions of chapters have appeared in journals: Chapter 4 as "Staging Overcoming: Narratives of Disability and Meritocracy in Reality Singing Competitions," *Journal of the Society for American Music* (2017): 184–214; Chapter 5 as "So You've Been Musically Shamed," *Journal of Popular Music Studies* 30 (2018): 1–30; and Chapter 6 as "Black Noise, White Ears: Resilience, Rap, and the Killing of Jordan Davis," *Current Musicology* 102 (2018): 115–89.

Prelude

Loving Music and Loving People

Love is not based on great works as unperformed abstractions.

—Carolyn Abbate[1]

Love is the core of it all. The rest is just sounding brass and tinkling cymbal.

—Cornel West[2]

People love music for how it sounds and how it feels. At least this is the way many of us, through our early years, fall *in* love with music: the ears magnetized by a croon on the radio, the broken heart soothed by a ballad on infinite loop, the limbs ensorcelled by the perfect groove, the deaf body attuned to the creative powers of vibrational experience. We come to love music for its palpable events, less so for its status as an unsounded object. True, people can declare a love of music without overt mention of performances, and instead with shorthand references to specific musicians, works, or genres. *I love Prince. I love* Cats. *I love K-pop.* With any of these loves, nonetheless, a sensory encounter is likely what once kindled the flame.

For me, it's the voice of Eva Cassidy. In high school, I came across her exquisite cover of "Autumn Leaves," which led me to discover her solo album *Live at Blues Alley*, which led me to an Internet search revealing she had died of cancer in 1996 at age thirty-three, just months after *Blues Alley*'s release. Ever since, I've never gone more than a few months without finding my way back to Cassidy, if only nowadays to stream a song or two, and falling in love all over again. You probably have musical treasures you call your own, along with vivid stories of how you chanced upon them.

So you probably also know how it feels to love music so much, it hurts. Hurts because music can be excruciatingly beautiful, quickening the breath and teasing out tears. Hurts because a musician you love is no longer alive to hear you declare how much they've meant to you. Hurts because a part of you wants a sublime harmony or high note to last forever, yet you realize the moment means something precisely because it is, as with the searing paradox of mortal existence, gone too soon. In the grandest scheme, maybe loving music can hurt because you're all but overwhelmed with gratitude for the sheer fact of music's existence in a universe that didn't owe us music, or really owe us anything at all.

We love music so much that we might talk about it as an animate, sentient being. Music theorist Joseph Straus explains how some scholars analyze a composition as if it were "a human body, a living creature with form and motion, and often with blood, organs, limbs, and skin as well."[3] We anthropomorphize music the way we anthropomorphize—well, just about everything. But does a musical work have dignity? Can it sense pain? Does it have rights? Of course not, one might reason. Yet think of the colloquialisms we use for music, especially when we believe music has been violated. An underrehearsed cover band made a *mockery* (dignity) of Led Zeppelin's classics. A singer *butchered* or *mangled* (pain) the "Star-Spangled Banner." An orchestra didn't quite *do justice* (rights) to the grandiosity of Mozart's Requiem. As art historian W. J. T. Mitchell points out, similar language and feelings pop up when people witness the "violation" and "mutilation" of visual art and physical objects—a painting slashed by a knife, a teddy bear with a torn arm, a sofa abandoned on the curb, a violin broken in two.[4]

As music vibrates our bodies sympathetically, it can move us to react empathetically. When we perceive our beloved music hurting, we hurt a little, too. It sounds illogical. We know music isn't truly an organism, so we should rest easy knowing it's free of pain receptors. In another sense, the fantasy is not strange at all. As a companion, music can do so much for us, mean so much to us, and even grant us a profound sense of self and humanity. We feel called to love and protect music, as parents would defend their young, or as lovers would guard each other.

Is it possible for our love and protection of music to go too far? Can such devotion ever do more harm than good? Can our intense allegiances to music distract, release, or hinder us from attending to matters of social justice?

Consider a 2012 *Washington Post* article by music critic Anne Midgette, who recalled an unpleasant experience at the Port Authority Bus Terminal in New York. She described hearing a recording of a Franz Schubert piano trio piped through overhead loudspeakers. "I've long heard that the Port

Authority is one of many public spaces across the country that uses classical music to help control vagrancy," Midgette noted. Upon hearing this music firsthand, she started to believe its efficacy. "Schubert's piano trios are among my favorite pieces in the universe," she declared, "but as I listened, I found that I wasn't relaxing; quite the contrary. The music sounded awful: tinny, hard-edged, aggressive. I wanted to get away."[5] Although Midgette prudently acknowledged that playing classical music "to 'civilize' a space" is a form of "supreme elitism," her article focused on the insults *to* this music. In short, she took issue with the reduction of Schubert to the status of sonic wallpaper, saying "what we're actually talking about is Muzak," while lamenting how the subpar speakers and acoustics could not do right by the repertoire she profoundly loved. "In that windowless, ugly space, with pigeons strutting across the grimy floor, announcements blaring unintelligibly over the loudspeaker and the sound system giving the music a harsh edge, as if impaling it on a jagged chunk of metal, my sympathies were all with the homeless people that such music is widely thought of as attempting to repel," Midgette concluded. "If I'd had a choice, it would have driven me away, too."[6] (Implied here is that Midgette couldn't choose to leave. With an eventual bus to catch, yet having arrived somewhat early at Port Authority "with enough time" so that she "actually noticed the music," she found herself ostensibly stuck.)

Midgette might be correct that some of the homeless people at Port Authority were irked by grating renditions of Schubert. Or maybe these concerns are only a fraction of daily crises involving the bare necessities of food, warmth, and shelter. Despite Midgette's sympathies, this *Washington Post* article dwelled far more on the metaphorical wounds inflicted on an "impaled" Schubert than on the material injuries and structural injustices perpetrated against homeless individuals. Not that compassion is a zero-sum game. One can feel pain on behalf of music while trying to feel and assuage the pain of people. But here's a useful hypothetical. If Anne Midgette had heard a high-fidelity, captivating rendition of Schubert at the Port Authority that day—say, an undistorted recording of his piano trios by the legendary Beaux Arts Trio—would she have thought to document her outrage about the recording's gentrifying utility? Would she have ended up writing an op-ed denouncing, as she astutely states, the "supreme elitism" of this anti-vagrancy practice? Or would she have been content to bask in the beauty of what she calls her "favorite pieces in the universe," even praising the good taste of Port Authority's administrators?[7]

It's only fair to ask the same questions of ourselves. Had I found myself in a similar situation—enjoying some recordings of Chopin or Eva Cassidy through a transit hub's crystal-clear loudspeakers, despite harboring vague suspicions of this music's anti-loitering functions—would I have thought to object? I'm not sure. I would like to think so. Yet chances are just as good that I would have ended up lulled into auditory bliss by music I thoroughly love.

Audible performances aren't the only manifestations of music that activate our protective instincts. Although the origins of our love for music may depend on, as musicologist Carolyn Abbate points out, how its performed "realities" profoundly speak to us, we can be ferociously defensive of the *idea* of music as well—namely, our differing ideas about what qualifies as good music, where this music should be played, under which circumstances, with what technologies, how and how loudly, and by and for whom.[8] Instincts to protect music (and one's own ideal of music) can crop up in the insistence that not a single sacred note of Beethoven's sonatas must ever be changed, or that someone who posthumously seeks to finish a composer's unfinished symphony is as presumptuous as "an archaeologist adding a missing arm of his own making to a recovered Venus."[9] Preservationist instincts toward music can come out more coarsely, as when a chorus of *shhhh!* descends on a fellow concertgoer whose vibrating cell phone has sorely punctured a pair of lovers' onstage duet. More grievously, a protectiveness of your favorite music could motivate you to defend and continue to patronize the music of a superstar who has been multiply accused of sex crimes. In all of these cases, it's not just about protecting music itself, but also about safeguarding one's entitlements to musical pleasures.

At times, it's as if people care more about music—and in particular about their own beloved music and musical ideals—than about fellow human beings. This attitude isn't unthinkable when we realize how love in general, and the fierce loyalty it engenders, can make us do things far out of the ordinary, often beyond the typical sweeps of our moral compasses. Chaotic minds, irrational actions, questionable ethics: these are ingredients of love stories writ large. Why would people's lifelong love affairs with music prove any less complicated?

Impassioned and vigilant, one can love music to the point of hurting or neglecting other people, whether directly or indirectly, consciously or not. Conversely, one's own enjoyment of music can come under fire. You might be "singing and dancing around the apartment" to the rhymes of Notorious B.I.G., or relaxing to a "bikram yoga CD" in your parked car, and someone might call the cops on you. It's what happened respectively in mid-2018 to Mary Branch and Ezekiel Phillips—both black, both playing music they loved.[10] Such cases bring up questions about why some people's displays of music loving face higher evidentiary thresholds of legitimacy and respectability. Here, with feasible elements of race and prejudice in play, one takeaway is how disputes involving music are rarely just about the music itself, even or especially when arguments flare over whether there's such a thing as "the music itself."[11] If, while listening to music you love, you find yourself shamed, chided, or reported to the authorities, then music is likely only one factor in a much larger, messier equation.

Loving Music Till It Hurts explores how we can love music to the point of hurting one another. It is a book about how such interpersonal hurt emanates in part from our fantasy that music itself can be hurt and therefore must be protected. Ultimately, this book is about how human relationships with music—relationships often founded on an aching love, yes, but also potentially rooted in ambivalence, pragmatism, dysfunction, or covetous intensity—resonate with the just and unjust relationships among people. Driving this book is a single question:

> How do we love music, even embrace it as vital to human thriving, without intentionally or unintentionally weaponizing this love—that is, without allowing such love to serve oppressive, discriminatory, and violent purposes?

Your instinct might be to read this question as a rhetorical one. Its aims are not achievable, you could say. And you'd likely be right, for humans have always found ways to make weapons out of tools, and music is a tool because it can do things. More than lovable, music is useful. It can appease or annoy, heal or harm, bring people together or break communities apart.

At the heart of this book, however, is a naive refusal to hear the preceding question as merely rhetorical. Taking an optimistic page from feminist and queer scholars such as Sara Ahmed, José Esteban Muñoz, and Michael Snediker, I want to think that a better world is possible—or recursively, at the very least, to think that a better world is thinkable.[12] Here, then, is my answer to the question.

> Love music and love people. If ever in doubt—or if forced to choose—choose people.

Orbiting this answer is a burning constellation of interrogative asterisks. Why prioritize people? Is it simply because people are mortal beings who feel pain—and sometimes need alleviation from suffering—whereas music does not? Why would we ever need to choose between music and people anyway? Can't we have it all? And must we love all people? What about the people who hurt us? Crucial considerations all around. More than insisting that we always blithely choose a love of people over a love of music, my answer is an invitation to contemplate the potential falsity of the choice itself. In other words, it's an opportunity to ask why there's ever doubt in the first place, and indeed who or what is even capable of making us choose or making us believe a choice does or doesn't exist. Plenty of internal and external forces—stubborn personal habits and loyalties, or powerful institutions and creeds—can seemingly present us with a choice between loving music and loving people. In this book, we will encounter examples of human beings who do appear to pick sides. Some choose music, opting to lovingly protect it even to the detriment of other people. Some choose people, letting musical concerns take a back seat. Some implicitly challenge the choice, resisting the either/or. And some, all the while, show amazing ways of channeling musical love to empower interpersonal love, and vice versa.

Humans have committed plenty of dubious or outright abominable deeds in the name of love. Going to war for the love of country. Persecution and genocide for the love of god. Crimes of passion for the love of your life. Concerning the deleterious consequences of love-borne actions, then, music isn't exceptional.

Or is it? Consider discourses of musical exceptionalism—writers' characterizations of music in exceptional, even mystical, terms. Music is indescribable and ineffable, invisible and ephemeral, transcendent and sublime. Our love of music, along with our awe at its power, can move us to talk about it in these high-minded terms. Equally revealing is that such love often remains implied rather than spoken aloud. Although numerous writers persuasively address the dangers and abuses of music, notably fewer do so through a critical lens of love. Many don't use the L-word at all, maybe because it comes across too sentimental, embarrassing, or obvious. Yet given that our love of music is part of what makes music worth fighting for and fighting over, it is curious how frequently love gets the silent treatment, not least in academia.

Six chapters in *Loving Music Till It Hurts* try to coax love out of the shadows, progressively shining light on the real and imagined tensions between loving music and loving people. I anchor my case studies primarily in the contemporary United States. By contemporary, I really mean since 2007, from the bursts of post-racial fantasies surrounding the election of Barack Obama to the pendular swing that handed nuclear codes to Donald Trump. I settled on this modest scope for a few reasons. First, because it makes enough room for close cultural readings—unpacking US-specific conceptions of music, race, sex, disability, meritocracy—without attempting giant leaps toward transcultural claims. Second, because this scope shows that the controversies explored here are ongoing, urgent, and (for readers living in the United States) close to home. And third, because musical exceptionalism shares prominent similarities with American exceptionalism, notably, what historian Donald Pease calls "the new American exceptionalism": a post-Cold War ethos that has doubled down on the nation's status as a "moral exception," the proverbial shining City upon a Hill.[13] Exceptionalism, whether national or musical, is inherently an ideology of power. For this reason, it can be dangerous, and calls for scrutiny.

My opening two chapters delve into people's enduring beliefs in music as a humanizing force: the first chapter moves fast, cycling through diverse examples to flesh out preliminary ideas; the subsequent chapter slows things down, mapping out a single story from multiple perspectives.

Chapter 1 demonstrates how people's love of music can enable myths of music as an instrument of edification and civilization. Some traditions, such as those of classical music, are alleged to ennoble, while other repertoire is conversely said to reveal its patrons' incivility. Although it sounds obvious that loving masterpieces doesn't make someone a good person (think of the Beethoven-loving Nazis), I emphasize here that this presumption of obviousness can itself pose problems. How immune are we really to the seductive myths of music-as-morality? Even if we claim immunity out loud, how might our verbal quandaries and silences about music loving nevertheless speak to our deep-seated vulnerabilities?

Chapter 2 examines a famous experiment conducted in the name of musical love and loss: the 2007 undercover busking effort by famed violinist Joshua Bell, recounted in a Pulitzer-winning *Washington Post* article by journalist Gene Weingarten. Playing Bach and other classical repertoire, the disguised Bell attracted few eager listeners. Many readers declared their love of this story, lamenting its proof of how easily beauty gets drowned out in our busy lives. Other responses to Weingarten fell into traps of intellectual elitism, rushing to proclaim that "obviously" this article was hokum and that no reader would be gullible enough to buy what Weingarten was selling. Three themes emerge from my critiques of musical and academic exceptionalism: one, how we mismeasure beauty and its scarcity; two, how we productively or harmfully imbue musicianship with humanizing values; and three, why lovable dreams of musical universalism (*we are all musical, music is everywhere*) may elude or even impede agendas of social justice.

Following these introductory critiques of music as a humanizing force, the book's middle pair of chapters turns to the power of music as a *de*-humanizing force—that is, the way people's love of "the music itself" encourages auditory and adjudicatory practices that minimize, hide, or wholly reject the relevance of performers' identities or needs.

Chapter 3 drops in on "blind" auditions, commonly upheld as a gold standard in appraisals of musical excellence. Using screens and anonymizing apparatus, judges evaluate auditionees on sound alone, thereby doing right by the music they love. But a hidden cost of such auditions, whether for the Boston Symphony Orchestra or the reality show *The Voice*, is the wholesale severing of musicianship from human identity at large. With auditionees out of sight, the conceits of meritocracy enable all parties to avoid talking about issues of discrimination altogether—that is, why anonymity is desirable or necessary to begin with. A short case study ventures outside the United States to consider the illustrious, nearly all-white and all-male Vienna Philharmonic Orchestra. Tellingly, recent criticisms of this orchestra have come overwhelmingly *from* the United States, with music lovers exporting American brands of liberal feminism and social justice to protest the ensemble's hiring practices.

Chapter 4 continues to chase down myths of meritocracy and the musical mystique across the stages of reality television competitions, which often feature disabled auditionees and their moving tales of overcoming adversity. Musical abilities in general and singing talents in particular are shown to normalize and humanize disabled contestants while once again silencing vital conversations about the exploitation, stigmatization, and corporate politics at work. One wrinkle I stress here is that critiques of "inspiration porn" are neither easy nor obvious: chronicles of overcoming can emotionally overcome consumers; heartwarming tales about disability can seemingly disable a beholder's emotional, intellectual, and rhetorical faculties. As we either re-sist or succumb to the tearfulness induced by lovable stories and gorgeous songs, we must chart tricky routes through the heady skepticism of Scylla and the naive waterworks of Charybdis.

My two closing chapters show how musicians and music lovers stand to face dehumanization in a crueler sense: subjection to public shaming, ha-rassment, and even physical violence—all because their production or con-sumption of music has violated others' expectations of what (good) music is or how it should sound.

Chapter 5 focuses on the modern epidemic of public shaming. In 2014, someone leaked the raw, out-of-tune vocals of pop star Britney Spears attempting a studio take of her song "Alien." Shame storms promptly followed. By connecting voice shaming to concomitant practices of sex shaming and slut shaming, I ask what we think we gain when we judge, po-lice, and dehumanize musicians at their worst moments. Do people shame musicians out of a putative love for music? Or is music simply an excuse, an accomplice? Given the deluge of leakable data today, some provocative analogies materialize between our myths of secure networks (a technical impossibility) and our idealizations of pitch-perfect (infallible, unassail-able) lyric voices. I invite readers to relisten to Spears's naked voice not as shameworthy detritus best left on the cutting room floor, but rather as an object of clickbait that always already implicates our own aural vulnerability and consumer complicity.

Chapter 6 closes the book with an extended investigation into how mu-sical judgments can kill—how someone can be killed while listening to music they love, and for refusing to turn it down when asked. In 2012, a forty-seven-year-old white man named Michael Dunn heard loud rap music coming from a nearby red car containing four black youths. Loud words were exchanged. Minutes later, Dunn fired ten bullets at the car and killed one of its passengers, seventeen-year-old high school student Jordan Davis. Dunn claimed Davis had threatened him with a shotgun. No such gun was ever found. Concerning the murder trial that followed, I show how Dunn's lawyer, Cory Strolla, leveraged racist stereotypes of rap to paint dehumanizing (un-civilized, savage, criminal) *and* superhumanizing (formidable, fearsome, brawny) portraits of these youths. As for Dunn, the defendant? Strolla depicted him as someone who himself loved music, including "any type of hip-hop," the stuff "that the kids listen to."[14] I supplement my research into this trial with materials that were either purposely excluded from or inadvertently overlooked by media coverage: Michael Dunn's jailhouse letters and phone calls, transcriptions of courtroom sidebars, pretrial documents, evidence technicians' reports, and 911 records. I end with brief recollections of my conversations with Jordan's parents, Ron Davis and Lucy McBath.

1

Misjudgments of Humanity

We write symphonies. We pursue innovation. [. . .] And above all, we value the dignity of every human life, protect the rights of every person, and share the hope of every soul to live in freedom.

—President Donald J. Trump, 2017 speech in Warsaw[1]

What can music tell us about people? Specifically, what can the music someone loves (or otherwise feels strongly about) reveal about that person's character and values? Plenty, insists the romantic. Pretty much nothing, scoffs the skeptic. Probably something but who really knows? shrugs the agnostic.

In a 2007 *New Republic* article, "The Musical Mystique," Richard Taruskin reviewed three books. Each book, in its own way, voiced a passionate defense of classical music and its role in the twenty-first century.[2] As Taruskin read these volumes, he recalled how

> the question that throbbed and pounded in my head was whether it was still possible to defend my beloved repertoire without recourse to pious tommyrot, double standards, false dichotomies, smug nostalgia, utopian delusions, social snobbery, tautology, hypocrisy, trivialization, pretense, innuendo, reactionary invective, or imperial haberdashery. On the evidence before me, the answer is no.

Following this litany, Taruskin described how some defenders of classical music evince a dangerous elitism that, in turn, perpetuates myths of this music as a civilizing and humanizing force. Western art music has long served ambitions to colonize land, educate "noble savages," edify children, and, increasingly today, rehabilitate prisoners.[3] Any genre of music, though, can generate mystique, so long as this music is perceived to have human and moral value. All told, the musical mystique is a kind of aesthetic moralism, a leap of faith (or dogma, per the -ism) bridging artistic taste with moral humanity.[4]

In practical terms, then, what are the consequences of overestimating music's ability to tell us things—that is, of judging people by their beloved music, and of mysticizing music as a second sight into human minds, bodies, and souls? We should know, logically speaking, that no music can sound out the full measure of a person. We're also taught that jumping to conclusions in general can be impolite, unethical, and perilous. But conventional wisdom isn't always enough to stop us from rushing to judgment. And to be clear, the validity of prejudging people, whether on the basis of music or other limited information, isn't dependent on whether the appraisal turns out to be right or wrong. Warnings of *don't judge a book by its cover* aren't appended with . . . *unless you happen to judge correctly.* Landing one lucky guess doesn't foreclose the broader hazards of continuous guesswork and stereotypes.

With a parade of vignettes, this chapter shows how our love of music can compel us to buy into its mystique, enticing us to attribute musical performances and ideas alike with preternatural powers of revelation. I underscore the immediately hurtful as well as systemically harmful ramifications of judging and misjudging people by their musical tastes, affinities, and abilities. I also ask why we are susceptible to mystiques if, as the word itself implies, we should rationally know better. The staying power of the musical mystique, I argue, is indebted to a trio of partners in crime. First in this trio is what I call the *musicological* mystique—the idea that knowledge about the musical mystique necessarily makes one immune to its overwhelming seductions. Second is the limitation of language when it comes to defining some of the big ideas around the musical mystique: *love, human,* and *music,* all of which invite poetic yet evasive tautology, as in our soaring declarations that *love is love,* or *people are people.* Last in this trio is the loud silence around love altogether in critical dialogues about music, insofar as ideas of intimacy, pleasure, and erotics have long been treated as irrelevant or even (in music theorist Marion Guck's terms) "embarrassing."

The Musical Mystique: Humanization, Dehumanization, Superhumanization

On the surface, there's nothing wrong with believing your beloved music and your moral center are somehow connected. You're entitled to derive a sense of self, self-love, and existential awareness from your musical craft or personal playlist. So far, so good. But the problem is we rarely stop with self-appraisal; we tend to judge other people, too.[5] What happens when someone else sees or hears your musicality as a precondition—a prerequisite—for your humanity? "Black music serves as durable cultural and social evidence that blacks have survived America," wrote the black jazz musician and activist William H. McClendon in 1976.[6] "[But] Blacks did not and never have needed to find themselves and learn of their humanity in order to produce music."[7] Alas, the same cannot be said, McClendon remarks, for the many white people who have become alerted to the fact of black humanity primarily through delightful encounters with jazz, blues, spirituals, and gospel music. A beautiful performance by a black musician can jolt a previously racist or indifferent listener into epiphanic acceptance of this musician's humanity. Yet surely the listener's change of heart must not derail the question of why any epiphany was ever required, much less the question of how, going forward, one should make amends for prior racist actions.[8]

Even if lovable music has the power to humanize, we cannot lose track of why the burdens of proof for humanity weigh more heavily on some individuals than on others to begin with.

To grasp the word *humanize*, we can bring in two of its lexical companions—*dehumanize* and *superhumanize*. I situate these terms in part within the vantages of moral philosophy and critical race theory. Alexander Weheliye, for example, has offered the phrase "pernicious logics of racialization" to describe a culture's "sociopolitical relations that discipline humanity into full humans, not-quite-humans, and nonhumans"—people treated humanely, people treated poorly, and people, such as slaves or detainees, treated with utmost cruelty.[9] An addition to Weheliye's catalog is the superhuman, an insidious construct for a pair of diametric reasons: one, because someone lionized as a superhuman lives above the law; two, because the superhuman, in some cases, is actually a dehumanizing label wrapped up in a bow (the preternaturally musical "Magic Negro," the "supercrip" who "overcomes" disability by dint of specialized proficiencies, and similar patronizing tropes that fetishize freakery and circle back to the not-quite-human).[10]

People have found countless ways to humanize, dehumanize, and superhumanize themselves and others through music. Humanize: by attaching a sense of self or self-worth to the music one loves, performs, or promotes. Dehumanize: by degrading, mistreating, or harming someone else for their perceived lapses in musical taste, ability, or decorum. Superhumanize (nearly always pernicious, despite the lofty prefix): by deifying, say, a brilliant conductor, thereby allowing such idol worship to mitigate or cover up his history of grave misconduct.

Let's begin with music's humanizing potential. Recall one of the most popular YouTube clips ever, singer Susan Boyle's 2009 audition for the reality competition show *Britain's Got Talent*. Judges and audience members initially sneered and rolled their eyes at this middle-aged woman who prefaced her performance by stating a desire to be as successful as the musical theater star Elaine Paige.[11] As Boyle began singing "I Dreamed a Dream" from *Les Misérables*, however, the room's condescending milieu melted into warm smiles and dropped jaws. The rest became viral-video history, with the web feasting on a real-life "ugly duckling" tale.[12] As observed by ethnomusicologist Katherine Meizel, motifs of the "noble savage" peppered the media's exaltation of Boyle's "natural voice" and romanticization of this amateur singer's "village background, her self-described virginity, and the mild brain damage she suffered at birth."[13] Or as a *Sun* writer characterized: "Untouched by human hand, this girl. Literally. Kicking 50, never had a boyfriend. Eyebrows you could knit into a jumper, dress sense nicked from the drag queens on the paper towel adverts. But the voice? Borrowed from heaven itself."[14] Despite judges and fans eventually showering Boyle with praise, the shock value of the narrative arc can make us wonder how people would have treated this woman had she *not* sung beautifully and elevated herself as someone deserving of human decency. Not that there was anything inherently wrong with celebrating Boyle; reality shows are, by their nature, premised on the sensationalism of unlikely triumphs. What's problematic is that people were able to prejudge Boyle terribly—for her appearance, class (perhaps discernible by her accent and dialect during her pre-audition remarks), and comportment—and then, after the big musical reveal, to anoint themselves as founding members of the Susan Boyle fan club. Amid the thunderous applause and consequent lovefest, all is forgiven, and earlier prejudice forgotten.

Again: someone's display of musicality *can* awaken others to this person's humanity. It just shouldn't be *necessary*.

With the musical mystique at work, a beautiful singing voice ended up validating Boyle in the eyes of her prior skeptics. Most listeners didn't know anything about Boyle before her audition, and this is why they prejudged her. Yet the humanizing powers of the musical mystique can just as easily creep into cases of people about whom a great deal is already known. Consider, in the arena of high-stakes politics, the Russian president Vladimir Putin, whose well-documented actions have been variously called authoritarian, cruel, and inhumane. In May 2017, Putin attended a "One Belt, One Road" summit hosted in Beijing. As he waited at the state guesthouse for the arrival of Chinese president Xi Jinping, Putin sat down at a grand piano and played excerpts of two Soviet pieces from the 1950s: Vasily Solovyov-Sedoi's "Evening Song" and Tikhon Khrennikov's "Moscow Windows." Putin played hesitantly, falteringly. By his own admission, he is an amateur, "someone who plays with two fingers."[15] Cameras were present to capture the minute-long performance. In a *New York Times* report, journalist Ivan Nechepurenko perceived in this impromptu pianism "a softer side of Mr. Putin, an authoritarian leader who has been in power since 1999 and has often appeared eager to be seen as manly."[16] (Nechepurenko's assumption is that piano playing doesn't qualify as "manly," because manliness is portrayed by the Internet's copious photos of Putin's judo training, weight lifting, hunting, and bare-chested horseback riding.)[17] A *Boston Globe* article similarly described how Putin, "known for his passion for the outdoors, showed off his softer side during a visit to China when he sat down to play the piano Sunday."[18] And a *Financial Express* piece bore the title, "Russian President Vladimir Putin Shows His Soft Skills, Plays Piano."[19] Several of these articles took care to note that the two pieces performed by Putin were "tunes from his childhood," as if this remembrance of songs of yesteryear were a lifeline to an innocent and vulnerable child nesting within the brawny adult body of a nefarious world leader.[20] Remarks about Putin's amateurism and how he "plays piano like a 3rd grader" compounded this fantasy of illusory infantility.[21] Some readers agreed with the sentimental gloss of Putin's musicality, whereas others rebuffed the reports as false narratives that were "normalizing" and "humanizing" the president by sole virtue of pianistic aptitude.[22] Comparisons to Adolf Hitler popped up on cue. Hitler loved music, loved theater, and loved to paint.[23]

Intentionally or not, we sometimes mysticize music as a humanizing force. What about music's dehumanizing force? In his book *Less Than Human*, philosopher David Livingstone Smith posits that dehumanization is not a kink in human relationships. It's a feature. Proof, argues Smith, is everywhere, from the way people climb corporate ladders by stepping on others, to the *homo sapiens* survivalist instincts of tribalism and natural selection, to human vocabularies in general (calling one another bitches, dogs, cockroaches, leeches, rats, snakes, pigs, and vermin).[24] If someone intends to dehumanize you, they clearly have plenty of tactical options. Musical judgments are one such option.

Staying in the twin realms of reality television and politics, let's rewind to January 2017 and Donald Trump's inauguration, which lacked the kinds of big-name performers who fêted predecessor Barack Obama during the 2009 and 2013 ceremonies. President Obama had welcomed the likes of Aretha Franklin, Herbie Hancock, Stevie Wonder, Beyoncé Knowles, and Bruce Springsteen. For President Trump's festivities, by contrast, even a Bruce Springsteen cover band backed out at the last minute.[25] Dozens of left-leaning news outlets pounced on the inauguration's sparse lineup as proof of the commander-in-chief's wholesale repulsiveness. Reports of performers' mass demurral held up these musicians, and by extension their music, as ethical barometers. But anti-Trumpers didn't just lean on music and musicians, or the lack thereof, for confirmation bias. Some people brashly derided and dehumanized the musicians who did end up agreeing to perform in Trump's honor.

One of these musicians was an especially easy target, the sixteen-year-old "classical-crossover" singer Jackie Evancho, who had risen to fame as the runner-up in the 2010 season of *America's Got Talent*. Upon accepting an invitation to sing the national anthem at the swearing-in ceremony, Evancho began to face extensive cyberbullying and accusations of being a "sellout, has-been, puppet, and pawn."[26] (Accusations of selling out were hypocritical given that commercial interests were probably no less instrumental for the musicians who declined to perform.) Evancho's defenders quickly fired back. In particular, people who admired both Evancho and Trump were able to argue that Trump is obviously a good person and a great leader *because* the talented Evancho agreed to sing for him. As musicologist Dana Gorzelany-Mostak has thoroughly documented, plenty of Evancho's fans already regarded this white Christian starlet as more than simply talented; men in particular have idolized her as a rare, angelic, saintly gift to music and to society at large. "Evancho's male fans [. . .] laud their idol's moral uprightness and the transformative potential her character and music confer upon them," observed Gorzelany-Mostak on the basis of her interviews with the singer's admirers. "Put simply, many male fans believe their love for Jackie Evancho makes them better men."[27] As for Jackie Evancho's own reasons for agreeing to perform at Trump's inauguration? In an interview on *Good Morning Britain*, the singer explained: "My reason for doing this has nothing to do with politics. It's all about the honor of performing for my country."[28] Minutes later, when asked if she had any parting remarks, Evancho repeated, almost word for word: "My decision has nothing to do with politics. It's all based off of the honor that I feel to perform for my country that I love."[29]

Numerous critics have called Donald Trump's policies inhumane. Whether or not you believe this to be true, musical mystiques come into play when we start believing that music—including Trump's ability to court performers, which ones, for what reasons—is germane to the accuracy of this criticism.

Besides our humanizing and dehumanizing judgments involving music, moral slippages prove no less precarious in cases of judgments that superhumanize. In late 2017, old scandals were beginning to rock the classical music world anew. One scandal involved James Levine, the famed conductor and then-director of the Metropolitan Opera. Several men had come forward to accuse Levine of sexual assault, citing his coercive relationships with them long ago. By December, the Met suspended Levine.[30] Within weeks, in January 2018, London's Royal Philharmonic Orchestra also cut ties with Swiss conductor Charles Dutoit after four women accused him of sexual assault, including rape.[31]

Damningly, allegations of Levine's and Dutoit's indiscretions had long been open secrets in classical music circles. In Levine's case, rumors reached back thirty-plus years.[32] Music critic Alex Ross, in a 2001 *New Yorker* article, had written off these rumors about the "affable, untouchable Levine" as products of pot-stirring antagonism:

> Creepier than the rumors [about Levine] themselves is the delight with which people in the music world have repeated them. Some have done so out of professional envy, some out of sheer malice. Levine has denied the rumors, but his most effective response has been his performances, which make all the gossip sound bitter and small.[33]

Sixteen years blew by, and the whispers about Levine stayed whispers. He remained untouchable. It took the ramming speed of #MeToo—a movement (originating with activist Tarana Burke in 2006 and catching a fierce second wind in 2017) that was already pushing into pretty much every other political, workplace, and entertainment sector—to thrust this heretofore deified man under glaring light. As soon as the Met announced Levine's suspension, Alex Ross took to Twitter to apologize for having so confidently doubted this conductor's multiple victims: "At the time, I thought that Levine was being victimized by false rumors. I was disastrously wrong, and am ashamed to have written this [2001 article]."[34] Ross's regret is important, but his initial defense of Levine is revealing all the same. As musicologist Linda Shaver-Gleason points out, among the most telling aspects of Ross's original article is how this prominent critic "had once considered Levine's *performances* as an appropriate response to accusations of impropriety [. . .]; he places music and moral behavior on the same scale, contrasting the smallness of the motivation behind the rumors against the implied immensity of Levine's performances."[35] Ross's 2001 statement invoked, furthermore, the figurative as well as literal capability of Levine's beautiful performances to quell any murmurs about this conductor's impropriety.[36] When the superhuman Levine is conducting, the audience has to hush; a maestro's hands command music and silence alike.

As I write this, the Levine case persists. He has continued to deny all wrongdoing, countersued the Met for unfair dismissal, and most recently, presented intimate letters sent to him by alleged victims decades ago. Levine is hoping some of these letters will show that certain relationships were consensual. For instance, the words "I love you" appear in a 1989 missive by Ashok Pai (nineteen years old at the time), who reported to the police in 2016 that the conductor had sexually abused him from the age of fifteen, driving him to feelings of shame and thoughts of suicide. A portion of Levine's legal complaint reads, "It is unimaginable that a person [Pai] would write that he desperately wants to see and loves the person who sexually abused or harassed him."[37]

Is it unimaginable? It is not unimaginable. It is not even uncommon. Victims of abuse can propound to feel love, or what they think is love, for their abusers.[38] So for Levine and his lawyers to weaponize love—to repurpose the dried ink of "I love you" into textbook gaslighting—is a perversely domineering move that simultaneously reveals considerable ignorance of how abuse works.

Look, the letter says "love." Love is love. How does one argue with love?

To this day, Levine and Dutoit enjoy plenty of defenders. "James Levine may be a sinner," stated a person's Letter to the Editor published in the *New York Times*, "but I am less shocked by his sins than by how we instantly throw overboard people who, in the course of their long careers, have made such immense contributions to the world of music and society."[39] I find it tempting to dismiss the author of this letter as a fringe voice. I might even wish to believe that no one, aside from the most conservative commenters on the most conservative websites, could be so foolish. But to attack Levine's and Dutoit's apologists neither negates their existence nor explains, in some cases, their distinguished credentials. Here's a take by music connoisseur and New York University emeritus professor of economics Melvyn Krauss in a *USA Today* op-ed:

> Lost in the brouhaha about sexual harassment are the interests of innocent third parties who can have an important stake in the battle between accuser and accused. When people like Charlie Rose, Bill O'Reilly, and Matt Lauer lose their jobs, millions of their viewers are affected. [. . .] One recent casualty has been the distinguished classical music conductor, Charles Dutoit, [who] was blackballed from concerts throughout the U.S. after being charged with sexual misconduct by four women. He vigorously denied the charges. [. . .] Now Americans are being deprived of Dutoit's considerable talents because of the country's sexual politics. [. . .] The classical music business already is on the rocks in the United States. The last thing it needs is a silent boycott of U.S. concert halls and opera houses by top European conductors and musicians.[40]

Krauss has called #MeToo's proponents "McCarthyites," and the movement as a whole "McCarthyism."[41] Here, his complaint about devalued concert tickets is clothed in logics of aesthetic utilitarianism. *Just think of all the beautiful music we will miss out on now that we have fired the Dutoits of our society,* he bemoans.

Superhumanized musicians show just how forcefully music can beguile us into magical thinking. Music's mystique can lead us to imagine that we know far more about ourselves—and about other people—than we actually do or ever could.[42] Now, you might agree with the excuses and rationalizations people have made on behalf of Levine and Dutoit. You might viscerally disagree. Or you might feel torn. From what these apologists have written, nevertheless, one thing is hard to deny: they love music a great deal. As do many of us, surely. And it is this head-over-heels love of music that lays some of the sharpest snares of the musical mystique. Although we might not always like to admit it, any of us can wander into these snares. We're only human, after all.

The Musicological Mystique; or, a Not-So-Obvious Accomplice

Loving great music does not, on its own, make me a good human being.

It sounds obvious. But it doesn't feel obvious—at least, not to me.

With questions of music and morality, dissonances arise between what sounds evident and what feels evident. Consider again the opening sentence, now prefaced with a personal claim to knowledge:

I know that loving great music does not, on its own, make me a good human being.

Another plausible, even obvious, claim. Yet is it true? Do I know better than to equate aesthetic appreciation with personhood? At best, I can say *I know I am supposed to know*, or *I think I might know*, or *I want to say I'm pretty sure I know*. I . . . I . . . I: the stretched-out syntax already betrays uncertainty, with pronouncements of knowledge buckling under the weight of wordy explanations. Because despite knowing I should probably know better, there's something about music—especially music considered great, canonic, important, lovely—that's capable of lulling me into moralist dreams.

Think of the Nazis. As exemplars of evil, they come up regularly in historians' efforts to demolish myths of musicality-as-decency. "If the Nazis taught us anything," Susan McClary writes, "it is that one may listen to Mozart and still act in barbaric ways."[43] Lawrence Langer brings up the issue with interrogative disbelief: "Given the 'mere factual truth' that the same individual is capable of loving Mozart and murdering children without recognizing any contradiction in his personality or being affected by it [. . .] how is one to respond?"[44] And Richard Taruskin likewise leans on skeptical queries to drive the point home: "Are we not tired of hearing that only those who respond to Beethoven are fully human? Do we still believe that no Nazi could have responded to Beethoven that way?"[45] All of these writers make the same excellent point. We—you and I—*should* be tired of correlations between the love of classical music (or any music) and ethical personhood. Yet these correlations apparently remain prevalent enough that writers still sense an urge to set the record straight.[46] For if it were conventional wisdom that loving music doesn't make you a good person, then no one would find it necessary to continually invoke the potent counterexamples of Wagner-adoring Adolf Hitler or aria-whistling Angel of Death Josef Mengele to begin with.[47] Put another way: Nazis constitute a reliable trump card for debunking fantasies of music as an ennobling force; nonetheless, the very trumpiness *of* the Nazi card is itself revelatory, for the gambit's enduring popularity raises the question of why the card needs to be played at all if the wisdoms therein are by now, in fact, so conventional.

One explanation may be that cautionary tales of music-loving Nazis haven't stuck. Nazi atrocities couldn't purge posterity's delusion about the musical mystique any more than they could persuade the world to expunge racism and fascism forever. Fast-forward to the neo-Nazis of the present day. In Charlottesville, Virginia during the summer of 2017, white nationalist rallies erupted around the city's plans to remove a statue of Confederate general Robert E. Lee. One of the leaders was white supremacist Richard Spencer.[48] As recounted by Bonnie Gordon, a professor of music at the University of Virginia: "Surreally, Richard Spencer, perhaps the most recognized music major in the country, is a 2001 graduate of the University of Virginia. And how did he use his majors in Music and English? He coined the term 'alt-right' and served as an impresario for the sick operatic rally staged here in Charlottesville."[49] Like Gordon, I find it "surreal" that Spencer had been a music major, disciplinarily no different from some of the college students whom I teach.[50]

But what exactly makes Spencer's curricular choices sound surreal? Is it because this man's college majors defy stereotypes of right-wingers as relatively dismissive of the value of arts and humanities?[51] Is it because we have a hard time imagining our own students could be neo-Nazis? If plain facts about Spencer's coursework *feel* surreal, then what can these feelings teach us about our grip on reality itself when we're wading through quagmires of music, morality, and education? "It's relatively easy to get college students to see the grotesque potential of some of the music they love, especially if it includes sounds mobilized by the likes of Stalin and Hitler," Gordon cautions. "But it is so much more work and so much more important to make our students hear the ways that racialized nationalism played and plays out today in our own spaces—politically and musically."[52]

I've therefore come to wonder how many people, including the lifelong practitioners and students of music among us, are truly immune to the seductions of the musical mystique. Hence my term *musicological* mystique, which speaks to the misconception that a knowledge of music—acquired not necessarily through formal music education, but through any channels— vaccinates us against music's contagious myths and moralist charms. You don't need to be a card-carrying musicologist to succumb to the musicological mystique, just as you don't need to be a musician to be enamored of the musical mystique.

Let's circle back to the instructive example of classical music, which enjoys a double-edged reputation as an elite and elitist artform. I spent much of my own early musical education performing and analyzing Western masterpieces, often labeled explicitly as such on the covers of score anthologies and history textbooks. Even upon learning to critique the canon through feminist, queer, racial, postcolonial, and disability frameworks, I find that much of this music, when I play or hear it nowadays, maintains an uncanny hold over me. It's not just an understandable ambivalence toward Richard Wagner's *Die Meistersinger*, Carl Orff's *Carmina Burana*, and other works known to have been treasured by the Nazis. Listening to virtually any classical repertoire can sometimes make me feel strangely respectable. Smart. Cultured. Educated. Civilized. I'd be loath to utter these descriptors out loud, for they sound extremely problematic. But the feelings, in all honesty, persist. To borrow ethnomusicologist Judith Becker's phrase, these feelings comprise my emotional "habitus of listening," an "embodied pattern of action and reaction [. . .] tacit, unexamined, seemingly completely 'natural.'"[53] Associations pile up, habits harden—not that all classical music hits me (or would strike you) the same way.[54] Palestrina's lamentations can reduce me to tears. Chopin's mazurkas send me to the moon. And *Für Elise* inevitably reminds me foremost of garbage trucks (looping the first thirty seconds of this Beethoven bagatelle) waking me up at 5:00 a.m. in Taipei, where I spent my earliest years and childhood summers.[55]

Can habits and habitus change? Yes. Do they change easily and quickly? By definition, no.

Here's another insight from Richard Taruskin, this time denouncing the mythical virtues of art for art's sake: "It is all too obvious by now that teaching people that their love of Schubert makes them better people teaches them nothing more than self-regard, and inspires attitudes that are the very opposite of humane."[56] I agree with every part of this sentence except the prefatory insistence of "all too obvious."[57] For a comparable choice of words, an article by philosopher Peter Kivy recalls a scene from the film *Schindler's List* in which a German soldier sits down at a piano to play some J. S. Bach while his comrades are slaughtering Jews. "The point of the scene is all too clear," Kivy remarks. "Love of Bach does not engender love of humanity, or of the good."[58] If, however, the faults of moralist music pedagogy are "all too obvious" or "all too clear," then why do these authors spill ink on the subject? Maybe a phrase such as "all too obvious" is itself just a semantic habit in academic writing. But maybe the habit is both a symptom and a cause of the ongoing musical miseducation under scrutiny. In a 2016 lecture at Texas A&M University, philosopher Cornel West picked on the word "obviously" as a mark of punditry.

> [W. E. B.] Du Bois talks about what will happen to America when America opts for the dusty desert of smartness and dollars. He says that in 1903, *Souls of Black Folk*. All you have to do is listen to any of the pundits on television. Keep in mind how many times they use the word "obviously." Obviously this, obviously, obviously, obviously. You say, no—it's not obvious to me.[59]

With any complex topic, claims of total obviousness can exacerbate problems—problems of communication, explication, empathy—even if the explanatory intentions are good. The musical mystique is no different. Not everyone knows what a small number of music scholars know, think they know, or think everyone else should already know.

Concerning the musical mystique, it's hard to articulate what we believe or what we know at all. It's even harder to know what others believe until they tell you outright. In November 2017, two hosts at Boston Public Radio, Margery Eagan and Jim Braude, interviewed Boston Symphony Orchestra director Andris Nelsons and congratulated him for having recently been named *Musical America*'s Artist of the Year. Following a laudatory discussion of the BSO's tour of Japan, Braude mentioned that many people in the United States had been talking about "sexual harassment in entertainment, in politics," especially with the uproar over former senator Al Franken's lewd offenses against television personality Leeann Tweeden.[60]

Braude then asked Nelsons: "Is that an issue in the orchestral world around the world? Is that an issue? Is it a problem? Has it been?"

"No," Nelsons replied.

"Really? No?" Braude pressed dubiously, as if taken aback by Nelsons's response.

"I think. I mean . . ."—and what followed was a paean to musical virtue, an expression of the musical mystique in a nutshell:

> When we [the Boston Symphony Orchestra] played [. . .] this Mahler symphony, and Rachmaninoff—it's a different world, and it feels so human and so right. [. . .] I just think that music and art can bring people together, and I would just wish that those who are very busy—and I understand that they are busy—if they could find the time, [then] they could realize how

important it is, other parts of life including music and art. I believe they would become better human beings.[61]

Nelsons's comments were met with total excoriation . . . as well as with total commendation. "ANYBODY who went to conservatory or worked in [the] professional classical realm knows that this is wrong and dangerous," tweeted percussionist Adam Sliwinski.[62] By contrast, a *Boston Globe* reader commented, "I agree 100% with Mr. Nelsons that music makes us better people, that it ennobles the soul and strengthens our humanity."[63] Verbal skirmishes raged on. Four days after the interview aired, the BSO issued a statement, nominally by Nelsons:

> During a recent interview with Jim Braude and Margery Eagan on WGBH's Boston Public Radio, I did not express myself as clearly as I would have liked when asked about sexual harassment in the classical music world. In my own experience working in the classical music industry for many years, I myself have not seen overt examples of sexual misconduct in my day-to-day work life. That being said, this kind of offensive behaviour, unfortunately, takes place in all fields, including the classical music industry. All of us in the field must remain vigilant and fight against all types of inappropriate and hurtful behaviour, and continue the essential work of creating a fair and safe work environment for all classical musicians. Though involvement in music and the arts can't cure all the ills of society, I do believe that the inspiration they provide has the potential to help us reflect at times on the better angels of our natures. Or put more simply by Beethoven—the genius composer of the Ode to Joy symphony, considered the universal anthem of brotherly/sisterly love—"Music can change the world."[64]

From the doubling down on better angels to the apocryphal Beethoven quotation, Nelsons's follow-up statement was only a slight improvement over his initial remarks.[65] And the statement became all the more troublesome when, within weeks of its issuance, a double whammy came in the breaking stories about James Levine and Charles Dutoit.

Classical music and musicians, to be fair, have no monopoly on the musical and musicological mystiques. Across and within cultures, the loose categories of folk music, popular music, world music, dance music, and court music are all lightning rods for value judgments.[66] We'd be hard pressed to find a hierarchical society that's able to suppress distinctions between high and low arts.[67] As far as mystiques go, then, classical music might seem like an easy target. Perennial laments today about the "death of classical music" characterize this tradition as "circling the drain," fragile and victimized; accordingly, to focus righteous fire on classical music would be to kick it while it's always already down.[68] But classical music is, if anything, the opposite of an easy target. Like Hollywood or the Catholic Church, the classical music business is a mighty fortress, the home of giants who have slept soundly for decades. It's just that when cultural titans such as Levine or Dutoit actually fall, the boom is so noisy we stand to forget the long and silent passages that came before.

When Language Gets Stuck—Love Is Love. Music Is Music. People Are People.

The musical mystique is a concoction of love, music, and the measures of humanity. Love invites yet defies language. Music drums up similar verbal tensions. Mix in our attempts to define humanity, and it's easy to become tongue tied.

At the 2016 Tony Awards, when Lin-Manuel Miranda walked onto the stage to accept the evening's Best Original Score award for *Hamilton*, he delivered a sonnet. Audience members began cheering and weeping when Miranda reached his final couplet:

> And love
> is love is love is love is love is love is love is love
> cannot be killed or swept aside.

Love is love is love . . . : grammatical transgression, syntactic short circuiting, percussive strikes winning out over metrical propriety. (Had the line run, "And love cannot be killed or swept aside," it would have adhered to a classic iambic pentameter.) As for the sonnet's concluding words:

> Now fill the world with music, love, and pride.[69]

Miranda dedicated his poem in part to his family, and in part to the victims and survivors of the Pulse nightclub massacre that had occurred just twenty hours earlier. It had been a busy "Latin Night" at this Orlando queer bar when a shooter opened fire, killing forty-nine people and wounding fifty-three others.[70] Both homophobia and racism were plausible motives. At the core of Miranda's message was to love and let love; to let queer people be people; and to let music keep peace.

It's interesting how language can get stuck on love. *Love is love*, for starters, is a beautiful thing to say. It's a tautology painted proudly on banners by people who have historically had to defend their love—say, interracial love, transcultural love, same-sex love. But opponents of such love can move the target and say that this love isn't love at all, but rather a sin, a perversion, a trick of corrupted minds and libidinous bodies. You can't convince anti-miscegenists and homophobes that they are against love. For as the writer Laura Kipnis puts it, "who would dream of being against love?"[71] Virtually no one. So in order for bigots to reconcile a pro-love and anti-gay stance, there's only one way forward: to rebrand any objectionable love as not true love at all.

Love isn't the only thing that tussles in tautology and moving targets. Music gets the same treatment. In his 1973 book *How Musical Is Man?*, ethnomusicologist John Blacking spelled out music as "humanly organized sound."[72] Music, according to this definition, is a quintessentially and exclusively human phenomenon. Music is what humans say or feel it is. Without humans, there wouldn't be music. A few years following the publication of Blacking's influential book, the academic journal *World of Music* devoted a double issue to the topic of "Universals/Le Problème des Universaux."[73] One article in this issue was authored by semiotician Jean-Jacques Nattiez, who, like Blacking, leaned on tautological conceits to delineate music via humanity:

> It is a human being who decides what is and is not musical, even when the sound is not of human origin. If we acknowledge that sound is not organized and conceptualized (that is, made to form music) merely by its producer, but by the mind that perceives it, then music is uniquely human.[74]

Nattiez's *if-(but-)then* statement played a trick on me the first few times I read it. It looks like such a logical and daresay obvious construction. Look more closely, however, and the sentence—when buffered by its preceding claim, "It is a human being who decides . . ."—is basically saying humans are the sole arbiters of pretty much everything. With our language, we get to say and judge what is or is not musical, ethical, beautiful, rational, delectable, laughable, peaceable. These subjective qualities are granted evidentiary weight by the fact that humans and their words exist. But the salient point is that humans are plural, disagree widely on what qualifies as music, and voice these disagreements to sociopolitical ends.

Even if the question of music's universality among humankind could be persuasively resolved one way or the other, what good would it do? It's not a rhetorical question. "[Music] is an important part of what makes us human as well as a vehicle for recognizing—and directly experiencing— our common humanity," suggests philosopher Kathleen Marie Higgins. "As varied as our music is, as varied as we are, we all sound human. If anything about music is universal, that certainly is."[75] Such claims may be true; maybe, according to evolutionary biology and MRI brain scans, we are all musical. Yet when was the last time an attempt to reach agreement succeeded on the basis of language that *we are all x*? Scientists have said that human beings share 99.9% identical DNA, so people sometimes use this popular factoid to push for anti-racism and for everyone to get along.[76] It doesn't work. As scholar Paula Ioanide has declared with regard to the "emotional politics of racism," feelings can trump facts.[77]

If you're a musician and people wish to dehumanize you on the basis of your skin color, gender identity, or religion, they can, once again, easily move the target and relabel your musical output as noise, trash, or whatever. In her work on anti-Semitism and the "music libel against the Jews," musi- cologist Ruth HaCohen observes how gentiles have, since the days of early Christianity, linked Jews with noise.[78] Or think of how the past and present reception of jazz, rap, and Afro-American genres in the United States tends to include complaints about this music as too cacophonous, too primitive, and too animalistic.[79] In the nineteenth century, the surgeon V. Josiah C. Nott, owner of nine slaves, speculated that "in animals where the senses and sen- sual faculties predominate, the nerves coming off from the brain are large, and we find the nerves of the Negro larger than those of the Caucasian."[80] Samuel A. Cartwright, the physician who coined "drapetomania" (the mental "disease" that mysteriously compels slaves to run away from plantations), likewise portrayed black musical ability in a condescending and animalizing manner.[81]

> The negro's hearing is better [. . .]. His imitative powers are very great. [. . .] Thus, music is a mere sensual pleasure with the negro. There is nothing in his music addressing the understanding; it has melody, but no harmony;

his songs are mere sounds, without sense or meaning—pleasing the ear, without conveying a single idea to the mind; his ear is gratified by sound, as his stomach is by food.[82]

Cartwright saw slaves as beasts of pure appetite.[83] His insistence on the solely imitative capabilities of musical slaves jibes with postbellum characterizations of black musical bodies. In the program notes for a 1910 Boston Symphony Orchestra performance of Antonín Dvořák's *New World Symphony*, Philip Hale remarked on the work's "Negro melodies" and noted the "peculiarly mimetic" abilities of the "American negro."[84] Such emphasis on imitation might bring to mind mimetic songbirds,[85] mimetic primates (hence the word *aping*), mimetic child prodigies who display freakishly "automatonic" or "mature" virtuosity,[86] mimetic Jews,[87] merely mimetic Autistic "savants,"[88] mimetic deaf musicians whose engagements with music are "reduced [...] to tactility and vibration,"[89] or mimetic East Asian "assembly-line" conservatory students "whose impressive arsenal of skills cannot fully compensate for the lack of an original mind."[90] In every example, attributions of "imitative powers" delimit the music-making subject as either bestial or machinic, to wit, not truly human.[91] Notice, too, how frequently disability and race come up in these variegated judgments of the musically human and the humanly musical. Both ableism and racism, after all, install social hierarchies by designating who is human, and who is treated as less than.

When people say *love is love*, they often do so in defense of relationships deemed taboo by societal norms and laws. When people say *music is music*, it's sometimes a plea to allow listeners to enjoy the music of their choice, and to leave aside any potentially unsavory details about the musician or the repertoire. And when people say *people are people*, they are appealing to a fairly recent internationalist framework of human rights. Being called a human or a person doesn't matter much if the label lacks accompanying protections and privileges. Human rights violations persist despite biological classifications of victims as humans, and for that matter, animal rights violations often arise via contradistinctions between human and non-human sentience.[92] Such slippages have led philosophers, legal scholars, and critical race theorists since the 1990s to take issue with the unwieldy universalism of the human rights framework itself.[93] "Today the *language* of human rights, if not human rights themselves, is nearly universal," law professors Austin Sarat and Thomas Kearns remark. "Governments everywhere [. . .] claim to believe in and respect the dignity of their citizens," even if such belief and respect don't bear out in practice.[94] Writers such as Sonu Bedi, Slavoj Žižek, Eric Posner, John Nelson, Chidi Anselm Odinkalu, and Abdullahi An-Na'im have posited alternatives and complements to the human rights framework; these include reason, rationalism, anti-racist policies, anti-torture initiatives, preemptive restrictions on governmental states of exception, and dismantling top-down ideologies of humanitarian foreign aid.[95]

People are people, then, really has little actionable value so long as certain humans are juridically reclassifiable as convicts, aliens, "illegals," and three-fifths humans.[96] Claims about "self-evident" human rights likewise conceal paradoxes because the very overstatements of certainty—obviousness—are undercut by the apparent need for a statement at all. Concerning the pervasive variations on "we hold these truths to be self-evident," historian Lynn Hunt asks: "If equality of rights is so self-evident, then why did this assertion have to [be] made and why was it only made in specific times and places?"[97] One answer is that the antecedent purposefully jumps the gun. Although rights are evidently *not* self-evident, people who claim otherwise are, with humane intentions, accelerating from zero to one hundred, hoping that raw rhetorical velocity can make up for lapses in veracity or enforceability.[98] It's wishful language.[99]

In the end, it would be easy to state that love, when weaponized or tarnished by immoral agendas, is no longer true love at all, but instead a corrupt emotional doppelgänger. Such a statement would be no more useful than an insistence that music, when deployed for torture by the CIA, is no longer music, but instead "noise" or "sheer sound."[100] No more useful than saying that a man who commits atrocious acts is best thought of as not human, but instead a "wild" animal or an "inhuman beast."[101] By throwing around definitional quick changes, we get to hang on to a few threads of a stable worldview: surely, love and music (and, some would say, humans) are basically good; whenever they're not, let's just start calling them by other names.

What's ultimately most revealing about our attempts to talk about (and around) love, music, and humanity is indeed how such language spins its wheels. And when all three terms enter the fray—when it comes to questions of *humans loving music*—our silences can be as telling as our words.

Coda: Loves That Dare Not Speak

> Though presumably we all came to our present positions through
> a strong attraction to music and to specific pieces, most theorists
> and musicologists, whether old or new, are not comfortable with
> "music loving." Or perhaps I should say I think that no one is com-
> fortable with "loving." We do not call ourselves music lovers; we call
> amateurs music lovers. My title [for this academic article, "Music
> Loving, or the Relationship with the Piece"] was difficult to settle on
> because I kept finding it embarrassing.
>
> —Marion Guck[102]

Conversations about music, morality, and humanity span millennia and
continents.[103] From the oft-cited treatises of the Ancient Greeks to today's
one-liners about music changing the world, from Venezuela's controversial music education program El Sistema to the multilingual songs of solidarity performed at the US-Mexico border, from Yo-Yo Ma's Silk Road
Project to China's recent bans on tunes that "harm public morality," from
the worshipping of Beethoven's Ninth Symphony to the paternalistic benevolence of humanitarian songs such as "We Are the World," from Tupac's
"killer rhymes" to Marilyn Manson's Satanism and innumerable alleged
scenarios involving music- or musician-incited violence—no words have
been spared.[104] But how often do these words spell out the roles of love in
our debates? Is music loving simultaneously too obvious and too abstract of
a concern?

I love music. Yet I don't think I've ever said out loud the words, "I'm a music
lover," at least not in the way people sometimes say, "I'm an animal lover,"
"I'm a foodie," "I'm a movie buff," or "I'm an oenophile." As Marion Guck
points out, the compound label of *music lover* tends to connote amateurism
and dilettantism. What's in a name, though, and who cares? Well, according
to Guck, musicologists and music theorists might care—the people who research, teach, and write about music for a living, and who expertly sublimate
their affections through histories, ethnographies, and analyses that show an
undeniable love of music (doting on its tiny details and huge implications)
while brushing away the need to say the embarrassing L-word outright. In
the 1990s, writers such as Guck blazed trails to incorporate love, pleasure,
carnality, queerness, and erotics into the musical academy. It has since become clear that silences around loving music sprang from multifaceted

anxieties about intellectual mastery, subjectivity, sentimentality, masculinity, and disability.[105] These silences became filled by the clarion interventions of scholars who dared speak truth to love.[106]

Although I say I love music, the course of this love hasn't always run smooth. My previous book, *Just Vibrations*, narrated how the onset of chronic illness unmoored me from music's safe harbors, leaving me adrift in existential and vocational angst. Nonstop neuropathic pain in my abdominal wall broke my ability to play piano, kept me holed up in my apartment, and shattered my sense of self.[107] Was I still a musicologist, given that I increasingly found myself backing out of conferences and professional commitments? Did I still love music, seeing as how I stopped going to concerts? Was music even meaningful anymore, to the extent that no manner of music therapy seemed to touch the pain?

In January 2016, an advance excerpt of *Just Vibrations* appeared in a *Washington Post* op-ed. I had submitted the short piece with the title, "I'm a Music Professor, But I No Longer Play Music. Here's Why." When the op-ed ran, I saw that my editor had changed the title to: "I'm a Musician Who Can't Play Music Anymore. I Feel Like I'm Letting My Heroes Down."[108] I was perplexed about the second half of this new header because the op-ed wasn't about my fear of disappointing heroes. It was about how societies' prevalent narratives of heroism and resilience (*what doesn't kill you makes you stronger*) elide the reality that, in some cases, people neither manage nor aspire to transmute trauma into creative production—and that these are stories worth telling, too.

In a way, I felt as though music had let *me* down. It's not like I could have raged at specific musical repertoire or instruments, but the feeling of betrayal by an erstwhile reliable ally—Music—wasn't much different from the feeling of being abandoned or lied to by another person. In the throes of pain, my bonds with musicality and humanity were fraying. It's as if I had, since an early age, stacked blocks of my identity upon a proud foundation of musical engagement, only to have this foundation toppled fast. Once a steady companion, music was no panacea. I tried to love it. Love just wasn't enough.

I have summarized this portion of *Just Vibrations* for the sake of transparency about the impetus behind *Loving Music Till It Hurts*: my personal run-ins with both the privileges and the perils of tethering personhood to music. For me, loving music wasn't just a love that, in academic discourse, dared not speak; it was also a love that I didn't realize needed articulating at all—not until I felt it slipping away. Since 2017, for what it's worth, I have found my way back to a better love of music, even back to the piano bench every once in a while. It has been a gradual and tentative rekindling, as expected of an attempt at reconnection after any sort of breakup. No, the relationship isn't yet all it once was. At least for the time being, however, I am able to say: it is enough.

Let's now head to the US capital to hear a single, sustained story. Within this story is a seemingly obvious moral about the importance of loving music. Except, as you can guess by now, such stories are rarely as lovely as they sound, and their morals never quite as straightforward as they appear. It's a story with the usual suspects from the present chapter: the musical mystique (in journalist Gene Weingarten's narrative), the musicological mystique (in some readers' responses), the traps of language, and the things—the people—we tend to overlook when the imperatives of music loving take top billing.

2

Princes and Paupers

Many years ago, on this very spot, there was a beautiful city of fine houses and inviting spaces, and no one who lived here was ever in a hurry. [. . .] Then one day someone discovered that if you walked as fast as possible and looked at nothing but your shoes you would arrive at your destination much more quickly. Soon everyone was doing it. [. . .] No one paid any attention to how things looked, and as they moved faster and faster everything grew uglier and dirtier, and as everything grew uglier and dirtier they moved faster and faster, and at last a very strange thing began to happen. Because nobody cared, the city slowly began to disappear. Day by day the buildings grew fainter and fainter, and the streets faded away, until at last it was entirely invisible. There was nothing to see at all.

—Alec, a perceptive boy, describing the derelict City of Reality in Norton Juster's *The Phantom Tollbooth*[1]

"What Is All This Teary Stuff Doing in My Eyes?"

On an ordinary Friday near the entrance to a subway station, an extraordinary violinist played beautiful music but received little ovation. Here stood a superstar capable of selling out Carnegie Hall. He was clutching a Stradivarius worth millions and performing a wonderful Bach chaconne. Yet out of the thousand-plus people who heard this man play, most breezed by. Over forty-three minutes, the violinist wasn't shown much love. He collected barely more than fifty dollars. Given his stellar merits, the math didn't add up.

This famous stunt involved the virtuoso Joshua Bell busking incognito in the arcade of the L'Enfant Plaza metro station in Washington, DC on January 12, 2007. Wearing casual clothes and a baseball cap, Bell performed indoors near an escalator during the morning rush. The social experiment was the brainchild of *Washington Post* columnist Gene Weingarten, who reported his findings in a lengthy article called "Pearls before Breakfast," which went on to receive the 2008 Pulitzer Prize for Feature Writing.[2] "In a banal setting at an inconvenient time," pondered Weingarten, "would beauty transcend?"[3] The answer, based on commuters' behaviors, was a hollow *no*.

Weingarten heard innocence lost in the postlapsarian shuffle of impatient feet. Maybe life wasn't always like this; maybe people aren't born this way. Several children indeed tried to stop and watch Bell's performance, only to be hurried along by their parents. One mother pulled off an athletic gawk-block that was virtuosic in its own right, "deftly [moving] her body between Evan's and Bell's, cutting off her son's line of sight," physically coming between enchanted child and enchanting spectacle.[4] Can any artist cast a spell potent enough to slow the migrations of the morning slog? Amid travels and travails, shouldn't we embrace live and lovely music as glorious respite from daily dramas? Or as Weingarten framed it: "If we can't take the time out of our lives to stay a moment and listen to one of the best musicians on Earth play some of the best music ever written; if the surge of modern life so overpowers us that we are deaf and blind to something like that—then *what else are we missing*?"[5] Weingarten's lead-up to his own question (relying on metaphors of disability as ignorance and inattentiveness) sought to shepherd readers toward a cardinal answer: what we're missing is an appreciation for beauty. Beauty itself, he implied, can go missing when life's labors get in the way.

Weingarten accentuated his lesson by stacking the odds against Bell. For starters, the covert gig took place on a workday when people were dashing to their jobs. Bell was asked to play in an entryway where commuters had to scoot along. Bach aside, the other repertorial choices of Manuel Ponce and Jules Massenet were likely unfamiliar to many passersby. And the acoustics, though described by Weingarten as "surprisingly kind," couldn't have been ideal, given the vicinity's fuss and bluster: the *whirs* of the escalator, the *whoompfs* of heavy glass doors, the *clacks* and *clops* of shoes, and the magnetostrictive *tzzz* of lights overhead.[6] In these regards, Bell was set up to bomb. During later interviews, the violinist even stated that the experiment "played out the way I thought it would,"[7] and Weingarten likewise voiced an early prediction that things "would happen this way."[8]

To ramp up the scandal of jilted brilliance, Weingarten raved about the virtuoso's physical beauty and musical finesse, calling Bell a "heartthrob" and "onetime child prodigy" whose violin "sobbed and laughed and sang—ecstatic, sorrowful, importuning, adoring, flirtatious, castigating, playful, romancing, merry, triumphal, sumptuous."[9] Weingarten cited like-minded adorers who have proclaimed that Bell "plays like a god" and "does nothing less than tell human beings why they bother to live."[10] For the purposes of the story, Bell's talent was unimpeachable, Bach's elegance absolute, and the pair's lovability axiomatic. In the experiment, the superhuman musician and music represented the definitive controls, the unerring centers around which variables came and went in the form of capricious passersby who gave up free lessons on "why they bother to live."

On the day after it published "Pearls before Breakfast," the *Washington Post* hosted a chatroom for readers to interact with Weingarten. In the chatroom's prefatory remarks, Weingarten stacked the deck once more, extending a targeted invitation to his most sympathetic base. "With little or no elaboration, more than 100 readers so far have told me that this story made them cry," he revealed. "It was not a reaction I anticipated, at least not so universally, and it has somewhat taken me aback. Can those of you who had this reaction try to explain it? [. . .] Weepers, please write in."[11] With selection bias in place, most of the participants who dropped in the chatroom were admirers of Weingarten and Bell. Over the next hour, "weepers" chimed in to emphasize their disenchantment with snubbers of beauty.[12] Some readers admitted an inability to make sense of their tears. "Why did this article make me cry?" asked a commenter, reflecting on the original *Washington Post* article. "I'm 32, male, working on Capitol Hill, hell I'm even a Republican. [. . .] Tell me Gene, what is all this teary stuff doing in my eyes, or is it just dusty in here?"[13] Another confused reader said: "I have no idea. I wasn't sad, or disgusted, or feeling like we lead wasted lives, or any of that banal BS. I was wiping my eyes thinking 'what the heck is wrong with me?' So, you tell me."[14] And one crier received validation for a no-frills answer: "I think the tears are from not knowing what's important and not using our important time on this earth wisely."[15]

Responded Weingarten: "Ooooh. Well put. Thank you, weepers. You are doing well."[16]

What's certain is how the story of an unheeded Bell produced a sensational touchstone. "Who could have predicted that Joshua Bell's 43-minute busking experiment in a D.C. Metro station would still be inspiring stories more than 10 years later?" asked journalist Laurie Niles in her coverage of a 2017 Kennedy Center multimedia event in honor of this violinist.[17] Bell, for his part, hasn't been able to live the story down either, insofar as writers continue to pepper him with questions about the incident. In a June 2016 interview, the *Music Times* mentioned the busking experiment straight out of the gates, to which Bell replied, maybe with a tinge of annoyance: "It's already eight [sic] years ago now and here I am still talking about it. It did strike a nerve with people."[18] As for Weingarten, he followed up the 2007 article with a 2014 piece titled "Setting the Record Straight on the Joshua Bell Experiment," in which he noted, "Hardly a month goes by that I don't get an e-mail from some priest or minister or rabbi or imam gratefully and graciously informing me that they have just delivered a sermon based on the events in my story; often, they include a copy of the sermon, and more often than not it is based on the erroneous summary."[19] Elsewhere in this *Post* postmortem, Weingarten remarked: "I thought I had written my final words on Joshua Bell and the Metro, but . . ."—and what came next was a point-by-point correction of errors committed by writers who had attempted to sum up the original article. Weingarten's list of errata included the following:

> Wrong. Two Bach pieces, one Massenet, one Schubert.
> Not "thousands" [of passersby] or anywhere near. Exactly 1,097.
> Seven people [the number of commuters who stopped for a while to listen], not six, but who's counting?
> Three days [the number of days between Bell's sold-out concert in Boston and the L'Enfant Plaza experiment], not two, but who's counting?[20]

In total, Weingarten came up with sixteen corrections. (And when it came to exact numbers, he was the one counting.)

Over the past decade, numerous retellings, embellishments, emendations, and oral extemporizations have imbued Weingarten's story with a legendary afterlife. It's no surprise that some religious leaders found the story appealing and useful, given how the original article resonates with Passionate overtones: just as Christian scriptures portrayed Jesus as an overlooked gift from God, so Bell, in commoner's garb, was depicted as preaching heavenly music that went ignored save for a perceptive, faithful few. Plenty of critics have sung the praises of Bell's celestial talents, and the violinist himself has said that the music he loves reveals "a sense of divine order in the world."[21] According to media reviews, Bell even went on to obtain an almost Christ-like redemption when, in 2014, he played a successful concert at DC's Union Station for over a thousand appreciative listeners. A do-over for Bell—or rather, according to his publicist Jane Covner, "a do-over for the people in Washington."[22] Announced the virtuoso as he greeted the atoned music lovers: "Wow. This is more like it!"[23]

Beyond its circulation in places of worship, the tale of Bell the busker has entered classrooms and bedrooms, for among its tributes is a 2013 illustrated children's book by Kathy Stinson and Dušan Petričić, *The Man with the Violin*, with an afterword by Bell himself. In this storybook, a fictional boy named Dylan, while walking through the city with his mom, hears a violinist's lovely performance.[24] But his mom doesn't let him stop to listen (Figure 2.1). Once they have arrived home and turned on the radio, however:

> A voice on the radio drones on and on until suddenly . . . Music! Telling a story that makes the apartment bigger and brighter, and Dylan shouts, "That's the man in the station!" The music fades. The voice on the radio says, "Today over a thousand people had the chance to hear one of the finest musicians in the world. Joshua Bell was playing some of the most elegant music ever written, on one of the most valuable violins ever made. Yet few people listened for even a minute. Dylan said, "I knew it! We should have stopped. We should have listened." [. . .] "Dylan, you're right." His mom turns up the radio. Loud and sweet, the music fills every corner of the apartment. And together Dylan and his mom dance. Together they listen.

It's a story that, in the tradition of many children's books, vindicates the youngster as an uncannily wise protagonist. Like Alec in Norton Juster's *The Phantom Tollbooth* (recall this chapter's epigraph), Dylan sensed something unnatural about the rush and din of the adults around him. He knew how to listen.

Figure 2.1. Kathy Stinson and Dušan Petričić, *The Man with the Violin*. Reproduced by courtesy of Kathy Stinson and with permission of Annick Press.

Some readers have found the *Washington Post* article obviously lovable and tearjerking. Others have, with no less conviction, found it obviously problematic. Recall how, in his 2007 *New Republic* review essay, "The Musical Mystique," musicologist Richard Taruskin admonished various defenders of classical music for "smug nostalgia, utopian delusions, social snobbery," and "imperial haberdashery."[25] Taruskin began this essay with an indictment of the Weingarten-Bell experiment, a fresh headline at the time. "But of course it was hardly an experiment," he wrote. "All concerned knew perfectly well that people at rush hour are preoccupied with other things than arts and leisure, and would not break their stride. But the fulfillment of the self-fulfilling prophecy gave Weingarten the pretext he sought [. . .] to cluck and tut."[26] I concur with Taruskin's view that a pompous "promulgation of mystique" drove Weingarten's experiment and its choice of hifalutin music. But Taruskin wandered into an adjacent trap. "Saddest for me was that the weblist of the American Musicological Society [AMS], my professional organization, added its meed of clucking and cackling [to Weingarten's article]," he sighed. "Scholars are supposed to be skeptical of spin and pose, but here we were piling on."[27] Why should Taruskin be superlatively sad about the complicity of his colleagues? He had already cited exchanges on the AMS weblist as evidence of academics' susceptibility to "spin and pose"—meaning he knew not everyone knows what he believes he so firmly knows. Indeed, Taruskin bought into the musicological mystique, a presumption that people who know things about music somehow have heightened resistances to the intoxications of the musical mystique.

Maybe the problems with Weingarten's experiment sound obvious to you as well. But as I asked in Chapter 1: do problems with the musical mystique ever feel obvious? Or might statements of obviousness be part of the problem here? Richard Taruskin has not been alone in his reprobation of the Joshua Bell experiment, which he went so far as to call "disgusting."[28] At a music colloquium where I shared my preliminary thoughts about Weingarten's article, an ethnomusicologist informed me that "anyone who reads the *Washington Post* knows Weingarten is a satirist," and therefore the Bell experiment cannot be treated as serious journalism.[29] An anonymous reviewer of my initial proposal for this book cautioned, "Pretty much everyone who thought about the Weingarten piece for more than 3 seconds thought it was baloney, and said so."[30] Another anonymous reviewer stated, "[The Weingarten experiment] has been written about endlessly; there is nothing new to be said about it."[31] Add these confident declarations to Taruskin's stratagem,

"All concerned knew perfectly well that people [. . .] would not break their stride," and I've started to notice some patterns in speechcraft.[32] Everyone, anyone, all concerned: these universalizing referents contradict from within, for the overstatement of obvious unanimity points to an understanding that not everyone is on the same page. As Weingarten even noted, his own coworkers had expected an opposite response from the DC commuters; they feared Bell would draw a huge audience and jam the metro station. Prior to greenlighting the experiment, the team of editors "discussed how to deal with likely outcomes. The most widely held assumption was that there could well be a problem with crowd control."[33]

Consequently, are those who claim that "everyone" could "perfectly" see through Weingarten's ploy really just hurrying to announce they know better than everyone else? Do these claims use the illusion of public accord to serve personal bluster?[34] A learned skepticism toward the musical mystique does not equate to an innate immunity against the sorts of enticing narratives that can put this very acuity to the test. My hunch is this: if Weingarten's article has deeply bothered some readers (not least esteemed musicologists), it did so not because the experiment was obviously repulsive, but rather because it remains subtly seductive. A piece like Weingarten's, for all of its shortcomings, is a tantalizing tale likely to ignite a battle between the sucker and skeptic who dance within each of us. It's a siren song of a story, at once beautiful and dangerous. And when we are exposed to this siren song, it can be far easier to stuff wax in our ears than to ask how and why we, as imperfect human beings, are enticeable by musical myths and mystiques to begin with.

I am fascinated by the rapidity (the tempo, as much as tone) with which some readers have excoriated Weingarten's moralistic article, and with which others have found themselves reduced to tears.[35] Using the Joshua Bell experiment as a keyhole, I wish to scan the musical mystique from the analytical vantage of velocity—literal and figurative, locomotive and discursive. In practices of critique, we tend to talk about rhetorical direction (where people are trying to go with their arguments) without paying as much attention to the metric of speed (the rate and certainty with which the arguments are voiced). What might we learn when we take critical velocities into account? How can snap judgments and fast feet illuminate the stakes of coveting or waiving music (frequently dubbed a "time-bound" or "temporal" art form)?[36] As a corrective to haste, this chapter will stroll through Weingarten's experiment multiple times, each time charting a different route, until a map of our relationships with the musical mystique takes shape.[37] My broadest aim is to break the illusions of universality when it comes to musical knowledge and appreciation. In the twenty-first century, the field of musicology has tread into theories of humans' musical sameness, including the idea that we are all, in some fashion, musical and musically appreciative. As well-intentioned as fantasies of human musical commonality may be, I ask whether these fantasies can end up stalling rather than promoting agendas of justice, love, and solidarity. As with the contemporary rush to trumpet a post-feminist, post-human, or post-racial age, elisions of difference might sound good yet do harm.

Weingarten's *Washington Post* article was published on April 8, 2007. It's worth taking stock of what was happening in the United States around this time. Technologically, politically, and economically, 2007 was a year of speed. In January, Apple CEO Steve Jobs announced the first iPhone, which hit US stores that summer and went international a few months later. Mobile broadband speeds shot up. Besides chips and bytes, an ethos of speed permeated the US electoral arena. Barack Obama announced his presidential candidacy in February. His campaign slogans of hope and change generated unrealistic expectations of swift reform. Meanwhile, in market sectors, the American subprime bubble was expanding at an alarming rate. Although numerous factors contributed to this bubble's burst and its precipitation of a financial meltdown, the pervasive metaphor of the bubble (now you see it, now you don't) led people to talk about the economic crisis as if it had a sudden and singular cause. All of this alacrity unfolded against the booming backdrop of social media: Facebook and YouTube had just rolled out to the public, and users had more means and incentives than ever to share news, opinions, and videos. (For its 2006 Person of the Year, *TIME* magazine had even come to the controversial decision of "You," explained on the cover of its December 25th issue as follows: "Yes, you. You control the Information Age. Welcome to your world."[38]) From Internet bandwidths to state primaries to market inflation, acceleration was paradoxically the new equilibrium.[39]

Once More, with Feeling

L'Enfant Plaza, another track.

One day at a subway station, a man suffered others' disregard. Given his status, he should have stood out, but instead went unheard. Coins tossed his way weren't enough. More so than most, this man needed some attention from those around him.

And it wasn't Joshua Bell.

For his *Washington Post* feature, Weingarten interviewed a shoe shiner named Edna Souza who said she wasn't surprised that so few commuters stopped for Bell. "Couple of years ago, a homeless guy died right there," Souza recalled, gesturing to a spot near the escalator. "He just lay down there and died. The police came, an ambulance came, and no one even stopped to see or slowed down to look."[40] This homeless man comes up in Souza's statement and then never receives another mention in the article. Like fleeting commuters, Weingarten rhetorically whooshes past the vagrant, using the tragic anecdote to fuel readers' outrage toward the neglect of Joshua Bell, the subway's unsung star. As Weingarten waxes lyrical about life's lusters lost, he takes aim at symbolic fatalities, not literal ones: the demise of beauty, the deaths of laborers' souls, and the extinction of aesthetic scruples in an age of mega-corps and machines.

Neither the commuters nor Weingarten could be bothered to reprogram their moral GPS when it came to an unidentified man adrift in the indifference of strangers, just a speck in a sea of melodious prose and scuffed-up shoes. Travelers follow train schedules; *Washington Post* writers abide by character limits. For Weingarten to expound on a nameless death would have taken up valuable semantic real estate. Lying in the story's and society's margins, then, the homeless man lived out his last days on the fringes of foot traffic, then died a footnote, an adjunct casualty who mainly served to verify passersby's stinginess toward Bell. Given the pandemic of urban homelessness in the United States—a problem so widely seen that some people might no longer see it at all—it's no wonder that the faces of actual impoverishment can't compete these days with the novelty of a prosperous star *pretending* to slum it as a struggling artist. "On that Friday in January," Weingarten reported, "Joshua Bell was just another mendicant."[41] We get what Weingarten was trying to say—notably, that a disguised Bell had to busk without the aid of his gilded reputation. But deigning to role-play as a street musician for one morning doesn't make a virtuoso "just another mendicant." It makes Bell the subject of an experiment that shrouds the lived realities of indigence versus privilege.

Sure, Weingarten's article isn't about the homeless crisis in southwest DC.[42] Given the author's focus on beauty and Bach, any prolonged exposure of a deceased homeless person would have appeared to miss the mark. For me now to focus on Edna Souza's anecdote could prompt accusations of exploitative overcorrection, of perpetuating tropes of poverty porn, and of patronizing the homeless individual as a mascot or martyr of societal negligence.[43] But Souza's remarks can't go unaddressed, because they do complicate our own attempts at answering Weingarten's question of *what else we are missing* when we don't stop for the beautiful music of someone like Joshua Bell. For what we're missing is not just beauty (of classical music or otherwise), but also its many opposites, from injury and injustice to atrocity and societal ugliness. "Ugly Laws," in fact, was the umbrella name for ordinances that, across the United States from the mid-nineteenth through mid-twentieth centuries, prohibited "unsightly" individuals—the homeless, the disheveled, the disabled— from appearing in public spaces.[44] These laws officially ruled ugly as sin, looking to purge open reminders of society's nonnormative denizens. Recall how, as Weingarten stressed, several parents sped along the curious kids who wanted to pause for Bell's performance. In daily life, parents also hurry children past homeless people on the streets because, according to elders, it's not nice to stop and stare.[45] For all the efforts to shield the eyes of youths, however, adults are sometimes the ones who play peekaboo with unpleasant realities.[46]

To be clear, Weingarten wanted a ritzy headliner from the start. Although he omitted the experiment's origin story from the *Washington Post* article, he explained in a subsequent NPR interview: "Well, a couple of years ago, I was coming out of the subway and I noticed there was a keyboard artist there. And I just thought he was terrific. But nobody was stopping, nobody was looking, nobody was giving him any money. And I thought, boy, you know, if Yo-Yo Ma himself were there, people would just pass him by. And so, after trying and failing to get Mr. Ma for a little bit of time, I finally decided that a violinist would be even better and managed to persuade the man I think is the best violinist in the world to do it."[47] In one respect, Weingarten's experiment was ingenious for the way it roped in a musical big shot to prove a point. But it also catered to the lowest common denominators of highbrow bias. Had Weingarten chosen to acquaint himself with the keyboardist whom he found so "terrific," he could have written an article with the same message about the beauties lost amid busy lives. Rather than interviewing this keyboardist, however—rather than paying tribute to the street musician who served as the muse for the eventual Pulitzer-winning idea—Weingarten sought out A-lister Joshua Bell. Weingarten, a respected journalist in his own right, could have repaid the underappreciated keyboardist with significant publicity, materially redressing the very neglect that he bemoaned, even if on a one-time basis. Yet undercover celebrities are a sexier sell, whether it's talk-show host Ellen DeGeneres getting a disguised soccer player David Beckham to peddle aftershave at Target, or supermodel Tyra Banks donning a fat suit to "experience" obesity (and to educate herself on what it's like to endure "laughter, stares, and nasty comments" from other people), or socialite Kim Kardashian wearing a frumpy costume on *Celebrities Undercover* to mingle with her fans and test their loyalties, or a physiognomically prosthetized Adele auditioning to be an Adele impersonator in front of actual impersonators.[48] Viewers of these antics await the moment when the masks come off and the commoners go gaga from a celebrity's gracious aura.[49]

What about Joshua Bell himself, the celebrity in the *Washington Post* experiment? Despite being a good sport and playing along, he performed unknowingly at the site of a homeless man's demise, then went on, in interviews, to lament the painful, awkward feelings of receiving, for once, no attention. Bell recalled that it was "not fun to play to an audience that's not a captive audience," and how the experience taught him to "really appreciate any sort of glance, or dollar, or a couple [dollars], you know, a comment here and there."[50] Although the grievances voiced by Bell make him an easy target for accusations of insensitivity, we have the option of reading more generously between his lines. If Weingarten's experiment sought to audit the viability of beauty, a fringe benefit came through in Bell's heightened awareness of people who can take neither accolades nor assets for granted. With Bell and the homeless man, one could scarcely imagine, as far as material privileges go, two figures from more different worlds. Different worlds, same coordinates; radically disparate means, vaguely similar pleas. *Can you hear me now? Will you look at me? Slow down for a second?*

No homeless person—no one at all—should have to delight passersby with musical abilities in order to receive some attention and care. People shouldn't need to prove themselves as productive stewards of beauty (to make aesthetic, bankable contributions to society) in order to be regarded as someone worth helping. Again, does this sound obvious? Or might these humanitarian claims feel self-evident to some people, and anathema to others?[51] One thing many Americans know intimately, like a lullaby seared into memory, is the meritocratic myth that justifies wealth and impoverishment alike: work hard and persevere, and you will get what you deserve. In terms of individual resilience, the meritocratic ethos ranks right up there with brazen claims that poverty is a "state of mind" and a lack of "richness in spirit," or that "the only disability in life is a bad attitude."[52] But disability, debility, and systemic inequalities throw wrenches into any pretense of institutional fairness. "Nowhere is the disabled figure more troubling to American ideology and history than in relation to the concept of work," points out Rosemarie Garland-Thomson. "Labor, the definitive creed of Puritan through contemporary America, transforms necessity into virtue and equates productive work with moral worth, idleness with depravity."[53] Homeless people are commonly branded as drains on society and emblems of abject poverty. Visibly disabled or not, they are marked as what scholars David Mitchell and Sharon Snyder call "nonproductive bodies," the "inhabitants of the planet who, largely by virtue of biological (in)capacity, aesthetic nonconformity, and/or nonnormative labor patterns [. . .] represent the nonlaboring populations—not merely excluded from, but also resistant to, standardized labor demands of productivity particular to neoliberalism."[54] Mitchell and Snyder define a neoliberal "biopolitics of disability," or "ablenationalism," as an insincere form of inclusionism "requir[ing] that disability be tolerated as long as it does not demand an excessive degree of change from relatively inflexible institutions, environments, and norms of belonging."[55] Such institutions will put up with—even self-congratulatorily laud and hungrily co-opt—deviants whose reappropriated bodies can prop up the status quo.[56]

Here's a textbook example of musical ablenationalism in action. In 2015, ABC News published a story called "Homeless Man Plays Piano So Beautifully It Might Earn Him a Job."

> A homeless man in Sarasota, Florida is going wildly viral after shocking people with his incredible musical skills. One passerby, Aurore Henry, took notice of the bearded mystery man as he sat at the piano effortlessly playing a beautiful rendition of Styx's "Come Sail Away." She was so impressed with his talents that she uploaded the video of his sidewalk serenade to her Facebook page where it now has a whopping 2.5 million views in just two days. [. . .] "This homeless man now has the opportunity to be something other than 'just a nuisance' to all the people downtown," she wrote. "Just took my breath away. Wow."[57]

The man, Donald Gould, was playing on one of several pianos installed downtown by the Sarasota Keys Piano Project, which described its goal of setting up instruments for "the public to play, explore, learn, practice, and most importantly, enjoy."[58] Prior to his life on the streets, Gould had served in the US Marine Corps; pursued a musical education at Spring Arbor University in Michigan; run out of money for tuition; begun working to support his family; lost his wife in 1998; developed substance abuse problems;

and surrendered his then-three-year-old son to Social Services.[59] Upon becoming an overnight Internet sensation, Gould was offered the chance to audition for a job at a local restaurant's piano bar. Grander gigs followed. Gould played the national anthem at a San Francisco 49ers game, appeared on a Japanese television show, and obtained a deal from Triple Pop Records in Austin, Texas.[60] He also received treatment for addiction and reconnected with his son. Without discounting the upsides of Gould's rapidly ameliorated life, we can still observe, right down to the fine print of capital-driven contracts (for performances, recordings, and media appearances), how fast the neoliberal machine revved its gears and made efficient use of a model mendicant.[61] Gould's apparent salvation via musical exhibition gave a pitch-perfect testimony to the primacy of individual merit, the kind-heartedness of art lovers, and the fertility of American Dreams. Music humanized Gould. In the eyes of admirers, he was judged to be someone worth saving, worth loving. His talent would have been a terrible thing to waste. But shouldn't we expect homelessness, hunger, poverty, and human rights to receive ethical and policy considerations irrespective of artistic abilities and clickbait premiums?

During music classes and colloquia, I have recounted the story of Donald Gould and shown YouTube clips of his 2015 keyboard performance of "The Star-Spangled Banner" at the San Francisco 49ers game.[62] Prior to playing the videos, I would take a timeout and invite viewers to pay attention not just to Gould's body and music but also to their *own* bodies and sounds: how they feel, sit, tense up, squirm, sigh, and let out other voluntary and involuntary vocalizations when observing Gould. I made these requests because, in the video, Gould hits plenty of wrong notes, experiences some memory lapses, and understandably appears nervous overall. Watching Gould's video, audience members would indeed variously chuckle, look bemused, cringe, grit their teeth, or appear unfazed. Judgments of musical ability would hardly be unusual coming from music students and scholars who are trained to lend critical ears and vocabularies to performative minutiae. Yet while it's easy to notice Gould's slip-ups, it's trickier to discern the larger purpose of such perceptiveness. How much good would it do to accuse Gould, an apparent amateur, of taking undeserved handouts and pity deals from professional record labels? Maybe what we can prioritize is the exposure of exploitative systems that would seize someone's musicality, no matter the actual proficiency, under false banners of aesthetic edification and patronage. For sponsors and employers, Gould was just *musical* enough—enough to convince some listeners (especially those partial to human interest tales) to buy the story, literally, with clicks and cash. At the same time, this amateur pianist was just *unmusical* enough—meaning that his portrayal as sufficiently undertrained enabled the media to play up narratives of the man as a "noble savage."[63]

Such music-industrial mystiques required a version of Gould who was broken yet amendable, Other yet assimilable. All told, the public fixation on Gould's "stunning" and "heart-stopping" pianism implicitly deemed this man deserving of care primarily by proxy of his threshold musicality (Figure 2.2).[64] Inspirational themes surrounding Gould's tale stand to distort public expectations and understandings of homeless individuals at large. Adoring fans could wonder: if someone like Gould could rise up through grit and talent, then shouldn't all homeless people and veterans try to do so?[65] Pseudo-inspirational provocations of "What's Your Excuse?" (the long-time unofficial motto for the Paralympics) celebrate resilience while shaming disabled and disenfranchised people who are perceived to lag behind their extra-extraordinary peers (more on this in Chapter 4).[66]

Donald Gould was not a "prodigy," as *People* magazine called him; that a homeless veteran can play piano—or, inversely, *that a piano student can end up a homeless veteran*—is utterly believable.[67] Musicians as a whole don't enjoy guarantees of financial stability, even if the scarce exceptions of major celebrities inspire skewed perceptions to the contrary. In turn, plenty of US veterans end up jobless and homeless from a dearth of support systems for military families at municipal, state, and federal levels.[68] So what would lead incredulous writers to fetishize Gould as a unicorn? The musical mystique is one culprit, baiting people toward romantic connections between musicality and moral humanity. But such mystique has an accomplice: the dehumanizing stigma attached to vagrancy. If you're homeless, you must be

Figure 2.2. (*Left*) ABC report on Donald Gould and (*right*) a before-and-after juxtaposition of Gould in the *Wounded Times*, a news and blog site devoted to issues of veterans and combat post-traumatic stress disorder.

uncultured and uncivilized . . . for why else would you have let go of culture and civilization, and the quintessential symbol thereof—the home?[69]

Gould isn't the only homeless person whose exhibition of musicality has courted outsized media attention.[70] A man named David Allen Welsh used to wander into a thrift store in Vancouver, British Columbia and sit down at an old piano to play for a while, "impressing customers with his piano improvisations, even moving them to tears."[71] One customer, James Maynard, told ABC News that "when [Welsh] started to play, I choked on my coffee."[72] Similar cases involving singing abilities abound in articles bearing titles such as "Homeless Man with Amazing Voice Sings John Legend, Stuns All of Us" and "Pedestrians Stop & Stare As Homeless Lady With Angelic Voice Walks down Street Singing."[73] Famously, in the early 2000s, the Juilliard-trained double bassist Nathaniel Ayers experienced homelessness, mental illness, and institutionalization. His talents were discovered by the *Los Angeles Times* columnist Steve Lopez, and their relationship became the subject of a film, *The Soloist*, starring Jamie Foxx (as Ayers) and Robert Downey Jr. (as Lopez).[74] Collectively, these sensational stories—which emphasize onlookers' stupefaction, enchantment, and eagerness to play promotional roles in the lives of homeless musicians—reify links between musical ability and salvageable humanity.

Assumptions about homeless people's allergy to all things civilized have underpinned commercial businesses' strategies of deterrence, namely, the growing number of stores, restaurants, and transport hubs that blast music to drive loiterers away. Recall, in this book's Prelude, Anne Midgette's story of hearing a "harsh" rendition of an "impaled" Schubert piano trio in New York's Port Authority. Classical music is indeed a popular choice for such strategies, and its representation of high culture tacitly names the specific populations it's meant to repel: the homeless, the would-be criminals, black and brown youths, and other people who are presumably up to no good.[75] Urban planners use the terms "hostile architecture" and "defensive architecture" with reference to designs of buildings and public spaces that discourage loitering, sleeping, or other activities unintended by the property's overseer.[76] Spikes on the ground are an egregious example (Figure 2.3), which has rightly elicited protests from people who see the design as an affront to the homeless. Less obvious yet more pervasive examples of deterrent design include park benches with vertical slats and armrests, which render horizontal repose either impossible or supremely uncomfortable.[77] Likewise, sound can be part of a space's hostile architecture. It can occasionally be blatant (the sonic equivalent of spikes), as in the case of the sustained

Figure 2.3. Deterrents in the form of (*left*) spikes and (*right*) benches with armrests.

high-pitched alarm that a Marks & Spencer store in East London deliberately blasted all night long in an attempt to ward off "rough sleepers."[78] Or it can be subtle and plausibly benign (akin to a bench's slats, ostensibly usable as arm rests), as with the 7-Elevens and Burger Kings that loop classical music around the clock.[79]

At the end of the day, I do find the musicality of someone like Donald Gould to be a beautiful thing. Perhaps what's most beautiful about the whole story is how vestiges of musicality stayed dormant in Gould—stayed in his muscle memory, neural circuitry—through a hard life of loss, addiction, and trauma. It's a story to love. Yet so lovable is the story of Gould's rescue that we might be reluctant to imagine what would have become of this man had he not proven his pianism to the world. Because to allow ourselves to imagine this alternate timeline is to admit we might already know the answer. And to know the answer is to feel further pressure to question the basis of our love of Gould and, more broadly, to question some uncomfortable consequences of our love of music.

We Are More Musically Alike, My Friends . . .

In minor ways we differ,
in major we're the same.

I note the obvious differences
between each sort and type,
but we are more alike, my friends,
than we are unalike.

We are more alike, my friends,
than we are unalike.

We are more alike, my friends,
than we are unalike.

—Maya Angelou, "Human Family"[80]

Let's say the cold January morning in 2007 at L'Enfant Plaza had gone differently. Joshua Bell, incognito, performed Bach. One by one, people slowed down as they drew near, pulling out their earbuds and putting phones on silent. No one dared to cough or rustle. Parents beamed as they watched their children transfixed by the spectacle. Comments about the mystery musician lit up the Internet. Within twenty minutes, camera crews for ABC and CNN were on the scene. Police roped off sections of 10th Street and D Street to quell vehicular noise; conductors halted all trains. As the Baroque chaconne's final notes rang out, they melted into the audience's stupefaction. Then, thunderous applause: Bell's identity was revealed. The story broke nationwide. Its message centered on how an undercover virtuoso relied on superb ability to reap rewards, and how what we all need is a little more beauty in our lives.

Even if this version of events had transpired in reality, it would not have signaled a happily ever after. If people were to stop for a meritorious musician but not for, say, a homeless man in need, then something would still be amiss. Let's say a musician pulled off a traffic-stopping miracle, but no one stopped to help those incapable of performing miracles. How beautiful does this world sound?

Stories like Joshua Bell's and Donald Gould's lean on the sensational delights of hearing music in unlikely places from unlikely people. Beautiful music and musical participation can come from anywhere, anyone. It's a lovely idea. In his 1998 book *Musicking*, Christopher Small gerunded *music* with a magnanimous description that blew typical metrics of participation wide open:

To music is to take part, in any capacity, in a musical performance, whether by performing, by listening, by rehearsing or practicing, by providing material for performance (what is called composing), or by dancing. We might at times even extend its meaning to what the person is doing who takes the tickets at the door or the hefty men who shift the piano and the drums or the roadies who set up the instruments and carry out the sound checks or the cleaners who clean up after everyone else has gone.[81]

Reading these words two decades following their publication, I continue to be startled by the capaciousness of Small's delineation. So broad, so attentive to performances' unsung aides. As a treatise, *Musicking* aimed to subvert Western art music's traditions of lionizing the solitary genius and the attendant ideas of art for art's sake. To this end, Small cautioned that "the verb *to music* is not concerned with valuation. It is *descriptive*, not *prescriptive*. It covers all participation in a musical performance [. . .]. Value judgments come later, if they come at all."[82] Hence Small's eventual hypothesis: "If everyone is born musical, then everyone's musical experience is valid."[83]

Despite the statement's spirit of egalitarianism, how often do these ideals bear out in practice? Think of audience members who might fawn over concerto soloists but don't always say thank you to the people taking tickets at the door, much less go out of their way to acknowledge the contributions of custodians and stagehands.

We are all musical is a generous, generative sentiment. It can empower individuals to claim stakes and participation in musical spheres even in the absence of "obvious" performance abilities.[84] But the dreams of this sentiment cannot alone forfend the waking realities of how *musician* is an identity shot through with negotiations of judgment, capability, literacy, belonging, and privilege. With music and musicality, value judgments don't "come later," as Small said, but rather are constantly crowding the stage. Conjecturing the validity of everyone's musicking role can end up sounding as gallant as claims that

> *musicality is a universally human capacity* (Theodore Gracyk).[85]
> *we are all (ethno)musicologists now* (Nicholas Cook).[86]
> *we're all Africans, really* (Meryl Streep).[87]
> *we are all mixed-race people* (Bill Clinton).[88]
> *we are all natives now* (Clifford Geertz).[89]
> *everyone's queer* (various).[90]
> *we are all disabled* (various).[91]
> *we are all posthuman* (various).[92]
> *we are all (im)migrants* (various).[93]
> *we're all Muslim, we're all Mexican, we're all women, we're all*
> *Americans; yes, and we are all gay and lesbian and bisexual and*
> *transgender and, goddamn it, we're all queer too* (Michael Moore).[94]

Much of this rhetoric shows good intentions, grasping at threads of pluralism to weave a quilt of solidarity.[95] Comparable cries of pan-allyship following terrorist attacks—"Je suis Charlie," "Je suis Nice," "We are Orlando"—spin out a *we are the world* ethos of internationalism that can sometimes look like exceptionalism in disguise.[96] Universalizing a label (be it migrant, Muslim, or musician) cannot, by utterance alone, speak into existence the justice devoutly wished (Figure 2.4).[97] Until the day Hollywood royalty Meryl Streep finds herself stopped and frisked in New York, or gets shot in the back while unarmed, her "we're all Africans, really" statement remains a mere overture to anti-discriminatory action. Today, the Out of Africa theory of paleoanthropology does posit a single origin of *Homo sapiens* and, as mentioned in the previous chapter, geneticists believe that humans share in excess of 99% DNA. Yet these empirical studies can't abate partisanship, tribalism, and hate crimes. In terms of persuasive intent and cavalier universals, the "all" of "we are all x" teeters precariously between the optimistic "all" of "Can we all get along?" and the reactionary "all" of "All Lives Matter." *Obviously* all lives

Figure 2.4. In December 2015, documentary filmmaker Michael Moore held up a "We Are All Muslim" sign in front of Trump Tower until the police came and asked him to leave.

matter. So obvious is the statement, however, that it confuses unobjection-able truism with anti-racist advocacy.

In cultural studies of music, Small's use of "musicking" has become a fa-miliar referent for expansive, even universal, conceptions of musicality. Gary Tomlinson invokes the term in his book *A Million Years of Music*: "We are, al-most all of us, musicians—everyone who can entrain (not necessarily dance) to a beat, who can recognize a repeated tune (not necessarily sing it), who can distinguish one instrument or one singing voice from another. I will often use an antique word, recently revived, to name this broader musical expe-rience. Humans are *musicking* creatures."[98] Interestingly, this definition of musicking closely echoes the first portion of Small's definition—performing, listening, dancing—while excluding its most radically inclusive portion, where Small gave a nod to ticket collectors, piano movers, and the hidden figures least likely to wear the mantle of "musicking creatures."[99] Even as Tomlinson, through his ambitious project, attempts to argue for global and evolutionary commonalities in human musicianship, he ends up bypassing Small's anti-hierarchical charge of musicking.[100] Nonetheless, Tomlinson and Small do share a lovely idea: we are more musically alike, my friends, than we are unalike.

Similar arguments have appeared in other scholars' recent efforts to advo-cate for transcultural bridges between people's musical propensities. The 2015 volume *Rethinking Difference in Music Scholarship*, coedited by musicologists Olivia Bloechl, Melanie Lowe, and Jeffrey Kallberg, includes essays that "take difference-based epistemologies of music to task for neglecting sameness and even universality as significant aspects of musical life."[101] *Difference*, strangely, is a familiar rubric in studies of culture. Academics have copious vocabularies to probe difference with regard to privilege, power, colonialism, appropriation, and distinction. *Sameness* sounds a little more awkward, right down to its suffixness. But sameness has some advantages. In his 2003 book *Representing African Music*, Kofi Agawu urged researchers to allow for musical inquiries based on "carefully defined sameness" instead of conven-tional theories of "difference," which have heretofore produced a "distorted, ideologically one-sided, and politically disadvantageous representation."[102] Agawu believes that many non-African scholars of African music, by their choices of transcription systems and critical frameworks, have traditionally played up the distinctive Africanness of this music, thereby risking a dis-course of exoticism, alterity, and unjust illustration. Asks Agawu rhetorically, "When was the last time an ethnomusicologist went out to hunt for sameness rather than difference?"[103] All in all, it doesn't take long for Agawu to arrive at a definitional conundrum, when he advises that an "ideology of difference must be replaced by an ideology of sameness so that—and this is somewhat paradoxical—we can gain a better view of difference."[104] Difference and sameness turn out to be two sides of the same currency in this marketplace of complicated musical ideas.

One escape route out of Agawu's paradox could involve changing the key variable from music to justice: what needs same-ing is the humane treatment of people irrespective of musical differences *or* similarities. Put another way, what we sorely need is practicable solidarity, not heuristic sameness. Regardless of music's and musicking's provable commonalities across populations, musicality shouldn't be used wholesale to legitimize or disqualify the humanity and civil entitlements of a person. After all, a cynical gloss of *all humans are musical* could extract an Orwellian shadow clause: *all humans are musical, but some are more musical than others.*[105] The post-comma half of the statement cannibalizes the setup, insofar as dreams of equality are swallowed by bleak realities of hierarchy.

For my part, I don't want to silence my own inner romantic entirely, the part of me that wishes to believe people might be more similar than they are different, musical and otherwise. In times of division, better we cling to visions of unity than to abandon all hope. But I can't help thinking that *we are all musical* misses the mark. As for an alternative? Perhaps *we are human—all music aside.*

But who counts as human, anyway? Like the problematic models of universal rights (the Human Rights Framework, as described in Chapter 1), frameworks of universal humanity and universal musicality can sometimes harm those whom they purport to help. Inspirational tales about musical engagement and music therapy overwhelmingly zoom in on marginalized, disenfranchised, and disabled individuals. People with dementia, Autistic people, d/Deaf people, and neurodiverse people do perform, appreciate, or benefit greatly from music. For some, music is a miraculous lifeline. But what about those who don't show much (or any) interest in music, or fail to benefit noticeably from music? What about Alzheimer's patients who don't respond to music therapy? Is there something wrong with them? Is their inability to be revivified—daresay rehumanized—by music a sign of being less human in the first place? Of course not. Yet a valorization of music's universality stands to further marginalize individuals for whom music doesn't play a major rehabilitative or edifying role. For this reason, the phrase *we are all* tends to triumph as rhetorical fantasy while floundering by way of actionable policy.

Being Musically Human: The Good, the Bad, and the Dangerous

> Music—certainly for musicians—is not something subject to simple definition. Rather, it is an object simultaneously of love and hate, of discipline and compulsion; both a "universal language" and a "secret society," all-consuming and all-rewarding, vocation and avocation, and more. [. . .] Any attempt to explain such facts will necessarily come face to face not only with questions of what music is, but of what it means to engage with and even to dedicate oneself to music— that is, to be in a serious way *musical.*
>
> —Nadine Hubbs[106]

According to sensational stories about people like Donald Gould, a spontaneous exhibition of musical ability can garner the attentive care of passersby. Tales of musicality as a golden ticket are enough to make us wonder whether the homeless man who died in L'Enfant Plaza might have lived if only he had shown some proof of talent—if only he had fulfilled the neoliberal tit-for-tat mandate for all citizens to give back to society in an appreciable way. It's somewhat of an unproductive fantasy, not just because we can't turn back time, but also because, for all we know, the man *was* musical. Indeed, in a follow-up essay to "Pearls before Breakfast," Gene Weingarten conceded that people are normally not even permitted to busk where Joshua Bell ended up playing. Weingarten sought to obtain "special, secret dispensation by directors of the transit system," asking Metro official Jack Requa to "loosen the rules" this one time. Requa explained that "busking in the Metro was not only against the rules, but against the law." To which Weingarten responded: "Uh, well, the *Washington Post* would have no objection if you made the same concession to any other news organization that happens to be proposing placing a world-class violinist in one of your stations as a sociological experiment!"[107] Against Weingarten's appeal to fame, the Metro yielded.

At first blush, then, the musical mystique seems to benefit people who are judged to be musically adept. Exceptional musical abilities can reap adulation, wealth, prestigious appointments, and the "special, secret dispensation" to busk where no one else may. More generally, being musical can net social, cultural, and material capital. Orchestra auditions, *American Idol*, and record companies reward those who demonstrate great musical skill. Musical extracurriculars and supplemental materials can be a boon on a student's college application. Beyond these quotidian examples, consider historical moments of extreme human precarity, including scenes of incarceration and subjugation where humanity is brought to die, even if some music survives. During the era of chattel slavery in the United States, Thomas Jefferson and other plantation owners "gave preferential treatment to certain slaves, based in part on their musical aptitude."[108] In the concentration camps of Auschwitz-Birkenau, musical Jews occasionally received favors in exchange for entertaining Nazi officers; music bought time, whereas non-musicians had less to wager.[109] From Austrian composer Arnold Schoenberg to Afghan rapper Sonita Alizadeh, musical laurels are conducive to requests for immigration, refuge, and asylum. Not that at-risk musicians need to be famous to obtain an advantage. As ethnomusicologist Benjamin Harbert has documented, a prisoner at Louisiana State Penitentiary recently incurred administrative favoritism when the music-loving warden learned that this inmate was an accomplished guitarist.[110] It wasn't a get-out-of-jail-free card, but surely every perk matters behind bars. For as writer Chris Waller observes, music in prisons "often comes tied to judgements by the regime about prisoners' conduct, with incentive systems [. . .] continuous with the mechanisms of carceral control, with its 'humanising' or 'therapeutic' effects being defined as a luxury to be earned through good behaviour."[111]

A questionable representation of music-as-salvation comes during the dramatic centerpiece in the 2002 film *The Pianist*, directed by Roman Polanski and based on the memoirs of Polish pianist and composer Władysław Szpilman (1911–2000). In 1944, while hiding in an abandoned house in Warsaw, Szpilman was discovered by a Wehrmacht officer, Wilm Hosenfeld.[112] Upon learning that Szpilman was a musician, Hosenfeld commanded him to play the piano. Szpilman obliged (as if he had a choice), performed some Chopin, and subsequently received periodic food drops of jam and bread from Hosenfeld. So famous is this story that it appears on the jacket of Szpilman's book. "On September 23, 1939, Władysław Szpilman played Chopin's Nocturne in C-sharp minor live on the radio as shells exploded outside—so loudly that he couldn't hear his piano," ran the synopsis. "In the end, his life was saved by a German officer who heard him play the same Chopin nocturne on a piano found among the rubble." Yet as philosopher Peter Kivy remarks, this blurb is misleading. Someone who skims it is supposed to deduce "a causal connection between the German officer hearing the Chopin nocturne and his saving [Szpilman's] life," and that "Chopin's Nocturne in C-sharp minor had the moral effect of deflecting a vicious Nazi killer of Jews from his intended purpose."[113] A slower and more thorough reading would arrive at a different conclusion. It becomes clear, on the basis of his extensive diary entries throughout military service, that Hosenfeld had grown disillusioned by and eventually antipathetic toward the National Socialists, and had discreetly begun aiding Polish Jews as early as 1939. In *The Pianist*'s depiction of the encounter between Szpilman (played by Adrien Brody) and Hosenfeld (Thomas Kretschmann), however, the beauty of Chopin is drenched in moonlit tension.[114] All we hear before and after Szpilman's performance is the shuffling of feet, the scraping of the piano bench, and other grating noises conveying unease. As Szpilman plays, the viewer obtains multiple close-ups of Hosenfeld's features—sharp jaw, light skin, blue eyes. Hosenfeld stares. He paces. He is transfixed by the music, for sure, but it's hard for a viewer to look past his imposing uniform and the pistol dangling from his hip. It's as if Szpilman's life were riding on a single performance.

Such a cinematic nail-biter plays up the possibility that being musical can save one's life. Even if this had been the case in the meeting between Szpilman and Hosenfeld, *musical ability's ability to save a human life* shouldn't be treated as the *end* to a felicitous survival tale, but rather as a cause for a sustained investigation into the broader dehumanizing circumstances that render some lives in dire need of saving in the first place.

As highlighted by narratives about music's moral and salvational power, being musical can be good. Just as importantly, being musical is *a* good. Like goods writ large, this good can be leveraged, traded, coveted, exploited, weaponized, and used against its owners.[115] By definition, anything of value can whip up disdain, greed, and envy. As a result, being called musical or a musician might *not* always be a net positive. Even the word "musical," as the musicologist Philip Brett once reminded us, has at times served as a euphemism for "gay."[116] Musicians more generally, if perceived as deviants or threats, can be targeted outright. Ethnomusicologist Martin Daughtry has written about cases in which, during US Operation Iraqi Freedom, "musicians and musical practices ended up performing the role not of *agent* but of *victim*: they were recipients of acts of violence, aggression, and silencing that were directed specifically toward music qua music."[117] As

Daughtry remarks, it can be "shocking" to see musicians singled out for abuse and violence.[118] At the same time, maybe it's not so shocking at all, given that musicians often play the role of joy bringers.[119] Like the combat medics and street medics who serve as aid bringers, musicians are fleshy, unarmored, destructible embodiments of morale, vigor, and other precious yet abstract values.[120] Over the last few years, the world has witnessed a surge in terrorist attacks on auditoriums, nightclubs, outdoor concerts, and music-saturated events (Paris, Orlando, Manchester, Las Vegas).[121] These were joyous occasions swiftly turned to nightmares, for their packed venues were spatially and affectively ideal for a rapid-fire rampage to lay waste to song and happiness. Alas, the tempting targetability of musical events is itself a brutal confirmation of music's good. In a modern age of semiautomatics, bumper stocks, and homebrewed bombs, terrorists stalk musical celebrations. Or rather, terrorists will stalk any place with lots of people where music might happen to play.

In the wake of terrorist attacks these days, mourners find solace by sharing this quotation by Leonard Bernstein.

> This will be our reply to violence: to make music more intensely, more beautifully, more devotedly than ever before.[122]

Bernstein made these remarks in response to news of John F. Kennedy's assassination in 1963. Touting musical beauty as societal salve, his uplifting words nevertheless rub some people today the wrong way. "This sentence is always, *always*, **ALWAYS** piously posted by musician friends after violent incidents," writes musicologist Jonathan Bellman with typographical crescendo. "As I've said many times before, I hate it; it always struck me as a musician's facile justification (and who better to reflect validity than the protean pianist, composer, conductor, scholar, and teacher Lenny?) for not canceling or rescheduling a gig."[123] Granted, not canceling or rescheduling a gig is the point. Bernstein's words resonate with the urge for beautiful mundanity whenever terror strikes. *Go about business as usual, live your life, attend concerts, do what you love, do what you ordinarily do*, leaders advise. *Otherwise, the terrorists win.* Such exhortations frame disruption as concession, normalcy as quiet victory. And musical beauty—as a sonic and symbolic testament to a populace's refusal to be silenced—can certainly play an important role in agendas of healing, restoration, and justice.

Beauty and justice, after all, have a mutual synonym in *fairness*, which connotes symmetry, balance, and equality. Yet literature, film, and pop culture have long highlighted rifts between aesthetes and activists—dewy-eyed stargazers versus steely-eyed advocates, flighty daydreamers versus boots-on-the-ground agents. Some writers object to these dichotomies. It is too commonly assumed, the literary scholar Elaine Scarry remarks, that "beauty, by preoccupying our attention, distracts attention from wrong social arrangements."[124] In her 1999 book *On Beauty and Being Just*, Scarry refutes this assumption by arguing that "far from damaging our capacity to attend to problems of injustice, [beauty] instead intensifies the pressure we feel to repair existing injuries."[125] How does beauty motivate such good will? Scarry hypothesizes that encountering a beautiful object can snap someone out of self-absorption, "radically decentering" our ego so that "we cease to stand even at the center of our own world."[126] For Scarry, beauty can move beholders to think beyond themselves and to care about others. Invoking caves, blossoms, paintings, and songs, Scarry's treatise zips along with exhilarating confidence in beauty as an analogue, instrument, and impetus for justice.[127] Like Leonard Bernstein, and like Lin-Manuel Miranda (recall, from Chapter 1, the final lines of his sonnet at the Tony Awards—"Now fill the world with music, love, and pride"—in response to the Pulse nightclub massacre), Scarry longs for "more and more" beautiful things to pop up around the world.[128] She even surmises that a beautiful object "prompts a copy of itself," in the way "it makes us draw it, take photographs of it, or describe it to other people."[129] With human stewardship, beauty begets beauty.

Geoffrey Galt Harpham, the former President of the National Humanities Center, has called Scarry's *On Beauty and Being Just* a "defiantly 'naïve' treatise," an exercise in theoretical flight. "Reading Scarry as she negotiates a difficult passage, as between beauty and justice, or wounding and creation, one often feels as if one is watching a sleepwalker," he writes. "Her admirers are those who do not want her to wake up."[130] I feel this tension outlined by Harpham. Part of me wants to believe in Scarry's radically hopeful words, in a version of our world in which the words ring true. But I don't always feel hopeful when I hear loving recommendations to fill the world with ever more beauty. Not when beauty, no matter how one defines it, is a thing of value. Not when beauty is therefore *a* good that's susceptible to theft, baiting, suppression, and weaponization. Mere calls for "more and more" beauty—by art lovers, Broadway stars, grieving survivors—do sound beautiful, yet remain fragile.

Coda: All the Beauty in the World

L'Enfant Plaza, a final trek.

Recall how Gene Weingarten kept Bell and Bach as aces in his pocket. He implied that if people wouldn't stop for such superlative music, then they must be blowing off beauty in all kinds of other ways. Beyond the elitist gimmick of Weingarten's musical choices, however, the experiment leaned subtly on a false corollary: that commuters who sweep past a street musician necessarily do so at the expense of savoring something beautiful—in brief, that these commuters, as cogs in the capitalist machine, live to work. A reality elided here is how people rush to work so they may earn a means to live, if by *live* we mean sustaining a good life for oneself and for loved ones. For some, there can be beauty in seeing a partner's beaming face upon hurrying home after work, even if it means regrettably skipping past a busker on the way. Or there can be beauty in hearing your kids talk about their school day while they munch on the food you've obtained with your consistent wage (which could require not being penalized or fired for tardiness). And even if you appear like someone who has outwardly let go of a chance to pause for a street musician, you might have felt inwardly gratified by the ephemeral encounter anyway, cherishing the private echoes of the brief musical episode well into the night. You might be someone who gets moved to tears by a majestic double rainbow or a plastic bag dancing in the wind, or maybe by a stranger's courtesy or an avian chorus or autumn's last leaves or all of the lovable things that don't come preauthorized on pedestals.

Has our world ever lacked either beauty or people who are willing to find, create, and appreciate beauty on their own terms?

Bewailing a dearth of beautiful objects or attentive beholders is an easy road, so it is the one frequently traveled by aesthetes who are understandably eager to share their love and expertise. But ecological models of scarcity and surplus can't be facilely transplanted onto concerns of art and beauty. Yes, we can always stand to watch and listen for beautiful objects, ideas, and moments. We should support artists and arts initiatives. Blanket claims about beauty's endangerment, however, are red herrings. Individually, people seek beautiful materials, memories, and companions in their own ways, at their own pace, and for manifold reasons. What's actually in short supply—what lies at the root of so much injury and injustice—is people's limited capacity or willingness to understand, tolerate, and dignify the different things that *other people* find beautiful. Think of all the strife that erupts when society's inhabitants fail to empathize or put up with one another's tastes and interests. It can be as innocuous as friends' late-night quarrels about favorite bands, fashions, cuisines, or video games. Or it can spiral into grave entanglements when persecution, oppression, and hate crimes break out from people's inability or disinclination to see beauty and humanity in this skin color or that sexual orientation, in this gender identity or that visible disability, in this god or that philosophy. Our purpose can't simply be to rake in ever more aesthetic delights for our personal consumption, or to stock up on beauty's quantities through capitalist models of expansion and production. A deeper purpose would start by recognizing the plurality of beauty and its patrons. It's good to share with other people the beautiful things we love. It's dangerous to assume that anyone's failure to value a particular item or standard of beauty is a sign of intellectual or moral deficit.

During a 2012 conference at Princeton University, musicologist Karol Berger presented a paper that caused a stir. A *New York Times* reporter in attendance, James Oestreich, perceived enough tension in the room "that a mere spark could have caused a conflagration."[131] In this presentation, later published as a short article, Berger urged his colleagues to serve as rigorous gatekeepers and curators of the musical canon. He recommended that colleagues "discriminate wisely" between "successful instances of a [musical] practice from the less successful ones," and warned that "if we do not recover and exercise our capacity for judgment, we shall suffocate under the mountains of trash that, worse than carbon dioxide, pollute our cultural environment."[132] In other words, Berger was asking people to judiciously safeguard the artworks that he deemed most worthy of attention, performance, and inquiry. Like Weingarten, he was apprehensive about our current state of musical appreciation. He even feared that abstaining from loaded words such as "masterpiece" and "trash" can send us down an anything-goes path of aesthetic relativism. Upon hearing and reading Berger's arguments, various scholars felt as if they (and the non-canonic music they devotedly study and love) were facing a direct attack by this call for the redoubled establishment of repertorial hierarchies. I understand where Berger is coming from, as he fears the dilution or outright extinction of the classical music he loves. I also sympathize with his critics, given Berger's apocalyptic language. "We are drowning in the flood of ever new products of what, whether you like Theodor Adorno or not, can only be called the music entertainment industry," Berger cautions.[133]

It's unlikely that embracing distinctions between people's tastes for art will cause the world (tomorrow, or in ten years, or even a thousand) to be stripped of beautiful sculptures and symphonies. If, in a thousand years, the world does in fact end, it will likely have been the result of rising sea levels, environmental calamity, nuclear war, imperialist hubris, and other catastrophes that we, through love and tolerance of one another, may have had the sole power to forestall. Our world isn't short on beautiful things to love. It's short on human acceptance of what others find beautiful and what others happen to love. Yes, trying to love others, and trying to love what others love, opens oneself up to the risks of rejection, heartbreak, and harm.[134] People are entitled to draw lines in the sand. If a white nationalist claims to find beauty in racial purity, I have no obligation to empathize with that view. If I feel safe enough to do so, I might carry on a conversation with this person to test whether our divide can be bridged. But just as someone's right to swing a fist stops at your face, so your duty to test someone else's worldviews or notions of beauty ceases at the point you reasonably feel targeted or unsafe. Power relations are key: perhaps the greater one's privilege—whether based in class, race, gender, or ability—the greater the responsibility to explore aesthetic values and standards outside one's comfort zone. If you have considerable financial means, disposable time, professional wherewithal, and social capital, then you can better afford to take these risks.

To end, here's a caveat. As with the universality of *we are all musical*, a sweeping claim about how *there's beauty everywhere* poses a danger. It can be embezzled by the privileged and hoarded as an excuse to shirk interpersonal responsibilities via the twisted justification of *well, if all people—even, say, poor people and refugees and minorities—have beauty in their respective lives, then obviously their situations can't be all that bad.* In any effort to connect beauty with justice, beauty runs the risk of being appropriated anew as moral ablution. Watch the slaves sing. Hear the homeless man play the piano. See noble savages dance. Admire the crafts and games and colorful garb of resilient children in Flint, Michigan laughing and living against the odds. Or, as Donald Trump Jr. marveled when reflecting on his 2018 visit to India: "You can see the poorest of the poor, and there is still a smile on a face."[135] True, poor and persecuted people may well have music and beauty and love in their lives, and they might say so if you asked them. Yet the private treasures of the oppressed don't exist for oppressors to plunder and to curate as yet another means to cleanse guilt and responsibility. Perils, then, do accompany

any effort to expand our criteria for what qualifies as beautiful. The danger is not, as Karol Berger proposed, that such expansion will lead us to drown in the aesthetic trash heaps of tomorrow. Rather, the danger is that aesthetics will become a false placeholder for ethics once more.

Music studies is a kind of ability studies. When we teach music history, theory, culture, politics, and criticism, we are usually teaching the achievements, aspirations, material contributions, and powerful performances of bodies, voices, and identities in full swing.[136] Even if, as instructors, we avoid diagnostic vocabularies of "masterpiece" or "trash," our pedagogical objects of interest are bound up in glowing implications of merit and aptitude: scores, recordings, viral videos, and anything else that is by definition exemplary as a result of being teachable examples.

The musical mystique has a faithful partner in crime, and its name is meritocracy. In debates about what music is good and what good music can do, the specter of merit is ever present. A popular enabler of musical meritocracy is the blind audition, which ostensibly tasks listeners with the adjudication of music by sound alone, with the performer's body and identity hidden from view. Joshua Bell's busking experiment was itself similar to such an audition, given how this famous violinist purposefully hid his face under a baseball cap. (As it happened, only one commuter, a woman named Stacy Furukawa, recognized him—and it was because she had seen him in concert just three weeks earlier.)

Myths of meritocracy enable presumptions of blind auditions as superlatively fair and obviously good.

Sometimes, neither presumption is true.

3

Moral Masquerades

Because the word [blind] bears such a burden of negative connotations and dreaded associations, it can hardly be said to have any neutral, merely descriptive meaning. *Blind* means darkness, dependence, destitution, despair. *Blind* means the beggar in the subway station. Look at him slouching there, unkempt, head bowed, stationary among the rushing crowd. Intermittently, an involuntary twitch jerks his arm upward, making the coin or two in his cup clink. Otherwise he is silent, apparently speechless.

—Georgina Kleege, author[1]

The Soles of Women Folk

Double-blind peer reviews in academia. Need-blind college admissions. Blind grading of students' homework. Blind wine tastings. Blind scorings of fashion, food, and singing on *Project Runway, Beat Bobby Flay*, and *The Voice* respectively. Colorblind castings for screen and stage. And classically, blind auditions for symphony orchestras.[2] Presiding over these institutions and procedures are expert adjudicators who proudly claim their desire and ability to look past skin color, sex, disability, and any other traits ostensibly legible through appearance. Judging blind is hailed as an obvious virtue: judicious like seer Tiresias, vigilant like crimefighter Daredevil, wise like poets Homer, Virgil, and Milton.

A note on terminology. Although some writers insist we can differentiate between "ableist" and "benign" metaphors of disability—say, the insult "blind as a bat" versus the ideal "justice is blind"—the word "blind" in phrases such as "blind review" and "blind audition" nonetheless associates blindness with lack of knowledge. Even if this lack of knowledge (lack of knowing an author's or auditionee's gender, for example) is ultimately meant to facilitate impartial judgment, the implication of informational dearth perpetuates, as philosopher Shelley Tremain remarks, the "ocular ableist metaphors" in a long history of "association between sight and knowledge in the Eurocentric philosophical tradition."[3] To be sure, debates about metaphors of disability are complicated and ongoing. For my own writing—when it comes to the subject of music auditions and peer reviews—I will choose, going forward, to substitute "blind audition" with "anonymous audition" for two reasons. First, because I wish to counter people's rhetorical tendencies to equate blindness with ignorance (regardless of whether this ignorance is deemed a net virtue). Second, because "anonymous" is more precise anyway, emphasizing the concealment of the performer's identity rather than the direct obstruction of juries' sensory faculties.

Anonymous orchestra auditions are fascinating. They purportedly allow juries to evaluate a candidate's musical proficiency on its own merits. Describing the rigorous auditions for the Boston Symphony Orchestra, journalist Geoff Edgers writes:

> Take the level of competition and scrutiny at a pro football tryout. Add a shield of secrecy rivaling Yale's Skull and Bones society. Then, to complete the drama, throw in the screen. It is a brown-polyester 33-foot-long barrier that slices the Symphony Hall stage in half. On one side sit 10 of the BSO's players, waiting to vote on sheets of paper. On the other sit the hopefuls, who trudge on and off the stage, one by one [. . .]. Everything in this audition process, from the secret ballots to the eight-hour stretches of Shostakovich excerpts, is driven by a puritanical fervor for a single, guiding principle. All that matters is the music.[4]

Until circa 1980, women made up no more than 12% of the musicians in many of the top-ranked US symphony orchestras, including the so-called Big Five: Boston Symphony Orchestra, New York Philharmonic, Chicago Symphony Orchestra, Philadelphia Orchestra, and Cleveland Orchestra.[5] Several music directors back then openly declared that women simply were not capable musicians, citing their "smaller techniques," low breath capacity, "temperamental" attitudes, demands for special treatment, and predisposition toward pregnancy.[6] In efforts to tamp down the mounting accusations of sexism and discrimination, orchestras began to adopt anonymous auditions in the 1970s. Women's numbers in orchestras surged. In 2000, a lengthy study published in the *American Economic Review* by Claudia Goldin and Cecilia Rouse concluded that the use of a screen during orchestra auditions increased

by 50% "the probability that a woman will be advanced from certain preliminary rounds."[7] But what comes after the preliminaries? Almost certainly, a
degree of deanonymization. With the Pittsburgh Symphony Orchestra, for
example, "the screen is removed for the semifinal and final rounds so that
committee members can observe musicians' technique—their fingering or
the way they grip the bow."[8] Implementing anonymous auditions for just
one round among multiple rounds, however, is a bit like patching up just one
leak in a ship riddled with holes. Each hole represents an opportunity for
potential prejudice to seep in. A single patch can slow the sink. But we might
wonder: why not apply the fixes all the way around?[9]

Anonymous orchestra auditions are not leakproof, anyway. Some jury
members say they can discern a performer's sex through the audible tells of
breath intake. And juries as a whole have underhanded, cronyistic ways of
gleaning the identities of candidates. It could be as simple as obtaining an il-
licit glimpse of the roster, or as insidious as having the accompanist send covert signals (coughs, chords) about a candidate's gender during an audition.[10]
With or without the explicit intention to cheat, moreover, jury members
might well recognize the playing styles of their own students.

Peeks, leaks, and nepotism aside, an anonymous audition can be ethically
fraught even if it could be technically enforced to perfection. Consider the
carpets that are sometimes rolled out to dampen the sounds of candidates'
footsteps during orchestra auditions—a workaround to prevent shoes (heels)
from betraying a candidate's gender. If appropriate carpets are not available,
a personnel manager can ask a female auditionee to take off her shoes; the
(male) manager might then walk alongside her to the stage to provide the
"compensating footsteps" so that her gender identity is not telegraphed by an
absence of ambulatory noise.[11] It's like a real-life case of "Mickey-Mousing"
(the mimetic syncing of onscreen action with musical accompaniment; imagine Mickey falling down the stairs to the sound of a staccato descending
scale). A cartoon analogy isn't even that outlandish here, given how these
anonymous orchestra auditions go to such comical lengths to bring bodies
under erasure, all in order to adjudicate them purely as vessels of musical
production. Women in particular are the ones who must sometimes literally tiptoe to their marks. Now imagine if a woman, during anonymous
auditions, declined to remove her shoes despite a stage manager's advice that
doing so would be for her own good. Imagine she found the charade a little
ridiculous and thus chose to risk being identified by her footfalls, and then
ended up, for whatever undisclosed reason, failing to advance to the next

round of auditions. Could she claim sexism or discrimination? Or could someone fire back with the familiar victim-blaming retort: *well, what (shoes) was she wearing?*

Polyester screens, carpet runners, and gendered footwear constitute an impressive theater of ethical levers and pulleys, a system of checks and balances to rule out foul play. From a distance, it looks fair. Get closer, and the sheer abundance of labor, apparatus, and procedural pizzazz might start to appear excessive.

Medical researchers today uphold "double-blind," placebo-controlled clinical trials as a gold standard. Key advantages include the elimination of bias and influence among all parties, even if the ethics of randomization itself—the ethics of conducting a trial in which, say, researchers know that half of their cancer patients (determined by computer algorithms or lottery) will receive a placebo—remains hotly contested.[12] Outside scientific and medical experiments, and upon entering the subjective realms of artistic evaluation, our metrics and morals become even murkier.[13] Although anonymous orchestra auditions, for instance, pose as meritocratic procedures that guarantee impartial judgment, they can counterproductively suppress conversations about *why* anonymizing operations are needed to begin with. Accused of discriminating against black violinists or female percussionists? Just throw up a screen and purport to listen solely for merit by cutting all human variables out of the equation. By nobly claiming to judge people on musical ability alone, by dehumanizing them for all intents and purposes, we defer obligations to talk about trickier matters of humanity and prejudice.

An anonymous review is a glorified Band-Aid for prejudice. It's good as a stopgap measure. But the wounds of systemic discrimination can fester if left untended. We like to think that looking past identity means we've done right by other people. Such imaginative fictions let us off the hook. Lest we congratulate ourselves too eagerly for endorsing anonymous auditions, maybe we should begin by admitting that they aren't so much a first response as a last resort—the least worst option in a world where biases prevail.

For how much do we trust justice to be blind anyway? Representations of Lady Justice commonly emphasize her impartiality with a bandage covering her eyes (Figure 3.1).[14] If Justice herself is blind, however, then why does she wear a blindfold? Does Justice, capable of sight, not trust herself to keep her eyes closed? Do those who are judged by her insist on the blindfold as insurance, the way that, in games of Hide and Seek, the Seekers are redundantly asked to close their eyes, cover their faces with hands, and even

Figure 3.1. Portrayals of Lady Justice in (*left*) Hans Gieng's statue on the Gerechtigkeitsbrunnen in Bern and (*right*) opening credits of Marvel's *Daredevil* series.

turn toward a tree while counting down, thereby enacting multiple failsafes? Such redundancy can be at once reassuring and suspicious. As *Boston Globe* columnist Jeff Jacoby points out, the oath sworn by US federal judges builds a veritable triad of assertions about "blind justice" and judicial dispassion, italicized here: "[I] do solemnly swear (or affirm) that I will administer justice *without respect to persons*, and do *equal right* to the poor and to the rich, and that I will faithfully and *impartially* discharge and perform all the duties incumbent upon me."[15] This threefold assertion may bring to mind the more well-known testimony of court witnesses who are asked to tell "the truth, the whole truth, and nothing but the truth."[16] In these juridical cases, the multi-promissory ritual raises the question of how absolute values of impartiality and truthfulness are supposed to benefit from repetition or attempted clarification. After all, under most circumstances, saying *I swear!* ten times hardly makes the speaker sound more trustworthy than saying it once.

Concerning Lady Justice's blindfold, disability scholar Georgina Kleege writes: "True, it's difficult to depict blindness in painting or sculpture without representing some unsightly deformity, unless the blindfold is actually a bandage hiding a gruesome wound. But it seems more likely that [Justice] has willingly renounced sight. She makes herself blind to extenuating circumstances. Presumably when Justice is off duty she can see."[17] Presumably. Yet we humans are the ones who created the mythical figure of Justice, and we could have chosen to anoint her as a flawless personification. We could have said, *Here's Lady Justice: she has promised to keep her eyes closed* or *Here's Lady Justice: her eyes are wide open, but she—a PERFECT BEING—has assured us of her impartiality*. Lady Justice's blindfold, it turns out, isn't about Lady Justice at all. It's about us. Is our own belief in the *ideal of impartiality* so shaky that we, the people, cannot bring ourselves to trust the mere sight of a sighted Justice? Lady Justice is, in a sense, the patron saint of anonymous auditions. She judges by audition, by listening. So the fact that we've made her wear a blindfold, if only to reassure ourselves of her fairness, should tell us something about humans' unrealistic expectations of blind justice writ large.

Relying on adjudicatory blindfolds can render us both complacent with and complicit in the unjust relationships, policies, and institutions that make demands for anonymous auditions in the first place. Put performers behind screens too habitually and we might forget why we need to do so. Preach too zealously the virtues of meritocracy and we could stumble into the traps of post-racial and colorblind fantasies. In this chapter, I map out the perks and pitfalls of anonymous auditions undertaken in the name of loving music and preserving fairness. I focus on the preeminent Vienna Philharmonic Orchestra (VPO) rather than on domestic US orchestras because the former, with its nearly all-white-male membership, has drawn intense criticism in the past two decades; pertinently, much of this criticism of the VPO has come *from* Americans rallying under third-wave feminist banners of gender equality, representation, and intersectionality. I am interested in how people rationalize, practice, and boast about the morality and exigency of anonymous judgments. By the end, I will propose a couple of alternatives to anonymization. Far from magic cure-alls, my proposals task us with small steps toward a future in which elaborate masquerades of impartiality are neither uncritically performed nor desperately needed.

Meritocracy—Power Ballad or Siren Song?

> If you work hard, if you get educated, if you're an honest person, you can make it in America.
> —Bill O'Reilly, former Fox News pundit[18]

> If you're willing to work hard, it doesn't matter who you are, or where you come from, or what you look like, or where [sic] you love. [. . .] You can make it here in America if you're willing to try.
>
> —Barack Obama, former US president[19]

On a 2014 episode of *The Daily Show with Jon Stewart*, conservative guest Bill O'Reilly attempted to convince liberal host Jon Stewart that white privilege no longer exists in the United States. As long as black people work hard, O'Reilly explained, they can succeed in this country. A left-leaning studio audience laughed and groaned at O'Reilly throughout his statements (Figure 3.2).

A couple of years before, Barack Obama had delivered his re-election victory speech, driving home values of diversity, persistence, and resilience. Each emphatic sentence won applause. O'Reilly and Obama: diametric fanbases, nearly interchangeable rhetorics. (Obama's speech included the confusing phrase "or where you love," perhaps a misspoken mashup of "or whom you love" and "or where you live." Individually, both made sense; a shout-out to "love" in particular would have served to remind people that Obama had come out in favor of same-sex marriage in 2012, and was the first sitting president ever to do so.) Mentions of love aside, Obama's and O'Reilly's spiels were the same.

Meritocracy is a power ballad of capitalism and neoliberalism. It emphasizes individual achievement and perseverance. We know the catchy lyrics of the American Dream by heart: do good work, aim high, and rise. As a national anthem, meritocracy is an earworm that loops nonstop during election season and its hope-laced campaigns for upward mobility.[20] Although, as far as *-ocracies* go, meritocracy isn't an official form of government (Singapore and its People's Action Party come close), it obliquely poses as *the* rule of governance in sectors of employment, education, and industry.[21] Just think of all the naturalist metaphors (biology, agriculture, physics) pervading the karmic slogans of meritocracy: survival of the fittest, the cream rises to the top, what goes around comes around, you reap what you sow, the weak gets weeded out, and the sky is the limit. In these popular

Figure 3.2. O'Reilly delivering the blow-by-blow bromides of the American Dream to Jon Stewart, who responds by performing dramatic poses that swing between the extremes of shock (*left*) and boredom (*right*) in quick succession.

sayings, images of heaven and earth depict meritocracy to be as incontro-vertible as the laws of matter and energy.[22] In short, the merits *of* meritoc-racy sound nearly self-evident. For its fervent proponents across US political parties, meritocracy is just, and it just is.

A common critique of meritocracy pegs it as a craven and bullish ideology favoring the already privileged—a retroactive, top-down justification of hier-archical status quo. Sociologists Stephen J. McNamee and Robert K. Miller Jr. call meritocracy a myth that belies social inequalities arising from genetics, inherited wealth, nepotism, and sheer luck. "The tenets of the American Dream comprise an ideology of inequality," they write. "For a system of inequality to be stable over the long run, those who have more must con-vince those who have less that the distribution of who gets what is fair, just, proper, or the natural order of things. The greater the level of inequality, the more compelling and persuasive these explanations must appear to be."[23] Psychologists would classify these explanations under System Justification Theory, which proposes that "individuals are motivated to justify and ra-tionalize existing social arrangements, defending and bolstering the status quo simply because it exists."[24] Motivations to defend the status quo are that much stronger if you're personally benefiting from its arrangements.

But American Dreams turn into nightmares if you find yourself on life's losing end. A dangerous corollary of rags-to-riches fantasies is that if you don't succeed, you must have only yourself to blame—an ugly turn that's es-pecially harmful when it comes to the underprivileged.[25] "Positive thinking has made itself useful as an apology for the crueler aspects of the market economy," warns activist Barbara Ehrenreich. "If optimism is the key to ma-terial success, and if you can achieve an optimistic outlook through the disci-pline of positive thinking, then there is no excuse for failure."[26] Meritocratic principles fall apart when they square off against the grim realities of dis-crimination, nepotism, and plain bad luck. Platitudes about American Dreams meet their match in platitudes about fickle fates: life's not fair, that's the way the cookie crumbles, shit happens, *c'est la vie, que sera sera*, it is what it is, and tautologies galore.[27] Among the tricks of meritocracy is how the individuals who face the most systemic discrimination and disenfranchise-ment (say, owing to skin color or gender expression) are often the ones most staunchly advised to keep their heads down, pump up the effort, and pull ahead by extra labor alone . . . in other words, to double down on one's faith in meritocracy even when this faith has failed to pay off.[28] It's like telling someone without boots to pull themselves up by their bootstraps, or goading a depressed person to cheer up, or asking an exhausted, broke, worn-down person whether they've tried trying harder.

Despite public familiarity with the ideals and mottos of meritocracy, a lesser-known fact is that the word originated from satire. Michael Young (1915–2002), a sociologist and politician, came up with the neologism for his 1958 book *The Rise of the Meritocracy*, which portrayed a dystopian British government adamant about stratifying society through extensive tests of intelligence and vocational aptitude.[29] In 2001, a year before his death, Young lamented in a letter to *The Guardian*: "I have been sadly disappointed by [. . .] *The Rise of the Meritocracy*. I coined a word which has gone into general circulation, especially in the United States and most recently found a prominent place in the speeches of Mr. [Tony] Blair. The book was a satire meant to be a warning [. . .]. If meritocrats believe, as more and more of them are encouraged to, that their advancement comes from their own merits, they can feel they deserve whatever they can get."[30] Young realized only belatedly that his creation had slipped out of his control; how poetic that true believers saw legitimate merit in meritocracy and, as such, co-opted the criteria of self-evident meritability to strip meritocracy of its subversive genesis.

To understand how a lexical joke could have taken such a serious turn, we need to grasp the sheer power of meritocracy to pass as downright commonsensical. "Meritocracy may rightly deserve condemnation," declares economist Amartya Sen, "but to define it in such thoroughly revolting terms makes it hard to understand how it can appeal to anyone and why it may have an expanding role in modern society."[31] Put differently, it's not helpful for critics of meritocracy to scoff at how anyone could possibly believe its lies, just as it's not helpful for critics of the musical mystique to insist people should just know better by now. Meritocracy, like the musical mystique, is an alluring song. It's *easy* to believe. Pretending that meritocracy's lies are obvious doesn't make them any less seductive.

In his 2016 book *Success and Luck: Good Fortune and the Myth of Meritocracy*, economist Robert H. Frank documented the common ways in which super-wealthy individuals, when recounting their paths to success, underestimate the role of luck and instead fixate on merit, effort, and grit.[32] But when it comes to meritocracy's myths, placing blame solely on "the 1%" isn't enough, especially if such blame distracts from the accountabilities of society's top 10% earners, or top 20%, or households that lead relatively comfortable existences.[33] Over hundreds of interviews with blue-collar workers across the United States and across France, sociologist Michèle Lamont has shown how some middle-lower-class laborers lean on meritocratic logic to draw distinctions between themselves and the poor(er).[34] Meritocratic beliefs, then, seem to facilitate stratification and inhibit solidarity at every income bracket. In the end, matter-of-factly exclaiming that meritocracy is a myth—that people don't always deserve what they get, and can't always get what they deserve—won't ensure an instant change of heart in anyone. People who buy the myth and people who reject it don't belong to discrete, unmalleable sets. We are each at risk of becoming fair-weather friends to our own psyches: when life is good, we claim credit to affirm self-worth; when life goes south, we curse bad luck or other people.

Frequent surveys of Americans' changing attitudes toward the American Dream should be taken with many grains of salt. Results are inevitably clouded by skewed samples, selective reporting, and variability in questions and terminologies.[35] Sometimes, faith in the Dream is reportedly strong. Other times, faith dwindles, owing to financial downturns, income disparities, gender wage gaps, and the pendular partisanship of election cycles. Money troubles aside, however, maybe we realize that the very terms of meritocracy can ask us to give up too much of what we hold dear. Hear again President Obama's rousing victory speech from 2012: "If you're willing to work hard, it doesn't matter who you are, or where you come from, or what you look like, or where you love . . . you can make it here in America if you're willing to try." Yet what if all of these *whos* and *wheres* and *whats* do matter to you? Some of us spend lifetimes sorting out who we are, learning where we've come from, coming to terms with what we look like, and seeking love and a place to call home. Aren't these the things that feel *most* real? If so, what kinds of work ethic and subjunctive rhetoric would demand that we even imagine redacting ourselves, piece by piece, all for the sake of . . . what? Wealth? Prestige? Bare survival?

As long as you / it doesn't matter who / you can: the rote syntax is meritocracy's Mad Libs, a can't-go-wrong template used roundly by yea-sayers such as Democratic presidents, Fox News pundits, robust pastors, and the incomparably wise moms and dads of after-school specials. Meritocracy's currency is hope. But we cannot presume the dream is free for all. The cost? *People*, plural. I mean the shades of humanity that make literally all the difference in the world.[36] Across party lines, the vocabularies for meritocracy urge willful and selective "blindness" toward nonessential aspects of identity.[37] What do we consider nonessential? Is putting tape over this or that part of a person the optimal way to go about life? Do meritocracy and anonymous evaluations do enough to counter discrimination?

Consider again the metaphor of blindness in phrases such as "blind audition" and "blind review," along with other adjectives derived from disability and illness (*deaf, crippled, lame, barren, cancerous*). Feminist theorist Naomi Schor, with reference to Susan Sontag's *Illness as Metaphor*, describes how there can be "a casual cruelty, an offhanded thoughtlessness, about metaphors of illness."[38] A likewise callous rhetoric permeates "metaphors of disablement and disfigurement," which "void words of their charge of pain and sorrow, dread and death, and invest them with the language of stigma and shame and burden them with negativity."[39] In a critique of ableist metaphors, Vivian May and Beth Ferri likewise argue that an "over-reliance on stale modes of address reifies disability as a problem," resulting in epistemic "sedimentation" that stalls anti-prejudicial agendas.[40] "Blind," however, is curious because it often operates not only spitefully (*blind as a bat*) and accusatorily (*you must be blind*) but also sentimentally (*love is blind*) and self-congratulatorily (*need-blind admissions*). Such dual significations affirm how sight itself is a faculty that wavers between connotations of power and the corruptions thereof. In societies that discourage people from staring at one another, notes Rosemarie Garland-Thomson, "vision is celebrated *and* scorned, pronounced to be manipulative, liberating, rapacious, pornographic, gendered, or dominating."[41] Although a term such as "retard" is met these days with gasps of outrage, the metaphor of "blind" has become prosaic.[42] Here, then, lies the hypocrisy: metaphors of blindness derive their legibility and utility from the stigmatization of blindness as an *abject* and *permanent* condition, but sighted individuals who participate in "blind reviews" or "blind auditions" do so as a *magnanimous* and *temporary* choice.[43] Upon the completion of such meritocratic evaluations, sighted jury members presumably return to business as usual, "blind" no more.

An anonymous audition gives judges a preemptive moral high ground. It is also an insurance plan. In the event an auditionee makes accusations of sexism or racism, the sound-porous screen suddenly becomes bulletproof glass, shielding judges from any collateral blame or lawsuits that might later fly their way. A blunter way to bat away accusations of prejudice is, of course, simply to state that you're not a sexist or a homophobe or a bigot. An employer who has an all-white workplace could declare that they are virtuously meritocratic, and that they are, in fact, so non-racist that they don't really see race at all, or see the need to keep talking about race. It's not an uncommon claim. "Colorblindness," as post-racial fantasy, is on the rise, often uttered in the same breath as the American Dream.

Colorblind and Loving It

Zac: Man, there were so many incredible, super-diverse movies last year [. . .] like *Moonlight, Lion, Hidden Figures*, and *Fences*.

Katie: So interesting. I never really thought about that. [. . .] Call me crazy, but I just don't see race. I guess I'm just the least racist person here. [. . .] This is going to sound nuts, but I don't see gender and I don't see sex. I just see people.

Grant: You don't see how men and women look different?

Katie: No, I just see, like, shapeless blobs walking around. [. . .] I just am so committed to equality. I'm just a good person.

Zac: Unless you're blind, you can tell that people have inherent differences.

Katie: Oh, I wouldn't know if I was blind or not. Because I don't see disabilities. I'm not a monster.

Mike: So if someone were in a wheelchair, you wouldn't be able to see the wheelchair?

Katie [hesitantly]: I have never seen a wheelchair.
                    —"I Don't See Race," *College Humor* skit[44]

It doesn't end well for Katie. After she boasts about how she doesn't even "see age," her friend Mike tries to stump her. "You have two older brothers," he declares. "Can you at least acknowledge that?" Without missing a beat, Katie replies: "Yes. And I believe both women are my same age." Exasperated, Mike finally asks: "Katie, why are you doing this?" Katie narrows her eyes and shoots agitated glances at each of her companions, then cracks under their icy stares: "Guys, come on! Okay? I just want to be able to do and say whatever I want, whenever I want, and I don't want to have to think about the world's problems!"[45]

An understanding of anonymous evaluations' failings can draw insight from critiques of colorblind ideology and its masquerades of false

egalitarianism. In his oft-quoted dissent to the 1896 Supreme Court decision in Plessy v. Ferguson, Justice John Marshall Harlan declared, "Our
Constitution is color-blind and neither knows nor tolerates classes among citizens."[46] Ever peculiar is how colorblindness has since been touted by people
who sit on seemingly opposite sides of arguments over civil rights, segregation, and affirmative action. Colorblindness is a discursive chameleon whose
versatility has allowed it to infiltrate every nook and cranny of social dialogue. Especially since the 2008 election of Barack Obama, American dreams
of "post-racial liberalism," "racial transcendence," and "colorblind universalism" have whitewashed the urgent realities of a color-bound society.[47] In
bids for enlightened facades, people who say they don't see race often confuse averred colorblindness with active anti-racism. In 2016, the director
Steven Spielberg, when asked for his opinions about the #OscarsSoWhite
controversy, replied: "Look, I have two black children, you know? I've been
colorblind my entire life. [. . .] When you just look at the films I've made,
and look at the people who've worked on those films—look at the diversity
within the crew, within the cast—I've always [had it]."[48] Spielberg also cited
the 2014 Academy Awards won by Lupita Nyong'o (Best Supporting Actress)
and 12 Years a Slave (Best Picture, Best Adapted Screenplay) as proof that
there isn't "inherent or dormant racism" simply by virtue "of the amount
[over 90% in 2016] of white Academy members."[49] Spielberg's words glisten
with unobjectionable veneer; absolutely, let's celebrate black awardees. But
the unobjectionability itself becomes a gesture of misdirection, pointing to
the shining star of Nyong'o to halt—rather than to advance—a conversation
about race. In the past decade, the most vindicatory of shining stars has been
Obama himself, whose own speeches and books have repeatedly embraced
the audacity of "colorblind" hope.[50]

Like anonymous orchestra auditions, the colorblind castings in
Hollywood, Broadway, and opera stumble into meritocracy's moral snares.[51]
So that we don't assume only old white male directors prematurely pat themselves on the back for colorblind ideals, listen to these empowered words by
Shonda Rhimes, who has created several television shows featuring black
female leads: "My friends and I don't sit around and discuss race. We're
post-civil rights, post-feminist babies, and we take it for granted we live in a
diverse world."[52] Yet far from accelerating toward "acceptance or progress,"
points out writer Angelica Jade Bastién, colorblind casting may "just as easily
be erasure wrapped up in benevolence."[53] Colorblind castings in plays and
musical theater are no less complicated. We can trace back the debates year

by year. In 2017, the estate of playwright Edward Albee denied permissions to an Oregon production of *Who's Afraid of Virginia Woolf?* because its director wished to cast a black actor in the role of Nick, a white character whose blonde hair and blue eyes are explicitly commented on in the play.[54] In 2016, controversy broke out when a Chicago production of Lin-Manuel Miranda's musical *In the Heights* cast a white man in the role of protagonist Usnavi, a character born in the Dominican Republic.[55] In 2015, the Metropolitan Opera announced it would stop using blackface for its performances of Giuseppe Verdi's *Otello*: "Although the central character in *Otello* is a Moor from North Africa, the Met is committed to color-blind casting, which allows the best singers possible to perform any role, regardless of their racial background."[56] Recent critics of colorblind casting have advocated for "color-conscious" casting—that is, casting strategies that remain mindful of how performers' color, race, and ethnicity can productively, even provocatively, recontextualize and refresh the script or libretto at hand.[57]

Away from the bright marquees of screen and stage, the alibis of colorblindness can prove deadly in courts, prisons, and systems of criminal justice. As Michelle Alexander insists in her 2010 book *The New Jim Crow*, the "officially colorblind" policies of mass incarceration, along with the seemingly inarguable goods of "law and order," mask the ways in which societal enforcements of apprehension, conviction, and imprisonment "function much like a racial caste system."[58] As a result, continues Alexander:

> It is not an overstatement to say the systematic mass incarceration of people of color in the United States would not have been possible in the post-civil rights era if the nation had not fallen under the spell of a callous colorblindness. [. . .] Saying that one does not care about race is offered as an exculpatory virtue, when in fact it can be a form of cruelty.[59]

If one must dream, then better to dream of a society in which color—as with gender, sexuality, musicality, neurodivergence—is neither a qualifier nor a disqualifier for humanity and humane affordance. Because regardless of whether it's remotely possible to be colorblind, a threshold awareness of this task's impossibility already runs the risk of making any *pretense* of plausibility somewhat irresponsible.

Beliefs in colorblindness engender refusals to hear out (much less participate in) what psychologist Derald Wing Sue calls "race talk," or conversations about racism, prejudice, and cultural difference.[60] In his writings about Jim

Crow, James Baldwin once defined racial segregation as a mode of "ignorance" and "apathy."[61] Likewise, what is modern colorblindness if not a kind of *psychic* segregation, one's mental efforts to compartmentalize people's identities? Colorblind fantasies aren't automatically racist. More importantly, they are far from sufficiently anti-racist. Colorblind auditions aren't definitively unjust. More importantly, they don't pledge sufficient commitments to racial justice.[62]

For a case study, let's consider one of the world's most famous orchestras, the Vienna Philharmonic. Compared to its European rivals, and certainly compared to US orchestras, the VPO happens to be among the least diverse in membership, yet also lately the most vocal about its commitments to diversity. What explains this contradiction?

Vienna Philharmonic So White

Philharmonic (n.): from the Greek, *philo* + *harmonika*—love of harmony, of music.

Founded in 1842, the Vienna Philharmonic is a hot commodity.[63] Scoring a ticket to a VPO concert has long been as difficult as nabbing a seat for the Super Bowl. Many seats at VPO performances are taken up by season subscribers. As of 2018, new subscriptions have had a wait list of up to thirteen years. A certain mystique and old-fashioned charm becloud the subscription process itself, which requires hopeful attendees to "[submit] a written letter on paper in the spring (March–May) of each year."[64] Alas, applicants should understand that "every year in the fall, the submitted subscription requests are answered, regrettably often with the information that no subscription is currently available."[65] Mystique likewise shrouds the VPO as a whole. Abiding by its proud tradition of "democratic self-administration," this philharmonic is governed by the "full orchestra membership," which confidentially discusses and votes on key decisions, statutes, and elections.[66]

No wonder that admirers of the VPO rely on appropriately orphic vocabularies to compliment the ensemble's "unique" style and sound.[67] "Not everyone agrees on precisely what it is," points out *New York Times* music writer Michael Cooper, "but many listeners say that they know it when they hear it."[68] Musical choices that distinguish the so-called *Wiener Klangstil* include tuning ($A^4 = 443$ Hz), period instruments, rhythmic nuances (accented second beat in a Viennese waltz), and other idiosyncrasies of historical performance practice.[69]

In the mid-1990s, the Vienna Philharmonic faced mounting criticisms of its all-white-male membership.[70] Although women have consistently outnumbered men as graduates of Austria's music schools, female musicians were not allowed even to audition for the VPO until 1996.[71] Much of the initial pressure confronting the VPO came from demonstrators in the United States—"not from the Kärntner Straße [a famed shopping street in central Vienna]," as a journalist put it, "but from Culver City, California."[72] From 1997 onward, members of the International Alliance for Women in Music (IAWM) and the National Organization for Women began showing up annually to protest VPO's big concerts in Orange County and in New York.[73] Protesters' numbers typically didn't exceed a few dozen, and the VPO had no trouble selling out its tickets regardless. Yet the Vienna Philharmonic's leadership showed signs of wishing to appease the protesters and to avoid bad press; reviews of the VPO's performances at, say, Carnegie Hall increasingly featured obligatory warnings about the ensemble's "male domination" alongside praise of these men's "technical excellence and musical sensitivity."[74]

Early on, one of the VPO's attempted quick fixes involved hiring a handful of adjunct female musicians specifically for its US tour. The strategy backfired. IAWM president Kris Burns blasted this gesture as "egregious tokenism," pointing out that the United States remains "the only place in the world where the Vienna Philharmonic faces open protest, and it is the only place where the orchestra uses women substitutes."[75] Twenty years following the VPO's vote to accept female members, the number of women in the 140-seat orchestra has risen from zero (in 1996) to ten (in 2016).[76] As for women conductors, that ceiling didn't shatter until November 2005, when Sydney-born Simone Young took the podium for two concerts at the Wiener Musikverein.[77]

No less fraught than the VPO's gender troubles are matters of ethnic and racial inclusivity. For the most part, the Philharmonic's spokespersons have failed to offer sensible explanations for the ensemble's nondiversity, apart from insinuations that white performers are just better. In a 1998 interview, Vienna Philharmonic chairman Clemens Hellsberg explained the challenge of finding suitable Japanese musicians, who make up a high percentage of music students and professional performers in Vienna:

> It's out of the question to say we do not accept Japanese. It is just that we have never found any who fit with our special style of playing. If they don't

have it [this special style], they won't be accepted, and to have studied in Vienna is no guarantee [. . .]. This is a matter of cultural tradition.[78]

Hellsberg's claims sound confusing. On the one hand, this former chairman was insisting that the VPO would never discriminate against Japanese candidates. On the other hand, he relied on the impossibly vague metric of "special style" in order to rationalize why, at the time, no Japanese musicians, even those who had undertaken their entire musical educations in Vienna's conservatories, had ever been successful in attaining membership. Muddy language says a lot. In a 2011 article that coined the now-popular phrase "white fragility," Robin DiAngelo pointed out that "incoherent talk is a function of talking about race in a world that insists race does not matter."[79] Drawing on the anti-racist writings of Eduardo Bonilla-Silva, DiAngelo elaborated, "Probing forbidden racial issues results in verbal incoherence—digressions, long pauses, repetition, and self-corrections."[80] Hellsberg's denial of racial prejudice looks awkward because the explications inevitably touch on race while trying to get as far away from the subject as possible.[81]

We have no reason to doubt VPO's prioritization of a Viennese "cultural tradition" and its "special style of playing."[82] But if we turn to the memoirs of a previous chairman, Otto Strasser, even the excuse of *it's about the music* falls apart.[83]

> I hold it incorrect that today the applicants [should] play behind a screen, an arrangement that was brought in after the Second World War to assure objective judgments. I continuously fought against it [when I became a member of the Philharmonic's board of directors] because I am convinced that to the artist also belongs the person [*daß zum Künstler auch der Mensch gehört*], that one must not only hear, but also see, to judge him in his entire personality. [. . .] Even a grotesque situation that played itself out after my retirement was not able to change the situation. An applicant qualified himself as the best, and as the screen was raised, there stood a—Japanese before the stunned jury [*stand ein—Japaner vor der verdutzten Jury*]. He was, however, not engaged, because his face did not fit with the *Pizzicato-Polka* of the New Year's Concert.[84]

Surprise: it was a—Japanese person all along (dramatic em dash in the original statement). Too bad the musician didn't have a "polka face" while playing this composition by Johann Strauss II, though it's hard to know how the jury could have discerned this physiognomic mismatch, given that they ostensibly saw him only after the performance had concluded.

It's not just the VPO's chairmen and maestros who have voiced desires to uphold whites-only policies in the name of beautiful and nationally authentic music.[85] In a 1996 hour-long program titled "Musikalische Misogynie" on the West German State Radio (WDR), sociologist Roland Girtler observed that "the Vienna Philharmonic would also never take a Japanese or such. If they took one, this also would somehow by appearances put in question the noble character of Viennese culture. But this is not racist!"[86] Similarly, the VPO's solo flutist Dieter Flury told the WDR that "if one thinks that the world should function by quota regulations [for race and gender], then it is naturally irritating that we are a group of white-skinned male musicians, that perform exclusively the music of white-skinned male composers. It is a racist and sexist irritation." In an appeal to cost-benefit analysis, Flury went on to say "it is worthwhile to accept this racist and sexist irritation, because something produced by a superficial understanding of human rights"—meaning quotas and diversity—"would not have the same standards"—meaning musical standards.[87]

Barring any egregious violations of anti-discrimination laws, the privately managed Vienna Philharmonic retains considerable autonomy in its hiring practices and its disclosures of information. Musicologist Fritz Trümpi remembers being rebuffed by the VPO's management in 2003 when he tried to access the Historical Archive of the Vienna Philharmonic (HAWPh) to investigate the orchestra's historical ties to National Socialism.[88] Although "a previous official history by Clemens Hellsberg from the early '90s contained a chapter about the Nazi period," recalled Trümpi years later, "the idea that external researchers could come and root around in their archive was long considered taboo."[89] Despite the HAWPh's purported status as "unrestricted" [*in keiner Weise behindert*], historians besides Trümpi have likewise reported running into brick walls in their attempts to gain entry.[90] I asked music scholar Sebastian Smallshaw, whose research deals with the VPO's autonomy following the Anschluss, to describe his various efforts to access the archives.

I phoned the [Vienna Philharmonic's] archive and asked to see minuted committee discussions from 1942 as well as private correspondence from the orchestra's then-chairman Wilhelm Jerger (who was well-connected with the Nazi establishment and had seized the chairmanship in an internal coup following the Anschluss). I think the immediate response was along the lines of "not just anybody can look at these files." I gave up after trying a couple more times [. . .]. Complaints about obstruction already spilled into the public domain back in 2007, when Fritz Trümpi was refused access to committee minutes for his dissertation. It took him 18 months and the backing of an influential Doktorvater, Oliver Rathkolb, to get the access he needed. But that didn't mean the archive was open for everyone, as [Bernadette] Mayrhofer, another Rathkolb student, was denied access at the same time that Trümpi was finally let in. Hellsberg calls this claim "absurd and scurrilous."[91]

Only in 2013 did Hellsberg himself commission a hand-selected group of scholars—which included Trümpi, Rathkolb, and Mayrhofer—to, as the VPO website states, "integrate the results of their research and publications, including newly found documents in the Vienna Philharmonic archives, into the orchestra's website."[92] Collective research has since demonstrated that, by 1942, sixty of the 123 active members of the Philharmonic had become members of the National Socialist German Workers' Party. Of the sixteen musicians expelled from the orchestra after annexation, six went on to be murdered in concentration camps, and two died prior to deportation.[93] Nine other VPO members, being "jüdisch Versippte" (people related to Jews by blood or marriage), lived under constant threat of having their provisional exemptions terminated.[94] After the war, as Rathkolb points out, "a quarter of the [Vienna Philharmonic] orchestra members," as former NSDAP adherents, "were suspended from active service, but the purge was confined predominantly to elderly musicians. The top priority was for the orchestra not to lose too many musicians, as this would have [come across] in its sound."[95] In sum, compulsory denazification was at odds with *Klangstil* preservation. Moral compromises were made in the name of music.

Such moral hedging continues today. Visit the VPO website's History section and you would see, in the middle of the page, a row of images tracing the orchestra's progression from the professed Golden Era (circa 1875–1898 under conductor Hans Richter) to the present. A dark, monochrome thumbnail for National Socialism—showing Nazi politician Baldur von Schirach surrounded by orchestra members with barely discernible faces—recedes amid the adjacent thumbnails, which, with their own dignified and romantic sepia tones, depict the clear-as-day portraits of Richter, composer-conductor Gustav Mahler (who led the orchestra between 1898 and 1901), and Philharmonic honorary member Leonard Bernstein (Figure 3.3).[96] On

Figure 3.3. (*Left to right*) Timeline of the Vienna Philharmonic with photos of Hans Richter, Gustav Mahler, Baldur von Schirach (with orchestra), and Leonard Bernstein.

the VPO website's National Socialism page, the first line reads: "In 1938, politics encroached upon the Vienna Philharmonic in the most brutal manner" [*1938 griff auf brutalste Weise die Politik ins philharmonische Geschehen ein*].[97] This sentence names "politics," *die Politik*, as the shadowy archvillain that preyed on and engulfed the defenseless Philharmonic.[98] In terms of postwar Austrian historiography more generally, much debate has whirled around representations of the country as the "first victim," rather than the first accomplice, of Hitler's expansionism.[99] Such narratives of victimhood (*Opferthese*, Victim Theory) argue for Austria's mitigated culpability with respect to the atrocities of the Second World War.[100] In this regard, the VPO's decades of silence on its National Socialist ties were patterned comfortably on Austria's longstanding blame of Nazi Germany as the originary and sole culprit of its time.

Instead of relinquishing its patriarchy and racial homogeneity, the public face of the Vienna Philharmonic has performed atonement by way of benefit concerts, residencies, donations, and statements about its mission "to communicate the humanitarian message of music into the daily lives and consciousness of its listeners."[101] In 2000, the Vienna Philharmonic played Beethoven's Ninth Symphony at the former Nazi concentration camp in Mauthausen, commemorating the fifty-fifth anniversary of the Austrian camp's liberation; in light of its exclusionary hiring practices and its history of Nazi entanglements, however, the VPO drew criticisms for daring to headline such an event at all.[102] In subsequent years, plagued by a spate of bad press about the VPO's deeds under National Socialism, administrators increased the visibility of the orchestra's charity work.[103] On its main website, the VPO began displaying heartwarming photos and videos of its musicians interacting with smiling youths of color in a São Paulo favela, smiling youths of color in post-Tōhoku-earthquake Tokyo, and smiling youths of color of low-income families in Lima. Apart from the white-savior optics, it's impossible to deny the admirable intentions of the VPO's service and outreach. But this almost-impossibility constitutes the kind of discursive impasse theorized by queer scholar Lee Edelman, who has worried about Western societies' "pervasive invocation of the Child as the emblem of futurity's unquestioned value."[104] Exhortations to "think of the children" and tautological clichés that "children are the future" can, for example, end up leveraging the primacy of youth welfare for pro-censorship, anti-abortion, and anti-gay agendas. For the VPO, several powerful alibis (Latin: *alius* + *ibi*, meaning *other* + *place*) temper its otherwise conservative and hermetic image. By undertaking noble deeds in distant locales, by emphasizing their dedication to children (as emblems of the future), and by documenting its Nazi past (which included awarding a Ring of Honor to Baldur von Schirach, who served as the leader of the Hitler Youth from 1931 to 1940), the Vienna Philharmonic has tried to turn the spotlight onto *other places* (ambassadorship abroad) and *other times* (future and past) so as to divert scrutiny from the inconvenient politics of the orchestra's here and now.[105] By finally opening up its dusty archives and by creating shiny new photo albums (shared publicly on sites such as Facebook) of its good activities in foreign lands, the orchestra manages to claim the dual virtues of transparency and philanthropy.[106]

These virtues do not resolve the dissonances between what the Philharmonic purportedly stands for and whom it looks (out) for. Consider the irony of this testimonial, appearing under "Impressions of Young People" on the Philharmonic's site, by seventeen-year-old musician Micaela dos Santos: "I was very excited that the Vienna Philharmonic came to Monte Azul and listened to our rehearsal. They were very nice and friendly. They invited us to listen to their rehearsal in the concert hall in São Paulo. I felt like I was in a magical place and when I saw the orchestra I dreamed of one day sitting at the first chair of the cello section and playing along with them."[107] It's a wonderful dream, albeit one that's undercut by the orchestra's 170-year record of white male membership. If her dream does comes true, and assuming no one else beats her to the punch, Micaela dos Santos would be the first woman of color ever to join the VPO.

Promotional strategies of the Vienna Philharmonic have involved the careful foregrounding and the backgrounding of particular topics, much like the diligently monitored opening and closing of stage curtains. In recent years, some of the VPO's social media posts have focused on auditions' physical curtains as evidence of impartiality. On November 28, 2014, the public Facebook page for the Philharmonic uploaded a series of captioned photos showing the jury setup (Figure 3.4). Auditions take place in the Vienna State Opera's Gustav Mahler Hall.[108] Candidates draw random numbers to determine the sequence of auditions. Each performer is evaluated on a scale of two to twenty points by a panel of twenty-five orchestra members who sit on the other side of the divider. (Expectedly, however, "at least the final round will be played without the curtain."[109]) One captioned photo shows the attendance of a few "guests [who] may experience the auditions behind the jury to see how incredibly difficult auditions are for everyone involved."[110] Although it's laudable for the Vienna Philharmonic to offer community members a behind-the-scenes peek at the otherwise closed session, the onlookers also serve the conspicuous role of *seeing* that the jury *cannot see* the performers—a role of corroboratory witnessing reminiscent of a gallery audience in a courtroom, or of the lucky spectators who are invited onto the stage during a magic show to confirm the absence of strings and the opacity of blindfolds. This VPO Facebook post was promptly picked up by Norman Lebrecht on his classical music blog *Slipped Disc*, which warned: "Do not be fooled by this splendid PR exercise. The final selection is without a screen, enabling old prejudices to be asserted."[111]

I share Lebrecht's skepticism. But not everyone regards the VPO's selectively anonymous auditions—the partial impartiality—as a bad thing.[112] A frequent *Slipped Disc* commenter named John Borstlap opined: "The VPO has been set-up as a private club and if it wants to remain that way, they should be allowed to have the freedom such position infers [sic]. [. . .] If they have the feeling that fat black lesbian violinists, fragile old Chinese trombone players and long-haired hippy percussionists do not quite produce the

Figure 3.4. Vienna Philharmonic audition with jury (*left*) and guest spectators (*right*). Photos by Jun Keller, VPO first violinist.

image of an old Viennese local classical orchestra, they should be free to take such feelings into account at auditions, however excellent the auditioners play."[113] Scanning this litany of stereotypes, we could easily dismiss Borstlap as a mere troll. Yet his point rings true: the Philharmonic *has* been free to remain, as multiple writers have termed it, a white male "bastion," connoting a holdout that's either (depending on one's politics) heroically embattled or atavistically enturtled.[114] To be clear, furthermore, the VPO is no longer all white and all male. Women make up about 10% of its membership. As for the presence of non-white musicians, here is another telling exchange on *Slipped Disc*.

FREDDYNC SAYS (November 29, 2016 at 4:04am):
And don't forget the token Asian player (in 1st violins) who also happens to be half German.

MAX GRIMM SAYS (November 29, 2016 at 6:56pm):
Count again. In the 1st Violins there is Jun Keller, born and raised in Germany to a German father and Japanese mother. Also in the 1st Violins is Wilfried Hedenborg, born and raised in Austria to an Austrian father and Japanese mother; his brother Bernhard plays in the cello section.

JOHN BORSTLAP SAYS (November 29, 2016 at 7:37pm):
Fortunately for the music, it is these players' upper half that are from German-speaking extraction.

A MUSICIAN IN MUNICH OF 100% ASIAN GENETIC MAKEUP SAYS (December 4, 2016 at 3:47pm):
What on earth is this supposed to imply?[115]

Not just one, but three (half-)Asians, meaning three bodies to rebut accusations of VPO's racial homogeneity. Indeed, the Philharmonic's leaders and fans do mention the memberships of these Asian musicians when questions of race arise. When pressed on the issue, then-chairman Clemens Hellsberg once declared that "there is no racism and no sexism in the orchestra," and that "in the first violin section we have two half-Japanese players."[116] This is true. Also true, however, is that almost 25% of the music students in Vienna are of Asian descent.[117]

Certain musicians have even speculated that the VPO will go only so far as to accept mixed-race candidates who can phenotypically pass for white. Elena Ostleitner, a musicologist who has studied the Vienna Philharmonic for over two decades, was informed by a woman back in 1995: "I auditioned for an orchestra, and I led in the point tabulations as long as I played behind a screen. Due to my name it was not apparent that I am an Asian. But when the screen was removed [for the final round], I was rejected without comment. Friends in the orchestra confirmed my assumption. They do not take foreigners, and if they do, then only those in which foreign appearance is not visible."[118] As the exculpatory cousin of the condemnatory one-drop rule, diversity and tokenization alike become extra fraught when multiracial bodies enter the fray. "As emblems of an imagined colorblind world," remarks LeiLani Nishime in the book *Undercover Asian*, "multiracial people are often used to bolster claims to a post-civil rights era," propping up liberal narratives of post-racial triumphalism.[119] Or as Michele Elam puts it in her book *The Souls of Mixed Folk*: "Not accidentally, the ascension of mixed race popularity has been enabled in the post-race, 'post soul' era [. . .]. Ethnic hybridity, we are told, heralds a liberating 'racelessness' (Naomi Zack), a step 'beyond race' (Ellis Cose), the 'end of racism' (Dinesh D'Souza), a gesture 'against race' (Paul Gilroy), a 'new racial order' (G. Reginald Daniel) freed of a supposedly irresistible essentialism (Walter Been Michaels)."[120] Mixedness, for some, signals utopia. Such optimism elides the inconvenient truths of colorism and colonialism, as well as how certain interracial acts of sexual reproduction have, throughout history, occurred nonconsensually and even violently.

Problems with the Vienna Philharmonic's racial and gendered homogeneity go beyond zero-sum questions of membership. It's not enough to shell out tokens to prove diversity, not least because "diversity" itself has become a tokenized buzzword.[121] In response to music critic Richard Morrison's 1992 claims in London's *The Times* about "the recurring anti-Semitism in [the Vienna Philharmonic's] history" and the article's accompanying caricature (Figure 3.5),[122] Hellsberg resorted to Semitic equivalents of *some of our members are (half-)Asians*. "Such representation is untenable in light of facts," Hellsberg remarked. "Even if you set aside the flawless relationship [*das einwandfreie Verhältnis*] with Otto Dessoff, Bruno Walter, David Oistrach, or Leonard Bernstein, to name but a few of the great Jewish artists beloved by the Philharmonic [. . .] indiscriminate accusations of anti-Semitism come up empty [*geht der undifferenzierte Vorwurf des Antisemitismus ins Leere*]."[123]

A drawn-out case of gender tokenization arose in 1997 when the board of the Vienna Philharmonic, for the first time since its founding in 1842, voted

Figure 3.5. *The [London] Times* (25 March 1992). Illustration by Adrian George; reprinted with permission. In our correspondences, George noted he was aiming for "a hint of [Herbert von] Karajan" in his portrayal of the conductor, and chose the cello as Hitler's instrument because "it seemed [like] a sinister pose."

to extend full membership to a woman, the harpist Anna Lelkes.[124] In an interview with the *Salzburger Nachrichten*, Lelkes explained:

I was hired Jan. 1, 1971, by the [Vienna] state opera, and three years later, in 1974, I was admitted informally into the philharmonic as a regular without full membership. I didn't exist officially until yesterday. My name was never mentioned in any program [. . .] and they always claimed, even in my presence, right under my own nose, that they didn't have a woman [in the orchestra]. [. . .] At the last meeting [when they took the vote to admit women], it really wasn't nice. What I had to listen to there really hurt me. Someone said: "There are no women in the Vienna Choir Boys and no pigs at the Lipizzaners [the Spanish Riding School in Vienna featuring dressage with white horses]." [. . .] I was not admitted unanimously, but with a big majority, as I heard. I had to leave the room before the vote. They were terribly frightened by the possibility of demonstrations by American women's rights activists. I believe that this pressure was decisive. And that's why they said, "OK, we have to give some proof that we are not that bad. We must stand up for 'equal employment opportunity for both genders,'" as they formulated it officially for the press.[125]

A few years later, in a 2003 interview with the Austrian weekly news magazine *profil*, a VPO member commented that the optimal number of women in the orchestra is zero: "Three women are already too many. By the time we have twenty percent, the orchestra will be ruined. We have made a big mistake, and will bitterly regret it."[126]

For all of its high honors, the Vienna Philharmonic may appear to be low-hanging fruit in terms of condemnable institutions. As far as accusations of discrimination go, perhaps the orchestra comes off as too easy of a target, with its conservative homogeneity clashing loudly with sanctified values of liberal pluralism. One could mercifully say, *We get it! Vienna Philharmonic—white men, little change, Nazi history, PR maneuvers—can we move on now?* Arguments for letting the Philharmonic off the hook include the following: the speculation that membership will incrementally change in time, with or without external intervention (presumption of inevitable mutability); the lament that things probably *won't* change very much, interventions be damned (the lost-cause fallacy); the synchronous sigh that boys will be boys (tautology and sexist apology); and reminders that the ensemble's productions of musical beauty could override or at least mitigate the orchestra's problematic ethics and politics.[127]

I've lately immersed myself in music performed by the Vienna Philharmonic. As I researched the ensemble's past, I listened to YouTube recordings of this orchestra's New Year's extravaganzas, BBC Proms concerts, and miscellaneous renditions of masterpieces (Beethoven's Seventh Symphony under Wilhelm Furtwängler, Mahler's Ninth Symphony under Leonard Bernstein, and so on). Achingly beautiful music. But the more I dug into the Philharmonic's infelicitous details, the more difficult it became to refrain from seeing the sea of white faces onstage. Even when I minimized my browser window and listened "blind," the musicians' homogeneity glinted in my mind's eye. Today, I think I have lost much of my appetite for this orchestra's performances. It's my right, and, as some people will believe, it's also my loss. I've wondered if I'm alone in my disenchantment. So I reached out to two leading experts on the Vienna Philharmonic, William Osborne and Fritz Trümpi. (Like Elena Ostleitner, both Osborne and Trümpi have researched the VPO since the 1990s, and both graciously read this chapter's drafts and lent their advice.) Most of the things I asked Osborne and Trümpi pertained to facts and figures. In the summer of 2017, however, I emailed each of them with a different sort of question on my mind. I wanted to know if they felt any love for the VPO's performances.

> Me: As someone who has extensively researched this orchestra, and who has discovered (and published widely about) its unpleasant politics and past, do you still listen to the Philharmonic's recordings? Attend their concerts? For pleasure, for research?[128]

Here's how Osborne and Trümpi responded.

> Osborne: The Vienna Philharmonic's exclusion of Asians, and its recent history of excluding women, makes it difficult [. . .]. This problem is exacerbated since there are reasons to suspect that the orchestra continues to discreetly discriminate against women. This makes it difficult for me to listen to the orchestra. To look past these issues and just enjoy the music is inevitably an exercise in dulling the conscience. A kind of moral deafness is created, a tacit acceptance of forms of chauvinism that have historically brought humanity enormous suffering. [. . .] I watch and listen to the orchestra as a historical exercise, but it is not something I enjoy.[129]

> Trümpi: During my research period on the VPO's Nazi and post-Nazi history, I had various phases where I lost the desire to listen to VPO's recordings and concerts. The time lag changed my approach somehow. I tend to listen to concerts with traditional (meaning "classical" or "romantic") repertoire from a historic perspective, which means I mainly focus on how it is played in a rather comparative way. This approach doesn't cause problems when I listen to concerts or recordings of the VPO. The historic perspective leads also to a certain distance [from] the orchestra officials' behavior regarding the orchestra's past. I try to depersonalize [my] former fierce and personal fights with some of them. There were always musicians in the orchestra who appreciated the research I did.[130]

There are as many ways to hear the Vienna Philharmonic as there are ways to critique it. Maybe I have been too immersed in my research to experiment adequately with alternate modes of listening. And what can and should VPO's critics do aside from pointing out the orchestra's shortcomings? Some musicians have called for boycotts of the VPO on the basis of its discriminatory policies.[131] Others disagree. "How would you like it," asked one concertgoer, "if Cleveland [Orchestra] gets boycotted because they don't have enough Black Americans in their orchestra? Or Asian Americans? Or homosexuals?"[132] Another wrote: "And how about all-women music groups? And I suspect the Israel Philharmonic employs only Jews. And so on. Live and let live."[133] Such slippery slope arguments in favor of laissez-faire music loving are hard to wrestle with. Yes, these defenders of VPO make a fair point. We have *lots* of moral, political, and legal causes to boycott *lots* of different musical entities. Yet isn't it revealing how people who go to bat for white men (such as those in the Vienna Philharmonic) suddenly begin sounding like champions for minorities (*what about the Black Americans, the Asians, the gays, the Jews*)? For where were these anti-racist, anti-homophobic, and social justice perspectives when the subject at hand was *not* about the embattlement and potential sanctioning of white men? Why does it take the jeopardization of white patriarchy to motivate people into voicing heuristic concerns for everyone else?

First, they came for the white men in power . . . that's not how the poem goes.[134]

Time Outs

As long as we're tasked with judging fellow human beings for purposes of employment, education, and financial allotment, the ethics of adjudication will continue to split opinions. Are we supposed to do away with anonymous auditions and reviews? Aren't they nevertheless the least worst of all our options? No and yes, respectively. If we intend to chug along with default anonymization, then maybe we can take active measures to stave off complacency and equality-mongering hubris. For a preliminary measure, adjudicators who participate in anonymous reviews—for orchestra auditions, academic articles, university admissions—can be encouraged to address the conscious and unconscious biases that allegedly justify the need for anonymization.[135] Do the decision makers understand why there's a giant screen or why names have been removed? Can these authorities draw up cognitive, historical, and institutional reference points so as to offer rationales beyond "blinders make things fair?"[136] No matter whether or how one chooses to partake in anonymous evaluations, adjudicators can inch toward best practices by improving their abilities to spot personal biases.[137]

Adjudicatory time outs could even take some notes from preoperative time outs in medicine. In recent years, I've spent a lot of time in doctors' offices. Prior to undergoing full-on neurectomies (surgical extractions of entrapped nerves), I paid visits to an anesthesiologist who performed trials of thermal ablations (using a superheated rod to burn away pathological nerves), cryotherapies (freezing nerves), injections (numbing them), and other jabby interventions. During these dreaded visits, while waiting in the offices at Dartmouth-Hitchcock Medical Center, I often stared at the colorful Time Out charts on the wall. On these charts were basic instructions for medical procedures: check the name of the patient; check site of operation; check allergies; and check that no surgical tools or foreign bodies have been left behind in the patient's cavities (Figure 3.6). Reading and rereading this list of seemingly self-evident tasks both reassured and unnerved me. Great! Doctors follow these rules, sometimes with double- and triple-checks. But wait! The checklist spells out, blow by blow, the exact kinds of human error that could transpire. In 2001, the physician Kenneth Kizer introduced the term "never event" to describe major surgical errors—wrong-site, wrong-patient, and wrong-procedure operations—that should *never occur . . .* or more accurately, should retrospectively *never have been allowed to occur.*[138] Notice how *never event* embodies the same oxymoronic charge as the word *colorblind*: just as a sighted person cannot be blind to race (all hopes and boasts aside), so surgeons' wishes of adverse never-ness are undermined by data showing that never events occur globally about 4000 times per year.[139] A similar wrinkle lies in the fact that, as of 2005, one day out of the year has been designated National Time Out Day by the Association of periOperative Registered Nurses and the Joint Commission. Although the advocates of Time Out Day emphasize that time outs should always be observed with maximum diligence, this claim is somewhat countervailed by the existence of a once-a-year special event. An explanation appears on the Joint Commission's page:

> The time out is *the last line of defense* before an adverse event happens. Every member of the surgical team from the tech to the nurse to the surgeon needs to be fully engaged. The team needs to be accountable for following the proper time out procedure and feel empowered to speak up if they see something that could result in a wrong site, wrong procedure, or wrong person surgery. Now is a great time to take a look at your current time out procedure and not only celebrate your successes, but to identify areas for improvement and encourage continuous compliance with safe surgery practices.[140]

In the preceding blurb, we could substitute medical personnel, patients, and surgeries with adjudicators (for auditions, admissions, prizes), candidates, and evaluations of all kinds—and the broad call for careful and humane practice would still apply. Before holding anonymous orchestra auditions, for example, the jury members could choose, at minimum, to sit down as a group and put into words the reason behind the screen on the stage. Answers might be obvious, and out-loud confirmations might sound redundant . . . yet no less redundant than quadruple-checking the birthdate of a patient undergoing a procedure with a very low mortality rate. Sure, a music audition, unlike surgery, doesn't pose an imminent life and death scenario. Yet matters of livelihood, sustenance, power, material equity, and healthcare do hinge on employment. Discrimination *can* be a life and death issue. It is not enough to append Equal Opportunity boilerplates to job postings (*we are committed to nondiscrimination during evaluations*), just as it is not enough for a surgical patient to receive informational pamphlets assuring that the doctors will do their best (*we are committed to not messing up during surgery*). For members of any adjudicatory or medical team, a vocal time out may well be the last line of defense before a sensitive procedure.[141]

Conducting implicit bias training and time outs are important. No less important—and likely more challenging—is approaching these preparatory measures with an open mind. If a committee member is asked to participate in an anti-discrimination workshop, they might grudgingly respond with, *But I'm pretty sure I know this stuff already!*, in the same way that surgical teams who ask for multiple verifications of a patient's name might think such rituals are a little redundant. (By the time I was undergoing my sixth nerve block, my anesthesiologist had seen me a dozen times, and we had long been on a first-name basis. Still, as I lay on the cushioned table, awaiting the cold pinch of fat needles filled with bupivacaine and methylprednisolone acetate, he asked me to state my name before the draping began.)

Each of us can probably learn something from anti-bias activities. We can also learn a great deal from the vehemence with which some people oppose these activities. In 2017, Duke University divinity professor Paul Griffiths quit his job after publicly scorning the school's diversity training workshops, calling these offerings a waste of time.[142] "[The workshops will] be, I predict with confidence, intellectually flaccid: there'll be bromides, clichés, and amen-corner rah-rahs in plenty," Griffiths declared in a mass email to Duke faculty. "When (if) it gets beyond that, its illiberal roots and totalitarian tendencies will show. Events of this sort are definitively anti-intellectual."[143] People, not least very smart people, don't like to hear that they can benefit from anti-bias training. Some hear these moderate recommendations as immoderate accusations of racism or sexism or homophobia.[144] Others may worry that participating in this training may reveal within them deep-rooted prejudices that they prefer to ignore altogether. Although Griffiths is correct that "diversity" training today can easily be co-opted as a public-relations tool, his objection—quitting a long-held job—was inordinately forceful.[145]

Anti-bias training is valuable even or especially where anonymous evaluations are concerned.[146] Although screens and redactions of identity can level the playing field on a case-by-case basis, they concurrently generate complacency and conceit, and therefore aren't viable as long-term substitutes for continuous practices of self-critique and awareness. For if people were not at least implicitly aware *of* their own implicit biases, then why would they see any need for anonymous evaluations to begin with? As Michelle Alexander writes at her most critically wishful: "Seeing race is not the problem. Refusing to care for the people we see is the problem. [. . .] We should hope not for a colorblind society but instead for a world in which we can see each other fully, learn from each other, and do what we can to respond to each other with love."[147]

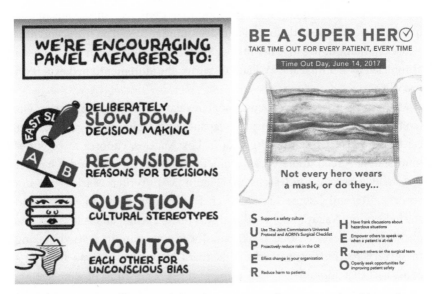

Figure 3.6. (*Left*) A rundown of considerations regarding unconscious bias and (*right*) the Time Out checklist of the Association of periOperative Registered Nurses.

Coda: Loud Reveals

> I really, really don't want to make being a woman an issue in the work that we [chefs] do. But it's just there [. . .] which is why, at this restaurant, the best way for people to enjoy the food is to not see who's making their food.
>
> —Niki Nakayama, chef[148]

At anonymous auditions, noise can erupt during the tiny windows of big reveals—the moments of deanonymization when screens are removed and bodies are exposed. Upon seeing candidates who don't look the way they sounded, jury members might be unable to keep their reactions quiet. Some might respond loudly, dramatically, irrationally. Recall Otto Strasser's complaint about the "grotesque situation" of the Vienna Philharmonic's "stunned jury" who saw a Japanese performer after the divider was removed. Or, likewise in the classical music world, a famous incident involved trombonist Abbie Conant. In a 1980 anonymous audition for the Munich Philharmonic Orchestra, Conant's performance led music director Sergiu Celibidache to gush, "That's who we want!" But when Conant stepped out from behind the screen, Celibidache—who had been expecting Herr Conant—exclaimed: "Was ist'n des! Sacra di! Meine Goetter! Um Gottes willen!"[149] Ugliness followed. Conant was hired and then demoted. She, alone among her male peers, was made to undergo degrading medical, physical, and musical examinations to prove her fitness. She went to court. All of this has been chronicled by her husband William Osborne, the aforementioned expert on the VPO.

Musical surprises aside, sensational revelations rule the culinary, viticultural, and advertising world.[150] Japanese chef Niki Nakayama, at her celebrated kaiseki restaurant n/naka in Los Angeles, chooses to cook behind sliding screen doors because diners' discovery of her gender has occasionally sparked condescension (Figure 3.7). Writer Maria Fontoura reports: "Recently, some big-name chef in Hawaii came to n/naka and started eating [Nakayama's] food and was really excited about it. After one of the servers revealed that [Nakayama] was a woman, he started making these very patronizing remarks: 'Oh, that's so cute! Oh, that's how girls cook. Isn't that adorable?'"[151] Or think of the *gotcha!* stunts of wine tasting. During the infamous 1976 gathering that came to be known as the Judgment of Paris, prestigious connoisseurs, in a "blind taste-off" of French and

Figure 3.7. Nakayama closes the sliding translucent *shōji* doors (*left*), which sufficiently obscure diners' sight of the kitchen (*right*) but still allow the reciprocal passage of sounds and scents. Screen captures by author.

Californian wines, ended up awarding top honors to the latter.[152] (One judge, Odette Kahn, editor of *Revue du vin de France*, felt so humiliated that she demanded the return of her score card.[153]) This scandalous outcome has since inspired plenty of copycat experiments. One informal experiment was devised in the mid-1990s by economist Steven Levitt, who, at a weekly dinner with the Harvard Society of Fellows, held a "blind wine tasting" with four bottles: Wine A (super expensive), Wine B (super expensive), Wine C ($8.00), and a devious Wine D (the same pour as Wine A, a duplicate thrown in for good measure).[154] Results showed negligible differences between mean ratings of the cheap Wine C versus the expensive wines, and even more damningly, the largest difference showed up between the scores of the secretly identical Wine A and Wine D. Most telling were people's reactions, as Levitt describes: "There was a lot of anger when I revealed the results, especially the fact that I had included the same wine twice. One eminent scholar stormed out of the room stating that he had a cold—otherwise he would have detected my sleight of hand with certainty."[155] Time and again, removals of anonymizing apparatus—a methodological control—can seemingly make evaluators *lose control* of their own faculties (their temper, their composure, their words).[156] Such moments of shock make for great publicity. Ever since the 1975 "double-blind" Pepsi Challenge and eventual Cola Wars, television commercials have zoomed in on happy guinea pigs exclaiming "No way!" upon learning they have just tasted a miraculously low-price, low-calorie, or low-sugar variant of junk food, or that they have just consumed a particular brand of beer, potato chips, peanut butter, or margarine (the first three words of *I Can't Believe It's Not Butter!* nicely capture the ethos of consumerist disbelief-turned-delight).[157] Car company Chevrolet's "Real People, Not Actors" ads, which saturated the commercial breaks during the

2016 Summer Olympics, featured focus-group participants saying ridiculous things such as, "Thanks for blowing our minds."[158] Today's rapid rise of judge-it-yourself "Reaction Videos" on YouTube has codified an entire Internet genre devoted to such judgments and their sensational aftermath.[159] Producers of these videos expose excitable test subjects to mystery potables, brands, and music, while devilishly instructing them: *Try it—and just wait till you find out what it really is!*

Given that anonymous evaluations pose as exemplars of meritocracy, it's no surprise that some people who are invested in such ideals react strongly when interlocutors pull back the curtains on meritocracy itself. Earlier, I referenced the author Robert Frank, who, in a 2016 *New York Times* piece, argued that talent and labor are neither necessary nor sufficient for prosperity if luck is gravely lacking.[160] On a Fox Business news segment in 2016, Frank was asked to defend this claim by an incensed host Stuart Varney, who griped: "Do you know how insulting that was, when I read that? I came to America with nothing 35 years ago. I've made something of myself, I think through hard work, talent, and risk-taking, and you're going to write in the *New York Times* that this is luck."[161] Varney, with a net worth of around $10 million, felt as though his accomplishments were under siege by Frank's very acknowledgment of luck as a factor of success.[162] Varney rushed to wrap the hypothesis around only himself (*n=1 millionaire*), then moaned that the fit was far too tight—a dangerous and familiar convergence of implacable egotism with white fragility. Frank, after all, wasn't belittling hard work. Hard work is not the enemy. Actual enemies come in the form of self-exculpation by way of denial: a willful refusal to recognize meritocracy's faults.[163]

Deanonymization can be galvanizing, and the subsequent reactions—whether a jury's "stunned" silence or an oenophilic professor "storm[ing] out of the room" or a millionaire's rant—speak volumes.[164] Anonymity masks people. Deanonymization can unmask people, even showing certain colors in turn.

Some of the loudest revelations today occur in one of our most popular platforms for musical auditions: reality television competitions. A show such as NBC's *The Voice* opens each season with what it calls Blind Auditions, during which four judges begin with their backs turned to the onstage auditionee. Even reality shows without formal anonymous auditions tend to feature sensational moments with performers who don't look the way they sound. Reality television trots out a celebratory parade of varied bodies, a human panoply of colors, shapes, sizes, abilities, and musicalities. In one respect, these programs make good on Michelle Alexander's call for "see[ing] each other fully," for loving and learning: viewers witness contestants from all walks of life and listen to their stories of overcoming adversity, discrimination, and disability.

But this hypervisibility of diversity comes with its own baggage. Extending the present chapter's critiques of meritocracy, Chapter 4 focuses on the beauty, power, and political predicaments surrounding narratives of disability on reality programs. Lovable chronicles of contestants overcoming hardships can overcome us, the viewers, in turn—emotionally, rhetorically, critically. When someone's moving story reduces us to a puddle of tears and leaves us at a loss for words, what are we to do? How do we reconcile that old warring duo within us, the skeptic and the sucker?

Before we press forward, a brief Interlude will aim to show how critiques of meritocracy, colorblindness, and anonymous auditions might bear on the aims and operations of the American Musicological Society, one of the leading US organizations for music scholarship.

Interlude

Loving Musicology Till It Hurts

In the years in which I have officially been a part of AMS [the American Musicological Society] and involved in musicological study, I have spoken with both junior and senior scholars of color, those with tenure, and those who have left the discipline. For every time I can congratulate a friend on landing a job, getting a grant, or giving a paper, it is overshadowed by moments when those same people have been disparaged, whitesplained to by another scholar, been on the receiving end of racist and sexist comments, felt marginalized in their departments and in the discipline. I include myself in this list. I have been demoralized, made to feel less than, and disrespected on the basis of my race and gender just as so many others have.

—Imani Mosley, in response to the publication of a
controversial article by Pierpaolo Polzonetti[1]

In February 2016, a professor named Pierpaolo Polzonetti published a short article in *Musicology Now*, the official blog of the American Musicological Society. Titled "*Don Giovanni* Goes to Prison: Teaching Opera behind Bars," this piece recounted the author's experience teaching an "opera history class for inmates" at the Westville Correctional Facility in Indiana.[2] Polzonetti's article opened a schism in the AMS. In the comments section of *Musicology Now* (and across other websites that picked up the story), accusations about Polzonetti's stereotypical depictions of black Westville inmates were parried by colleagues who applauded the author's good intentions; complaints about the article's perpetuation of Western art music's white-savior narrative were matched by sincere admiration of Polzonetti's efforts to share classical masterpieces with prisoners; and charges against Polzonetti's "elitist" and "patronizing" rhetoric were met with astonishment toward the very articulation of these charges.

In short, some readers found the article obviously abominable, while others found it obviously noble. Ableist vocabularies of visual and aural deficit peppered the indignation across this thread. People used phrases such as "blind to difference," "blind spots," "blind political correctness," "willfully tone-deaf," "turn a deaf ear," and "disturbing, essentializing, and tone-deaf piece of writing."[3] Across the aisle, commenters lobbed these metaphors of blindness and deafness to emphasize their opponents' hopeless lack of acuity and intellect. Multiple critics of Polzonetti focused on how he reductively described rap as a genre with "blatant lyrics" and a "pounding beat":

> They [the prisoners] opened their minds and ears to music that sounded exotic to many of them. Eighteenth-century oratorios and operas can appear meaningless or dull to listeners mostly accustomed to the blatant lyrics and pounding beat of rap music.[4]

Some people pointed out that rap does tend to have blatant lyrics and pounding beats. Others rebutted by saying that certain classical repertoire contains these elements as well. Musicologist Robert Fink went so far as to declare that "in 2016, referring to rap music as 'blatant lyrics and pounding beats' is the musicological equivalent of using the N-word. It has the effect of invalidating anything else you say."[5] It's worth mentioning that Polzonetti didn't specify that the inmates "mostly accustomed to" rap were black, even though the demographics of US incarceration would support this assumption. All the more reason, then, that some readers objected to how Polzonetti did explicitly delineate the blackness of an inmate who spoke in a "frightening" tone:

> One man commented that we are supposed to laugh at the betrayed stupid woman [the jilted Donna Elvira] in the presence of her cunning seducer [Don Giovanni]. A second student, an African-American man with a long beard, immediately pointed his finger at the first, shouting that it is never funny when a woman suffers. "Never!" he repeated three times in a frightening crescendo.

Polzonetti went on to publish an expanded version of the blog post in the journal *Musica Docta*, where he graciously included a prefatory footnote thanking "colleagues and participants in this debate for the animated discussion on the blogosphere," which convinced him "to change the wording of [the] text in a few critical points."[6] Here are some of the critical changes:

> They [the prisoners] opened their minds and ears to music that sounded ~~exotic~~ unfamiliar to many of them. Eighteenth-century oratorios and operas can appear meaningless or dull to ~~listeners mostly accustomed to the blatant lyrics and pounding beat of rap music~~ today's listeners not accustomed to this genre of music. [. . .] A second student~~, an African-American man with a long beard,~~ immediately pointed his finger at the first, shouting that it is never funny when a woman suffers. "Never!" he repeated three times in a frightening crescendo.[7]

Polzonetti's edits tried to address several problems. "Blatant lyrics and pounding beat" was removed, along with the racial marker for the shouting man.[8] But colorblinding and erasure aren't perfect solutions; indeed, the *Musica Docta* article ended up entirely devoid of words such as "black" or "African American"—perhaps a gesture of overcorrection prompted by the scathing pushback from the initial blog post's readers.

As musicologist Imani Mosley remarked in her response to Polzonetti's blog post, few scholars of color spoke out publicly about the controversy. Some did so under pseudonyms, and some shared thoughts only via private posts on social media. (Mosley had shared her own response with friends on Facebook; despite invitations to publish it on *Musicology Now*, she declined out of understandable concerns about her status as a junior scholar. I am quoting and citing her here with permission.) Why did the responses to Polzonetti—on issues of race, racism, white-savior narratives—come overwhelmingly from white AMS members? Because the AMS membership is overwhelmingly white. Yet there is a societal expectation that people of color speak out—serve as educators, peacebrokers—when matters of racism come up. This expectation is itself a problem. People of color are already tasked with confronting, explaining, and enduring racism in their daily lives. It's an inescapable labor. Concerning the collective responses to Polzonetti's essay, maybe the question shouldn't be why there were so few voices of color tackling this specific controversy (emergency damage control), but why so few voices of color exist within musicology in the first place (long-term reforms and initiatives).

What practical steps can be taken by the American Musicological Society to empower and envoice its marginalized members? How can the AMS better lend platforms to scholars of color *outside* moments of crisis? Several years ago, the AMS began adopting a quasi-anonymized abstract selection procedure for its annual meetings. After filling most of the spots on a conference program via anonymous evaluations, the committee members could choose to reveal the names of all abstracts' authors in order to complete the remaining selections. According to the August 2015 AMS Newsletter:

> The Program Committee may now choose a range, from 0 to 24, of paper slots to reserve for the time in the deliberations when author names are revealed (which comes at the very end of the process). Stated another way: the committee can now opt to fill all 216 paper slots without revealing the names, or can determine a number to leave open until the names are revealed. The Louisville committee chose to keep the maximum number of slots (24) open, which were filled after the authors' names were revealed.

In the second round, the committee's deanonymization extends an extra chance—presumably to big-name scholars who didn't make the first cut. After all, the only additional data provided by this bonus round are names; *name recognition*, therefore, is what informs the committee members' second-stage decisions. This safeguard sounds logical. Shouldn't the proposal of a famous professor—whose intellectual merits might not be adequately communicable in a 350-word abstract—receive a lifeline and some benefit of the doubt? Surely, the reasoning goes, this scholar will deliver a stellar, well-attended, impactful, seasoned paper when the time comes.[9]

But the reasoning is imperfect. If the AMS Program Committee members do wish to deanonymize submissions for an extra round of selection, then in this second round, could they grant opportunities to scholars who are underprivileged or underrepresented in the field? Racial minorities, contingent faculty, underfunded graduate students, and disabled colleagues may have the least access to professional resources, yet stand to benefit the most noticeably from presenting their work on the national AMS stage. Contrast this with the circumstances of a senior scholar who has already presented at AMS a couple of dozen times, and who will likely have abundant invitations to publish their paper irrespective of its exposure at a conference. Does AMS wish to be affirmative and color-conscious? If so, the program committee's policies are one place to start.

I reached out to members and chairs of recent years' AMS program committees to ask how the policy of quasi-anonymization began. From a handful of correspondences, I learned about how various senior scholars, since the early 2000s, had begun complaining about the occasional rejection of their abstracts, with some members threatening to boycott the AMS annual meetings if mollifying measures were not introduced. At the time, leaders of the AMS could have responded by saying that senior scholars who feel entitled to special consideration should purportedly know how to craft abstracts with an above-average chance of acceptance. Or they could have pointed out that senior scholars receive plentiful opportunities to participate as conference panelists, respondents, and session chairs anyway. Or that senior scholars, especially those at wealthy institutions, are less likely than other colleagues to need to submit proof of active participation at a conference in order to qualify for travel funding. Or that a disproportionately large number of marginalized AMS members and scholars of color have already quietly left the organization and the field without sending threats of mass boycott on their way out the door. Or that—at a minimum, even if it's not quite true—anonymous abstract reviews without deanonymization make things somewhat fair, so let's stick with pure meritocracy for now.[10] Instead, the leadership agreed with their most prestigious colleagues, and changed the rules to bolster their chances.

Any hope of achieving an affirmative AMS will ideally welcome the help *of* some prestigious colleagues who would willingly relinquish their own gains under a policy that favors underprivileged and underrepresented members— members who entered the discipline presumably out of a certain love for its intellectual pursuits, and out of a certain faith in the possibility of acceptance. For a famous white scholar to certify that they neither want nor need special consideration (and that they would, at the expense of improving their own odds, prefer a radically inclusive procedure attentive to class, race, rank, disability) sends a brilliant flare of allyship to young and marginalized colleagues who are, despite their low visibility in the discipline, constantly surveying the field and gauging its hospitability. True, an affirmative model of AMS abstract selection would come with challenges. How would program committee members know, by name alone, which applicants are minorities? Students? People with low income? With disabilities? Would applicants voluntarily identify themselves in these ways? Would these identifications require verification? Could a senior scholar claim to feel underrepresented or disenfranchised owing to a diminishing ratio of program offerings, over the last few decades, in their area of expertise? Although these questions don't have hard and fast answers—and every committee may improve on past approaches—they can at least begin to work toward resource redistribution and institutional reforms.

Make no mistake: hemming and hawing over the practicalities of any race- or class-affirmative policy is a familiar stalling tactic. As the author Ta-Nehisi Coates observes with regard to the systemic compensation for historic crimes against African Americans: "Broach the topic of reparations today and a barrage of questions inevitably follows: Who will be paid? How much will they be paid? Who will pay?"[11] For some of the people firing off the interrogative barrage, Coates says, the hope is that the sheer mention of logistical headaches might move plaintiffs to drop the case altogether. But belief in the just cause must precede blueprints for action; any anticipated challenges of fulfilling the cause aren't an excuse to abandon pursuit.

Many scholars surely enter the discipline of musicology with hopes that their love for its topics and communities would somehow be reciprocated. For scholars who have felt marginalized by musicology and by the AMS on the basis of color, gender, disability, class, or employment status, the pain of unrequited love can become too much, and leaving the field ends up being the most sensible option. Even someone who loves musicology with all her heart can't be expected to stay in the relationship if it has shown itself, time and again, to be unjust.

I began with Imani Mosley's insightful reactions to Pierpaolo Polzonetti's article, and I end with them. "Would the people so up in arms, rushing to Polzonetti's defense, listen to what I have to say, acknowledge my feelings? Or would I be another whiny, petulant junior scholar?" Mosley asked. "This hurts me so much because I love this field with all of my heart. I have it in *ink on my skin*. And I know how meaningful and enriching the work can be to both the practitioners and to society. This is not what I want the world to see when they look at *us*." By "ink on my skin," Mosley was referring to her tattoos of Benjamin Britten (the subject of her dissertation) and Johann Sebastian Bach. Proof of love indeed.

And by "us"? That's the open question.[12]

4

Feeling Overcome

With head held high, a twenty-one-year-old man strides into a room and sees four celebrity judges. Identifying himself as a Cuban immigrant living in Florida, he speaks with a stutter—haltingly, laboriously, unsteadily. But as he goes on to sing, he does so fluidly and effortlessly and confidently. The judges compliment his beautiful voice and positive vibe. A couple of them even tell him that he should just sing all the time. As grateful tears stream down this auditionee's face, a resounding quartet of *yeses* sends him through to the next round of the competition.

With assistance, a twenty-six-year-old woman walks cautiously onto a large stage. She does not identify herself to four judges who are, for the moment, turned away from her. Hearing her musical cue, the woman sings marvelously, winning applause from the studio audience. After the performance, she tells the judges—who have since swiveled around in their chairs to face her—that she cannot see them because of her glaucoma. One judge asks her why she has chosen to try out for the show. She says she was attracted to its format: how the judges initially could not see her, just as she could not (and still cannot) see them. Her response elicits delighted chuckles from the judges and audience members. A "double-blind" audition, a rare promise of parity . . . maybe.

With uneven gait, a man of unknown age makes his way into a gigantic auditorium to greet four judges and an audience of hundreds. His limbs appear unusual in length and form. When asked how old he is, he replies that he is not sure: as a child, he was rescued from an Iraqi orphanage by a woman who became his adoptive mother. As he sings, his performance draws cheers and tears. Afterward, one judge commends this contestant for his courage. Another judge says he won her over as soon as he stepped onto the stage. He is voted through unanimously. The crowd goes wild.

Supercrip Stories

Tales of overcoming have dominated reality competitions since this television genre took global flight at the turn of the millennium. The three preceding vignettes describe the respective auditions of Lazaro Arbos on *American Idol* (2013), Andrea Begley on *The Voice UK* (2013), and Emmanuel Kelly on *The X Factor Australia* (2011) (Figure 4.1). These singers have joined the vast ranks of reality contestants with wide-ranging disabilities—disabilities that rarely go unremarked on the shows, but rather become illuminated as the crux of inspirational, lovable stories. Such auditionees in recent years include Luca Patuelli (a breakdancer with arthrogryposis), Jack Carroll (a

Figure 4.1. (*Top*) Lazaro Arbos on *American Idol* (2013), (*bottom left*) Andrea Begley on *The Voice UK* (2013), and (*bottom right*) Emmanuel Kelly on *The X Factor Australia* (2011). Screen captures by author.

fourteen-year-old comedian with cerebral palsy), Justin LeBlanc (a Deaf fashion designer), Connor Doran (a virtuoso kite flier with epilepsy), and Liu Wei (an armless boy who plays piano with his toes).[1] Through demonstrations of specialized abilities, disabled individuals exemplify the rags-to-riches ideals of reality competitions more broadly.[2] For hopeful contestants dealing with impairments, strife, loss, poverty, or trauma, the meritocratic dream coheres in a tempting belief that talent, ambition, and hard work can prevail over all adversity.

Producers of reality competitions expertly play up disability narratives to maximize emotional impact and popular appeal. Before showing an audition, a program usually offers glimpses into the contestant's life via on-site interviews, off-site footage, and solicited materials such as childhood photos and home videos. Accompanying these mini-biopics are stirring musical underscores and the contestant's reflective voice-overs. Cross-fades, slow motion, and other visual effects conjure sympathetic, sentimental auras. Some series go to even greater lengths to ramp up the theatrics. On his lengthy *X Factor Australia* audition segment, Emmanuel Kelly is first shown walking through a backstage area filled with machine-generated fog, which dramatically sets up his subsequent onstage declaration that he was born in an Iraqi battle zone (think: fog of war). During Kelly's audition, home viewers see abundant close-ups of the weeping, transfixed faces of the judges and studio audience. Later, as the judges praise the performance, we hear triumphant background music—the song "Kings and Queens" by Thirty Seconds to Mars—which drops a thumping bass just as a beaming Kelly receives his final *yes* vote and walks off the stage into the outstretched arms of his ecstatic mother and similarly disabled brother.

Inspirational auditions like Kelly's boast high viral potential and become eagerly shared among friends and coworkers as heartwarming pick-me-ups. But insofar as reality competitions cash in on these token appearances by contestants with impairments, the format may end up treating adversity in exploitative, reductive ways. Disability, neatly packaged, enables producers to turn stories of plight into profit. Recall, from Chapter 2, David Mitchell's and Sharon Snyder's idea of "ablenationalism." Mitchell and Snyder have likewise pointed out how disability frequently serves as a "narrative prosthesis," a construct "used throughout history as a crutch upon which literary narratives lean for their representational power, disruptive potentiality, and analytical insight."[3] Narratives of overcoming disability are prone to sliding from good-natured celebration into patronizing lionization. Media hyperexposure of "savants" and "supercrips" erects problematic hierarchies within disability communities, implicitly devaluing impaired individuals who are not deemed sufficiently *extra*-extraordinary.[4] (The flawed yet pervasive slippage: If *this* blind contestant can dance so beautifully, shouldn't all blind people manage—or at least attempt—to do so? Or, thinking back again to Chapter 2: If the homeless pianist Donald Gould can overcome his circumstances, then why can't all homeless people give this path a chance?)

Supercrip stories can further fetishize the extraordinarily ordinary, lauding disabled people for accomplishing feats that fall within easier reach of able-bodied individuals.[5] On reality competitions, specific talents (musical performance, dance, fashion design, culinary arts) sparkle as golden foils for otherwise down-on-their-luck contestants. In these arenas, then, there are actually two narrative prostheses at work: first, contestants' disabilities, which are extensively captured, distorted, and simplified by reality television's presentational strategies; and second, the contestants' valorized abilities that, when cast in a compensatory light, function as putative counterweights to physical, neurological, or social deviance.

Stories of disability and overcoming supply reliable comfort food to the millions of viewers who consume reality shows as part of their weekly media diets. Mixing sentimental narratives with sensational performances yields feel-good television, plotting out predictable trajectories that culminate in thunderous applause and messages of hope. Granted, not all viewers buy into reality television at face value. Many express skepticism toward the format's narrative conceits, complain about producers' ulterior motives, wonder whether judges' responses are scripted, and venture theories about rigged votes.[6] Exacerbating such speculation are the shows' ubiquitous product placements (Coca-Cola, Subway, Starbucks), which heighten consumers' cynical impression that reality shows may be selling out in general, valuing commercial appeal over authentic talent.[7]

But here's what is so potent about reality television and its overcoming narratives: even viewers who protest the shady business of these programs are sometimes the same people who tune in faithfully, contribute to online discussions, and take time to upload videos of their favorite contestants. The fanbase of *American Idol*, describes ethnomusicologist Katherine Meizel, "negotiates the product/text puzzle in a scenario where awareness of manufacture, as a central theme of the show, is high, but somehow belief remains strong as well. It is one of *American Idol*'s most intriguing properties that viewers can maintain a skeptical attitude about the show and its processes, and yet still sit down in front of the television every Tuesday with their AT&T phones at the ready to log their votes."[8] Despite the knowledge that reality television doesn't offer unfiltered reality or absolutely fair procedures, fans appear socially and monetarily willing to embrace the shows. One reason is that overcoming narratives have tremendous ability to instill feelings of love, compassion, empathy, and spiritual conviction. Producers of reality shows bank precisely on the timeless appeal of human interest stories—on how even if people see through these stories, this means they are at least watching and bumping up ratings.

In disability studies to date, scholars have critiqued overcoming narratives mainly with analyses of their representational strategies, cultural contexts, and semantic nuances (in films, television shows, plays, memoirs, and news reports), in effect probing what the texts *mean* and how they signify.[9] In this chapter, I travel a parallel path, one that touches on what overcoming narratives *do* and how they act on the people who consume them. I'm interested here in feeling as much as I am in meaning. With reality competitions, stories of overcoming proffer inspirational tropes that stand to *overcome* audiences in turn. By bringing viewers' bodies, agencies, emotions, and perceptual faculties into focus, tales of uplift can be so viscerally compelling that they leave us at a loss for satisfactory criticisms. Before we know it, waterworks undam, sending us grasping at words and groping for tissues. For even if some overcoming narratives might come off corny and contrived, the fact remains that they have extraordinary powers to charm and disarm, undermining viewers' self-determination and efforts at adjudication. Triumphant tales can seem grand yet also cheap in multiple senses of the word—formulaic (cheaply conceived), easily manufactured (cheap in labor costs), and manipulative (cheap shots to bleeding hearts). At the same time, viewers might take pleasure in exactly this loss of control, allowing themselves to suspend judgment upon surrendering to an irresistible montage. Overcoming narratives therefore have the ability to leave consumers feeling ambivalent and, in some ways, disabled (discursively, critically, even physiologically). Beyond identifying the resonances of vulnerability, precarity, and resistance in disability and its metaphors, I'm invested in how these affects play out at the interface between disabled performers and the spectators who celebrate or criticize them.

As the approximate midpoint of *Loving Music Till It Hurts*, this chapter grapples with reality shows' songs and stories, which can be lovable yet suspect, tearjerking yet bothersome. Reality shows hinge on judgments—by the celebrity judges, by studio audiences, by voting viewers. More pro-foundly, they hinge on (recalling Chapter 1) the sensational *mis*judgments of humanity—the initial jeers heaped on the likes of Susan Boyle, and then the triumphant performance that proved doubters wrong. Indeed, of all the talents featured on reality shows, singing ability has long stood out as a com-pelling and romanticized corrective for disability.[10] Singing competitions highlight the lyric voice as a natural instrument, a catch-all vehicle for hu-manity, sincerity, and an ably communicative body. For performers with mobility impairments, the singing voice ostensibly overcomes kinesthetic limits and the challenges of *space*, filling up auditoriums and projecting into viewers' living rooms across the country; for performers who speak with a stutter but sing fluently, signs of crip *time* (delays and temporal vicissitudes related to disability) likewise sound smoothed over.[11] Beautiful singing can inspire discourses of transcendence and ineffability, yet also fulfill an ironically normalizing function in cases of already extraordinary bodies. To the extent reality competitions glorify lyric proficiency as evidence of a contestant's normalcy, they simultaneously conceal, mitigate, or draw at-tention away from impairments at hand, potentially curbing rather than generating much-needed conversations *about* disability. Whereas matters of disability are liable to leave audiences at a loss for words (out of anxieties about, say, political correctness), people may feel relatively at ease using safe, standard vocabularies to pass technical judgments on voice alone, on "the music itself." A normalish-sounding song, in other words, offers listeners a comfortable point of critical fixation. Autonomously conceived, musical ability is a lovely thing to put on its own pedestal, enabling representations and assessments of performers as though disability were inconsequential. Across these exercises in imagination and elision, however, it is ultimately ableism and prejudice that most urgently need overcoming.

Voice Alone

Reality singing competitions sell an endearing promise: perform beauti-fully enough, and maybe the world will love you. But in these competitions, it is no secret that contestants' longevity depends on far more than vocal ability. Image, personality, marketability, and intangibles all come into play.[12] More accurately, this is an *open* secret—for while judges, hosts, contestants, and fans know that adept singing alone cannot ensure victory, they still

sometimes talk about vocal prowess as if it were an isolatable, reigning crite-
rion. As described in Chapter 3's examples of anonymous auditions, people's
emphasis on the importance of musical ability champions a brand of meritocracy that responsibly prioritizes measurable talent over appearance and
artifice. In reality shows, fan-voting systems dangle a utopian brand of ultimate democracy, spinning out false yet comforting justifications for who
wins and who loses.

Valorization of vocal merit is the central gimmick of *The Voice*, which
premiered in 2011 and delivered a twist on the formulas of its generic
predecessors.[13] With two cycles per calendar year (winter and fall), the lucrative show kicks off each season with several episodes of Blind Auditions.
Four celebrity coaches sit in electronic swivel chairs and start by facing away
from the onstage performer, who performs a song with prerecorded accompaniment.[14] Coaches who like what they hear can hit a button to turn around
in their chairs before the audition ends. Contestants advance in the competition if they coax at least one chair turn. But Blind Auditions make up only the
first round of *The Voice*. Like the Vienna Philharmonic, like most symphony
orchestras that begin with auditions behind screens, *The Voice* removes the
element of anonymity in subsequent rounds (Chapter 3). Even prior to the
show's televised Blind Auditions, prospective contestants must first perform in full view for producers at the Open Call Auditions and the Callback
Auditions. At the producers' discretion, these contestants must then "voluntarily submit to and complete a background check" and to "examinations
to be conducted in Los Angeles, CA, by medical professionals selected by
and paid for by the Producer."[15] Only after this preliminary visual, legal, and
medical scrutiny does a tiny pool of remaining contestants get to sing for the
celebrity coaches at the Blind Auditions. How anonymous is this procedure,
then, if lawyers have combed through your life's records to ensure that your
presence on the show will not be a liability? Or if physicians have listened to
your heartbeat, scanned your organs, peered into your bodily cavities, and
literally seen you inside and out?

Once a *Voice* contestant has finally made it onto a televised Blind Audition,
the coaches usually end up snatching more screen time than the singer. In
close-up shots, coaches variously scrunch up their cheeks, crease their eyes,
purse their lips, mouth words to one another, and keep their hands hovering
above their all-important buttons as if in agony over whether to take a chance
on the unseen contestant (Figure 4.2). Such agony, conveyed not just by
coaches' faces but also by their gesticulating bodies, is itself a spectacle to

Figure 4.2. (*Left*) *The Voice* coach Usher looks as though he were having a hard time deciding whether to push his button for Season 4 auditionee Caroline Glaser (2013), and (*right*) Season 5 auditionee Matthew Schuler quickly manages to tempt four judges to turn around (2013). Screen captures by author.

behold—an odd kind of music-induced hurt, as these adjudicators resolve whether certain disembodied voices are lovable enough, worthy enough for a leap of faith. More so than other reality singing shows, in short, *The Voice* places listening on display. As auditionees perform music, the coaches *perform audition*, putting on a melodrama of taut aurality and tantalizing ambivalence.

Although coaches on *The Voice* often maximize suspense by waiting until the end of an audition to hit their button (or not), they do choose, on rare occasions, to turn around as soon as a contestant begins singing. Season 5 contestant Matthew Schuler made headlines by simultaneously winning all four judges just seconds into his rendition of "Cough Syrup," a song by Young the Giant.[16] An early chair turn represents exceptional praise, signaling a coach's high confidence in the singer. It epitomizes the belief that stardom can reside in a voice's infinitesimal grain (timbre, tone, color) irrespective of the performer's endurance, consistency, technical range, and dramatic arc.[17] Such preemptive judgment is curious not least because it is typically *sight* that we describe as a no-lag faculty, and *hearing* as a process that unfolds over time.[18] (The speed of light, the blink of an eye, love at first sight: it's no coincidence that idioms of instantaneity rely overwhelmingly on optical and ocular metaphors.) Yet despite music's status as a temporal art, singing can compel snap judgments, reducing appraisals of excellence to a few good vibrations. In the case of *The Voice*, coaches have pride at stake. Swiftly endorsing a great voice allows them to appear confident and knowledgeable, like busy talent scouts who are so good at their jobs that the first line of a demo tape is all they need to hear. (During *The Voice* auditions, moreover, the sooner coaches turn around for a contestant, the more strongly they can claim afterward that they believed in this singer from the beginning—a notable advantage if multiple coaches end up fighting to recruit the same person.) Thus while Blind Auditions on this show may eschew the trappings of visual prejudice, they ironically encourage a degree of hasty judgment and even guesswork.

A *Voice* coach's chair turn produces a miniature audiovisual spectacle on its own, activating a deliciously reverberant *whoosh* and lighting up a column of square panels from chair to stage. But even this technological luster pales in comparison to the variously delighted, enthralled, or flabbergasted faces of coaches as they turn to see a singer. Blind Auditions on *The Voice* bank on moments when these celebrities display utter surprise toward the purported mismatch between a contestant's voice and appearance. Although preconceptions of sex, race, and physical attractiveness all come into play, coaches rarely address these touchy topics of human identity and appearance head on. Euphemisms, code words, deflective humor, physical affection (a hug between coach and contestant), stock praise, and speechless amazement obviate the need to detail the reasons for such surprise. During the Blind Auditions for Season 9 (2015), contestant Jordan Smith performed Sia's warhorse of a song "Chandelier" and received four chair turns. Upon swiveling around, coach Gwen Stefani kicked up one leg over her head and nearly fell out of her seat, exclaiming "What? Whaaaaat?" Once the song ended, Stefani ran to the stage and threw her arms around Smith (Figure 4.3). "Oh my god," she cried, "you shocked me! You do not look like your voice, FYI."[19] *The Voice* did not show Stefani specifying—for our information!—the rationale for shock. Was Stefani shocked because she hadn't expected Smith to be white? Young? Male? And if any or all of these factors were in play, then why didn't the other three coaches look remotely fazed when they turned around? Recall the loud unblindings described at the end of Chapter 3: the outrage of oenophiles during the 1976 Judgment of Paris, the shock of the Munich Philharmonic jury during trombonist Abbie Conant's 1980 anonymous audition, and a famous diner's patronizing remarks about Niki Nakayama and her kaiseki restaurant. Big reveals, revelatory reactions.

With regard to Jordan Smith, critics and journalists didn't fare much better when trying to articulate this singer's alleged voice-body mismatch. "With his demure glasses and cardigan and that baby face," wrote one reviewer, "it's hard to believe such amazing range, power, and even a little rocker edge could come out of Jordan!"[20] Another writer described Smith as "sort of regular-looking: pale and doughy, a bit hunched, wearing glasses that contract his eyes into wet-looking seeds."[21] Short of pinpointing Stefani's train of thought,

Figure 4.3. (*Top left and right*) Coach Gwen Stefani and contestant Jordan Smith on NBC's *The Voice*, and (*bottom from left to right*) the expressions of coaches Blake Shelton, Pharrell Williams, and Adam Levine upon turning around.

we can nevertheless observe how an adjudicator's own song and dance might gesture to the biases, stereotypes, and identity politics that remain verbally masked even after deanonymization takes place. A gushing remark such as "you do not look like your voice, FYI" leaves the insinuations (nebulized around a simile-teasing *like*) suspended mid-dialogue, a suspension easily forgotten by the time viewers find themselves aww-ing over a heartwarming hug between the thunderstruck celebrity and the starstruck contestant.

Ebullient yet vague praise likewise reigns supreme when contestants defy racial stereotypes. In the second season of *X Factor USA* (2012), a black auditionee named Willie Jones walked onto the stage and was hailed by judge Demi Lovato as "very Fresh Prince of Bel-Air" (Figure 4.4). As Jones began to perform, audience members' jaws began to drop, for he had chosen to sing Josh Turner's 2005 country hit, "Your Man" (Figure 4.4). After the audition, judge L. A. Reid gushed to Jones, "You are an absolute original." Added judge Britney Spears, as vaguely as possible: "I was very surprised. I wasn't expecting that. [. . .] It's very original of you to do what you just did."[22] And in Season 8 of *America's Got Talent* (2013), black auditionee Travis Pratt, in a countertenor range, sang a Giacomo Puccini aria, "O mio babbino caro," that left the audience visibly flabbergasted. Judge Howard Stern told Pratt, "This

Figure 4.4. (*Left*) Willie Jones on *X Factor USA* eliciting (*middle and right*) expressions of surprise.

is the most outrageous audition I have ever seen. [. . .] You are a freak, but I mean it, like, in a good way."[23] What was so freaky? What exactly had people been expecting out of these black contestants? Rap? Funk? R&B? (Yes.) Tellingly, the purported novelty of Willie Jones and Travis Pratt took them only so far, as they were both cut from their respective shows mere weeks into the season. Good for a playing-against-type cameo, then right out the door.

At his audition, Pratt was hailed as a "freak" perhaps because the judges weren't comfortable calling him "black"—that is, naming his blackness (and apparently mismatched voice) as the part of his identity that caused apparent shock and awe.[24] Like the common phrase "that's so crazy!," the commendation "you're a freak!" is a time-buying rhetorical device. (We could even think of "freak" as the ableist cousin of the weirdly empty word "interesting," which, as literary theorist Sianne Ngai points out, is "particularly handy as a euphemism, filling the slot for a judgment conspicuously withheld [. . .] like sticking a Post-It in a book."[25]) For a number of systemic reasons, black people are a minority in US country music and classical music circles. Yet the outsized "enfreakment" of those who do travel in these circles probably isn't helping the cause of diversification.[26] At times, the performances and judgments on reality shows will indeed elicit gasps and exclamations. On other occasions? Quiet, streaming tears.

Refrain: "What Is All This Teary Stuff Doing in My Eyes?"

Blind women who run at Olympic pace, talented jazz musicians with Tourette's syndrome, deaf heart surgeons, or famous actors with a stutter are the usual stuff of these narratives. In each case, ability trumps disability, creating a morality tale about one person's journey from disease to cure, from inhumanity to humanity. These accounts fit with the masquerade because they exaggerate the disability of their heroes, suggesting that it is a mask that can be easily removed to uncover the real human being beneath. But they also exaggerate in the process the connection between humanness and ability, giving happy relief and assurance to those who consider themselves healthy.

—Tobin Siebers[27]

Although reality competitions have blossomed into an international phenomenon—with *Idol, Voice, Got Talent, So You Think You Can Dance,* and *X Factor* variants spanning dozens of countries—shows in the United States offer an opportune lens to critique overcoming narratives rooted in the meritocratic ideals of the American Dream.[28] Reality television, like the American Dream, is brimming with contradictions. It is both real and unreal, ordinary and extraordinary, transparent and opaque. Especially in the wake of earthshaking events, people compare their so-called new reality *to* reality television as a means of making sense of what seems senseless. Put differently, when people feel overcome by a lack of historical precedents to explain the bizarre present, they often lean on the analogies of entertainment media.

Among the most influential reality series is *American Idol*, which premiered on June 11, 2002, exactly nine months after the Twin Towers fell on September 11, 2001. As noted by Katherine Meizel, the show offered a post-9/11 "microcosmic arena where discourses of American music and correlating, intertwined narratives of American identity are belted into a microphone and judged by millions."[29] Al-Qaeda's attacks jolted Americans into the realization that anything is possible. *American Idol* promised viewers the same thing, except with immanent optimism instead of imminent terror: anything *is* possible, from fame and glory to healing and hope. More broadly, it's worth remembering how *American Idol* burst onto the Fox Network during a year when executives were wringing their hands about how to balance the profits, ethics, and optics of television programming for a post-9/11 consumer culture.[30] "On September 11, the everydayness of television itself was suddenly disrupted by news of something completely 'alien' to the usual patterns of domestic TV," recalls communications scholar Lynn Spigel. "The nonstop commercial-free coverage, which lasted for a full week on major broadcast networks and cable news networks, contributed to a sense of estrangement from ordinary life."[31] Yet by the weekend of September 15, news anchors were telling viewers to "return to the 'normal' everyday schedule of television entertainment," in the same way politicians began calling for "a return to normalcy" and "normal levels of consumerism."[32] Ratings—and capitalism—couldn't afford to crumble.

When *American Idol* crowned its first winner, Kelly Clarkson, on September 4, 2002, dual specters of terror and nationalism coalesced and came full circle. Just days after her victory, Clarkson received an invitation to perform the "Star-Spangled Banner" for a commemorative event at the Lincoln Memorial in Washington, DC. In the week leading up to September 11, 2002, controversies flared. Some people accused Clarkson and her management company of, as the *New York Times* put it, "turning a day of national mourning into a giant promotional opportunity."[33] Clarkson reportedly tried to back out of the engagement. In the end, however, she sang with neither much fanfare nor backlash. Amid the torrent of think pieces, remembrances, and coverage of other commemorative events, Clarkson's straightforward performance of the national anthem barely received any press coverage. For Clarkson and her managers, this was the best outcome. After all, in virtually every regard, she was already perfect as an inaugural American Idol. She had come from a family of modest means. She had worked as a telemarketer and a cocktail waitress. She had faced multiple rejections from record labels. And she overcame these adversities on a show that was, in its own right, a parable of overcoming the strife of modern times.

Reality singing competitions weave a rich tapestry of audiovisual spectacle. Emotions run high amid montages of contestants' tribulations, sentimental background music, dazzling acts, and trickling tears of pathos and pride. As performers, judges, and audience members cry, their faces serve as visual loci of identification for the home viewers who may be moved to mirror these sobs in kind (Figure 4.5). In an influential essay, "Film Bodies: Gender, Genre, and Excess," Linda Williams classified pornography, melodrama, and horror as "body genres" for the way they move "the body of the spectator [to be] caught up in an almost involuntary mimicry of the emotion or sensation of the body on the screen," resulting in "an apparent lack of proper esthetic distance, a sense of over-involvement in sensation and emotion."[34] Alongside these three body genres, the modern reality competition perhaps deserves an honorary fourth spot. It hews closely to melodrama, but its nominal framing as *reality* ups the ante with real people, high stakes, huge cash prizes, and record deals.

Figure 4.5. (*Left*) Tears from coach will.i.am on *The Voice UK* (2014), and (*right*) tears from contestant Stacy Francis on *X Factor USA* (2011). Screen captures by author.

With today's public growing ever more mindful of reality television's controlled artifice and power over fans, it can be gratifying for consumers to witness someone losing apparent control on a show. Teary outbursts, laughing fits, and spontaneous altercations expose the famous faces on these programs as humanly susceptible to emotional whims.[35] Disabled or nondisabled, a contestant who appears "genuine" can win strong favor with judges and fans.[36] "Hard work, happiness, familial moments, tears, stress, laughter, and joy add to each contestant's authenticity," Amanda McClain points out with regard to *American Idol*, "paradoxically adding to their celebrity by being normal."[37] Contestants' displays of emotion and exertion make an attractive mix of vulnerability and confidence—the confidence to *appear* vulnerable, to let go, to bare tender souls to a live audience of millions.

Stories of overcoming are easy to love. They arouse, uplift, invigorate. Inspirational though they may be, however, these tales can come across as exploitative maneuvers that unfairly take consumers' intellectual faculties hostage. For how does one objectively judge a singer who has confessed to recently losing her mother or losing her sight? How and why would one nitpick technical shortcomings when confronting a hopeful, tearful contestant determined to stand as living proof of survival against all odds? A contestant's tearjerking story might send viewers scurrying for emotional sanctuary. And even though it's easy to be cynical and dismissive when contemplating these stories in the abstract, it proves considerably more difficult when hearing a specific tale with vivid stakes and faces attached. A touchy-feely story compels us simultaneously to raise our defenses and to let them down. No one wants to be taken for a sap, but there isn't much virtue in shutting down sympathy altogether.

As with our susceptibility to the musical mystique, our vulnerability to overcoming narratives is a reminder that we are human, and only human (Chapter 1). We might let a contestant's story and song wash over us one evening, then suddenly find ourselves crying uncontrollably, uncharacteristically. Recall the "weepers" who live-chatted with Gene Weingarten about the Joshua Bell experiment (Chapter 2). Many of these readers confessed they were crying without really knowing why. "I was wiping my eyes thinking 'what the heck is wrong with me,'" one person told Weingarten in the chatroom. "Why did this article make me cry?" wondered another. Follow the comment threads under any YouTube video featuring a reality show contestant's feat of overcoming, and we would find a similar pattern: viewers' declarations of crying, along with confusion about one's own tears. Implicit in these confessions is that crying shows an embarrassing lack of control. Yet people's eagerness to describe the inexplicability of their tears signals a concomitant awareness that maybe crying isn't so bad.

Scholars probably cry as much as anyone else, despite academia's connotations of critical and stoic inquiry. For both research and recreational purposes, I have watched hundreds of hours of reality competitions, and taken in more overcoming stories than I can count. And some of these stories still make me cry, even as I try not to let my tears interfere with my task of scribbling down notes. I can't help it. I might chide myself for crying, then take comfort in knowing that at least I'm crying in the privacy of my living room. But why should scholars be expected to be tear-free even in public professional settings? At the 2000 conference for the Modern Language Association, disability scholars Elizabeth J. Donaldson and Catherine Prendergast both cried during their panel when they related stories of their loved ones with schizophrenia. They went on to write an article titled "There's No Crying in Disability Studies!" Spontaneous tears can be embarrassing, inappropriate, "unprofessional," and yet ultimately revelatory. "Our bodies, and our minds, do not always conform to prescribed norms and regulations," remark Donaldson and Prendergast. "Crying when one wishes not to cry is both a bodily refusal and an inability to contain or to be contained by these rules. There is a certain power in transgression; abject bodies and abject emotions can reveal the fault lines of foundational concepts of what the body should be or should do."[38] In an academic gathering, the encroachment of tears can swiftly shatter the illusion of disembodied thought. Bodies don't always fall in line even in one's devotion to a life of the mind.

Narratives of overcoming permeate reality competitions and tug at heartstrings. But how real are these narratives? Producers meticulously extract sellable stories from their contestants. For starters, proof of artifice can be found in the fine print of a show. Release forms lay out the executives' far-reaching liberties to control, concoct, and knowingly misrepresent any aspect of a contestant's image, sound, and backstory. To audition for *America's Got Talent*, for example, contestants must sign a legal agreement containing this clause: "My appearance, depiction, and portrayal in connection with the Program or in any aspect or phase thereof (including, without limitation, the interview and audition process), may be disparaging, defamatory, embarrassing or of an otherwise unfavorable nature, may expose me to public ridicule, humiliation or condemnation, and may portray me in a false light."[39] Contracts further bar contestants from ever denying or denouncing the ways in which they have been factually or fictionally portrayed by a program. Contestants who violate these stipulations stand to owe millions of dollars ($5 million is a common figure) in liability. Given the high stakes of top-grossing reality shows, contracts are expectedly filled with absolutist language that neatly closes loopholes in the producers' favor: "including but not limited to," "throughout the universe in perpetuity," "for any reason or for no reason at all," and other stern jargon can shackle participants between a boilerplate and a hard place.

Draconian, daresay Faustian, contracts are occupational hazards in the entertainment industry. At times, however, excessive publicity about reality television's terms and conditions can threaten the wholesome, family-friendly image of these talent-scouting shows. During the first season of *American Idol* in 2002, Los Angeles music attorney Gary Fine obtained the show's release agreement from a contestant and leaked its contents on the Internet (more on leaks in Chapter 5). A scandal broke out as news sites and blogs ripped into the contract's severity, notably a clause that granted producers "the unconditional right throughout the universe in perpetuity to use, simulate or portray [. . .] my name, likeness (whether photographic or otherwise), voice, singing voice, personality, personal identification or personal experiences, my life story, biographical data, incidents, situations and events which heretofore occurred or hereafter occur."[40] Here, the word "simulate" gave producers the legal prerogative to mold contestants however they wished. For viewers invested in their favorite contestants' musical talents, no less distressing was the inclusion of "singing voice" as a variable deemed fair game for dissemblance and manipulation. If a reality show about singing is allowed to fake the voices of its singers, then what vestiges of verifiable meritocracy remain?

To expedite on-site auditions, several reality competitions today make their release agreements available online. While these contracts are not confidential per se, they hide in plain sight: first, because contestants who sign the forms are unlikely to read them carefully, if at all; and second, because casual viewers of these programs have little reason to go looking for this paperwork. Poring over the legal minutiae of one's favorite reality show can be a disillusioning exercise. The realities of fakery on these shows are inconvenient truths that most fans don't care to face. Release agreements, after all, paint a suspicious image of shows, arguably setting out terms of subjugation masquerading as avuncular concern and mutual welfare. Contractual prices of admission can be so high because, according to a reality show's paternalistic conceits, participants receive a shot at something supposedly priceless—namely, celebrity. Contestants, the subtext goes, should be willing and downright grateful for the chance to be rescued from lives of obscurity, mediocrity, and, in some cases, disability. As much as a reality program may depict its competitors pulling themselves up by their bootstraps through talent and hard work, viewers are reminded at every turn—via interviews with thankful contestants, the testimonials of proud family members, and the host's sentimental announcements—that the show is responsible for furnishing these lucky breaks to begin with.

To shore up their role as purveyors of opportunity, reality competitions favor participants with attractive overcoming stories. Producers scope out auditionees' backgrounds from the outset. Prospective contestants for *America's Got Talent* must fill out a questionnaire asking the following:

> Who in your life do you want to make the most proud and why?
> What obstacles have you overcome in pursuing your act?
> Please describe a major event that has affected your life.[41]

Such questions work to extract tales of struggle. Common obstacles reported by contestants include physical impairments, mental illness, injuries, near-death experiences, unemployment, impoverishment, eviction, divorce, single parenthood, familial alienation, domestic abuse, substance abuse, bereavement, professional rejection, and loss of faith. Even with persistent talk of talent and technique, reality shows' barrage of human interest stories sends an imperative message to fans and hopeful auditionees alike: merit alone isn't enough. Shows all but explicitly tell contestants that a good story is mandatory.

Even if you have to make one up.

Triumphant Fictions

On reality competitions, sensationalist performances defy belief—at least, this is what clickbait headlines need viewers to believe. Audition clips for *Idol, Got Talent*, and similar programs bear titles and captions such as

> You won't believe the sound of this girl's voice!
> Everyone laughed at him but you won't believe what happens next . . .
> Simon [Cowell] didn't believe he is from Earth!

Titular claims of unbelievability typically point up a disconnect between audiences' modest expectations and the spectacular performance that follows. Disabled, disheveled, homeless, and very young or very old contestants might strike viewers as "incredible" because of societal expectations around what these individuals can or cannot do. As with the "shocking" pianism of the homeless Donald Gould (Chapter 2), reality show contestants' "unbelievable" performances are met with spectators' vocal and physiognomic expressions of disbelief in kind.

On some occasions, a contestant's extraordinary performance will elicit actual disbelief, even outright accusations of fakery. In 2012, a woman named Aida Yurijivna Nikolaychuk auditioned for *X Factor Ukraine* with the song "Lullaby," written by Russian singer-songwriter Polina Gargarina. During the performance, Nikolaychuk's voice was so in tune that the judges suspected she was lip-synching to a recorded track. One judge shook her head dubiously; another scooped out his ear piece; and throughout the audition, they whispered to one another with utmost concern. Nikolaychuk was eventually signaled by a judge to stop, and was then asked to sing the same song a cappella to prove her voice was live. She obliged . . . and her unaccompanied live vocals ended up sounding just as pristine. As the audience burst into applause, the judges unanimously voted her through to the next round.[42] Months later, Nikolaychuk won the entire season.

Nikolaychuk's case is unusual in the way it aroused doubts about the authenticity of her voice. More frequently, viewers' doubts pertain to the authenticity of a contestant's *story*. Backlash can be severe when fans suspect contestants of feigning their emotions or lying about their life circumstances.[43] Take the case of singer Alice Fredenham, who, during her 2013 audition for *Britain's Got Talent*, confessed to her serious stage fright. On camera, she wrung her hands, spoke timidly, and wiped tears from her eyes no fewer than nine times. She went on to sing "My Funny Valentine" and received high praise from the judges for a winning exhibition of nerves overcome. Unfortunately, fans later cried fraud upon seeing Fredenham "looking confident" during her appearance on another show, *The Voice UK*, which aired around the same time as this *Britain's Got Talent* episode. The *Daily Mail* reported viewers who believed that Fredenham's "apparent shyness on *Britain's Got Talent*, filmed *three months after* her audition for *The Voice*, was nothing more than a cynical ploy to win votes."[44] To be clear, it didn't matter to some viewers whether Fredenham was, beyond a doubt, deliberately faking. Rumors sufficed to sour people's enthusiasm (Figure 4.6).[45] For all the sympathy that honest tears elicit, then, phony crying can strike fans as both awkward and insulting. A fraudulent show of emotion can fuel public disdain not simply for its deceit, but also because such fakery vexingly calls attention to the artifice of reality television's melodramatic programming in general.[46] It turns a lovably "Unbelievable!" performance into an ambivalent object that genuinely challenges the viewer's assumptions of what kinds of stories can or cannot be believed.

Given the well-known currencies of overcoming narratives on reality shows, hopeful contestants have ample incentives to embellish or outright

Figure 4.6. A nervous-looking Alice Fredenham on *Britain's Got Talent* (2013) as she wrings her hands (*left*) and cries (*right*). As judges praise Fredenham, the show underscores the sentimental moment with "Somewhere Over the Rainbow." Screen captures by author.

fabricate stories of woe. Sometimes, people get caught. Scandals in past years have included two unrelated instances of contestants, on *America's Got Talent* and *American Idol* respectively, lying about having sustained severe injuries in the line of military duty. One of these cases was Timothy Poe, who, in his 2012 audition for *America's Got Talent*, declared that he had suffered a broken back and brain damage from a grenade explosion while serving in Afghanistan.[47] On the show, he explained how his injuries have caused him to speak with a stutter, but how he doesn't stutter when he sings, thanks to his work with a speech therapist. Poe's performance of "If Tomorrow Never Comes" by Garth Brooks won a standing ovation from the audience and the judges (Howie Mandel, Sharon Osbourne, and Howard Stern). Mandel told him, "Everything about you is amazing—I have to say: you, sir, are a phenomenal talent," while Osbourne praised Poe for his "rich, beautiful tone."[48] Later, when Poe returned backstage and proclaimed his excitement about his successful audition, the show's host Nick Cannon gushed, "Man, that was awesome. And I don't know if you just noticed, but this whole sentence that you just said, you didn't stutter one bit."

"That's amazing!" Poe replied.

Within days, military records came out attesting that although Poe had served in the Minnesota National Guard, there were no reports that he was ever injured in combat. The media blew up, accusing Poe of playing the "disabled vet card" and putting on a stutter.[49] Veterans and military personnel were among those who most vigorously sought to expose him. Poe claimed to suffer problems of self-delusion, apologizing tearfully during interviews with ABC News and the *New York Post*. He also confessed that, despite his earlier claims of never having sung before, he had in fact sung in a band. In light of this new information, judge Howie Mandel went on to complain in an interview:

> On so many levels it is so irritating. The truth is, especially at this time in our lives, in this country, I am so thankful for anybody, in any service, for whatever they are doing, and wherever they are stationed. And when [Poe] showed up with this story that he never sang before and the stuttering was part of a brain injury, he captured the hearts and minds and ears of all of America. It certainly helped him in this competition. [. . .] Last week he was publicly praised and honored. Now he is publicly humiliated and he deserves to be publicly humiliated. [. . .] I feel violated. Other service people

feel violated. [. . .] We should not be judging at all on a back story. Whatever the judges do will be based on the talent and whatever he does in Vegas.[50]

Unsurprisingly, Poe was eliminated from *America's Got Talent* during its Vegas callback week. In that episode, however, none of the judges mentioned the scandal. Instead, they concluded out loud, for the cameras, that Poe was not a good enough *singer* to move on in the competition—the same singer whom they had once praised for his "phenomenal talent" and "rich, beautiful tone." Here, we see the rationalizations of meritocracy cutting both ways. By playing up the priority of vocal merit, judges and producers had a convenient excuse to eliminate Poe without addressing any stories of disability, deception, and special dispensation that were otherwise being foregrounded in the news and social media. They didn't need to talk about Poe the person at all. Just about the music itself.

When fans reckon contestants are lying about impairments or injuries, the resulting anxieties serve up reminders of how easily overcoming narratives can scramble one's cognitive filters and faculties. Skepticism aside, tales of adversity and achievement may ultimately be narratives that people *want* to believe. Without accepting a contestant's poignant story wholesale, consumers recognize the value of believing in its believability (compare this, say, to the situation of a person who tells a loved one suspected of lying: *I want to believe you, I really do*). Although we could file this mindset under bad faith, it jibes with a staple feeling: hope.[51] Clichéd as they are, sentimental stories are formidable and, at times, seemingly irresistible. Aptly named, overcoming narratives overcome us in turn, dampening our eyes and giving us chills. As they flood us with feelings, they leave us raw, tender, beside ourselves, *despite* ourselves.

If the overcoming stories on reality shows can occasionally cause fans to feel disempowered and disillusioned, these competitions' voting allowances have sought to restore viewers with a sense of power and meritocracy. Every major American reality singing contest in recent years—*The Voice, X Factor,* and *American Idol*, along with the variety show *America's Got Talent*—has allowed viewers to vote for their favorite contestants. America decides. Such participatory agency, granted, is egalitarian only in theory, and only if we ignore that people's voting capabilities vary. A viewer's ability to vote depends on financial status (calling and texting plans cost money), place of residence (connection speeds and services differ across the country), and disposable time (some viewers can afford to spend more hours voting than others). Each individual fan can indeed cast multiple votes and is outright encouraged by shows to do so, since every call or text fills the coffers of the programs and their partnering service providers. Given the commercialist bent of such voting, fans have theorized conspiracies about miscounts, "power-dialing" (voting via enhanced technical apparatus), producers' interference, and flat-out vote tampering.[52] With so much suspicion in the mix, meritocracy seems but a dream. Yet even if "viewers may question the level of agency actually afforded them in the innovative *Idols* voting processes," observes Katherine Meizel, "the *implications* of agency remain crucial."[53]

Voting aside, among the central draws of a reality competition is how it affords viewers a fantasy of community, an opportunity to feel together— crying and emoting and being overcome along with contestants, judges, studio audience members, and other fans watching across the nation. Before YouTube and DVR, this opportunity typically meant tuning in to a live show. Today, fans further claim participatory agency through the everyday sharing of videos, memes, and tweets. Although the concept of virality dominates contemporary descriptions of digital circulation, the writers Henry Jenkins, Sam Ford, and Joshua Green remark that an uncritical reliance on this met-aphor impedes understandings of how media objects spread. A model of virality, they say, implies that "the spread of ideas and messages can occur without users' consent and perhaps actively against their conscious resist-ance."[54] But while it is important to recognize consumers as active, genera-tive, and cognizant agents, my larger point pertains to how some examples of media can seem so powerful and pervasive that they do appear capable of self-replication. A lovable, clever, or hilarious video *virtually* begs to be passed along to friends and coworkers. We share this material almost *as though* we were overcome by a need to do so.

Given the rapid rates of media circulation, the last thing a modern con-sumer might want is to feel left out or left behind. Accelerated online dialogues and twenty-four-hour news cycles have intensified societal pressures to keep up with the headlines, to share a timely clip on Facebook, and to latch onto a story before its moment has passed. Amid all this speed, however, we can forget to account for the temporal idiosyncrasies—in some cases, the slowness—that result from, among other things, disability and neurodiversity. In rushing to praise or to lambast a reality contestant's voice or narrative, we might forget to take the necessary time to think and talk through disability itself, including vital issues of how different people live according to different parameters, requirements, and sensations of time.

Slow Stigma

Conversations about disability feature plentiful references to time and duration: medical diagnoses of lifespan, philosophical forays into finitude, and disclaimers about the always-temporary nature of able-bodiedness—should one live long enough.[55] People with disabilities are commonly stigmatized as unable to meet deadlines, "bound" in asexual or presexual states, "stunted" in physique and intellect, or otherwise "trapped" in slow bodies and minds.[56] By exhibiting deviance, disabled individuals also get stared at, reified, catalogued, and contained—stuck—in strictures and stereotypes. Especially where mobility and speech impairments are concerned, disability leads to discrimination and exclusion in terms of not just space (unaccommodating architecture and terrain) but also time (daily schedules and temporal norms).

Many reality shows have spotlighted contestants who speak with impediments—slowly, unevenly—yet sing fluently.[57] Notwithstanding the controversial Timothy Poe on *America's Got Talent*, recent examples include Carlos Guevara on *The X Factor USA* and Harrison Craig on *The Voice Australia*. Another high-profile case was Lazaro Arbos on Season 12 of *American Idol*, which premiered in January 2013 and featured judges Mariah Carey, Randy Jackson, Keith Urban, and Nicki Minaj (Figure 4.7).[58] In the episode, Arbos stutters as he answers Carey's basic questions about his name and place of residence. At this point, the show cuts to Arbos's backstory

Figure 4.7. Lazaro Arbos tears up (*left*) while he receives praise (*right*) from the *American Idol* judges (2013). The hashtag overlay reads "#idolinspire." Screen captures by author.

through a montage of childhood photos and a recorded interview with his parents, who speak in Spanish about their son's difficult assimilation into American life. The montage concludes with Arbos saying to the camera, with optimism but apparent effort, "You can't let things get you down, 'cause you have to keep going"—setting the stage for a lyrical display of overcoming.

Following is a transcript of Arbos's exchange with the judges before and after his performance. For the first half, during which Arbos speaks on many occasions, I plot enunciations along a scaled time graph to visualize the temporal flux in play. More so than typical text representations of stuttering's phonics (namely, with repeated consonants and dashes, such as "L-L-Lazaro"), this scaled graph aims to represent the relative pacing of the dialogues (Figures 4.8a and 4.8b).

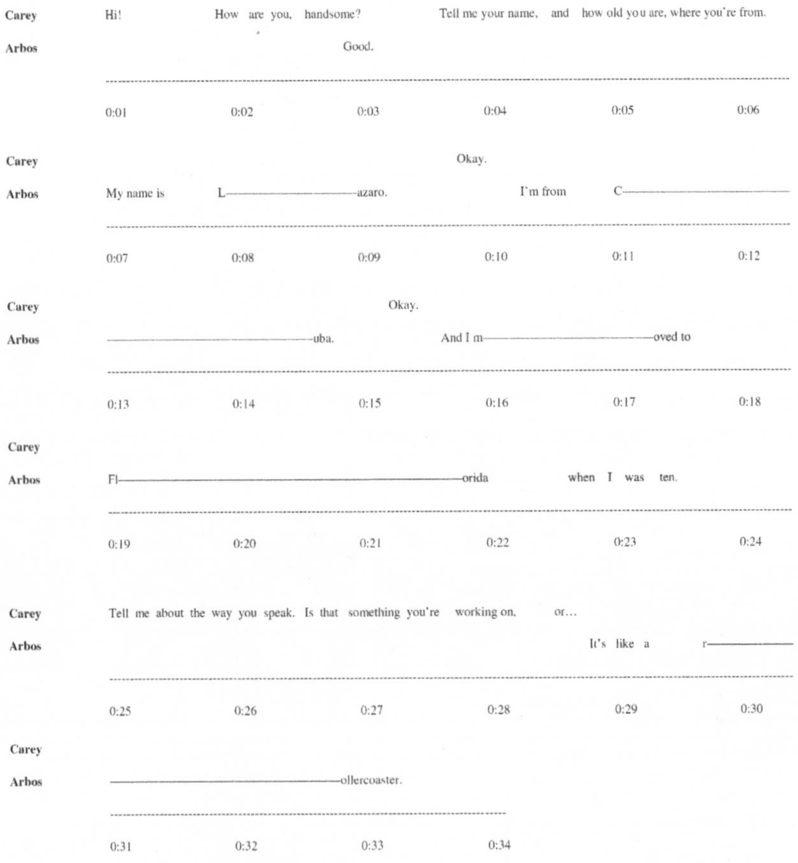

Carey	Hi!		How are you, handsome?		Tell me your name, and how old you are, where you're from.	
Arbos				Good.		
	0:01	0:02	0:03	0:04	0:05	0:06
Carey				Okay.		
Arbos	My name is	L————azaro.			I'm from	C————
	0:07	0:08	0:09	0:10	0:11	0:12
Carey			Okay.			
Arbos		————uba.		And I m————oved to		
	0:13	0:14	0:15	0:16	0:17	0:18
Carey						
Arbos	Fl————orida				when I was ten.	
	0:19	0:20	0:21	0:22	0:23	0:24
Carey	Tell me about the way you speak. Is that something you're working on, or...					
Arbos					It's like a r————	
	0:25	0:26	0:27	0:28	0:29	0:30
Carey						
Arbos	————ollercoaster.					
	0:31	0:32	0:33	0:34		

Figure 4.8a. Arbos's audition.

0:35 to 2:35—*Montage and voice-overs by Arbos and his parents, who relate Arbos's backstory. Interview footage is intercut with pictures of Arbos as a child.*

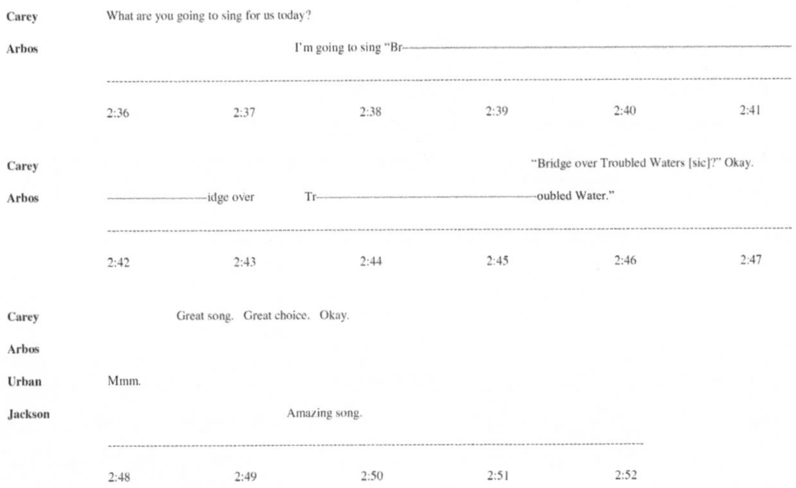

	2:36	2:37	2:38	2:39	2:40	2:41
Carey	What are you going to sing for us today?					
Arbos			I'm going to sing "Br———————————————————————			

	2:42	2:43	2:44	2:45	2:46	2:47
Carey					"Bridge over Troubled Waters [sic]?" Okay.	
Arbos	————idge over	Tr———————————————————			——oubled Water."	

	2:48	2:49	2:50	2:51	2:52
Carey		Great song. Great choice. Okay.			
Arbos					
Urban	Mmm.				
Jackson			Amazing song.		

Figure 4.8b. (continued).

2:52 to 3:55—*Arbos performs Simon and Garfunkel's "Bridge over Troubled Water."*

3:56 to end (transcript):

JACKSON: Wow, wow.

URBAN: You should sing all the time.

CAREY: Randy, what do you think?

JACKSON: Very pleasant. Really, really nice, man. Love your voice. It's amazing that, like, the stammering doesn't happen when you sing. So, Keith just said, just sing all the time.

MINAJ: Your story is very, very inspiring. I think you brought a really great vibe into the room, so . . .

URBAN: I love your tone. I love the way you sing. I love that you did that song. That's one of my all-time favorite songs. It's just so—it just elicits so much emotion.

ARBOS: Thank you.

CAREY: I think you have a beautiful voice . . .

ARBOS (TO CAREY): I love you so much.

CAREY: Thank you. So let's vote!

JACKSON: I feel like this is going to be unanimous, guys, so should we do it together?

CAREY: I'm ready.

JACKSON: One, two, three . . .

ALL JUDGES: Yes!

As Arbos approaches the judges to thank them, a background track begins to play The Script's "Hall of Fame," the chorus of which goes, "Standing in the hall of fame / And the world's gonna know your name."

Arbos's singing bore no discernible traces of disability. His performance of a Simon and Garfunkel standard was fluid, mostly in tune, and stylistically conventional (with controlled vibrato, clear diction, and minimal melismas). And although Arbos sang a cappella, he did so in strict time—on the beat, enunciations snapped to grid, the pulses of phrases marked out by his subtly swaying body and gesticulating hands.

Predictably, the judges lavished praise on Arbos's "very, very inspiring" story and proficient singing. A rhetorical flub came out, however, in Urban's and Jackson's tongue-in-cheek recommendation that Arbos should "just sing all the time." Maybe these two judges meant to say simply that because Arbos sings well, he should perform frequently to share this gift with others. More likely, Urban and Jackson were alluding to Arbos's speech impediment (without naming it explicitly) and noting that because Arbos does not stutter when he sings, he could presumably overcome the practical inconveniences of disfluency if only he could habitually sing to communicate with others. Of course, Urban and Jackson weren't being literal, since it's not realistic for any-one to sing through daily dialogues, as if inhabiting the magic bubble of an opera or a Broadway musical. Although intended as an off-hand compliment, then, this comment evinced a familiar ableist mindset. Urban and Jackson didn't just blithely posit a facetious "cure" to a complex condition; they also evoked an ideal scenario deemed pitifully unattainable (as in, too bad you obviously *can't* sing all the time, at least not without drawing unwanted at-tention).[59] In the least generous terms, their statements come across as self-serving, to wit: *You* should *sing* all the time so that *we* (and others) don't have to *hear* you stammer.

In certain genres of popular music, as Laurie Stras reminds us, a "damaged voice continues to be accepted, even preferred," as in the case of "the gravel-voice of the rock singer" or "the subtle hoarseness of the jazz vocalist."[60] An aesthetics of damage can indeed convey authenticity, integrity, and overcoming. But Arbos, whose speech disability was already explicit, arguably won over the judges not because he sang exceptionally well, but by singing well—just normally—*enough*. His performance gave his auditors a conversational lifeline, a comprehensible aesthetic experience that they knew how to talk about and fixate on *apart* from Arbos's speech (which, based on Mariah Carey's awkward questions and comportment, did not seem to be a topic that the judges wanted—or were equipped—to address in depth). Disability can pose a critical quagmire to anyone who lacks the vocabulary, patience, and understanding to confront it. Rosemarie Garland-Thompson uses the phrase "shared disability illiteracy" to describe how "most people don't know how to *talk* about disability or how to *be* disabled," even though disability pervades the "human lifecycle and our encounters with the environment."[61] Especially when coming up against a disability that involves speech and communication, able-bodied people may feel relatively powerful in terms of verbal and physical ability, yet somewhat powerless in their rhetorical capacity to address the deviance in question. Public discomfort with the facts and fictions of disability shows up in little signs here and there: grasping at politically correct terms to minimize one's air of insensitivity or ignorance; looking differently at people who look different (the inquisitive squint, the averted gaze); or straining the ears to understand someone's atypical speech, trying to make out the words while trying not to look as though there were much trying involved.[62]

No, the capacity for disability to make nondisabled people uneasy does not mitigate the realities of ableism and able-bodied privilege. Yet by contemplating how disability can disable its beholders, and how overcoming stories can overcome consumers—emotionally, physiologically, cognitively— we gain deeper knowledge of the ways in which power gradients unexpectedly shift and shake alongside disability's upheaval of expectations. If disabled bodies can "seem dangerous because they are perceived as out of control," as Garland-Thomson says, then a contestant's fluent vocal performance reins in this danger with a safely controlled voice.[63] Skilled singing provides a generous target for calculated criticisms and congratulations regarding pitch, tone, and easily denoted musical parameters. The fluent singing of an otherwise disfluent performer demonstrates power by virtue of vocal ability, but also returns adjudicatory power to the listening critic. As much as we may idealize the singing voice as a thing of lyric flight—free, transcendent, out there—the voice ends up functioning here as an anchor, grounding a performance in concrete metrics and rubrics, here and now. So whereas disabled characters in literature, film, music, and freak shows have often served as exploited foils to reaffirm readers' and spectators' sense of a normal self, the stereotypes of savants and supercrips valorize these individuals as sufficiently conventional and conversable through their performances of relatable, appraisable abilities.[64]

On a larger scale, the story of Lazaro Arbos points to the plural identities tangled up in understandings of normalcy, disability, and overcoming. *American Idol* showed Arbos grappling with not just his stutter, but also his immigrant status (coming from communist Cuba to capitalist United States) and language barriers (Spanish to English). In the pre-audition interviews, Arbos's mother remarked that her son's stutter became more pronounced when he moved to Florida and faced the requirements of speaking in a new language; Arbos himself recounted that he felt lonely at school in part because of his difficulties communicating with classmates. Similar intersectional concerns abounded in the journey of *X Factor Australia*'s Emmanuel Kelly, shown trying to overcome not simply his physical disabilities, but furthermore his former orphaned status and his Iraqi origins (no small feat amid climates of Islamophobia). Xenophobia, as much as ableism, has long stewed in the shadows of the American Dream. The exclusionist conceit is that the Dream should be reserved for true Americans, whatever that means. For immigrants confronting stigma and ethnic stereotypes, even a spot on a show called *American Idol* can neither guarantee the status of national belonging nor forfend accusations of seizing or stealing unmerited gains.

At the end of the day, despite the numerous controversies around reality competitions, many contestants nonetheless express gratitude for the opportunities to share their talents with enormous and appreciative audiences.[65] There's nothing wrong with celebrating the abilities of musicians who live with (and have in some ways overcome) impairments, illnesses, and adversity. Complications arise when claims of meritocracy silence crucial conversations about disability and inclusion. Judges, fans, and even contestants themselves sometimes describe musical aptitude as a sufficient or necessary source of cure, consolation, or recompense. Highlighting certain talents as miracle correctives additionally risks implying that disabled people who do not display obvious, marketable talents are somehow more hopelessly disabled and less deserving of attention and compassion (recall Chapter 2). As reality shows raise up singing ability as facile proof of pseudo-normalcy, this emphasis on the lyric voice consistently threatens to bring disability under re-erasure, obscuring the practical, political, and lived realities of oppression.

All Stories Aside?

> Like any great love, great art requires great sacrifice. This cliché is especially prevalent among musicians, who are taught narratives of sacrifice and overcoming from Beethoven's deafness and Schumann's crippled hand to Robert Johnson's visit to the crossroads and Kurt Cobain's suicide. As musicians, we rely on our bodies to express our art, and when our bodies fail us, or rather fail our expectations by becoming impaired or incapacitated, we return to these narratives, seeking comfort and community in romanticized tropes of tragic artists. But those caught by physical limitations must find a way to live with them—not to overcome and triumph, as the consoling disabled-hero narrative has it, but rather to live with the new and changing structures of our lives.
>
> —M. Celia Cain[66]

In spring 2015, I taught a class on music and media with a unit on reality shows. At one point, students watched videos of Emmanuel Kelly, Lazaro Arbos, and other contestants with disabilities. By the time we got to Timothy Poe—the *America's Got Talent* contestant accused of faking a stutter and military injury—I felt the room growing jaded. As millennials, most of these students were already savvy to reality television's formulas and falsehoods. But viewing so many clips in close succession (capped off with Poe's scandal, no less) was leading some people in the class to roll their eyes as soon as a contestant started recounting *any* tale of adversity. Students began lamenting how contestants unapologetically play the sympathy card, how producers manipulate viewers, and how the programs' clichés sow cynicism in consumers. Halfway through the unit, several students looked as if they weren't even listening to contestants' stories anymore. Perhaps they believed they knew these narrative conventions so well that there was no need to pay attention. And were these the lessons I wanted my students to learn? Hypervigilance, defaulted skepticism, emotional hardening? For my part, having researched reality shows for the past several years, I likewise instinctively find myself these days trying to resist feeling overcome when watching an auditionee's backstory and performance.

Celia Cain's epigraph reminds us that overcoming narratives have long pervaded the biographies of artists, musicians, and writers. Romantic tropes prop up the tortured creative soul whose authentic greatness springs from embattlement and suffering. In an age of reality television, such stories have become more visible than ever. Lovable chronicles of overcoming on these shows can take both cheap and costly shots at our defenses, pulling at our heart strings and loosening our purse strings. In turn, it's easy for discerning consumers to slam these stories for their coercive conceits. But recognizing the exploitativeness of overcoming narratives does not automatically immunize a viewer against their power. As with our vulnerability to the musical mystique, our relationships with persuasive tales of overcoming are anything but simple: we might love to hate the shows; hate that we love them; feel ashamed for loving them; admit them as guilty pleasures; or profess to "hate-watch" them.[67] Vulnerability and resilience are recurrent, problematic themes in representations of people with disabilities. Here, I've emphasized how these themes can apply just as intensely to nondisabled people who encounter disability's stories and manifestations.[68]

Today, there's reason to be ever mindful of how disability gets packaged, distorted, sanitized, and mobilized to commercial and ideological ends. Abundant overcoming narratives simplify disability by pitching certain achievements and capabilities as compensatory remedies, which, in an effusively celebratory mode, might halt conversations about disability altogether. Curiously, aside from cases of performers with speech impediments, most of reality shows' disabled singing contestants are actually not presented as dealing with impairments related to vocal ability. Few contestants who appear on these shows purport to have hearing loss (or Deaf gain), throat damage, reduced lung capacity, amusia, muteness, or conditions that bear directly on singing and musical talent.[69] On the one hand, then, it shouldn't come as a surprise when someone who is blind, poor, or grieving demonstrates proficient singing. On the other hand, it's easy to assume that hardship, pain, and any misfortune can take a toll on one's voice, materially as well as metaphorically—on one's will and ability to sing at all. Given the voice's implications of natural expression, an adequate singing voice can resound, to optimistic ears, as instant proof of disability overcome, as wholesale triumph over an afflicted body.

With grace and caution, there are productive, respectful ways to weave inspiration and sentimentality into disability discourse. Wendy Chrisman writes, "If we consider all the circumstances in which we might truly need inspiration, perhaps we can envision the need for recuperating inspirational narratives: the inspiration needed to confront a struggle, to seek justice, to right wrongs, to set examples of encouragement."[70] Catherine Prendergast similarly rejects the assumption that "an inquiry that boils down to pathos must somehow fail to reach the political. [. . .] The field [of Disability Studies] would be most advanced by participating in the circulation and recirculation of emotion, rather than trying to arrest it."[71] But for every nuanced article, we can find plenty of objectionable statements about inspiration. Psychiatrist Darold Treffert, in his work on "savant syndrome," flies close to appropriative territory. He insists:

"Acquired" savants are normal (neurotypical) persons who, having previously shown no particular special savant skills or abilities, suddenly, *after* a head injury, stroke, or other brain disease or disorder, develop art, music or math skills, for example, sometimes at a prodigious level. These cases heighten the possibility that savant capabilities—a little *Rain Man* perhaps—might be buried, but dormant, within us all. If so, it also presents the related question as to how one might access such dormant potential without having a head injury, stroke or other central nervous system catastrophe.[72]

As ambitious as these musings might be, Treffert frames inspiration selfishly. People with disabilities can inspire others, but they do not live to edify the nondisabled. (Case in point: after hearing Emmanuel Kelly's tale of hardship on *X Factor Australia*, judge Natalie Bassingthwaighte cradled her head in her hands and sighed, "It just makes everything that you worry about seem so pathetic." In a response to this episode, disability activist Stella Young fired back, "Natalie Bassingthwaighte, disabled people don't exist to remind you to be less shallow."[73]) Critiques of "inspiration porn" have appeared in recent memoirs and reflections, such as Young's article "We're Not Here for Your Inspiration" and Harilyn Rousso's book *Don't Call Me Inspirational: A Disabled Feminist Talks Back*.[74] Maybe witnessing oppression, adversity, and deficits in societal and architectural accommodation should inspire the nondisabled not just to do well, but foremost to do good—that is, not to fuel one's personal ambitions and merits, but to fight for a more compassionate world where the hurdles in these paths to overcoming aren't so copious and prohibitive in the first place.

As media consumers, as academics, and as music lovers, we have reason to remain wary of how stories of overcoming on *American Idol* or *The Voice* sway our perceptions of a performer's musical abilities. Trying to set these stories aside, we might pick on the notion that the audition of Lazaro Arbos was a little off-pitch, at times shaky and lacking control. But maybe we pick on things like pitch and tone and timing because these are the technical elements that are easiest and safest to talk about, the musical dimensions for which we have authoritative and precise technical vocabularies. Emotional stories, by contrast, are messier and touchier, more human and hazardous. Perhaps, then, the burden falls on listeners to learn to listen differently; to listen to difference differently; and to reflect on the stakes, costs, and incentives for either upholding or uprooting standards of aesthetic merit.

Any suspicions we've developed lately toward ideals of musical autonomy (art for art's sake) should translate to similar disavowals of autonomous musical ability.[75] If we believe that artwork is made meaningful by living acts of creation, reception, and revision, then we should be equally inclined to believe that no artistic ability can meaningfully exist without considerations of the artist and the audience. Yet on reality shows, judges continue to express praise and critique as if they could separate song from singer, performance from story, and disability from musical ability. When Emmanuel Kelly performed John Lennon's "Imagine" on *X Factor Australia*, judge Guy Sebastian told him: "Emmanuel, you're a great singer. And I'm not saying that because you've had a hard life, [but] because it's the thing to say. Compared to the other people here, *regardless of your story*, you've got a beautiful gift, and you moved everyone in this room."[76] On a 2011 episode of *China's Got Talent*, judge Annie Yi offered similar comments to a twelve-year-old Mongolian boy who was mourning the death of his parents: "*No matter what your story is*, Da Mu, the most important thing is that you truly sang the song very well."[77] And on a 2013 episode of *X Factor USA*, judge Simon Cowell told Carlos Guevara, an auditionee with Tourette syndrome: "You know what I like about you is that you're not a victim. You know, I mean, you've got this, you know, this issue, but most importantly, you haven't let that stop you doing what you've dreamt of doing. *Forget about all of that*, you've actually got a great voice."[78]

> Regardless of your story.
> No matter what your story is.
> Forget about all of that.

Are human stories things to be disregarded, no-mattered, forgotten? Are people any more reducible to their singing abilities than they are to their disabilities? We can try to set stories momentarily aside for the sake of objectivity (in the name of fairness, professionalism, and meritocracy), but the very imagination of ability *or* disability as detachable carries the risk of leaving humanity behind. Stories matter; they matter so long as we believe people matter.

So this was what I ended up proposing to my students on the last day of our unit on reality shows. After offering them many examples of overcoming narratives—during which some students scoffed, some watched with apparent interest, and one student fought back tears (occasionally giggling at herself as she did so, maybe out of concern that she would be teased by her classmates)—I told them that they, to a large extent, get to decide how they wish to take in and take on these stories. Down the line, as they watch reality shows on their own, they can assume that every contestant is a potential Timothy Poe, and turn a stone heart to emotional tales. Maybe this will make them feel smart, strong, and in control. Alternatively, they can aim to give contestants the benefit of the doubt and conceive of how, despite the overt exploitativeness of reality programs, there's value in allowing oneself to be moved—moved to tears and, more importantly, even moved to actions that promote disability rights and justice.

Coda: Boyle Revisited . . . and the Girl Who Rolled Her Eyes

> I also suffered from what psychologists call cognitive difficulties. Even at a young age, I often knew the answers to questions, but I couldn't seem to get what I was thinking out of my head and into my mouth. [. . .] My singing silenced the bullies, but better than that, it silenced the demons inside me. When you've been jeered at, told to shut up, sit still, stop being silly, there's a cacophony of noise constantly rolling around inside your head. When I was singing, it was peaceful.
>
> —Susan Boyle, in her autobiography *The Woman I Was Born to Be*[79]

"And how old are you, Susan?" Simon Cowell asked the woman in the gold-lace dress.

"I am 47," she replied. Susan Boyle's biographer, John McShane, reminds us what happened next:

> Cowell, at the time 49 himself, rolled his eyes. A mixture of laughter and groans could be heard from the audience behind him. A cruel wolf-whistle came from somewhere in the crowd. The people watching in the theatre, and the millions who later saw Susan Boyle's audition in their homes, must have feared they were watching car-crash television.[80]

It wasn't a car crash. It was a triumph. On the *Britain's Got Talent* stage, Susan Boyle overcame other people's prejudicial attitudes toward her and, as she later revealed, overcame her own struggles and anxieties.

But Boyle wasn't the only person who became famous that day. Amid the fairy-tale audition, a villainess was also born, a teenager who had sat in the studio audience. People nicknamed her "1:24 Girl," given that she shows up at approximately the 1′24″ mark in one of the first YouTube videos of Boyle's audition.[81] By the time the video racked up 120 million views, "1:24 Girl" had become the target of a massive online hate campaign. The reason? Simply because a close-up of this teen shows her scoffing and rolling her eyes when Boyle, prior to singing, declares the dream of being a professional singer (Figure 4.9). One commenter stated, "Talk about never judging a book by its cover—anybody else feel like punching the chick at 1:24 in the face?"[82] Another said, "I wanted to kick her ass."[83] YouTubers, Redditors, and Boyle fans came together to find out this audience member's name, and the

Figure 4.9. Jennifer Byrne, a.k.a. 1:24 Girl, smiling (*left*) and rolling her eyes (*right*) in the *Britain's Got Talent* audience at the Glasgow SECC. Screen captures by author.

vigilante swarm soon managed to identify her as eighteen-year-old Jennifer Byrne. It's almost as if, to balance the scales of poetic justice, people's love for Boyle required a counterweight via a hate for Byrne.

Abusive messages and death threats followed. "It was a split-second reaction that changed my life. All I did was roll my eyes and I'm targeted by a hate campaign for months," Byrne told reporters. "I just can't believe how I have been targeted by total strangers around the world who don't even know what kind of person I am. [. . .] They could have filmed 100 people around me with exactly the same expressions."[84] Byrne recalled the moment she first saw herself on television:

> We were all sitting watching it and then suddenly my face popped up. I couldn't believe it. All my pals started texting saying they'd seen me. But even then I said to my mum, "Why did they show me looking like that?" Within a few days people started messaging me on the internet with some really nasty stuff. They were saying things like "Let's get the bitch" and "We'll hunt her down and slap her." It was really upsetting to see such horrible things being said about you. Over the weeks and months it got worse and worse. One day I was on the train and somebody recognised me and started to try to film me on their mobile phone.[85]

Spokespersons for *Britain's Got Talent* and eventually Susan Boyle herself spoke out in Byrne's defense, pointing to the many audience members who were indeed skeptical and making similarly derisive faces at that exact moment. Byrne was just unlucky enough to get caught on camera.[86] She was singled out as a spectatorial scapegoat, a convenient target onto which viewers could project and unburden their own guilt of prior prejudice. Byrne's nightmare resulted from what psychoanalyst Sigmund Freud would call "the narcissism of minor differences" (*der Narzissmus der kleinen Differenzen*), the theory that "communities with adjoining territories, and related to each other in other ways as well" are precisely the ones most likely to "[engage] in constant feuds and in ridiculing each other."[87] Although Byrne's haters might like to believe they are nothing like this young woman, their fierce disavowals may paradoxically confirm otherwise.

It is both unbelievable and utterly believable that a hate campaign could so ruthlessly victimize someone based on a split-second eye roll. In today's screen-grab, GIF-happy Internet culture, every frame and pixel can launch you into fame or ruin.

In his 2015 book *So You've Been Publicly Shamed*, Jon Ronson recounts the stories of various people whose lives have been destroyed because of a single off-color tweet or some tiny instance of poor judgment. Virtually anyone can find themselves on the receiving end of a cybermob's pitchforks, from the celebrities who live their lives in the limelight to the obscure commoner whose faux pas makes them infamous overnight. Importantly, Ronson admits that he sees himself not just in the targets of public shaming, but also in the people who tear these targets apart.[88] Sure, we might prefer to believe that we're nothing like either Byrne *or* her attackers. We might also wish to believe we're resistant to the manipulative powers of overcoming narratives, inspiration porn, implicit biases, and the musical mystique. But reality—human fallibility—begs to differ.

Enter the Princess of Pop.

5

The Worst You've Ever Sounded

Some musicians like to think of themselves as carried on the waves of the public's sympathy, lapped in its love, but the love is double-faced. The popular idol is greeted as he enters with acclaim by the audience because he is, for its sake, about to expose himself to the danger of public humiliation. At any moment the singer's voice may crack on a high note, the pianist fall off his stool, the violinist drop his instrument, the conductor give a disastrous cue and irretrievably confuse the orchestra.

—Charles Rosen[1]

"Poor Britney Spears"
is not the beginning of a sentence
you hear often uttered in my household.

—Tony Hoagland, "Poor Britney Spears,"
beginning of the poem[2]

In summer 2014, the Internet sprang a musical leak. Suddenly circulating on YouTube was a video featuring the allegedly raw, non-Auto-Tuned sounds of Britney Spears singing a new album track called "Alien."[3] Spears's voice in this recording was noticeably off key and off kilter, like something meant to be overwritten, forgotten, abandoned on the cutting room floor. In the video's comment threads, viewers' strident pronouncements of aching ears and melting brains swirled in a chorus of mockery. Haters pounced on the denuded voice and offered it as evidence of the star's artistic deficits.[4] Although track producer William Orbit tried to run damage control by saying that Spears had failed to warm up prior to the leaked run-through, people gloated nonetheless by labeling the pop diva's voice as "diabolical," "like a strangled cat," and, predictably, as "alien."[5] Such dehumanizing characterizations whipped through a firestorm of pearl-clutching *gotcha!* journalism.

But how shocking was the leak, anyhow? Long before the "Alien" fiasco, critics had relentlessly accused Spears of lapses in vocal ability by variously knocking her failure to sing in tune, satirizing her vocal fry, or pitting her against one-time arch-frenemy Christina Aguilera.[6] A leak of Spears's unprocessed voice probably didn't tell listeners much beyond what they already knew, whether about Spears or the music industry at large. After all, writers have bewailed Auto-Tune in general as a "crutch" that conditions singers into "lazy" vocal habits; when freed from the disciplined pressures to hit and hold their notes with precision, recording artists who rely excessively on the technology may feel content to let their pitch—observe here the doubling down on metaphors of disability and impairment (recall Chapters 3 and 4)—"atrophy" and "wobble."[7] Despite the collective charades of disgust and disbelief over Spears's "Alien" leak, then, it's a safe bet that people's heads were neither literally nor (and this is key) *figuratively* exploding.

"Leak" is an alarm, a toxin, a media buzzword. To shout "leak!" is to say "look here!" or "listen here!"—a forceful yank of the gaze and jerk of the ear. Headlines about the Panama Papers, Ashley Madison, Anonymous, WikiLeaks, US-Russian collusion, Facebook, and revenge porn reliably set off clamor on social media.[8] By their nature, leaks surprise. Media scholar Wendy Chun and filmmaker Sarah Friedland, however, offer a skeptical reading of public responses to leakage, observing that "what is surprising about all of these recent leaks [in the news] is not their existence, but rather our surprise at them," in part "because *new media are not simply about leaks: they are leak.* New media work by breaching, and thus paradoxically sustaining, the boundary between private and public."[9] In other words, it's surprising when people feel (or act) surprised by leaks, because leaks, along with bugs, kinks, and glitches, are intrinsic to the architecture of new media. Without the possibility of leakiness, no container and no inter-user channels can be said to exist.

But let's take this recursion one level deeper. Should it come as a surprise when Chun, Friedland, and other savvy writers voice surprise toward others' surprise toward leaks? If so, is *this* surprising as well? Despite the rabbit-hole conceit, I am posing these questions seriously. Hard questions. Questions that we might be unable to fully wrap our minds around. Yet this confusion speaks precisely to the allure of leaks: whatever their true shock value, leaks tempt people into performative spirals of introspection, all the while short-circuiting the intellectual, affective, and moral integrity of our own leakable bodies and of the body politic.[10] Put another way, leaks involving other people rarely involve *only* other people. Leaks are about all of us. And any of us can leak.

My case study will be Britney Spears, who, since the turn of the twenty-first century, has been one of the most publicly shamed and lucratively leaked-about celebrities in American popular culture.[11] Sensationalist journalism has reduced Spears to her highest highs and her lowest lows. Just as "new media are leak," as Chun and Friedland put it, so we could say *Spears is leak*; her persona is the sum of what she has leaked, the glitz and the dirt.[12] Besides the "Alien" leak, fans and haters alike have prodded every pixel of Spears, split every hair, floated every hypothetical pathology, archived every frame of lip-sync fail, dissected every relationship, and guesstimated every pound lost or gained. Critics have gossiped openly about her virginity and sexual activity since she was a teenager. Paparazzi have even come up with dirty tricks to snap and sell photos of her genitals. Scrutiny of Spears has routinely banked on her Othering and dehumanization: as an alien, freak, or "cult member" (the shearing of her own hair in 2007); as an animal (rabid meltdowns, cagey hermeticism, physical confrontations with her camera-wielding hounders); as an impostor (with putative delusions about, among other things, her vocal proficiency and her entitlements to fame); and as slutty white trash. Public voice shaming and slut shaming of this singer have played out as intersectional bloodsports, filled with sexist, ableist, and classist jabs. In the end, Spears's "Alien" problem was equal parts mundane smut and jarring cautionary tale, reverberating with people's trenchant anxieties about beauty standards, the illusion of privacy, and the loves lost amid musical scandals in this age of ubiquitous leaks.

Dehumanizing the Diva: Animal Control and White Trash Royalty

My ears just bled.

— Matt Thompson, commenting on Spears's out-of-tune "Alien" leak[13]

Discourses of *it hurts me to have to hear this* have been around for a while. In the eighteenth century, physicians and philosophers exhaustively theorized "the idea that music could overstimulate a vulnerable nervous system, leading to illness, immorality and even death."[14] With recourse to notions of female hysteria and to the Enlightenment "cult of sensibility," researchers of this period warily eyed certain styles of music not just as moral vices (à la Plato) but also as legitimately pathogenic or pathological. In a 1900 issue of *The Medical Magazine*, J. Herbert Dixon warned readers that girls who practiced piano excessively could suffer "the baneful influence of the continual vibrations on the organ of Corti [in the cochlea], and so on the brain," with symptoms including "headaches, neuralgia, nervous twitchings, hysteria, melancholia, madness."[15] In past and present rhetorics of aural harm, the ear is framed as a conduit, the organ that allows foreign sonic substances to slip through. Ears, in this formulation, aren't merely anatomical channels through which external sounds may leak inward; ears themselves, as permeable media, *are* metonymic leaks. As scholars of sound studies like to point out, humans have eyelids but have no "earlids."[16] Normative and unimpaired ears, according to these writers, are chronically receptive, hence persistently leaky.

Social media platforms today have amplified and accelerated people's claims about offensive sounds and offendable ears.[17] Upon the leak of Spears's non-Auto-Tuned vocals for "Alien," listeners lined up to file for damages in the court of mob justice. "PROTECT your ears," an Australian website cautioned with regard to this "hideously painful leaked studio clip."[18] YouTube viewers similarly shared laments such as "My ears, my precious ears, they can't take it anymore!"[19] while critics dissed Spears's voice as "toxic to the ears" and "pretty shocking."[20] Public uproar pointed to the singer's vocals as an extraordinary sonic invasion of exceptionally delicate cochleae. To be sure, the "Alien" leak sat in good company. Around this time, it was just one specimen in a thriving Internet business of voice shaming. One trend has involved "isolated vocals," through which someone tries to strip a singer's (typically live in concert) voice from accompanying sounds (backup vocals, instruments, synths, audience noise), then posts this bare-bones voice online for listeners to admire or, more often, to ridicule. It's the acoustic equivalent of pulling the rug out from under someone, as the editing yanks away the bass and other sonic buffers in order to cause a potentially embarrassing fall from grace. Surges in computer and mobile audio-editing apps have lowered the price of entry into practices of musical tinkering.[21]

Women are disproportionately shamed by these curations of isolated vocals, whether it's Mariah Carey struggling with "All I Want for Christmas Is You" at a 2014 Rockefeller Center holiday performance, Katie Price flubbing a duet of "A Whole New World," Courtney Love rocking "Celebrity Skin," or Linda McCartney belting out "Hey Jude."[22] Conversely, the isolation of male artists' vocals is more commonly submitted as testaments to these men's "genius": Michael Jackson, David Bowie, Kurt Cobain, Marvin Gaye, Freddie Mercury, and Paul McCartney (with occasional nods to divas such as Adele and Beyoncé).[23] Nothing about this gendered double standard comes as a shock. Acoustically zooming in on a woman's blemished voice calls to mind the tabloid gambit of visually zooming in on women's bodies: the encircling of engagement rings (or absence of engagement rings), baby bumps (or not), augmented breasts (or not), or Botoxed faces (or not), frequently with an actual arrow pointing at the gawk-worthy piece of flesh (Figure 5.1). Vocal and photographic croppings alike bank on the irresistibility of note-by-note, pixel-by-pixel voyeurism.[24]

A leak of a famous performer's vocal foibles can conceivably make the singer appear fallibly human and relatable. Don't we all have bad voice days, bad hair days, and days when pretty much everything seems to go wrong? Yet because celebrities are supposed to be larger than life, any signs of ordinariness may paradoxically make them appear all the more extraordinary and inhuman. Examples of this paradox readily catch our eyes at the grocery store's magazine racks—namely, the *Us Weekly* feature, "Stars: They're Just Like Us!," which, upon its launch in April 2002, began showing "suddenly

Figure 5.1. (*Left*) Cover of *In Touch* magazine and (*right*) candid photograph of Rachel Bilson with emphasis on and close-up of nothing (ringlessness).

[...] the beautiful extraterrestrials pumping gas, schlepping FedEx packages, and tying their shoes."[25] Along with *People, In Touch, National Enquirer,* and other gossip rags, *Us Weekly* has hiked up the supply and demand for photographing celebrities in their natural habitats, with stars rendered familiar (*look, it's Jennifer Lopez carrying her OWN luggage*) to the point of uncanniness (*. . . which is sooo weird!*).

In this lucrative market, paparazzi embark on safaris. More accurately, they conduct capture and release programs: ambush the star at the supermarket, snap some pictures, and then let her retreat to a hiking trail where she can be photographed and monetized anew. In 2008, journalist David Samuels spoke of how the paparazzi agency X17 would task its photographers to "[wait] 12 or 14 hours a day, six or seven days a week" near Britney Spears's home, in hopes "that one day Britney will roll her car into a ditch, or be taken away again strapped to a gurney."[26] With paparazzi routinely catching this singer off guard, numerous candid photos of Spears have given her the appearance of a startled, disgruntled animal over the years (Figure 5.2). No wonder the American poet Tony Hoagland, in "Poor Britney Spears," leaned into easy animal comparisons by calling the star "my adorable little monkey / prancing for your candy," while taking bonus digs at her "slim javelin of talent" and "recklessly little protective clothing."[27]

A rock-bottom week for Spears in early 2007 can illuminate the paparazzi's guerilla tactics and the tabloids' animalization of celebrities. On February

Figure 5.2. Candid photos (*left and right*) of Spears.

16, Spears was caught using an electric razor to shave her own head in a Ventura Boulevard hair salon. She appeared, according to Samuels's multi-abjecting summary, "at once vulnerable and wildly alienated, the expression one might expect to see on the face of a young cult member who had just set fire to her birth certificate on the sidewalk."[28] Public responses likewise overwhelmingly linked this act of self-shearing with insanity and freakery. Surely, people said, Spears's willful disposal of her gold locks was a cry for help.[29] Yet the close shave turned out to be merely the warm-up act to a greater scandal a few days later, when an X17 team tracked the singer to the house of her then-husband Kevin Federline. Spears had hoped to see her children, who at the time were under Federline's care. But she was denied entry. So she drove away to a nearby Jiffy Lube, the paparazzi still hot on her trail. What happened next made instant headlines. "She took her hat off, and she was bald," recalled paparazzo Daniel "Dano" Ramos. "She was breathing like a bull. It was like smoke was coming out of her nostrils."[30] Spears then leapt out of the car and screamed, "Motherfuckers!" while brandishing an umbrella and using it to strike the door of a paparazzo's car. If Spears behaved like a "bull," though, maybe it's because the paparazzi choreographed themselves like bullfighters. As Dano has explained, paparazzi work optimally in "triangle" formations so that the celebrity has nowhere to turn.[31] With the savage grace of matadors, paparazzi manufacture arenas where celebrities may feel—and act—like cornered animals.[32]

In her first concert tour after the umbrella showdown (as well as after a gauntlet of rehab, divorce, custody battles, a death in the family, and other hardships), Spears aptly played on themes of caginess and cagedness. Called *The Circus Starring Britney Spears*, each concert opened with the 2008 namesake song "Circus," with Spears descending from the ceiling in an interlocking pair of glittery hoops, invoking one part burlesque dancer, one part ensnared beast (Figure 5.3). With hardly a breath in between, Spears would transition from "Circus" into the 2007 song "Piece of Me," featuring her inside yet another cage, this one gold and rectangular. In case anyone could miss the blunt symbolism of cages in multiple shapes and colors, the lyrics for "Piece of Me" take explicit aim at the insatiable photographers who stalk the stars: "I'm Mrs. Oh-My-God-That-Britney's-Shameless! / I'm Mrs. Extra-Extra-This-Just-In! / I'm Mrs. She's-Too-Big-Now-She's-Too-Thin! / I'm Mrs. You-Want-a-Piece-of-Me?" Ironically, or all too fittingly, Spears's post-show obligations have often included photo ops with VIP ticketholders—presumably superfans dying to get a piece of her. Listen, however, to the way Felicia Culotta, the

Figure 5.3. Spears performing "Piece of Me" in her *Circus* tour. Screen capture by author.

coordinator of a Las Vegas VIP package, characterized this artist to the eager meet-and-greeters: "Britney plays off energy. If you go in scared of her, she is going to be scared of you. So don't be scared of her. She's very normal."[33] Don't Culotta's remarks sound as though she were talking about a skittish creature at a petting zoo? Even this well-intentioned message of *Britney: she's just like us!* rang with dehumanizing and infantilizing insinuations, affirming that Spears is sufficiently *unlike* normal people to warrant the caveat of alikeness in the first place.

If Culotta's words come across as condescending, they nevertheless align with Spears's daily control by a squad of agents, lawyers, public relations specialists, and family members. Sure, most celebrities rely on managers. Spears's micromanagement, though, is next level. Following her breakdowns in 2007 and an emergency visit to a psychiatric hospital in 2008, the singer has remained under court-ordered conservatorship. This means Spears "cannot make key decisions, personal or financial, without the approval of her conservators: her father, Jamie Spears, and an estate lawyer, Andrew M. Wallet. Her most mundane purchases, from a drink at Starbucks to a song on iTunes, are tracked in court documents as part of the plan to safeguard the great fortune she has earned but does not ultimately control."[34] Since 2008, rumblings about this paternalistic conservatorship have fed concurrent rumors about Spears's mental and moral incapacities. Is the star incompetent? Depressed? Profligate? Reckless? Hanging by a thread?

Tabloids' dehumanizing portraits of Britney Spears have been virtuosically intersectional, concentrating on everything from the star's gender (womanhood, girlhood, hyper-femininity, unfemininity) and sexuality (dating men, kissing Madonna) to matters of disability (psychological ails, physical injuries) and faith (Baptist upbringing, atheism, "dabbling" in Hinduism).[35] And unlike some white musicians—whose color and race might go unremarked via the cultural hegemonies of white privilege—Spears and her whiteness have received colorful coverage because it has been nominally inextricable from "white trash" narratives, which sit discursively adjacent to stamps of animality and incivility.[36]

Raised in a modest household in Kentwood, Louisiana, with its population of just over 2000, Spears has been this rural town's most famous export. As a teenager, she blossomed into a picture-perfect and photo-ready exemplar of the American Dream: rags to riches, dairy farms to Big Apple penthouses. But as scandals began piling on, critics were quick to dredge up her white-trash roots. In January 2004, when Spears married (and, fifty-five hours later, divorced) her childhood friend Jason Alexander, *Guardian* writer Kathryn Flett called the singer "a white trash girl who, after years of high-gloss polish in the Business of Show, is currently reverting to type," as evidenced by "a seven-minute, $70 ceremony at a Las Vegas chapel."[37] *Reverting* to type— implying a return to a white-trash upbringing. Subsequently, in fall 2004, Spears married rapper Kevin Federline and, a year after that, gave birth to her first child. Concerning this arduous period in Spears's life, *Rolling Stone* writer Vanessa Grigoriadis declared:

[Spears] is not a good girl. She is not America's sweetheart. She is an inbred swamp thing who chain-smokes, doesn't do her nails, tells reporters to "eat it, snort it, lick it, fuck it" and screams at people who want pictures for their little sisters. [. . .] Federline gave Britney license to fully embrace her white-trash side—walking into gas-station restrooms barefoot, dumping ashtrays out hotel windows, wearing novelty tees like I'M A VIRGIN, BUT THIS IS AN OLD SHIRT and, most notably, not strapping the kids into car seats.[38]

Sociologist Karen Bettez Halnon described Spears and Federline along similar lines, calling them the "quintessential 'super trash' romance" whose nuptials confirmed that "Spears was no longer a cute and innocent virgin but rather a not-so-intelligent, beer-drinking, trucker-hat wearing, cigarette-smoking, sexually charged, white-trash princess."[39] Notice how, for these authors, white trashiness is multifariously yoked to indecency (shouting, cursing, bad parenting), dirtiness (unkempt nails, uncovered feet), substance use (smoking, drinking), sluttiness (loss of virginal status), and animality ("a swamp thing," in Grigoriadis's words). Notice additionally how, like sluttiness, white trashiness gets summoned as a sticky quality in spite of wealth and fame.[40] Once white trash, always white trash—this is what writers imply when they harp on Spears "reverting to," "fully embrac[ing]," and "backslid[ing] into" white-trash status, as if it were a malady prone to remission and relapse.[41] As much as people love feasting on stories of overcoming (Chapter 4), they reserve plenty of appetite for the opposite: stories of abject failure, not least those involving sexualized, sexist, or misogynist fantasies of a woman returning to her rightful place, whether it's white-trash roots or some other besmirched subject position.[42] For although plenty of male musicians receive praise for recuperating or "owning" their white-trash identity—Eminem, Kid Rock, and the "King of White Trash Culture," Elvis Presley—female musicians and celebrities such as Spears, Madonna, Miley Cyrus, Anna Nicole Smith, Jessica Simpson, Paris Hilton, and Lindsay Lohan have stood to face reprobation for the slightest hint of trashiness.[43] As with the shaming of isolated vocals, the double standard burns brightly.[44]

To her critics, a white-trash woman is shamefully unwomanly. Just as crucially, a white-trash woman is *shameless about the shamefulness* of her unwomanly vices. Among the most "significant stigma symbol[s] of so-called white trash status," notes Halnon, is the expression "just don't give a fuck," which "refers to a kind of indignation, to outward displays of not caring."[45] Unsurprisingly, Spears's white-trash, "don't give a fuck" reputation has leaped across national borders and languages. Canada's premier newspaper *Globe and Mail* once called out Spears's "trailer-trash vulgarity."[46] In the United Kingdom, Spears has been deemed a "chav," referring to an unsocialized young person in sportswear.[47] And in Uriangato, Mexico, where Spears's CDs and plastic dolls were flying off store shelves at the turn of the millennium, anthropologist Hilary Parsons Dick met local informants who referred to the singer as "*una gabacha sinvergüenza*," or "a shameless white-trash woman."[48] Ascriptions of unapologetic shamelessness are a small skip and hop away from permissions to shame unapologetically. If someone is perceived as shameless (ergo unshameable), then eager shamers obtain implicit license to fire at will.

As Britney Spears has tumbled from one "rock bottom" to the next, people have expressed both admiration and resentment that she indeed seemingly "doesn't give a fuck" anymore—about a wardrobe malfunction during a Vegas concert, about lukewarm reviews of her 2016 album *Glory*, or about "starv[ing] herself down" for a performance.[49] In a *Rolling Stone* decennial retrospective on Spears's 2007 *Blackout* album, Rob Sheffield described the work as "an avant-disco concept album about getting famous, not giving a fuck, getting divorced, not giving a fuck, getting publicly mocked and despised and humiliated [. . .] [b]ut mostly it's an album about not giving a fuck."[50] Even if Spears exudes a kind of blunt insouciance, she typically doesn't bring this attitude onto the stage, where, over thousands of shows, she has vigorously danced and sung in front of screaming fans. At the same time, her empowered stage presence might belie her disempowerment behind the scenes. During concerts, her cage props can ooze kink and sex. When the curtains fall, however, the bondage is real. Between the physical flanks of paparazzi and the legal boilerplates of conservatorship, Spears has been tightly steered, zoned, and controlled for most of her life.

All the more newsworthy, then, when the tight ship springs a leak or veers off course. Some of the most sensational moments in Spears's career have involved the singer's apparent inability either to control her body (lashing out with an umbrella, messing up choreography, gaining weight, suffering nip slips) or to control her voice (the "Alien" leak, lip-sync fails, giving "the worst interview of the year," telling "liars" to "kiss [her] lily white southern Louisiana ass," and mysteriously fading in and out of a British accent).[51] In addition to body shaming and voice shaming, Spears has faced fat shaming and slut shaming in spades. Euphemisms for *fat* and *slut* jointly traffic in accusations about, once again, the deficit of control: a woman dubbed fat has "really let herself go" or "given up" on herself; a woman dubbed slut is "loose" or all too ready to "give it up."[52] But whereas Spears has been slammed for failing to be a good singer and a good girl, critics count precisely on her out-of-control, leaky moments to produce news, bait clicks, elicit gasps, and crank the money mill.

In short, the media has relied on concomitant narratives of Spears losing her voice (singing ability), losing her body (unrealistic thinness), and *loosening* her body (virginity) over a strenuous career.

Leaks, Sluts, and Shit

If she wants to make a career comeback
and her agent pushes her into the MTV awards show
but she can't lose the weight beforehand

and so looks chubby in a spangled bikini
before millions of fanged, spiteful fans and enemies,

then gets a little drunk while getting her nerve up
so botches a step in the dance routine
which makes her look, one critic says,
like a "comatose piglet,"

well, it wasn't by accident, was it,
that she wandered into that glitterati party
of late 20th century striptease celebrity?
                    —Hoagland, "Poor Britney Spears," middle of poem[53]

On September 10, 2007, a Britney Spears fan named Chris Crocker rocketed to YouTube fame with his two-part video, "Leave Britney Alone!" Voicing teary concern for Spears's wellbeing, Crocker pushed back against the critics who were roundly panning Spears's opening act at the MTV Video Music Awards the day before.[54] Out of fear that Spears might wither under the media's vicious attacks, Crocker implored, "Do we really want to see a twenty-five-year-old woman leave behind two children and die? Have we learned nothing from Anna Nicole Smith [who died in February 2007 from a drug overdose]?"[55] Crocker repeatedly dignified Spears as "a human" and castigated the people who were treating her inhumanely: "I know it's hard to see Britney Spears as a human being. But trust me, she is. [. . .] All you people care about is readers and making money off of her. She's a human! Leave Britney alone!"

Reviewers of Spears's performance at the Video Music Awards (VMAs) complained about the singer's sloppy dance moves, lethargic tempo, and weight. Her "tight body was long gone," noted one critic; so were "those abs of yore."[56] In the book *Fat Shame*, Amy Farrell reflects on the ways "the story of [Spears's] downfall—which includes questionable parenting techniques, violent behavior, and drug and alcohol binges—is largely told through a narrative about her fat body. [. . .] The *New York Daily Post* said that Spears [at the 2007 VMAs] was 'stuffed into a spangled bra and hot pants and jiggled like Jell-O,' while *E! Online* described the horror of the 'bulging belly she was flaunting.' "[57] Writers effectively depicted Spears's flesh as *leaking* out of her two-piece. These depictions drew validation from a *New York Times* report that revealed how Spears, an hour before curtains up at the VMAs, had "decided not to wear the custom-fitted corset designed for the performance, opting for a black bikini-style costume that revealed more of her body."[58] And here's where fat shaming crashed into slut shaming: some people claimed they took issue not with Spears's size per se, but rather with the fact that Spears, at *that* size, dared to wear such a sexy get-up. "She isn't fat," admitted a blog commenter. "But she isn't fit enough to be wearing (or not wearing) what she is."[59] *Us Weekly* editor Janice Min gave her professional opinion along similar lines: "In that ensemble, you just can't have an ounce of anything extra. Many women wouldn't eat for days if they were wearing that."[60] Translation: what right did Britney have, as someone who was no longer pencil thin (and, moreover, as a new mother of two)—what right did she have to wear anything other than a head-to-toe potato sack? Did she have no shame?

In society's narratives of respectable womanhood, a subtle yet crucial quirk distinguishes fat shaming from slut shaming. Fat-centered narratives often work as boomerangs, circling between misfortune and redemption based on weight fluctuations. "Just as fatness narrates [Spears's] downfall, a newly thin body is what later becomes the motif for her comeback," notes Farrell.[61] A kindred and contemporaneous example was Monica Lewinsky, who, as a guest star in the 1999 ad for the American weight loss program Jenny Craig, exemplified "a 'dieting narrative' that moves the primitive, impulsive fat woman into a new status of civilized and controlled."[62] In 1998, condemnation of Lewinsky's affair with President Bill Clinton relied not just on reports of the couple's "kinky sex," but also on a "mutual fatness [that] marked them as already culpable [. . .] [as] two people who were impulsive, whose bodily cravings were out of control."[63] In recent years, Lewinsky herself has come out as a bold advocate against what she calls a "marketplace [of] public humiliation" driven by sex shaming, fat shaming, and just interpersonal shaming in general. "You're looking at a woman who was publicly silent for a decade," announced Lewinsky at the beginning of her 2015 TED Talk. "Overnight I went from being a completely private figure to a publicly humiliated one worldwide. I was branded as a tramp, tart, slut, whore, bimbo, and, of course, 'that woman.' I was seen by many but actually known by few. And I get it. It was easy to forget that 'that woman' was dimensional, had a soul, and was once unbroken."[64]

As the case of Lewinsky attests, it's hard to shed a reputation of lasciviousness. In the public eye, as Wendy Chun and Sarah Friedland declare, the "slut is the woman who is repeatedly and habitually open and opened. [. . .] The slut 'asks for it'—that is, she brings penetration and exposure upon herself through her openness and thus constant vulnerability."[65] Merciless models of sexism operate under the corollary *once a slut, always a slut*. Like white trashiness, sluttiness sticks. Its unretractability is buoyed by misconstruals of virginity (the presumed irrevocability of its loss) and compounded by misunderstandings of affirmative sexual consent (a single *yes* meaning *yes, definitely and indefinitely*).[66] In the Internet era, the permanence of one's slut branding is anchored by the quasi-permanence of naked pictures and their weaponized medium, revenge porn. An implicit tag of slut shaming is "Once It's There, It's There to Stay" because, as Chun and Friedland explain, "once you've exposed yourself as a slut—as a consenting spectacle, as shameless—you deserve no protection, no privacy. [. . .] [C]onsent once, circulate forever."[67] Once someone gives herself up to the public eye, in other words, she—and her photographic documentation—will stay fair game for tabloids and trolls. (Tellingly, "giving it up," with its deflowering and subdom connotations, is the paparazzi's code phrase for celebrities who are "good sports" and who cop to being "attention whores.")[68]

No-going-back principles of sluttiness have clung to Britney Spears ever since the release of the music video for her 1998 debut mega-single, "(Hit Me) Baby One More Time," in which she dressed the part of a sexy Catholic schoolgirl. Writers frequently point to this song as a millennial pop touchstone. Diane Pecknold remarks that if American pop's "new teen girl sound of the 2000s and 2010s [. . .] can be imagined as having an inaugural moment, it would surely be in the opening 'Oh baby, baby' of Britney Spears's 1998 hit '. . . Baby One More Time'" and its "distinctive vocal fry."[69] Ann Powers, invoking comparisons to aliens, likewise observes how Spears burst from a chrysalid in this "catchy electro-pop come-on" expertly produced by Swedish songwriter Max Martin: "With her gorgeous flesh and tiny voice—its metallic tone perfectly suited for manipulation—Spears presented from the beginning as a hybrid: half shopping mall American, half creature from another planet. Her body, voice, and projected emotions were youthful but washed clean of any adolescent awkwardness."[70] With the phrase "washed clean of any adolescent awkwardness," Powers is referring to the music video's meticulous production values. Every angle, frame, cut, costume change, vocal inflection, and audiovisual sync is rigorously accounted for, resulting in a sanitized and glossy spectacle. But might there be something awkward—even disturbing—about such presentational Purell? Could the "clean" surface of ". . . Baby One More Time" be as unnerving as, say, the bright, white, hyper-sterile, impossibly spotless rooms featured in numerous science fiction thrillers? Sometimes, don't the most polished surfaces send the most muddied signals?

Case in point: a few months after the release of the music video for ". . . Baby One More Time," Spears graced the cover of *Rolling Stone* while wearing an open blouse, polka-dot panties, and a bra. Her left hand gripped a pink phone, and her right hand clutched a plush doll of Tinky Winky the Teletubby. Like the choreography and iconography of ". . . Baby One More Time," this cover shoot was fastidiously styled and airbrushed, or "washed clean," to use Powers's words. Yet the "cleanliness" of the photo shoot couldn't mask the mixed signs therein: the purple plushie toy said *girl*, the pink phone said *teenager*, the shiny black bra and cleavage said *woman*, and the multi-item caption—"Inside the Heart, Mind, & Bedroom of a Teen Dream"—authorized voyeuristic entry into this celebrity's inner life and dwelling. The feature story itself began in a way that made good on the cover's tease: "Britney Spears extends a honeyed thigh across the length of the sofa, keeping one foot on the floor as she does so. [. . .] The BABY PHAT logo of Spears' pink T-shirt is distended by her ample chest, and her silky white shorts—with dark blue piping—cling snugly to her hips."[71]

To be clear, Teen Dreams aren't kids anymore. Like other adolescent stars, Britney Spears "performed awakening" on the world stage, surprising and even scandalizing people with her displays of sexuality and skin.[72] The music video for ". . . Baby One More Time" literalizes awakening by opening with a daydreaming Spears, who, upon the salvational *ding!* of the 3 p.m. school bell, snaps out of her stupor and hurries into the hallway, where she leads a dance number replete with gyrations, shimmies, back flips, and high kicks. She exhibits coming of age by dramatically coming *to life*, transforming from a languid, silent pupil into a hyperenergetic, vocal ringleader (Figure 5.4).

Figure 5.4. Music video for ". . . Baby One More Time." Screen captures by author.

Prior to the meteoric debut of ". . . Baby One More Time" and the alluring magazine shoots, a preteen Britney Spears had sung in Baptist church choirs, participated in pageants, and frolicked in the G-rated *New Mickey Mouse Club*. Once a teenage Spears became a household name, however, she arrived seemingly at a point of no return, cementing into a precocious sex icon and eventually a presumed slut. Diane Sawyer, in a 2003 interview with Spears, held up the singer's photo shoots in *Esquire* and *Rolling Stone*, and asked incredulously, "What happened to your clothes? What's this about? No kidding. What is it about?"[73] Musicologist Melanie Lowe, who conducted focus groups with adolescent girls, describes how she found herself "overwhelmed" by these girls' intense reactions to the mere mention of Britney Spears, whom they described as "slutty," "trashy," and "slore [portmanteau of slut plus whore] slore slore slore slore slore whore!"[74] In a 2006 pull-no-punches invective against Spears and Lindsay Lohan, Bette Midler called these millennial celebrities "wild and woolly sluts."[75] And in 2015, Naomi Wolf, author of the bestseller *The Beauty Myth*, penned a *Guardian* op-ed imploring "young women" to "give up vocal fry" while naming Britney Spears as a famous fryer; this trendy speech mannerism, to the ears of Wolf, "sound[s] like ducks quacking" and forfeits authority.[76] (The animal simile is condescending enough, but Wolf makes it clearer, with a bonus comparison, that she also associates vocal fry with a certain looseness or wantonness: "'Vocal fry' is that guttural growl at the back of the throat, as a Valley Girl might sound if she had been shouting herself hoarse at a rave all night.")[77] Insults lobbed at Spears and Spears-alikes . . . and the preceding comments are just the ones made by female (and, in some cases, self-identified feminist) critics! Plainly, slut shaming of Spears hasn't come solely from men and anonymous Internet trolls. It has been an equal-opportunity sport, admitting participants of all genders and ages.

If fat-shaming and slut-shaming narratives have respectively depicted Spears as redeemable (via weight loss) and incorrigible (as a loose woman), the case of voice shaming has fallen somewhere in between. From a reviewer's excoriation of her "pathetically lip-synched" 2007 performance at the VMAs to YouTubers' jeers at the "Alien" leak, the critical history of Britney Spears has played out as a history of listeners doubting her vocal talents.[78] But a speculative *pre*history is where greater intrigue lies: fans insist that Spears, far from being an essentially bad singer, is a victim of having her voice *taken* from her. Sitting in fans' crosshairs are industry forces, in particular Jive Records, the American label that signed the star from 1997 through 2011. Some say Jive "ruined" Spears's voice by forcing her to sing persistently in a salacious yet insalubrious "baby voice" with vocal fry.[79] Such claims are corroborated by compilations on YouTube offering glimpses into the vocal chops of Spears in her youth.[80] In a fan-made montage called "The Hidden Potential of Britney Spears," we see the singer performing as a finalist on *Star Search* in 1992, crooning Christmas carols at a Miss New Orleans pageant in 1996, and singing capably on multiple other occasions. By pointing to these examples, and by pointing to Jive as a corporate archvillain that drained the light out of a starlet's budding voice, fans have continuously attempted to absolve Spears's present-day vocal infelicities.

In the comment threads for videos such as "The Hidden Potential of Britney Spears," "Britney Spears (REAL VOICE)," or "BRITNEY SPEARS HAS LOST HER VOICE FOREVER! (PROOF)," laments about Spears losing her voice to Jive resonate with a slew of familiar narratives about the kleptovocal vices of music industries past and present. Wistful remarks about Spears's once-untainted and now-irretrievable voice bring to mind the way musicians sometimes pine for the "lost voice" of castrati, and rue, notwithstanding the ethics of castration, the dearth of audio recordings by these lyric "angels."[81] Or take the example of opera singer Maria Callas, who, by her forties, had begun exhibiting symptoms of vocal damage. Despite critics' harsh reviews, as musicologist Laurie Stras points out, "[Callas's] vocal deterioration (in pathological terms) was seen by her loyal fans as an inevitable outcome of physical self-abuse brought on by the pressures of stardom," and her "public persona as tragic heroine allowed, and continues to allow, her audience to connect a personal history with an otherwise indeterminate sound of damage."[82] In literary narratives, vocal damage plus dreams of fame have served up deadly cocktails for women who virtually sing themselves into the grave, whether it's the doomed Antonia in Jacques Offenbach's 1881 opera *Les Contes d'Hoffmann* or the consumptive, coughing Satine in Baz Luhrmann's 2001 film musical *Moulin Rouge!* Although one could reason that it's better for a chanteuse to have sung and perished than never to have sung at all—better to vocally "[rebel] against a domestic/paternal order that would silence her," as Heather Hadlock surmises with regard to Offenbach's Antonia—the double bind of silence-or-singing-equals-death is an unfair choice, a rock and a hard place deceptively upsold as open pasture.[83]

Fans of Britney Spears, by blaming Jive and its theft of the star's voice, are essentially running a two-pronged defense. First, they could say that Spears has an authentic and proficient voice hibernating beneath the thick layers of industry influence. Second, they could say that even if Spears can never recover her pre-Jive talent, her current voice is beautiful as it is, warts and all. Just as some art collectors appreciate, even favor, paintings with patina—the oxide coating that, as anthropologist Shannon Lee Dawdy puts it, conveys value via the "requisite crust and haze of time"—so fans cherish Spears's summative patina, the layers of tabloid smear and the stubborn crust of performative habits accumulated over the years.[84] Now let's go further and imagine this patina as not solely metaphorical but also physiological: the oft-rumored scars lining Spears's larynx, or the nodules and polyps along the vocal folds. In terms of laryngeal damage and the prospect of phonomicrosurgery, Spears sits in good company. Tales of mixed success (Adele) and outright horror stories (Julie Andrews) abound.[85] Especially for female singers, a common and noticeable symptom of throat impairment is the onset constriction of range. Some divas—albeit, not Spears—are famous for hitting high notes. Yet just as they are lauded for successfully soaring to the peaks of their tessitura, these women may be denounced with equal zeal if or when they fall short. Virtuosos such as Idina Menzel, Demi Lovato, Christina Aguilera, and Mariah Carey have been tsk-ed and shamed for "whiffing" climactic notes as well as for preventatively transposing melodies into lower registers.[86] But what this kneejerk scolding perpetually overlooks is that any accrued limitations in vocal register might owe to how these singers, as literally as possible, *give their voices* to listeners over the course of their careers—sometimes belting out high notes so loudly, exhaustively, and detrimentally that the worn-and-torn throat is left with hardly any more voice to give.

Music industries, insatiable fans, and a host of external forces aren't the only things that can crack a pop star's voice. For pubescent and adolescent girls, developmental rites of passage come with internal pressures and natural changes that stand to make, unmake, and remake the voice. Diane Pecknold, a scholar of gender and popular music, and Barbara DeMaio, a professional soprano and voice teacher, respectively characterize these bodily changes:

> In the teen girl voice, the physical failures of closure and transition associated with the mutations of puberty—the rasps, breaks, breathiness, straining, and other failures to connect or cohere—sonically project an infinite state of restless becoming whose endpoint is never determined. [. . .] This thoroughgoing transformation produces a litany of control problems: insecure pitch, noticeable register breaks, breathiness or huskiness, temporary range limitations, voice cracking, and hoarseness.[87]

> As young women grow into puberty and beyond there are many changes in the larynx; children are not miniature adults. Along with the development of the lamina propria there is a hardening of the arytenoid cartilages, mentioned earlier; while the arytenoids are hardening, the vocal folds cannot close cleanly, causing the breathy sound common in young girls due to the mutational chink (so-called because it is a product of the voice as it mutates during puberty) or gap in the vocal folds that can extend into adulthood. The thyroid-arytenoid muscle strengthens and lengthens as it develops, favoring the development of a strong, healthy chest voice. At the same time, the cricothyroid muscle also develops, extending the "head voice."[88]

Pecknold's and DeMaio's nuanced descriptions make a girl's road to vocal maturity sound like a sonic minefield. For girls, as Laurie Stras observes, "what is actually [vocal] development can sound like aberration. [. . .] These voices *by their nature* were liable to sound out of control, at least occasionally."[89] And it's not just girls' voices that can sound aberrant; discourses *about* these voices, by virtue of their inherent complexity and specialized vocabulary, mirror the mystique at play. Words such as "lamina propria," "thyroid-arytenoid," "crico-thyroid," and "mutational chink"—though familiar to voice teachers, students, and physicians—may sound like the stuff of science fiction, delineating young women-in-training as little aliens. (I was uninformed about this terminology until a knowledgeable colleague guided me toward pertinent literature.)

Along with the pressures exerted by Jive, then, morphological idiosyncrasies shaped, skewed, and challenged the vocal development of a young Britney Spears. It's hard to say how this singer would have fared had she received alternate forms of training and different industry mandates. For the record, though, Spears herself has rarely shown any delusions about bodily or vocal perfection. After her panned performance at the 2007 VMAs, Spears called herself a "fat pig" while crying backstage.[90] And in their 2003 ABC interview, when Diane Sawyer asked Spears if she likes her own voice, the singer looked stunned.

"Do I *like* my voice?" Spears echoed, briefly pausing as if taken aback by the forthright and rudimentary question. "Um, I'll be completely honest. I think my voice is . . . okay? I like the feeling that I get when I sing. It's not so much my voice. But I would love to have a voice like Christina [Aguilera's] [or] like Whitney [Houston's]."[91]

For all of the media's chronic speculations about her ditziness and mental instability, Spears hasn't needed others to tell her she's not the best singer or the thinnest performer or the most saintly celebrity in the world. Not that evidence of self-awareness has ever stopped people from loving to explain all things Britney Spears to Britney Spears. Leave Britney alone? Not a chance.

Fake News (Voice Edition)

When she started singing that ageless song ["Amazing Grace"] with such clarity and beauty, she sounded astonishing, like a young Aretha Franklin, soulful and pure. In my mind that's what her "real" voice sounds like, a wholesome, powerful sound, not like the breathy, super-produced pop voice given to her by record producers.

—Lynne Spears[92]

It gets more complicated.

In the YouTube comment threads for "Alien NO AUTOTUNE," Spears's diehard defenders have clashed with haters. Wave after wave of insults, shaming, and name calling. Equally prevalent in the comments, however, is a debate that has little to do with whether the singing is good or bad, in tune or not. It's a debate about whether the sounds of Spears's voice in the leaked video—and, by extension, the leak itself—are even real. Several viewers came forward to insist that the voice was manipulated to sound out of tune.

You can clearly hear the autotune lowering the notes and making them flat. i cant belive people are this stupid.[93]

This is not real this is fake promise i know britnye does not sing like that[94]

This has obviously been edited by someone too make her voice sound worse.[95]

If, as these commenters argue, a voice these days can easily be Auto-Tuned into sounding on pitch, then a voice can be detuned and faked into sounding off pitch. Some people's superlative truth claims plunged straight into personal attacks. Others opted to focus instead on technicalities. One commenter invited listeners to notice how pitches "change in every part" and that "some of the notes were just forced (by means of editing) to make [Spears's] voice off key!"[96] Another remark siphoned authority from music theory: "The person who made [the video] put auto tune on the vocals but in the wrong key which causes it to sound like this. If you understand music theory and scales you will understand."[97] But even if tuning and detuning were to leave audible tells—an infinitesimal buzz, a timbral twang—these tells have remained indeterminate enough to stall consensus. I've included screen grabs from a few threads (Figure 5.5). Notice the common semantic ploy (think back to Chapter 1) in the otherwise varied claims of veracity or fakery: the amplification of statements by "clearly," "obviously," "so," "promise," and other intensifiers, all overstating epistemic confidence in the

Figure 5.5. Viewers' comments for YouTube videos of the "Alien" leak. Screen captures by author.

face of underwhelming evidence one way or the other. This promissory ping-ponging of *fake news! 100% real! swear it's false! I* PROMISE *it's real!* messily scattered the burden of proof across party lines.

Although a few commenters saw a silver bullet in producer William Orbit's statement about the leak simply being Spears's warm-up, not everyone was convinced. For all we know, fans argued, the "admission" by Orbit doesn't discount the possibility that he spoke hastily for the sake of putting out a fire; maybe Orbit hadn't heard the leak firsthand at all. In sum, the alleged leak of "Alien" led certain listeners to attack Spears as a faker and a meritless singer, whereas others defended Spears by saying the leak itself was fake and had no merit. Together, people knew they probably would never ascertain the absolute truth, yet they participated in the back-and-forths anyway. No one had reason to concede.[98]

In 2017, I presented excerpts of this Spears paper at a few places. During these opportunities, I asked audience members to experiment with relistening to both the lyrics and the tuning of the "Alien" leak. I wondered aloud whether we could shift the onus of aesthetic appreciation from Spears's flawed, purportedly deceptive voice to our own fallible, deceivable ears. Here are the song's opening lyrics.

> There was a time I was one of a kind,
> lost in the world doubting me, myself, and I—
> was lonely then
> like an alien.
>
> I tried but I never figured it out
> why I always felt like a stranger in a crowd,
> but that was then,
> like an alien.
>
> But the stars in the sky look like home; take me home.
> And the light in your eyes lets me know I'm not alone.
>
> Not alone, not alone, not alone,
> not alone, not alone, not alone,
> not alone, not alone, not alone,
> not alone, not alone, not alone.

On the surface, the lyrics are straightforward. The protagonist, presumably Spears or her stage persona, has found a companion who relieves her loneliness. But what if we can't trust our first reading and listening of the song? As Spears sings about alienation, each refrain contains twelve iterations of "not alone" plus one lead-in. Although the words overtly celebrate companionship—"the light in your eyes lets me know I'm not alone"—the sheer repetitiveness of "not alone" belies its denotations. For why would someone need to chant "not alone" a whopping total of fifty-one times throughout the song, if not to reassure herself or to persuade others of her not-aloneness? The way we might hear it, each successive "not alone" recants its own assertion, unraveling the speech act from within. Yet only by taking into account the multiple instances of "not alone"—only by patiently listening in full, and relistening over time—would someone gain access to this alternate interpretation. With diametric interpretations resounding, maybe the truth sits in the middle, somewhere between the desperate denials of aloneness and the naivety of a newfound paramour as panacea.

If the lyrics of "Alien" can be read against their own grain, then Spears's voice (its tone, tuning, timbre) has the potential to be creatively reheard in kind. In my presentations, I typically played three versions of "Alien" to facilitate a listening exercise: first, the official album version; second, the alleged leaked version; and lastly, a synchronized playback of the first version superimposed over the second. Superimposing the two tracks created audible frictions between the in-tune voice and the out-of-tune voice, with a result vaguely reminiscent of the "thick" aesthetics achieved by vocal layering techniques in hip-hop.[99] Although my experiment in superimposition was nowhere near as sophisticated or laborious as professionals' sound-engineering wizardry, I wanted my combination of Spears's two-voicedness to drive home a principle upheld by certain philosophies of compassion and restorative justice: that we are all probably more than the sum of the best and the worst we've ever sounded, musically and otherwise.[100] Time and again, Spears has been broken into *her* best and worst pieces—sonically and graphically, by the clean croppings of Auto-Tune versus embarrassingly isolated vocals, by the airbrushed magazine covers versus the most unflattering candid photos. We, the public, have always had choices in terms of what to do with these pieces. Smelt them into ammunition? Craft them into art anew? Leak them? Leave them alone?

During my presentations, I found it fascinating to watch the facial expressions and body language of my audience members, especially when I played for them the leaked version of "Alien." As people listened to Spears falling conspicuously flat on sustained words such as "sky" and "home" in the first refrain, some faces would contort into winces, smiles, or suppressed laughter; heads would shake; butts would squirm in chairs. What is it, though, about a few flat pitches that can animate listeners' bodies into living GIFs? Are these behaviors performative? Conditioned? Fake? Granted, in formal music education, we're usually taught to think of performative flaws as impurities, whether it's coming up short when singing a high note, pinching an adjacent key on the piano, or croaking a low A-flat on a tenor saxophone. A visual score, an oral template, or a teacher's demo lays out an aspirational and clean rendition, and for purposes of musical reproduction, all obvious errors are toxins, the grime that leaks into an otherwise ideal system. But in musical performances, not least those with improvisatory traditions, is there nonetheless something toxic about hygienic perfectionism and its demands on bodily discipline? Insofar as disciplined musical ability is something that builds up *in your system*—your muscles, nerves, circuitry, calloused skin, vocal folds—we can't claim it's normal or natural for a voice to sound always in tune, or for a thumb to strike every ivory dead center. Discipline makes us capable of amazing feats. But discipline is also bound to Foucauldian control and its warnings of consequent punishment.[101] Stated differently, are pitch norms in (tonal) music any more or less toxic than, say, gender norms, or able-bodied norms, or the racialized norms of respectability politics (soon to be discussed in Chapter 6)? Any more or less political? Certainly for some musicians, it can be second nature to obsess over the worst few seconds of a performance, perhaps just a single fudged note or a forgotten lyric, despite smooth sailing everywhere else. And all it takes is one leak to bring would-be shamers out of the woodwork.

In terms of collective fallibility, leaks are great equalizers. Everything— everyone—is leakable, physically and metaphorically, corporeally and infor- mationally. No one should feel immune to the surveillance of Big Brother, the hell of revenge porn, the blackmail of ransomware, and the plethora of phishing ploys that, like antibiotic-resistant bacteria, engage in arms races with your latest version of antivirus software. No one has inalienable rights to privacy, and no one is exempt from the alienation that breaches of pri- vacy can precipitate. To this point, the chant in Spears's "Alien" rings true: the singer is correct when she professes to be "not alone, not alone, not alone," seeing as how her susceptibility to leakage is a key way in which the stars *are* just like us. Although people take special notice when a leak pertains to a celebrity, we have to remember that leaks can *make* someone a celebrity. With today's prevalence of hacking technologies, a leak could happen to you, even if it sounds like the sort of thing that only happens to other people. (We are all other people's other people.) An anonymous source could dump the entirety of your digital existence onto the Internet—bare-skinned selfies, web history, medical records, dirty laundry, skeletons in the closet—and open you up to body shaming, sex shaming, voice shaming, humiliation, hate mail, and even the threat of physical violence.

Say *data leak* or *data dump* enough times, and these words start summoning images of the natural yet embarrassing leaks and dumps of the human body. Corporeal discharges and scatology are grossly appropriate for conceptualizing privacy's discontents.[102] We know that everyone poops and that everyone has crap to manage. But people learn, internalize, and project abjection. For though we all have actual shit inside us, we sometimes shit on others when they don't seem to have their shit together (disarray), when they lose their shit in public (outburst), when their shit hits the fan (crisis), or when they shit their pants.[103] Or the urinary equivalent: during a 2005 performance in San Diego, Black Eyed Peas singer Fergie visibly wet her shorts, a "most unattractive moment" (in her own words) that people haven't let her live down.[104] Indeed, in February 2018, when another Internet tsunami of shaming washed over Fergie's "sexy sendup" of the "Star-Spangled Banner," some listeners were quick to bring up the 2005 pee incident; her sultry rendition of the national anthem was so shamelessly "out there"— leaking outside the boundaries of respectable taste—that commenters seized on the opportunity to reminisce about the literal leaks of her past.[105] Yet aren't bodily emissions, ejections, and confessions the things that make us commonly human as well as humanly common? Instead of flinging leaks and shit in people's faces, can we help others save face? Can we better differentiate between consequential, generative, maybe game-changing leaks—those brought to light by Chelsea Manning, Edward Snowden, the silence breakers of #MeToo, and whistleblowers—and frivolous, faux-shocking smears? Instead of understanding leakability in terms of individual risk, how might we approach the issue with a nod to collective responsibility?

Before I attempt to answer these questions, a literary comparison from the nineteenth century bears mentioning. As I researched Britney Spears, my mind has repeatedly wandered to George du Maurier's *Trilby*. In this bestselling 1895 novel, a man named Svengali is a Jewish—and, some argue, anti-Semitically caricatured—hypnotist who manipulates the titular heroine

Trilby, bidding her to sing her way to stardom.[106] Originally tone deaf, Trilby becomes an excellent chanteuse under Svengali's Auto-Tune enchantment. At the novel's climax is a calamitous London performance during which Trilby, temporarily freed from Svengali's spell, reverts to singing out of tune. She is humiliated.

One detail typically omitted in accounts of *Trilby* is that du Maurier does give the heroine a kind of celestial voice during her mortifying nadir on the London stage. Facing a jeering audience in a proto-Apollo Theater, the singer doesn't have her own Chris Crocker to plead, "Leave Trilby alone!" . . . so she takes matters into her own hands.

> [Trilby] had not got further than this [part of the performance] when the whole house was in an uproar—shouts from the gallery—shouts of laughter, hoots, hisses, catcalls, cock-crows. She stopped and glared like a brave lioness, and called out: "[W]hat have *I* done, I should like to know?" And in asking these questions the depth and splendor of her voice were so extraordinary—its tone so pathetically feminine, yet so full of hurt and indignant command, that the tumult was stifled for a moment. It was the voice of some being from another world—some insulted daughter of a race more puissant and nobler than ours; a voice that seemed as if it could never utter a false note. Then came a voice from the gods in answer: "Oh, ye're Henglish, har yer? Why don't yer sing as yer *hought* to sing—yer've got *voice* enough, any'ow! why don't yer sing in *tune*?"
>
> "Sing in *tune*!" cried Trilby. "I didn't want to sing at all—I only sang because I was asked to sing—that gentleman [Svengali] asked me—that French gentleman with the white waistcoat! I won't sing another note!"[107]

According to historian Daniel Pick, Svengali is the ultimate "alien hypnotist," an embodiment of Victorian mass paranoia toward psychopathology and illusions of free will.[108] But in her shining and lucid moment on the London stage, Trilby is the one who channels the powerful "voice of some being from another world," even temporarily silencing the clamor against her. Facing hecklers and trolls, our heroine taps into a voice that is proudly alien in its unshameability. Stripped of an artificially beautified voice, she nevertheless finds *a* voice, which she promptly uses to shush and shame her haters. Irrespective of Svengali's magical pitch correction and conservatorship-like management, Trilby shows that she had a voice all along. It just didn't happen to be a people-pleasing, pitch-perfect *singing* voice. And that was fine by her.

In a 2008 memoir, Lynne Spears, mother of Britney Spears, accused a man named Osama "Sam" Lutfi of acting as her daughter's puppet master. Lynne explicitly called Lutfi "Svengali" in the book.[109] Trying to shame and blame a singular Svengali-in-Chief within Spears's inner circle, however, can be a disingenuous and hypocritical game. Is the archvillain Lutfi? Jive? Mother Lynne, author of a tell-all memoir? Father Jamie, conservator? Music critics? Paparazzi? *Us Weekly*? Or us, the public? Celebrity, by definition, cannot exist without public celebration and complicity. People who attack or defend Spears for her scandals are joining an overall attention-granting chorus that sustains the diva's fame and infamy.

So is it even possible, I have asked myself, to write a chapter about Spears without reproducing the media's scrutiny of her life, body, and voice? Doesn't the dialectical academese of what queer theorist Eve Kosofsky Sedgwick called "paranoid reading"—here's a case for X, now here's a case against X—resemble the fickle syntax, as Spears sings in "Piece of Me," of *She's-Too-Big-Now-She's-Too-Thin*?[110] Was the best thing *I* could've done just to leave Britney alone? As I prepared the PowerPoint slides for my oral presentations on this research, for example, I found myself instinctively and repeatedly Googling terms such as "Britney Spears, Weight Gain" to find tabloids' "then and now" images of the singer. On the one hand, I was scouring the Internet's photos to provide conference audiences with visual examples of fat shaming. On the other hand, the search itself replicated the very problems I was seeking to combat and deconstruct. After all, Google terms are tracked, tallied, and archived, so every user's search for mentions of Spears's size incrementally boosts the subject as a search-worthy, auto-fillable keyword.[111]

I left a trace.

Coda: A Leak-Proof Planet; or, Maybe the Least We Can Do Is Nothing

First we made her into an object of desire,
then into an object of contempt.
Now we want to nominate her
as an object of compassion?

Are you sure we know what the hell we're doing? [. . .]
With one of my voices I shout, "Jump, Jump, you little whore!"

With another I turn down the lights and say,
"Put on some clothes and go home, sweetheart."
    —Hoagland, "Poor Britney Spears," end of poem[112]

Does Spears deserve compassion and love? I think so. Am I sure I know what the hell we're doing when it comes to enabling or rectifying cultures of shame and dehumanization? Definitely not.

Given the subject matter of leaks, I should have seen an obligatory post-script coming—because leaks and celebrities are the gifts that keep on giving, the never-ending purveyors of scandal. Just when I thought I had satisfactorily said my piece about Britney Spears, another alleged leak entered the news in summer 2017. This time, it featured Spears's non-Auto-Tuned vocals for the 2004 chart-topping jam "Toxic."[113] But in contrast to the it's-so-bad uproar over the "Alien" leak, the "Toxic" leak spawned dominant narratives of how surprisingly *good* Spears sounded. Headlines read, "You Have to Listen to Britney Spears Singing 'Toxic' without Auto-Tune: Mind. Blown" in the *Huffington Post*; "Britney Spears's 'Toxic' sans Auto-Tune Will Blow Your Mind" in *InStyle Magazine*; and "Britney Spears: Raw Vocals for 'Toxic' LEAKED!" in *The Hollywood Gossip*.[114] Expressions of praise, delight, and exploding heads came fast. Naturally, skeptics weren't far behind. One doubter remarked that "Toxic without autotune [was] just Toxic being sung by an impersonator of Britney."[115] Other listeners went so far as to specify that parts of the so-called leaked version featured the voice of Cathy Dennis, one of the songwriters for "Toxic."[116] Skeptics of the skeptics, however, wouldn't hear of such theories, choosing instead to embrace the leak as a full-throated redemption of the "Alien" fiasco three years prior.

Leaks involving Britney Spears's life, voice, and body will keep coming. If not Britney, then someone else.

But I wish to end on a more optimistic note by turning our attention toward the one thing in the world that is leak proof—or, at least, the one thing that's best *imagined* as leak proof: the world itself. Meaning planet Earth. Barring future frontiers of galactic colonization or alien visitation, we, the earthlings, are stuck with one another for now, and, as the fatalist quip goes, no one's getting out of here alive. Envisioning Earth as a closed system can prompt awareness of individual vulnerability as well as mutual accountability. To think about one's leakable self is to worry about private flourishing. To think about our leak-proof planet is to keep the public good—interpersonal, infrastructural, environmental—in mind.

Here are the first words of economist Amartya Sen's 1981 treatise, *Poverty and Famines*: "Starvation is the characteristic of some people not *having* enough food to eat. It is not the characteristic of there *being* not enough food to eat."[117] Although a framework of resource entitlement sounds self-evident, the writer Uttara Choudhury reminds us that these "opening lines of [Sen's] study startled the world" upon initial publication.[118] Maybe the startling power had to do with the force of the sentences' double gesture: with one hand, Sen pointed implicitly at individual and systemic culprits (the people and organizations inhibiting the fair, humane allocation of food); with the other, he pointed at the entire planet, alerting us to how, in terms of nutrition and caloric sustenance, there has long been an embarrassment of sum provisions, which in turn have been embarrassingly maldistributed. In a prefatory stroke, Sen zoomed in on the procedural minutiae of food waste while zooming way out for a bird's-eye (or alien-ship's) view of our global biosphere and its faulty human stewardship. More profoundly, Sen was saying that our world doesn't have to be this way. Tragically *and* happily, all the food needed to end famine has long existed. In the same vein, if we conceive of the world's interpersonal relationships as a closed and conservationist system, then we cannot afford to blow our outbursts on facetious targets. Is wasting indignation any more justifiable than wasting food? Can we find worthier investments for the time and energies squandered on petty practices of shaming, dehumanization, and alienation? To adapt Sen's formulation: alienation is the characteristic of some people not *having* humane affordances; it is not the characteristic of there *being* not enough humanity to go around.

Ecological vocabularies of scarcity need to be tested against the respective costs of human sustenance and dehumanizing offenses. How much does it cost each of us to treat one another with greater dignity and love, even a sense of shared destiny? Do we fallaciously apply algorithms and scenarios of material dearth (oil, coal, rare earth elements) to our affective transactions? Think of the Free Hugs Campaign, or advocacy for random acts of kindness, or the Jennifer Lopez song "Love Don't Cost a Thing." Initiatives and phrases like these ask people to approach peers, strangers, and even opponents with surplus decency rather than anxieties about just returns or the *schadenfreude* of just desserts.

Maybe such generosity is not always the answer. Maybe reparative ideals sometimes feel more desirable than they are achievable. Either way, though, what passes for outrage these days doesn't automatically give the outraged a free pass. Saying a song hurts the ears doesn't mean you're a good listener. Judging someone as slutty, fat, or trashy can reveal more about the adjudicator's faults than the target's failings. A 2008 *Jezebel* article summed up the reflexive predicament in its title: "Who's Crazier: Britney Spears or the Rest of Us for Giving a Shit?"[119] The question's rhetorical pitch implies that we might all be crazy. Or the conciliatory inverse: none of us are crazy—certainly not as shamefully, haplessly, inhumanly crazy as the pejorative, often ableist, label itself indicates.

From her days on *Star Search* to her night of head shaving, from her big breaks to the breakdowns, Spears has been a lightning rod for controversy and thus a divining rod for societies' toxic wells of shaming and blaming. But leaks, misclicks, and wayward emails can happen to anyone. Maybe tomorrow, you accidentally blast to your department's listserv an innocent yet mortifying nude selfie, or an old video of you singing terribly in the shower, or some other private yet harmless artifact never meant for others' eyes and ears. You might think you're in a waking nightmare. And what then? It could feel like the end of the world . . . until the realization dawns that you are, in fact, not alone, not alone, not alone: that your private apocalypse is one in a million, and that it would be much less chronically apocalyptic if only more members of this million-strong public had the good sense to lend a loving and helping hand or, at the very least, had the grace to do nothing—and to leave you alone.

What if someone refuses to leave you alone? What if, one evening, a stranger notices the music playing from your car stereo—music you love, music he hates—and assumes the worst about you? And what if he comes looking for trouble, not merely with an intent to shame, but with a desire to take forceful and even violent action?

For this book's final chapter, I tread into a case of a musical judgment turned deadly: how an unarmed black teen's loud rap music activated a white man's fear, rage, and prejudice; how this prejudice led to murder; and how this murder went on to be defended as a preemptive strike by a "never-been-called-a-racist" adult against a loud, foulmouthed "thug" who appeared simultaneously superhuman (strong and threatening beyond his years) and subhuman (incapable of speaking civilly or listening to reason).

Michael Dunn shot and killed Jordan Davis in Jacksonville, Florida on Black Friday of 2012. This was just twenty days following Barack Obama's clutch re-election. Liberals were celebrating while conservatives were wallowing and calling for the Republican National Committee to perform an "autopsy" report of their party. "We sound increasingly out of touch," the resulting ninety-seven-page report stated. "If we want ethnic minority voters to support Republicans, we have to engage them and show our sincerity."[120] (Among the autopsy's suggestions, under a section titled "African Americans—Recommendations," was the following: "The RNC and State Parties should make every effort to feature and use diverse committee members."[121])

Meanwhile, black Americans had other things to worry about. With the rise of camera-equipped mobile phones, shaky videos showing police brutality and everyday racism were blazing across social media. And results of actual autopsies were making the evening news, showing the bodies of unarmed black people who had been shot in the back, shot while kneeling, shot while on the ground, shot while already lifeless. Cries of rage, fury, and "Black Lives Matter" were fast ascending to a fever pitch.

Soon, a flashpoint: Ferguson.

6

Jordan Russell Davis

I speak out of direct and particular anger at an academic conference, and a white woman comes up and says, "Tell me how you feel but don't say it too harshly or I cannot hear you." But is it my manner that keeps her from hearing, or the threat of a message that her life may change?

—Audre Lorde, on being tone-policed by a colleague[1]

I am a black woman over six feet tall. My laugh sounds like an exploding mouse. I squeak loudly and speak quickly when I get excited. I like knock in my trunk and bass in my music. [. . .] I am especially attuned to how my sonic footprint plays into how I live and if I should die. As a black woman, the bulk of my threat is associated with my loudness.

—Regina Bradley, on the "sonic disrespectability" of Sandra Bland[2]

Cops and Demons

Around noon on August 9, 2014 in Ferguson, Missouri, a white police officer named Darren Wilson fatally shot Michael Brown, an unarmed black teenager. Later, when facing a grand jury, Wilson testified to Brown's formidable, animalistic attributes:

And when I grabbed him [Brown], the only way I can describe it is I felt like a 5-year-old holding onto Hulk Hogan. [. . .] The only way I can describe it—it looks like a demon. [. . .] As he is coming towards me, I tell [him], keep telling him to get on the ground, [but] he doesn't. I shoot a series of shots. [. . .] At this point, it looked like he was almost bulking up to run through the shots, like it was making him mad that I'm shooting at him. And the face that he had was looking straight through me, like I wasn't even there, [like] I wasn't even anything in his way. Well, he keeps coming at me after that again. During the pause I tell him to get on the ground, get on the ground; he still keeps coming at me, gets about 8 to 10 feet away. At this point I'm backing up pretty rapidly. I'm backpedaling pretty good because I know if he reaches me, he'll kill me. [. . .] I saw the last one [bullet] go into him. And then when it went into him, the demeanor on his face went blank; the aggression was gone. It was gone—I mean, I knew he stopped. The threat was stopped.[3]

"Demon" wasn't the "only way" Darren Wilson could have described eighteen-year-old Michael Brown. But the criminalizing epithet helped this officer dodge indictment. For how else should Wilson have reacted when staring down a resilient beast that can charge through bullets? In the courtroom, the locutionary gambit of *only way—demon* (no alternative words) slid into the self-defense justification of *only choice—kill* (no alternative actions).[4] Aside from allegedly slinging "fuck," "pussy," and other curse words around, this teenager had, according to Wilson, simply uttered "grunting, like, aggravated sound[s]."[5] To the ears and eyes of this cop, Brown was nonverbal (made inchoate noises), nonaural (didn't listen to orders), nonvisual (looked straight through Wilson).[6] Nonhuman.

Wilson's testimony painted Brown as a thug with impenetrable skin and impenetrable ears. Impenetrable—meaning organs resistant to supersonic bullets and clarion instructions alike. Dehumanizing and deadly consequences spawn from these myths of black bruteness. Multiple studies have shown the tendencies of white research subjects to overestimate the size, speed, and age of black people. Such "formidability bias," scientists argue, can expectedly "[promote] participants' justifications of hypothetical use of force against Black suspects of crime."[7] Take the tragedy of twelve-year-old Tamir Rice, who, while playing with an Airsoft toy gun in a Cleveland park on November 22, 2014, was shot and killed by police officer Timothy Loehmann.[8] In his signed statement to investigators, Loehmann declared that Rice "appeared to be over 18 years old and about 185 pounds."[9] Later, in defending Loehmann's use of lethal force, Cleveland Police Patrolmen's Association president Steve Loomis likewise urged the public not to trust their own eyes when it came to photos and videos of this preteen: "He's menacing. He's 5-feet-7, 191 pounds. He wasn't that little kid [. . .] you're seeing in pictures. He's a twelve-year-old in an adult body."[10]

Or was he just a twelve-year-old in a black body?

Racist demonstrations of formidability bias similarly broke out in the aftermath of George Zimmerman's 2012 shooting of unarmed seventeen-year-old Trayvon Martin in Sanford, Florida. Zimmerman's supporters complained about the news' circulation of a photo showing a grinning and "much younger" Martin (Figure 6.1).[11] One defiant reader sent a *Washington Post* journalist a more "honest" picture that was making the rounds on the Internet, a picture of an "up-to-date" Martin with face tattoos and a sizeable frame.[12] Except, it turns out, this wasn't Trayvon Martin (b. 1995) at all; it was a photo of the rapper Jayceon Terrell Taylor (better known as The Game, b. 1979).[13] Such blatant examples of fake news are usually easy to debunk. Subtler cases of pictorial deceit, however, can prove more elusive yet no less toxic. In April 2012, for instance, people accused Fox News of darkening Trayvon Martin's skin with Photoshop, a facile manipulation that, as one critic put it, approximated "journalistic lynching" via colorist stigma.[14] (Several readers likened this case of colorism to the doctored image of O. J. Simpson on a 1994 cover of *TIME* magazine.)[15] Darker, blacker, meaner, stronger.

Formidability myths go beyond overestimations of how resilient black bodies *look* (exteriorities). These myths concurrently enable underestimations of black bodies' capacity to *feel* (interiorities). In a 2014 study, researchers found that white children, beginning as early as age seven, believe their black peers to possess reduced susceptibility to physical pain.[16] Much injustice has historically sprung from white denials of black nociception. "Pain bias," sometimes called the "racial empathy gap,"

Figure 6.1. (*Left*) Trayvon Martin (5′11″, b. 1995, at age sixteen) and (*right*) rapper The Game (6′4‴, b. 1979).

is complicit in the societal normalization of black trauma.[17] Physicians today prescribe lower and fewer doses of pain medication to black patients, including black children.[18] Police use more severe physical force on dark-skinned bodies.[19] Therapists, through buy-in of the Strong Black Woman trope, disproportionately trivialize black women's requests for mental health-care.[20] Or we could think back to the era of US chattel slavery, during which white doctors forced black women to undergo childbirth without anesthetic chloroform, even when infants had to be delivered "with the aid of the blunt hook."[21] Slaveholders' assumptions that black women were generally "strong enough to endure any pain" further warranted their subjection to every other abuse, including rape.[22] Past and present, fantasies of black painlessness have fanned racist attitudes, actions, and policies. Certainly, *being* bulletproof, like Marvel superhero Luke Cage, could be the devout wish of black people who face police and precarity. Being *perceived* as bulletproof is the mortal fear.[23]

Overestimations of physical and emotional resilience can be curses in disguise.[24] "Stop calling me RESILIENT," insisted activist Tracie Washington in her iconic 2005 flyers, which she nailed to telephone poles throughout New Orleans in response to the US media's coverage of Hurricane Katrina. "Because every time you say, 'Oh, they're resilient,' that means you can do something else to me" (Figure 6.2).[25] Don't explain to me what you think I can survive, proclaimed Washington; ask me what my sunken city needs.[26] Washington's message is a reminder that to mythologize black bodies

Figure 6.2. A flyer by Tracie L. Washington, Louisiana Justice Institute.

as *indomitable* is to reify systems of racist *domination*. Put differently, professing to know what someone is capable of can risk sliding into neoliberal presumptions of what the person can be subjected to—pain, labor, tribulation, trauma.

Obviously, black people are resilient. It's just that, historically speaking, bad things happen when white people overeagerly celebrate, fetishize, or exploit the obviousness of this notion (recall Cornel West's critique of "obviously" in Chapter 1). Sure, if you're white, go ahead and admire Strong Black Women, so long as you remember that their strength isn't for you to test, in the same way their hair isn't yours to touch.

Formidability bias and pain bias together entail an overestimation of black people's strength, size, age, and resilience—characteristics of physical excess. As a music scholar, I've lately wondered how biases about physical excess might intersect and compound with analogous prejudices about black sonic excess. Black people face accusations of protesting too forcefully (Black Lives Matter, "uppity-ism," the Angry Black Woman), laughing too boisterously (the 2015 Napa Valley wine train skirmish), playing music too loudly ("Jeep Beats" and racial epithets), and shouting in the movie theater.[27] For resentful listeners, black noise is like dirt; it is, to paraphrase the anthropologist Mary Douglas, sonic "matter out of place."[28] And dirt is an apt simile because, beginning in the nineteenth century, scientific discourses of American hygiene have churned out stigmas of nonwhite bodies as "dirty" and "impure"—which, as the historian Carl Zimring points out, are viciously hypocritical, given how environmental racism (the inequitable allocation of waste and toxins) overwhelmingly harms communities of color.[29] Indictments of black sonic impurities ultimately hinge on the following twin assumptions: black bodies *make* noise; and black ears can *take*—embrace, withstand, shrug off—noise. Diagnoses of black ears and policings of black noise have often accompanied insidious policies, from the Antebellum South's pseudo-medical treatises about the auditory "nerves of the Negro"[30] to the present-day fiascos that generate memes of #LaughingWhileBlack, #SingingWhileBlack, and #TalkingWhileBlack.[31] Some of these hashtags are meant to be humorous. Far from mere funny business, though, prejudices about black noise can pose grave consequences. Stereotypes about "the 'deep' black voice, the 'noisy' neighborhood, [and] the 'loud' music," notes the race theorist Jennifer Lynn Stoever, expose "incidents of racist listening [that] cannot be dismissed, laughed off, or chalked up to white ignorance and/or innocence."[32] Altogether, stereotypes of black physical excess and black sonic excess implicate the threatening physicalities of black sound and, in turn, the threatening sounds of black physicality.

In this final chapter of *Loving Music Till It Hurts*, I bear witness to how white misimaginations of black skin, black ears, and black voices in the United States have subtly yet severely abetted racist ideologies that dehumanize, discredit, or outright destroy black life. In the chapter's first half, I tug at knotty cultural stereotypes of black resilience and sonic excess. Why are certain expressions of black empowerment deemed respectable, whereas other expressive modes face denunciation and censorship? And how can black-coded musical genres—say, rap, a lynchpin in culture wars— construct and deconstruct myths about the formidability of black bodies? I arrange these primers on resilience, respectability, and rap to triangulate a case study in the chapter's latter half, the 2014 criminal trial *People of the State of Florida v. Michael David Dunn*. Nicknamed the "Loud Music Trial," this case involved a white software developer named Michael Dunn who, one evening at a Florida gas station, noticed rap music coming from a parked SUV. Dunn approached the SUV and asked the black youths inside the vehicle to turn their music down. When they refused, Dunn launched into a heated argument with one of the boys, a high school student named Jordan Russell Davis. The confrontation ended with Dunn pulling out a handgun, unloading ten rounds, and shooting Davis through the heart.

As a high-profile case, *People v. Dunn* received abundant news coverage in 2014 and served as the main subject of a 2015 documentary called *3½ Minutes, 10 Bullets*.[33] I have drawn insights from these sources as well as from my own multiple viewings of the complete trial footage.[34] I'm also supplementing this research with materials that eluded mainstream coverage: Dunn's jailhouse letters and phone calls (largely omitted from the trial's formal proceedings); stenographers' transcriptions of courtroom sidebars (inaudible to gallery members and not picked up by the documentary team's microphones); and discovery documents, evidence technicians' reports, and 911 records (now publicly available).

Jordan Davis was seventeen years old, 145 pounds, 5'11", and unarmed. Michael Dunn was forty-seven years old, 250 pounds, 6'4", and armed. Yet according to Dunn's testimony, Davis had "threatened my life like a *man*" and became "*louder and louder* and more violent and more violent" with every word.[35] Or as Dunn told the police: "I didn't know he was seventeen. I thought he was a full-grown man. I thought they all were. And in my mind they were all going to get out of this truck and shoot me or beat me or kill me."[36] Like Michael Brown, Trayvon Martin, and Tamir Rice (forever eighteen, seventeen, and twelve), Jordan Davis was seen and heard as formidable beyond his years. Perceptions of loud blackness metamorphosed into fictions of criminal threat. Physical and sonic excess made flesh. Flesh unmade by bullets. "I had no choice but to defend myself," said Dunn. "It was life or death."[37] Only choice—kill.

More on *People v. Dunn* soon. First, one of the case's essential themes; or, how resilience became the new black.

What Doesn't Kill You . . .

> When a sweet grandmotherly sort has to tell you how black people once were chained in iron masks in the canebrake, to keep them from eating the cane while they harvested it, and that these masks were like little ovens that cooked the skin off their faces—when you hear that grandmotherly voice and realize she once was a girl who might have been your girl, and someone caused this pain on her lips and nobody did anything about it but keep living—this gives you a tendency to shout.
>
> —Ralph Wiley, *Why Black People Tend to Shout*[38]

In his 1855 autobiography *My Bondage and My Freedom*, Frederick Douglass dreamt of music breaking chains. "I have sometimes thought," he wrote, "that the mere hearing of those [slave] songs would do more to impress truly spiritual-minded men and women with the soul-crushing and death-dealing character of slavery, than the reading of whole volumes of its mere physical cruelties."[39] With one wistful sentence, Douglass fantasized—while admitting his fantasy's naivety—that slaves' sorrowful, beautiful melodies might somehow move slaveowners to show mercy, grant freedom, and recognize black humanity.

But the music of slaves did not inspire white epiphanies. Some masters assumed slaves sang out of joy (the Myth of the Happy Slave), proving an amenability to captivity and manual labor.[40] Others saw chattel value and resilience in this singing, such that talented slaves often fetched higher auction prices.[41] And signs of resilience meant, to borrow the language of Tracie Washington's post-Katrina flyers, that something else could be done to slaves—more demands for labor, more disciplinary lashes, more subjection to rape, more cruel tests of how much these black bodies could take before they broke their backs, or burned out, or could sing no more.

As a triumphalist ideal, resilience *is* resilient.[42] Its virtues are, on the surface, unimpeachable. As journalist Krishnadev Calamur asked with regard to state responses to terrorism, "Would [anyone] oppose the idea of resilience so a city or a community bounces back stronger from the terror inflicted upon it?"[43] Likewise, would anyone tell a resilient disabled contestant on *America's Got Talent* to get off the stage and to cease complicity in the patronage of supercrip inspiration porn (Chapter 4)? Would anyone rush to instruct the doctors, social workers, and activists of Flint, Michigan to abstain from celebrating the city's "exemplary kids" who have survived lead toxins and even channeled hardship into chromatic art (Figure 6.3)?[44] Probably not. But these questions—premised on *reductio ad absurdum* killjoy caricatures— are misleading.[45] Because as with the institutional lip services paid to diversity, inclusivity, and equality, the self-evident merits of resilience can

Figure 6.3. (*Left*) *TIME* magazine cover with headline: "The storms keep getting stronger. **And so do we**" (25 September 2017); (*right*) Water Bottle Chandelier (photo by Doug Pike) created by children of Flint, Michigan, and gifted to the city's Hurley Medical Center. With regard to the chandelier, Dr. Mona Hanna-Attisha wrote, "Our Flint kids are more than resilient: they are exemplary. [. . .] Like our exemplary kids, we are turning a tragedy into something beautiful."

lull us into uncritical cheer, threatening to derail deeper investigations into the social norms, injustices, and precarities that require some populations to be extra-resilient in the first place.[46] Consider the fraught intersections of race, disability, gender, and class in the example of US military veterans who seek medical and financial benefits. Troops nowadays undergo regimented Comprehensive Soldier Fitness (CSF) programs and comparable forms of "resilience training."[47] Again, it would be hard to oppose CSF's stated goal of "equipping and training our Soldiers, Family members, and Army Civilians to maximize their potential and face the physical and psychological challenges of sustained operations."[48] Studies have shown, however, that the perceived success of such training comes partly from how it discourages troops from *reporting* trauma—that is, how resilience programs dissuade their participants from grousing, from showing weakness, and from demanding their share of veterans' resources from the government. Low-ranking officials who ask for healthcare or otherwise display vulnerability are, notes feminist scholar Brianne Gallagher, "repeatedly called 'PTSD sissies' by higher ranking officials" and subsequently shamed into silence.[49] Black troops—especially black women, who enlist at far higher rates than black men and white women alike—stand to face even greater obstacles, as they must crawl through thickets of stereotypes on the path to aid: the gangsta/er, the Strongman, the Strong Black Woman, the Welfare Queen, the angry loud minority, and other racist molds that presume soldiers of color as either feeling no need to complain at all, or having no right to complain as much as they do.[50]

Kneejerk appeals to resilience are problematic not only in terms of acute trauma—a battle injury, a natural disaster, a terrorist attack—but also when it comes to people dealing with slow-burning injustices, degenerative conditions, and inhumane circumstances weathered over time. Toxicity can hide in plain sight, as with cases of environmental racism in Warren County or Flint or Standing Rock. Ecological and financial adversities further animate what Lauren Berlant terms "slow death," the "physical wearing out of a population" through debilitative labor and a never-ending carousel of daily crises.[51] How can we tell if hard conditions are stimulating someone's growth or simply depleting that person's finite reserves of will and fight? How do we know if a reliably punctual but chronically exhausted worker will soon be set for life or has been marked for early death? Phoenix rising or stagnant ash? Dewy visions of resilience confuse bare life—the bare condition of (still) being alive—with humane living.[52] Critical theorist Judith Butler frames it this way: "It seems that we survive precisely in order to live, and life, as much as it requires survival, must be more than survival in order to be livable."[53] Teaching people how to be resilient is good. But the pedagogy itself turns sour if, as urban ecologist Maria Kaika declares, the preaching of resilience is twisted into a form of "immunology [that] vaccinate[s] people and environments alike so that they are able to take *larger* doses of inequality and environmental degradation in the future."[54] In medicine, after all, a round of vaccination neither guarantees a patient's invulnerability nor automatically concludes the healthcare provider's terms of responsibility.[55] The same goes for individual resilience, which neither promises a good life nor obviates the need for statewide reforms.

Embedded in celebrations of resilience are assumptions about what resilience should sound like. Respectable resilience is Senator Elizabeth Warren and her Nevertheless-She-Persisted recitation of a letter by Coretta Scott King on C-SPAN—a recitation that was confident in tone yet moderate in volume.[56] Unrespectable resilience is, per this chapter's epigraph, Audre Lorde speaking "harshly" at a conference and getting scolded by a white woman.[57] Respectable resilience is the Strong Black Woman who shoulders mountains with nary a complaint. Unrespectable resilience is the Angry Black Woman who's "overbearing, attitudinal, bitter, mean, and hell raising."[58] Respectable resilience is Oprah Winfrey, rising from poverty and becoming a mogul whose iconic shout, loud though it may have been on her talk show, was music to people's ears because such vocal excitation sometimes carried promises of cars to white folk.[59] Unrespectable resilience was Sandra Bland, whose shouts carried only promises of insubordination.[60] Respectable resilience was the Nina Simone who pushed through discrimination and received a scholarship to Juilliard. Unrespectable resilience was the Nina Simone who went on to sing "Mississippi Goddam" to burn racism to the ground. Respectable resilience can be black. Unrespectable resilience, too black.[61]

On August 8, 2015, a pair of unrespectable black voices sounded off against white ears at a Seattle rally for US presidential candidate Bernie Sanders. Two women named Marissa Janae Johnson and Mara Jacqueline Willaford jumped the barricade, rushed onto the stage, and seized the microphone. Ignoring the audience's cries of surprise and dismay, Johnson began by stating some unsavory facts about the city's colonialist roots. She called out white supremacy, police misconduct, and the disproportionate rate of black students' suspension in Seattle's schools. She also called for four-and-a-half minutes of silence for Michael Brown, who had been killed almost exactly one year ago. (Four-and-a-half minutes—because Brown's bleeding facedown body, half-covered by a sheet and roped off by yellow tape, had been left to lie for four-and-a-half hours on Ferguson's sunbaked street as the horrified residents of the neighborhood gathered and helplessly looked on.) At first, Marissa Johnson received a smattering of applause for palatable declarations such as "Bernie Sanders, welcome to Seattle!" and "Black Lives Matter!" But once she brought up Michael Brown and began naming white racism in earnest, the audience turned audibly hostile. Johnson and Willaford were met with boos, "shame!," calls for arrest, and racial slurs lobbed by Sanders's fans.[62] "I think it is unfortunate because, among other things, I wanted to talk about the issues of black lives," said Sanders after the rally came to a premature end. "They [Johnson and Willaford] didn't want to hear anything."[63]

True, Sanders might have been, as copious pundits explained to Johnson and Willaford over the next several days, black Americans' "best option" given that he had even "marched with Martin Luther King."[64] In a subsequent press release, Sanders himself proclaimed that when it came to "the need to fight racism, there is no other candidate for president who will fight harder than me."[65] In blunter terms, Hamilton Nolan at *Gawker* condescendingly told Johnson and Willaford, "Don't piss on your best friend."[66] All the more perplexing, however, that black people's best friend—a man who had marched with King—stood silently next to these two young women as they faced hisses and "n-word carpet-bombing" by his Seattle audience.[67]

In the media coverage, Johnson and Willaford weren't hailed as resilient, brave, or heroic. For weeks, they received death threats and rape threats, were called "thugs" and "hood rats," endured tone-policing lessons, and received invitations onto news programs only to answer questions mired in antinomies and false dichotomies: . . . *why interrupt the most progressive candidate? . . . if you don't support Bernie Sanders, then which nominee* do *you support? . . . shouldn't you at least* listen *to what Bernie has to say?*[68] It didn't seem to occur either to Sanders or to reporters that perhaps Black Lives Matter protestors would disrupt the rally not *despite* but *because* he was discernible as one of the strongest hopes for anti-racist and economic reform. Nor did most critics entertain the possibility that this interruption of Sanders's stump speech communicated more than stock talking points, already neatly summarized anyway on the candidate's campaign website, ever could.[69]

And what happened to Sanders's website the day after Johnson's and Willaford's disruption? It discreetly added a hyperlinked item to the candidate's list of issues: racial justice (Figure 6.4).[70]

Given the angry reactions of the white liberal Seattle crowd, a gesture of black interpellation by Johnson and Willaford was apparently too radical, too loud. It wasn't only an issue of decibels. For even as Johnson and Willaford fell completely mute to observe four-and-a-half minutes of silence in memory of Michael Brown, the audience hollered:

> We don't care!
> Assholes!
> All lives matter! All lives matter!
> How dare she call me a racist!
> You are out of line!
> Get off the stage!
> You had your say!
> Call security!

And one attendee, in direct response to Johnson's insistence on a moment of silence for Brown, shot back,

> We've already done it![71]

We've already done it. Done what? Mourned appropriately? Shed enough tears? Moved on from Ferguson? Healed?[72]

INCOME AND WEALTH INEQUALITY	INCOME AND WEALTH INEQUALITY
CREATING DECENT PAYING JOBS	CREATING DECENT PAYING JOBS
A LIVING WAGE	RACIAL JUSTICE
REAL FAMILY VALUES	A LIVING WAGE
CLIMATE CHANGE & ENVIRONMENT	REAL FAMILY VALUES
REFORMING WALL STREET	CLIMATE CHANGE & ENVIRONMENT
GETTING BIG MONEY OUT OF POLITICS	REFORMING WALL STREET
	GETTING BIG MONEY OUT OF POLITICS

Figure 6.4. Bernie Sanders's website on (*left*) August 8, 2015, and on (*right*) August 9, 2015.

Johnson and Willaford forced a captive audience to stew in a crucible of cognitive dissonance. Surely one can't vote Democrat *and* be called a racist. Surely one can't be nominally pro-Black Lives Matter and yet have screamed for security to remove two black women from the stage.[73] Surely Michael Brown was commemorated sufficiently throughout 2014; 2015 was supposed to be about looking forward to the 2016 election and the new presidency of 2017. During the Sanders rally, such ideological discord was made audible when the rally organizers twice started up music over the loudspeakers, as if attempting either to drown out Johnson and Willaford or, in awards show fashion, to play them off the stage. In both instances, the music of choice was "Glory," a song by John Legend and Common. The first blast of "Glory" came when the women initially climbed onto the stage; the second blast hit at the exact moment Johnson accused Sanders of failing to put forward a comprehensive platform for criminal justice reform. But the organizers' clumsy co-optation of "Glory" was ironic at best, baneful at worst. As the theme song for the 2014 film *Selma*, it had been performed to notoriously tearjerking effect at the 2015 Academy Awards.[74] "Glory" goes like this:

> [*Sung by Legend*] One day when the glory comes,
> It will be ours, it will be ours.
> Oh, one day when the war is won,
> We will be sure, we will be sure. [. . .]
> [*Rapped by Common*] That's why Rosa sat on the bus.
> That's why we walk through Ferguson with our hands up.
> When it go down we woman and man up
> They say, "Stay down," and we stand up.

Given how readily "Glory" came on the loudspeakers, it's safe to assume that organizers had purposefully cued up the song for the Sanders rally, presumably with an intention to drive home the point, once again, that Sanders had marched with Dr. King and is therefore black people's shining hope. Yet to watch Johnson and Willaford attempt to make their own voices heard over a blaring playback of a song about civil rights, about strong black women, and about Ferguson and Michael Brown—to watch these two women perform a resilient immovability against a furious chorus trying to shout them into silence—was, if anything, to witness the enduring necessity of an *un*respectable movement for black lives.[75]

Figure 6.5. Johnson (*left*) and Willaford (*right*). Photo by Alex Garland.

In an interview with *Real Change* a couple of months after the protest, Marissa Johnson wore a black hoodie that sported the words, "NOT YOUR RESPECTABLE NEGRO." A riff on James Baldwin.[76] As for Mara Willaford's attire on the day of the protest? A T-shirt emblazoned with "BULLETPROOF" in gold letters (Figure 6.5).[77]

A riff on a powerful, perilous fantasy.

Bulletproof Rap

> Black people are a minority in the country they built. The legacy of
> that building has remanded them to the basement of America. There
> are only two conscious ways to escape the basement: (1) Appeal to
> the magnanimity of white people. (2) Become super-human.
>
> —Ta-Nehisi Coates[78]

Harlem after dark. A black man in a hoodie, with heart of gold and skin of steel, peers out from behind a tree.[79] He's preparing to break into a stash house to reclaim some stolen money. As he leaves his hiding spot, he puts on a pair of headphones and kicks up "Bring da Ruckus" at full volume. *BRING DA MOTHERFUCKIN' RUCKUS.* He rips off the door of a nearby car to use it as a shield, then busts through the front doors of the stash house. *I COME ROUGH, TOUGH LIKE AN ELEPHANT TUSK.* Men with semiautomatics charge at him and open fire. But the shots bounce off the man's skin, their idle ricochets sounding like metal meeting metal. *I WATCH MY BACK LIKE I'M LOCKED DOWN. HARDCORE-HITTIN' SOUND, WATCH ME ACT BUGGED AND TEAR IT DOWN.* More goons strike him with fists, pipes, and machetes, all to no avail. *CHECK IT, MY METHOD ON THE MICROPHONE'S BANGIN', WU-TANG SLANG, I'LL LEAVE YOUR HEADPIECE HANGIN'.* The hoodied man takes the cash he came for, leaving unconscious bodies in his wake. Thus concludes a breathless scene from an early episode of the Netflix series *Luke Cage*, with the Wu-Tang Clan's rapid-fire rhymes accompanying the show's fantasy of bulletproof blackness.[80]

Although Cage's invincibility is the stuff of Marvel fiction, this hero's choice of music reverberates with several virtues and vices familiarly attributed to rap: hypermasculinity, belligerence, resilience, and even invulnerability. Like Cage, a listener might feel tough when jamming to a loud, brash, percussive rap song.[81] Surely, though, rap—or any music—can't physically toughen your skin.

Or can it? Decades of studies in music therapy, cognition, and psychology have affirmed music's ability to alter moods, emotions, hormonal balance, and brain chemistry.[82] More recently, scholars have further shown how auditory stimuli can skew our perceptions of our own bodily exteriors. Authors of a 2014 *PLOS ONE* article, "The Marble-Hand Illusion," set out to investigate "whether the brain can update its knowledge about the material properties of the body by inducing an illusory perception of the material of the hand. We gently hit participants' right hand with a small hammer, and manipulated the auditory feedback so that each time the hammer hit the hand, participants heard the sound of a hammer against a stone."[83] In sum, the authors demonstrated how the human brain can be tricked, via audiotactile synchrony, into updating its "knowledge" about what one's skin is made of and hence what it's capable of withstanding.[84] Subjects reported "feeling stiffer, heavier, harder, less sensitive, unnatural," and involuntarily "showed enhanced Galvanic skin response (GSR) to threatening stimuli."[85] Along with complementary studies of GSR, bass frequencies, loud noises, and auditory perception, the "Marble-Hand Illusion" posits that the sounds we hear can actually modulate our dermal resilience.[86] All this is to say, whereas no sonic stimuli can make you a literally bulletproof Luke Cage, certain sounds can still do more than merely make you feel *like* Luke Cage.[87]

Especially when its volume and bass are cranked up, rap is a culturally reliable signifier of formidability. Fight scenes, chase scenes, and action set pieces in television and film commonly play out to rap.[88] Many athletes say they include rap in their pregame "get-hyped" playlists, as with Lebron James's practice of blasting Wu-Tang Clan's "Bring the Pain" and Jay-Z's "Reservoir Dogs" in the locker room, "pump[ing] up the volume loud enough to send vibrations through a nearby dry-erase board."[89] RAP MUSIC MAKES ME FEEL INVINCIBLE is a motto splashed across apparel.[90] Lyrics of rap songs typically spin out fantasies of empowerment, anti-authoritarianism, and even omnipotence.[91] And myths of rap-imbued resilience are sustained by tantalizing stories of unbreakable rappers. Atlanta's Yung Mazi, who had proudly reported being struck by bullets ten times earlier in life, tweeted out "God made me bulletproof" after another failed attempt on his life in December 2016.[92] (On August 7, 2017, he was shot yet again—and, this time, killed. For a while, however, news of his death elicited doubt, as if someone's luck in surviving a bullet on a prior occasion could be a realistic indicator of that person's intrinsic ability to survive another. "Is it true? Atlanta rapper Yung Mazi dead?" asked one journalist. "It was hard to believe at first because Mazi had been shot in the past numerous times, including in the head, and lived to tell about it."[93]) More famously, Tupac Shakur was hailed as "invincible" when he survived five shots in 1994; his legendary reputation only intensified when he was shot four more times and killed in 1995, at which point some fans still refused to believe he could be deceased.[94] Other rappers known to have survived gunshot wounds include 50 Cent, Ol' Dirty Bastard, and The Game (shown in Figure 6.1 vis-à-vis Trayvon Martin).[95]

Sounds of rap are bound to images of resilience. But resilience, as I've underscored here, is a double-edged sword. If people discern formidability in your rap-blaring, trunk-thumping ways, then they might see you as a threat. And if these nearby people happen to be police or armed private citizens, then the threat level of your sonic footprint can suddenly become a threat unto yourself—especially if you're black. For in spite of the racial heterogeneity of contemporary rap's artists and consumers, musicologist Loren Kajikawa reminds us that most of today's American "listeners still perceive rap as a 'black' genre."[96] One problem therefore lies in the privilege of "white fans [to] claim hip-hop as 'their' style" without "liv[ing] with the consequences of being stereotyped as 'thugs' or 'hos.' They can partake in the music or fashion of the hip-hop industry without worrying that they will be targeted and killed."[97] Ethnomusicologist Ingrid Monson, writing about jazz, has similarly protested how "it often seems that the only aspects of African American culture that non-African Americans really want access to are the fun parts: music, dancing, sex, and sports."[98] But fun parts are only half of the story, because equally tempting are the sad parts of black culture, the tragedies that bleed beauty out of blackness: stirring documentaries about slavery, songs of strange fruit, Afro-pessimist poetry, and other testaments to black resilience—myriad art and artifacts that white people can consume without making concurrent moves to dismantle the injustices that necessitate the resilience of black bodies to begin with.[99]

It's no surprise, then, that narratives of "black music" generally unfold as narratives of black resilience.[100] From spirituals to blues to rock to funk to gospel to hip-hop (along with crip hop, homo hop, and countercultures within countercultural genres), writers tend to chronicle black musicianship through themes of empowerment, resistance, and creative impulses born from adversity.[101] "Through all the sorrow of the Sorrow Songs there breathes a hope—a faith in the ultimate justice of things," wrote W. E. B. Du Bois about the music of slaves. "The minor cadences of despair change often to triumph and calm confidence."[102] Musicologist Eileen Southern, who named Du Bois as a role model, published histories and anthologies highlighting the persistence of black musical traditions and repertoire—worksongs, spirituals, ragtime, blues—in the face of systematic oppression.[103] Or take bebop, which poet Amiri Baraka exalted for its "willfully harsh, *anti-assimilationist* sound,"[104] and which jazz scholar Scott Deveaux characterized as "a rebellion by black musicians against a white-controlled capitalist hegemony."[105] When framed within narratives of overcoming, black music is seemingly never allowed just to be, but must always formidably, laboriously be *against*.

Even when the repertoire in question isn't as openly incendiary as, say, "Fuck tha Police," black music's reputation of againstness can pigeonhole black members of society as automatic activists, mavericks, or otherwise threats to the status quo. Some black people have therefore found sonic life hacks that project respectability and innocuousness. In his 2010 book *Whistling Vivaldi*, social psychologist Claude Steele shared the anecdote of a male graduate student who would "[whistle] popular tunes from the Beatles and Vivaldi's *Four Seasons*" while walking down the street in order to appear educated and "knowledge[able] of white culture, even 'high white culture.'"[106] With Steele in mind, ethnomusicologist Alisha Lola Jones has taken her own informal surveys of black men in her Chicago community, and found that respondents had varying strategies for appearing nonthreatening. Some men "hum," some "sing softly" or walk with "soft" mannerisms, and some indeed "rap loudly," albeit with the important purpose of sending "subtle alarms to let people know we are approaching."[107] Such musical virtue signaling would sound comical if it weren't so necessary in light of societal prejudices against dark-skinned bodies.

Retta, a comedian and actress, has tried to find humor in musical-racial stereotypes nonetheless. She has a joke that happens to feature Vivaldi. "I love classical music," she begins. "Don't get me wrong. I'm still black. I still kick the bass and pump up the volume." As her audience chortles, Retta continues:

> It's just that when I'm in my car and the windows are closed, you wouldn't know [that I love classical music]. So I'm driving down the street. I stop at a light. An older couple pulls up next to me. Now keep in mind, all they can hear is the bass, and they see me. [*Vocally percusses into the microphone*] *Puh-puh, puh, puh. Puh-puh, puh, puh, puh-puh puh.* [*Winks at audience*] Now the woman on the passenger side, she looks across at me and she's like, "Ugh, it's that rap music again." That's when I let down my power windows. [*Sings Vivaldi's "Gloria," RV 589*] *Laudamus te. Laudamus te. Benedicimus te. Adoramus te. Glorificamus te.* Bitch![108]

In the sixty seconds that it takes for Retta to tell this story of classical music clapback, multiple morals emerge. Don't judge music by its thumping bass-line, because classical music thumps, too (recall this book's Interlude). Don't judge a black woman by her muffled music, because she might surprise you by revealing that she's listening to a Baroque choral favorite. Better yet, don't judge her by her playlist at all; she shouldn't have to out herself as a classical music buff to appear respectable and to avoid dirty looks.

Beyond the occasional side-eye from someone in the next car over, condemnations of rap come up in academic writing and everyday conversations. Ethnomusicologist Cheryl Keyes recalls a colleague who "concluded that rap music could not be considered music because its text did not consist of a sequence of tempered pitches, [but] rather spoken or speech-like text."[109] In a 2003 *City Journal* article, the linguist John McWhorter declared that rap, far from having any "political engagement" or "revolutionary potential," reinforces a "thuggish" stereotype that "retards black success."[110] In their controversial 2007 manifesto for black respectability, *Come On, People*, Bill Cosby and Alvin Poussaint excoriated "young black males spewing angry, profane, and women-hating rap music that plays on the worst stereotypes of black people."[111] In 2017, law professors Amy Wax and Larry Alexander penned an op-ed castigating the American decline of "bourgeois culture," citing, as one culprit, "the anti-'acting white' rap culture of inner-city blacks."[112] And in 2018, jazz giant Wynton Marsalis told a *Washington Post* editor that rap and hip-hop are "more damaging" to society "than a statue of Robert E. Lee."[113]

I have no problem with people who knowledgeably criticize misogynist, homophobic, and bellicose strains within various examples and subgenres of rap.[114] My beef is with people who criticize rap primarily in the context of— and as a means of derailing—conversations about anti-black racism. Rap has long been an easy target in games of "whataboutism."[115] Got a problem with white privilege? Well, what about rap and its supposed corruption of black youths? Accusing cops of shooting unarmed black people? Yeah, but what about gangsta rap's glorification of "black-on-black" violence?[116]

Here's a clear example. In October 2016, when *Access Hollywood* leaked the infamous hot-mic recording of Donald Trump saying "grab 'em by the pussy" to Billy Bush on a bus, a Trump campaign adviser named Betsy McCaughey appeared on CNN to dish out her opposition research. "I abhor lewd and bawdy language. I don't listen to rap music," she explained. Rather than addressing Trump's "pussy" remark (or "P-word," as she put it), however, McCaughey began reading from her notes. "Hillary Clinton expresses that she finds language on that [*Access Hollywood*] bus horrific, but in fact she likes language like this. Quote, 'I came to slay, bitch; when he F me good, I take his ass to Red Lobster.'" As the rest of the CNN panel erupted in puzzled laughter— "Did [Clinton] *say* that?"—McCaughey triumphantly explained: "That happens to be a line from Beyoncé, her favorite performer, whom she says she idolizes and would like to imitate. So you know what I'm saying to you? There's a lot of hypocrisy."[117] Aside from McCaughey's misclassification of Beyoncé's "Formation" as rap, the derailment illuminated how the perceived unrespectability of *some* black music can be whittled into oblique excuses for *any* white offense. For as long as rap has served up a symbol of black resilience, white people have found durable ways to weaponize rap against black people and black culture.[118] Indeed, part of society's moral panic about rap has hinged on the fallacy that a rap lover necessarily, proactively, and literally wishes to commit the violence or improprieties described in certain rap lyrics. Note, however, that people do not fallaciously assume that anyone who sings along to Wolfgang Amadeus Mozart opera *Don Giovanni* in his car is a sexual predator.[119] It's a double standard of selective literalism, which in turn oils the social machinery of racialized hypocrisy. Because no less so than opera or other mediums of stylized art, rap is, as Henry Louis Gates Jr. puts it, "a contemporary form of signifying" that "complicates or even rejects literal interpretation." With its "virtuosic sense of wordplay," rap amounts to a "postmodern version of an African American vernacular tradition that stretches back to chants, Toasts, and trickster tales."[120]

None of this implies that if you're not a fan of rap, then you must loathe black people. But this question of causation and correlation tends to arise whenever rap-related discriminatory incidents make the news. In 2006, *Slate* author John Cook published an article that asked point-blank: "If you don't like rap, are you a racist?" Cook went to great lengths to justify his predictable answer of "no."[121] As in, no, you're not a racist if, as Cook glibly stated, "the number of black artists in your iPod falls too far below 12.5% of the total."[122] But the rhetorical question itself—"If you don't like rap, are you a racist?"—is already a distraction, baiting the reader away from the circumstantial peculiarities of how people might find themselves in a situation where they are being accused of racism in the first place. Specifically, Cook's article tried to defend singer Stephin Merritt, who has long faced charges of racism. Merritt has lamented how it's "shocking that we're not allowed to play coon songs anymore," advocated for the use of derogatory metrics like "quadroon and octoroon," voiced sweeping contempt for hip-hop, and supported "Zip-A-Dee Doo-Dah"—from the brashly racist 1946 Disney film *Song of the South*—as a "great song."[123] Altogether, do these views make Merritt a racist? Depends on how low we set the bar. Or maybe the bar for racism is the wrong apparatus entirely. Maybe the focus should be on the bar for *anti-racism*, such that the operative question changes from *Can this person pass for a non-racist?* into *What anti-racist actions has that person ever taken?* In societies beset by racial injustices and race-motivated violence, affirmative anti-racism is what counts.

On its own, loving rap doesn't anoint you as a champion of anti-racism. And you're not a de facto racist if rap isn't your cup of tea. But say that, one night, a man hears a rap song coming from the car of four black youths. He mutters to his fiancée, "I hate that thug music," and she replies, "Yes, I know." Later, while sitting in jail awaiting trial for murdering one of these unarmed youths, the man writes letters in which he rages against the "gangster-rap, ghetto talking thug 'culture' that certain segments of society flock to," and letters saying "if more people would arm themselves and kill these fucking idiots when they're threat[en]ing you, eventually they may take the hint and change their behavior."[124] This man's extreme dislike of rap would have only been one warning sign. Add it to a growing pile of supporting evidence, however, and a frightful picture of prejudice begins to emerge.

In this case, it wouldn't be too soon to cry racist. It would already have been too late.

People v. Dunn (I): The Trial

> It was not about the music. It was really about the inability of Michael Dunn to see those boys as human beings—to see them as somebody worthy of existing.
>
> —Lucia (Lucy) McBath, mother of Jordan Davis[125]

People of the State of Florida v. Michael David Dunn
February 6–15, 2014
Honorable Russell L. Healey
Attorneys appearing on behalf of the State of Florida: Angela Corey, John Guy, Erin Wolfson
Attorney appearing on behalf of the defendant: Cory Strolla
Notable witnesses: Tevin Thompson, Tommie Stornes, Leland Brunson, Steven Smith, Rhonda Rouer

People started calling it the "Loud Music Trial," and the name stuck (Figures 6.6a, 6.6b, 6.6c).[126] Because it was about loud music. Except it wasn't, said Lucy McBath, along with others who called the murder a racialized act and an outright "21st-century lynching."[127] It was about self-defense, claimed Michael Dunn's attorney, Cory Strolla. Except the black youths were unarmed and posed no threat, rebutted the State. So it was about the racist ramifications of Stand Your Ground, said liberal pundits and the victim's parents. Except "Stand Your Ground played zero role," retorted National Rifle Association benefactor David Kopel.[128] It should be about evidence, not emotion, Strolla instructed the jury.

Except you could see all of the worst possible emotions draped shawl-like over the face of McBath as she sat mutely in the second row during the trial,

Figure 6.6a. (*Left*) Michael Dunn (defendant); (*right*) Jordan Davis (victim).

Figure 6.6b. (*Left to right*) Judge Healey, John Guy (State), Erin Wolfson (State), Cory Strolla (defense).

Figure 6.6c. (*Left to right*) Key witnesses Tevin Thompson, Tommie Stornes, Leland Brunson, Steven Smith, Rhonda Rouer. Screen captures from *3½ Minutes, 10 Bullets*.

and you could hear breathless fear and fury vibrating in the quiet voices of the boy's father and three friends who took the stand to testify in the name of the law even as the laws of this country had failed to forestall the calamity of yet another young black life buried.

In *People of the State of Florida v. Michael David Dunn*, overstated syntax of all-or-nothing—it was all about this, it wasn't about this at all—reflected people's inability to comprehend the horrific incident. *People v. Dunn* was about aboutlessness, that is, the senselessness belied by the otherwise sensibly organized veneer of a legal docket.[129]

Every concept introduced so far in this chapter—formidability bias, sonic excess, resilience, respectability, and rap's racial stigmas—played a vital role in *People v. Dunn*'s juridical minutiae. Over the course of my research, I began to recognize a pernicious pattern in the rhetorical strategies of Dunn's lawyer, Cory Strolla, both in and outside the courtroom. Strolla, I argue, mounted a cunning defense of Michael Dunn by emphasizing the purported signs of Jordan Davis's sonic excess: the *loud voice* of Davis, in his heated argument with Dunn, signaled an unrespectable black body against which the defendant stood his ground; Davis's *loud music* gave Strolla the means to set off a sonic smokebomb in the courtroom, sending up clouds of doubt over Davis's three surviving friends and their testimonies about what they could have heard (that is, feasibly heard *over* the high-decibel rap playing at the time of the verbal confrontation and subsequent murder). Strolla effectively took the rap that these boys loved and sharpened it into a veritable weapon of litigation. In doing so, he implicitly placed formidable black bodies and black music on trial, perversely summoning blackness itself to answer for a crime of anti-black racism.

And that's only the half of it. Because as much as Strolla criminalized blackness, he tried to censor it as well—by disavowing the case as a "black and white issue," by calling for the jury's colorblind dispassion (recall Chapter 3), by touting that Dunn has "never been accused of racism," and by incessantly accusing the prosecution of playing the "race card."[130] At first blush, the simultaneous criminalization and censorship of blackness might seem like a procedural paradox: the former gambit highlights; the latter erases. What *People v. Dunn* ends up affirming, however, is that this two-pronged attack qua legal defense is not an exception in the broader plight and plunder of black America. It has been the norm.

Facts of the Case

Around 7:30 p.m. on November 23, 2012 in Jacksonville, Florida, four black youths—Jordan Davis, Tommie Stornes, Leland Brunson, and

Tevin Thompson—pulled up to a Gate gas station (8251 Southside Boulevard) in a red Dodge Durango SUV. Stornes, the driver, headed into the store to buy some gum and cigarettes. It was Black Friday, the day after Thanksgiving.

Meanwhile, Michael Dunn and his fiancée, Rhonda Rouer, had come to town to attend the wedding of Dunn's son. At the wedding reception, Dunn and Rouer each consumed a couple of drinks, then decided to leave early so they could walk their puppy back at the hotel. On the drive back to the Sheraton, Dunn and Rouer stopped their black Volkswagen Jetta at the Southside Boulevard Gate gas station to purchase wine and chips. Both of them noticed loud music coming from the Dodge Durango, which had its rear windows rolled down. The music playing was Lil Reese's rap song "Beef."[131] Dunn parked in the spot immediately to the right of the Durango, even though several other spaces were available nearby. Rouer took twenty dollars, exited the Jetta, and entered the store.

Dunn, who remained in the Jetta, noticed the Durango had tinted windows. He rolled down his own window and asked the youths in the SUV to turn down their music. Tevin Thompson, in the front passenger seat, obliged and turned it off. But Jordan Davis, sitting in the backseat with his best friend, Leland Brunson, told Thompson not to listen to this stranger. So Thompson turned the music back on. Dunn and Davis started to swap heated words. Before long, Stornes returned to the Durango, unaware of how and why an argument was taking place; he prepared to drive away. Before he could do so, Dunn retrieved a loaded handgun from his glove compartment and, without warning, fired three rounds into the Durango. Stornes, panicking, backed up his car and peeled away. Yet Dunn kept firing. Seven more bullets, making it ten in total, nine of which hit the car. Jordan Davis was struck in the legs, lungs, and aorta. Stornes kept driving until he reached a crowded plaza adjacent to the gas station.

Rhonda Rouer had heard the gunshots while standing at the checkout counter inside the store. When she came out to the parking lot, Dunn told her to get into the car. They returned to their hotel, where they ordered pizza, walked their dog, drank some wine, watched television, and eventually went to sleep. In the morning, Dunn and Rouer headed home to Satellite Beach, Florida, about a two-and-a-half-hour drive from Jacksonville. At 10:30 a.m., the police showed up at Dunn's house. They had been tipped off by a young witness who had spotted and memorized Dunn's license plate at the scene of the crime. Dunn was arrested for the murder of Jordan Davis.[132]

Defendant's Testimony (Dunn's Version of the Events)

When Dunn rolled down his window, he told the boys in the Durango to "turn that down, please."[133] One of them turned the music completely off. Dunn said, "thank you," then rolled his window back up.[134] But he started hearing someone say, "F him and F that" in a "mean-spirited" tone.[135] And then the music came back on, "probably a little bit less loud than it was [before]."[136]

At this point, "it got ugly," and "every time this young man [Jordan Davis] is speaking, it's louder and louder, and more violent and more violent."[137] Davis was "amping up," yelling forcefully enough to be audible over "that thumping noise" of the rap music.[138] Soon, Davis was saying repeatedly, "I should fucking kill that motherfucker."[139] Dunn felt "flabbergasted" and thought to himself, "I—I—I must not be hearing this right."[140] And then he heard, "in an even more elevated voice: 'I should fucking kill that mother-fucker'—and now [Davis is] screaming."[141] So Dunn lowered his window again. Out of the "corner of [his] eye," he saw "a young man [Tommie Stornes] walk by" and return to the Durango.[142] Dunn could also now see into the Durango's rear passenger seat, where there sat "two young men with menacing expressions."[143] Granted, the "guy [Davis] in the rear passenger was the one doing the threatening. The other guy [Brunson] was just looking mean."[144] Davis appeared "enraged," and even though Dunn couldn't be sure what the boys' intentions were, he "quite frankly" didn't "want to find out."[145] Having seen the way they were behaving, Dunn "thought everybody in the car was a thug or a gangster."[146] Davis did not "speak to [Dunn] like a child" or "act like a child" or "threaten [Dunn's] life like a child."[147] He threatened Dunn's life "like a man."[148]

Dunn said to the youths, "Are you talking about me?"[149] At this point, Davis "reached forward and picked something up and slammed it against the [Durango] door."[150] Dunn saw "sticking above, like, the windowsill, about four inches of a barrel."[151] He could hear "metal hit the door" and the sound of "a thump."[152] To Dunn, the dark object looked like a "12-gauge [shotgun], maybe 20."[153] Davis said to Dunn, "I'm going to fucking kill you," which led Dunn to "fear for [his] life."[154] Dunn saw Davis begin to open the Durango's rear door. He even heard that "door unhinge."[155] After the door was cracked open, Davis told Dunn, "You're dead, bitch," and as Davis's head "clear[ed] the window frame," the young man said to Dunn, "This shit's going down now."[156] So Dunn retrieved a gun from his own glove compartment and retorted, "You're not going to kill me, you son of a bitch," then fired three shots.[157] As the Durango started backing up, Dunn unleashed another three shots because he had "tunnel vision" and was "still fighting for [his] life."[158] Even once the Durango was driving away, Dunn fired yet more shots into the back of the SUV (Figure 6.7).[159] He "was worried about a blind firing situation where [the youths] would, you know, shoot over their heads or whatever and hit [him or Rouer]."[160]

When Rouer returned to the car, Dunn told her what had happened. Rouer got "very upset."[161] En route to their hotel, Dunn "tried to get out the fact that [the youths] were threatening [him]," and "tried to get out the fact that they were advancing on [him]," and "tried to get out the fact that they were armed."[162] But Rouer was "hysterical," "hysterical," "hysterical."[163] She couldn't "understand self-defense."[164] She was in no "condition that night to take care of herself."[165] Once inside their room at the hotel, Dunn continued to be fearful: "We were staying at the—at a hotel that has, like, a club room at the top floor, and we were there looking out the windows, like a waking

Figure 6.7. Durango with nine ballistic markers. Markers [4][5][6] indicate the first three shots, which Dunn fired into Jordan Davis's passenger-side rear door. As Stornes, the driver, backed up the Durango, Dunn fired shots [7][8][9]. Shots [1] [2][3] hit the rear of the Durango as it was speeding away. One of Dunn's ten shots missed the Durango.

nightmare. Every car was a red SUV, I mean, to us."[166] Despite his paranoia about retaliation, Dunn had left his gun in the Jetta's glove box—in hindsight, an "irrational" decision.[167] Despite his fear of threats around every corner, Dunn took their puppy outside to "go potty."[168] Despite reeling from the incident, Dunn ordered pizza because Rouer wanted it, as "she was upset and her stomach was in knots."[169]

Early next morning, Dunn and Rouer drove home. Rouer alternately suffered "fits of silence" and "fits of sobbing."[170] During the drive, Dunn called his neighbor Ken Lescallett, a federal law enforcement official. Dunn was hoping that he and Lescallett could go to their hometown sheriff and "tell them what happened" in Jacksonville "and, you know, hopefully they would listen to my side."[171]

Shortly after arriving home, Dunn found the police at his door. He did not resist arrest. He did not raise his voice. And had he ever raised his voice to Jordan Davis? "When I said, 'You're not going to kill me, you son of a bitch,' I may have had a little inflection in that," Dunn admitted. "But other than that? No."[172]

At his police intake interview, and later in court, Dunn swore he had seen the youths with a weapon. In his own speculative words, it was "some kind of industrial object, a pipe, something that would look very much like a barrel."[173] When asked at the police station whether this alleged weapon in the Durango could "have been [his imagination]," however, Dunn replied: "It cert— [*slight pause*] well, no. [*slight pause*] I mean, anything's possible, I guess."[174]

Witness Testimonies

Tevin Thompson (front passenger seat of Durango)
Before going out on Black Friday, the four friends went to Tevin Thompson's house to change their clothes. They were "dressing up" in order "to go pick up some girls."[175] Later in the evening, they stopped at the Gate gas station on Southside Boulevard because they wanted gum "so [their] breath would smell good."[176] After Stornes went into the store, Michael Dunn pulled into the station and parked "immediately next to" the Durango, so close to its passenger side that Thompson couldn't have "exited the Durango through [his] door" even if he had tried.[177] Dunn told them, "I can't hear myself think," appearing "upset, a little angry."[178] Thompson turned down the music. Davis told him to turn it back up. Thompson did. Davis said "f[uck] you" to Dunn

but did not "threaten [Dunn] in any way."[179] Davis was not "screaming" or "yelling loudly" or "enraged" or "mad," nor was he "so upset [that] he began cursing and screaming at Michael Dunn."[180] Moments later, Dunn pulled out a gun and said "angrily" to Davis, "Are you talking to me?"—and then fired at him.[181] As Davis lay dying, he could be heard "gasping for air."[182]

Tommie Stornes (driver of Durango)

After buying cigarettes and gum in the store, Stornes came out and "danced a little bit to the song that was playing."[183] He had barely reentered his car when Dunn raised his gun and started shooting. So Stornes "threw [his] car in reverse," backing up just "enough for [him] to drive away without hitting anything."[184] Although he was "in a panic," he tried to "check on the status of everybody else in the car" by "call[ing] everyone's name."[185] Thompson and Brunson responded, but Davis did not. Stornes looked to the back seat and could see Davis leaning against Leland Brunson.

Leland Brunson (rear passenger seat of Durango)

Before Dunn's car pulled up next to the Durango, Brunson was "happy," Thompson was "happy," Stornes was "happy," and Davis was "happy."[186] Fast-forward to the moment Dunn asked the boys to turn down their music. Davis said "f[uck] you" to Dunn.[187] He was "pointing at [Dunn]" with his right hand, and had his other arm propped behind Brunson's seat (Figure 6.8).[188] Davis did "put his hand on the car door handle" during the argument, but he never opened the door.[189] After Stornes returned to the car, Thompson turned down the music again. It's at this point that Brunson heard Dunn say to Davis, "Are you talking to me?"[190] Davis replied, "Yeah, I'm talking to you."[191] Immediately, Dunn reached into the Jetta's glove compartment, pulled out a gun, "cocked it back," "aimed it out of the window" toward Davis, and "started firing."[192] Brunson ducked down and "tried to pull [Davis] down" as well, but as he did so, "[Davis] just fell into [his] lap."[193] Brunson "patted [Davis] down in the upper body," and when he "reached and touched [Davis], blood appeared."[194] Brunson couldn't retrieve his phone from his pants pocket to call 911 because Davis was slumped over his legs.

Steven Smith (eyewitness)

Smith, a general contractor who lives in Bryceville, Florida (west of Jacksonville), pulled into the Gate gas station around 7:30 p.m. and entered

Figure 6.8. Brunson was the only witness who had clearly seen Davis's bodily position and gestures during the confrontation. He mimed Davis's movements in court (right arm, left arm). Screen captures by author.

the store to buy a fountain drink. He had noticed a red Dodge Durango and its music. Once inside the store, he joked to the clerk, "I wish they'd turn [the music] up. It's my favorite song."[195] Smith was "being a smart aleck," and the clerk "kind of laughed."[196] Upon exiting the store, Smith "was about to make a turn and walk towards [his own] truck door" when he heard someone yell: "No, you're not going to talk to me that way!"[197] It was a male voice coming from a parked Jetta. Smith turned his head in time to see a man inside the Jetta fire a gun at the Durango. Smith didn't see "anyone in the red Dodge Durango brandish any sort of weapon."[198]

Rhonda Rouer (Dunn's fiancée)
Rouer noticed music coming from the Durango as she and Dunn pulled into the gas station. She could hear the bass, but it wasn't so loud that anything "in the [Jetta was] rattling from the bass."[199] Dunn said to Rouer, "I hate that thug music."[200] Rouer replied, "Yes, I know."[201] She then gave Dunn a kiss, took twenty dollars, and went into the store. Moments later, Rouer "heard pop, pop, pop."[202] And then "another pop, pop, pop."[203] She heard the cashier say, "There was a guy and he has a gun!"[204] Rouer exited the store and entered the Jetta. On the way to their hotel, Dunn never mentioned a "weapon of any kind in that SUV."[205] No mention of a "stick," "shotgun," "barrel," or "lead pipe."[206] Once back in their room, they ordered pizza because "Michael thought we just needed to eat something."[207] That night, Dunn didn't say anything about "the boys [having] a weapon."[208] And during the next morning's trip home, Dunn still didn't mention "a weapon of any kind" in the SUV.[209]

Dunn, while driving, *received* a call from his neighbor Ken Lescallett, who was checking to see if he and Rouer wanted to join him later "for an evening out."[210] (Dunn and Lescallett chatted on speaker phone.) Dunn told Lescallett that Rouer was "not feeling well" and that they were coming home early.[211] In this phone conversation, Dunn never "mention[ed] that he had been involved in a shooting in Jacksonville."[212]

Verdict and Aftermath

On February 15, 2014, the jury reached a guilty verdict on three counts of attempted second-degree murder—Dunn's attempts on Thompson, Brunson, and Stornes respectively—and one count of shooting deadly missiles. But this jury could not reach an agreement on the most serious count: the first-degree murder of Jordan Davis. So Judge Russell Healey declared a mistrial on this particular charge.

In September 2014, Michael Dunn was retried for murder in the first degree. He did not have enough money to rehire Cory Strolla; this time, he was represented by a public defender named Waffa Hanania. At the conclusion of this retrial, Dunn was found guilty. After receiving a life sentence from Judge Healey, a cuffed and orange-clad Dunn walked to the front of the courtroom to read a prepared statement:

> I want the Davis family to know that I truly regret what happened. I'm sorry for their loss. And if I could roll back time and do things differently, I would. I was in fear for my life and I did what I thought I had to do. Still, I am mortified that I took a life, whether it was justified or not.[213]

Despite news articles declaring that Dunn "apologized during his sentencing hearing," it was more of a nonapology—a self-serving sorry-not-sorry that kept Dunn at the center (*I, I, I'm, I, I, I, I, I, I, I*), neglected to mention Jordan Davis (reduced to *a life*), and hedged without shame (*I did what I thought I had to do . . . whether it was justified or not*).[214]

On November 17, 2016, a three-judge panel denied Dunn's appeal to Florida's First District Court. As I write this, Dunn is serving a life sentence in prison without eligibility for parole. One source reports that Dunn is trying to appeal once again.[215]

People v. Dunn (II): "She Is Trying to Put Race to Have Emotion into the Jury"

The difference from the rock and roll beat is that rap sounds aggressive—almost angry—even when it is not profane.
—Bill Cosby and Alvin Poussaint, *Come On, People: On the Path from Victims to Victors*[216]

I'm the victim. I'm the victor, but I was the victim too. [. . .] It made me think of the old TV shows and movies where, like, how the police used to think, when a chick got raped, "Oh, it's her fault, because of the way she was dressed." So it's my fault because I asked them to turn their music down.
—Michael Dunn (Duval County Jail inmate) in a phone call to his then-fiancée, Rhonda Rouer[217]

"They defied my orders," Dunn said to the cops when they came knocking on his door the day after the incident. "What was I supposed to do if they wouldn't listen?"[218] Nothing about Davis wielding a shotgun. Just grumblings about disobedience. Chillingly casual words capped by a rhetorical question: What is a white man supposed to do when black boys defy his orders?

It wasn't until his police intake interview—nearly twenty-four hours after the shooting—that Dunn began to claim he had seen the youths with any kind of weapon. But in court, Dunn's defense attorney, Cory Strolla, did everything he could to put threatening words in Jordan Davis's mouth and to plant a posthumous gun in Davis's hands. Strolla relied on a broad matrix of exculpatory strategies. First, he argued that Jordan Davis was "enraged," foulmouthed, armed, and responsible for escalation.[219] Second, he discredited key witnesses, including the prosecution's forensics experts, the crime scene investigators, Davis's three friends, onlooker Steven Smith, and even Rhonda Rouer. (Once Rouer voiced the damning revelation that Dunn had never told her about any weapon in the Durango, Strolla turned on her, condescendingly dubbing her a "hysterical" woman "on prescription medication.")[220] Third, Strolla solicited character witnesses—family members, friends—who painted Dunn as a "gentle man,"[221] a "very nice guy,"[222] and someone with a "very calm demeanor."[223] Fourth, he attempted to strip color from juridical consideration, arguing that Dunn was so non-racist and colorblind that he would have lacked prejudicial motive to act with deadly force had he not reasonably perceived an imminent threat. And fifth, Strolla hypothesized a scenario in which the youths *did possess* a gun, *ditched* this gun from the Durango after Davis was shot, and *returned to retrieve* the firearm before police could sweep the area.

Strolla's fourth and fifth strategies emphasized respectively Dunn's colorblind virtue and Davis's weapon-toting vice—namely, that while Dunn *did not see Davis's blackness at all, he could clearly see Davis as armed and dangerous.* With Florida's tensions still boiling from the acquittal of George Zimmerman (the killer of Trayvon Martin) six months earlier, Strolla understandably wanted to nudge his jury's attention as far away from race as possible. One of the defense's ploys involved Dunn's denial of ever saying, contrary to Rouer's testimony, "I hate that thug music." So heavy-handed was this denial, however, that one might wonder whether Dunn had been coached by Strolla to disavow the word "thug" altogether. Here are some of Dunn's statements.

JOHN GUY (ASSISTANT STATE ATTORNEY): You don't recall saying, "I hate that thug music"?

DUNN: No. If I ever said anything, I would have called it "rap crap." "Thug music" isn't a term I would use.[224]

[*several minutes later*]

GUY: And what did you say to [Rouer]? You didn't say, "I hate that thug music." What did you say?

DUNN: I didn't say this, but if I had said anything I would have characterized it as "rap crap," not "thug music." That's not a term I'm familiar with.[225]

[*toward end of cross-examination*]

GUY: And you said that you don't use the phrase "thug music," do you?

DUNN: It doesn't seem to be a familiar term. If I was going to refer to it, I'd call it "rap crap."[226]

Stated ad nauseam, "rap crap" was the defense's PG-rated euphemism of choice. Note also the verbatim repetition of the words "familiar [term]," which, when articulated in tandem with the referent (*thug*), undercut the very claim of nonfamiliarity.[227] Compared to "thug music," the phrase "rap crap" may sound tame and color neutral—derogatory enough to come off believably disapproving, but not so epithetic as to reek of inexcusable bigotry.[228] Dunn's alleged ignorance of the word "thug" could have passed muster had it not been demonstrably false. As the State pointed out during closing statements, Dunn said "thug" during his police intake interview and even used the word several times in his letters from jail.[229] Ironically, then, the defense's "rap crap" gambit fell flat, for all it did was point up Dunn's dishonesty.

What Strolla didn't seem to grasp was that the more he tried to deny the shooting as a "black and white issue," the more blackness and whiteness—spoken into existence by paradoxical allegations of irrelevance—necessarily muscled their way to the fore.[230] If race isn't a factor, then why take such great pains to pretend your client has never even heard of the word "thug"?

One of Strolla's most puzzling and desperate attempts at deracination came out in an objection during the prosecution's closing statement, delivered by Assistant State Attorney Erin Wolfson. (As far as courtroom norms go, closing statements are an unusual time for an interruption from opposing counsel.)

ERIN WOLFSON: [Dunn] heard loud thumping music when they pulled in. He heard two young—he saw two young men with menacing expressions, Jordan Davis and Leland Brunson, but yet he told detectives, "I don't know how many kids were in that car." He used the word "kids" the day after he shot into that SUV. It was only six months later, I think, when [Dunn] wrote his statement, that he writes, "I glanced back and saw the rear windows were down and the back seat was occupied by two very menacing-looking black *men*."

STROLLA: Your Honor, if we can object and just approach?

THE COURT (JUDGE HEALEY): Yes, sir.

Judge Healey, Strolla, and Wolfson began a sidebar conversation that was inaudible to the gallery and beyond the range of the microphones and cameras in the courtroom. But a court stenographer was present to transcribe the exchange.

THE COURT: Yes?

STROLLA: Again, I just think, at this point, the State—I know [Wolfson] is reading from the letter in evidence, but I would say, at this point, *she is trying to put race to have emotion into the jury*, so I would object for that and move for a mistrial, Your Honor.

THE COURT: I don't know how to respond to that. She is reading from a document that is a document in evidence—I think [entered] without an objection—that was authored by *your* client [Dunn]. There is nothing wrong with reading it and she has not, in my observations, evoked any emotion about race. She is just stating a fact. The fact of the matter is there were two black fellows in the back seat [. . .] so your objection is overruled for the same reasons. The Motion for Mistrial is denied.[231]

Two crucial points came up in this hushed sidebar. First, police records show that Dunn initially described the youths as "kids" before inflating them, in his written account, into "menacing-looking black men" (read: formidable and resilient adults). Second, Strolla's phrase "she is trying to put race to have emotion into the jury" is a word salad, a jumble that conflates the mere mention of blackness with inappropriate appeals to emotion. Notice how Strolla's bizarre articulation was contagious, in that it likewise left Judge Healey grasping for adequate words (*I don't know how to respond to that*)— for how does one respond to an objection with no legal basis? Recall, from Chapter 3, Robin DiAngelo's quotation about white fragility and colorblind illusions: "Incoherent talk is a function of talking about race in a world that insists race does not matter."[232] The flustered interruption by Strolla, replete with odd verbs and prepositions, was a crystalline and litigious manifestation of such incoherence.

Strolla's efforts to downplay race reached beyond the courtroom walls. After attorneys' closing statements, and as the jury began deliberations, Strolla held a press conference and took questions from reporters, who inquired about race, racism, and *People v. Dunn*'s comparability with the Trayvon Martin case. Strolla offered multiple "matters of fact."

I want to be very clear. Nobody from my office, or Mr. Dunn, has brought race into this, period. Matter of fact, I filed a pre-trial motion to keep it out, because we don't want to taint that jury; we want to *keep it clean*. And, matter of fact, I never identified a single witness by either the color of their skin or their gender. [. . .] Matter of fact, Mr. Dunn [. . .] does believe there's a subculture. Mr. Dunn does believe that there are kids and youth out there that listen to this, what we call, gangster rap or violent lyrics, and they see violent things on TV and then try to imitate it because they think that's fun, or they think that's cool, or they think that's the way you're supposed to act. [. . .] As a matter of fact, again, I can't tell you how many times [Dunn's] said this isn't a black and white issue. It's what he would call a "subculture thug" issue, and again, that doesn't go to race. [. . .] He's never been racist. He's never been accused of racism. As a matter of fact, the guys in the car even testified on cross-examination that that night [Dunn] never said anything racial, he never said anything of violence or disrespect, or even raised his voice.[233]

Let's "keep it clean," people—meaning let's keep the taint of blackness at bay.[234] It's a "subculture thug issue" that "doesn't go to race"—meaning anyone (black or white) can be a thug, and it's the thug behavior (not the color of thugs) that irked Michael Dunn. And true, no one heard Dunn shout "anything racial" that night—meaning the night he unloaded ten bullets on four unarmed black youths. Not saying "thug" or the "N-word," however, hardly proves absence of racial animus.[235]

During the same press conference, a reporter pointed out that Dunn's own jailhouse letters, some of which had come to public attention, contained "what we [would] interpret as racial animus."[236] Replied Strolla: "Don't forget, they [the prosecutors] introduced one letter. They had all of his letters. And again, they had thousands of hours of phone calls. And you didn't hear one. So they piecemealed what they wanted."[237] Strolla's comment here was at best disingenuous, and at worst deceitful, on three fronts—but no one at the press conference called him out on this mendacity. First, court documents show an estimated total of 180 hours, not "thousands of hours," of jailhouse phone calls.[238] Second, Strolla made the situation sound as if the prosecution had lucked out on a uniquely flagrant jailhouse letter amid a heap of otherwise disappointingly benign and inconsequential correspondences. In actuality, a pre-trial document from January 24, 2014, "Order Denying Defendant's Motion," reveals a far more mundane reason for the State's underreliance on Dunn's letters and calls: the "lack of resources and staff available to listen to" the massive volume of oral communications, and a concomitant lack of wherewithal for the timely transcriptions and necessary redactions of the handwritten letters.[239] And third, Strolla himself was the one who filed a pretrial motion to disallow references to jailhouse calls and letters in court proceedings; this preemptive move all but confirmed Strolla's own recognition that the correspondences' disclosure could potentially damage Dunn.[240] Consequently, the State attorneys hadn't been cherry-picking the *worst* of what Dunn wrote. These prosecutors, working under the practical constraints of time and personnel, had presented the scant materials that they could reasonably review and responsibly accommodate.[241]

Now that we're free from the time crunch of the court proceedings, let's take up Strolla's implicit dare. Let's comb through Dunn's jailhouse letters, which were released to the public by the January 24, 2014 court order, and see the racial and racist comments therein.

Letter from Dunn to his grandmother (February 20, 2013)

> I'm really not prejudiced against race, but I have no use for certain cultures. This gangster-rap, ghetto talking thug "culture" that certain segments of society flock to is intolerable. They espouse violence and disrespect towards women.[242]

Another letter from Dunn to his grandmother (May 7, 2013)

> I don't know if I should feel like I'm a victim of reverse-discrimination or a political prisoner. Either way, the state of Florida is screwing me over! ☺ [. . .] The blacks seem to be calling the shots in the media and the courts. [. . .] I don't know if I mentioned my latest "neighbor" to you. This one talks through the air vent to the juveniles (15–17 yr old murderers + thieves) and says: "Whas up my niggah?" It's hard to understand him as it sounds like he has marbles in his mouth.[243]

Letter from Dunn to Michelle (May 20, 2013)

> I'm still here in thugville. [. . .] I've never been exposed to thugs like they have here. The jail is chock-full of blacks and they all appear to be thugs, along the lines of 90% of the inmates. [. . .] I'm sitting here, stewing in my own juices—waiting for my day in court and plotting my revenge against the system for all the civil rights violations. ☹[244]

Letter from Dunn to Rhonda Rouer (June 23, 2013)

> I got a new neighbor yesterday. [. . .] I overheard the mental health people talking to him and he claims to be suicidal. [. . .] I haven't spoken to him yet, but I was thinking to suggest an easy way to die would be to ask a car load of thugs to turn their stereo down! ☺[245]

Letter from Dunn to his daughter (July 12, 2013)

> It is spooky how racist everyone is up here, and how biased towards
> blacks the courts are. The jail is full of blacks and they <u>all</u> act like
> thugs. [. . .] This may sound a bit radical, but if <u>more</u> people would
> arm themselves and kill these fucking idiots when they're threating
> [sic] you, eventually they may take the hint and change their beha-
> vior. As it is, going to jail is like a badge of honor for them.[246]

Dunn's letters comprised more than racist rants. Quotidian musings, smiley
faces, frowny faces, and terms of endearment punctuated the scrawl. Letters
were addressed to "Sweetheart," "Baby," and "Darling," and signed off with
"Love you all!" and "Love, Dad" (Figure 6.9).[247] One missive included a ri-
sotto recipe that Dunn had hand-copied from a Stone Barrington book.[248]
Beneath the veneer of good humor in his letters and calls, however, Dunn's
racism bubbled to the surface in fits and starts—pervasive yet casual, blatant
yet banal.

   Dunn's self-identification as a victim was rather virtuosic and perturb-
ingly intersectional for its sheer variety of attempted metaphors. He likened
himself to a victim of civil rights violations, a target of reverse racism, a
political prisoner, and even a survivor of sexual assault, per his phone call
(epigraphed earlier) in which he compared himself to a "chick [who] got
raped."[249] Such preposterous analogies demonstrated his nominal familiarity

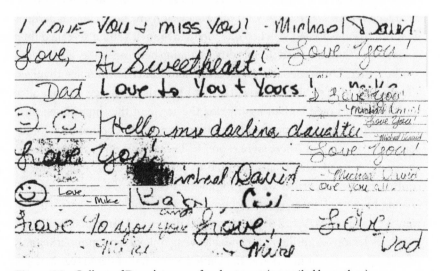

Figure 6.9. Collage of Dunn's terms of endearment (compiled by author).

with multifaceted systems of oppression, violence, and victim blaming. Yet he rhetorically co-opted these systems, stitching them into the white mantle of a martyr. Tellingly, Dunn didn't see himself as a racist. He saw racism only in others. "No wonder people are afraid to tell [black people] to pick up their pants," said Dunn in another jailhouse call to Rouer. "I'm not a racist. *They're* racist. What is with this subculture that feels entitled to exert their will? The only thing I can think of is the culture. I mean, this MTV culture—the gangster rap. *And where are their dads*?"[250]

I don't know where Dunn's disdain for "MTV culture" came from. But Dunn must have learned and internalized his vehement anti-black racism from somewhere, someone. Maybe it was his upbringing in general, given the explicit and unapologetic racism in his letters to family members.[251] Or maybe he was channeling the likes of Bill Cosby, who, during his infamous "Pound Cake" speech at the 2004 NAACP awards ceremony, inveighed: "I'm talking about these people who cry when their son is standing there in an orange suit. Where were you when he was two? [. . .] *And where is his father?*"[252] (It's possible Dunn had once picked up a copy of Cosby's and Poussaint's aforequoted book, *Come On, People*, seeing as how its subtitle—*On the Path from Victims to Victors*—bears similarities with Dunn's choice of words: "I'm the victor, but I was the victim too."[253]) I've even wondered whether Dunn had ever seen the 1991 film *Boyz n the Hood*, given the coincidence between its climactic scene and Dunn's eerily analogous claim that he had seen *a menacing black person* with *a shotgun* in *a red car* with *heavily tinted windows* (Figure 6.10). Had I been the prosecutor, I might have liked to ask Michael Dunn if he had indeed seen *Boyz n the Hood* (say, on cable television one night), and if perhaps he was the one who had watched one too many movies about so-called thug "subcultures" and thus had trouble differentiating between reality and fiction.

Altogether, Dunn's letters, phone calls, and court testimonies divulged a fearful loathing of black people. During his initial interview at the police station, Dunn noted he had hastily fled the scene of the shooting because he was feeling "afraid"—not merely afraid of the youths coming back for revenge, but also afraid "there were more."[254] Dunn went on to describe how, even once he and Rouer had returned to their hotel room that night, he continued "shitting bricks waiting for another carload of thugs to come."[255] During his retrial, he clarified, "I know it's not rational, but every car that went by was a red SUV, full of people out to kill me."[256] Dunn imagined black people as legion—a resilient, formidable, vengeful, violent, monolithic unit perpetually on the hunt. (If ever the United States has suffered "car loads of

Figure 6.10. *Boyz n the Hood* (1991, dir. John Singleton). Lloyd Avery II (1969–2005) portrayed the shotgun-wielding member of Ferris's gang. Screen captures by author.

people" terrorizing civilians after dark, we would have to look no further than to the notorious night rides of the Ku Klux Klan, whitecappers, and bald knobbers.) Given Dunn's embattled ego, it makes sense that he went about everyday life armed to face the worst. On the basis of the search warrants filed into the trial's discovery documents, detectives retrieved from Dunn's Jetta a handgun (legally owned with a concealed carry license), a magazine with eighteen live 9mm rounds, a .22LR suppressor, three Stoney Point rifle pads, a gun tote, and a pair of nunchucks (Figure 6.11).[257]

In the end, despite the overwhelming evidence of Dunn's racism, Strolla's defense strategies worked . . . at least temporarily. A mistrial, after all, was called on the first-degree murder count in February 2014. Perhaps this is why, during Dunn's retrial later that year, the new public defense counsel Waffa Hanania saw fit to keep up the charade of denying race's relevance. The maneuver succeeded once before; maybe it could succeed again. So in her closing arguments, Hanania declared:

> The other guys [Brunson, Stornes, Thompson] in the car don't say Mr. Dunn ever cursed—that it was Mr. Davis who was the first one to throw around a racial term. [. . .] And let me just say right now, ladies and gentlemen, this is not about race. [. . .] Would anyone be saying that it was about race if someone had said, "Hey, I hate that country music," or "that redneck music," even? No. This isn't even about the loud music. [. . .] Mr. Davis is the one that got angrier and angrier. [. . .] Jordan Davis tells Tevin Thompson, "F that [*quietly*] N-word. Turn the music back up." And again, obviously, real words were used, not euphemisms, like we're using here in court, because we're in a courtroom, and it's not polite.[258]

INVENTORY AND RECEIPT
(SEARCH WARRANT)

FOUR (4) 9mm SHELL CASINGS; FRONT W.NDSHIELD (MUSSER)
ONE (1) FIREARM MAGAZINE; GLOVE BOX (SMITH)
EIGHTEEN (18) 9mm LIVE ROUNDS FROM MAGAZINE; GLOVE BOX (SMITH)
THREE (3) RIFLE PADS; FROM TRUNK (SMITH)
ONE (1) BERETTA GUN TOTE; FROM TRUNK (SMITH)
ONE (1) PAIR OF NUNCHUCKS; FROM BACKSEAT (SMITH)
ONE (1) MODEL FS22 .22LR FAKE SUPPRESOR; TRUNK (MUSSER)

DATED this 7TH day of DEC., 2012, _m. a. Musser 61159_
Officer

RETURN
(SEARCH WARRANT)

STATE OF FLORIDA   )
COUNTY OF DUVAL   )

    Received this Search Warrant on the 7Td day of
DEC., 2012, and executed and served the same in Duval
County, Florida, on the 7TH day of DEC, 2012, by
searching the premises described therein and by taking into my
custody the property described in the above Inventory and Receipt
and by having read and delivered a copy of this Search Warrant and
Inventory and Receipt to   LEFT IN VEHICLE

I, m.A. MUSSER 61159 , the officer by whom the
Warrant was executed, do swear that the above Inventory and Receipt
contains a true and detailed account of all the property taken by
me on said warrant.

m.a. musser 61139
Officer

Sworn to and subscribed before me
this 17 day of December, 2012.

LP Haddock

Judge, Circuit Court of the Fourth
Judicial Circuit, in and for Duval
County, Florida.

Figure 6.11. Search warrants in *People v. Dunn.*

"Polite" is another word for "respectable." Or, given that "respectable" has increasingly taken on racialized connotations, "polite" is a *polite word for* "respectable." And if we listen to the polite word "N-word" whispered by Hanania, the ventriloquistic accusation—"Davis tells Tevin Thompson, 'F that N-word' "—backfired. Her conspicuous moderation of tone and volume imbued the word "N-word" with paradoxical resonance. Hanania's need to remind the jury that "obviously, real words were used" further controverted the claim of obviousness.

Equally specious was Hanania's rhetorical question, a feint posing as axiom: "Would anyone be saying that it was about race if someone had said, 'Hey, I hate that country music,' or 'that redneck music,' even?" By doubling down on her example of country music with a substitutive epithet (*redneck*), Hanania laid out her cards unambiguously: no one, she was ready to bet, would even think about race had this case involved a dispute over a stereotypically white musical genre.[259] But her very presumption relied on the conflation of whiteness with racelessness—a logic that, in itself, roosts in the ethos of white supremacy.[260] For if one finds it hard to imagine a fatal encounter resulting from the salvo, "I hate that country music," maybe it's because we don't hear black people voicing righteous fury toward country music at nearly the same rate with which white people have disparaged rap.[261]

Let us, then, see Hanania's hypothetical scenario to its conclusion, inverting all variables on the table. A 145-pound, seventeen-year-old unarmed white kid, sitting in a car with three unarmed white friends, is playing loud country music and minding his own business. A forty-seven-year-old, 250-pound black man pulls up in a car that contains multiple weapons and weapon accessories—guns, ammo, nunchucks, you name it. He tells his fiancée, "I hate that redneck music." When his fiancée heads into the store, the man initiates a harsh dialogue with the boys, and within minutes, unloads ten bullets and kills the seventeen-year-old. At the police station, this black man cries self-defense. He had feared for his life, feared that truck loads of retaliatory white teens would show up at his hotel. Awaiting trial, he writes letters from jail about how he wishes more people would arm themselves and kill rednecks. (Not that it's about blacks versus whites; it's a "subculture redneck issue," he insists.) In trial, though, this defendant denies familiarity with the phrase "redneck music" or even the word "redneck." If he had said anything to his fiancée, he would have said "country crap."

Come to think of it, Hanania's right. No prosecutor, in this scenario, would feel compelled to make the case explicitly about race . . . because explicit statements about race wouldn't be necessary to launch a successful case against this defendant. Systems of social, legal, and carceral anti-black racism would do all of the requisite incrimination. Stated another way: given the past trends of biased news reportage and juridical outcomes for interracial crimes, prosecutors would not need to identify the color of this defendant's skin to obtain a litigious advantage; the plain and visible fact of the man's blackness would suffice. First, he would be branded as a deranged killer (with an inexplicable revulsion toward country music, no less). Second, in light of the arsenal recovered from his car, he would be labeled a terrorist, even someone who wished to start a race war.[262] Finally, considering Florida's record of capital punishment for black-on-white crimes, he would receive not a life sentence—as Dunn did—but, in all likelihood, a death sentence.[263]

People v. Dunn (III): Smokescreen and Silence

[There are] YouTube videos of these guys [the youths in the Durango], and they're all gangster rappers. [. . .] You know, 'cause when the police said that these guys didn't have a record, I was like, you know, I wonder if they're just flying under the radar. 'Cause they were bad.

—Michael Dunn, jailhouse call to Rouer[264]

Jordan Davis loved rap music, and he loved playing it loudly. Yet at the Southside Boulevard gas station, he and his friends did not have the right to play music as loudly as they wanted.[265] By all accounts, they were violating the municipal noise ordinances of Jacksonville.[266] Urban noise pollution, after all, is a real problem, one that touches on accessible spaces, sensory accommodation, and neurodiversity.[267] With *People v. Dunn*, however, the defense attorneys' moves to criminalize Davis's loud voice and loud music amounted to games of whataboutism. Yes, let's have conversations about noise pollution and civic policy. But just as urgently, let's rectify the systemic problems of gun proliferation, Stand Your Ground, and racist formidability biases so that societies may keep black children alive long enough to participate in these conversations. The way things turned out, we are left to pursue a dialogue standing over the body of Jordan Davis rather than with any chance to include his voice in the mix.

Davis's loud music was unquestionably a catalyst for the fatal encounter, as it drew Dunn's attention to the Durango to begin with. Disruptive and abrasive though it may have sounded to Dunn, however, the rap music itself was not a weapon.[268] Actually, that's not true. In *People v. Dunn*, Davis's music did serve as a figurative weapon. It just so happens that defense attorney

Cory Strolla was the one who ended up wielding it. Strolla, through the first trial, harped on the loudness of the youths' music to build a case for reasonable doubt. With the burden of proof on the State, Strolla aimed to persuade the jury that—with loud music saturating the entire Gate gas station soundscape—Tommie Stornes, Leland Brunson, Tevin Thompson, and bystander Steven Smith could neither have heard Dunn's alleged threats to Davis nor have known for certain that Davis didn't threaten Dunn in return. In cross-examination, Strolla asked the three youths to admit what they could not "hear," could not "[lip] read," and could not perceive or accurately recall because of musical interference, distance, lighting, and agitated states of mind.[269] "Isn't it true that the music was so loud that the windows and mirrors were vibrating in that SUV?" Strolla asked Thompson. "Isn't it true the music was so loud you could not hear everything Jordan Davis said?"[270] With these questions, Strolla turned the music against the youths and chipped away at their sensory credibility. He depicted these young black bodies as quasi-disabled: perceptually deficient, mnemonically lapsed, and informationally dubious.

By contrast, Michael Dunn sought sympathy in court by disclosing putative disabilities of his own, namely hearing loss and ear pain. "Growing up in the [Florida] Keys, scuba diving is a big part of life, and I actually have damage to my right ear," Dunn testified. "I don't know what the percentage is, but I do have a loss of hearing in my right ear and consequently my left ear kind of compensates for it."[271] On the stand, Dunn was asked by Strolla to clarify whether the youths' "loud thumping [music]" had caused him "any discomfort." He responded, "It did in my left ear, my sensitive ear."[272] Dunn's disability shored up his status as victim; the youth's beloved music physically hurt him and was so loud that, in Dunn's words, his "eardrum was vibrating" at the gas station.[273] None of this explains why Dunn chose to park so close to the Durango or why he rolled down his Jetta's windows (thus exposing his ears to the music at full blast), especially given his understanding that Rouer would be in the store for only a couple of minutes to fetch a bottle of wine.[274]

In court, Strolla went after more than just the acuity of Davis's friends. He outright assailed their characters with repeated snipes at their musical and vocal propensities. During cross-examination, for example, Strolla asked Tommie Stornes about his aspirations as a musician and music producer. "Isn't it true about a week after the shooting, you created a song about Jordan Davis?" asked Strolla.

Stornes said "yes," and confirmed the song was titled "Jordan Davis."[275]

Strolla swooped in with baited praise: "And you're smart enough to know marketing [that] when people were looking up Jordan Davis's name, your song could pop up? [. . .] And isn't it true you posted [the song] so that you could try to make money from Jordan Davis?"[276] Stornes denied these insulting charges. "No, sir," he quietly replied. But Strolla pressed on: "Even though you titled the song 'Jordan Davis'?"[277] No doubt, Strolla was trying to peg Stornes as a money-hungry opportunist who would coldly exploit the death of a friend.[278]

In closing statements, Strolla likewise attempted to delineate Tevin Thompson as a cold, unfeeling person: "Listen to the 911 calls. They're in evidence. [. . .] 'Can you send the ambulance? My friend's shot.' And you will hear zero panic in [Thompson's] voice, almost zero distress."[279] Here is a transcript of the call to which Strolla was referring. (Audio is available online.)[280]

THOMPSON: May I please have the ambulance, please?

9-1-1 OPERATOR: Someone's sick or hurt?

THOMPSON: Somebody's been shot.

9-1-1 OPERATOR: Where at?

THOMPSON: The Gate gas station on Baymeadows Road, South Side.

9-1-1 OPERATOR: Who shot him?

THOMPSON: We have no idea. Please, can you just bring help, please, now.

9-1-1 OPERATOR: Do you know what they look like?

THOMPSON: No, ma'am, I do not. The police are here. But please, can you just bring help.

9-1-1 OPERATOR: Okay, there's an ambulance on the way. You don't know who shot him?

THOMPSON: No, ma'am.

To Strolla's ears, Thompson's voice conveyed "zero distress." Or was it a voice barely held together, with shock and terror bursting at the seams? How do you *want* a black kid to sound when calling 911, maybe for the first time in his life? Scream more loudly? Cry more convincingly? Can we think of tragic precedents that would disincentivize a black teen from calling the authorities to report any violent crime?[281] To suspicious white ears, Thompson might have sounded too respectable on the phone, with a surplus of "may I" and "please" and "ma'am." Neither Thompson's vocal mannerisms nor Stornes's musical entrepreneurship had any evidentiary bearing on Dunn's murder of

Davis.[282] But what Strolla did was to place Davis's friends on trial by proxy, to paint these black youths as emotionless, heartless thugs (without, naturally, uttering the T-word out loud). For if they were thugs, then maybe Jordan Davis was a thug, too. And if Jordan was a thug, then for all we know, this thug had a shotgun.[283]

Besides denouncing the youths' black voices and demolishing the credibility of their black ears, Strolla sang the praises of Dunn's white ears, the "damage to [his] right ear" notwithstanding. Friendly character witnesses took the stand to describe the demeanor of Dunn at the wedding that he and Rouer had attended on the afternoon of Black Friday. At the wedding reception, according to Strolla's leading questions, Dunn didn't "push over the DJ table or tell that guy to turn it down," or "storm out of there when he played music that the kids listen to," such as "any type of hip-hop or any kind of music like that."[284] Despite the fact that not pushing over a DJ table at a wedding sets an absurdly low bar for decorum and basic human decency, Strolla sought to establish Michael Dunn as a general patron of music and an ally to musicians. Dunn's ears could tolerate, even celebrate, loud music—including the loud hip-hop "that the kids listen to." Strolla elevated Dunn's image through the musicophilic equivalent of Some of His Best Friends Are Black (Some of His Favorite Music Is Black).

During cross-examination, John Guy did not press Dunn on the details of his aural impairments or disability, nor did he ask Dunn how or whether he, with his sensitive ears, could have tolerated loud music at his son's wedding or at similar events. Instead, Guy tried to rope the loud music back to the State's advantage, interrogating Dunn about how he could have heard Davis's alleged threats over the Durango's booming stereo.[285] Dunn, however, slyly worked these questions to his favor by inverting their premise. As he had already testified, the fact (or falsity) that he could distinctly hear Davis over the high-volume rap went to prove just how loudly this teenager had been screaming threats. Dunn further launched into an explanation of how he could "certainly" hear Davis "because the bass isn't, there's no mid-range, there's no—there's no instruments or voices, it's just low bass, and I, he is so excited and angry, I hear him over that, with my window up."[286] Guy and his co-counsels neglected to put pressure on Dunn's convoluted account, which would have fallen apart with even a brief listening exercise. Contrary to Dunn's description of the music in question (all bass, no vocals), the rap song playing at the time, Lil Reese's "Beef," consists of nonstop vocals.

Was Dunn lying? Did he misremember? Did some of Lil Reese's lines—such as "Run up on ya with that fuckin' pipe"—lead Dunn to imagine a pipe in Davis's hands?[287] (Recall that Dunn testified to seeing Davis with a vague weapon; in his own speculative words, it was "some kind of industrial object, a pipe, something that would look very much like a barrel."[288]) For that matter, did Dunn hear other lyrics from the rap song—"Fuck nigga, you don't want no beef / You shoot one, I'm shootin' ten / 300, we take yo' life / Savage shit, bitch say that twice"—as words coming out of *Davis's* mouth? During his intake interview, after all, Dunn casually said to the police: "I don't know if they're singing or what. But they're saying, 'Kill him.' So I put my window down again, and I said, 'Excuse me, are you talking about me?' "[289] By his own admission, Dunn had perceived the youths as just potentially singing along to the car stereo. He had no reason to believe they were singing *about* him. But in Dunn's perspective, Davis, by talking the talk (the Lil Reese lyrics), was rap personified—a black teen embodying and envoicing "thug subculture" itself.

Even as Cory Strolla exploited the details of the youths' loud rap music, this defense strategy paled next to a complementary ploy that he undertook toward the end of the initial trial: the weaponization of silence. In his closing arguments, Strolla first reminded the jury that the youths, when Dunn started shooting, had sped away from the Gate parking lot and circled around a nearby shopping plaza before returning to the gas station for help. Based on in-store surveillance time stamps and phone records of 911 calls, calculated Strolla, "that truck was gone for three minutes."[290] Upon stating this estimate, Strolla fell silent and directed his gaze at a clock on the courtroom wall. And waited.

.

"One minute," said Strolla, after exactly one minute had passed. He was pacing back and forth in front of the court clerk's table. People in the gallery sporadically coughed and cleared their throats.

.

"Two minutes," said Strolla, after another minute went by. He walked up to his lectern, licked a finger, and flipped through his notes.

.

"There were no weapons found in that truck in the three minutes," said Strolla after the minutes were up. "Where was the truck? It left the scene."[291]

Strolla's forced silence felt painfully long by virtue of the awkward and anomalous speechlessness. That was his intention. He was trying to simulate the "ample time" in which the boys could have ditched a "firearm or pipe" (or whatever weapon Dunn claimed to have seen) from the Durango, "because they're a hundred yards away [from the Gate gas station] in a dark parking lot," where there would have been plenty of opportunities to toss weapons into "the dumpsters," "the roofs," or "the bushes."[292] For 180 seconds, Strolla wanted the jury to fidget, to second-guess their instincts, to imagine how the black youths could have plausibly disposed of a shotgun. Yet the moment of compulsory silence in the courtroom was perverse if we stop to think about one of the only things that had been incontrovertibly transpiring during those three minutes: Jordan Davis was dying. All we know for sure—something no one in the courtroom could dispute—is that those were three of the last minutes of Jordan's life. Far from serving as a moment of silence for Davis, Strolla's wordlessness was poisoned by insinuations of black criminality.

Think back to the 2015 Bernie Sanders rally in Seattle. Protesters Marissa Johnson's and Mara Willaford's demands for four-and-a-half minutes of silence in memory of Michael Brown were met with noisy refusals and racial epithets. It failed as far as literal silence was concerned. But their attempt to impel silence succeeded as an irruption of respectability politics. In *People v. Dunn*, Cory Strolla's demand for three minutes of silence succeeded. But it was a moral failure, insofar as it herded imaginations toward racist stereotypes of armed and devious black people. And it's hard to fault the State for not objecting to Strolla's gambit. How does one verbally object to silence—that is, something that sounds like nothing? Any State request for a sidebar with the judge in the middle of Strolla's silence would simply have prolonged the moment of mandatory quietude in the courtroom, thereby affording the jury even more time to imagine what shady actions the youths could have committed in those few minutes.

People v. Dunn was a trial saturated with sonic footprints and innuendos: loud music, a "hysterical" fiancée, the (un)voicing of "thug," the armchair diagnosis of a teen's "zero distress" speech in a 911 call, the smokescreen of rap, the silence, and, above all, the formidable, threatening voice of the now-deceased black teenager who, if you believe Michael Dunn, started it all. Lucy McBath, Jordan's mother, has wondered: "In my mind I keep saying, 'Had [Jordan] not spoke back, spoke up, would he still be here?'"[293] In other words, if Jordan hadn't played music so loudly, hadn't raised his voice to a white man, hadn't been disrespectful, had been more sonically respectable . . . would he have lived to see another Thanksgiving? Most likely. But if staying silent versus speaking out comprised the razor-thin line between staying alive and being murdered, then Davis's encounter with Dunn would have been a *near*-death experience regardless—still far too close for comfort.

Say Rhonda Rouer had found the right bottle of wine a bit faster that night and had come out of the store thirty seconds sooner, and that she and Dunn decided to drive away before things turned violent. Jordan Davis would have lived. Yet it wouldn't have foreclosed the eventuality of Davis crossing paths with another Dunn on another evening at another gas station, or Dunn hearing another black kid play a different rap song someplace else, some other day.

Because many Michael Dunns walk the earth. And many Jordan Davises lie beneath it.

Coda: Miracles

> The first words out of the doctor's mouth was, "I'm sorry, Mr. Davis, I was not able to revive." [. . .] And something just came out of me that apparently was so—I think you have a sound inside of you that, when it comes out, when people hear it, they know something is wrong. And the policeman, who's 6′5″, 250 pounds, started crying; the chaplain, she started crying. So the sound must have been something else.
>
> —Ron Davis[294]

> I just started screaming. [. . .] I couldn't think, I couldn't breathe. All of those fears just came crashing down on me at one time.
>
> —Lucy McBath[295]

Jordan Davis is survived by family. He is also survived by the ones who survived: Tevin Thompson, Tommie Stornes, and Leland Brunson, whose testimonies helped put Michael Dunn behind bars. But that the flesh of these young men came out unbroken doesn't mean their spirits emerged unscathed. Thompson described his aftershocks to a writer for *Rolling Stone* magazine: "Can't get my work done, laying awake all night, never coming out of my room. It plays in my head a lot."[296] Stornes likewise stated: "I wake up still in the situation. Anywhere I go, I'm nervous, feeling like someone's gonna do something to me."[297] And Tanya Booth-Brunson spoke on behalf of her son, Leland Brunson: "[On his eighteenth birthday, Leland] went over to Jordan's house and just sat on his bed and cried. They were supposed to have a huge party together. Now, he doesn't even hardly leave the house. The light's gone out of his eyes."[298]

Thompson, Stornes, and Brunson lived through enormous odds. Just look at the projectile trajectories through the Durango, including one showing a bullet that clipped the overhead visor and could have missed the skull of Stornes, in the driver's seat, only by inches (Figure 6.12). It is a miracle that no one else in the car died. And no less miraculous is that Jordan Davis, the only child of Lucy McBath and Ron Davis, was ever born:

> McBath was riddled with uterine fibroids that made bringing a fetus to term almost impossible. She'd miscarried twice and delivered a stillborn son by the age of 34; then she got pregnant with Jordan. Her surgeon put her on ironclad bed rest for eight months till her due date, staged a radical procedure to partition the fetus from the huge tumor trying to squash it—and still she almost died in labor. For a week after his birth, she lay at death's door with a rabid case of septicemia, half-conscious, bloated on antibiotics and bearing the kind of pain they couldn't numb. "She was moaning all the time, couldn't hardly speak—they sent for the chaplain a couple times," says Ron [Davis]. When she somehow came through it, though, there was Jordan: the happy, healthy boy she'd suffered to meet.

Again, talk about resilience. Or don't. Instead, talk about how long it took to bear a life, and how fast a stranger's fear and rage snuffed it out.

Lucy McBath and Ron Davis screamed when they learned their son had died. A little over a year later, these parents would sit silently in the same

Figure 6.12. Projectile trajectory markers.

room as the man who had killed their son. Prior to the opening statements for Michael Dunn's first trial, Judge Russell Healey called McBath and Davis into the courtroom to receive private instructions (recorded in the pretrial transcripts) about comportment. "We have you, I think, seated [in] the second row just so there's—in case there was some sort of an emotional response," Healey told them. "If a tear comes to your eye, I understand. Hopefully you'll have a tissue or something and just wipe your eye. If it gets to a point where you're somewhat overcome, you will probably need to leave the courtroom."[299] Healey acknowledged that his demands would be easier said than done (Figure 6.13).

With tears discreetly welling and evaporating, McBath and Davis stayed glued to that second row as the trial unfolded.[300] They listened to Dunn denigrate Jordan as a rageful, foulmouthed, violence-prone, shotgun-wielding delinquent. They listened to Dunn's family and friends describe the defendant as a peace-loving, music-loving fellow. They heard not one, not two, but five eyewitnesses (Smith, Stornes, Thompson, Brunson, and Dunn) deliver graphic accounts of their son's final moments. They listened to Cory Strolla criminalize Jordan's friends and damn them as loud, unruly, and unfeeling. Amid these denunciations of black noise, the black silence in that courtroom went unheard. How did Ron Davis, when unexpectedly

Figure 6.13. Ron Davis and Lucia McBath (second row, left and right of frame).

called by opposing counsel to testify, *not* holler hate as Strolla tried to muddy the waters?[301] How did Lucy McBath *not* wail as she listened to repeated chronicles of her son's death? How is it that someone can bemoan black sonic excess, but neglect to recognize a pair of bereaved black parents who compressed all the grief in the world into impossibly respectable exteriors?[302] It's the aural equivalent of survivorship bias, whereby every audible scream is rigorously shushed, yet every scream unscreamed is taken for granted.

At Michael Dunn's sentencing on October 17, 2014, Lucy McBath stood up to give her victim impact statement. Between sobs and gasps, she shared loving memories of her son. Toward the end of her statement, McBath fixed her gaze on Dunn, then addressed him directly for the first time. "I choose to forgive you, Mr. Dunn, for taking my son's life," she said, breathless from weeping. "I pray to God to have mercy on your soul."[303] As a woman of faith, McBath later explained that God had spoken to her and moved her to extend mercy even to her greatest enemy, perhaps in hopes that rehabilitation and transformation may one day visit upon Dunn through others' gestures of grace. For all of her anger toward her son's killer in particular, however, McBath has since called out the broader faults of institutional racism, lax gun laws, and what she calls the "legal lynching" enabled by Stand Your Ground.[304] She has channeled private mourning of a lost child into public critiques of systemic ails. In doing so, McBath was extending a legacy of radical black compassion, honoring the examples set by Shirley Sherrod's forgiveness of the NAACP (and even of Breitbart News), by bell hooks's meditations on love as salvation, by Martin Luther King Jr.'s famous sermon on "loving your enemies," and by Frederick Douglass, who went so far as to imagine how a cruel slaveowner—had he "been brought up in a free state, surrounded by the just restraints of free society"—might have turned out "as humane and respectable as are members of society generally."[305] A capacious benefit of the doubt, a faith that people can be more than the worst of what they've done. Or as Cornel West puts it: "To come from a people who were denigrated, enslaved, and despised, and still place love in the center of life is to be part of a miracle."[306]

McBath's decision to forgive Dunn verges on the miraculous, pulsing forth, as it did, from a heart crushed by inconceivable sorrow (Figure 6.14).[307] Such forgiveness was also profound in how it embodied the ethics of "just mercy" advocated by lawyer Bryan Stevenson, who reasons that "it's when mercy is *least* expected that it's most potent," and therefore "the most meaningful

Figure 6.14. (*Left*) Lucia McBath speaking at rally against gun violence (photo by Gemma Purkiss), and (*right*) Ron Davis holding a photo of Jordan Davis (*JET*).

recipients of our compassion" may be the people "who haven't even sought it."[308] But McBath has admitted the exhaustion of clutching fury in one hand while conferring forgiveness in the other. "Forgiving Michael Dunn doesn't negate what I'm feeling and my anger," she told Ta-Nehisi Coates. "And I am allowed to feel that way."[309] Yes, McBath is allowed to be an angry black woman without being an Angry Black Woman. She can choose to remain, when the spotlight glows too hot, a bereaved black mother rather than step forward as the inexhaustible face of bereaved black motherhood. She should be able to display resilience—whether by remaining silent in the courtroom, or by orating through a megaphone—without people seizing on her signs of resilience as an unlimited license to ask more of her, or *to do something else to her*. She can show clemency; she can withdraw in devastation. Because she is more than one thing.[310] She is the complexity and the complexion that the Michael Dunns of the world do not see. She radiates a spectrum of humanity that a prejudicial society needs to embrace, but might not yet deserve.

Over the course of researching *People v. Dunn*, I had the privilege of becoming friends with Lucy McBath and Ron Davis, who work today as fierce activists for social and racial justice. Even between their busy schedules—with Lucy running for Congress in 2018, and Ron traveling the world with humanitarian programs—they insisted on making time to read drafts of this chapter, to collaborate on public lectures, and to raise funds for their respective youth scholarship foundations in Jordan's name.[311] (Lucy went on to win her race in Georgia, defeating Republican incumbent Karen Handel to become a Democratic member of the US House of Representatives.)

Some of the most powerful things I ascertained from Lucy and Ron came from simple anecdotes, little details casually shared over meals or over the phone. From Lucy, I learned that she and Jordan used to play music together while driving around; that Jordan was afraid of guns; that Jordan saw his own likeness in Trayvon Martin; and that, even with the pain that comes with remembrance, she appreciates opportunities today to reminisce about her son.[312] From Ron, I learned that he and Lucy check in with each other once every couple of weeks; that Jordan's favorite song was The Brothers Johnson's 1977 cover of "Strawberry Letter 23" (written by Shuggie Otis, 1971), because Ron used to play it for him in the car; that Jordan also loved the Temptations, Sly and the Family Stone, Chief Keef, and Rick Ross; and that Ron is thankful he had the chance to take Jordan on a vacation to Las Vegas in 2011, a year before the murder.[313]

During a 2018 visit to Dartmouth College, where I teach, Ron told me something that left me speechless.[314] He said he believed that Michael Dunn, who is serving a life sentence, could—rather, will—one day change. Dunn, insisted Ron, will reckon with his racism and emerge a better man, whether it's in five years, or ten, or twenty.[315] When that day comes, Ron will want to visit Dunn in prison. Not a day sooner.[316] To my ears, such faith in goodness indeed sounded nothing short of miraculous, seeing as how Dunn has never, to my knowledge, offered any public indication of repentance.

Both Ron and Lucy vividly remember the day Dunn received his sentence. There's a video of Lucy walking down the steps of the courthouse to explain, in front of an array of cameras, why she chose forgiveness. "I believe that Michael Dunn had not been raised the way we were raised, the way we were raising Jordan," she declared, squinting into the early afternoon sun.[317] A reporter asked her what she had seen in Michael Dunn's face when she had addressed him in court and informed him of her forgiveness.

Lucy took a few seconds to think it over.

Then, with a slight shrug, she said, "Nothing."[318] Ron, standing next to her, nodded in agreement.

Lucy McBath and Ron Davis gave Jordan life. Dunn stole that life. Meaning he stole everything from these parents. But maybe plunderers cannot wholly take what they cannot see, and cannot silence the voices they hear only as noise. Meaning Dunn couldn't take away a mother's mercy, a father's grace, or all of the values these two parents shared with their child from his cradle to his grave.

Postlude

Songs without Words

I'd rather not chronicle my demise. When you're young [. . .] you start to believe that you have to suffer to be an artist. I've graduated from that school.

—Lauryn Hill[1]

The Beautiful from the Terrible

As a child, Frederick Douglass was once jolted awake at dawn by the shrieks of Aunt Hester as she suffered horrible lashes at the hands of slaveowner Captain Anthony. In his first autobiography, *Narrative of the Life of Frederick Douglass* (1845), the abolitionist recalled:

> No words, no tears, no prayers, from his gory victim, seemed to move his iron heart from its bloody purpose. The louder she screamed, the harder he whipped; and where the blood ran fastest, there he whipped longest. He would whip her to make her scream, and whip her to make her hush.[2]

In a subsequent memoir, *My Bondage and My Freedom* (1855), Douglass narrated the story again. And in this retelling, Hester had a voice.

> Each blow, vigorously laid on, brought screams as well as blood. "Have mercy; Oh! have mercy," she cried; "I won't do so no more"; but her piercing cries seemed only to increase his fury. [. . .] Language has no power to convey a just sense of its awful criminality.[3]

Hester's screams and pleas, in turn, shocked a hidden, cowering Douglass into silence. "I was hushed, terrified, stunned, and could do nothing," he remembered. So he said nothing. He rightly feared that her fate "might be mine next."[4]

Hester was resilient insofar as she survived Captain Anthony's "thirty or forty stripes," even though Douglass saw "she could scarcely stand, when untied."[5] Yet it's not so much that her skin was strong enough to keep her alive, but rather that the slaveowner, in his cruelty, was cautious enough not to let her die. As scholar Jasbir Puar has observed in her work on "the right to maim," *let live* and *will not let die* are not the same thing.[6] To let live, at its best, can be merciful. To refuse to let die, at its worst, is the definition of torture.

Hester's scream has haunted modern theorists of race and slavery.[7] Christina Sharpe introduced her book *Monstrous Intimacies* by describing Aunt Hester's beating as an "extraordinarily rendered scene of ordinary brutality" because, despite the acute horror of Douglass's words, the episode was not an exception to—but rather a feature of—the chronic brutalities of slavehood.[8] In her book *Scenes of Subjection*, likewise in the introduction, Saidiya Hartman invoked Hester by announcing a *refusal* to quote or to "reproduce Douglass's account of the beating of Aunt Hester."[9] For Hartman, Hester's abuse is overquoted today to the point of authorial complicity in "the ease with which such scenes are usually reiterated, the casualness with which they are circulated, and the consequences of this routine display of the slave's ravaged body."[10] And in his book *In the Break*—again, in the opening pages— Fred Moten critiqued Hartman's purposeful non-account of Aunt Hester as a provocative yet ultimately "illusory" gesture, a "refusal of recitation that reproduces what it refuses."[11] More authors have since conducted astute readings of Moten's reading of Hartman's reading of Douglass's hearing of Aunt Hester's cries of pain.[12] The interpretive chain continues to lengthen, every link tethered to that terrible primal scream. It's a scream that became the screams of Sybrina Fulton and Tracy Martin (parents of Trayvon Martin), the screams of Lesley McSpadden and Michael Brown Sr. (parents of Michael Brown), of Lucy McBath and Ron Davis.

Became music, too. Or at least this is one way Moten urges his readers to hear Hester. He finds something to salvage in Douglass's blood-stained narrative: black suffering, scattering a seed that survives, sprouting into a poetics of things yet to come, then blossoming into melodious impulse, so that "shriek turns speech turns song."[13] Obliquely, remarks Moten, black musical traditions owe a debt to Hester. Or as he explained during a 2016 panel discussion with Saidiya Hartman: "Anybody who thinks that they can understand how terrible the terror has been without understanding how beautiful the beauty has been against the grain of that terror is wrong; there is no calculus of the terror that can make a proper calculation without a reference to that which resists it."[14] Meaning we can't understand what terror is without understanding the things that resist it. Beauty—music—may be one such thing.

I concede the humanizing power of rescuing music from an abject scene of inhumane torment. It is enticing to cradle Hester's screams as a generative force. But this enticement clashes with another desire—namely, the desire to sacrifice all of the posthumous pain-paved beauty for an alternate history in which Hester was never made to scream in the first place.

Time travel isn't real. We cannot jump back centuries to wrench the whip from Anthony's hands. We cannot save Hester anymore; she does not need saving anymore. Yet perhaps our willingness to bargain with ghosts of the past already says something. It says, despite the impossibility of a deal, we have come to the table. It says we will sit at the table, and our fantasy of defying the logics of space and time will not be doused by pragmatist claims that no treaties will be drawn today. It says we will honor Hester not simply by appreciating the music her screams might have wrought, but also by fighting for a reality in which no slave—or no one at all—will be made to scream like that again.

Readings of Aunt Hester's scream are so profound and profuse that there seems, on the one hand, nothing new left to say about it, yet on the other, an endless responsibility to keep saying things anew. Ethnomusicologist Michael Heller describes this tension as a "double-movement toward and away from signification."[15] Heller locates power in Hester's raw sound: "Through its immense volume, her scream cuts into the bodies of those within earshot. The symbolic rape of Hester's beating is resisted and inverted as her scream functions as a sonic penetration against her attacker, a penetration the master cannot control."[16] Hester's scream was beyond the master's control. Beyond the control of posterity as well, given how writers have wrestled uncomfortably with Douglass's story.

Beyond, too, the control of Hester herself, who, subjected to agony, could not possibly have suppressed her screams. Hester's "most piercing" scream, as with many screams unleashed in response to pain, was surely loud, but not necessarily loud enough.[17] Had it been humanly possible, she might have wished to scream infinitely more loudly—loudly enough not just to wake young Douglass, but also to wake the whole plantation, the whole country or the whole world, to communicate the magnitude of incommunicable anguish, to overwhelm the senses of her abuser and jolt him into unlikely sympathy, or, failing this appeal to the slaveowner's better angels, to repel him with a supernatural wall of sheer vibrational force. In other words, one of Hester's only viable, visceral responses to pain and bondage was, in that moment, to scream as stridently as she could; it was solely a limitation in breath and physiology, not a limitation in desire, that must have prevented her from screaming more loudly still.

Writers habitually lionize the scream as the amplitudinal apex of human sonic production.[18] We stand to be so shaken by the already exceptional potency of screams, however, that we forget how each audible scream may only be a fraction of the decibels desperately wished. In this sense, a scream—not least a scream of suffering—is only sounding out a shadow of itself. It tells a partial story, though its palpable powers might convince listeners otherwise.

The Beautiful without the Terrible

So it is with music. Music tells partial stories. Some stories are reliable, others mendacious. Even music without words will whisper to us a mashup of truths and falsehoods about ourselves and about other people. We frequently treat music—in particular the music we have strong feelings about—as if it were a mystical window into minds, bodies, and souls.

Music guarantees no such miraculous second sight. Yet music's existence itself is something of a miracle. Because the universe didn't owe us music. The universe has never owed us anything. So maybe we, the inhabitants, owe each other nothing. Or maybe, as Stefano Harney and Fred Moten say, "we owe each other everything."[19] We who, even with incalculable potential to do right by others, have historically found devastating ways to perpetrate terror and weaponize beauty. To fellow human beings, we might owe love: with, through, or in the company of music.

Or—all music aside.

As a teacher, I have experimented with how it sounds and how it feels to set music aside. In early 2017, I offered an undergraduate seminar on music and activism. Given that classes began two weeks prior to Donald Trump's inauguration, my students were keen to talk about politics, yet weren't always instinctually linking their arguments to music per se. Despite my syllabus's slate of musical case studies and audio examples—protest songs, rousing speeches, censored recordings, campaign-trail performances—it quickly became clear that, at times, the students simply wanted to discuss the Muslim ban, healthcare platforms, borders, refugees, and human rights violations. In preparation for each class, I knew that a speedy online search of, say, *Trump* plus *protest* plus *song* (with a filter for the last seven or thirty days) could have easily pulled up a cornucopia of analyzable videos ripe for the critical reintegration of music into our weekly conversations. But such pinpoint tactics, whenever I attempted them, felt simultaneously forced and facile. I mean, it *was* a music class. It was my responsibility to keep dialogues on topic by asking questions like, "And how can we better understand this social issue through musical examples?" At the same time, however, I was afraid of sounding like a broken record: *but what about music? Music? Music?*

At the start of the term, I thought I was failing as a music instructor whenever students ventured into lengthy non-musical tangents. I eventually grew more comfortable letting music go. So what if music receded from our classroom conversations every once in a while?

One day, something changed again. On campus, news broke about the death of a graduating senior. During a class meeting that immediately followed the announcement of this tragedy, several of my students were speechless with grief. Some of them had been friends with this senior. So instead of discussing the week's readings and adopting any pretense of business as usual, we devoted time to music—just listening to music, without much talk. And for the next class, I informed them, they could likewise come prepared to share a piece of music they loved; they could bring musical instruments or sheet music, or just have a recording cued up. Indeed, later that week, the class meeting was simply a jam session. Students sang, played, listened. I sat at the piano, something I rarely do these days, to accompany a couple of elegiac ballads chosen by the students.

During the term, then, we occasionally let music go; other moments, we let music in, and loved it till things hurt, or hurt less. Depending on what was happening around the world and in their own lives, students went from lamenting how music couldn't do anything—in the face of upheavals everywhere—to believing that the sounds of music could feel like everything, upheavals be damned.

Toward the end of the term, I sketched on the chalkboard a summary of loving music and the dilemmas of this love (Figure 7.1).

Round and round, parenthetical *but-but-buts* chug like the little engines that could. No promises of any fast track to epiphany. Staring at the illustration, I find it impossible to absorb all three statements at once.[20] My gaze goes in circles; my mind spins as well.

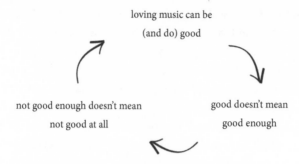

Figure 7.1. Illustration for a class on music, ethics, and activism.

On some days, I feel as if music and musical education don't matter much. School shootings, humanitarian crises, and political tremors shake my confidence in the relevance of what I do. Other days, music can be the apex of unfettered joy, as when I attend a student's exquisite recital or witness a scintillating classroom discussion.[21] I don't want to excise the radically wishful parts of myself (or of my students) that most desperately need to believe in music's powers for good, even or especially when colossal pressures threaten to extinguish this bright belief altogether.

As I continue to teach and think about music, an array of lessons shimmers on the horizon. If anything, writing *Loving Music Till It Hurts* has led me to realize just how much I have left to learn about music, love, and being a person in a world so potentially beautiful yet perpetually flooded with constant breaking news saying everything is terrible. Writing this book has also guided me to a trio of longer-term goals. Perhaps your own goals, upon reading this book, will be similar to mine. Perhaps you chart a path of your own.

First, I would like to learn to admit freely, without shame or guilt, my susceptibility to the musical mystique. I can verbalize, with reference to the examples in this book, why this mystique can be problematic and even dangerous. But it hardly means my mind and body are now impenetrable by lines of dangerous thinking, particularly when I'm reading heartwrenching human interest stories, watching tearjerking clips of reality show auditions, or listening to some sublime recording that hastens me to presume the performer's decent character. Fruitful conversations about the musical and musicological mystiques can begin, I think, largely through acknowledgments of mutual vulnerability rather than through the stubborn pretense of immunity.

Second, I would like to appreciate how the qualities that lure me into traps of the musical mystique—qualities such as music's indescribable craft, soul-shaking beauty, overwhelming power—are exactly the sorts of qualities that might lead me to believe, even if naively, in the power of people to be (or become) generous and empathetic. Although music probably can't be a primary, much less sole, vehicle for such a hopeful stance, our love of music can remind us of our human capacity to love, period. All the better if this love more frequently spreads to, or intersects with, a love of other people. Thankfully, there are role models: people who have witnessed or directly suffered the consequences of misjudgments, iniquities, or violence, yet have fought for better worlds—through music or otherwise—often with anti-ableist, anti-racist, anti-sexist, and anti-homophobic actions. I'm thinking of the trajectories of activists such as Lucy McBath, who, as the mother of a child murdered while playing loud music, now serves in the US Congress as a fierce proponent of gun control and civil rights. I'm also thinking of people such as Susan Boyle, who, knowing what it's like to face prejudice, sheltered "1:24 Girl" Jennifer Byrne as this teen was receiving death threats for rolling her eyes during Boyle's audition; or people such as Monica Lewinsky, who, after a decade of silence, has recently reemerged to speak out passionately against today's maelstroms of public shaming. Any of these women could have chosen to say nothing. Instead, their own hurt became calls for tolerance, reform, and love.

Lastly, then, I would like to declare my debt to anyone who has—through the unenviable impetus of private pain—inspired, written, performed, or otherwise fostered music for a greater public good. Far be it from me or others to wonder whether this beautiful music has been worth the hurt, or to claim to understand you through tropes of the resiliently suffering artist, or to take your labors of love for granted. May those of us who stand to love your musical labors work that much harder alongside you toward a future where the beautiful can be emancipated from the terrible, and indeed, where the terrible is a rarity rather than some romantic necessity. Granted, maybe this kind of harmonious future is virtually unthinkable. Or think of it another way. Maybe such a future is no less unthinkable than the unlikely fact that the things we call music, love, and humanity already exist.

As I write this, it's February. Spring is imminent—then summer—then before too long, autumn, my favorite season, when leaves in New England sing a thousand shades.

I will listen to Eva Cassidy today.

Notes

Prelude

1. Carolyn Abbate, "Music—Drastic or Gnostic?," *Critical Inquiry* 30 (2004), 505.
2. Cornel West with David Ritz, *Living and Loving Out Loud: A Memoir* (New York: SmileyBooks, 2009), 232.
3. Joseph N. Straus, *Extraordinary Measures: Disability in Music* (New York: Oxford University Press, 2011), 103.
4. Consider analogous cases of "offending images," such as Chris Ofili's controversial 1996 dung-encrusted painting *The Holy Virgin Mary*. Pointing to this artwork, W. J. T. Mitchell asks: "What is it about people that makes them so susceptible to being offended by images? And why is the response to the offensive image so often a reciprocal act of violence, an 'offending of the image' by destroying, vandalizing, or banning it from view?" (*What Do Pictures Want? The Lives and Loves of Images* [Chicago: University of Chicago Press, 2005], 125–26).
5. Anne Midgette, "Blasting Mozart to Drive Criminals Away," *Washington Post* (20 January 2012), http://www.washingtonpost.com/lifestyle/style/blasting-mozart-to-drive-criminals-away/2011/10/11/gIQAgDqPEQ_story.html?utm_term=.194a743958e6.
6. Midgette, "Blasting Mozart."
7. Midgette, "Blasting Mozart."
8. See Peter Kivy, *De Gustibus: Arguing about Taste and Why We Do It* (New York: Oxford University Press, 2015), 1–5.
9. This comment comes from Paul Henry Lang with respect to Deryck Cooke's "completion" of Gustav Mahler's Symphony No. 10; quoted in David Trippett, "Editing Unfinished Music by a Great Composer Is Controversial—But Sometimes It Needs to Be Done," *The Conversation* (11 February 2019), http://theconversation.com/editing-unfinished-music-by-a-great-composer-is-controversial-but-sometimes-it-needs-to-be-done-108632.
10. See Mary Branch, "I'm a Black Doctor. My Neighbors Called the Cops on Me for Listening to Biggie," *Washington Post* (28 May 2018), http://www.washingtonpost.com/opinions/my-white-neighbors-called-the-cops-on-me-for-listening-to-hip-hop/2018/05/28/54930d04-4fbe-11e8-af46-b1d6dc0d9bfe_story.html?utm_term=.ad3b3265c347; and Breanna Edwards, "White Woman Calls Cops on California Man Chilling in His Car Listening to Yoga CD," *The Root* (13 July 2018), http://www.theroot.com/white-woman-calls-cops-on-california-man-chilling-in-hi-1827586286. Or take the example, earlier that year, of Larry Moneta (Vice President of Student Affairs at Duke University), who berated a black barista and her white coworker for

playing an "inappropriate" rap song in a campus cafe, then went on to lodge formal complaints that resulted in the termination of these two employees. See Monique Judge, "Trap Music Gets 2 Baristas Fired from a Duke University Coffee Shop after School VP Complains," *The Root* (9 May 2018), http://www.theroot.com/trap-music-gets-2-baristas-fired-from-a-duke-university-1825903769. Larry Moneta has since faced accusations of bigotry on other fronts. Michelle Li, president of Duke's Asian Students Association, criticized Moneta's social media posts that mocked China's junk food and living conditions: "It's obvious to us from the posts that they are, at best, very culturally insensitive and, at worst, very racist" (Bre Bradham and Nathan Luzum, "Larry Moneta Takes 'Hiatus' from Facebook after 'Insensitive' Posts Spark Student Backlash," *Chronicle* [13 December 2018], http://www.dukechronicle.com/article/2018/12/duke-university-administrator-larry-moneta-takes-hiatus-from-facebook-after-insensitive-posts-spark-student-backlash).

11. See, for example, Scott Burnham, "Theorists and 'The Music Itself,'" *Journal of Musicology* 15 (1997), 316–29; Berthold Hoeckner, *Programming the Absolute: Nineteenth-Century German Music and the Hermeneutics of the Moment* (Princeton, NJ: Princeton University Press, 2002), 1–4; and Carl Dahlhaus, *The Idea of Absolute Music*, translated by Roger Lustig (Chicago: University of Chicago Press, 1989).

12. See Sara Ahmed, *The Promise of Happiness* (Durham, NC: Duke University Press, 2010); José Esteban Muñoz, *Cruising Utopia: The Then and There of Queer Futurity* (New York: New York University Press, 2009); and Michael Snediker, *Queer Optimism: Lyric Personhood and Other Felicitous Persuasions* (Minneapolis: University of Minnesota Press, 2009). Snediker, for example, summarizes the one-step-removed concept of "queer optimism" as "a form of meta-optimism: it wants to think about feeling good, to make disparate aspects of feeling good thinkable" (*Queer Optimism*, 3).

13. Donald E. Pease, *The New American Exceptionalism* (Minneapolis: University of Minnesota Press, 2009), 20, 8.

14. Closing Arguments, *People of the State of Florida v. DUNN MICHAEL DAVID*, Case No. 16-2012-CF-011572-AXXX-MA (2014), 2959, emphasis added; and Testimony by Alexandria Molinaro, *People v. Dunn. People of the State of Florida v. DUNN MICHAEL DAVID, Case No. 16-2012-CF-011572-AXXX-MA* (2014), 2683, http://lawofselfdefense.web.unc.edu/files/2014/10/Alexandria-Molinaro.pdf. Citations of this case (all dated 2014) are hereafter abbreviated as *People v. Dunn*. Full witness transcripts are available at http://lawofselfdefense.web.unc.edu/selected-cases/michaeldunn/dunn-trial-witness-transcripts.

Chapter 1

1. Anthony Tommasini, "Trump Is Wrong If He Thinks Symphonies Are Superior," *New York Times* (30 July 2017), http://www.nytimes.com/2017/07/30/arts/music/trump-classical-music.html.

2. Richard Taruskin, "The Musical Mystique," *New Republic* (22 October 2007), http://newrepublic.com/article/64350/books-the-musical-mystique. Taruskin's essay jointly

reviewed the following books: Julian Johnson, *Who Needs Classical Music? Cultural Choice and Musical Value* (New York: Oxford University Press, 2002); Joshua Fineberg, *Classical Music, Why Bother? Hearing the World of Contemporary Culture through a Composer's Ears* (New York: Routledge, 2006); and Lawrence Kramer, *Why Classical Music Still Matters* (Berkeley: University of California Press, 2009).

3. On music, "civility," and civilization, see Kira Thurman, "Singing the Civilized Mission in the Land of Bach, Beethoven, and Brahms: The Fisk Jubilee Singers in Nineteenth-Century Germany," *Journal of World History* 27 (2016), 443–71; Edmond Strainchamps and Maria Rika Maniates, with Christopher Hatch, *Music and Civilization: Essays in Honor of Paul Henry Lang* (New York: Norton, 1984); Hans T. David, "The Cultural Functions of Music," *Journal of the History of Ideas* 12 (1951), 423–39; Mary DuPree, "Beyond Music in Western Civilization: Issues in Undergraduate Music History Literacy," *College Music Symposium* 30 (1990), 100–105; Ivan Supičič, "Aesthetics of Music—Particularity and Universality," *The World of Music* 25 (1983), 16–25; Nicholas Tochka, "To 'Enlighten and Beautify': Western Music and the Modern Project of Personhood in Albania, c. 1906–24," *Ethnomusicology* 59 (2015), 398–420; Matthew Riley, "Civilizing the Savage: Johann Georg Sulzer and the 'Aesthetic Force' of Music," *Journal of the Royal Music Association* 127 (2002), 1–22; and Bennett Zon, "Disorienting Race: Humanizing the Musical Savage and the Rise of British Ethnomusicology," *Nineteenth-Century Music Review* 3 (2006), 25–43.

4. For varied considerations of music, morality, and moralism, see Charles Trainor, "Fielding and the Morality of Music," *Neophilologus* 97 (2013), 775–83; Anna Chęćka-Gotkowicz, "Peter Kivy's Discursive 'Weakness': The Problem of Moral Entanglement of Music," *Miscellanea Anthropologica et Sociologica* 16 (2015), 77–85; Leon Botstein, "Music, Morality, and Method," *Musical Quarterly* 81 (1997), 339–43; Halbert H. Britan, "Music and Morality," *International Journal of Ethics* 15 (1904), 48–63; and So Jeong Park, "Music as a Necessary Means of Moral Education: A Case Study from Reconstruction of Confucian Culture in Joseon Korea," *International Communication of Chinese Culture* 2 (2015), 123–36. See also Ian Power, "Why Does This Mozart Piece Make Me Cry Even Though It's Stupid and Probably Evil?," *Medium* (11 January 2019), http://medium.com/@ianpoweromg/why-does-this-mozart-piece-make-me-cry-even-though-its-stupid-and-probably-evil-80c63c60fc7f.

5. As philosopher Peter Kivy writes, we are "indisputably, disputatious animals," not least when musical taste is concerned (*De Gustibus*, x).

6. William H. McClendon, "Black Music: Sound and Feeling for Black Liberation," *Black Scholar* 7 (1976), 21.

7. McClendon, "Black Music," 22.

8. See Greg Tate, ed., *Everything but the Burden: What White People Are Taking from Black Culture* (New York: Broadway Books, 2003). On how blackface minstrelsy arose in part from white people's perverse fascination with black culture, see Eric Lott, *Love and Theft: Black Minstrelsy and the American Working Class* (New York: Oxford University Press, 1993), 38–62.

9. Alexander G. Weheliye, *Habeas Viscus: Racializing Assemblages, Biopolitics, and Black Feminist Theories of the Human* (Durham, NC: Duke University Press, 2014), 3.

10. See Cerise L. Glenn and Landra J. Cunningham, "The Power of Black Magic: The Magical Negro and White Salvation in Film," *Journal of Black Studies* 40 (2009), 135–52; and José Alaniz, *Death, Disability, and the Superhero: The Silver Age and Beyond* (Jackson: University Press of Mississippi, 2014), 26–68. Rosemarie Garland-Thomson defines "freakery" as a "category of corporeal otherness" and of "generalized embodied deviance" ("Introduction: From Wonder to Error—A Genealogy of Freak Discourse in Modernity," in *Freakery: Cultural Spectacles of the Extraordinary Body*, edited by Rosemarie Garland-Thomson [New York: New York University Press, 1996], 10).

11. See John McShane, *Susan Boyle: Living the Dream* (London: John Blake Publishing Ltd, 2010), xiv.

12. Belinda Luscombe, "Susan Boyle: Not Quite Out of Nowhere," *TIME* (23 April 2009), http://content.time.com/time/arts/article/0,8599,1893282,00.html.

13. Katherine Meizel, *Idolized: Music, Media, and Identity in American Idol* (Bloomington: Indiana University Press, 2011), 30.

14. Quoted in McShane, *Susan Boyle*, 41.

15. Anastasia Tsioulcas, "Putin Plays the Piano, with Perhaps Unintentional Undertones," NPR (15 May 2017), http://www.npr.org/sections/thetwo-way/2017/05/15/528451430/putin-plays-the-piano-with-perhaps-unintentional-undertones.

16. Ivan Nechepurenko, "In Beijing, Vladimir Putin Plays Two Piano Tunes from His Childhood," *New York Times* (14 May 2017), http://www.nytimes.com/2017/05/14/world/europe/vladimir-putin-piano-one-belt-one-road-beijing.html.

17. An excellent montage of Putin's hypermasculine optics can be found at "Vladimir Putin Doing Manly Things," *CBS* (n.d.; last accessed 8 March 2018), http://www.cbsnews.com/pictures/vladimir-putin-doing-manly-things.

18. Associated Press, "Putin Sits Down at Piano in China, Plays Soviet Songs," *Boston Globe* (14 May 2017), http://www.bostonglobe.com/news/world/2017/05/14/putin-sits-down-piano-china-plays-soviet-songs/LYHC3zHPriZcYcNJqLKQQN/story.html.

19. FE Online, "Russian President Vladimir Putin Shows His Soft Skills, Plays Piano as He Waits for Chinese President Xi Jinping," *Financial Express* (15 May 2017), http://www.financialexpress.com/world-news/watch-russian-president-vladimir-putin-shows-his-soft-skills-plays-piano-as-he-waits-for-chinese-president-xi-jinping/668909.

20. See Nechepurenko, "In Beijing."

21. Paul Resnikoff, "Vladimir Putin Plays Piano Like a 3rd Grader," *Digital Music News* (15 May 2017), http://www.digitalmusicnews.com/2017/05/15/vladimir-putin-plays-piano-china.

22. Comments under *The New York Times* (@nytimes), tweet (14 May 2017), http://twitter.com/nytimes/status/863928551111888896. See also Katherine Brooks, "No, Putin's Piano Recital Doesn't Make Him Any 'Softer,'" *Huffington Post* (15 May 2017), http://www.huffingtonpost.com/entry/no-putins-piano-recital-doesnt-make-him-any-softer_us_5919b8cfe4b0031e737f3437.

23. In 1990, attorney Mike Godwin coined "Godwin's Law" to capture the preponderance of *reductio ad Hitlerum* impulses in the Internet era (with thanks to Michael Casey for bringing this to my attention): "As an online discussion grows longer, the probability of a comparison involving Nazis or Hitler approaches 1" ("Meme, Counter-meme," *Wired* [1 October 1994], http://www.wired.com/1994/10/godwin-if-2). Adapting Godwin's Law for debates about the musical mystique, we could say with fair confidence: *As an online discussion about great music and monstrous men grows longer, the probability of a comparison involving Nazis or Hitler approaches 1.*

24. David Livingstone Smith, *Less Than Human: Why We Demean, Enslave, and Exterminate Others* (New York: St. Martin's Press, 2011), 21.

25. See Jason Newman, "Bruce Springsteen Cover Band Drops Out of Trump Inauguration Party," *Rolling Stone* (16 January 2017), http://www.rollingstone.com/music/news/bruce-springsteen-cover-band-drops-out-of-donald-trump-party-w461203;   and Kelly-Ann Mills, "Russia's President Putin Fails in Attempt to Play Piano while Waiting for Chinese Leader—and Blames 'Bad Tuning,'" *Mirror* (15 May 2017), http://www.mirror.co.uk/news/world-news/russias-president-putin-fails-attempt-10427986.

26. Dana Gorzelany-Mostak, "Hearing Jackie Evancho in the Age of Donald Trump," *American Music* 35 (2017), 467. See also Jia Tolentino, "Jackie Evancho, Trump's Inauguration, and the Politics of Childhood," *New Yorker* (19 January 2017), http://www.newyorker.com/culture/jia-tolentino/jackie-evancho-and-the-politics-of-childhood.

27. Dana Gorzelany-Mostak, "The Curse of 'O mio *bambino* caro': Jackie Evancho as Prodigy, Diva, and Ideal Girl," in *Voicing Girlhood in Popular Music: Performance, Authority, Authenticity*, edited by Jacqueline Warwick and Allison Adrian (New York: Routledge, 2016), 128.

28. "Jackie Evancho on Performing at Donald Trump's Inauguration—Full Interview," YouTube (20 January 2017), http://www.youtube.com/watch?v=n7NdSL1eNrE, ~3:01.

29. "Jackie Evancho," ~4:31. See also Caroline McCoy, "Don't Attack Musicians Who Want to Perform at Trump's Inauguration," *Washington Post* (18 January 2017), http://www.washingtonpost.com/posteverything/wp/2017/01/18/dont-attack-musicians-who-want-to-perform-at-trumps-inauguration/?noredirect=on&utm_term=.7806e870c012.

30. See Michael Cooper, "Met Opera Suspends James Levine after New Sexual Abuse Accusations," *New York Times* (3 December 2017), http://www.nytimes.com/2017/12/03/arts/music/james-levine-met-opera.html. For a comprehensive recent report of sexual harassment in classical music, see Anne Midgette and Peggy McGlone, "Assaults in Dressing Rooms. Groping During Lessons. Classical Musicians Reveal a Profession Rife with Harassment," *The Washington Post* (26 July 2018), http://www.washingtonpost.com/entertainment/music/assaults-in-dressing-rooms-groping-during-lessons-classical-musicians-reveal-a-profession-rife-with-harassment/2018/07/25/f47617d0-36c8-11e8-acd5-35eac230e514_story.html?tid=ss_tw&utm_term=.f8cb0b627d08.

31. See Tom Huizenga, "Charles Dutoit Facing New Sexual Assault Accusations, Royal Philharmonic Cuts Ties," NPR (11 January 2018), http://www.npr.org/sections/deceptivecadence/2018/01/11/577378738/londons-royal-philharmonic-ends-its-relationship-with-conductor-charles-dutoit.

32. See Ben Miller, "On Knowing and Not Knowing about James Levine," Atavist (7 December 2017), http://van-us.atavist.com/silence-breaking.

33. Alex Ross, "Metropolitan Lives," New Yorker (5 November 2001), http://www.newyorker.com/magazine/2001/11/05/metropolitan-lives. Perhaps it's significant that Ross wrote this apologia a mere couple of months after the terrorist attacks of September 11, 2001, which spawned strongly worded dialogues about the salvational power of music, art, beauty, and returning to "life as usual." See Joel B. Eisen, "The Trajectory of 'Normal' after 9/11: Trauma, Recovery and Post-Traumatic Societal Adaptation," Fordham Environmental Law Journal 14 (2003), 499–561.

34. Alex Ross (@alexrossmusic), tweet (4 December 2017), http://twitter.com/alexrossmusic/status/937701099976327173?lang=en.

35. Linda Shaver-Gleason, "The Morality of Musical Men: From Victorian Propriety to the Era of #MeToo," lecture delivered at Utah State University (26 January 2018), 11, emphasis in original, http://hcommons.org/deposits/objects/hc:18044/datastreams/CONTENT/content.

36. An additional consideration, as William Robin points out, is how some people had initially tried to dismiss rumors of Levine's sexual misconduct on the basis of the rumors' implicit homophobia; calling gay men pedophiles has been a mainstay in anti-gay attitudes and legislation. As Robin notes, "what's monstrous is that Levine—like [Kevin] Spacey—was able to use homophobia as a cover for his crimes, ultimately giving ammo to homophobes" (@seatedovation, tweet [4 December 2017], https://twitter.com/seatedovation/status/937842848946409472). See also Joseph Fischel, "How Calling Kevin Spacey a Pedophile Hurts the Gay Community," Slate (1 November 2017), http://www.slate.com/blogs/outward/2017/11/01/how_calling_kevin_spacey_a_pedophile_hurts_the_gay_community.html.

37. Melissa Klein, "James Levine Using 'Love' Letter to Discredit Alleged Victim," New York Post (16 June 2018), http://nypost.com/2018/06/16/james-levine-using-love-letter-to-discredit-alleged-victim.

38. See Judith Herman, Trauma and Recovery: The Aftermath of Violence—from Domestic Abuse to Political Terror (New York: Basic Books, 1997); Catherine Donovan and Marianna Hester, Domestic Violence and Sexuality: What's Love Got to Do with It? (Bristol, UK: Policy Press, 2015); and Heather Fraser, "Narrating Love and Abuse in Intimate Relationships," British Journal of Social Work 33 (2003), 273–90; cf. Joshua D. Pilzer, Hearts of Pine: Songs in the Lives of Three Korean Survivors of the Japanese "Comfort Women" (New York: Oxford University Press, 2012). With thanks to an anonymous reviewer for guiding me to Herman's work.

39. Quoted in Shaver-Gleason, "Morality of Musical Men," 11.

40. Melvyn Krauss, "In the #MeToo Era, the Audience Deserves a Voice," USA Today (18 January 2018), http://www.usatoday.com/story/opinion/2018/01/18/when-metoo-stretches-too-far-classical-music-world-audience-loses-melvyn-krauss-column/1018659001.

41. Melvyn Krauss, "Running Scared at the Met," *Music Matters* (1 March 2018), http://www.musicmattersblog.net/blog/2018/3/1/running-scared-at-the-met.

42. In this way, our human attachment to music is saturated with what literary scholar Lauren Berlant would call "cruel optimism" (*Cruel Optimism* [Durham, NC: Duke University Press, 2011]). Lovers of music naturally wish to safeguard their optimism about the music they love. Yet this love can impede personal flourishing, interpersonal care, and the pursuit of truth and justice.

43. Susan McClary, "Foreword: Humanizing the Humanities," in William Cheng, *Just Vibrations: The Purpose of Sounding Good* (Ann Arbor: University of Michigan Press, 2016), xix.

44. Lawrence Langer, *The Holocaust and the Literary Imagination* (New Haven, CT: Yale University Press, 1975), 8–9. See also Joseph J. Moreno, "Orpheus in Hell: Music in the Holocaust," in *Music and Manipulation: On the Social Uses and Social Control of Music*, edited by Steven Brown and Ulrik Volgsten (New York: Berghahn Books, 2006), 264–86; Amy Lynn Wlodarski, *Musical Witness and Holocaust Representation* (Cambridge: Cambridge University Press, 2015), 164–70; and James Berger, *After the End: Representations of Post-Apocalypse* (Minneapolis: University of Minnesota Press, 1999).

45. Richard Taruskin, "Is There a Baby in the Bathwater? (Part II)," *Archiv für Musikwissenschaft* 63 (2006), 326. See also Michael H. Kater, "Introduction," in *Music and Nazism: Art under Tyranny, 1933–1945*, edited by Michael H. Kater and Albrecht Riethmüller (Laaber, Germany: Laaber, 2003), 10.

46. Musicologist William Robin, critiquing the longstanding fantasy that "great music made people better," points out: "The moral angle is bust—it's unjust and untrue to claim that classical music is inherently better than any other kind of music—but a fire still burns. Talk to anyone who performs, composes, promotes, or organizes anything in this field [of classical music] and the blaze is palpable" ("Classical Music Isn't Dead," *The New Yorker* [29 January 2014], http://www.newyorker.com/culture/culture-desk/the-fat-lady-is-still-singing); see also Tamara Levitz, "The Musicological Elite," *Current Musicology* 102 (2018), 9–80.

47. See Juliane Brauer, "How Can Music Be Torturous? Music in Nazi Concentration and Extermination Camps," *Music & Politics* 10 (2016), http://dx.doi.org/10.3998/mp.9460447.0010.103.

48. On the coining of "alt-right," see Benjamin Wallace-Wells, "Is the Alt-Right for Real?," *New Yorker* (5 May 2016), http://www.newyorker.com/news/benjamin-wallace-wells/is-the-alt-right-for-real.

49. Bonnie Gordon, "In the Aftermath of Charlottesville," *Musicology Now* (8 September 2017), http://musicologynow.ams-net.org/2017/09/in-aftermath-of-charlottesville.html. Gordon's comparison of Spencer's rally to an "operatic" spectacle resonates with past writers' various comparisons between Richard Wagner's monumental music dramas and Adolf Hitler's titanic atrocities. Carl von Ossietzky, the German pacifist and Nobel Peace Prize recipient, stated (three weeks after Hitler was sworn into office) that Germany would become "for a second time a Wagner opera" (quoted in Berthold Hoeckner, "Wagner and the Origin of Evil," *Opera Quarterly* 23 [2007], 161). See also Les Back, "Voices of Hate, Sounds of Hybridity: Black Music and the Complexities of Racism," *Black Music Research Journal* 20 (2000), 127–49.

50. Additional critiques of music and musicology associated with, inflected by, or mired in Nazi ideology can be found in Pamela M. Potter, "What Is 'Nazi Music'?," *Musical Quarterly* 88 (2005), 428–55; Pamela M. Potter, *Art of Suppression* (Berkeley: University of California Press, 2016), 1–47; Anne C. Shreffler, Boris von Haken, and Christopher Browning, "Musicology, Biography, and National Socialism: The Case of Hans Heinrich Eggebrecht," *German Studies Review* 35 (2012), 289–318; and Michael Meyer, "The Nazi Musicologist as Myth Maker in the Third Reich," *Journal of Contemporary History* 10 (1975), 649–65.

51. See Sopan Deb, "Trump Proposes Eliminating the Arts and Humanities Endowments," *New York Times* (15 March 2017), http://www.nytimes.com/2017/03/15/arts/nea-neh-endowments-trump.html.

52. Gordon, "In the Aftermath of Charlottesville."

53. Judith Becker, *Deep Listeners: Music, Emotion, and Trancing* (Bloomington: Indiana University Press, 2004), 71. On habitus, see Pierre Bourdieu, *Outline of a Theory of Practice*, translated by Richard Nice (Cambridge: Cambridge University Press, 2013); see also Suzanne G. Cusick, "Feminist Theory, Music Theory, and the Mind/Body Problem," *Perspectives of New Music* 32 (1994), 8–27 (esp. 9–10).

54. Rose Rosengard Subotnik, reflecting on her skills in musical listening and analysis, asks: "[W]hat in almost forty years of serious musical study had overlaid my child-hood love of classical music with such burdensome feelings of anxiety and obliga-tion?" ("Afterword: Toward the Next Paradigm of Musical Scholarship," in *Beyond Structural Listening? Postmodern Modes of Hearing*, edited by Andrew Dell'Antonio [Berkeley: University of California Press, 2004], 281). See also Loren Kajikawa, "The Possessive Investment in Classical Music: Confronting Legacies of White Supremacy in U.S. Schools and Departments of Music," in *Seeing Race Again: Countering Colorblindness across the Disciplines*, edited by Kimberlé Williams Crenshaw, Luke Charles Harris, Daniel Martinez HoSang, and George Lipsitz (Berkeley: University of California Press, 2019), 155–74.

55. See Mina Yang, *Planet Beethoven: Classical Music at the Turn of the Millennium* (Middletown, CT: Wesleyan University Press, 2014), 27; and Matt Hickman, "Taiwan Garbage Trucks: Classical Music Accompanies Collection," *Huffington Post* (6 December 2017), http://www.huffingtonpost.com/2012/01/09/taiwan-garbage-trucks-music_n_1195020.html.

56. Taruskin, "Is There a Baby in the Bathwater? (Part II)," 327.

57. Taruskin has attempted to defend his use of the word "obviously" in an essay on music, ethics, and Nazis. See Richard Taruskin, *The Danger of Music and Other Anti-Utopian Essays* (Berkeley: University of California Press, 2009), 164–65.

58. Peter Kivy, "Musical Morality," *Revue internationale de philosophie* 4 (2008), 397. For another take on this scene, see Michael H. Kater, *The Twisted Muse: Musicians and Their Music in the Third Reich* (New York: Oxford University Press, 1997), 3–4. See also Kivy, *De Gustibus*, ix–x.

59. Jasmine Baker, Mark Haslett, and Scott Morgan, "Cornel West at A&M-Commerce: Transcript," *KETR* (7 October 2016), http://ketr.org/post/

cornel-west-am-commerce-transcript. West continues: "I want to hear an argument. Where is the evidence? It's a signifier of being part of the in-crowd in the culture of smartness. I do not come from a tradition that elevates smartness. Why? Because there are a whole lot of smart vicious white supremacists."

60. See Samantha Cooney, "All the Women Who Have Accused Sen. Al Franken of Sexual Misconduct," *TIME* (6 December 2017), http://time.com/5042931/al-franken-accusers.

61. Full interview available in "A News Quiz Made with Love," *Boston Public Radio (WGBH)* (17 November 2017), ~45:00 mark. See also Mark Shanahan, "BSO's Andris Nelsons Says Sexual Harassment Isn't a Problem in Classical Music," *Boston Globe* (20 November 2017), http://www.bostonglobe.com/lifestyle/names/2017/11/20/bso-andris-nelsons-says-sexual-harassment-isn-problem-classical-music/RS4BiGKOcT4nLUWP9szsGP/story.html; and Lisa Hirsch, "Andris Nelsons, Further to Previous," *Iron Tongue of Midnight* (21 November 2017), http://irontongue.blogspot.com/2017/11/andris-nelsons-further-to-previous.html.

62. Shanahan, "BSO's Andris Nelsons."

63. Shanahan, "BSO's Andris Nelsons." In a study of Christian music in contemporary society, Jonathan Arnold declares, "Music has always been an essential expression, not only of what it is to be a religious believer, but what it is to be human" (*Sacred Music in Secular Society* [Farnham, UK: Ashgate, 2014], 151).

64. Hirsch, "Andris Nelsons."

65. On Beethoven's "deeply rooted belief that great music can move the world," see Lewis Lockwood, *Beethoven's Symphonies: An Artistic Vision* (New York: W. W. Norton & Company, 2015), 223. See also Joseph Horowitz, *Moral Fire: Musical Portraits from America's Fin de Siècle* (Berkeley: University of California Press, 2012), 194–95.

66. See John J. Sheinbaum, *Good Music: What It Is and Who Gets to Decide* (Chicago: University of Chicago Press, 2019), 216–37.

67. See Frederick Lau, "'Center or Periphery?' Regional Music in Contemporary China," *International Communication of Chinese Culture* 2 (2015), 31–47; Katherine Butler Schofield, "Reviving the Golden Age Again: 'Classicization,' Hindustani Music, and the Mughals," *Ethnomusicology* 54 (2010), 484–517; and Nishlyn Ramanna, "Shifting Fortunes: Jazz in (Post)apartheid South Africa," *South African Music Studies* 33 (2013), 159–72; cf. Steven Skaggs and Carl R. Hausman, "Toward a New Elitism," *The Journal of Aesthetic Education* 46 (2012), 83–106.

68. Mark Vanhoenacker, "Requiem: Classical Music in America Is Dead," *Slate* (21 January 2014), http://www.slate.com/articles/arts/culturebox/2014/01/classical_music_sales_decline_is_classical_on_death_s_door.html. *Washington Post*'s classical music critic Anne Midgette retorted that the *claim* of classical music's death is itself an "easy target" for refuters; the *Slate* article, Midgette notes, is "low-hanging fruit. If you're a thinking person, it's child's play to blow holes in an article like this" ("Classical Music: Dead or Alive?," *Washington Post* [30 January 2014], http://www.

washingtonpost.com/news/style/wp/2014/01/30/classical-music-dead-or-alive/
?utm_term=.5eecdf059ed8). Music historian Charles Rosen famously quipped
that "the death of classical music is perhaps its oldest living tradition" (*Critical
Entertainments: Music Old and New* [Cambridge, MA: Harvard University Press,
2000], 295). See also Norman Lebrecht, *Who Killed Classical Music? Maestros,
Managers, and Corporate Politics* (Secaucus, NJ: Carol Pub. Group, 1997); Steven
Pinker, *The Blank Slate: The Modern Denial of Human Nature* (New York: Viking,
2002), 400–401; Robert J. Flanagan, *The Perilous Life of Symphony Orchestras: Artistic
Triumphs and Economic Challenges* (New Haven, CT: Yale University Press, 2012);
and Andrea Moore, "Neoliberalism and the Musical Entrepreneur," *Journal of the
Society for American Music* 10 (2016), 33–53 (esp. 37–38).

69. For a transcript of Lin-Manuel Miranda's sonnet, see Katey Rich, "Watch Lin-Manuel
    Miranda's Emotional Tony Awards Acceptance Sonnet," *Vanity Fair* (12 June 2016),
    http://www.vanityfair.com/culture/2016/06/lin-manuel-miranda-tony-speech.

70. See Sarah Hankins, "After Pulse: An Introduction," *Ethnomusicology Review* 20
    (2016), http://www.ethnomusicologyreview.ucla.edu/content/after-pulse.

71. Laura Kipnis, *Against Love: A Polemic* (New York: Vintage Books, 2003), 3.

72. John Blacking, *How Musical Is Man?* (Seattle: University of Washington Press,
    1973), 3.

73. See Special Issue, "Universals/Le Problème des Universaux," *World of Music* 19, No.
    1 & 2 (1977).

74. Jean-Jacques Nattiez, "Under What Conditions Can One Speak of the Universality of
    Music?," *World of Music* 19 (1977), 92–105, quoted in Dario Martinelli, "Introduction
    (to the Issue and to Zoomusicology)," *Trans: Revista transcultural de música* 12
    (2008), http://www.sibetrans.com/trans/articulo/93/introduction-to-the-issue-and-
    to-zoomusicology. Some objections to Nattiez's circumscription of music as uniquely
    human have come from writers (such as Martinelli) who point out the musical output
    of and communications between nonhuman animals such as whales, dolphins,
    and birds.

75. Kathleen Marie Higgins, *The Music Between Us: Is Music a Universal Language?*
    (Chicago: The University of Chicago Press, 2012), 2, 184.

76. See Noah A. Rosenberg, Jonathan K. Pritchard, James L. Weber, Howard M. Cann,
    Kenneth K. Kidd, Lev A. Zhivotovsky, and Marcus W. Feldman, "Genetic Structure of
    Human Populations," *Science* 298 (2002), 2381–85.

77. Paula Ioanide, *The Emotional Politics of Racism: How Feelings Trump Facts in an Era of
    Colorblindness* (Stanford, CA: Stanford University Press, 2015).

78. Ruth HaCohen, *The Music Libel against the Jews* (New Haven, CT: Yale University
    Press, 2011).

79. See Robin D. G. Kelley, "Kickin' Reality, Kickin' Ballistics: Gangsta Rap and
    Postindustrial Los Angeles," in *Droppin' Science: Critical Essays on Rap Music and Hip
    Hop Culture*, edited by William Eric Perkins (Philadelphia: Temple University Press,
    1996), 117–58.

80. V. Josiah C. Nott, "Two Lectures on the Natural History of the Caucasian and Negro
    Races," in *The Ideology of Slavery: Proslavery Thought in the Antebellum South,*

1830–60, edited by Drew Gilpin Faust (Baton Rouge, LA: Louisiana State University Press, 1981), 223.

81. Samuel A. Cartwright, "Diseases and Peculiarities of the Negro Race," *De Bow's Review* XI (1851), available via *PBS* at http://www.pbs.org/wgbh/aia/part4/4h3106t. html.

82. Quoted in Mark M. Smith, *Listening to Nineteenth-Century America* (Chapel Hill: University of North Carolina Press, 2001), 69. See also James Kennaway, *Bad Vibrations: The History of the Idea of Music as a Cause of Disease* (New York: Routledge, 2016), 117–19; and William C. Davis, *Look Away! A History of the Confederate States of America* (New York: Free Press, 2002), 131–32.

83. Although chattel-era ethnology produced an especially glaring brand of aesthetic racism, its reductionist impulses have since continued to percolate through representations of black musicality. Some modern representations are conspicuously retrograde (not far from Cartwrightian opinions), as with the work of psychologist Richard Lynn, who argued in a 2006 book that Africans possess a "strong sense of rhythm" at the expense of authentic "musical abilities" (*Race Differences in Intelligence: An Evolutionary Analysis* [Augusta, GA: Washington Summit Publishers, 2006], 56).

84. Quoted in Horowitz, *Moral Fire*, 221. Horowitz obtained the writings of Philip Hale from Jean Ann Boyd, "Philip Hale, American Music Critic, Boston, 1889–1933" (PhD diss., University of Texas at Austin, 1985).

85. See Rachel Mundy, *Animal Musicalities: Birds, Beasts, and Evolutionary Listening* (Middletown, CT: Wesleyan University Press, 2018), 1–3, 17–19.

86. On how child prodigies discomfit spectators, see Carolyn Abbate, *In Search of Opera* (Princeton, NJ: Princeton University Press, 2001), 198.

87. See Jay Geller, "The Aromatics of Jewish Difference; or, Benjamin's Allegory of Aura," in *Jews and Other Differences: The New Jewish Cultural Studies*, edited by Jonathan Boyarin and Daniel Boyarin (Minneapolis: University of Minnesota Press, 1997), 203–56; and Steven Weitzman, "Mimic Jews and Jewish Mimics in Antiquity: A Non-Girardian Approach to Mimetic Rivalry," *Journal of the American Academy of Religion* 77 (2009), 922–40.

88. For a critique of savant stereotypes, see Joseph Straus, "Idiots Savants, Retarded Savants, Talented Aments, Mono-Savants, Autistic Savants, Just Plain Savants, People with Savant Syndrome, and Autistic People Who Are Good at Things: A View from Disability Studies," *Disability Studies Quarterly* 34 (2014), http://dsq-sds.org/article/view/3407/3640; see also Arnie Cox, "Embodying Music: Principles of the Mimetic Hypothesis," *Music Theory Online* 17 (2011), http://www.mtosmt.org/issues/mto.11.17.2/mto.11.17.2.cox.html; and Blake Howe and Stephanie Jensen-Moulton, "Introduction: On the Disability Aesthetics of Music," *Journal of the American Musicological Society* 69 (2016), 525–30.

89. Jessica Holmes, "Expert Listening beyond the Limits of Hearing: Music and Deafness," *Journal of the American Musicological Society* 70 (2017), 173. See also Jeannette DiBernardo Jones, "Imagined Hearing: Music-Making in Deaf Culture," in *The Oxford Handbook of Music and Disability Studies*, edited by Blake Howe, Stephanie

Jensen-Moulton, Neil Lerner, and Joseph Straus (New York: Oxford University Press, 2016), 54–72; and Anabel Maler, "Musical Expression among Deaf and Hearing Song Signers," in *The Oxford Handbook of Music and Disability Studies*, edited by Blake Howe, Stephanie Jensen-Moulton, Neil Lerner, and Joseph Straus (New York: Oxford University Press, 2016), 73–91.

90. Grace Wang, *Soundtracks of Asian America: Navigating Race through Musical Performance* (Durham, NC: Duke University Press, 2015), 65. As Mina Yang likewise notes: "Asians have the technique, Westerners have the heart, the soul. The image of Asians as automatons, robots without souls, appears frequently in the Western imagination, standing in as an effigy conjured up by the Western resentment of Asia's growing prosperity" ("East Meets West in the Concert Hall: Asians and Classical Music in the Century of Imperialism, Post-Colonialism, and Multiculturalism," *Asian Music* 38 [2007], 14).

91. This isn't to say that musical mimesis is an *a priori* subhuman skill set, but rather that representations of musical ability as *merely* mimetic tend to oversimplify the performative, affective, and social capabilities in play. See, for example, Manolete Mora, *Myth, Mimesis and Magic in the Music of the T'boli, Philippines* (Quezon City: Ateneo de Manila University Press, 2005).

92. Literary scholar Colleen Glenney Boggs lays out the fallacy as follows: "One has rights by virtue of being human, and one is human by virtue of having rights. By that definition, animals lack rights because they are animals, but all too easily, those who lack rights, such as the abused detainees [in Abu Ghraib], are animalized" ("American Bestiality: Sex, Animals, and the Construction of Subjectivity," *Cultural Critique* 76 [2010], 99).

93. On the human rights framework, see Nancy Glass, Jacquelyn Campbell, Veronica Njie-Carr, and Terri-Ann Thompson, "Ending Violence against Women: Essential to Global Health and Human Rights," in *Routledge Handbook in Global Public Health*, edited by Richard Parker and Marni Sommer (New York: Routledge, 2011), 236–43.

94. Austin Sarat and Thomas R. Kearns, "The Unsettled Status of Human Rights: An Introduction," in *Human Rights: Concepts, Contests, Contingencies*, edited by Austin Sarat and Thomas R. Kearns (Ann Arbor: University of Michigan Press, 2001), 2.

95. See Sonu Bedi, *Rejecting Rights* (Cambridge: Cambridge University Press, 2009); Eric Posner, *The Twilight of Human Rights Law* (New York: Oxford University Press, 2014); Slavoj Žižek, "Against an Ideology of Human Rights," in *Displacement, Asylum, Migration: The Oxford Amnesty Lectures 2004*, edited by Kate E. Tunstall (New York: Oxford University Press, 2006), 56–85; John O. Nelson, "Against Human Rights," *Philosophy* 65 (1990), 341–48; Chidi Anselm Odinkalu, "The Role of Case and Complaints Procedures in the Reform of the African Regional Human Rights System," *African Human Rights Law Journal* 1 (2001), 225–46; and Abdullahi A. An-Na'im, "The Legal Protection of Human Rights in Africa: How to Do More with Less," in *Human Rights: Concepts, Contests, Contingencies*, edited by Austin Sarat and Thomas R. Kearns (Ann Arbor: University of Michigan Press, 2001), 89–116.

96. See Robert Courtney Smith, "'Don't Let the Illegals Vote!': The Myths of Illegal Latino Voters and Voter Fraud in Contested Local Immigrant Integration," *Russell Sage Foundation Journal of the Social Sciences* 3 (2017), 148–75.

97. Lynn Hunt, *Inventing Human Rights: A History* (New York: W. W. Norton, 2007), 19–20.

98. Scholars, humanitarians, and politicians continue to disagree over not just the terms of international human rights instruments, but also the usefulness of these global(ized) treatises in the first place. As legal scholar Eric Posner points out, "the use of 'human rights' in English-speaking books has increased 200-fold since 1940, and is used today 100 times more often than terms such as 'constitutional rights' and 'natural rights'" (*Twilight of Human Rights Law*, 6). Despite this uptick in human rights discourse (in formal documents as well as everyday parlance), cautions Posner, human rights violations have *not* commensurately diminished.

99. A knowledge *of* human rights language, to be sure, can hurt as easily as it can help. As a common yet insidious example, if you're a black or brown person and your vehicle is pulled over by a cop, you could say, "I know my rights." Stating this is indeed within your legal rights. Yet the statement is no guarantee that you will be treated justly; the defiant utterance might even anger and incite retaliatory actions from the police officer. See NAACP, "Know Your Rights: What to Do If You're Stopped by the Police," available at http://action.naacp.org/page/-/Criminal%20Justice/Racial_Profiling_Know_Your_Rights_Supplement_6-12-12.pdf.

100. See Suzanne Cusick, "Musicology, Torture, Repair," *Radical Musicology* 3 (2008), http://www.radical-musicology.org.uk/2008/Cusick.htm; and Marie Thompson, *Beyond Unwanted Sound: Noise, Affect and Aesthetic Moralism* (New York: Bloomsbury Academic, 2017), 1–3.

101. Susan Brison, *Aftermath: Violence and the Remaking of a Self* (Princeton, NJ: Princeton University Press, 2002), 86, 89; and Shirli Gilbert, *Music in the Holocaust: Confronting Life in the Nazi Ghettos and Camps* (New York: Oxford University Press, 2005), 5.

102. Marion Guck, "Music Loving, or the Relationship with the Piece," *Music Theory Online* 2 (1996), http://www.mtosmt.org/issues/mto.96.2.2/mto.96.2.2.guck.html, par. 7. See also Marion Guck, "A Woman's (Theoretical) Work," *Perspectives of New Music* 32 (1994), 28–43; Vivian Luong, "Rethinking Music Loving," *Music Theory Online* 23 (2017), http://mtosmt.org/issues/mto.17.23.2/mto.17.23.2.luong.html; and Terry Castle, *The Apparitional Lesbian: Female Homosexuality and Modern Culture* (New York: Columbia University Press, 1993), 200–38. Castle's first and final sentences in the chapter on Fassbaender reveal a lot: "To 'come out' as the fan of a great diva is always an embarrassing proposition—as difficult in its own way, perhaps, as coming out as a homosexual. [. . .] If I have, however crudely, inspired a desire to hear, or hear again, the singing of Brigitte Fassbaender, I am glad: in the presence of such brave and tender artistry, there is nothing in the end to fear, and much—oh, so very much—to love" (200, 238).

103. For examples of case studies and anecdotes about ethical dilemmas in musicology and ethnomusicology, see Kay Kaufman Shelemay, "The Impact and Ethics

of Musical Scholarship," in *Rethinking Music*, edited by Nicholas Cook and Mark Everist (New York: Oxford University Press, 1999), 531–44; Theodore Levin, with Valentina Süzükei, *Where Rivers and Mountains Sing: Sound, Music, and Nomadism in Tuva and Beyond* (Bloomington: Indiana University Press, 2006), 41–44; Anthony Seeger, "Theories Forged in the Crucible of Action: The Joys, Dangers, and Potentials of Advocacy and Fieldwork," in *Shadows in the Field: New Perspectives for Fieldwork in Ethnomusicology*, second edition, edited by Gregory Barz and Timothy J. Cooley (New York: Oxford University Press, 2008), 271–88; and Andrew Dell'Antonio and Elizabeth J. Grace, "No Musicking about Us without Us!" *Journal of the American Musicological Society* 69 (2016), 553–59.

104. See Yang, *Planet Beethoven*, 1–4, 145–65; Geoffrey Baker, *El Sistema: Orchestrating Venezuela's Youth* (New York: Oxford University Press, 2014); Robert Fink, "Resurrection Symphony: El Sistema as Ideology in Venezuela and Los Angeles," *Action, Criticism, and Theory for Music Education* 15 (2016), 33–56; Yana Stainova, "Musical Slums: Playing for Your Life in Venezuela's El Sistema," *ReVista: Harvard Review of Latin America* (Winter 2016), http://revista.drclas.harvard.edu/book/musical-slums; Elena dell'Agnese, "'Welcome to Tijuana': Popular Music on the US-Mexico Border," *Geopolitics* 20 (2015), 171–92; Yang, "East Meets West," 18–22; "The Day the Music Died: China Blacklists 120 Songs for 'Morality' Violations," *Wall Street Journal* (12 August 2015), http://blogs.wsj.com/chinarealtime/2015/08/12/the-day-the-music-died-china-blacklists-120-songs-for-morality-violations; David Howes, "'We Are the World' and Its Counterparts: Popular Song as Constitutional Discourse," *International Journal of Politics, Culture, and Society* 3 (1990), 315–39; Esteban Buch, *Beethoven's Ninth: A Political History*, translated by Richard Miller (Chicago: University of Chicago Press, 2003); Alexander Rehding, *Beethoven's Symphony No. 9* (New York: Oxford University Press, 2018); Michael G. Mauskapf, "Enduring Crisis, Ensuring Survival: Artistry, Economics, and the American Symphony Orchestra" (PhD diss., University of Michigan, 2012), 193–247; Chuck Philips, "Gangsta Rap: Did Lyrics Inspire Killing of Police?," *Los Angeles Times* (17 October 1994), http://articles.latimes.com/1994-10-17/entertainment/ca-51308_1_police-officer; and Robert Wright, "'I'd Sell You Suicide': Pop Music and Moral Panic in the Age of Marilyn Manson," *Popular Music* 19 (2000), 365–85. Another important case pertaining to music-incited violence is the trial of singer-songwriter Simon Bikindi, who was charged with (among other items) public incitement to commit genocide. See Jason McCoy, "Making Violence Ordinary: Radio, Music and the Rwandan Genocide," *African Music* 8 (2009), 85–96; and Susan Benesch, "Inciting Genocide, Pleading Free Speech," *World Policy Journal* 21 (2004), 62–69. With thanks to Ted Levin for introducing me to this case.

105. See Fred Everett Maus, "Masculine Discourse in Music Theory," *Perspectives of New Music* 31 (1993), 264–93; Elisabeth Le Guin, *Boccherini's Body: An Essay in Carnal Musicology* (Berkeley: University of California Press, 2006); and Straus, *Extraordinary Measures*.

106. Examples of scholars writing (obliquely, dreamily, passionately, critically) about loving music—and about the wisdoms and quandaries such love can bring—include

Michael Steinberg and Larry Rothe, *For the Love of Music: Invitations to Listening* (New York: Oxford University Press, 2006); Suzanne Cusick, "On a Lesbian Relationship with Music: A Serious Effort Not to Think Straight," in *Queering the Pitch: The New Gay and Lesbian Musicology*, second edition, edited by Philip Brett, Elizabeth Wood, and Gary C. Thomas (New York: Routledge, 2006), 67–84; Wayne Koestenbaum, *The Queen's Throat: Opera, Homosexuality, and the Mystery of Desire* (New York: Poseidon Press, 1993); Mitchell Morris, "Reading as an Opera Queen," in *Musicology and Difference: Gender and Sexuality in Music Scholarship*, edited by Ruth A. Solie (Berkeley: University of California Press, 1993), 184–200; Monica B. Pearl, "The Opera Closet: Ardor, Shame, Queer Confessions," *Prose Studies* 37 (2015), 46–65; Judith Peraino, *Giving Voice to Love: Song and Self-Expression from the Troubadours to Guillaume de Machaut* (New York: Oxford University Press, 2011); Elisabeth Le Guin, "One Bar in Eight: Debussy and the Death of Description," in *Beyond Structural Listening? Postmodern Modes of Hearing*, edited by Andrew Dell'Antonio (Berkeley: University of California Press, 2004), 233–51; Kay Kaufman Shelemay, *A Song of Longing: An Ethiopian Journey* (Urbana: University of Illinois Press, 1991); and Scott Burnham, *Mozart's Grace* (Princeton, NJ: Princeton University Press, 2013); cf. James Q. Davies, "On Being Moved/Against Objectivity," *Representations* 132 (2015), 79–87. On Roland Barthes's ideas of (close) reading as loving, see Barbara Engh, "Loving It: Music and Criticism in Roland Barthes," in *Musicology and Difference: Gender and Sexuality in Music Scholarship*, edited by Ruth A. Solie (Berkeley: University of California Press, 1993), 66–79; and Mitchell Morris, "On Gaily Reading Music," *repercussions* 1 (1992), 48–64. See also Daniel J. Levitin, *The World in Six Songs: How the Musical Brain Created Human Nature* (New York: Dutton, 2008), 229–89; Matthew Del Novo, *Art Music: Love, Listening, and Soulfulness* (New Brunswick, NJ: Transaction Publishers, 2013), 125–49; and John Powell, *Why You Love Music: From Mozart to Metallica—the Emotional Power of Beautiful Sounds* (New York: Little, Brown and Company, 2016), 214–30.

107. See William Cheng, *Just Vibrations: The Purpose of Sounding Good* (Ann Arbor: University of Michigan Press, 2016), 20–36.

108. William Cheng, "I'm a Musician Who Can't Play Music Anymore. I Feel Like I'm Letting My Heroes Down," *Washington Post* (20 January 2016), http://www.washingtonpost.com/posteverything/wp/2016/01/20/im-a-musician-who-cant-play-music-anymore-i-feel-like-im-letting-my-heroes-down/?utm_term=.0d98d63c8576.

Chapter 2

1. Norton Juster, *The Phantom Tollbooth* (New York: Yearling, 1961), 117–18.

2. The Pulitzer citation stated: "Gene Weingarten of *The Washington Post*. For his chronicling of a world-class violinist who, as an experiment, played beautiful music in a subway station filled with unheeding commuters" (*Pulitzer Prizes* [7 April 2008], http://www.pulitzer.org/winners/gene-weingarten).

3. Gene Weingarten, "Pearls before Breakfast: Can One of the Nation's Great Musicians Cut through the Fog of a D.C. Rush Hour? Let's Find Out," *Washington Post* (8 April 2007), http://www.washingtonpost.com/lifestyle/magazine/pearls-before-breakfast-can-one-of-the-nations-great-musicians-cut-through-the-fog-of-a-dc-rush-hour-lets-find-out/2014/09/23/8a6d46da-4331-11e4-b47c-f5889e061e5f_story.html.

4. Weingarten, "Pearls before Breakfast."

5. Weingarten, "Pearls before Breakfast," italics added.

6. Weingarten, "Pearls before Breakfast."

7. Philip Trapp, "Violinist Joshua Bell Talks Viral Video Fame, New Album and Shares Exclusive Playlist," *Music Times* (26 June 2016), http://www.musictimes.com/articles/71382/20160626/joshua-bell-violinist-viral-video-new-album-exclusive-playlist-subway.htm.

8. Kojo Nnamdi, "A Washington Original: Gene Weingarten," *WAMU* (30 December 2010),http://thekojonnamdishow.org/shows/2010-12-30/washington-original-gene-weingarten- rebroadcast.

9. Weingarten, "Pearls before Breakfast."

10. Specifically, Weingarten recounts how "*Interview* magazine once said [Bell's] playing 'does nothing less than tell human beings why they bother to live,'" and how when "composer John Corigliano accepted the Oscar for Best Original Dramatic Score [for *The Red Violin*], he credited Bell, who, he said, 'plays like a god'" (Weingarten, "Pearls before Breakfast").

11. Gene Weingarten, "Too Busy to Stop and Hear the Music," *Post Magazine* (9 April 2007), http://www.washingtonpost.com/wp-dyn/content/discussion/2007/04/06/DI2007040601228.html.

12. For analyses of comparable admissions and exhibitions of tearfulness in musical contexts (via discourses of gender, masculinity, confession, and performativity), see Suzanne Cusick, "'There Was Not One Lady Who Failed to Shed a Tear': Arianna's Lament and the Construction of Modern Womanhood," *Early Music* 22 (1994), 21–41; James H. Johnson, *Listening in Paris: A Cultural History* (Berkeley: University of California Press, 1996), 53–68; and Kira Thurman, "Singing the Civilizing Mission in the Land of Bach, Beethoven, and Brahms: The Fisk Jubilee Singers in Nineteenth-Century Germany," *Journal of World History* 27 (2016), 443–71.

13. Gene Weingarten, "Too Busy." Implicit in this person's voluntary list of identifications is that adult men who work in DC and vote Republican don't cry. I've written elsewhere about the curious phenomenon of men (in Internet forums) confessing to crying in response to music, while also gratuitously announcing they are crying *despite* being men—a humble brag about vulnerability as masculinity (see William Cheng, *Sound Play: Video Games and the Musical Imagination* [New York: Oxford University Press, 2014], 57–92). See also Patrick R. Miller, "The Emotional Citizen: Emotion as a Function of Political Sophistication," *Political Psychology* 32 (2011), 575–600.

14. Weingarten, "Too Busy."

15. Weingarten, "Too Busy."

16. Weingarten, "Too Busy."

17. Laurie Niles, "Joshua Bell: The Man with the Violin," *Violinist* (21 January 2017), http://www.violinist.com/blog/laurie/20172/20998.

18. Trapp, "Violinist Joshua Bell." By the time this June 2016 interview aired, it had actually been nine and a half years—not merely eight—since the January 2007 experiment.

19. Gene Weingarten, "Setting the Record Straight on the Joshua Bell Experiment," *Washington Post* (14 October 2014), http://www.washingtonpost.com/news/style/wp/2014/10/14/gene-weingarten-setting-the-record-straight-on-the-joshua-bell-experiment/?utm_term=.167728785d98.

20. Weingarten, "Setting the Record Straight."

21. Bob Faw, "Joshua Bell," *PBS* (10 October 2014), http://www.pbs.org/wnet/religionandethics/2014/10/10/october-10-2014-joshua-bell/24323. Bell elaborated: "There is no other explanation for [Bach's] music. For me music has been in a sense my religion, and it is what brings me closest to God or truth or whatever you want to call it."

22. Tessa Berenson, "World-Famous Violinist Joshua Bell Performs in Union Station," *TIME* (30 September 2014), http://time.com/3450389/violinist-joshua-bell-performs-in-union-station.

23. Jessica Contrera, "Joshua Bell's Metro Encore Draws a Crowd," *Washington Post* (30 September 2014), http://www.washingtonpost.com/lifestyle/style/joshua-bells-metro-encore-draws-a-crowd/2014/09/30/c28b6c50-48d5-11e4-a046-120a8a855cca_story.html?utm_term=.4972e5b14b13.

24. Kathy Stinson and Dušan Petričić, *The Man with the Violin* (Toronto, ON: Annick Press, 2013).

25. Taruskin, "The Musical Mystique."

26. Taruskin, "The Musical Mystique."

27. Taruskin, "The Musical Mystique."

28. Taruskin, "The Musical Mystique."

29. Audience member, colloquium at UNC Chapel Hill (21 April 2017).

30. Anonymous reader report, Oxford University Press.

31. Anonymous reader report, National Endowment for the Humanities.

32. Taruskin, "The Musical Mystique," emphasis added.

33. Weingarten, "Pearls before Breakfast."

34. Critiquing the fetishisms of universals in the music academy, James Currie declares that "too overbearing a sense of certainty and identification with how a musicological project can function politically threatens to delimit severely what musicologists will let themselves see; through an over-insistence on telling us how we should respond, it may even circumscribe the possibility of being taken unawares by something in the music that might be politically *more* effective" ("Music after All," *Journal of the American Musicological Society* 62 [2009], 197, emphasis in original).

35. With the vigor of a play-by-play sportscaster, Bruno Latour articulates the one-upmanship of critique as follows: "Do you see now why it feels so good to be a critical mind? You are always right! When naïve believers are clinging forcefully to their objects, claiming that they are made to do things because of their gods, their poetry, their cherished objects, you can turn all of those attachments into so many fetishes

and humiliate all the believers by showing that it is nothing but their own projection, that you, yes you alone, can see. But as soon as naïve believers are thus inflated by some belief in their own importance, in their own projective capacity, you strike them by a second uppercut and humiliate them again, this time by showing that, whatever they think, their behavior is entirely determined by the action of powerful causalities coming from objective reality they don't see, but that you, yes you, the never sleeping critic, alone can see" ("Why Has Critique Run Out of Steam? From Matters of Fact to Matters of Concern," *Critical Inquiry* 30 [2004], 238–39).

36. See Joan Stambaugh, "Music as a Temporal Form," *Journal of Philosophy* 61 (1964), 265–80; and Estelle Ruth Jorgensen, *The Art of Teaching Music* (Bloomington: Indiana University Press, 2008), 126; cf. John Powell, "What Is Temporal Art? A Persistent Question Revisited," *Contemporary Aesthetics* 13 (2015), http://hdl.handle.net/2027/spo.7523862.0013.009.

37. On resisting neoliberal haste, see Maggie Berg and Barbara K. Seeber, *The Slow Professor: Challenging the Culture of Speed in the Academy* (Toronto, ON: University of Toronto Press, 2016); and Margaret Price, *Mad at School: Rhetorics of Mental Disability and Academic Life* (Ann Arbor: University of Michigan Press, 2011).

38. "Person of the Year: You," *TIME* (25 December 2006), http://content.time.com/time/covers/0,16641,20061225,00.html. Runners-up were Mahmoud Ahmadinejad, Hu Jintao, Kim Jong-il, and James Baker.

39. See Carol Vernallis, "Accelerated Aesthetics: A New Lexicon of Time, Space, and Rhythm," in *The Oxford Handbook of Sound and Image in Digital Media*, edited by Carol Vernallis, Amy Herzog, and John Richardson (New York: Oxford University Press, 2013), 707–31. On the acceleration of humor (via the metric of jokes or laughs per minute, LPM) in television comedies, see Ken Jennings, *Planet Funny: How Comedy Took Over Our Culture* (New York: Simon & Schuster, 2018), 77–78; with thanks to Linda Shaver-Gleason for introducing me to this book.

40. Weingarten, "Pearls before Breakfast."

41. Weingarten, "Pearls before Breakfast."

42. Arguing about what something is or is not "about," as some philosophers and linguists point out, necessarily bears a political charge, affirming or denying the topical priorities, affordances, and attachments in play. See Stephen Yablo, *Aboutness* (Princeton, NJ: Princeton University Press, 2014).

43. On poverty porn and poverty tourism, see Kyle Powys Whyte, Evan Selinger, and Kevin Outterson, "Poverty Tourism and the Problem of Consent," *Journal of Global Ethics* 7 (2011), 337–48; and Eveline Dürr and Rivke Jaffe, "Theorizing Slum Tourism: Performing, Negotiating and Transforming Inequality," *European Review of Latin American and Caribbean Studies* 93 (2012), 113–23.

44. See Susan Schweik, *The Ugly Laws: Disability in Public* (New York: New York University Press, 2010). And as Rosemarie Garland-Thomson writes: "If there was no danger that one's eyes would be drawn to such sights, there would be no need for the law. Ugly laws aid ladies and gentlemen in the job of monitoring their own impulses and bodily functions by preventing them from embarrassing evidence of their own visual stimulation. [. . .] The worry is that our capacity to turn away from such sights

is not secure enough that we can resist the temptation to violate the American social code against staring. Like anti-prostitution laws, ugly laws are intended to save us from ourselves" (*Staring: How We Look* [New York: Oxford University Press, 2009], 73).

45. See Garland-Thomson, *Staring*, 5–6.

46. For a critique of how institutions capitalize on the presumed welfare of children (actual and hypothetical) as alibis, shields, and failsafes for harmful social policies, see Lee Edelman, *No Future: Queer Theory and the Death Drive* (Durham, NC: Duke University Press, 2004).

47. "Commuter Concerto Helps Writer Net Pulitzer," NPR (7 April 2008), http://www.npr.org/templates/story/story.php?storyId=89443778.

48. See Mike Larkin, "Spend It like Beckham!," *Daily Mail* (17 September 2011), http://www.dailymail.co.uk/tvshowbiz/article-2038408/David-Beckham-goes-undercover-Target-sell-aftershave-Ellen-DeGeneres.html; and "Tyra Banks Experiences Obesity through Fat Suit," ABC (4 November 2005), http://abcnews.go.com/GMA/BeautySecrets/story?id=1280787. See also Kiri Blakeley, "Stop with the Stupid Fat Suit Experiments, Please," *Forbes* (26 October 2011), http://www.forbes.com/sites/kiriblakeley/2011/10/26/stop-with-the-stupid-fat-suit-experiments-please; Nicole Eggenberger, "Kim Kardashian Wears Bad Fake Teeth, Frizzy Wigs on Celebrities Undercover," *US Magazine* (19 March 2014), http://www.usmagazine.com/entertainment/news/kim-kardashian-bad-fake-teeth-frizzy-wig-celebrities-undercover-2014193; and Daniel Kreps, "Watch Disguised Adele Prank Adele Impersonators," *Rolling Stone* (21 November 2015), http://www.rollingstone.com/music/news/watch-disguised-adele-prank-adele-impersonators-20151121.

49. Other cases of famous musicians performing undercover include Brandy, who sang in a subway car to little avail; Erykah Badu, who earned $3.60 busking anonymously in New York; and Sting, who made £40 busking in a London Tube station. See Bobbie Whiteman, "'Can a Sistah Get One Fan?' Brandy Goes Incognito as She Belts Out a Song in a New York Subway Car . . . and Everyone Ignores Her," *Daily Mail* (14 July 2015), http://www.dailymail.co.uk/tvshowbiz/article-3161312/Brandy-goes-incognito-belts-song-New-York-subway-car-ignores-her.html; Jen Carlson, "Erykah Badu Made $3.60 Busking in Times Square," *Gothamist* (15 October 2014), http://gothamist.com/2014/10/15/video_erykah_badu_made_360_busking.php; and "Sting Busked to Improve Confidence," *Irish Examiner* (1 May 2005), http://www.irishexaminer.com/breakingnews/entertainment/sting-busked-to-improve-confidence-200567.html.

50. "Joshua Bell's 'Voice of the Violin,'" NPR (11 April 2007), http://www.npr.org/templates/story/story.php?storyId=9528118.

51. See Susan Schweik, "Begging the Question: Disability, Mendicancy, Speech and the Law," *Narrative* 15 (2007), 58–70; and Sunny Taylor, "The Right Not to Work: Power and Disability," *Monthly Review* 55 (2004), http://monthlyreview.org/2004/03/01/the-right-not-to-work-power-and-disability.

52. Stuart Varney stated: "The image we have of poor people as starving and living in squalor really is not accurate. Many of them have things; what they lack is the

richness of spirit" (quoted in Jeremy Holden, "Finding Just Enough Food to Not Be Poor Enough," *Truthout* [1 February 2012], http://truthout.org/articles/finding-just-enough-food-to-not-be-poor-enough). Ben Carson, U.S. Secretary of Housing and Urban Development, likewise once declared: "I think poverty to a large extent is also a state of mind. You take somebody who has the right mindset. You can take everything from them and put them on the street, and I guarantee you, in a little while, they'll be right back up there. And you take somebody with the wrong mindset. You can give them everything in the world—they'll work their way back down to the bottom" (quoted in Jose A. DelReal, "Ben Carson Calls Poverty 'A State of Mind' during Interview," *Washington Post* [24 May 2017], http://www.washingtonpost.com/news/post-politics/wp/2017/05/24/ben-carson-calls-poverty-a-state-of-mind-during-interview/?utm_term=.687600080f74). See also Alisa Tanaka, "Dear Scott Hamilton: A Bad Attitude Is Not the Only Disability," *The Mighty* (27 June 2016), http://themighty.com/2016/06/dear-scott-hamilton-a-bad-attitude-is-not-the-only-disability.

53. Rosemarie Garland-Thomson, *Extraordinary Bodies: Figuring Physical Disability in American Culture and Literature* (New York: Columbia University Press, 1997), 46–47. Garland-Thomson continues: "As modernization proceeded, the disabled figure shouldered in new ways society's anxiety about its inability to retain the status and old meanings of labor in the face of industrialization and increasing economic and social chaos. American individualism is most clearly manifest in the conviction that economic autonomy results from hard work and virtue, while poverty stems from indolence and moral inferiority" (47).

54. David Mitchell and Sharon Snyder, *The Biopolitics of Disability: Neoliberalism, Ablenationalism, and Peripheral Embodiment* (Ann Arbor: University of Michigan Press, 2015), 211.

55. Mitchell and Snyder, *Biopolitics of Disability*, 14. See also Jasbir Puar, *Terrorist Assemblages: Homonationalism in Queer Times* (Durham, NC: Duke University Press, 2007), 1–36.

56. On the neoliberal co-optation of "diversity," see Sara Ahmed, *On Being Included: Racism and Diversity in Institutional Life* (Durham, NC: Duke University Press, 2012); and Jeff Chang, *We Gon' Be Alright: Notes on Race and Resegregation* (New York: Picador, 2016).

57. Eliza Murphy, "Homeless Man Plays Piano So Beautifully It Might Earn Him a Job," ABC News (1 July 2015), http://abcnews.go.com/Lifestyle/homeless-man-plays-piano-beautifully-earn-job/story?id=32166650. The lyrics of Styx's 1977 hit song "Come Sail Away" yearn for lost dreams, past lives, and salvation through faith—an apt thematization of the circumstances of the pianist, David Gould (thus appealing all the more to Gould's fans).

58. "Sarasota Keys Return to Downtown," *Arts and Cultural Alliance* (18 January 2016), http://www.sarasotaarts.org/community/sarasotakeys.

59. Adam Cellini, "Homeless Musician Finds Receptive Audience on Streets of Sarasota," ABC News (30 June 2015), http://www.mysuncoast.com/entertainment/news/featured/homeless-musician-finds-receptive-audience-on-streets-of-sarasota/article_ddaf749a-1f6c-11e5-9f44-03eeab4 adabb.html.

60. Melanie Michael, "Homeless Piano Man Gets Recording Contract, Asks Jimmy Fallon for a Duet," WFLA (10 May 2016), http://wfla.com/2016/05/10/homeless-piano-man-gets-recording-contract-asks-jimmy-fallon-for-a-duet. See also "Donald Gould One Year After Being Discovered on the Streets of Downtown Sarasota," ABC 7 Sarasota (5 May 2016), http://www.youtube.com/watch?v=Qxi4AxaWnE0.

61. Ted Williams is another example of someone who went from homeless to famous through others' discovery of his "golden voice"—in this case, a baritone and broadcast-friendly *speaking* voice (for radio, commercials, and announcements). See Ted Williams, with Bret Witter, *A Golden Voice: How Faith, Hard Work, and Humility Brought Me from the Streets to Salvation* (New York: Gotham Books, 2012). For an analysis of a composer who "was careful to use the aura granted by his hoboing to construct his image as an outsider correcting societal and musical ills," see S. Andrew Granade, *Harry Partch: Hobo Composer* (Rochester, NY: University of Rochester Press, 2014), 2. On busking and street performers, see Lily E. Hirsch, "'Playing for Change': Peace, Universality, and the Street Performer," *American Music* 28 (2010), 346–67; Joseph Williams, "Busking in Musical Thought: Value, Affect, and Becoming," *Journal of Musicological Research* 35 (2016), 142–55; and William Boyer, "Public Hearings: Sonic Encounters and Social Responsibility in the New York City Subway Systems" (PhD diss., New York University, 2014). See also Robert R. Desjarlais, *Shelter Blues: Sanity and Selfhood among the Homeless* (Philadelphia: University of Pennsylvania Press, 1997); and Teresa Gowan, *Hobos, Hustlers, and Backsliders: Homeless in San Francisco* (Minneapolis: University of Minnesota Press, 2010).

62. See "Sarasota Homeless Man Plays National Anthem at NFL Game," YouTube (15 September 2015), http://www.youtube.com/watch?v=Oasd_AStets.

63. On the "noble savage" and the fetish of musical amateurism, see Meizel, *Idolized*, 30–31. See also Laurie Stras, "The Organ of the Soul: Voice, Damage, and Affect," in *Sounding Off: Theorizing Disability in Music*, edited by Neil Lerner and Joseph N. Straus (New York: Routledge, 2006), 173–84; and Alex S. Porco, "Throw Yo' Voice Out: Disability as a Desirable Practice in Hip-Hop Vocal Performance," *Disability Studies Quarterly* 34 (2014), http://dsq-sds.org/article/view/3822/3790.

64. See "Homeless Man Stuns Passersby by Playing Styx's 'Come Sail Away' on Street Piano," *Bored Panda* (2016), http://www.boredpanda.com/homeless-man-plays-piano-styx-come-sail-away-donald-gould-sarasota-keys; and "Watch Heart-Stopping Moment Homeless 'Piano Man' Performs National Anthem at Football Game," *Inside Edition* (15 September 2015), http://www.insideedition.com/headlines/11920-watch-heart-stopping-moment-homeless-piano-man-performs-national-anthem-at-football-game.

65. See Jan Grue, *Disability and Discourse Analysis* (New York: Routledge, 2015), 118; Samantha Bassler, "'But You Don't Look Sick': Dismodernism, Disability Studies and Music Therapy on Invisible Illness and the Unstable Body," *Voices: A World Forum for Music Therapy* 14 (2014), http://voices.no/index.php/voices/article/view/802/668; and Angie the Antitheist, "Athletic Inspiration Porn Is No Excuse to Shame Me for My Disability," *Everyday Feminism* (13 May 2016), http://everydayfeminism.com/2016/05/disability-inspiration-porn.

66. Marc Rice, "Paralympics Ad Campaign: 'What's Your Excuse?,'" *Associated Press* (13 July 1995), http://apnews.com/2c4450efb1493657768b75efedd93d4d.

67. Caitlin Keating, "Homeless Piano Prodigy Lands Recording Contract, Asks Jimmy Fallon for a Duet: 'I Never Saw Anything like This Ever Happening,'" *People* (17 May 2016), http://people.com/celebrity/homeless-piano-prodigy-gets-recording-contract-asks-jimmy-fallon-for-a-duet.

68. Through predeployment "resilience training," veterans have been urged to buck up and to manage post-service life in self-sufficient terms (so as to minimize their requests for governmental aid).

69. See Jean Calterone Williams, "The Politics of Homelessness: Shelter Now and Political Protest," *Political Research Quarterly* 58 (2005), 497–509; and Barrett A. Lee, Sue Hinze Jones, and David W. Lewis, "Public Beliefs about the Causes of Homelessness," *Social Forces* 69 (1990), 253–65.

70. Images in Figure 2.2 come from "Homeless Piano Man Wows Internet," YouTube (1 July 2015), http://www.youtube.com/watch?v=ER0IKu86qNI; and "Homeless Veteran Plays National Anthem at NFL Game," *Wounded Times* (16 September 2015), http://www.combatptsdwoundedtimes.org/2015/09/florida-piano-playing-homeless-veteran.html.

71. Liz Fields, "Homeless Man's Music Moves Listeners to Tears at a Thrift Store," ABC News (1 December 2013), http://abcnews.go.com/US/homeless-mans-music-moves-listeners-tears-thrift-store/story?id=21057869.

72. Fields, "Homeless Man's Music."

73. Kimberly Yan, "Homeless Man with Amazing Voice Sings John Legend, Stuns All of Us," *Huffington Post* (1 August 2014), http://www.huffingtonpost.com/2014/08/01/homeless-man-sings-john-legend_n_5639380.html; and Beverly L. Jenkins, "Pedestrians Stop & Stare as Homeless Lady with Angelic Voice Walks down Street Singing," *Inspire More* (9 January 2018), http://www.inspiremore.com/radio-homeless-woman-singer.

74. See Matthew W. Hughey, *The White Savior Film: Content, Critics, and Consumption* (Philadelphia: Temple University Press, 2014).

75. See Lily E. Hirsch, *Music in American Crime Prevention and Punishment* (Ann Arbor: University of Michigan Press, 2012), 12–28; and Jonathan Sterne, "Sounds Like the Mall of America: Programmed Music and the Architectonics of Commercial Spaces," *Ethnomusicology* 41 (1997), 22–50.

76. See Sarah Johnsen, Suzanne Fitzpatrick, and Beth Watts, "Homelessness and Social Control: A Typology," *Housing Studies* (2018), 1–21.

77. Robert Rosenberger, "How Cities Use Design to Drive Homeless People Away," *Atlantic* (19 June 2014), http://www.theatlantic.com/business/archive/2014/06/how-cities-use-design-to-drive-homeless-people-away/373067.

78. Diane Taylor, "Homeless People Demand M&S Apology over Deterrent Alarm," *Guardian* (26 July 2017), http://www.theguardian.com/society/2017/jul/26/homeless-people-demand-ms-apology-over-deterrent-alarm.

79. Images in Figure 2.3 come from Rosenberger, "How Cities Use Design."

80. Maya Angelou, "Human Family," in *The Complete Collected Poems of Maya Angelou* (New York: Random House, 1994), 225.

81. Christopher Small, *Musicking: The Meanings of Performing and Listening* (Hanover, NH: Wesleyan University Press, 1998), 9, emphasis in original.

82. Small, *Musicking*, 9, emphasis in original.

83. Small, *Musicking*, 13.

84. In a hardbound volume as beautifully and lovingly produced as the music explored therein, Stephen Wade describes the importance of finding music in everyday settings: "*The Beautiful Music All around Us* brings to life largely unheralded individuals—domestics, farm laborers, state prisoners, schoolchildren, cowboys, housewives and mothers, loggers and miners—whose music has become part of the wider American musical soundscape" (*The Beautiful Music All around Us: Field Recordings and the American Experience* [Urbana: University of Illinois Press, 2012], jacket interior).

85. Theodore Gracyk, *Listening to Popular Music: Or, How I Learned to Stop Worrying and Love Led Zeppelin* (Ann Arbor: University of Michigan Press, 2007), 5.

86. Nicholas Cook, "We Are All (Ethno)musicologists Now," in *The New (Ethno) musicologies*, edited by Henry Stobart (Lanham, MD: Scarecrow Press, 2008), 48–70.

87. See Benjamin Lee, "We're All Africans Really," *Guardian* (11 February 2016), http://www.theguardian.com/film/2016/feb/11/meryl-streep-berlin-film-festival-diversity-were-all-africans-really.

88. See Rebecca Carroll, "People Who Don't 'See Race' Are Erasing Black People and Their Contributions," *Guardian* (15 February 2016), http://www.theguardian.com/commentisfree/2016/feb/15/bill-clinton-we-are-all-mixed-race-erases-black-people.

89. Clifford Geertz, *Local Knowledge: Further Essays in Interpretive Anthropology* (New York: Basic Books, 1983), 151.

90. See Leila J. Rupp, "Everyone's Queer," *OAH Magazine of History* 20 (2006), 8–11; and Jenna Wortham, "When Everyone Can be 'Queer,' Is Anyone?," *New York Times* (12 July 2016), http://www.nytimes.com/2016/07/17/magazine/when-everyone-can-be-queer-is-anyone.html.

91. Disability scholars and activists often point out that all people will experience disability at some point in life—that is, if they live long enough. See Robert McRuer, *Crip Theory: Cultural Signs of Queerness and Disability* (New York: New York University Press, 2006), 200; and Michael Bérubé, "Afterword: If I Should Live So Long," in *Disability Studies: Enabling the Humanities*, edited by Sharon L. Snyder, Brenda Jo Brueggemann, and Rosemarie Garland-Thomson (New York: Modern Language Association of America, 2002), 337–43.

92. See N. Katherine Hayles, *How We Became Posthuman: Virtual Bodies in Cybernetics, Literature, and Informatics* (Chicago: University of Chicago Press, 1999); and Rosi Braidotti, *The Posthuman* (Cambridge: Polity Press, 2013).

93. See Gregory Feldman, *We Are All Migrants: Political Action and the Ubiquitous Condition of Migrant-hood* (Stanford, CA: Stanford University Press, 2015).

94. Video of speech available at "Michael Moore: 'We're All Muslim, All Gay, All Trans, All Queer,'" YouTube (20 January 2017), http://www.youtube.com/watch?v=nqFhc5V-TX4. See also Michael Moore, "Sign the Statement. #WeAreAllMuslim," http://michaelmoore.com/WeAreAllMuslim.

95. Image in Figure 2.4 comes from Jessica Chasmar, "Michael Moore Holds 'We Are All Muslim' Sign in Front of Trump Tower," *Washington Times* (17 December 2015), http://www.washingtontimes.com/news/2015/dec/17/michael-moore-holds-we-are-all-muslim-sign-in-fron.

96. See George Yúdice, "We Are *Not* the World," *Social Text* 31–32 (1992), 202–16.

97. On claims about music as a "universal language," see George List, "Concerning the Concept of the Universal and Music," *World of Music* 26 (1984), 40–49; Linda Shaver-Gleason, "Is Music a Universal Language?," *Not Another Music History Cliché!* (4 January 2018), http://notanothermusichistorycliche.blogspot.com/2018/01/is-music-universal-language.html; and Hoeckner, *Programming the Absolute*, 1–4. On the universal appeal of Beethoven's symphonies, Lewis Lockwood writes: "In a sense, when we listen to Beethoven now, we are all descendants of the Łódź ghetto dwellers [who performed Beethoven's music in the concentration camp]. On tragic occasions, after civic and national tragedies such as 9/11 or comparable events, we want to hear the *Eroica* and the Fifth Symphonies, and we want to gather together for the reassertion of human brotherhood that is brought home by performances of the Ninth" (*Beethoven's Symphonies*, 229–30). On music in the Polish ghettos, see Gilbert, *Music in the Holocaust*, 21–54; and Gila Flam, *Singing for Survival: Songs of the Lodz Ghetto, 1940–45* (Urbana: University of Illinois Press, 1992).

98. Gary Tomlinson, "Evolutionary Studies in the Humanities: The Case of Music," *Critical Inquiry* 39 (2013), 647; and Gary Tomlinson, *A Million Years of Music: The Emergence of Human Modernity* (New York: Zone Books, 2015), 23, emphasis in original. See also Steven Mithen, *The Singing Neanderthals: The Origins of Music, Language, Mind, and Body* (Cambridge, MA: Harvard University Press, 2006).

99. For other uses of "musicking," see Daniel Albright, *Musicking Shakespeare: A Conflict of Theatres* (Rochester, NY: University of Rochester Press, 2007); and Suzel A. Reily and Katherine Brucher, *The Routledge Companion to the Study of Local Musicking* (New York: Routledge, 2018).

100. Here is an example—from the musicological academy—of how selective exclusionism can hide in plain sight amid well-intentioned rhetorics of inclusionism. In February 2017, the American Musicological Society's Board of Directors issued a "Statement Opposing Executive Order Banning Immigrants and Refugees," which voiced opposition to President Donald Trump's calls for border entry policies that amounted to a Muslim ban: "We the Board of Directors of the American Musicological Society urgently request that the Trump administration withdraw its Executive Order of 27 January 2017 suspending entry of all refugees to the United States for 120 days, barring Syrian refugees indefinitely, and blocking entry into the United States for 90 days for citizens of seven predominantly Muslim countries: Iran, Iraq, Libya, Somalia, Sudan, Syria, and Yemen. This travel ban is inconsistent with freedom of inquiry, with basic principles of law, and with our

nation's tradition of welcoming talented individuals from all nations to study and teach in the United States" (Board of Directors of the American Musicological Society, "Statement Opposing Executive Order Banning Immigrants and Refugees," *American Musicological Society* [1 February 2017; revised 2 February 2017], http:// www.ams-net.org/AMS-condemns-executive-order.php). A colleague, Kendra Preston Leonard, shared this post on Facebook and opposed the wording of its final sentence: "Only 'talented individuals' who come here to 'study and teach'?" (1 February 2017, quoted with permission). Upon seeing Leonard's complaint, some people responded by pleading that we shouldn't quibble over a small and singular adjective (*talented*), and that such nitpicky infighting distracts us from the real Big Bads out there. Others, however, pointed out that the statement's inclusion of the qualifier *talented* embodies—even if unintentionally—the very seeds of xenophobic dogma concerning whose lives do or do not matter. "Brown non-citizen here," wrote musicologist Erika Supria Honisch under Leonard's post. "I'm not sure the tradition has actually been to invite strangers to learn from them. It's a nice idea, but (as I'm reminded every time I re-enter) I have my work visa not because Homeland Security thinks that I should become a citizen but precisely because that agency was persuaded I am a 'talented individual' whose intellectual capital is of value" (1 February 2017, quoted with permission). To its credit, the AMS Board quickly emended the statement. AMS executive director Robert Judd wrote: "Thanks to all the AMS friends who've expressed views on the recent statement from the board of directors. Since the board did not intend to suggest exclusion, they have agreed that the recommendation to remove the word 'talented' is good, and the statement has been edited accordingly." As tiny as the edit may have been, it swung the message from *welcome, if . . .* toward *welcome, all*. For critiques of lip-serviced "diversity" as the new "normal," see Lennard Davis, *The End of Normal: Identity in a Biocultural Era* (Ann Arbor: University of Michigan Press, 2013).

101. Olivia Bloechl, with Melanie Lowe, "Introduction: Rethinking Difference," in *Rethinking Difference in Music Scholarship*, edited by Olivia Bloechl, Melanie Lowe, and Jeffrey Kallberg (Cambridge: Cambridge University Press, 2015), 4. This volume pays tribute to and expands on the landmark text, Ruth Solie, ed., *Musicology and Difference: Gender and Sexuality in Music Scholarship* (Berkeley: University of California Press, 1993).

102. Kofi Agawu, *Representing African Music: Postcolonial Notes, Queries, Positions* (New York: Routledge, 2003), 168.

103. Agawu, *Representing African Music*, 64. For a critique *of* musicological critiques of essentialism, see Guthrie P. Ramsey Jr., "The Pot Liquor Principle: Developing a Black Music Criticism in American Music Studies," *Journal of Black Studies* 35 (2004), 210–23.

104. Agawu, *Representing African Music*, 67; cf. Kofi Agawu, "Tonality as a Colonizing Force in Africa," in *Audible Empire: Music, Global Politics, Critique*, edited by Ronald Radano and Tejumola Olaniyan (Durham, NC: Duke University Press, 2016), 334–55; and Martin Scherzinger, "Notes on a Postcolonial Musicology: Kofi Agawu and the Critique of Cultural Difference," *Current Musicology* 75 (2003), 223–50.

105. For an analysis of this *Animal Farm* counter-logic in neoliberal US contexts, see Linda Williamson Nelson and Maynard T. Robison, "Which Americans Are More Equal and Why: The Linguistic Construction of Inequality in America," *Race, Gender and Class* 20 (2013), 294–306.

106. Nadine Hubbs, *The Queer Composition of America's Sound: Gay Modernists, American Music, and National Identity* (Berkeley: University of California Press, 2004), 65, emphasis in original.

107. Weingarten, "Too Busy to Stop."

108. Bonnie Gordon, "What Mr. Jefferson Didn't Hear," in *Rethinking Difference in Music Scholarship*, edited by Olivia Bloechl, Melanie Lowe, and Jeffrey Kallberg (Cambridge: Cambridge University Press, 2015), 120.

109. In her autobiography, *Playing for Time* (and in a film with the same title), composer-pianist Fania Fénelon recounted how musicians in the concentration camps of Auschwitz-Birkenau were allowed to obtain dispensations in exchange for entertaining Nazi officers. Fania Fénelon with Marcelle Routier, *Sursis pour l'orchestre*, translated by Judith Landry (New York: Atheneum, 1977). For a critique of Fénelon's narrative, see Susan Eischeid, *The Truth about Fania Fénelon and the Women's Orchestra of Auschwitz-Birkenau* (London: Palgrave MacMillan, 2016); see also Kater, *Twisted Muse*, 104–5; and Lily Hirsch, *A Jewish Orchestra in Nazi Germany: Musical Politics and the Berlin Jewish Culture League* (Ann Arbor: University of Michigan Press, 2010).

110. Benjamin Harbert, unpublished interview with Bud Wilkerson (7 November 2012) at Louisiana State Penitentiary, quoted with permission. Angola inmates who participate in the penitentiary's gospel group sometimes perform for communities outside the prison walls; as Harbert points out, this is a way for Angola's administration to "[perform] reform of its prison by capitalizing on the expression of redemption in music" ("I'll Keep on Living after I Die: Musical Manipulation and Transcendence at Louisiana State Penitentiary," *International Journal of Community Music* 3 [2010], 73). Such artistic displays, in other words, may lead spectators to *overestimate* the extent to which Angola's inmates, all musicking aside, receive humane treatment and enjoy civil coexistence on a daily basis. In reality, once shuttled away from the stage or altar, these prisoners suffer chronic chaos, violence, and an 85- to 90-percent prerelease death rate. See also Melissa Schrift, "The Angola Prison Rodeo: Inmate Cowboys and Institutional Tourism," *Ethnology* 43 (2004), 331–44.

111. Chris Waller, "'Darker Than the Dungeon': Music, Ambivalence, and the Carceral Subject," *International Journal for the Semiotics of Law* 31 (2018), 277.

112. Władysław Szpilman, *The Pianist: The Extraordinary Story of One Man's Survival in Warsaw, 1939–1945*, translated by Anthea Bell (New York: Picador, 1999).

113. Kivy, "Musical Morality," 398.

114. In the film, Szpilman plays excerpts from Chopin's Ballade No. 1 for Hosenfeld instead of a Chopin nocturne.

115. For a sweeping view of "the social status and role of the musician" in Western societies, see Ivo Supičić, *Music in Society: A Guide to the Sociology of Music* (Stuyvesant, NY: Pendragon Press, 1987), 195–219.

116. See Philip Brett, "Musicality, Essentialism, and the Closet," in *Queering the Pitch: The New Gay and Lesbian Musicology*, second edition, edited by Philip Brett, Elizabeth Wood, and Gary C. Thomas (New York: Routledge, 2006), 9–26.

117. J. Martin Daughtry, *Listening to War: Sound, Music, Trauma, and Survival in Wartime Iraq* (New York: Oxford University Press, 2015), 259, emphasis in original.

118. Daughtry, *Listening to War*, 259.

119. See Patrick F. Gillham and Gary T. Marx, "Complexity and Irony in Policing and Protesting: The World Trade Organization in Seattle," *Social Justice* 27 (2000), 212–36; and Daphne Carr, "Sound Protocols: Street Medic Care for Sonic Energy Injury," paper presented at CUNY's Graduate Students in Music Conference (10 March 2017).

120. Musicians can also be targeted for their perceived cultural, political, and/or religious ideologies, as with the case of the murder of Pakistani Sufi singer Amjad Sabri. See Anastasia Tsioulcas, "Why Was a Prominent Muslim Musician Gunned Down in Pakistan?," NPR (26 June 2016), http://www.npr.org/2016/06/26/483231557/why-was-a-prominent-muslim-musician-gunned-down-in-pakistan.

121. See Alyssa Rosenberg, "Why Terrorists Attack Concert Halls," *Chicago Tribune* (24 May 2017), http://www.chicagotribune.com/news/opinion/commentary/ct-manchester-concert-terrorist-attacks-20170524-story.html.

122. Todd A, "This Will Be Our Reply to Violence," *Medium* (8 July 2016), http://medium.com/hey-todd-a/this-will-be-our-reply-to-violence-223e12fc9910.

123. Jonathan Bellman, "All Hands," *Dial M for Musicology* (29 June 2018), http://dialmformusicology.com/2018/06/29/06-29-18-all-hands, emphases in original.

124. Elaine Scarry, *On Beauty and Being Just* (Princeton, NJ: Princeton University Press, 1999), 39.

125. Scarry, *On Beauty and Being Just*, 39.

126. Scarry, *On Beauty and Being Just*, 77. Scarry explains: "Radical decentering might also be called an opiated adjacency. A beautiful thing is not the only thing in the world that can make us feel adjacent; nor is it the only thing in the world that brings a state of acute pleasure. But it appears to be one of the few phenomena in the world that brings about both simultaneously: it permits us to be adjacent while also permitting us to experience extreme pleasure, thereby creating the sense that it is our own adjacency that is pleasure-bearing. This seems a gift in its own right, and a gift as a prelude to or precondition of enjoying fair relations with others" (78–79). See also Richard Shusterman, *Pragmatist Aesthetics: Living Beauty, Rethinking Art* (Oxford: Blackwell, 1992), 139–68.

127. Barry Shank theorizes music's political powers via metaphors, analogies, and abstractions reminiscent of Scarry's bold leaps in logic (as well as the sociomusical treatises of Jacques Attali and Jean-Luc Nancy): "Musical listening brings to our awareness patterns of tension and release, a tolerance for dissonance, the pleasures of delayed resolution, the relative independence of multiple layers that twine the knots of our experience [. . .]. Music's ability to focus our attention on those patterns [. . .] encourages us to sharpen our perceptions of the intricate relations of difference that constitute our world" (*The Political Force of Musical Beauty* [Durham, NC: Duke University Press, 2014], 244).

128. Scarry, *On Beauty and Being Just*, 5.

129. Scarry, *On Beauty and Being Just*, 4, 3.

130. Geoffrey Galt Harpham, "Elaine Scarry and the Dream of Pain," *Salmagundi* 130–131 (2001), 203, 228.

131. James Oestreich, "The World According to One Musicologist," *New York Times* (15 February 2012), http://www.nytimes.com/2012/02/16/arts/music/after-the-end-of-music-history-conference-at-princeton.html.

132. Karol Berger, "The Ends of Music History, or: The Old Masters in the Supermarket of Cultures," *Journal of Musicology* 31 (2014), 198, 189, 196. For a response to Berger's article, see Richard Taruskin, "Agents and Causes and Ends, Oh My," *Journal of Musicology* 31 (2014), 272–93.

133. Berger, "Ends of Music History," 195–96; cf. Richard Leppert, "Music 'Pushed to the Edge of Existence' (Adorno, Listening, and the Question of Hope)," *Cultural Critique* 60 (2005), 92–133.

134. See María Lugones, "Playfulness, 'World' Travelling, and Loving Perception," *Hypatia* 2 (1987), 3–19; Judith Butler, *The Psychic Life of Power* (Stanford, CA: Stanford University Press, 1997); and Kelly Oliver, *Witnessing: Beyond Recognition* (Minneapolis: University of Minnesota Press, 2001), 23–49, 217–24. With thanks to an anonymous reviewer for pointing me to Oliver's work.

135. Kamala Thiagarajan, "Donald Trump Jr. Is Impressed by the 'Smile on a Face' of India's Poor," NPR (21 February 2018), http://www.npr.org/sections/goatsandsoda/2018/02/21/587604741/donald-trump-jr-is-impressed-by-the-smile-on-a-face-of-indias-poor.

136. Jay Timothy Dolmage captures the dangerous normalization of ableism (and lost cause fallacies) beautifully: "Because people say that 'of course the university is ableist'—and this form of apologia is particularly nuanced in that it releases the person who says it from doing anything at all about this ableism. There is a shift to admitting that at the very least the university is an elitist space, but it comes joined with dismissing responsibility for doing anything about this elitism, or even interrogating its fairness. So what makes it so hard for people to both admit that the university is ableist, and to admit that this is a bad thing? [. . .] There are certainly academics and other stakeholders who would say 'of course the university is racist' and leave it at that, but it is understood that this is a response that reinforces the racism. Making this racism the center of a conversation means taking responsibility for it and committing to change" (*Academic Ableism: Disability and Higher Education* [Ann Arbor: University of Michigan Press, 2017], 38).

Chapter 3

1. Georgina Kleege, *Sight Unseen* (New Haven, CT: Yale University Press, 1999), 19–20, emphasis in original.

2. See Michèle Lamont, *How Professors Think: Inside the Curious World of Academic Judgment* (Cambridge, MA: Harvard University Press, 2009), 53–106; Julie R.

Posselt, *Inside Graduate Admissions: Merit, Diversity, and Faculty Gatekeeping* (Cambridge, MA: Harvard University Press, 2016); David Gooblar, "Should We All Be Grading Blind?," *Chronicle Vitae* (4 November 2015), http://chroniclevitae.com/news/1186-should-we-all-be-grading-blind; Craig Sutton, "Why Are Low-Income High Achievers So Underrepresented at Elite Schools?," *Washington Post* (18 December 2015), http://www.washingtonpost.com/opinions/closing-the-income-gap-at-elite-colleges/2015/12/18/90f91054-a057-11e5-a3c5-c77f2cc5a43c_story.html?utm_term=.b35f9beddcaf; and Weingarten, "Pearls before Breakfast."

3. Shelley L. Tremain, *Foucault and Feminist Philosophy of Disability* (Ann Arbor: University of Michigan Press, 2017), 32. See also Jay Timothy Dolmage, "Between the Valley and the Field: Metaphor and Disability," *Prose Studies* 27 (2005), 108–19.

4. Geoff Edgers, "6 Minutes to Shine," *Boston Globe* (4 September 2005), http://archive.boston.com/news/globe/magazine/articles/2005/09/04/6_minutes_to_shine. See also Jennie Dorris, "Mike Tetreault's BSO Audition," *Boston Magazine* (July 2012), http://www.bostonmagazine.com/2012/06/boston-symphony-orchestra-audition.

5. Claudia Goldin and Cecilia Rouse, "Orchestrating Impartiality: The Impact of 'Blind' Auditions on Female Musicians," *American Economic Review* 90 (2000), 717.

6. Goldin and Rouse, "Orchestrating Impartiality," 719. See also Chia-Jung Tsay, "Sight over Sound in the Judgment of Music Performance," *PNAS* 110 (2013), 14580–85.

7. Goldin and Rouse, "Orchestrating Impartiality," 738.

8. Caroline Abels, "Symphony Auditions: Where Only the Strong Survive," *Pittsburgh Post-Gazette* (30 May 1999), http://old.post-gazette.com/magazine/19990530auditions1.asp. Abels further reports: "Some musicians in the PSO believe strongly in being able to see candidates, but others believe the screen should be up for the semifinals and finals, to prevent bias at every stage. In fact, there is a debate now within the orchestra over whether to use the screen in all rounds. [. . .] When the screen comes down for the semifinals and finals, committee members sometimes talk to candidates. [Concertmaster Andres] Cardenes told a few of them to play 'Death of Tybalt' lower in the bow, using heavier strokes. Instruction such as this gives the committee a chance to learn more about the players and see how quickly they are able to adapt. Cardenes also asked candidates the make of their violin."

9. Jane Bowyer Stewart, describing the initial blind auditions for the National Symphony Orchestra, notes how "the process arguably creates a true meritocracy. [. . .] Letters of recommendation? Rave reviews? Irrelevant. It's all about *how you play today*." Yet, as Stewart points out, "For the final round at the NSO, the Music Director arrives and the curtain comes down. The committee learns your name and even sees your résumé" ("Behind the Curtain: Auditioning for the NSO," *National Symphony Orchestra* [4 July 2016], http://nsomusicians.org/blog/2016/7/4/behind-the-curtain, emphasis in original).

10. See Abels, "Symphony Auditions"; and Christine Ammer, *Unsung: A History of Women in American Music* (Portland, OR: Amadeus Press, 2001), 258–59.

11. Goldin and Rouse, "Orchestrating Impartiality," 721. See also Marianne Bertrand and Sendhil Mullainathan, "Are Emily and Greg More Employable Than Lakisha

and Jamal? A Field Experiment on Labor Market Discrimination," *American Economic Review* 94 (2004), 991–1013; William A. Darity Jr. and Patrick L. Mason, "Evidence on Discrimination in Employment: Codes of Color, Codes of Gender," *Journal of Economic Perspectives* 12 (1998), 63–90; Curt Rice, "How Blind Auditions Help Orchestras to Eliminate Gender Bias," *Guardian* (14 October 2013), http://www.theguardian.com/women-in-leadership/2013/oct/14/blind-auditions-orchestras-gender-bias; Yassmin Abdel-Magied, "What Does My Headscarf Mean to You?," *TED* (27 May 2015), http://www.ted.com/talks/yassmin_abdel_magied_what_does_my_headscarf_mean_to_you/transcript; Claire Cain Miller, "Is Blind Hiring the Best Hiring?," *New York Times* (25 February 2016), http://www.nytimes.com/2016/02/28/magazine/is-blind-hiring-the-best-hiring.html?_r=0&mtrref=undefined&gwh=BDB31ED44DA5DE14BFAC213B2302E19D&gwt=pay; and Jonathan Marshall, "'Blind Auditions' Putting Discrimination on Center Stage," *SF Gate* (10 February 1997), http://www.sfgate.com/business/article/Blind-Auditions-Putting-Discrimination-on-2855410.php.

12. See Joseph Millum and Christine Grady, "The Ethics of Placebo-Controlled Trials: Methodological Justifications," *Contemporary Clinical Trials* 36 (2013), 510–14.

13. On the pros and cons of double-blind peer review, see Nils Petter Gleditsch, "Double-Blind but More Transparent," *Journal of Peace Research* 39 (2002), 259–62.

14. Few artists depict Justice without a blindfold. For analysis, see Gregory G. Colomb, *Designs on Truth: The Poetics of the Augustan Mock-Epic* (University Park: Pennsylvania State University Press, 1992), 50–51.

15. "Texts of the Oaths of Office for Supreme Court Justices," *Supreme Court* (Version 2014.2), http://www.supremecourt.gov/about/oath/textoftheoathsofoffice2009.aspx. See also Jeff Jacoby, "Lady Justice's Blindfold," *Boston Globe* (10 May 2009), http://archive.boston.com/bostonglobe/editorial_opinion/oped/articles/2009/05/10/lady_justices_blindfold.

16. See Brendan Koerner, "Where Did We Get Our Oath?," *Slate* (30 April 2004), http://www.slate.com/articles/news_and_politics/explainer/2004/04/where_did_we_get_our_oath.html.

17. Kleege, *Sight Unseen*, 25–26. See also Amanda Cachia, "Talking Blind: Disability, Access, and the Discursive Turn," *Disability Studies Quarterly* 33 (2013), http://dsq-sds.org/article/view/3758/3281.

18. Bill O'Reilly on *The Daily Show with Jon Stewart* (15 October 2015), http://www.cc.com/video-clips/4u4hqr/the-daily-show-with-jon-stewart-bill-o-reilly.

19. "President Barack Obama Victory Speech 2012: Election Remarks from Chicago Illinois," *YouTube* (7 November 2012), http://www.youtube.com/watch?v=ddx8t6zGWxA.

20. Beyond formal evaluations and auditions, people talk constantly about merit and meritocracy, even if they don't always use such clinical terms. Merit's near-synonyms include excellence, value, and ability, along with, as Michèle Lamont has observed (with regard to the lingo of academic reviewers), "craftsmanship," "depth," "attention to details," "soundness," "rigor," "solidity," and "quality" (*How Professors Think*, 168).

21. See Kiat-Jin Lee, "The Semiotics of Singapore's Founding Myths of Multiracialism and Meritocracy," *American Sociologist* 42 (2011), 261–75.

22. Andrea Moore has observed people's similar tendencies toward discursive normalization when it comes to neoliberal ideals of musical entrepreneurship: "Neoliberal economic programs and policies have a symbiotic relationship with the discursive processes by which their aims are 'naturalized' in public rhetoric" ("Neoliberalism and the Musical Entrepreneur," 36); cf. Dale Chapman, "The 'One-Man Band' and Entrepreneurial Selfhood in Neoliberal Culture," *Popular Music* 32 (2013), 451–70.

23. Stephen J. McNamee and Robert K. Miller Jr., *The Meritocracy Myth*, second edition (Lanham, MD: Rowman & Littlefield, 2009), 3. See also Lawrence R. Samuel, *The American Dream: A Cultural History* (Syracuse, NY: Syracuse University Press, 2012), 9–13; and Manuel Peña, *American Mythologies: Semiological Sketches* (Burlington, VT: Ashgate, 2012), 1–23.

24. Erin B. Godfrey, Carlos E. Santos, and Esther Burson, "For Better or Worse? System-Justifying Beliefs in Sixth-Grade Predict Trajectories of Self-Esteem and Behavior across Early Adolescence," *Child Development* 90 (2019), 180–95.

25. See Melinda D. Anderson, "Why the Myth of Meritocracy Hurts Kids of Color," *Atlantic* (27 July 2017), http://www.theatlantic.com/education/archive/2017/07/internalizing-the-myth-of-meritocracy/535035.

26. See Barbara Ehrenreich, *Bright-Sided: How the Relentless Promotion of Positive Thinking Has Undermined America* (New York: Metropolitan Books, 2009), 8. On films' representations of meritocracy and its discontents, see Gordon B. Arnold, *Projecting the End of the American Dream: Hollywood's Visions of U.S. Decline* (Santa Barbara, CA: Praeger, 2013), 1–19.

27. On how tautology can "function as conservative proverbs or short-hand renderings of an epic worldview defined by necessity and institutional consistency rather than turbulent change and randomness," see Paul Allen Anderson, "'The Game Is the Game': Tautology and Allegory in *The Wire*," *Criticism* 52 (2010), 375.

28. Such exhortations are often voiced in self-help books by (pre)advantaged individuals. For controversial and well-known examples, see Sheryl Sandberg, *Lean In: Women, Work, and the Will to Lead* (New York: Alfred A. Knopf, 2013); and Ivanka Trump, *Women Who Work: Rewriting the Rules for Success* (New York: Portfolio, 2017).

29. Michael Young, *The Rise of the Meritocracy, 1870–2033: An Essay on Education and Equality* (London: Thames and Hudson, 1958).

30. Michael Young, "Down with Meritocracy," *Guardian* (28 June 2011), http://www.theguardian.com/politics/2001/jun/29/comment. For analysis, see Catherine Liu, *American Idyll: Academic Antielitism as Cultural Critique* (Iowa City: University of Iowa Press, 2011), 29.

31. Amartya Sen, "Merit and Justice," in *Meritocracy and Economic Inequality*, edited by Kenneth Joseph Arrow, Samuel Bowles, and Steven N. Durlauf (Princeton, NJ: Princeton University Press, 2000), 8. Sen writes elsewhere in this essay that "meritocracy may have many virtues, but clarity is not one of them," in part because the "notion of merit is fundamentally derivative, and thus cannot but be qualified and contingent" on people's disparate views of a "good society" (5).

32. Robert H. Frank, *Success and Luck: Good Fortune and the Myth of Meritocracy* (Princeton, NJ: Princeton University Press, 2016).

33. See Richard V. Reeves, *Dream Hoarders: How the American Upper Middle Class Is Leaving Everyone Else in the Dust, Why That Is a Problem, and What to Do about It* (Washington, DC: Brookings Institution Press, 2017).

34. Michèle Lamont, *The Dignity of Working Men: Morality and the Boundaries of Race, Class, and Immigration* (Cambridge, MA: Harvard University Press, 2000). See also Thomas Piketty, *Capital in the Twenty-First Century* (Cambridge, MA: Belknap Press of Harvard University Press, 2014), 417–18; Lionel S. Lewis, *Scaling the Ivory Tower: Merit & Its Limits in Academic Careers* (New Brunswick, NJ: Transaction Publishers, 1998); and Paul Kamolnick, *The Just Meritocracy: IQ, Class Mobility, and American Social Policy* (Westport, CT: Praeger, 2005).

35. In 2014, a *New York Times* survey revealed that 64 percent of respondents believed the American Dream to be within reach, down from 71 percent in 2012, and from 81 percent in 2007 during the months prior to the stock market meltdown ("Poll Finds a More Bleak View of American Dream," *New York Times* [10 December 2014], http://www.nytimes.com/interactive/2014/12/10/business/dealbook/document-poll-finds-a-more-bleak-view-of-american-dream.html). On problematic poll data about meritocracy, see also McNamee and Miller Jr., *The Meritocracy Myth*, 14.

36. See Martha Minow, *Making All the Difference: Inclusion, Exclusion, and American Law* (Ithaca, NY: Cornell University Press, 1991).

37. As Kenneth Paul Tan concisely puts its, meritocracy purports "to 'isolate' merit by treating people with fundamentally unequal backgrounds as superficially the same" ("Meritocracy and Elitism in a Global City: Ideological Shifts in Singapore," *International Political Science Review* 29 [2008], 8).

38. Naomi Schor, "Blindness as Metaphor," *differences: A Journal of Feminist Cultural Studies* 11 (1999), 76.

39. Schor, "Blindness as Metaphor," 77. See also Paul de Man, *Blindness and Insight: Essays in the Rhetoric of Contemporary Criticism* (Minneapolis: University of Minnesota Press, 1983); Susan Sontag, *Illness as Metaphor* (New York: Farrar, Straus and Giroux, 1978); and Susan Sontag, *AIDS and Its Metaphors* (New York: Farrar, Straus and Giroux, 1989).

40. Vivian M. May and Beth A. Ferri, "Fixated on Ability: Questioning Ableist Metaphors in Feminist Theories of Resistance," *Prose Studies* 27 (2005), 124.

41. Garland-Thomson, *Staring*, 25, emphasis added.

42. Georgina Kleege provides this list of "blind" metaphors: "In fact, when you stop to listen, the word [blind] is far more commonly used in its figurative than its literal sense. And it comes up so often: blind faith, blind devotion, blind luck, blind lust, blind trust, blind chance, blind rage, blind alley, blind curve, blind-nail flooring, blind date (more dangerous than you think), duck blind, window blind, micro-mini blind (when open, they're hard to see), blind taste test, double-blind study, flying blind, following blind, blind leading the blind, blind landing, color blind (in the racial sense, a good thing), blind submission, blind side, blind spot, blindfold, blindman's bluff, three blind mice (have you ever seen such a sight in your life?). Pick up any book

or magazine and you will find dozens of similes and metaphors connecting blindness and blind people with ignorance, confusion, indifference, ineptitude" (*Sight Unseen*, 21).

43. "To most people blindness means total, absolute darkness, a complete absence of any visual experience," writes Georgina Kleege. "Though only about 10 percent of the legally blind have this degree of impairment, people think the word should be reserved to designate this minority" (*Sight Unseen*, 14). See also Mark Paterson, "'Looking on Darkness, Which the Blind Do See': Blindness, Empathy, and Feeling Seeing," *Mosaic: An Interdisciplinary Critical Journal* 46 (2013), 159–77.

44. "I Don't See Race," YouTube (8 April 2017), http://www.youtube.com/watch?v=5qArvBdHkJA.

45. "I Don't See Race."

46. "Plessy v. Ferguson, 163 U.S. 537 (1896)," available at http://chnm.gmu.edu/courses/nclc375/harlan.html.

47. Tim Wise, *Colorblind: The Rise of Post-Racial Politics and the Retreat from Racial Equity* (San Francisco: City Lights Books, 2010), 27–36.

48. Scott Feinberg, "Steven Spielberg Supports Diversity in Academy, 'Not 100 Percent Behind' Current Plan, Calls for Limits on Oscar Campaigning (Exclusive)," *Hollywood Reporter* (11 February 2016), http://www.hollywoodreporter.com/race/steven-spielberg-supports-diversity-academy-864310. For critique, see Rebecca Carroll, "People Who Don't 'See Race' Are Erasing Black People and Their Contributions," *Guardian* (15 February 2016), http://www.theguardian.com/commentisfree/2016/feb/15/bill-clinton-we-are-all-mixed-race-erases-black-people?CMP=share_btn_fb.

49. Feinberg, "Steven Spielberg."

50. See Wise, *Colorblind*, 11–15. See also Tim Wise, *Between Barack and a Hard Place: Racism and White Denial in the Age of Obama* (San Francisco: City Light Books, 2009).

51. See Brandi Wilkins Catanese, *The Problem of the Color[blind]: Racial Transgression and the Politics of Black Performance* (Ann Arbor: University of Michigan Press, 2011), 12–13.

52. Matthew Fogel, "'Grey's Anatomy' Goes Colorblind," *New York Times* (8 May 2005), http://www.nytimes.com/2005/05/08/arts/television/greys-anatomy-goes-colorblind.html.

53. Angelica Jade Bastién, "The Case against Colorblind Casting," *Atlantic* (26 December 2015), http://www.theatlantic.com/entertainment/archive/2015/12/oscar-isaac-and-the-case-against-colorblind-casting/421668.

54. See Michael Paulson, "A Black Actor in 'Virginia Woolf'? Not Happening, Albee Estate Says," *New York Times* (21 May 2017), http://www.nytimes.com/2017/05/21/theater/a-black-actor-in-virginia-woolf-not-happening-albee-estate-says.html

55. See Morgan Greene, "A White Actor Is Cast in 'In the Heights,' Setting Off a Complicated Debate," *Chicago Tribune* (14 August 2016), http://www.chicagotribune.com/entertainment/theater/ct-latino-casting-porchlight-in-the-heights-ent-0815-20160814-story.html.

56. Brakkton Booker, "Metropolitan Opera to Drop Use of Blackface-Style Makeup in 'Otello,'" NPR (4 August 2015), http://www.npr.org/sections/thetwo-way/2015/08/04/429366961/metropolitan-opera-to-drop-use-of-blackface-style-makeup-in-otello. Observe how even the title, "Blackface-Style Makeup," sounds like semantic whitewashing. ("Blackface-style makeup"—that's just blackface.)

57. See Jessica Gelt, "Authenticity in Casting: From 'Colorblind' to 'Color Conscious,' New Rules Are Anything but Black and White," *Los Angeles Times* (13 July 2017), http://www.latimes.com/entertainment/arts/la-ca-cm-authenticity-in-casting-20170713-htmlstory.html; see also Michael K. Brown, Martin Carnoy, Elliott Currie, Troy Duster, David B. Oppenheimer, Marjorie M. Shultz, and David Wellman, *Whitewashing Race: The Myth of a Color-Blind Society* (Berkeley: University of California Press, 2003), 193–222.

58. Michelle Alexander, *The New Jim Crow: Mass Incarceration in the Age of Colorblindness* (New York: New Press, 2012), 183.

59. Alexander, *New Jim Crow*, 240–41. Tim Wise uses the term "illuminated individualism" to capture the truism that "we are made up of many identities, and that these matter" (*Colorblind*, 157). See also R. L. Segato, "The Color-Blind Subject of Myth; or, Where to Find Africa in the Nation," *Annual Review of Anthropology* 27 (1998), 129–51.

60. Derald Wing Sue, *Race Talk and the Conspiracy of Silence: Understanding and Facilitating Difficult Dialogues on Race* (Hoboken, NJ: John Wiley & Sons, 2015).

61. James Baldwin, *I Am Not Your Negro: A Major Motion Picture Directed by Raoul Peck*, compiled and edited by Raoul Peck (New York: Vintage Books, 2017), 40.

62. See Ian David Moss, "On the Cultural Specificity of Symphony Orchestras," *Create Equity* (4 October 2017), http://createquity.com/2017/10/on-the-cultural-specificity-of-symphony-orchestras.

63. The Vienna Philharmonic initially functioned as a "loose association that recruited members from the Court Opera (*Hofoper*)," which became the State Opera (*Staatsoper*) in 1918 (Fritz Trümpi, *The Political Orchestra: The Vienna and Berlin Philharmonics during the Third Reich*, translated by Kenneth Kronenberg [Chicago: University of Chicago Press, 2016], 27). As Trümpi further notes, "the Vienna Philharmonic had no official organizational form until 1908," when "the orchestra for the first time decided on association bylaws, because it had unexpectedly inherited a meeting or society house (*Gesellschaftshaus*), greatly increasing its assets" (27). Today, the VPO's distinguished membership continues to draw directly from members of the Vienna State Opera.

64. "Information on the Subscription Concerts of the Vienna Philharmonic," *Vienna Philharmonic* (n.d.; last accessed 15 July 2018), http://www.wienerphilharmoniker.at/language/en-US/Homepage/Konzerte/Karteninformation.

65. "Information on the Subscription Concerts."

66. "The Vienna Philharmonic," *Vienna Philharmonic* (n.d.; last accessed 15 July 2018), http://www.wienerphilharmoniker.at/orchestra/tradition. See also D. Kern Holoman, *The Orchestra: A Very Short Introduction* (New York: Oxford University Press, 2012), 21–29.

67. See William Osborne, "Vienna Phil Update: Philharmonic Daughters and Secret Histories" (30 December 2012), http://www.osborne-conant.org/vpo-update-2012. htm.

68. Michael Cooper, "A Sound Shaped by Time and Tools," *New York Times* (30 July 2014), http://www.nytimes.com/2014/08/03/arts/music/what-makes-the-vienna-philharmonic-so-distinctive.html.

69. See Eric Martin Usner, "'The Condition of Mozart': Mozart Year 2006 and the New Vienna," *Ethnomusicology Forum* 20 (2011), 413–42 (esp. 429–30); "Wiener Klangstil (Viennese Musical Tradition)," *Department of Music Acoustics* (n.d.; last accessed 15 July 2018), http://iwk.mdw.ac.at/?page_id=16&sprache=2; Robert Philip, *Performing Music in the Age of Recording* (New Haven, CT: Yale University Press, 2014); 74–75, 90–100, 160–62; Robert Philip, *Early Recordings and Musical Style: Changing Tastes in Instrumental Performance, 1900–1950* (Cambridge: Cambridge University Press, 1992), 78–79, 116–18, 125–27, 191–93; and Trümpi, *Political Orchestra*, 3.

70. James R. Oestreich, "Music; Keeping That Vienna Sound (and Everything Else) As Is," *New York Times* (26 September 1999), http://www.nytimes.com/1999/09/26/arts/music-keeping-that-vienna-sound-and-everything-else-as-is.html?pagewanted=all.

71. See Kris Burns, "Press Release" (12 February 2003), available at http://www.osborne-conant.org/iawminfo.htm. On the Vienna Lady Orchestra, which formed in 1867 (twenty-five years after the founding of the VPO) and "sparked a veritable craze for women's orchestras" in Europe as well as in the United States, see Anna-Lise P. Santella, "Modeling Music: Early Organizational Structures of American Women's Orchestras," in *American Orchestras in the Nineteenth Century*, edited by John Spitzer (Chicago: University of Chicago Press, 2012), 57.

72. Bernard Holland, "Feminist Protests and Vienna Musicians," *New York Times* (3 March 1997), http://www.nytimes.com/1997/03/03/arts/feminist-protests-and-vienna-musicians.html. See also Pauline Oliveros, *Sounding the Margins: Collected Writings 1992–2009*, edited by Lawton Hall (Kingston, NY: Deep Listening Publications, 2010), 14–15.

73. As the IAWM website explains: "The IAWM was formed in 1995 from the merger of three organizations that arose during the women's rights movements of the 1970s to combat inequitable treatment of women in music: the International League of Women Composers (ILWC), founded in 1975 by Nancy Van de Vate to create and expand opportunities for women composers of music; the International Congress on Women in Music (ICWM), founded in 1979 by Jeannie Pool to form an organizational basis for women-in-music conferences and meetings; and American Women Composers (AWC), Inc., founded in 1976 by Tommie Ewart Carl to promote music by American women composers" ("About Us," *International Alliance for Women in Music* [n.d.; last accessed 18 July 2018], https://iawm.org/about-us).

74. Anthony Tommasini, "Critic's Notebook: Glorious, Yes, but Resisting Today's World; the Vienna Philharmonic Returns, Virtually a Male Bastion," *New York Times* (15 March 1999), http://www.nytimes.com/1999/03/15/arts/critic-s-notebook-glorious-yes-but-resisting-today-s-world-vienna-philharmonic.html.

75. Burns, "Press Release."

76. See William Osborne, "Some Notable Progress for Women, but a Blind Eye to the Exclusion of Asians" (29 December 2015), http://www.osborne-conant.org/vpo-update-2015.htm.

77. See "Simone Young to Conduct Vienna Philharmonic," *Sydney Morning Herald* (9 November 2005), http://www.smh.com.au/entertainment/art-and-design/simone-young-to-conduct-vienna-philharmonic-20051109-gdmeqv.html.

78. William Osborne, "Why Did the Vienna Philharmonic Fire Yasuto Sugiyama?" (n.d.; last accessed 10 July 2018), http://www.osborne-conant.org/sugiyama.htm. On the perceived exceptionalism of Austro-German symphonic repertoire more generally, see Douglas W. Shadle, *Orchestrating the Nation: The Nineteenth-Century American Symphonic Enterprise* (New York: Oxford University Press, 2016), 1–4.

79. Robin DiAngelo, "White Fragility," *International Journal of Critical Pedagogy* 3 (2011), 65.

80. DiAngelo, "White Fragility." See also Eduardo Bonilla-Silva, *Racism without Racists: Color-Blind Racism and the Persistence of Racial Inequality in America*, fourth edition (Lanham: Rowman & Littlefield, 2014), 115–18.

81. See Michael Horowitz, "Tischgespräche: Dieses Mal mit Clemens Hellsberg," *Kurier* (9 December 2011), http://kurier.at/lifestyle/tischgespraeche-dieses-mal-mit-clemens-hellsberg/751.490.

82. Scholars have long documented Westerners' skepticism toward East Asian musicians' ability to perform and interpret Western art music (authentically, persuasively, holistically). Mari Yoshihara writes: "Japanese violinist Hiroko Yajima remembered well her first tour in the United States in 1965 as a member of a student orchestra. The orchestra, comprised mostly of college and some high-school students at the Toho School of Music in Tokyo, had meticulously rehearsed Arnold Schoenberg's *Transfigured Night* for the performance at the New York World's Fair. For decades following this performance, Felix Galimir, a world-famous violinist from Vienna who later became one of her mentors, repeatedly told the story about how astonished he was by the performance of this group of 'cute, young Japanese students in identical black and white outfits.' He could not believe that 'a student orchestra from Japan could possibly play Schoenberg at such a level.' Galimir was not only impressed by their impeccable technique but was also particularly surprised by the way in which the Japanese students, presumably so 'foreign' to the cultural and musical ideas of the Second Viennese School, had truly grasped the 'essence' of this extremely difficult piece with its changing rhythm and sonority and played it so convincingly. A few years later, when Yajima was a student at Juilliard, she and two other Japanese students performed the Schubert Piano Trio in B-flat Major at a recital sponsored by the Schubert Society. The young trio members, having been trained by Galimir, were quite confident about their mastery of the piece and had a wonderful time performing, as it had never even occurred to them that anything other than their playing would matter to the audience. The audience—especially the Viennese—did praise their playing, repeatedly telling them that they 'did not think that Japanese could play Schubert like this'" (*Musicians from a Different Shore: Asians and Asian Americans in Classical Music* [Philadelphia: Temple University Press, 2007], 187–88). Several comparable examples are recounted in Wang, *Soundtracks of Asian*

America. See also Eric Hung, "Performing 'Chineseness' on the Western Concert Stage: The Case of Lang Lang," *Asian Music* 40 (2009), 131–48; Bonnie C. Wade, *Composing Japanese Musical Modernity* (Chicago: University of Chicago Press, 2014), 59–95; and Yang, "East Meets West."

83. This Otto Strasser shouldn't be confused with another Otto Strasser (1897–1974), who had explicit ties to (and ideological breaks from) Adolf Hitler and was author of *Hitler and I,* translated by Gwenda David and Eric Mosbacher (Boston: Houghton Mifflin, 1940).

84. Osborne, "Why Did the Vienna Philharmonic Fire Yasuto Sugiyama?" The original German passage reads: "Für unrichtig halte ich, daß der Bewerber hinter einem Vorhang spielt; eine Einrichtung, die nach dem Zweiten Weltkrieg eingeführt wurde, um eine objektive Beurteilung zu gewährleisten. Ich habe dagegen, besonders als ich später Vorstand der Philharmoniker wurde, stets angekämpft, weil ich der Überzeugung bin, daß zum Künstler auch der Mensch gehört, den man nicht nur hören, sondern auch sehen muß, um ihn in seiner gesamten Persönlichkeit beurteilen zu können. [. . .] Sogar eine Groteske, die sich nach meiner Pensionierung abspielte, hat keine Änderung bewirkt. Ein Bewerber qualifizierte sich als Bester, und als sich der Vorhang hob, stand ein—Japaner vor der verdutzten Jury. Den engagierte man dennoch nicht, weil sein Gesicht nicht zum Neujahrskonzert und zur Pizzicato-Polka gepaßt hätte" (Otto Strasser, *Und dafür wird man noch bezahlt: Mein Leben mit den Wiener Philharmonikern* [Munich: Deutscher Taschenbuch Verlag, 1978], 21).

85. See William Osborne, "The Special Characteristics of the Vienna Philharmonic's Racial Ideology," http://www.osborne-conant.org/posts/special.htm. See also Michael White, "The Nazi Musicians Who Changed Their Tune," *Telegraph* (11 March 2013), http://www.telegraph.co.uk/culture/music/classicalmusic/9922592/The-Nazi-musicians-who-changed-their-tune.html

86. Quoted in William Osborne, "Symphony Orchestras and Artist-Prophets: Cultural Isomorphism and the Allocation of Power in Music," *Leonardo Music Journal* 9 (1999), 69. See also Roland Girtler, "Mitgliedsaufnahme in den Noblen Bund der Wiener Philharmoniker als Mannbarkeitsritual," in *Gesellschaft und Musik: Wege zur Musiksoziologie,* edited by Wolfgang Lipp (Berlin: Duncker & Humblot, 1992), 497–504; Elena Ostleitner, *Liebe, Lust, Last und Leid* (Vienna: Bundesministerium für Unterricht und Kunst, 1995); Clemens Hellsberg, *Demokratie der Könige: Die Geschichte der Wiener Philharmoniker* (Zurich: Schweizer Verlagshaus, 1992), 624–650; and Bernadette Mayrhofer and Fritz Trümpi, *Orchestrierte Vertreibung: Unerwünschte Wiener Philharmoniker: Verfolgung, Ermordung und Exil* (Vienna: Mandelbaum, 2014).

87. Francesca Jackes, "All White on the Night: Why Does the World-Famous Vienna Philharmonic Feature So Few Women and Ethnic Minorities?," *Independent* (4 March 2010), http://www.independent.co.uk/arts-entertainment/music/features/all-white-on-the-night-why-does-the-world-famous-vienna-philharmonic-feature-so-few-women-and-ethnic-1915666.html. See also Joshua Kosman, "Vienna Philharmonic Must Answer for Exclusion," *SF Gate* (20 February 2011), http://www.sfgate.com/entertainment/article/Vienna-Philharmonic-must-answer-for-exclusion-2474252.php; and Osborne, "Some Notable Progress."

88. Trümpi recounts: "As late as 2003, [Clemens] Hellsberg, in his capacities as chairman of the orchestra and head of the archive, denied my request to examine the archive's holdings. The reason given was that the minutes mentioned 'many very personal problems of and with the individual members and all-too-human internal arguments and artistic differences, including with conductors,' so 'their publication would most assuredly not be in the interest of our association'" (*Political Orchestra*, 7).

89. Fritz Trümpi, "The Vienna Philharmonic's Nazi Past: Lifting the Veil of Deliberate Ignorance," *Guardian* (16 March 2013), http://www.theguardian.com/commentisfree/2013/mar/16/vienna-philharmonic-nazi-past.

90. George Markus, "Zur Forderung nach einer kritischen Aufarbeitung der Geschichte dieser Institution," *Kurier* (31 December 2012), http://kurier.at/kultur/das-neujahrskonzert-abschaffen/2.212.193. See also Zwölftöner (Sebastian Smallshaw), "Philharmonic Archives and the Austrian Art of Remembering," *Von heute auf morgen* (3 January 2013), http://vonheuteaufmorgen.blogspot.com/2013/01/philharmonic-archives-and-austrian-art.html#more.

91. Sebastian Smallshaw, email correspondence with author (2 September 2017). Trümpi notes that Rathkolb was not his Doktorvater but rather his Co-Supervisor.

92. "The Vienna Philharmonic under National Socialism (1938–1945)," *Vienna Philharmonic*, http://www.wienerphilharmoniker.at/orchestra/history/national-socialism.

93. See Bernadette Mayrhofer, "Vertreibung von Wiener Philharmonikern aus dem Orchester nach 1938 und die versäumte Reintegration nach 1945," *Zeitgeschichte* 34 (2007), 72–94; Trümpi, *Political Orchestra*, 101; Hella Pick, *Guilty Victim: Austria from the Holocaust to Haider* (London: I. B. Tauris, 2000), 91–93; Oliver Rathkolb, *The Paradoxical Republic: Austria, 1945–2005* (New York: Berghahn Books, 2010); Sam H. Shirakawa, *The Devil's Music Master: The Controversial Life and Career of Wilhelm Furtwängler* (New York: Oxford University Press, 1992), 250–53, 277–80; and Kerry Skyring, "The Vienna Philharmonic Reveals Its Nazi Past," *Deutsche Welle* (12 March 2013), http://p.dw.com/p/17vWV; see also Raymond Holden, *The Virtuoso Conductors: The Central European Tradition from Wagner to Karajan* (New Haven, CT: Yale University Press, 2005), 203–24. For comparisons with the Berlin Philharmonic, see Abby Anderton, "'It Was Never a Nazi Orchestra': The American Re-education of the Berlin Philharmonic," *Music & Politics* 7 (2013), http://dx.doi.org/10.3998/mp.9460447.0007.103; and Erik Levi, *Music in the Third Reich* (New York: St. Martin's Press, 1994), 210–19.

94. See Rathkolb, *Paradoxical Republic*, 204.

95. Rathkolb, *Paradoxical Republic*, 203.

96. See Petroc Trelawny, "The New Year Tradition with a Dark History," *BBC* (1 January 2015), http://www.bbc.com/news/magazine-30536313; James Oestreich, "Waltzing Right Past History in Austria," *New York Times* (5 January 2014), http://www.nytimes.com/2014/01/06/arts/music/the-vienna-philharmonic-celebrates-the-new-year-twice.html?mcubz=0; and Oliver Rathkolb, *Führertreu und Gottbegnadet: Künstlereliten im Dritten Reich* (Vienna: ÖBV, 1991).

97. "Vienna Philharmonic under National Socialism (1938–1945)."

98. On the "pathetic fallacy," see Richard Taruskin, *The Oxford History of Western Music*, vol. 1 (New York: Oxford University Press, 2005), xxvi–vii and 221.

99. See Sonja Niederacher, "The Myth of Austria as Nazi Victim, the Emigrants and the Discipline of Exile Studies," *Austrian Studies* 11 (2003), 14–32; and Trümpi, *Political Orchestra*, 104.

100. See Susanne Cohen-Weisz, *Jewish Life in Austria and Germany since 1945: Identity and Communal Reconstruction* (New York: Central European University Press, 2015), 101–2.

101. "The Message of Music," *Vienna Philharmonic* (n.d.; last accessed 4 July 2018), http://www.wienerphilharmoniker.at/orchestra/tradition.

102. See James Schmidt, "'Not These Sounds': Beethoven at Mauthausen," *Philosophy and Literature* 29 (2005), 146–63; Thomas Dombrowski, "Ein Thesaurus des Gedenkens," *Der Standard* (4 May 2000); and William Osborne, "Bomb Scares and Concentration Camp Memorial Concerts" (5 April 2000), http://www.osborne-conant.org/posts/bomb.htm.

103. See Terry Teachout, "Orchestras and Nazis," *Commentary Magazine* (14 June 2017), http://www.commentarymagazine.com/articles/orchestras-and-nazis.

104. Edelman, *No Future*, 3–4. See also Mauskapf, "Enduring Crisis," 193–247.

105. See Michael H. Kater, *Composers of the Nazi Era: Eight Portraits* (New York: Oxford University Press, 2000), 129–30; and Trümpi, *Political Orchestra*, 147. On the etymology of "alibi," see William Cheng, "Taking Back the Laugh: Comedic Alibis, Funny Fails," *Critical Inquiry* 43 (2017), 533.

106. Justin Davidson, "How Can the Vienna Philharmonic Change without Changing?," *New York Magazine* (4 March 2014), http://nymag.com/arts/classicaldance/classical/reviews/vienna-philharmonic-2014-3.

107. "Social Responsibility of the Vienna Philharmonic," *Vienna Philharmonic*, http://www.wienerphilharmoniker.at/orchestra/social-responsibility. On the website's German-language version, the testimonial reads: "Es hat mich sehr begeistert, dass die Wiener Philharmoniker zu uns nach Monte Azul kamen und uns beim proben zuschauten. Ich fand es wunderbar, mit ihnen in Kontakt zu sein. Sie haben uns eingeladen, bei ihrer Probe im Konzertsaal von São Paulo zuzuhören. Ich habe mich gefühlt, als wäre ich an einem verzauberten Ort, sah das Orchester und träumte davon, eines Tages dort oben am ersten Pult der Celli zu sitzen und mit ihnen zu spielen.—Micaela dos Santos, 17."

108. Vienna Philharmonic/Wiener Philharmoniker, photo (1) by Jun Keller (uploaded 28 November 2014), Facebook, http://www.facebook.com/ViennaPhilharmonic/photos/a.761606443917167.1073741880.320213934723089/761608477250297/?type=3&theater.

109. Vienna Philharmonic/Wiener Philharmoniker, photo (2) by Jun Keller (uploaded 28 November 2014), Facebook, http://www.facebook.com/ViennaPhilharmonic/photos/a.761606443917167.1073741880.320213934723089/761608477250297/?type=3&theater.

110. Vienna Philharmonic/Wiener Philharmoniker, photo (2) by Jun Keller.

111. See comment thread for Norman Lebrecht, "Pictures at an Audition for the Vienna Philharmonic," *Slipped Disc* (30 November 2014), http://slippedisc.com/2014/11/pictures-at-an-audition-for-the-vienna-philharmonic.

112. Images in Figure 3.4 from Vienna Philharmonic/Wiener Philharmoniker, photo (1) by Jun Keller.

113. Lebrecht, "Pictures at an Audition for the Vienna Philharmonic" (comment by John Borstlap).

114. See Jane Perlez, "Vienna Philharmonic Lets Women Join in Harmony," *New York Times* (28 February 1997), http://www.nytimes.com/1997/02/28/world/vienna-philharmonic-lets-women-join-in-harmony.html?mcubz=0; and Tommasini, "Critic's Notebook."

115. Comment thread for Norman Lebrecht, "How Many Women in the Vienna Philharmonic," *Slipped Disc* (28 November 2016), http://slippedisc.com/2016/11/how-many-women-in-the-vienna-philharmonic.

116. Jackes, "All White on the Night."

117. Jackes, "All White on the Night."

118. Ostleitner, *Liebe, Lust, Last und Leid*, 6.

119. LeiLani Nishime, *Undercover Asian: Multiracial Asian Americans in Visual Culture* (Urbana: University of Illinois Press, 2014), 7, 12.

120. Michele Elam, *The Souls of Mixed Folk: Race, Politics, and Aesthetics in the New Millennium* (Stanford, CA: Stanford University Press, 2011), xiv. Discourses of Asian mixedness intersect with (and can be as problematic as) discourses of pan-Asian "multiculturalism." See Deborah Wong, *Speak It Louder: Asian Americans Making Music* (New York: Routledge, 2004), 132–33, 308–13.

121. See Ahmed, *On Being Included*, 51–82.

122. Richard Morrison, "Empires Fall but the Band Plays On," *London Times* (25 March 1992).

123. "Eine derartige Darstellung ist in Anbetracht der Fakten unhaltbar: Selbst wenn das einwandfreie Verhältnis zu Otto Dessoff, Bruno Walter, David Oistrach oder Leonard Bernstein, um nur einige der großen jüdischen Künstler zu nennen, welche von den Philharmonikern geliebt wurden [. . .] geht der undifferenzierte Vorwurf des Antisemitismus ins Leere" (Hellsberg, *Demokratie der Könige*, 502).

124. Quotation in Figure 3.5 comes from Adrian George, email correspondence with author (2 August 2018). George ended up gifting the original drawing to "a Jewish friend of mine, a music critic who was terminally ill, [who] wanted the original drawing very much."

125. Heinz Roegle, "Notes on 26 Years as Official Nonentity (Interview with Anna Lelkes)," transcribed by Jan Herman and translated from German by Mike Wiessner, *Los Angeles Times* (5 March 1997), http://articles.latimes.com/1997-03-05/news/mn-35044_1_vienna-philharmonic-orchestra.

126. Jackes, "All White on the Night."

127. For a critique of the lost-cause argument, see Elaine Scarry, "Beauty and the Scholar's Duty to Justice," *Profession* (2000), 21–31.

128. Author, email to William Osborne (August 15, 2017); author, email to Fritz Trümpi (August 15, 2017).

129. William Osborne, email to author (August 18, 2017).

130. Fritz Trümpi, email to author (August 16, 2017).

131. See Jan Herman, "Taking on the Vienna Philharmonic: Composer-Activist Plays the Internet for Women's Rights," MSNBC (20 January 2000), http://www.osborne-conant.org/Taking-on.htm; Norman Lebrecht, *The Maestro Myth: Great Conductors in Pursuit of Power* (New York: Citadel Press, 2001), 288; and Andrew R. Barnard, "In Defense of the Vienna Philharmonic: A Response to Norman Lebrecht," *Classical Commentator* (3 January 2015), http://www.theclassicalcommentator. com/in-defense-of-the-vienna-philharmonic-a-response-to-norman-lebrecht. See also Leonard Bernstein, "Something Called Terrorism," with introduction by Carol J. Oja and Mark Eden Horowitz, *American Scholar* (1 September 2008), http:// theamericanscholar.org/something-called-terrorism.

132. Uffeviking, "Vienna Philharmonic: Slow to Change Its Tune," *Good Music Guide* (2007), http://www.good-music-guide.com/forum/index.php/topic,13375.15/wap2. html.

133. Harry Collier, "Vienna Philharmonic: Slow to Change Its Tune," *Good Music Guide* (2007), http://www.good-music-guide.com/forum/index.php/topic,13375.30/wap2. html.

134. See Martin Niemöller, "First They Came for the Socialists," *Holocaust Encyclopedia* (n.d.; last accessed 24 June 2018), http://www.ushmm.org/wlc/en/article. php?ModuleId=10007392.

135. See Mahzarin R. Banaji and Anthony G. Greenwald, *Blindspot: Hidden Biases of Good People* (New York: Delacorte Press, 2013).

136. See Mark Lilla, "The End of Identity Liberalism," *New York Times* (18 November 2016), http://www.nytimes.com/2016/11/20/opinion/sunday/the-end-of-identity-liberalism.html; Walter Benn Michaels, Charles W. Mills, Linda Hirshman, and Carla Murphy, "What Is the Left without Identity Politics?," *Nation* (16 December 2016), http://www.thenation.com/article/what-is-the-left-without-identity-politics; and Leon Wieseltier, "Against Identity," *New Republic* (27 November 1994), http:// newrepublic.com/article/92857/against-identity.

137. In its February 2017 Newsletter, the American Musicological Society announced that its Board of Directors would undertake "a workshop for unconscious bias" at its April convening. In tandem, the AMS website added a page called "Resources for Unconscious Bias Training" containing links to informational literature, audiovisual materials, and training activities. See "News from the AMS Board," *AMS Newsletter* (February 2017), 12, available at http://www.ams-net.org/newsletter/ AMSNewsletter-2017-2.pdf. See also "Resources for Unconscious Bias Training," *American Musicological Society* (2017), http://www.ams-net.org/committees/cre/ unconsciousbias.php.

138. See Alan Lembitz and Ted J. Clarke, "Clarifying 'Never Events' and Introducing 'Always Events,'" *Patient Safety in Surgery* 3 (2009), http://www.ncbi.nlm.nih.gov/ pmc/articles/PMC2814808; and Winta T. Mehtsun, et al., "Surgical Never Events in the United States," *Surgery* 153 (2013), 265–72.

139. See "Johns Hopkins Malpractice Study: Surgical 'Never Events' Occur At Least 4,000 Times Per Year," *Johns Hopkins Medicine* (19 December 2012), http://www. hopkinsmedicine.org/news/media/releases/johns_hopkins_malpractice_study_ surgical_never_events_occur_at_least_4000_times_per_year.

140. "National Time Out Day, June 8, 2016," *Joint Commission* (13 June 2017), http://www.jointcommission.org/national_time_out_day_2016, emphasis added.

141. Concerning a similar recommendation for improving equity and curbing discrimination in philosophy, see Sally Haslanger, "Changing the Ideology and Culture of Philosophy: Not by Reason Alone," *Hypatia* 23 (2008), 210–23.

142. Adam Beyer, "Divinity School Professor Resigns after Dispute with Colleagues about Diversity Training, Calling It a 'Waste,'" *Duke Chronicle* (9 May 2017), http://www.dukechronicle.com/article/2017/05/divinity-school-professor-resigns-after-dispute-with-colleagues-about-diversity-training-calling-it-a-waste.

143. Beyer, "Divinity School Professor Resigns."

144. German Lopez, "Research Says There Are Ways to Reduce Racism. Calling People Racist Isn't One of Them," *Vox* (15 November 2016), http://www.vox.com/identities/2016/11/15/13595508/racism-trump-research-study.

145. See Chang, *We Gon' Be Alright*, 9–32.

146. Images in Figure 3.6 come from "Understanding Unconscious Bias," YouTube (17 November 2015), http://www.youtube.com/watch?v=dVp9Z5k0dEE; and "National Time Out Day," *AORN* (14 June 2017), http://www.aorn.org/timeout2017.

147. Alexander, *New Jim Crow*, 244.

148. "Niki Nakayama," *Chef's Table* (S1E3, 2015), Netflix Original, ~22:00.

149. Malcolm Gladwell, *Blink: The Power of Thinking without Thinking* (New York: Back Bay Books, 2005), 246. See also William Osborne, "'You Sound Like a Ladies' Orchestra': A Case History of Sexism against Abbie Conant in the Munich Philharmonic" (1994), http://www.osborne-conant.org/ladies.htm; and Monique Buzzarté, "We Need a Man for Solo Trombone: Abbie Conant's Story," *Journal of the International Alliance for Women in Music* (1996), 8–11, http://iawm.org/stef/articles_html/buzzarte_conant.html.

150. Images in Figure 3.7 come from "Niki Nakayama."

151. "Niki Nakayama." See also Maria Fontoura, "Meet Niki Nakayama, One of the World's Only Female Kaiseki Chefs,"*Wall Street Journal* (8 August 2014), http://www.wsj.com/articles/meet-niki-nakayama-one-of-the-worlds-only-female-kaiseki-chefs-1407509705.

152. See George M. Taber, *Judgment of Paris* (New York: Scribner, 2005).

153. See Maria Godoy, "The Judgment of Paris: The Blind Taste Test That Decanted the World," NPR (24 May 2016), http://www.npr.org/sections/thesalt/2016/05/24/479163882/the-judgment-of-paris-the-blind-taste-test-that-decanted-the-wine-world.

154. See Steven D. Levitt and Stephen J. Dubner, *Think like a Freak* (New York: HarperCollins, 2014), 42–43.

155. Steven D. Levitt, "Cheap Wine," *Freakonomics Blog* (16 July 2008), http://freakonomics.com/2008/07/16/cheap-wine.

156. For a comparable case of unblinding (and utter surprise) involving composer Rebecca Clarke's Violin Sonata at a 1919 competition, see Liane Curtis, "Rebecca Clarke and Sonata Form: Questions of Gender and Genre," *Musical Quarterly* 81 (1997), 393–429; and Nancy B. Reich, "Rebecca Clarke: An Uncommon Woman," in *A Rebecca Clarke Reader*, edited by Liane Curtis (Bloomington: Indiana University Press, 2004), 10–18.

157. See Matthew Yglesias, "Sweet Sorrow," *Slate* (9 August 2013), http://www.slate.com/articles/business/rivalries/2013/08/pepsi_paradox_why_people_prefer_coke_even_though_pepsi_wins_in_taste_tests.html.

158. Spencer Kornhaber, "The Reality of Those 'Real People, Not Actors' Ads," *Atlantic* (15 August 2016), http://www.theatlantic.com/entertainment/archive/2016/08/real-people-not-actors-chevrolet-olympics-ad-interview/495863. With thanks to Linda Shaver-Gleason for directing me to these entertaining Chevy ads.

159. See Cheng, "Taking Back the Laugh," 541–42.

160. See Robert H. Frank, "Are You Successful? If So, You've Already Won the Lottery," *New York Times* (20 May 2016), http://www.nytimes.com/2016/05/22/upshot/are-you-successful-if-so-youve-already-won-the-lottery.html?mcubz=0.

161. Quoted in Jesse Singal, "Why Americans Ignore the Role of Luck in Everything," *New York Magazine* (12 May 2016), http://nymag.com/scienceofus/2016/05/why-americans-ignore-the-role-of-luck-in-everything.html. For the full segment, see "Luck Is the Real Key to Success?," *Fox Business* (7 May 2011), http://video.foxbusiness.com/v/3887675/?#sp=show-clips.

162. "Stuart Varney Net Worth," *The Richest* (retrieved 28 June 2017), http://www.therichest.com/celebnetworth/celeb/journalist/stuart-varney-net-worth.

163. Floyd Cobb II and Nicole M. Russell, "Meritocracy or Complexity: Problematizing Racial Disparities in Mathematics Assessment within the Context of Curricular Structures, Practices, and Discourse," *Journal of Education Policy* 30 (2015), 631–49.

164. Unblindings could be considered a subspecies of what Henry Jenkins has termed the "wow climaxes" of contemporary media—the moments in television, film, games, and sports that make viewers say, "Wow!" (*The Wow Climax: Tracing the Emotional Impact of Popular Culture* [New York: New York University Press, 2007]).

Interlude

1. Imani Mosley, "MN" (19 February 2016), 4, quoted with permission.

2. Pierpaolo Polzonetti, "*Don Giovanni* Goes to Prison: Teaching Opera behind Bars," *Musicology Now* (16 February 2016), http://musicologynow.ams-net.org/2016/02/don-giovanni-goes-to-prison-teaching_16.html. For commentary, see Jonathan Bellman, "Scholar Teaches behind Bars; Is Sent to Woodshed," *Dial M for Musicology* (16 February 2016), http://dialmformusicology.com/2016/02/16/scholar-teaches-behind-bars-is-sent-to-woodshed; and Norman Lebrecht, "Musicologist Went to Jail—and Got Torn to Pieces," *Slipped Disc* (18 February 2016), http://slippedisc.com/2016/02/musicologist-went-to-jail-and-got-torn-to-pieces. For a revised and extended version of the *Musicology Now* post, see Pierpaolo Polzonetti, "*Don Giovanni* Goes to Prison: Teaching Opera behind Bars," *Musica Docta: Rivista digitale di Pedagogia e Didattica della musica* 6 (2016), 99–104. In this article's acknowledgments, Polzonetti stated: "I thank my colleagues and participants in this debate for the animated discussion on the blogosphere [of *Musicology Now*]. The feedback I received convinced me to change the wording of my text in a few critical

points, hoping that the present contribution in *Musica Docta* will no longer divert its readers' attention from its central argument and its main purpose, which is an invitation to social action through the dissemination of opera culture among imprisoned men and women and other unconventional audiences, especially among the underprivileged members of our society" (99).

3. Polzonetti, "*Don Giovanni*" (in *Musicology Now*).

4. Polzonetti, "*Don Giovanni*" (in *Musicology Now*).

5. Polzonetti, "*Don Giovanni*" (in *Musicology Now*).

6. Polzonetti, "*Don Giovanni*" (in *Musica Docta*), 99.

7. Polzonetti, "*Don Giovanni*" (in *Musica Docta*), 99, 103.

8. Even with no racism or racialism intended, characterizations of rap as containing "blatant lyrics and pounding beat" carry denotations of excessive decibels. "Blatant" was coined by Edmund Spenser in *The Faerie Queen* (1596) when describing a "blatant beast." Etymologists have speculated that the word was an alteration of *bleating* (calling to mind goats and sheep), with likely inspiration from the Latin *blatire* (v., to babble).

9. Daniel Goldmark, "Louisville Program Selection," *AMS Newsletter* XLV:2 (August 2015), http://ams-net.org/newsletter/AMSNewsletter-2015-8.pdf, 25.

10. Paying lip service to meritocracy does not guarantee material equity. Across three experiments, Emilio J. Castilla and Stephen Benard found that "when an organization is explicitly presented as meritocratic, individuals in managerial positions favor a male employee over an equally qualified female employee by awarding him a larger monetary reward," meaning that meritocracy can sometimes pose as a useful front for discrimination ("The Paradox of Meritocracy in Organizations," *Administrative Science Quarterly* 55 [2010], 543).

11. Ta-Nehisi Coates, *We Were Eight Years in Power* (New York: BCP Literary, 2017), 178.

12. Mosley, "MN," 4, emphasis added.

Chapter 4

1. These contestants appeared respectively on *So You Think You Can Dance Canada* (2010), *Britain's Got Talent* (2013), *Project Runway* (2013), *America's Got Talent* (2010), and *China's Got Talent* (2010).

2. On *American Idol* and the American Dream, see Christopher Bell, *American Idolatry: Celebrity, Commodity and Reality Television* (Jefferson, NC: McFarland, 2010), 157–58; Amanda McClain, *American Ideal: How American Idol Constructs Celebrity, Collective Identity, and American Discourses* (Lanham, MD: Lexington Books, 2011), 41–43; and Meizel, *Idolized*, 16–50.

3. David T. Mitchell and Sharon L. Snyder, *Narrative Prosthesis: Disability and the Dependencies of Discourse* (Ann Arbor: University of Michigan Press, 2000), 49.

4. On stereotypes, terminologies, and metaphors of savants and supercrips, see Brian Watermeyer, "Claiming Loss in Disability," *Disability & Society* 24 (2009), 91–102;

Sharon L. Snyder and David T. Mitchell, "Introduction: Ablenationalism and the Geo-Politics of Disability," *Journal of Literary & Cultural Disability Studies* 4 (2010), 113–25; Brendan Burkett, Mike McNamee, and Wolfgang Potthast, "Shifting Boundaries in Sports Technology and Disability: Equal Rights or Unfair Advantage in the Case of Oscar Pistorius," *Disability & Society* 26 (2011), 643–54; Wendy L. Chrisman, "A Reflection on Inspiration: A Recuperative Call for Emotion in Disability Studies," *Journal of Literary & Cultural Disability Studies* 5 (2011), 173–84; and Straus, "Idiots Savants," *Disability Studies Quarterly* 34 (2014), http://dsq-sds.org/article/view/3407/3640.

5. Coined by Rosemarie Garland-Thomson, the term "normate" refers not simply to a person who identifies as nondisabled, but furthermore to "the constructed identity of those who, by way of the bodily configurations and cultural capital they assume, can step into a position of authority and wield the power it grants them" (*Extraordinary Bodies: Figuring Physical Disability in American Culture and Literature* [New York: Columbia University Press, 1997], 8).

6. See Henry Jenkins, *Convergence Culture: Where Old and New Media Collide* (New York: New York University Press, 2006), 59–92; and Richard Rushfield, *American Idol: The Untold Story* (New York: Hyperion, 2011), 86–87.

7. See Jenkins, *Convergence Culture*, 90.

8. Meizel, *Idolized*, 21.

9. See M. F. Norden, *The Cinema of Isolation: A History of Physical Disability in the Movies* (New Brunswick, NJ: Rutgers University Press, 1994); Lennard Davis, *Bending over Backwards: Disability, Dismodernism, and Other Difficult Positions* (New York: New York University Press, 1994); and Johnson Cheu, "De-generates, Replicants, and Other Aliens: (Re)defining Disability in Futuristic Film," in *Disability/Postmodernity: Embodying Disability Theory*, edited by Mairian Corker and Tom Shakespeare (London: Continuum, 2002), 198–212.

10. For (primarily) celebratory readings of the lyric voice in song and opera, see Carolyn Abbate, "Opera; or, the Envoicing of Women," in *Musicology and Difference: Gender and Sexuality in Music Scholarship*, edited by Ruth A. Solie (Berkeley: University of California Press, 1993), 225–58; Mary Ann Smart, ed., *Siren Songs: Representations of Gender and Sexuality in Opera* (Princeton, NJ: Princeton University Press, 2000); and Jane Bernstein, ed., *Women's Voices across Musical Worlds* (Boston: Northeastern University Press, 2004); cf. William Cheng, "Hearts for Sale: The French *Romance* and the Sexual Traffic of Musical Mimicry," *19th-Century Music* 35 (2011), 115–46.

11. On "crip time" and activist perspectives on accommodating people's diverse pacing and temporal needs, see Price, *Mad at School*, 61–63; Julie Cosenza, "SLOW: Crip Theory, Dyslexia and the Borderlands of Disability and Ablebodiedness," *Liminalities: A Journal of Performance Studies* 6 (2010), 1–22; Irving Kenneth Zola, "Self, Identity and the Naming Question: Reflections on the Language of Disability," *Social Science and Medicine* 36 (1993), 167–73; and Cheng, *Just Vibrations*, 44–46.

12. See Simon Cowell, *I Don't Mean to Be Rude, But . . . : Backstage Gossip from "American Idol" & the Secrets That Can Make You a Star* (New York: Broadway Books, 2003), 5–7.

13. The U.S. series *The Voice* is based on *The Voice of Holland*, a Dutch reality singing competition that premiered in 2010.

14. On *The Voice*, the judges are called "coaches" because they work closely with contestants throughout the competition.

15. NBC's *The Voice*, "Eligibility Requirements" (2015), http://www.nbcthevoice.com/auditions/eligibility.

16. Following the audition of Andrea Begley on *The Voice UK*, coach Danny O'Donoghue recalled, "I knew straightaway from the first line of that song. I was like, 'This is something special,' because the mood just changed in the room. That's what a megastar is" ("Andrea Begley—Angel," YouTube [30 January 2014], http://www.youtube.com/watch?v=fLx0KnstmVk).

17. See Roland Barthes, *Image, Music, Text*, translated by Stephen Heath (London: Fontana, 1977), 179–89.

18. On the "audiovisual litany," which "idealizes hearing (and, by extension, speech) as manifesting a kind of pure interiority," see Jonathan Sterne, *The Audible Past: Cultural Origins of Sound Reproduction* (Durham, NC: Duke University Press, 2003), 15.

19. "The Voice 2015 Blind Audition—Jordan Smith: 'Chandelier,'" YouTube (21 September 2015), http://www.youtube.com/watch?v=vHR4oOIcVZo.

20. Samantha Lear, "Jordan Smith's 'The Voice' Premiere Blind Audition Was the Actual Most Shocking Ever," *Wet Paint* (22 September 2015), http://www.wetpaint.com/jordan-smith-the-voice-audition-sia-chandelier-1441618.

21. Suzannah Showler, "*The Voice* from Above," *Slate* (14 December 2015), http://www.slate.com/articles/arts/culturebox/2015/12/god_religion_and_jordan_smith_on_the_voice.html.

22. "Willie Jones 2," YouTube (22 June 2015), http://www.youtube.com/watch?v=jdwnHkNj1fM.

23. "Travis Pratt," YouTube (14 June 2013), http://www.youtube.com/watch?v=CEaMaEb6HIo.

24. On a visceral aversion to the word "freak," see Eli Clare, *Exile and Pride: Disability, Queerness, and Liberation* (Durham, NC: Duke University Press, 2009), 81–118.

25. Sianne Ngai, "Merely Interesting," *Critical Inquiry* 34 (2008), 786.

26. See David Hevey, "The Enfreakment of Photography," in *The Disability Studies Reader*, edited by Lennard J. Davis (New York: Routledge, 2006), 367–78.

27. Tobin Siebers, *Disability Theory* (Ann Arbor: University of Michigan Press, 2008), 114, emphasis added. See also Stefan Honisch, "'Music . . . to Cure or Disable': Therapy for Whom?," *Voices: A World Forum for Music Therapy* 14 (2014), http://voices.no/index.php/voices/article/view/793/658.

28. On reality television in cross-cultural perspectives, see Tasha Oren and Sharon Shahaf, eds., *Global Television Formats: Understanding Television across Borders* (New York: Routledge, 2012); Koos Zwaan and Joost de Bruin, eds., *Adapting Idols: Authenticity, Identity and Performance in a Global Television Format* (Burlington,

VT: Ashgate, 2012); and Amir Hetsroni, ed., *Reality Television: Merging the Global and the Local* (New York: Nova Science Publishers, 2010).

29. Meizel, *Idolized*, 9–10.

30. See Nathan Gardels and Mike Medavoy, *American Idol after Iraq: Competing for Hearts and Minds in the Global Media Age* (Malden, MA: Wiley-Blackwell, 2009).

31. Lynn Spigel, "Entertainment Wars: Television Culture after 9/11," *American Quarterly* 56 (2004), 237.

32. Spigel, "Entertainment Wars," 237.

33. Alex Kuczynski, "Traces of Terror: The Singer; 'Idol' Star Rethinks 9/11 Role," *New York Times* (7 September 2002), http://www.nytimes.com/2002/09/07/us/traces-of-terror-the-singer-idol-star-rethinks-9-11-role.html.

34. Linda Williams, "Film Bodies: Gender, Genre, and Excess," *Film Quarterly* (1991), 4, 5. See also Kendall L. Walton, "Projectivism, Empathy, and Musical Tension," *Philosophical Topics* 26 (1999), 407–40; and Jerrold Levinson, *Contemplating Art: Essays in Aesthetics* (New York: Oxford University Press, 2006), 220–36.

35. Just as reality shows' viewers might find pleasure in noticing cracks in a program's veneer, so operagoers, as Carolyn Abbate notes, might feel especially moved when hearing an unintended, unexpected crack in a singer's voice ("Music: Drastic or Gnostic?," 535).

36. See Matthew Wheelock Stahl, "A Moment like This: *American Idol* and Narratives of Meritocracy," in *Bad Music: The Music We Love to Hate*, edited by Christopher Washburne and Maiken Derno (New York: Routledge, 2004), 212–32; Charles Fairchild, "Building the Authentic Celebrity: The 'Idol' Phenomenon in the Attention Economy," *Popular Music and Society* 30 (2007), 355–75; Dana Heller, "'Calling Out around the World': The Global Appeal of Reality Dance Formats," in *Global Television Formats: Understanding Television*, edited by Tasha Oren and Sharon Shahaf (New York: Routledge, 2012), 39–55; McClain, *American Ideal*, 25–32; and Meizel, *Idolized*, 77–79.

37. McClain, *American Ideal*, 94. A contestant's "amateur" status also contributes to the image of authenticity and the narrative of overcoming. The rules of *Idol* and similar shows stipulate that contestants may not be signed with any record labels at the time of their auditions, but even ex-contracted contestants can nevertheless receive flack for being "too experienced" for the competition (see Rushfield, *American Idol*, 105–12).

38. Elizabeth J. Donaldson and Catherine Prendergast, "Disability and Emotion: 'There's No Crying in Disability Studies!,'" *Journal of Literary & Cultural Disability Studies* 5 (2011), 129–35; and Nick Hodge, "Unruly Bodies at Conference," *Disability & Society* 29 (2014), 655–58. In an earlier book, I observed how the Internet is full of teary disclosures by men, who, upon encountering beautiful recordings of game music, declare something along the lines of, "I'm a man, but I'm crying" (Cheng, *Sound Play*, 81–82).

39. Marathon Productions, "*America's Got Talent*, Season 10 Release Form" (2015), http://www.americasgottalentauditions.com/wp-content/uploads/Personal-Release-Website-Fillable.pdf.

40. Quoted in Eric Olsen, "Slaves of Celebrity," *Salon* (18 September 2002), http://www.salon.com/2002/09/18/idol contract.

41. "Performance Questionnaire," *America's Got Talent* (2013), http://americasgottalentauditions.com/wp-content/uploads/AGT8-VTR-YES-FAQ-FINAL.pdf.

42. "X-Factor Ukraine Aida Nikolaichuk," YouTube (15 July 2012), http://www.youtube.com/watch?v=TPoWDDFRmgg.

43. See Bell, *American Idolatry*, 170–72.

44. Alasdair Glennie, "'Shy' *Britain's Got Talent* Contestant Alice Fredenham Accused of Faking Her Stage Fright as She's Seen Looking Confident in Low Cut Top on *The Voice*," *Daily Mail* (19 April 2013), http://www.dailymail.co.uk/tvshowbiz/article-2311837/Britains-Got-Talentcontestant-Alice-Fredenham-accused-faking-stage-fright-shes-seen-looking-confident-bubbly-The-Voice.html, emphasis added. As the title of this *Daily Mail* article suggests, public criticisms of Fredenham displayed problematic signs and vocabularies of slut-shaming.

45. Images in Figure 4.6 come from "Alice Fredenham Singing 'My Funny Valentine'—Week 1 Auditions," YouTube (13 April 2013), http://www.youtube.com/watch?v=IChJ6eO3k48.

46. To this point, contestants who incorporate melismas into their singing are sometimes accused of putting on fancy airs and, in effect, *over*-singing. As Katherine Meizel notes, critics who lament the prevalence of vocal embellishments in *American Idol* performances imply that "there is *too much* body in the voice, berating *Idol* contestants for their 'vocal gymnastics.' [. . .] The general practice of melisma has, in recent years, been widely maligned by music critics. The magazine *Blender* has called it one of the '50 Worst Things to Happen to Music' and explains it as an '*Idol*-promulgated school of vocal histrionics.' The description of the practice as *histrionic* demonstrates a peculiarly Western, and potentially gendered, understanding of melisma as something disordered—or as a sign of disorder—and even unnatural" (*Idolized*, 66–67, emphasis in original).

47. The other case was Matt Farmer (*American Idol*, season 12), who invented a story about military injuries and thereafter issued a public apology for lying. See "Matt Farmer, *American Idol*'s 2013 Timothy Poe," *Guardian of Valor* (2013), http://guardianofvalor.com/matt-farmer-american-idols-2013-timothy-poe. To gain eligibility, some contestants have also lied or omitted details about criminal records and personal scandals. See "*American Idol* Contestant Jermaine Jones Booted over Criminal Charges," *Rolling Stone* (14 March 2012), http://www.rollingstone.com/music/news/american-idol-contestant-jermaine-jones-booted-over-criminal-charges-20120314.

48. The full audition can be viewed at "America's Got Talent 2012—Tim Poe, Singer/War Veteran," YouTube (5 June 2012), http://www.youtube.com/watch?v=hiItdgDxfMs.

49. See Bryant Jordan, "*Talent* Contestant's Afghan Wounds in Question," *Military* (6 June 2012), http://www.military.com/daily-news/2012/06/06/talent-contestants-afghan-wounds-in-question.html.

50. Jacqueline Cutler, "*America's Got Talent*: Tim Poe 'Deserves to Be Publicly Humiliated,' Says Howie Mandel," *Screener TV* (8 June 2012), http://screenertv.com/news-features/americas-got-talent-tim-poe-deserves-to-be-publicly-humiliated-says-howie-mandel.

51. See Daniel Todd Gilbert, *Stumbling on Happiness* (New York: Alfred A. Knopf, 2006); and Tali Sharot, Christoph W. Korn, and Raymond J. Dolan, "How Unrealistic Optimism Is Maintained in the Face of Reality," *Nature Neuroscience* 14 (2011), 1475–79.

52. As Richard Rushfield points out, "The question of whether *Idol* is 'fixed' remains the subject of perennial rumors and Internet theories," given fans' endless "talk of busy signals, crossed numbers, and changed vote totals" (*American Idol*, 179).

53. Meizel, *Idolized*, 216, emphasis in original. Fans may also derive feelings of agency by voting in ways that snub the meritocratic operations of a show. They could, for example, "Vote for the Worst" to subvert a program's expected metrics. See Jenkins, *Convergence Culture*, 91.

54. Henry Jenkins, Sam Ford, and Joshua Green, *Spreadable Media: Creating Value and Meaning in a Networked Culture* (New York: New York University Press, 2013), 18.

55. See Michael Bérubé, "Afterword: If I Should Live So Long," in *Disability Studies: Enabling the Humanities*, edited by Sharon L. Snyder, Brenda Jo Brueggemann, and Rosemarie Garland-Thomson (New York: Modern Language Association of America, 2002), 337–43.

56. See James Charlton, "Peripheral Everywhere," *Journal of Literary & Cultural Disability Studies* 4 (2010), 195–200; Tobin Siebers, *Disability Theory* (Ann Arbor: University of Michigan Press, 2008), 132–75; and Tom Shakespeare, *The Sexual Politics of Disability: Untold Desires* (London: Cassell, 1996). We might also recall, when physicist Stephen Hawking passed away, the controversial portrayals of his death as a romanticized act of "being freed" from his wheelchair. See Jessica Roy, "Erasing Stephen Hawking's Disability Erases an Important Part of Who He Was," *Los Angeles Times* (16 March 2018), http://www.latimes.com/science/sciencenow/la-sci-sn-stephen-hawking-disability-rights-20180316-story.html.

57. Abilities of fluent singing despite impediments in speech have been well documented but remain only partially understood by speech pathologists, music therapists, and cognitive scientists. See Catherine Y. Wan, et al., "The Therapeutic Effects of Singing in Neurological Disorders," *Music Perception* 27 (2010), 287–95; and Minae Inahara, "The Rejected Voice: Towards Intersubjectivity in Speech Language Pathology," *Disability & Society* 28 (2013), 41–53. See also Andrew Oster, "Melisma as Malady: Cavalli's *Il Giasone* (1649) and Opera's Earliest Stuttering Role," in *Sounding Off: Theorizing Disability in Music*, edited by Neil Lerner and Joseph N. Straus (New York: Routledge, 2006), 157–71.

58. Images in Figure 4.7 come from "American Idol Audition for Lazaro Arbos," YouTube (17 January 2013), http://www.youtube.com/watch?v=WG4YaVPffrI.

59. For a critique of "cure narratives," see Bassler, "But You Don't Look Sick."

60. Laurie Stras, "The Organ of the Soul: Voice, Damage, and Affect," in *Sounding Off: Theorizing Disability in Music*, edited by Neil Lerner and Joseph N. Straus (New York: Routledge, 2006), 174. See also Alex S. Porco, "Throw Yo' Voice Out: Disability as a Desirable Practice in Hip-Hop Vocal Performance," *Disability Studies Quarterly* 34 (2014), http://dsq-sds.org/article/view/3822/3790.

61. Rosemarie Garland-Thomson, "Disability Bioethics: From Theory to Practice," *Kennedy Institute of Ethics Journal* 27 (2017), 332, emphasis in original.

62. See Garland-Thomson, *Staring*; see also Erving Goffman, *The Presentation of Self in Everyday Life* (Garden City, NY: Doubleday, 1959).

63. Garland-Thomson, *Extraordinary Bodies*, 37.

64. See Frank Bogdan, *Freak Show: Presenting Human Oddities for Amusement and Profit* (Chicago: University of Chicago Press, 1990); and David Gerber, "The 'Careers' of People Exhibited in Freak Shows: The Problem of Volition and Valorization," in *Freakery: Cultural Spectacles of the Extraordinary Body*, edited by Rosemarie Garland-Thomson (New York: New York University Press, 1996), 38–54.

65. See Susan Boyle, *The Woman I Was Born to Be: My Story* (New York: Atria Paperback, 2010); Andrea Begley, *I Didn't See That Coming: My Story* (London: BBC Books, 2013); and "Exit Interview: Rion Paige—The X Factor USA," YouTube (6 December 2013), http://www.youtube.com/watch?v=-GYNAufW67A.

66. M. Celia Cain, "Of Pain, Passing and Longing for Music," *Disability & Society* 25 (2010), 747.

67. Darren Franich, "The Rise of Hate-Watching: Which TV Shows Do You Love to Despise?," *Entertainment Weekly* (16 August 2012), http://www.ew.com/article/2012/08/16/newsroom-smash-glee-hatewatch.

68. See Emily Hutcheon and Bonnie Lashewicz, "Theorizing Resilience: Critiquing and Unbounding a Marginalizing Concept," *Disability & Society* 29 (2014), 1383–97.

69. In 2016, a deaf singer named Mandy Harvey auditioned for Season 12 of *America's Got Talent* and received a "Golden Buzzer" (which allows a contestant to advance directly to the live finals, bypassing the intermediary Judge Cuts round). Harvey was born hearing, sang throughout childhood, and became deaf by the age of eighteen. She continued to practice singing with the aid of visual tuners, muscle memory, and vibrational perception. Although her performances on *America's Got Talent* garnered enormous praise, they also drew ire and even death threats from d/Deaf people who believed she was promoting oralism. See Mandy Harvey and Mark Atteberry, *Sensing the Rhythm: Finding My Voice in a World without Sound* (New York: Howard Books, 2017).

70. Chrisman, "A Reflection on Inspiration," 179.

71. Catherine Prendergast, "And Now, A Necessarily Pathetic Response: A Response to Susan Schweik," *American Literary History* 20 (2008), 241–42. See also Howard Sklar, "'What the Hell Happened to Maggie?': Stereotype, Sympathy, and Disability in Toni Morrison's 'Recitatif,'" *Journal of Literary & Cultural Disability Studies* 5 (2011), 137.

72. Darold A. Treffert, *Islands of Genius: The Bountiful Mind of the Autistic, Acquired, and Sudden Savant* (Philadelphia: Jessica Kingsley, 2010), xvii, emphasis in original.

73. Stella Young, "There Is No X-Factor in Patronising Judgement," ABC Australia (20 September 2011), http://www.abc.net.au/rampup/articles/2011/09/20/3321673.htm.

74. Stella Young, "We're Not Here for Your Inspiration," ABC Australia (2 July 2012), http://www.abc.net.au/news/2012-07-03/young-inspiration-porn/4107006; and Harilyn Rousso, *Don't Call Me Inspirational: A Disabled Feminist Talks Back* (Philadelphia: Temple University Press, 2013), 158.

75. See Max Paddison, "Music as Ideal: The Aesthetics of Autonomy," in *The Cambridge History of Nineteenth-Century Music*, edited by Jim Samson (Cambridge: Cambridge University Press, 2001), 318–42.

76. "Emmanuel Kelly, "*The X Factor* 2011 Auditions," YouTube (29 August 2011), https://www.youtube.com/watch?v=W86jlvrG54o, emphasis added.

77. "China's Got Talent 2011 12-yr-old Mongolian Boy Singing 'Mother in the Dream,'" YouTube (6 June 2011), http://www.youtube.com/watch?v=lY7ChkI6c8A, emphasis added, author's translation. Annie Yi's statement in the original Mandarin was: 「不管你的故事怎麼樣, 達木最重要是你歌唱的真的很好。」

78. "Carlos Guevara's Struggles Won't Hold Him Back," YouTube (18 September 2013), http://www.youtube.com/watch?v=3rUWDvuBOHY, emphasis added.

79. Susan Boyle, *The Woman I Was Born to Be: My Story* (New York: Atria Paperback, 2010), 39, 65. On Boyle's disabilities, see also Alice Montgomery, *Susan Boyle: Dreams Can Come True* (New York: Overlook Press, 2010), 11; and Dave Calvert, "'A Person with Some Sort of Learning Disability': The Aetiological Narrative and Public Construction of Susan Boyle," *Disability & Society* 29 (2014), 101–14.

80. McShane, *Susan Boyle*, xiii.

81. It should be noted that viewers of these clips could not even have known whether the reactions of "1:24 Girl" really occurred at the 1:24 mark—that is, whether this footage was doctored or spliced during post-editing (or came from a different performance entirely).

82. Rory Reynolds, "Susan Boyle Audience Member Blasts BGT Producers for Hate Campaign," *Deadline* (8 November 2009), http://www.deadlinenews.co.uk/2009/11/08/11258-2113.

83. "Susan Boyle—Britain's Got Talent 2009 Episode 1—Saturday 11th April," YouTube (11 April 2009), http://www.youtube.com/watch?v=RxPZh4AnWyk.

84. Steve Smith, "Agony of TV Teenager Filmed Sneering during Susan Boyle's Debut," *Daily Record* (22 November 2009), http://www.dailyrecord.co.uk/news/real-life/exclusive-agony-of-tv-teenager-filmed-1042797.

85. Quoted in McShane, *Susan Boyle*, 104.

86. See Smith, "Agony of TV Teenager."

87. Sigmund Freud, *Civilization and Its Discontents*, translated by James Strachey (New York: W. W. Norton, 2010), 41. See also Siebers, *Disability Theory*, 44–45.

88. See Jon Ronson, *So You've Been Publicly Shamed* (New York: Riverhead Books, 2015), 286.

Chapter 5

1. Rosen, *Critical Entertainments*, 9–10.

2. Tony Hoagland, "Poor Britney Spears," *American Poetry Review* 38 (2009), 47.

3. See Eliana Dockterman, "Listen to Britney Spears Singing 'Alien' without Autotune," *TIME* (9 July 2014), http://time.com/2969757/britney-spears-alien-autotune. Video accessible at "Alien NO AUTOTUNE Britney Spears FULL," YouTube (10 July 2014),

http://www.youtube.com/watch?v=MUdKrtsrCBI. "Alien" was the first track on Spears's eighth studio album, *Britney Jean* (2013).

4. On controversies over Auto-Tune, vocoders, and other voice-altering technologies, see Cheng, *Sound Play*, 123–28; Mark Katz, *Capturing Sound: How Technology Has Changed Music*, revised edition (Berkeley: University of California Press, 2010), 50–52; Robin M. James, "Deconstruction, Fetishism, and the Racial Contract: On the Politics of 'Faking It' in Music," *New Centennial Review* 7 (2007), 45–80; and Kay Dickinson, "'Believe'? Vocoders, Digitalised Female Identity and Camp," *Popular Music* 20 (2001), 333–47.

5. Cameron Adams, "Are Y'all Ready to Hear What Britney Spears Sounds Like without AutoTuned Vocals? Sure?," *News* (9 July 2014), http://www.news.com.au/entertainment/music/are-yall-ready-to-hear-what-britney-spears-sounds-like-without-autotuned-vocals-sure/news-story/be8dc05879522bb6d4d87c11ec8c9692; Jess Denham, "Britney Spears Sings 'Alien' without Auto-Tune in Embarrassing Leaked Audio Clip," *Independent* (9 July 2014), http://www.independent.co.uk/arts-entertainment/music/news/britney-spears-sings-alien-without-auto-tune-in-embarrassingly-brilliant-leaked-audio-clip-9595316.html; and King of the Clouds, comment on "Alien NO AUTOTUNE Britney Spears FULL," YouTube (video uploaded on 10 July 2014; comment posted in 2016), http://www.youtube.com/watch?v=MUdKrtsrCBI.

6. Deena Weinstein has pointed out how critics diss Spears's songs as a "paradigm of bad music" that's easy "to kick around" ("Rock Critics Need Bad Music," in *Bad Music: The Music We Love to Hate*, edited by Christopher J. Washburne and Maiken Derno [New York: Routledge 2004], 304).

7. See Sonya Silver, "Autotune. Simple Irony, Really," *Gearslutz* (11 January 2010), http://www.gearslutz.com/board/the-moan-zone/455796-autotune-simple-irony-really.html; Alex Pappademas, "Love Letter to Auto-Tune, Final Installment," *New York Times* (12 August 2011), http://6thfloor.blogs.nytimes.com/2011/08/12/love-letter-to-auto-tune-final-installment; Nick Holmes and Kevin Core, "Pitch Perfection? The 'Flawless' Vocal and the Rise of Auto-Tune," BBC (17 May 2013), http://www.bbc.com/news/entertainment-arts-22514705; and Mark Judge, "Britney, Auto-Tune, and Female Imperfection," *Acculturated* (12 August 2014), http://acculturated.com/britney-auto-tune-and-female-imperfection.

8. See Ronson, *So You've Been Publicly Shamed*; and Daniel J. Solove, *The Future of Reputation: Gossip, Rumor, and Privacy on the Internet* (New Haven, CT: Yale University Press, 2007).

9. Wendy Hui Kyong Chun and Sarah Friedland, "Habits of Leaking: Of Sluts and Network Cards," *differences: A Journal of Feminist Cultural Studies* 26 (2015), 4, emphasis in original.

10. Gregory Currie, "Imagination and Simulation: Aesthetics Meets Cognitive Science," in *Mental Simulation: Evaluations and Applications*, edited by Martin Davies and Tony Stone (Oxford: Blackwell, 1995), 161.

11. See Christopher R. Smit, *The Exile of Britney Spears: A Tale of 21st-Century Consumption* (Chicago: Intellect, 2011); Stan Hawkins and John Richardson,

"Remodeling Britney Spears: Matters of Intoxication and Mediation," *Popular Music and Society* 30 (2007), 605–29; Sean Redmond, "Pieces of Me: Celebrity Confessional Carnality," *Social Semiotics* 18 (2008), 149–61; and Melanie Lowe, "Colliding Feminism: Britney Spears, 'Tweens,' and the Politics of Reception," *Popular Music and Society* 26 (2003), 123–40.

12. Pop music scholarship aside, Spears makes cameos in academic articles on topics ranging from international policy to search engine algorithms, from gay marriage to school dress codes. See Jenna Pitchford, "The 'Global War on Terror,' Identity, and Changing Perceptions: Iraqi Responses to America's War in Iraq," *Journal of American Studies* 45 (2011), 695–716; Brian Hayes, "Computing Science: The Britney Spears Problem," *American Scientist* 96 (2008), 274–79; Robert R.M. Verchick, "Same-Sex and the City," *The Urban Lawyer* 37 (2005), 191–99; Sandra Weber, "Boxed-In by My School Uniform," *Counterpoints* 220 (2004), 61–65; and Mark Leonard, "Diplomacy by Other Means," *Foreign Policy* 132 (2002), 48–56. In these articles that otherwise have little to do with Spears, the authors name-drop the singer as a versatile stand-in for assorted values and vices: celebrity, sexiness, sluttiness, craziness, whiteness, and Americanness. Is it strange that "Britney Spears" appears in a book called *Hybridity: Or the Cultural Logic of Globalization* (by Marwan M. Kraidy [Philadelphia: Temple University Press, 2005], 15), or in an article titled "Manishevitz and Sake, the Kaddish and Sutras: Allen Ginsberg's Spiritual Self-Othering" (Craig Svonkin, *College Literature* 37 [2010], 166–93)? Or does the nature of mega-celebrity actually compel the inverse question: why *wouldn't* Spears come up in a hermeneutics of Ginsberg?

13. Matt Thompson, comment on "Alien NO AUTOTUNE Britney Spears FULL," YouTube (video uploaded on 10 July 2014; comment posted in 2016), http://www.youtube.com/watch?v=MUdKrtsrCBI.

14. Quoted in Kennaway, *Bad Vibrations*, 23.

15. Kennaway, *Bad Vibrations*, 76.

16. Hillel Schwarz, "Inner and Outer Sancta: Earplugs and Hospitals," in *The Oxford Handbook of Sound Studies*, edited by Trevor Pinch and Karin Bijsterveld (New York: Oxford University Press, 2012), 279.

17. These days, Facebook, YouTube, Twitter, Reddit, and comparable upvote-dependent platforms incentivize and facilitate the broadcasting of personal yet mass-standardized reactions (see Jenkins, Ford, and Green, *Spreadable Media*, 153–94).

18. Adams, "Are Y'all Ready."

19. Taylor Best, comment on "Alien NO AUTOTUNE Britney Spears FULL," YouTube (video uploaded on 10 July 2014; comment posted in 2016), http://www.youtube.com/watch?v=MUdKrtsrCBI.

20. Lyndsey Parker, "Producer William Orbit Defends Auto-Tune-Free Britney Spears Song Leak," *Yahoo* (9 July 2014), http://www.yahoo.com/music/bp/producer-william-orbit-defends-auto-tune-free-britney-spears-song-leak-211307690.html.

21. See Jamie Lendino, "The Best Audio Editing Software of 2018," *PC Mag* (12 February 2018), http://www.pcmag.com/roundup/356915/the-best-audio-editing-software.

22. See Harriet Gibsone, "Raw Power: Why Mocking the Isolated Vocals of Courtney Love Is Misogynistic," *Guardian* (10 October 2014), http://www.

theguardian.com/music/musicblog/2014/oct/10/raw-power-why-mocking-isolated-vocals-of-courtney-love-is-misogynistic.

23. See "Isolated Vocal Tracks—17 Voices That Marked the Last Century," *Ground Guitar* (2017), http://www.groundguitar.com/isolated-vocal-tracks-17-voices-that-marked-the-last-century.

24. See Hilary Weaver, "Jennifer Aniston Says She Can't Escape Baby-Bump-Rumor Photos," *Vanity Fair* (30 November 2016), http://www.vanityfair.com/style/2016/11/jennifer-aniston-says-she-cant-escape-baby-bump-rumor-photos.

25. Ruth Graham, "One of *Us*," *Slate* (22 September 2016), http://www.slate.com/articles/life/the_next_20/2016/09/the_invention_of_us_weekly_s_stars_they_re_just_like_us_feature.html.

26. David Samuels, "Shooting Britney," *Atlantic* (April 2008), http://www.theatlantic.com/magazine/archive/2008/04/shooting-britney/306735.

27. Hoagland, "Poor Britney Spears."

28. Samuels, "Shooting Britney."

29. Women with shaved heads, points out Patrick Barkham, "emerge in art as either frightening or frightened" ("The Bald Truth," *Guardian* [20 February 2007], http://www.theguardian.com/world/2007/feb/20/gender.music). In science fiction, bald women also tend to come off both/either alien and/or alienated: Ripley in *Alien 3*, Furiosa in *Mad Max: Fury Road*, Eleven in *Stranger Things*, and Jack in *Mass Effect 2*, to name a few.

30. Samuels, "Shooting Britney."

31. Samuels, "Shooting Britney."

32. Vanessa Grigoriadis delivers a play-by-play of the thrilling "Britney detail" as follows: "A Britney chase is more fun than a roller coaster, but with the chance that the experience could cause lasting harm. 'Britney is the most dangerous detail in Hollywood,' says [Harvey] Levin of TMZ. There are twenty paps in the core Britney detail, a bunch of hilarious, slightly scary thugs who use expert drag-racing skills to block off new guys who try to get in the mix. It's like a game of Frogger, with everyone jostling to be the first car behind Britney, the better to shoot all over her when she stops (and then watch their feet, because several have found themselves on crutches after she speeds away)" ("The Tragedy of Britney Spears," *Rolling Stone* [21 February 2008], http://www.rollingstone.com/music/news/the-tragedy-of-britney-spears-rolling-stones-2008-cover-story-20080221).

33. Serge F. Kovaleski and Joe Coscarelli, "Is Britney Spears Ready to Stand on Her Own?," *New York Times* (4 May 2016), http://www.nytimes.com/2016/05/08/arts/music/is-britney-spears-ready-to-stand-on-her-own.html?_r=1.

34. Kovaleski and Coscarelli, "Is Britney Spears Ready to Stand on Her Own?"

35. Jeannette Walls, "Oops, Spears Switched Religions Again," *Today* (18 January 2006), http://www.today.com/popculture/oops-spears-switched-religions-again-wbna10696063.

36. For a reflexive critique of "unmarked whiteness" (and how academic presumptions of white unmarkedness might paradoxically reify the implicit workings of white privilege), see Ruth Frankenberg, "The Mirage of an Unmarked Whiteness," in *The Making*

and Unmaking of Whiteness, edited by Birgit Brander Rasmussen, Eric Klinenberg, Irene J. Nexica, and Matt Wray (Durham, NC: Duke University Press, 2001), 72–96.

37. Kathryn Flett, "She Did It Again," *Guardian* (20 August 2005), http://www. theguardian.com/theobserver/2005/aug/21/features.review97.

38. Grigoriadis, "The Tragedy of Britney Spears."

39. Karen Bettez Halnon, *The Consumption of Inequality: Weapons of Mass Distraction* (New York: Palgrave Macmillan, 2013), 122, 124. For a lexical and social history of "white trash," see Matt Wray, *Not Quite White: White Trash and the Boundaries of Whiteness* (Durham, NC: Duke University Press, 2006); and Matt Wray and Annalee Newitz, eds., *White Trash: Race and Class in America* (New York: Routledge, 1997).

40. Olivia Oliver-Hopkins, "'I's Got to Get Me Some Education!' Class and the Camp-Horror Nexus in *House of 1000 Corpses*," in *Sontag and the Camp Aesthetic: Advancing New Perspectives*, edited by Bruce E. Drushel and Brian M. Peters (Lanham, MD: Lexington Books, 2017), 158.

41. Russell Meeuf, "Class, Corpulence, and Neoliberal Citizenship: Melissa McCarthy on *Saturday Night Live*," *Celebrity Studies* 7 (2016), 143. See also Kimberly Bachechi, "Our Icons: Ourselves; Britney Spears, Justin Timberlake, Kevin Federline, and the Construction of Whiteness in a Post-Race America," *Celebrity Studies* 6 (2015), 164–77.

42. See Kate Manne, *Down Girl: The Logic of Misogyny* (New York: Oxford University Press, 2018), 78–105.

43. See Hamilton Carroll, *Affirmative Reaction: New Formations of White Masculinity* (Durham, NC: Duke University Press, 2011), 101–27; Bachechi, "Our Icons: Ourselves," 173–74; and Gael Sweeney, "The King of White Trash Culture: Elvis Presley and the Aesthetics of Excess," in *White Trash: Race and Class in America*, edited by Matt Wray and Annalee Newitz (New York: Routledge, 1997), 249–66.

44. Infamously, when Rebecca Black's "Friday," dubbed the "Worst Song Ever," popped up on YouTube in 2011, viewers didn't just attack the music; they called Black "ugly, fat, terrible, the worst person in the world" (Elias Leight, "Life after 'Friday': Rebecca Black's Journey Back to the Charts," *Rolling Stone* [17 April 2017], http://www. rollingstone.com/music/music-features/life-after-friday-rebecca-blacks-journey-back-to-the-charts-117179). One could try to shrug off the attacks as misogynist trolling. But the fact remains that people read into then-thirteen-year-old Black's "grating voice" as a metonym for this teenager's personhood, as if her musical failings were somehow yoked to broader failings. Jokes and japes rapidly turned to death threats and rape threats against Black. According to police investigators, the threats "were related to getting the music [of "Friday"] off the Internet or they would kill her" (Daily Mail Reporter, "Teen YouTube Sensation Rebecca Black under Police Protection after Receiving Death Threats," *Daily Mail* [20 April 2011], http://www.dailymail.co.uk/news/article-1378865/Rebecca-Black-police-protection-receiving-death-threats.html). Even though the people who made these threats might say they were just kidding, the assaultive remarks were overtly launched in the name of aesthetic cleansing. Wipe that ugly music from the web, or else. For a critique of criticisms of Rebecca Black, see Diane Pecknold, "'These

Stupid Little Sounds in Her Voice': Valuing and Vilifying the New Girl Voice," in *Voicing Girlhood in Popular Music: Performance, Authority, Authenticity*, edited by Jacqueline Warwick and Allison Adrian (New York: Routledge, 2016), 77–98 (esp. 80); see also Danielle Keats Citron, *Hate Crimes in Cyberspace* (Cambridge, MA: Harvard University Press, 2014).

45. Halnon, *The Consumption of Inequality*, 112. Halnon furthermore offers a typology of white-trash characteristics and caricatures, including the "redneck," the "drunk," the "wifebeater," the "lot lizard," the "mullet man," the "smokin' mama," the "vacuous tart," the "stripper," the "super-hot scammer," and the "Jerry Springer Show Freak" (97–110).

46. Sarah Hampson, "No Sex Please. I'm Not Britney," *The Globe and Mail* (16 July 2005), http://www.theglobeandmail.com/arts/no-sex-please-im-not-britney/article18241016.

47. Milly Williamson, "Female Celebrities and the Media: The Gendered Denigration of the 'Ordinary' Celebrity," *Celebrity Studies* 1 (2010), 119.

48. Hilary Parsons Dick, "*Una Gabacha Sinvergüenza* (A Shameless White-Trash Woman): Moral Mobility and Interdiscursivity in a Mexican Migrant Community," *American Anthropologist* 119 (2017), 224.

49. Stephen M. Silverman, "Britney Spears Says She Was at 'Rock Bottom' in Rehab," *People* (29 May 2007), http://people.com/celebrity/britney-spears-says-she-was-at-rock-bottom-in-rehab; and Anna Holmes, "In Defense of the Badly-Behaved Britney Spears," *Jezebel* (17 August 2007), http://jezebel.com/290011/in-defense-of-the-badly-behaved-britney-spears.

50. Rob Sheffield, "Britney Spears' 'Blackout': A Salute to Her Misunderstood Punk Masterpiece," *Rolling Stone* (30 October 2017), http://www.rollingstone.com/music/news/rob-sheffield-on-britney-spears-blackout-punk-masterpiece-w510038.

51. Amber Ryland, "Britney Spears: Overwhelmingly the Worst Interview of the Year in Chicago—'It Was a Struggle For Her to Form a Sentence,'" *Radar Online* (23 December 2013), http://radaronline.com/exclusives/2013/12/britney-spears-worst-interview-of-year-chicago; and Sara Hammel, "Britney Spears: 'Kiss My A—!,'" *People* (2 December 2010), http://people.com/celebrity/britney-spears-fights-back-kiss-my-a.

52. See Feona Attwood, "Sluts and Riot Grrrls: Female Identity and Sexual Agency," *Journal of Gender Studies* 16 (2007), 233–47.

53. Hoagland, "Poor Britney Spears."

54. See "Britney Spears—Gimme More Live at MTV VMA's 2007," YouTube (28 January 2013), http://www.youtube.com/watch?v=udDlSRgyxMc; and John Maynard, "In VMA Comeback, Britney Makes All the Wrong Moves," *Washington Post* (10 September 2007), http://www.washingtonpost.com/wp-dyn/content/article/2007/09/09/AR2007090902135.html.

55. "Leave Britney Alone (Complete)," YouTube (11 August 2011), http://www.youtube.com/watch?v=WqSTXuJeTks.

56. Sheila Marikar, "Why Was Britney So Bad?," ABC News (10 September 2007), http://abcnews.go.com/Entertainment/story?id=3582432.

57. Amy Erdman Farrell, *Fat Shame: Stigma and the Fat Body in American Culture* (New York: New York University Press, 2011), 121.

58. Jeff Leeds, "Spears's Awards Fiasco Stirs Speculation about Her Future," *New York Times* (13 September 2007), http://www.nytimes.com/2007/09/13/arts/music/13brit. html.

59. Associated Press, "Was Media Unfair to Call Britney Spears Fat?," *Today* (10 September 2007), http://www.today.com/popculture/was-media-unfair-call-britney-spears-fat-wbna20713930.

60. Quoted in Associated Press, "Was Media Unfair?" For writings on voice, body, and body image (via the case study of Karen Carpenter and anorexia nervosa), see George McKay, "Skinny Blues: Karen Carpenter, Anorexia Nervosa and Popular Music," *Popular Music* 37 (2018), 1–21; Freya Jarman-Ivens, *Queer Voices: Technologies, Vocalities, and the Musical Flaw* (New York: Palgrave MacMillan, 2011), 59–94; and Mitchell Morris, *The Persistence of Sentiment: Display and Feeling in Popular Music of the 1970s* (Berkeley: University of California Press, 2013), 118–42.

61. Farrell, *Fat Shame*, 122.

62. Farrell, *Fat Shame*, 122.

63. Farrell, *Fat Shame*, 122. Critiquing the media's scrutiny of Britney Spears's physical and mental fitness, Brenda Weber writes: "[Spears's] 2007 weight gain of between 20 and 40 pounds signaled in media accounts not just a private life and a career out of control, but a mind unhinged. [. . .] The thin body is always one step closer to a Western ideal of empowered rational individualism and increasing upward class mobility, whereas the heavy body is made all the more abject through a madness brought on by a bodily disorder that culminates in an alienation from the self and a perpetual residency in the class codes of 'poor white trash'" ("Stark Raving Fat: Celebrity, Cellulite, and the Sliding Scale of Sanity," *Feminism & Psychology* 22 [2012], 346).

64. Monica Lewinsky, "The Price of Shame," *TED Talks* (2015), transcript available at http://www.ted.com/talks/monica_lewinsky_the_price_of_shame/transcript?language=en.

65. Chun and Friedland, "Habits of Leaking," 10.

66. Laura M. Carpenter, *Virginity Lost: An Intimate Portrait of First Sexual Experiences* (New York: New York University Press, 2005), 57–61.

67. Chun and Friedland, "Habits of Leaking," 3.

68. Samuels, "Shooting Britney."

69. Pecknold, "These Stupid Little Sounds in Her Voice," 84.

70. Ann Powers, *Good Booty: Love and Sex, Black & White, Body and Soul in American Music* (New York: HarperCollins, 2017), 302.

71. Steven Daly, "Britney Spears, Teen Queen: Rolling Stone's 1999 Cover Story," *Rolling Stone* (15 April 1999; published online 29 March 2011), http://www.rollingstone.com/music/news/britney-spears-teen-queen-rolling-stones-1999-cover-story-20110329.

72. Powers, *Good Booty*, xxi. Ann Powers uses the phrase "perform[ing] awakening" to describe Miley Cyrus's provocative (and, according to many critics, shockingly sexual) performance with Robin Thicke at the 2013 MTV Video Music Awards.

Concerning this arch-twerker, Powers writes: "Reaching sexual maturity at a time when pop's culture of pleasure and sensual awareness had never been more frankly explicit, Cyrus did the sensible thing. She performed awakening, the same way she'd performed awkward adolescence for years on prime time" (xxi). Emily White has noted the curious language of the phrase "sexual awakening," almost "as if before the moment of adolescence kids were asleep but now they live in a psychological morning" (*Fast Girls: Teenage Tribes and the Myth of the Slut* [New York: Scribner, 2002], 24)—that is, as if kids were not even humanly cognizant until puberty jolts them into vigilance and social participation. On girl groups and coming-of-age rituals (social, musical, performative), see Jacqueline Warwick, *Girl Groups, Girl Culture: Popular Music and Identity in the 1960s* (New York: Routledge, 2007). See also Jacqueline Warwick and Allison Adrian, "Introduction," in *Voicing Girlhood in Popular Music: Performance, Authority, Authenticity*, edited by Jacqueline Warwick and Allison Adrian (New York: Routledge, 2016), 1–11; and Alexandra Apolloni, "The Lollipop Girl's Voice: Respectability, Migration, and Millie Small's 'My Boy Lollipop,'" *Journal of Popular Music Studies* 28 (2016), 460–73.

73. "Britney Spears 'Primetime Interview with Diane Sawyer (Part 1)' HD," YouTube (4 September 2013), http://www.youtube.com/watch?v=qROlbBPwDG0.

74. Melanie Lowe, "Colliding Feminisms: Britney Spears, 'Tweens,' and the Politics of Reception," *Popular Music and Society* 26 (2003), 137, 124.

75. Sheila Marikar and Jonann Brady, "Bette Calls Britney a Wild and Woolly Slut," ABC News (8 December 2006), http://abcnews.go.com/Entertainment/story?id=2707901&page=1.

76. Naomi Wolf, "Young Women, Give Up the Vocal Fry and Reclaim Your Strong Female Voice," *Guardian* (24 July 2015), http://www.theguardian.com/commentisfree/2015/jul/24/vocal-fry-strong-female-voice. Critics both laud and lament Spears as an archetypal fryer. One person has gone so far as to claim that Spears "invented" vocal fry with her raspy moans and rattles in "Baby One More Time" ("Britney Inventions," *Tumblr* [24 October 2013], http://britneyinventions.tumblr.com/post/64960448604/vocal-fry-is-a-singing-technique-first-developed), while others concede how, at the very least, this debut single employed vocal fry "anachronistically" (Thom Dunn, "What Is 'Vocal Fry,' and Why Doesn't Anyone Care When Men Talk Like That?," *Upworthy* [28 July 2015], http://www.upworthy.com/what-is-vocal-fry-and-why-doesnt-anyone-care-when-men-talk-like-that) and "quite a long time before the term became popularised" (Alex Matsuo, "10 Most Irritating Female Celebrity Voices," *The Richest* [13 March 2015], http://www.therichest.com/expensive-lifestyle/entertainment/10-most-irritating-celebrity-vocal-fry-offenders).

77. Wolf, "Young Women." A few days after Wolf published her piece, the *Guardian* printed a response by historian Erin Riley, who argued that vocal fry is just an excuse that gives people yet another reason not to listen to women. "Before vocal fry, there were complaints about overuse of the word 'like.' Before that, there was upspeak," Riley points out. "But history shows once vocal fry is no longer the excuse, there'll be another. It is the listeners, not the speakers, who are the problem" ("Naomi Wolf Misses the Point about 'Vocal Fry': It's Just an Excuse Not to Listen to Women,"

Guardian [27 July 2015], http://www.theguardian.com/commentisfree/2015/jul/28/naomi-wolf-misses-the-point-about-vocal-fry-its-just-an-excuse-not-to-listen-to-women).

78. "Britney a Bust," *New York Post* (10 September 2007), http://nypost.com/2007/09/10/britney-a-bust.

79. Mia Renee, "The Curious Case of Britney Spears' 'Baby Voice,'" *Miareneecole.com* (2016), http://miareneecole.com/2016/10/11/the-curious-case-of-britney-spears-baby-voice; and James Dinh, "The Curious Case of Britney Spears's Voice: Where Did It Go?," *She Knows* (10 July 2014), http://www.sheknows.com/entertainment/articles/1043415/the-curious-case-of-britney-spears-voice-where-did-it-go.

80. See "The Hidden Potential of Britney Spears," YouTube (3 March 2018), http://www.youtube.com/watch?v=v8xdYEO4ukw.

81. Patrick Barbier, *The World of the Castrati: The History of an Extraordinary Operatic Phenomenon* (London: Souvenir Press, 1996), 242; and J. S. Jenkins, "The Lost Voice: A History of the Castrato," *Journal of Pediatric Endocrinology and Metabolism* 13 (2000), 1503–18.

82. Stras, "Organ of the Soul," 178.

83. Heather Hadlock, *Mad Loves: Women and Music in Offenbach's* Les Contes d'Hoffmann (Princeton, NJ: Princeton University Press, 2000), 13.

84. Shannon Lee Dawdy, *Patina: A Profane Archaeology* (Chicago: University of Chicago Press, 2016), 13.

85. See Andrea Mandell, "Adele Has 'Damaged' Vocal Cords, Cancels Final Shows," *USA Today* (30 June 2017), http://www.usatoday.com/story/life/music/2017/06/30/adele-has-damaged-vocal-cords-cancels-final-shows/103334582; and Justin Wm Moyer, "How Julie Andrews's Voice Was Stolen by a Medical Disaster," *Washington Post* (19 March 2015), http://www.washingtonpost.com/news/morning-mix/wp/2015/03/19/how-julie-andrewss-voice-was-stolen-by-a-medical-disaster/?utm_term=.672b4581a9f1.

86. Jon Caramanica, "Review: Mariah Carey and Her Can't-Look-Away Debut in Las Vegas," *New York Times* (7 May 2015), http://www.nytimes.com/2015/05/08/arts/music/review-mariah-carey-and-her-cant-look-away-debut-in-las-vegas.html.

87. Pecknold, "These Stupid Little Sounds," 78, 79.

88. Barbara Fox DeMaio, "Girls and Puberty: The Voice, It Is a-Changin'; A Discussion of Pedagogical Methods for the Training of the Voice through Puberty," in *Voicing Girlhood in Popular Music: Performance, Authority, Authenticity*, edited by Jacqueline Warwick and Allison Adrian (New York: Routledge, 2016), 104.

89. Laurie Stras, "Voice of the Beehive: Vocal Technique at the Turn of the 1960s," in *She's So Fine: Reflections on Whiteness, Femininity, Adolescence and Class in 1960s Music*, edited by Laurie Stras (Burlington, VT: Ashgate, 2010), 36, emphasis in original.

90. Alice Vincent, "A Decade Later: How Britney Moved on from Her Year of Hell," *Telegraph* (16 February 2017), http://www.telegraph.co.uk/music/artists/miming-through-the-heartbreak-the-story-behind-britney-spearss-t.

91. "Britney Spears 'Primetime Interview.'"

92. Lynne Spears, *Through the Storm: A Real Story of Fame and Family in a Tabloid World* (Nashville, TN: Thomas Nelson, 2008), 91.

93. iLike Pepsi, comment on "Britney Spears—Alien (No AutoTune)."

94. Divas Addixt, comment on "Britney Spears—Alien (No AutoTune)."

95. Graham Simmons, comment on "Britney Spears—Alien (No AutoTune)."

96. Psylon21 (Figure 5.5).

97. Let's Mash It Up! (Figure 5.5).

98. In a review of Spears's 2016 album *Glory*, Lindsay Zoladz points to a silver lining in this star's lack of a "traditionally virtuosic" voice, which has, throughout her career, provided "oddly, a stylistic boon: she was free to stretch it out like taffy, pitch it down to a low, alien moan, or smash it into a million crystalline pieces" ("Leaving Britney Alone," *Ringer* [30 August 2016], http://theringer.com/britney-spears-glory-album-vmas-42701dddac4c#.7g4wyj60r).

99. Adam Krims, *Rap Music and the Poetics of Identity* (Cambridge: Cambridge University Press, 2000), 54–55, 73–75.

100. See Cheng, *Just Vibrations*, 10–11; and Bryan Stevenson, *Just Mercy: A Story of Justice and Redemption* (New York: Spiegel & Grau, 2014), 17–18.

101. Michel Foucault, *Discipline and Punish: The Birth of the Prison* (New York: Random House, 1975); see also Katherine Bergeron and Philip V. Bohlman, eds., *Disciplining Music: Musicology and Its Canons* (Chicago: University of Chicago Press, 1992).

102. At the 2014 Grammy Awards, Lorde performed her chart topper "Royals" (which won the night's Song of the Year) and, alongside the down-tempo sultry vocals, broke out some "weird dance moves" that reportedly "freak[ed] people out" (Justin Massoud, "Lorde Breaks Out Some Weird Dance Moves for 'Royals' at 2014 Grammys," K945 [26 January 2014], http://k945.com/lorde-weird-dance-moves-royals-2014-grammys-video; and Tanya Chen, "Lorde's Grammy Performance Proved Her Dancing Continues to Freak People Out," *Buzzfeed* [26 January 2014], http://www.buzzfeed.com/tanyachen/lordes-grammy-performance-proved-her-dancing-continues-to-fr?utm_term=.guvjRrvj7#.poVAZ0QAz). Within hours, someone uploaded a video titled "LORDE WITHOUT AUTOTUNE—Royals—Grammys 2014," YouTube (26 January 2014), http://www.youtube.com/watch?v=7uzR0ZoZPjU. But it wasn't a *gotcha!* clip of isolated vocals; rather, it was an over-the-top satire that, as Diane Pecknold describes, "replaced Lorde's vocals with a track of unintelligible growls, choking gasps, throat clearing, and even farts" ("These Stupid Little Sounds," 92). In this conspicuously fake leak, the insertion of farts is especially revealing. Besides their intended comedic effect, the scatological sounds played on viewers' anxieties over not knowing what to make of then-seventeen-year-old Lorde's dancing, singing, girling body—an out-of-control body whose choreographies defied easy legibility.

103. Cindy LaCom, who lives with multiple sclerosis, offers a personal, visceral account: "Shit is filthy, and it represents contagion in ways that many physical and cognitive disabilities do not. [. . .] But when people discover that I might shit my pants or pass gas through an open fistula on my buttocks as a consequence of my Crohn's, conversation stops cold and verbal constipation becomes the order of the

day" ("Filthy Bodies, Porous Boundaries: The Politics of Shit in Disability Studies," *Disability Studies Quarterly* 27 [2007], http://dsq-sds.org/article/view/11/11). Susan Wendell similarly notes that "people with disabilities can and sometimes do make each other 'the Other,' for example by despising those who have less control over their bodily functions. [. . .] Failure to control the body is one of the most powerful symbolic meanings of disability" (*The Rejected Body: Feminist Philosophical Reflections on Disability* [New York: Routledge, 1996], 61). See also Margrit Shildrick, *Leaky Bodies and Boundaries: Feminism, Postmodernism, and (Bio)ethics* (New York: Routledge, 1997), 13–61.

104. Kayla Caldwell, "'The Most Unattractive Moment of My Life!' Fergie Opens Up about the Now-Infamous Moment She Wet Herself Onstage," *Daily Mail* (13 November 2014), http://www.dailymail.co.uk/tvshowbiz/article-2834060/The-unattractive-moment-life-Fergie-opens-infamous-moment-wet-onstage.html. Concerning the urination episode, Fergie explained that she and her fellow musicians were running late to the concert, such that she had been left with no time to visit the restroom before the show: "I'm running on and we jump and do 'Let's Get It Started,' and I get crazy and I jump and I run across the stage and my adrenaline was going and gosh" (Caldwell, "Most Unattractive Moment"). I thank Jacqueline Warwick for bringing this Fergie incident to my attention.

105. Chris Willman, "Fergie Sexes Up National Anthem at NBA All-Star Game and America Isn't Having It," *Variety* (18 February 2018), http://variety.com/2018/music/news/fergie-nba-all-star-game-national-anthem-1202704177.

106. Gayle Wald, "How Svengali Lost His Jewish Accent," *Sounding Out!* (26 September 2011), http://soundstudiesblog.com/author/gaylewald1.

107. George du Maurier, *Trilby* (New York: Harper and Brothers Publishers, 1894), 378–79, emphasis in original.

108. Daniel Pick, *Svengali's Web: The Alien Enchanter in Modern Culture* (New Haven, CT: Yale University Press, 2000), 221.

109. Spears, *Through the Storm*, 168.

110. Eve Kosofsky Sedgwick, "Paranoid Reading and Reparative Reading, or, You're So Paranoid, You Probably Think This Essay Is about You," in *Touching Feeling: Affect, Pedagogy, Performativity* (Durham, NC: Duke University Press, 2003), 123–51.

111. On academic shame in the age of Google, see Benjamin Walton, "Quirk Shame," *Representations* 132 (2015), 121–29.

112. Hoagland, "Poor Britney Spears," emphasis in original.

113. "[LEAKED] Britney Spears—Toxic (Raw Vocals)," YouTube (6 June 2017), http://www.youtube.com/watch?v=BPzZR4CMFQ0.

114. Cavan Sieczkowski, "You Have to Listen to Britney Spears Singing 'Toxic' without Auto-Tune," *Huffington Post* (7 June 2017), http://www.huffingtonpost.com/entry/britney-spears-toxic-no-auto-tune_us_59381280e4b01fc18d3f69d0; Isabel Jones, "Britney Spears's 'Toxic' sans Auto-Tune Will Blow Your Mind," *InStyle* (6 June 2017), http://www.instyle.com/news/britney-spears-toxic-without-auto-tune; and Simon Delott, "Britney Spears: Raw Vocals for 'Toxic' LEAKED!,"

Hollywood Gossip (9 June 2017), http://www.thehollywoodgossip.com/videos/
britney-spears-leaked-raw-vocals-for-toxic-better-than-autotune.

115. Manuster, comment on "Britney Spears—Toxic (without Auto-Tune)—NEW
VOCALS (ALTERNATE VERSION)," YouTube (video uploaded 12 July 2017; comment posted in 2017), http://www.youtube.com/watch?v=J-NrcIXz0VQ.

116. See "Cathy Dennis—Toxic (Demo for Britney Spears)," YouTube (10 January 2011),
http://www.youtube.com/watch?v=Bhwn-7Pm9Bg.

117. Amartya Sen, *Poverty and Famines: An Essay on Entitlement and Deprivation*
(Oxford: Clarendon Press, 1981), 1, emphasis in original.

118. Uttara Choudhury, "Amartya Sen: The Enlightened Economist," *Braingainmag.com*
(2011), http://www.braingainmag.com/amartya-sen-the-enlightened-economist.
htm.

119. Slut Machine, "Who's Crazier: Britney Spears or the Rest of Us for Giving a Shit?"
Jezebel (4 January 2008), http://jezebel.com/340504/whos-crazier-britney-spears-
or-the-rest-of-us-for-giving-a-shit.

120. Henry Barbour, Sally Bradshaw, Ari Fleischer, Zori Fonalledas, and Glenn McCall,
"Growth & Opportunity Project," paid for by the Republican National Committee
(2013), available at http://assets.documentcloud.org/documents/624581/rnc-
autopsy.pdf, 7.

121. Barbour et al., "Growth & Opportunity Project," 17, 18, 19, 22, 78, 79, 81.

Chapter 6

1. Audre Lorde, "The Uses of Anger: Women Responding to Racism," in *Sister
Outsider: Essays and Speeches* (Berkeley, CA: Crossing Press, 2007), 125.

2. Regina N. Bradley, "SANDRA BLAND: #SayHerName Loud or Not at All,"
Sounding Out! (16 November 2015), http://soundstudiesblog.com/2015/11/16/
sandra-bland-sayhername-loud.

3. *State of Missouri v. Darren Wilson*, Grand Jury Volume V (16 September 2014), 212,
225, 227–28, 228–229, available at http://www.documentcloud.org/documents/
1370494-grand-jury-volume-5.html. See also Jake Halpern, "The Cop," *New Yorker*
(10/17 August 2015), http://www.newyorker.com/magazine/2015/08/10/the-cop;
and Raphael Travis Jr., *The Healing Power of Hip Hop* (Santa Barbara, CA: ABC-CLIO,
2016), 102–4.

4. Dorian Johnson, who had been walking with Michael Brown, witnessed the alterca-
tion. He recalled that Brown, after being struck by Wilson's first bullet, announced,
"I don't have a gun" (*State of Missouri v. Darren Wilson*, Grand Jury Volume IV [10
September 2014], 123).

5. *State of Missouri v. Darren Wilson*, Vol. V, 227. Wilson testified that Brown had said,
"Fuck what you have to say," "What the fuck are you going to do about it" (209), and
"You are too much of a pussy to shoot me" (214).

6. Wilson claimed he had "[told Brown] to get on the ground, get on the ground," and
that "less than one minute" passed between "[seeing Brown] walking down the

street until Michael Brown is dead in the street" (*State of Missouri v. Darren Wilson*, Vol. V, 272).

7. John Paul Wilson, Nicholas O. Rule, and Kurt Hugenberg, "Racial Bias in Judgments of Physical Size and Formidability: From Size to Threat," *Journal of Personality and Social Psychology* 113 (2017), 59.

8. Loehmann claimed he had "ordered Tamir [Rice] three times to show his hands before opening fire," though several witnesses later came forward to say they had heard no warnings at all (Brandon Blackwell, "Witnesses Did Not Hear Cleveland Police Officer Order Tamir Rice to Show His Hands before Shots Fired," *Cleveland.com* [13 June 2015], http://www.cleveland.com/metro/index.ssf/2015/06/witnesses_did_not_hear_clevela.html#incart_maj-story-1).

9. Timothy Loehmann, statement to investigators (signed and dated 30 November 2015), available at http://i2.cdn.turner.com/cnn/2015/images/12/01/officer.loehmann.statement.pdf.

10. Jeremy Stahl, "Cleveland Police Union Boss Says Awful Thing about Tamir Rice Again," *Slate* (25 April 2016), http://www.slate.com/blogs/the_slatest/2016/04/25/steve_loomis_says_awful_thing_about_tamir_rice_again.html. The move to criminalize Rice didn't simply come from police officers. In an article for CNN, legal analyst Philip Holloway recommended that people "turn to the specific facts," which include the following: "Tamir Rice, while being a mere 12 years old, appeared much older" ("Tamir Rice's Death: A Lawful Tragedy," *CNN* [28 December 2015], http://www.cnn.com/2015/12/28/opinions/holloway-tamir-rice-case/index.html). For Holloway to classify Rice's "older" appearance as "fact" is all the more problematic given Holloway's legal credentials.

11. Jonathan Capehart, "Playing 'Games' with Trayvon Martin's Image," *Washington Post* (6 February 2013), http://www.washingtonpost.com/blogs/post-partisan/wp/2013/02/06/playing-games-with-trayvon-martins-image/?utm_term=.60ff66326d38.

12. Capehart, "Playing 'Games.' "

13. See Katie Sanders, "A Real Photo of Trayvon Martin? Chain Email Makes False Claim," *Politifact* (17 July 2012), http://www.politifact.com/florida/statements/2012/jul/17/chain-email/real-photo-trayvon-martin-chain-email-says-so.

14. Marc NC, "Graphic Evidence of the Racism of Fox News: Racial Photoshopping," *News Corpse* (11 April 2012), http://www.newscorpse.com/ncWP/?p=6851. See also Nick Summers, "Fox News Coverage of the Trayvon Martin Case Criticized," *Daily Beast* (21 March 2012), http://www.thedailybeast.com/fox-news-coverage-of-the-trayvon-martin-case-criticized.

15. See Deirdre Carmody, "*Time* Responds to Criticism over Simpson Cover," *New York Times* (25 June 1994), http://www.nytimes.com/1994/06/25/us/time-responds-to-criticism-over-simpson-cover.html.

16. See Rebecca A. Dore, Kelly M. Hoffman, Angeline S. Lillard, and Sophie Trawalter, "Children's Racial Bias in Perceptions of Others' Pain," *British Journal of Developmental Psychology* 32 (2014), 218–31; and Sophie Trawalter, Kelly M. Hoffman, and Adam Waytz, "Racial Bias in Perceptions of Others' Pain," *PLOS ONE* 7 (2012), http://doi.org/10.1371/journal.pone.0048546. Authors

summarized their findings as follows: "Five-, 7-, and 10-year-olds first rated the amount of pain they themselves would feel in 10 situations such as biting their tongue or hitting their head. They then rated the amount of pain they believed two other children—a Black child and a White child, matched to the child's gender—would feel in response to the same events. We found that by age 7, children show a weak racial bias and that by age 10, they show a strong and reliable racial bias" (n.p.).

17. See Lisa Wade, "The Racial Empathy Gap," *Pacific Standard* (26 September 2013), http://psmag.com/social-justice/racial-empathy-gap-race-black-white-psychology-66993; and Jason Silverstein, "I Don't Feel Your Pain," *Slate* (27 June 2013), http://www.slate.com/articles/health_and_science/science/2013/06/racial_empathy_gap_people_don_t_perceive_pain_in_other_races.html. See also Matteo Forgiarini, Marcello Gallucci, and Angelo Maravita, "Racism and the Empathy for Pain on Our Skin," *Frontiers in Psychology* 2 (2011), 1–7. Instructive though it may be, "racial empathy gap" can nevertheless sound too neutral, absolvent, clinical, and bilateral, as if people of different races simply happen to lack empathy across color lines, and as if dark-skinned bodies aren't overwhelmingly the ones paying for such a lack—paying, at times, with their lives. Perhaps a more honest term would be *racist* empathy gap.

18. See John Hoberman, *Black and Blue: The Origins and Consequences of Medical Racism* (Berkeley: University of California Press, 2012); Kelly M. Hoffman, Sophie Trawalter, Jordan R. Axt, and M. Norman Oliver, "Racial Bias in Pain Assessment and Treatment Recommendations, and False Beliefs about Biological Differences between Blacks and Whites," *PNAS* 113 (2016), 4296–301; and Ruth Graham, "I Don't Feel Your Pain," *Boston Globe* (15 June 2014), http://www.bostonglobe.com/ideas/2014/06/14/don-feel-your-pain/cIrKD5czM0pgZQv7PgCmxI/story.html.

19. See James W. Buehler, "Racial/Ethnic Disparities in the Use of Lethal Force by US Police, 2010–14," *American Journal of Public Health* 107 (2017), 295–97.

20. Lindsey M. West, Roxanne A. Donovan, and Amanda R. Daniel, "The Price of Strength: Black College Women's Perspectives on the Strong Black Woman Stereotype," *Women & Therapy* 39 (2016), 390–412.

21. Marie Jenkins Schwartz, *Birthing a Slave: Motherhood and Medicine in the Antebellum South* (Cambridge, MA: Harvard University Press, 2006), 167. In contrast to their poor treatment of black women, the same physicians usually "expressed 'a good deal of solicitude' for the white woman [. . . and] acted to relieve whatever discomfort she was experiencing" (166). See also Joanna Bourke, "Pain Sensitivity: An Unnatural History from 1800 to 1965," *Journal of Medical Humanities* 35 (2014), 301–19; and Rachel Dudley, "Toward an Understanding of the 'Medical Plantation' as a Cultural Location of Disability," *Disability Studies Quarterly* 32 (2012), http://dsq-sds.org/article/view/3248/3184.

22. Jean Wyatt, "Patricia Hill Collins's *Black Sexual Politics* and the Genealogy of the Strong Black Woman," *Studies in Gender and Sexuality* 9 (2008), 60. See also Robert Staples, "The Myth of the Black Matriarchy," *Black Scholar* 1 (1970), 8–16.

23. Empirical studies of "formidability bias" and "pain bias" are complemented by research on the "superhumanization bias" and the "Magic Negro myth." White research subjects have, in some cases, gone so far as to express beliefs in black people's

ability not only to withstand pain, but also to "suppress hunger or thirst" (Adam Waytz, Kelly Marie Hoffman, and Sophie Trawalter, "A Superhumanization Bias in Whites' Perceptions of Blacks," *Social Psychological and Personality Science* 6 [2015], 356).

24. For a similar example, Ana María Ochoa Gautier has noted Alexander von Humboldt's nineteenth-century documentations of the physical resilience and indecency of the Colombian *bogas*, the Magdalena River's boat rowers. As Ochoa Gautier points out, Humboldt's "positive impression of their tremendous physiques and 'demonstration of human force' [...] was muted by the sounds they made," evidenced by this Prussian explorer's "repeated use of negative adjectives of excess" such as "barbarous, lustful, angry" (*Aurality: Listening and Knowledge in Nineteenth-Century Colombia* [Durham, NC: Duke University Press, 2014], 31–32).

25. Quoted in Tom Slater, "The Resilience of Neoliberal Urbanism," *Open Democracy* (28 January 2014), http://www.opendemocracy.net/opensecurity/tom-slater/ resilience-of-neoliberal-urbanism.

26. In Washington's plea of "Stop calling me RESILIENT," then, "calling" is as much of a keyword as "RESILIENT." To call someone something is to exert implicit control over description, designation, and diagnosis.

27. See Phoebe Robinson, *You Can't Touch My Hair and Other Things I Still Have to Explain* (New York: Random House, 2016), 134–58; Cheng, "Taking Back the Laugh"; Akeema Duff, "Why Black People Tend to Shout," *Odyssey* (27 December 2016), http://www.theodysseyonline.com/why-black-people-tend-to-shout; and Ronald Radano, "Hot Fantasies: American Modernism and the Idea of Black Rhythm," in *Music and the Racial Imagination*, edited by Ronald Radano and Philip V. Bohlman (Chicago: University of Chicago Press, 2000), 459–80. On the racial politics of "Jeep Beats" and vehicular (black) noise, see Mary Dery, "Public Enemy: Confrontation," in *That's the Joint! The Hip-Hop Studies Reader*, edited by Murray Forman and Mark Anthony Neal (New York: Routledge, 2004), 407–20; Paul C. Jasen, *Low End Theory: Bass, Bodies and the Materiality of Sonic Experience* (New York: Bloomsbury Academic, 2016), 6–7; Robin D. G. Kelley, "Kickin' Reality, Kickin' Ballistics: Gangsta Rap and Postindustrial Los Angeles," in *Droppin' Science: Critical Essays on Rap Music and Hip Hop Culture*, edited by William Eric Perkins (Philadelphia: Temple University Press, 1996), 134–35; Tricia Rose, *Black Noise: Rap Music and Black Culture in Contemporary America* (Hanover, NH: Wesleyan University Press, 1994), 61–62; and Art M. Blake, "Audible Citizenship and Audiomobility: Race, Technology, and CB Radio," in *Sound Clash: Listening to American Studies*, edited by Kara Keeling and Josh Kun (Baltimore: Johns Hopkins University Press, 2012), 87–109. For historical perspectives on automobile sound systems, see David Z. Morris, "Cars with the Boom: Identity and Territory in American Postwar Automobile Sound," *Technology and Culture* 55 (2014), 326–53.

28. In her groundbreaking book on the metaphors and materialities of hygiene (and its opposites), anthropologist Mary Douglas defined dirt as "matter out of place," or anything that "offends against order" (*Purity and Danger: An Analysis of Concepts of Pollution and Taboo* [New York: Routledge, 1966], 44, 2); see also Deborah Kapchan,

"Listening Acts: Witnessing the Pain (and Praise) of Others," in *Theorizing Sound Writing*, edited by Deborah Kapchan (Middletown, CT: Wesleyan University Press, 2017), 283. On dirt and blackness, see Frantz Fanon, *Black Skin, White Masks*, translated by Charles Lam Markmann (London: Pluto Press, 2008), 82–86, 146–47; see also Alan Read, ed., *The Fact of Blackness: Frantz Fanon and Visual Representation* (Seattle, WA: Bay Press, 1996).

29. See Carl A. Zimring, *Clean and White: A History of Environmental Racism in the United States* (New York: New York University Press, 2015), 3–5. See also Rachel D. Godsil, "Remedying Environmental Racism," *Michigan Law Review* 90 (1991), 394–427; Laura Pulido, "Rethinking Environmental Racism: White Privilege and Urban Development in Southern California," *Annals of the Association of American Geographers* 90 (2000), 12–40; J. Tom Boer, Manuel Pastor Jr., James L. Sadd, and Lori D. Snyder, "Is There Environmental Racism? The Demographics of Hazardous Waste in Los Angeles County," *Social Science Quarterly* 78 (1997), 793–810; and Joan A. Casey et al., "Race/Ethnicity, Socioeconomic Status, Residential Segregation, and Spatial Variation in Noise Exposure in the Contiguous United States," *Environmental Health Perspectives* 125 (2017), http://doi.org/10.1289/EHP898.

30. V. Josiah C. Nott, "Two Lectures," 223. See also Mark M. Smith, *How Race Is Made: Slavery, Segregation, and the Senses* (Chapel Hill: University of North Carolina Press, 2006), 33–34; and Kennaway, *Bad Vibrations*, 117–19.

31. See Jeff Chang, *We Gon' Be Alright: Notes on Race and Resegregation* (New York: Picador, 2016), 69–70; and Bethania Palma Markus, "Singing While Black: Oakland Choir Threatened with 'Nuisance' Fines after Tech Workers Enter Neighborhood," *Raw Story* (15 October 2015), http://www.rawstory.com/2015/10/singing-while-black-oakland-choir-hit-with-nuisance-fines-after-tech-workers-enter-neighborhood. See also CTVNews.ca Staff, "Fun Police? Montreal Man Says He Was Given $149 Ticket after Singing While Driving," *CTV News* (22 October 2017), http://www.ctvnews.ca/canada/fun-police-montreal-man-says-he-was-given-149-ticket-after-singing-while-driving-1.3643552.

32. Jennifer Lynn Stoever, *The Sonic Color Line: Race and the Cultural Politics of Listening* (New York: New York University Press, 2016), 277.

33. *3½ Minutes, 10 Bullets* (dir. Marc Silver, HBO Documentary Films, 2015).

34. All cameras in the courtroom belonged to the documentary filmmakers of *3½ Minutes, 10 Bullets*. Full recordings of the trial and the retrial are available online and are cited in this chapter accordingly. I am grateful to Ron Davis, who has worked closely with the *3½ Minutes, 10 Bullets* team, for helping obtain access and permissions to original footage.

35. Testimony by defendant, *People v. Dunn*, 2959, emphasis added.

36. "Michael Dunn Trial. Day 5. Part 6. Police Interrogation Tape Played," YouTube (11 February 2014), http://www.youtube.com/watch?v=2y8v6pRtSOQ, ~4:35:00.

37. Testimony by defendant, *People v. Dunn*, 2958.

38. Ralph Riley, *Why Black People Tend to Shout: Cold Facts and Wry Views from a Black Man's World* (New York: Penguin Books, 1991), 1.

39. Frederick Douglass, *My Bondage and My Freedom* (New York: Miller, Orton & Mulligan, 1855), 98.

40. See Frederick Douglass, "Happy Slaves," *North Star* (28 April 1848); Wilma King, *Stolen Childhood: Slave Youth in Nineteenth-Century America* (Bloomington: Indiana University Press, 1995), 84–85; and Shane White and Graham J. White, *The Sounds of Slavery: Discovering African American History through Songs, Sermons, and Speech* (Boston: Beacon Press, 2005), 55–57. On the mishearing or nonhearing of slaves' music, see also Gordon, "What Mr. Jefferson Didn't Hear"; and Saidiya V. Hartman, *Scenes of Subjection: Terror, Slavery, and Self-Making in Nineteenth-Century America* (New York: Oxford University Press, 1997), 35.

41. Ronald Radano strikes a balance between purely defeatist and purely celebratory accounts of slave music. Although the musical talents of a slave gave slaveowners "yet another way to make money [. . .] by hiring him or her out for local dances and balls," this talent nonetheless "partially exceeded the realms of markets and exchange" insofar as the musicality resided within—and originated solely from— the slave body ("On Ownership and Value," *Black Music Research Journal* 30 [2010], 366).

42. In technical terms, resilience (Latin, *resiliens*) describes the capacity of a thing to rebound to its original state following the application of deformational force. Urban researchers have begun using the phrase "resilience machine" to describe environmentalists' surging preoccupation with discourses and models of resilience. "Resilience is replacing sustainability in everyday discourses," observes Simin Davoudi, "in much the same way as the environment has been subsumed in the hegemonic imperatives of climate change" ("Resilience: A Bridging Concept or a Dead End?," *Planning Theory & Practice* 13 [2012], 299). Even though resilience can be a worthwhile metric and goal, some writers argue that the concept implicitly drops the onus of survival on endangered locations and their inhabitants, all the while failing to address the systemic ills that enable this endangerment in the first place.

43. Krishnadev Calamur, "The Problem with Calls for 'Resilience,'" *Atlantic* (24 March 2017),   http://www.theatlantic.com/international/archive/2017/05/manchester-attack/527832.

44. The quotation in Figure 6.3 comes from Mona Hanna-Attisha, "Flint Kids: Tragic, Resilient, and Exemplary," *American Journal of Public Health* 107 (2017), 652.

45. Writing about the neoliberal complex of music, sexism, and racism, Robin James describes resilience as follows: "Instead of expending resources to *avoid* damage, resilience discourse *recycles damage into more resources*. Resilience discourse thus follows a very specific logic: first, damage is incited and made manifest; second, that damage is spectacularly overcome, and that overcoming is broadcast and/ or shared, so that: third, the person who has overcome is rewarded with increased human capital, status, and other forms of recognition and recompense, because: finally, and most importantly, this individual's own resilience boosts society's resilience. The work this individual does to overcome their own damage generates surplus

value for hegemonic institutions" (*Resilience & Melancholy: Pop Music, Feminism, Neoliberalism* [Alresford, UK: Zero Books, 2015], 7, emphasis in original).

46. Unsurprisingly, one of the first fields to examine human resilience was child psychology, as researchers in the mid-twentieth century sought to analyze how youths could or could not thrive under adverse circumstances. See Ingrid Schoon, *Risk and Resilience: Adaptations in Changing Times* (Cambridge: Cambridge University Press, 2006), xiii–xv; Mark de Bruijne, Arjen Boin, and Michel van Eeten, "Resilience: Exploring the Concept and Its Meanings," in *Designing Resilience: Preparing for Extreme Events*, edited by Louise K. Comfort, Arjen Boin, and Chris C. Demchak (Pittsburgh: University of Pittsburgh Press, 2010), 13–32; and Ann S. Masten and Jenifer L. Powell, "A Resilience Framework for Research, Policy, and Practice," in *Resilience and Vulnerability: Adaptation in the Context of Childhood Adversities*, edited by Suniya S. Luthar (Cambridge: Cambridge University Press, 2003), 1–27.

47. In 2010, US veteran-turned-antiwar-activist Ethan McCord spoke about how "the military refused to grant him a medical discharge and instead discharged him with a pre-existing personality disorder, a distinction that precludes him from receiving disability benefits from the military" (Sarah Lazare and Ryan Harvey, "WikiLeaks in Baghdad," *Nation* [29 July 2010], http://www.thenation.com/article/wikileaks-baghdad). A staff sergeant, upon hearing this request for mental healthcare, called McCord a "pussy" and told him to "to get the sand out of [his] vagina."

48. "Comprehensive Soldier Fitness: Building Resilience and Enhancing Performance," *U.S. Army Reserve* (n.d.; last accessed 16 February 2018), http://www.usar.army.mil/Featured/Resources/Comprehensive-Soldier-Fitness.

49. Brianne Gallagher, "Burdens of Proof: Veteran Frauds, PTSD Pussies, and the Spectre of the Welfare Queen," *Critical Military Studies* 2 (2016), 4. As Gallagher further notes, the military ultimately "attempts to become more 'cost effective' within neoliberal regimes of value by creating new diagnoses that evade the temporal logic of 'post' traumatic stress from combat experience" (3).

50. See Julia Melin, "Desperate Choices: Why Black Women Join the U.S. Military at Higher Rates Than Men and All Other Racial and Ethnic Groups," *New England Journal of Public Policy* 28 (2016), 14 pages; and Dawn Marie Dow, "Negotiating 'The Welfare Queen' and 'The Strong Black Woman': African American Middle-Class Mothers' Work and Family Perspectives," *Sociological Perspectives* 58 (2015), 36–55. In studying the biased criminalization of poor black women, Ann Cammett outlines the complicated case of veteran Shanesha Taylor, who, as a homeless, unemployed, single mother of three, had to present herself at her 2014 legal proceedings "as someone who did not resemble the image that many have of poor black mothers—the omnipresent Welfare Queen—an irresponsible, lazy mother who is somehow scamming the system" ("Welfare Queen Redux: Criminalizing Black Mothers in the Age of Neoliberalism," *Southern California Interdisciplinary Law Journal* 25 [2016], 385). Stereotypes of the "underserving welfare queen," points out Brianne Gallagher, also haunt the medical-military bureaucracies of the Veteran's Administration and its mismanagement of financial and medical provisions ("Burdens of Proof," 2).

51. Berlant, *Cruel Optimism*, 95.

52. See Giorgio Agamben, *Homo Sacer: Sovereign Power and Bare Life*, translated by Daniel Heller-Roazen (Stanford, CA: Stanford University Press, 1998).

53. Judith Butler, "Bodily Vulnerability, Coalitions and Street Politics," in *The State of Things*, edited by Marta Kuzma, Pablo Lafunete, and Peter Osborne (London: Koenig Books, 2012), 165. See also Nancy Scheper-Hughes, "A Talent for Life: Reflections on Human Vulnerability and Resilience," *Ethnos: Journal of Anthropology* 73 (2008), 25–56.

54. Maria Kaika, "'Don't Call Me Resilient Again!' The New Urban Agenda as Immunology . . . or . . . What Happens When Communities Refuse to Be Vaccinated with 'Smart Cities' and Indicators," *Environment & Urbanization* 29 (2017), 98, emphasis added. Kaika draws on the work of Roberto Esposito, who has argued that "the idea of immunity, which is needed for protecting our life, if carried past a certain threshold, winds up negating life" (*Terms of the Political: Community, Immunity, Biopolitics*, translated by Rhiannon Noel Welch [New York: Fordham University Press, 2013], 61).

55. Recent studies have shown the deleterious effects of racial microaggressions on physical and mental health. Although people who weather racist encounters could be deemed resilient, their repeated tolerance of such stressors may lead to measurable negative effects on the body. See David R. Williams and Selina A. Mohammed, "Racism and Health I: Pathways and Scientific Evidence," *American Behavioral Scientist* 57 (2013), https://www.ncbi.nlm.nih.gov/pubmed/24347666. See also Derald Wing Sue et al., "Racial Microaggressions in Everyday Life," *American Psychologist* 62 (2007), 271–86.

56. See Amy B. Wang, "'Nevertheless, She Persisted' Becomes New Battle Cry after McConnell Silences Elizabeth Warren," *Washington Post* (8 February 2017), http://www.washingtonpost.com/news/the-fix/wp/2017/02/08/nevertheless-she-persisted-becomes-new-battle-cry-after-mcconnell-silences-elizabeth-warren/?utm_term=.8e6548e4f252.

57. Lorde, "Uses of Anger," 125. Respectable resilience is also black people who are told that they're "so articulate and well-spoken," or that they can pass as white on the telephone (Danielle S., "I Used to Be a Respectable Negro, But Then I Woke Up," *Mamademics* [1 May 2015], http://mamademics.com/i-used-to-be-a-respectable-negro-but-then-i-woke-up; see also Randall Kennedy, *Sellout: The Politics of Racial Betrayal* [New York: Pantheon Books, 2008], 144–85).

58. Wendy Ashley, "The Angry Black Woman: The Impact of Pejorative Stereotypes on Psychotherapy with Black Women," *Social Work in Public Health* 29 (2014), 28.

59. On the majority-white audience of *The Oprah Winfrey Show*, and on Oprah's giveaways of cars and other goods, see Katrina Bell McDonald, *Embracing Sisterhood: Class, Identity, and Contemporary Black Women* (Oxford: Rowman & Littlefield, 2007), 169.

60. See Ted Scheinman, "The Mythical Virtues of Non-Violent Resistance," *Pacific Standard* (28 July 2015), http://psmag.com/news/sandra-bland-and-the-myth-of-black-obedience.

61. Respectable resilience is a semantic cousin of "grit" (the word itself connoting a clenching of teeth), which speaks to the ability of strong and silent types who can weather pain, who can grin and bear it, who can Keep Calm and Carry On. See Angela Duckworth, *Grit: The Power of Passion and Perseverance* (New York: Scribner, 2016); Paul Tough, *How Children Succeed: Grit, Curiosity, and the Hidden Power of Character* (New York: Houghton Mifflin Harcourt, 2012); and Linda Kaplan Thaler and Robin Koval, *Grit to Great: How Perseverance, Passion, and Pluck Take You from Ordinary to Extraordinary* (New York: Crown Business, 2015). On the Internet age's problematic (and neoliberally nostalgic) repurposing of the World War II British poster "Keep Calm and Carry On," see Owen Hatherley, *The Ministry of Nostalgia* (London: Verso, 2016). With thanks to Dale Chapman for introducing me to Hatherley's book.

62. See Marcus Harrison Green and James Trimarco, "Marissa Janae Johnson Changed the 2016 Presidential Election. And She's Not Finished," *Seattle News* (22 December 2015), http://archive.seattleweekly.com/news/962375-129/marissa-janae-johnson-changed-the-2016.

63. Peter Andrew Hart, "Bernie Sanders Shut Down by Black Lives Matter Protesters in Seattle," *Huffington Post* (10 August 2015), http://www.huffingtonpost.com/entry/bernie-sanders-black-lives-matter_us_55c68f14e4b0923c12bd197e, emphasis added.

64. Storycorps, "Not Sorry: The Woman Who Interrupted Bernie Sanders in Seattle," *KUOW* (29 February 2016), http://kuow.org/post/not-sorry-woman-who-interrupted-bernie-sanders-seattle.

65. Zachary Davies Boren, "Bernie Sanders: Democratic Presidential Candidate Kicked off the Stage by Black Lives Matter Protesters," *Independent* (9 August 2015), http://www.independent.co.uk/news/world/americas/us-elections/bernie-sanders-democratic-presidential-candidate-kicked-off-the-stage-by-black-lives-matter-10447101.html.

66. Hamilton Nolan, "Don't Piss on Your Best Friend," *Gawker* (10 August 2015), http://gawker.com/dont-piss-on-your-best-friend-1723074461.

67. Green and Trimarco, "Marissa Janae Johnson." See also Pramila Jayapal, "Guest Editorial: Why Saturday's Bernie Sanders Rally Left Me Feeling Heartbroken," *The Stranger* (9 August 2015), http://www.thestranger.com/blogs/slog/2015/08/09/22671957/guest-editorial-why-saturdays-bernie-sanders-rally-left-me-feeling-heartbroken; and Ijeoma Oluo, "Bernie Sanders, Black Lives Matter and the Racial Divide in Seattle," *Seattle Globalist* (9 August 2015), http://www.seattleglobalist.com/2015/08/09/bernie-sanders-black-lives-matter-race-divide-in-seattle/40394.

68. Rianna Hidalgo and Martha Tesema, "Silence Is Broken," *Real Change* (7 October 2015), http://realchangenews.org/2015/10/07/silence-broken. See also "Bernie Sanders 'Black Lives Matter' Protester [Interview]," YouTube (11 August 2015), http://www.youtube.com/watch?v=-ajWs3z8rs0.

69. Bernie Sanders, "On the Issues" (n.d.; last accessed 16 February 2018), http://berniesanders.com/issues.

70. See Sydney Brownstone, "Bernie Sanders Adds Racial Justice Platform to Website, Says He's 'Disappointed' by Seattle Rally Interruption," *The Stranger* (9 August 2015),

http://www.thestranger.com/blogs/slog/2015/08/09/22671362/bernie-sanders-adds-racial-justice-platform-to-website-says-hes-disappointed-by-seattle-rally-interruption.

71. See "Black Lives Matter Demonstration at Bernie Sanders Westlake Event Seattle (unedited)," YouTube (10 August 2015), http://www.youtube.com/watch?v=oV-ZSP0zAuI.

72. As Jennifer Lynn Stoever points out, silence "offers black people no guaranteed refuge from state and police violence," as shown by the October 2015 incident at Spring Valley High School in South Carolina involving a young black girl who was "accused by her teacher of refusing to leave class after using her cell phone; she quietly stared forward at her desk until her school's 'resource officer' grabbed and violently pulled her to the ground, desk and all" (*Sonic Color Line*, 3). Another high-profile example of unrespectable black silence (and gestural defiance) is football player Colin Kaepernick kneeling during the national anthem.

73. Some attendees, after the event, tried to reconcile this cognitive dissonance by spreading unsubstantiated rumors that these women were hired by Sarah Palin. See Marissa Janae Johnson, "1 Year Later: BLM Protester Who Interrupted Bernie Sanders' Rally Discusses the Moment and the Movement," *The Root* (9 August 2016), http://www.theroot.com/1-year-later-blm-protester-who-interrupted-bernie-sand-1790856353.

74. See Lindsey Weber and Dan McQuade, "Chris Pine Cries through 'Glory' on Behalf of Us All," *Vulture* (23 February 2015), http://www.vulture.com/2015/02/chris-pine-cries-through-glory-for-us-all.html.

75. About a month after the Sanders rally in Seattle, CNN's Don Lemon criticized BLM protesters who, like Johnson and Willaford, were intent on being loud. Lemon asked how social justice for black people could come about "without [them] being involved in the political or the legislative process." He added, "It doesn't just happen from yelling" ("Don Lemon to Black Lives Matter: Why Are You Yelling?," YouTube [3 September 2015], http://www.youtube.com/watch?v=q0sqaDYAW50). Lemon's statement was factual, of course. Social change doesn't just come from yelling. But it's a misleading accusation, because no one can accurately say that anything ever *just* comes from any one thing.

76. Hidalgo and Tesema, "Silence Is Broken." See James Baldwin, *I Am Not Your Negro* (New York: Vintage, 2017), based on the 2016 documentary *I Am Not Your Negro* (dir. Raoul Peck), based in turn on Baldwin's unfinished manuscript, *Remember This House*.

77. Figure 6.5 comes from Oluo, "Bernie Sanders." In 2016, Walmart made the controversial decision to stop selling "Bulletproof: Black Lives Matter" T-shirts after this retail corporation received a written complaint from the US Fraternal Order of Police. See Mary Papenfuss, "Walmart Ditches 'Bulletproof: Black Lives Matter' T-Shirt after Police Protest," *Huffington Post* (21 December 2016), http://www.huffingtonpost.com/entry/walmart-bulletproof-black-lives-matter_us_585aab22e4b0eb586484c12f.

78. Ta-Nehisi Coates, "To Raise, Love, and Lose a Black Child," *Atlantic* (8 October 2014), http://www.theatlantic.com/politics/archive/2014/10/to-raise-love-and-lose-a-black-child/381189.

79. Cage's skin, which possesses powers of cellular regeneration, is not actually made of steel; *skin of steel* is just a metaphor.

80. *Luke Cage*, Season 1, Episode 3.

81. See Abi Noda, "Why I Listen to Rap" (18 December 2013), http://abinoda.com/why-i-listen-to-rap.

82. See, for example, Hajime Fukui and Kumiko Toyoshima, "Influence of Music on Steroid Hormones and the Relationship between Receptor Polymorphisms and Musical Ability: A Pilot Study," *Frontiers in Psychology* 4 (2013), http://www.ncbi.nlm.nih.gov/pmc/articles/PMC3848314.

83. Irene Senna, Angelo Maravita, Nadia Bolognini, and Cesare V. Parise, "The Marble-Hand Illusion," *PLOS ONE* 9 (2014), http://doi.org/10.1371/journal.pone.0091688.

84. Senna et al., "Marble-Hand Illusion."

85. Senna et al., "Marble-Hand Illusion."

86. See, for example, Dennis Y. Hsu et al., "The Music of Power: Perceptual and Behavioral Consequences of Powerful Music," *Social Psychological and Personality Science* 6 (2015), 75–83. Anthropologists, psychologists, and music cognition specialists would be among the first people to warn that we're far from fully unraveling humans' complex mind-body connections. Nevertheless, significant empirical and ethnographic data have begun to demonstrate that sounds, especially loud and percussive sounds, can induce biochemical states that measurably increase the human body's psychological and dermal resilience.

87. Outside the controlled settings of laboratories, ethnographers have observed similar phenomena of sound-induced resilience, notably in forms of religious-musical trancing and drumming. As Judith Becker remarks, trances—from the "Sun Dance ritual of the Lakotas to the self-flagellation of Shi'a Muslims to the self-stabbing of the Balinese *bebuten* trances"—feature people who "perform feats of physical endurance that are unthinkable in ordinary body-mind states of consciousness" ("Music, Trancing, and the Absence of Pain," in *Pain and Its Transformations: The Interface of Biology and Culture*, edited by Sarah Coakley and Kay Kaufman Shelemay [Cambridge, MA: Harvard University Press, 2007], 166). Balinese trancers, for example, "not only do not feel pain when stabbing themselves but also rarely display any resultant physical trauma such as open, bleeding wounds" (Judith Becker, *Deep Listeners: Music, Emotion, and Trancing* [Bloomington: Indiana University Press, 2004], 148).

88. Rap—like any music—is not a monolith, but the apparent recognizability of its generic characteristics might impel perceptions and discourses that generalize it as such. Adam Krims's work on rap divided it into multiple subgenres, including party rap, gangsta rap, mack rap, and reality rap (*Rap Music*, 54). On defining and redefining rap, see also Loren Kajikawa, *Sounding Race in Rap Songs* (Berkeley: University of California Press, 2015), 4–6.

89. Michael Wallace, "Heat Pump Up the Volume, Rout Mavs," *ESPN* (30 March 2012), http://www.espn.com/nba/dailydime/_/page/dime-120329/daily-dime. See also Ken McLeod, *We Are the Champions: The Politics of Sports and Popular Music* (Burlington, VT: Ashgate, 2011), 38–58, 155–57.

90. See Colin Newcomer, "Rap Music Makes Me Feel Invincible Shirt from Print Liberation," *T-Roundup* (28 January 2011), http://www.troundup.com/rap-music-makes-me-feel-invincible-shirt-from-print-liberation.

91. See Justin Roberson, "25 Rap Songs That Make Us Want to Punch Someone in the Face," *Complex* (8 May 2013), http://www.complex.com/music/2013/05/25-rap-songs-that-make-us-want-to-punch-someone-in-the-face.

92. Associated Press, "Rapper Yung Mazi, Who Survived Multiple Shootings, Dies in Another," *USA Today* (7 August 2017), http://www.usatoday.com/story/life/music/2017/08/07/rapper-yung-mazi-who-survived-multiple-shootings-dies-another/547077001.

93. Jessica McBride, "Yung Mazi Dead: 5 Fast Facts You Need to Know," *Heavy* (7 August 2017), http://heavy.com/entertainment/2017/08/yung-mazi-killed-dead-shot-death-is-photos-video-suspect-young.

94. See Jeremy Prestholdt, "The Afterlives of 2Pac: Imagery and Alienation in Sierra Leone and Beyond," *Journal of African Cultural Studies* 21 (2009), 197–218; and George Kamberelis and Greg Dimitriadis, "Collectively Remembering Tupac: The Narrative Mediation of Current Events, Cultural Histories, and Social Identities," in *Afterlife as Afterimage: Understanding Posthumous Fame*, edited by Steve Jones and Joli Jensen (New York: Peter Lang, 2005), 143–70 (esp. 153). Curiously, it is conceivable Tupac might not have been killed that night had his car not been stopped by the Las Vegas police for loud music (sonic disturbance); this police stop occurred only fifteen minutes before the shooting.

95. "26 Rappers Who Have Been Shot," *Ranker* (n.d.; last accessed 16 February 2018), http://www.ranker.com/list/rappers-who-have-been-shot/ranker-hip-hop.

96. Loren Kajikawa, "Hip-Hop History in the Age of Colorblindness," *Journal of Music History Pedagogy* 5 (2014), 120.

97. Kajikawa, "Hip-Hop History," 119. See also Bill Yousman, "Blackophilia and Blackophobia: White Youth, the Consumption of Rap Music, and White Supremacy," *Communication Theory* 13 (2003), 366–91; and Tate, *Everything but the Burden*.

98. Ingrid Monson, "Jazz as Political and Musical Practice," in *Musical Improvisation: Art, Education, and Society*, edited by Gabriel Solis and Bruno Nettl (Urbana: University of Illinois Press, 2009), 32.

99. See Mark Anthony Neal, *What the Music Said: Black Popular Music and Black Public Culture* (New York: Routledge, 1999), 85–99.

100. On the definitions and (in)definability of "black music," see Doris Evans McGinty, "Black Scholars on Black Music: The Past, the Present, and the Future," *Black Music Research Journal* 13 (1993), 1–13. Concerning "musical blackness," see Kyra D. Gaunt, *The Games Black Girls Play: Learning the Ropes from Double-Dutch to Hip-Hop* (New York: New York University Press, 2006), 37–55. For a dive into voice's "acousmatic blackness," see Nina Sun Eidsheim, "Marian Anderson and 'Sonic Blackness' in American Opera," *American Quarterly* 63 (2011), 641–71. And on the historical initiatives of "black music inquiry" and "ostensibly [. . .] 'black' projects," see Guthrie P. Ramsey, Jr, "Who Hears Here? Black Music, Critical Bias, and the Musicological Skin Trade," *Musical Quarterly* 85 (2001), 1, 2.

101. Mark Anthony Neal warns that rap's signs of resistance may, as with any artform, buckle under the weight of market interests, a peril he describes as a "tumultuous marriage between black cultural production and mass consumerism" (*What the Music Said*, 17); see also Paul Gilroy, *Darker Than Blue: On the Moral Economies of Black Atlantic Culture* (Cambridge, MA: Belknap Press of Harvard University Press, 2015), 120–121; Josh Kun, "The Sound of Blacknuss: Rapping Master/ Counternarratives of the Hip Hop Imagi-Nation," *repercussions* 3 (1994), 5–49; and Theresa A. Martinez, "Popular Culture as Oppositional Culture: Rap as Resistance," *Sociological Perspectives* 40 (1997), 265–86. On "B/black music" implicitly or explicitly narrated through black resilience, see, for example, J. Jefferson Cleveland and William B. McClain, excerpt from *Songs of Zion*, in *Readings in Black American Music*, second edition, edited by Eileen Southern (New York: W. W. Norton, 1983), 298–301; LeRoi Jones (Amiri Baraka), *Blues People: Negro Music in White America* (New York: Harper Perennial, 2002), 17–121; Samuel A. Floyd Jr., *The Power of Black Music: Interpreting Its History from Africa to the United States* (New York: Oxford University Press, 1995); Guthrie P. Ramsey, Jr, *Race Music: Black Cultures from Bebop to Hip-Hop* (Berkeley: University of California Press, 2003); Maureen Mahon, *Right to Rock: The Black Rock Coalition and the Cultural Politics of Race* (Durham, NC: Duke University Press, 2004), 33–58; Josh Kun, *Audiotopia: Music, Race, and America* (Berkeley: University of California Press, 2005), 88–94; Charles Hiroshi Garrett, *Struggling to Define a Nation: American Music and the Twentieth Century* (Berkeley: University of California Press, 2008), 10–11; Marcus Reeves, *Somebody Scream! Rap Music's Rise to Prominence in the Aftershocks of Black Power* (New York: Farrar, Strauss & Giroux, 2009); Shana Redmond, *Anthem: Social Movements and the Sound of Solidarity in the African Diaspora* (New York: New York University Press, 2013), 261–88; Tammy L. Kernodle, "Diggin' You Like Those Ol' Soul Records," *American Studies* 52 (2013), 181–204; and Lakeyta M. Bonnette, *Pulse of the People: Political Rap Music and Black Politics* (Philadelphia: University of Pennsylvania Press, 2015). For additional reflections on the essentialist trappings of music and blackness, see Mark Katz, *Groove Music: The Art and Culture of the Hip-Hop DJ* (New York: Oxford University Press, 2012), 9–11; Karl Hagstrom Miller, *Segregating Sound: Inventing Folk and Pop Music in the Age of Jim Crow* (Durham, NC: Duke University Press, 2010); Imani Perry, *Prophets of the Hood: Politics and Poetics in Hip Hop* (Durham, NC: Duke University Press, 2004), 10–18; Cheryl L. Keyes, *Rap Music and Street Consciousness* (Urbana: University of Illinois Press, 2002), 6–13; and Richard Crawford, "On Two Traditions of Black Music Research," *Black Music Research Journal* 6 (1986), 1–9.

102. W. E. B. Du Bois, *The Souls of Black Folk: Essays and Sketches* (Chicago: A. C. McClurg, 1903), 175.

103. See Eileen Southern, *The Music of Black Americans: A History*, third edition (New York: W. W. Norton, 1997); and Eileen Southern and Josephine Wright, *Images: Iconography of Music in African-American Culture, 1770s–1920s* (New York: Garland, 2000).

104. Jones (Baraka), *Blues People*, 181, emphasis in original.

105. Scott Deveaux, *The Birth of Bebop: A Social and Musical History* (Berkeley: University of California Press, 1997), 4. On the politics of ambivalent claims about bebop's (non)politicality, see Eric Porter, *What Is This Thing Called Jazz? African American Musicians as Artists, Critics, and Activists* (Berkeley: University of California Press, 2002), 54–100. With thanks to Michael Heller for this reference.

106. Claude M. Steele, *Whistling Vivaldi: How Stereotypes Affect Us and What We Can Do* (New York: W. W. Norton, 2010), 6.

107. Alisha Lola Jones, "'We Are a Peculiar People': Meaning, Masculinity, and Competence in Gendered Gospel Performance" (PhD diss., University of Chicago, 2015), 4.

108. "Retta—Classical Music," *Comedy Central: Premium Blend*, Season 3, Episode 12 (22 February 2000), http://www.cc.com/video-clips/p3901a/premium-blend-classical-music.

109. Cheryl L. Keyes, "Sound, Voice, and Spirit: Teaching in the Black Music Vernacular," *Black Music Research Journal* 29 (2009), 14.

110. John H. McWhorter, "How Hip-Hop Holds Blacks Back," *City Journal* (Summer 2003), http://www.city-journal.org/html/how-hip-hop-holds-blacks-back-12442.html.

111. Bill Cosby and Alvin Poussaint, *Come On, People: On the Path from Victims to Victors* (Nashville, TN: Thomas Nelson, 2007), 119. On rap, religion, and the naivety of neat divisions between (morally) "good" rap and "bad" rap, see Anthony B. Pinn, "Making a World with a Beat: Musical Expression's Relationship to Religious Identity and Experience," in *Noise and Spirit: The Religious and Spiritual Sensibilities of Rap Music*, edited by Anthony B. Pinn (New York: New York University Press, 2003), 1–7.

112. Amy Wax and Larry Alexander, "Paying the Price for Breakdown of the Country's Bourgeois Culture," *Philadelphia Inquirer* (9 August 2017), http://www.philly.com/philly/opinion/commentary/paying-the-price-for-breakdown-of-the-countrys-bourgeois-culture-20170809.html.

113. Jonathan Capehart, "Jazz Musician Wynton Marsalis Says Rap and Hip-Hop Are 'More Damaging' Than a Statue of Robert E. Lee,'" *Washington Post* (22 May 2018), http://www.washingtonpost.com/blogs/post-partisan/wp/2018/05/22/jazz-musician-wynton-marsalis-says-rap-and-hip-hop-are-more-damaging-than-a-statue-of-robert-e-lee/?noredirect=on&utm_term=.d38aca27556e.

114. See Keyes, *Rap Music and Street Consciousness*, 104–21, 186–209; Michael P. Jeffries, *Thug Life: Race, Gender, and the Meaning of Hip-Hop* (Chicago: University of Chicago Press, 2011), 77–111; and Tricia Rose, *The Hip Hop Wars: What We Talk about When We Talk about Hip Hop—and Why It Matters* (New York: Basic Books, 2008), 75–94. Ta-Nehisi Coates harpoons the massive hypocrisy of causational arguments when it comes to rap and societal virtues: "Ronald Ferguson, a Harvard social scientist, has highlighted that an increase in hip-hop's popularity during the early 1990s corresponded with a declining amount of time spent reading among black kids. But gangsta rap can be correlated with other phenomena, too—many of them positive. During the 1990s, as gangsta rap exploded, teen pregnancy and the murder rate among black men declined. Should we give the blue ribbon in

citizenship to Dr. Dre?" (*We Were Eight Years in Power*, 27). On the educational potential of rap, see Susan Hadley and George Yancy, eds., *Therapeutic Uses of Rap and Hip-Hop* (New York: Routledge, 2012).

115. See Danielle Kurtzleben, "Trump Embraces One of Russia's Favorite Propaganda Tactics—Whataboutism," NPR (17 March 2017), http://www.npr.org/2017/03/17/520435073/trump-embraces-one-of-russias-favorite-propaganda-tactics-whataboutism.

116. See Torri Stuckey, "'What about Black-on-Black Crime?' What about Pink Polka Dotted Unicorns?," *Huffington Post* (6 December 2017), http://www.huffingtonpost.com/torri-stuckey/what-about-blackonblack-c_b_10905534.html.

117. Erin Gloria Ryan, "Donald Trump's Lackeys Blame Women and Blacks for How He Talks about Women," *Daily Beast* (11 October 2016), http://www.thedailybeast.com/donald-trumps-lackeys-blame-women-and-blacks-for-how-he-talks-about-women.

118. For a comparable study, see also Benjamin R. Teitelbaum, *Lions of the North: Sounds of the New Nordic Radical Nationalism* (New York: Oxford University Press, 2017), 61–88.

119. See Richard Will, "*Don Giovanni* and the Resilience of Rape Culture," *Journal of the American Musicological Society* 71 (2018), 218–22; Liane Curtis, "The Sexual Politics of Teaching Mozart's *Don Giovanni*," *NWSA Journal* 12 (2000), 119–42; and Bonnie Gordon, "What *Don Giovanni*, an Opera about a Charismatic Rapist, Can Teach Us about Donald Trump," *Slate* (21 October 2016), http://www.slate.com/blogs/browbeat/2016/10/21/what_don_giovanni_an_opera_about_a_charismatic_rapist_can_teach_us_about.html.

120. Henry Louis Gates Jr., "Foreword," in *The Anthology of Rap*, edited by Adam Bradley and Andrew DuBois (New Haven, CT: Yale University Press, 2010), xxiv, xxv.

121. John Cook, "Blacklisted: Is Stephin Merritt a Racist Because He Doesn't Like Hip-Hop?," *Slate* (9 May 2006), http://www.slate.com/articles/arts/music_box/2006/05/blacklisted.html.

122. Cook, "Blacklisted."

123. See Jonathan Sturgeon, "Is Magnetic Fields' Stephin Merritt a Racist Troll, Literary Celebrittante, or Both?," *Flavorwire* (31 March 2015), http://flavorwire.com/511904/is-stephin-merritt-a-racist-troll-literary-celebrittante-or-both; and David Carr, "One Man's Musical Tastes as Fodder for a Flame War," *New York Times* (18 May 2006), http://www.nytimes.com/2006/05/18/arts/music/18rock.html.

124. Testimony by Rhonda Rouer, *People v. Dunn*, 2306; and Michael Dunn's jailhouse letters to grandmother (20 February 2013) and to daughter (12 July 2013). Unless otherwise stated, all jailhouse letters cited hereafter have been obtained from the Law Offices of John M. Phillips, available at http://floridajustice.com/michael-dunns-letters-from-jail. John Phillips was hired by Jordan's parents, Ron Davis and Lucy McBath, to file civil suits against Dunn prior to the commencement of criminal trial proceedings. These suits were settled confidentially in January 2014. See John Cavazos, "Civil Lawsuits against Michael Dunn Settled," News

4 Jax (4 January 2014), http://www.news4jax.com/news/florida/duval-county/ civil-lawsuits-against-michael-dunn-settled.

125. Lucia McBath, "Lucia McBath: I Chose to Forgive My Son's Murderer," *Vimeo* (2016), http://vimeo.com/152631582.

126. Images in Figures 6.6a, 6.6b, and 6.6c come from the cover of *Jet* (14 January 2013); screen captures from *3½ Minutes, 10 Bullets*; and Natalege Whaley, "What's Happening in the Jordan Davis Case?," BET (17 October 2014), http://www.bet. com/news/national/photos/2014/02/what-s-happening-in-jordan-davis-case. html.

127. According to reporter Dave Schneider, the media made the case "about loud music. 'Loud music trial begins.' 'Loud music trial continues. This wasn't a 'loud music trial.' This was a 21st-century lynching" (quoted in *3½ Minutes, 10 Bullets*, ~1:00:15). See also Steve Swayne, "Music Is Power: Michael Dunn, Jordan Davis, and How We Respond When People Turn Up the Volume," *Pacific Standard* (5 March 2014), http://psmag.com/social-justice/music-power-volume-sound-michael-dunn-jordan-davis-75929.

128. David Kopel, "Stand Your Ground Had Nothing to Do with the Dunn Verdict in Florida," *Washington Post* (17 February 2014), http://www.washingtonpost.com/ news/volokh-conspiracy/wp/2014/02/17/stand-your-ground-had-nothing-to-do-with-the-dunn-verdict-in-florida/?utm_term=.b86acee547e9.

129. I use the term "youth" in accordance with the United Nations' definition of any person between fifteen and twenty-four years of age. The UN and UNESCO make this designation for "statistical consistency across regions," for clarifying scholarship eligibilities, and without prejudice against alternate definitions of youth by Member States. See United Nations Educational, Scientific and Cultural Organization, "What Do We Mean by 'Youth'?," http://www.unesco.org/new/en/social-and-human-sciences/themes/youth/youth-definition.

130. "Michael Dunn Trial—Cory Strolla—Press Conference," YouTube (13 February 2014), http://www.youtube.com/watch?v=OCJm1xvCX2s, ~12:37. On the history and uses of the "race card," see, for example, Tali Mendelberg, *The Race Card: Campaign Strategy, Implicit Messages, and the Norm of Equality* (Princeton, NJ: Princeton University Press, 2001); and George J. Sefa Dei, Nisha Karumanchery-Luik, and Leeno Luke Karumanchery, *Playing the Race Card: Exposing White Power and Privilege* (New York: Peter Lang, 2004).

131. See Alexander Nazaryan, "Murdered While Black: New Documentary Slams 'Stand Your Ground,'" *Newsweek* (20 November 2015), http://www.newsweek. com/murdered-while-black-new-documentary-slams-stand-your-ground-law-396777; Desire Thompson, "Rest in Peace: Today Would Have Been Jordan Davis' 21st Birthday," *Vibe* (16 February 2016), http://www.vibe.com/2016/02/ jordan-davis-twenty-first-birthday; and Susan Cooper Eastman, "Florida Jury Selected for Loud Music Murder Trial," *Reuters* (6 February 2014), http://www. reuters.com/article/us-usa-florida-shooting-dunn/florida-jury-selected-for-loud-music-murder-trial-idUSBREA1516L20140206.

132. The witness who memorized Dunn's license plate was named Shawn Atkins. See Testimony by Shawn Atkins, *People v. Dunn*, 1419–20.

133. Testimony by defendant, *People v. Dunn*, 2855.

134. Testimony by defendant, *People v. Dunn*, 2856.

135. Testimony by defendant, *People v. Dunn*, 2858.

136. Testimony by defendant, *People v. Dunn*, 2859.

137. Testimony by defendant, *People v. Dunn*, 2860, 2959.

138. Testimony by defendant, *People v. Dunn*, 2968, 2861.

139. Testimony by defendant, *People v. Dunn*, 2862.

140. Testimony by defendant, *People v. Dunn*, 2861, 2862.

141. Testimony by defendant, *People v. Dunn*, 2862.

142. Testimony by defendant, *People v. Dunn*, 2863.

143. Testimony by defendant, *People v. Dunn*, 2863.

144. Testimony by defendant, *People v. Dunn*, 2955.

145. Testimony by defendant, *People v. Dunn*, 2968, 2973.

146. Testimony by defendant, *People v. Dunn*, 2985.

147. Testimony by defendant, *People v. Dunn*, 3020.

148. Testimony by defendant, *People v. Dunn*, 3020.

149. Testimony by defendant, *People v. Dunn*, 2864.

150. Testimony by defendant, *People v. Dunn*, 2866.

151. Testimony by defendant, *People v. Dunn*, 2867.

152. Testimony by defendant, *People v. Dunn*, 2867.

153. Testimony by defendant, *People v. Dunn*, 2867.

154. Testimony by defendant, *People v. Dunn*, 2869, 2870.

155. Testimony by defendant, *People v. Dunn*, 2872.

156. Testimony by defendant, *People v. Dunn*, 2872, 2875.

157. Testimony by defendant, *People v. Dunn*, 2876.

158. Testimony by defendant, *People v. Dunn*, 2884, 2887.

159. Figure 6.7 shows an evidence photograph reproduced in CNN Wire, "Michael Dunn Found Guilty of 1st-degree Murder in Loud-Music Trial," *Fox Denver* (1 October 2014), http://kdvr.com/2014/10/01/michael-dunn-found-guilty-of-1st-degree-murder-in-loud-music-trial.

160. Testimony by defendant, *People v. Dunn*, 2890.

161. Testimony by defendant, *People v. Dunn*, 2926.

162. Testimony by defendant, *People v. Dunn*, 2895.

163. Testimony by defendant, *People v. Dunn*, 2894, 2907, 2926. To be clear, Dunn acknowledged Rouer as "hysterical" on three separate occasions during his testimony. He also said she was a "wreck" and was "hyperventilating" (2897, 2899).

164. Testimony by defendant, *People v. Dunn*, 2926.

165. Testimony by defendant, *People v. Dunn*, 3015.

166. Testimony by defendant, *People v. Dunn*, 2897.

167. Testimony by defendant, *People v. Dunn*, 2990.

168. Testimony by defendant, *People v. Dunn*, 2899.

169. Testimony by defendant, *People v. Dunn*, 2901.

170. Testimony by defendant, *People v. Dunn*, 2910.

171. Testimony by defendant, *People v. Dunn*, 2909.

172. Testimony by defendant, *People v. Dunn*, 2904.

173. Testimony by defendant, *People v. Dunn*, 2956.

174. "Michael David Dunn—Police Interview Uncut—Part 1," YouTube (24 July 2013), http://www.youtube.com/watch?v=MWlzUHtUOyY.

175. Testimony by Tevin Thompson, *People v. Dunn*, 1629.

176. Testimony by Tevin Thompson, *People v. Dunn*, 1632.

177. Testimony by Tevin Thompson, *People v. Dunn*, 1635, 1636.

178. Testimony by Tevin Thompson, *People v. Dunn*, 1637–38.

179. Testimony by Tevin Thompson, *People v. Dunn*, 1640.

180. Testimony by Tevin Thompson, *People v. Dunn*, 1677, 1681.

181. Testimony by Tevin Thompson, *People v. Dunn*, 1683.

182. Testimony by Tevin Thompson, *People v. Dunn*, 1690.

183. Testimony by Tommie Stornes, *People v. Dunn*, 1796.

184. Testimony by Tommie Stornes, *People v. Dunn*, 1800.

185. Testimony by Tommie Stornes, *People v. Dunn*, 1801, 1803.

186. Testimony by Leland Brunson, *People v. Dunn*, 1717.

187. Testimony by Leland Brunson, *People v. Dunn*, 1719–20.

188. Testimony by Leland Brunson, *People v. Dunn*, 1722. Figure 6.8 comes from "Michael Dunn Retrial—Day 2, Part 2," YouTube (26 September 2014), http://www.youtube.com/watch?v=MV4Bbi0IgdE. I have included stills from the retrial instead of the original trial because Brunson's gestures were slightly clearer the second time around.

189. Testimony by Leland Brunson, *People v. Dunn*, 1721. According to the youths' testimonies, Dunn had parked his Jetta so close to the Durango that, if Davis had tried opening the Durango's door, it would almost certainly have dinged the Jetta's rear door. No scratches or marks, however, were found on the Jetta during subsequent inspection.

190. Testimony by Leland Brunson, *People v. Dunn*, 1725.

191. Testimony by Leland Brunson, *People v. Dunn*, 1725.

192. Testimony by Leland Brunson, *People v. Dunn*, 1726, 1727.

193. Testimony by Leland Brunson, *People v. Dunn*, 1727.

194. Testimony by Leland Brunson, *People v. Dunn*, 1729.

195. Testimony by Steven Smith, *People v. Dunn*, 1336.

196. Testimony by Steven Smith, *People v. Dunn*, 1336.

197. Testimony by Steven Smith, *People v. Dunn*, 1339. Direct examination: "Can you use your voice to try to convey to the jury the volume of that person's voice?" Smith, more loudly: "YOU'RE NOT GOING TO TALK TO ME THAT WAY!"

198. Testimony by Steven Smith, *People v. Dunn*, 1341.

199. Testimony by Rhonda Rouer, *People v. Dunn*, 2306.

200. Testimony by Rhonda Rouer, *People v. Dunn*, 2306.

201. Testimony by Rhonda Rouer, *People v. Dunn*, 2306.

202. Testimony by Rhonda Rouer, *People v. Dunn*, 2308.

203. Testimony by Rhonda Rouer, *People v. Dunn*, 2309.

204. Testimony by Rhonda Rouer, *People v. Dunn*, 2309.

205. Testimony by Rhonda Rouer (rebuttal), *People v. Dunn*, 3063.

206. Testimony by Rhonda Rouer (rebuttal), *People v. Dunn*, 3063.

207. Testimony by Rhonda Rouer, *People v. Dunn*, 2316.

208. Testimony by Rhonda Rouer (rebuttal), *People v. Dunn*, 3063.

209. Testimony by Rhonda Rouer (rebuttal), *People v. Dunn*, 3064.

210. Testimony by Rhonda Rouer (rebuttal), *People v. Dunn*, 3060, 3062.

211. Testimony by Rhonda Rouer (rebuttal), *People v. Dunn*, 3061.

212. Testimony by Rhonda Rouer, *People v. Dunn*, 3061.

213. "Jordan Davis—Michael Dunn Sentencing, Part 2 (Michael Dunn Speaks)," YouTube (17 October 2014), http://www.youtube.com/watch?v=J1XyyrZ3MPY.

214. Rick Neale, "Michael Dunn at Sentencing: 'I Am Mortified I Took a Life,'" *Florida Today* (17 October 2014), http://www.floridatoday.com/story/news/crime/2014/10/17/michael-dunn-sentencing-mortified-took-life/17433269.

215. Bridgette Matter, "Action News Jax Investigation Reveals Michael Dunn Is Being Held in Oregon Prison," Action News Jax (10 October 2017), http://www.actionnewsjax.com/news/local/action-news-jax-investigation-reveals-michael-dunn-is-being-held-in-oregon-prison/622728736.

216. Cosby and Poussaint, *Come On, People*, 145.

217. Michael Dunn, jailhouse calls to Rhonda Rouer, available as "Dunn Call 7" and "Dunn Call 8" at http://www.jacksonville.com/news/2014-02-17/story/listen-state-attorneys-office-releases-michael-dunn-jailhouse-phone-calls. See also Scott Johnson, "Jail Calls of Michael Dunn's Conversations Released," News 4 Jax (14 February 2014), http://www.news4jax.com/news/local/jail-calls-of-michael-dunns-conversations-released_20151107153725123.

218. Paul Solotaroff, "A Most American Way to Die," *Rolling Stone* (25 April 2013), http://www.rollingstone.com/culture/news/jordan-davis-stand-your-grounds-latest-victim-20130425.

219. Defense closing arguments, *People v. Dunn*, 3416.

220. Defense closing arguments, *People v. Dunn*, 3371; and Testimony by Rhonda Rouer (rebuttal), *People v. Dunn*, 3065.

221. Testimony by Randy Berry, *People v. Dunn*, 2570.

222. Testimony by Frank Thompson, *People v. Dunn*, 2588.

223. Testimony by Beverly Berry, *People v. Dunn*, 2578.

224. Testimony by defendant, *People v. Dunn*, 2941.

225. Testimony by defendant, *People v. Dunn*, 2945.

226. Testimony by defendant, *People v. Dunn*, 2997.

227. Verbatim repetition in testimonies tends to sound suspicious. Common and generalizable examples include "I plead the Fifth," "I don't recall," "Not to my recollection," and other evasive maneuvers. Dunn's strict repetition of key terms (*thug, familiarity*) may indicate memorization by way of witness preparation. Some writers have called witness preparation a necessarily "dark" and "dirty" dimension of the United States adversary system, and its ethics remain murky and

underdefined. See Bennett L. Gershman, "Witness Coaching by Prosecutors," *Cardozo Law Review* 23 (2002), 829–63; and William M. McErlean, Dennis P. Stolle, and Monica R. Brownewell Smith, "The Evolution of Witness Preparation," *Litigation* 37 (2010), 21–26.

228. Phonemically, of course, the phrase "rap crap" doesn't sound anything like the phrase "thug music." (Interestingly, the State did not raise this point—either despite or because of its obviousness.) Indeed, as far as clever rhymes go, "rap crap" is quite memorable. How likely is it that Rouer misheard or misremembered "rap crap" as "thug music," especially given that she acknowledged his remark and responded with, "Yes, I know" (Testimony by Rhonda Rouer, *People v. Dunn*, 2306)?

229. Prosecution closing statements (rebuttal), *People v. Dunn*, 3421.

230. "Michael Dunn Trial—Cory Strolla—Press Conference."

231. Prosecution closing arguments, *People v. Dunn*, 3328–29, emphasis added. For video, see "Michael Dunn Trial—Day 6—Part 2 (Prosecution Closing Arguments)," YouTube (12 February 2014), http://www.youtube.com/watch?v=B8aME1ooGlM, ~1:11:47.

232. DiAngelo, "White Fragility," 65. See also Robin DiAngelo, *White Fragility: Why It's So Hard for White People to Talk about Racism* (Boston: Beacon Press, 2018).

233. "Michael Dunn Trial—Cory Strolla—Press Conference," ~11:00, emphasis added. But Ron Davis, Jordan's father, disagreed. "With [Dunn] saying 'thug music,' how can you as a juror not think that this was about race?" said Davis in a CNN interview. "Because before you even met Jordan, before you even looked at Jordan, looked at his clothes, or anything else, you heard rap music, and so you assumed it was all African Americans in the car, and you said, 'I hate that thug music.' So it is about race" ("Black Juror from Michael Dunn Trial States It Wasn't about Race and He Was a Nice Guy," YouTube [24 February 2014], http://www.youtube.com/watch?v=q3UTFGI1OYc, ~6:35).

234. In 2007, Joe Biden famously landed in hot water when he described Barack Obama as "clean." See Zimring, *Clean and White*, 220–21; and Coates, *We Were Eight Years in Power*, 122.

235. Perhaps the vehement certainty with which Strolla asserted Dunn's unracistness is precisely what merits suspicion. We've heard such superlative disavowals before from the likes of Donald Trump, who has repeatedly called himself the "least racist person" (Eugene Scott, "Six Times President Trump Said He Is the Least Racist Person," *Washington Post* [17 January 2018], http://www.washingtonpost.com/news/the-fix/wp/2018/01/17/six-times-president-trump-said-he-is-the-least-racist-person/?noredirect=on&utm_term=.418705398b11).

236. "Michael Dunn Trial—Cory Strolla—Press Conference," ~12:37.

237. "Michael Dunn Trial—Cory Strolla—Press Conference," ~12:50.

238. *People v. Dunn*, "Order Denying Defendant's Motion to Determine Confidentiality of Court Records and Motions for Protective Order Sealing Certain Court Records and Limiting the Disclosure of Discovery Materials Granting Intervenors' Motion to Set Aside Orders, to Direct Clerk Not to Seal Documents, to Unseal and Unredact Documents, to Refrain from Further Ex Parte Communications, and

Otherwise Enforce the Appellate Court Order of December 18, 2013, Granting in Part and Denying in Part Intervenor Post-Newsweek Stations Florida, Inc.'s Motion to Unseal Documents, Direct the State to Produce Documents Discussed at Ex Parte Hearing, and Direct the Clerk Not to Block Public Access to Files Absent an Order of Court" (24 January 2014), 4, item 5.

239. *People v. Dunn*, "Order Denying Defendant's Motion," 4, item 5.

240. Judge Healey justified his decision on the motion as follows: "On January 16, 2014, Defendant filed the instant 'Motion to Determine Confidentiality of Court Records and Motion for Protective Order Sealing Certain Court Records and Limiting the Disclosure of Discovery Materials.' In this Motion, Defendant seeks to protect 'any and all "jailhouse" conversations of the Defendant, including but not limited to any and all discussions, phone calls, and/or visitations.' In support of his Motion, Defendant argues that such closure is required to prevent a serious and imminent threat to the fair, impartial, and orderly administration of justice, to protect a compelling governmental interest, and to comply with established state and federal constitutional law and cases" (*People v. Dunn*, "Order Denying Defendant's Motion," 5–6, item 10); Healey denied the motion on the basis that the "Defendant failed to present any evidence showing that the disclosure of the jail calls 'would jeopardize the safety' of any of the victims or witnesses" (10, item 23). See also Susan Cooper Eastman, "Trial Opens for Florida Man Who Killed Black Teen over Loud Music," *Reuters* (3 February 2014), http://www.reuters.com/article/us-usa-florida-shooting-dunn/trial-opens-for-florida-man-who-killed-black-teen-over-loud-music-idUSBREA121AU20140203.

241. Here is one jailhouse letter that was actually entered into evidence. From Dunn to Rouer: "I had a visit from a Mr. Lockett—he's Mitch Stone's partner, and friends with Corey [sic] Strolla. He mentioned in passing that I had made no mention of a gun to you, based on your testimony to the prosecutors. He asked what I had told you, and I then realized that we hadn't really discussed what happened, as we were more concerned with whether or not anyone was hurt. Let me assure you, just as I told the detectives who first interviewed me in Melbourne, [redacted] and later Mitch Stone—there was a weapon. I cannot say for sure what it was, as I only saw the top portion of the barell [sic]—to me it looked like a shotgun" (Michael Dunn, jailhouse letter to Rhonda Rouer [Wednesday, 5 December 2012]). Wolfson brought up the contents of this letter in closing statements: "The first time [Dunn] mentioned [the gun] to [Rouer] is in a letter [from] December 5th, 2012, and this letter is in evidence and he says, 'He mentioned in passing that I made no mention of a gun to you, based on your testimony with the prosecutors'" (Prosecution closing statements, *People v. Dunn*, 3315).

242. Michael Dunn, jailhouse letter to grandmother (20 February 2013).

243. Michael Dunn, jailhouse letter to grandmother (7 May 2013).

244. Michael Dunn, jailhouse letter to Michelle (20 May 2013). I spoke with Ron Davis (Jordan's father) about this letter, but we were unable to confirm the identity of Michelle or her relationship to Dunn. On the basis of Dunn's repeated use of the word "mom" (as opposed to "my mom") in the letter, however, it is very likely that

Michelle is Dunn's sibling. Moreover, this Michelle should not be confused with Michelle Reeves, the name of a witness who had been working at a dry cleaners in the Southside Plaza.

245. Michael Dunn, jailhouse letter to Rhonda Rouer (23 June 2013).

246. Michael Dunn, jailhouse letter to daughter (12 July 2013).

247. Michael Dunn, jailhouse letter to Rhonda Rouer (2 July 2013); Michael Dunn, jailhouse letter to Rhonda Rouer (5 December 2012); Michael Dunn, jailhouse letter to daughter (26 June 2013); Michael Dunn, jailhouse letter to sibling (2 February 2013); and Michael Dunn, jailhouse letter to daughter (12 July 2013).

248. Michael Dunn, jailhouse letter to Rhonda Rouer (4 July 2013).

249. Dunn, jailhouse call to Rouer, "Dunn Call 8."

250. Quoted in *3½ Minutes, 10 Bullets*, ~55:56, emphasis added.

251. One of Michael Dunn's neighbors also spoke with the Davis family's lawyer and offered disturbing details about Dunn. See "Michael Dunn's Neighbor Speaks to Davis Lawyer John Phillips (Highlights)," YouTube (13 February 2014), http://www. youtube.com/watch?v=aocMpoAs59o.

252. Full transcript of the "Pound Cake" speech can be accessed at "Dr. Bill Cosby Speaks," *Reuters* (n.d.; last accessed 18 February 2018), http://www.rci.rutgers.edu/ ~schochet/101/Cosby_Speech.htm.

253. Michael Dunn, jailhouse calls to Rhonda Rouer, available as "Dunn Call 7" and "Dunn Call 8" at http://www.jacksonville.com/news/2014-02-17/story/listen-state-attorneys-office-releases-michael-dunn-jailhouse-phone-calls. See also Scott Johnson, "Jail Calls of Michael Dunn's Conversations Released," News 4 Jax (14 February 2014), http://www.news4jax.com/news/local/jail-calls-of-michael-dunns-conversations-released_20151107153725123.

254. "Michael Dunn Trial. Day 5. Part 6. Police Interrogation Tape Played."

255. "Michael Dunn Trial. Day 5. Part 6. Police Interrogation Tape Played."

256. "Michael Dunn Retrial—Day 5—Part 1 (Dunn Testifies)," YouTube (30 September 2014), http://www.youtube.com/watch?v=bCa2i8F_YTI, ~1:43:45.

257. Inventory and Receipt (Search Warrant), in "Dunn Discovery Documents," 83 (page 24 of Warrants).

258. "Michael Dunn Retrial—Day 5—Part 5 (Defense Closing Arguments)," YouTube (30 September 2014), http://www.youtube.com/watch?v=uxvBu0b66uo, ~10:00.

259. Delineating country music in monolithic terms is no more appropriate than painting rap with a broad brush. For intersectional studies of class, race, sexuality, and subgenres in country music, see, for example, Nadine Hubbs, *Rednecks, Queers, and Country Music* (Berkeley: University of California Press, 2014); and Travis Stimeling, *Cosmic Cowboys and New Hicks: The Countercultural Sounds of Austin's Progressive Country Music Scene* (New York: Oxford University Press, 2011).

260. Jennifer Lynn Stoever notes how the putative invisibility and "inaudibility of whiteness does not mean it has no sonic markers, but rather that [. . .] dominant listening practices discipline us to process white male ways of sounding as default, natural, normal, and desirable" (*Sonic Color Line*, 12). See also Derald Wing Sue, "The Invisible Whiteness of Being: Whiteness, White Supremacy,

White Privilege, and Racism," in *Addressing Racism: Facilitating Cultural Competence in Mental Health and Educational Settings*, edited by Madonna G. Constantine and Derald Wing Sue (Hoboken, NJ: Wiley & Sons, 2006), 15–30; Richard Delgado and Jean Stefancic, eds., *Critical White Studies: Looking behind the Mirror* (Philadelphia: Temple University Press, 1997); Ashley Doane and Eduardo Bonilla-Silva, *White Out: The Continuing Significance of Racism* (New York: Routledge, 2003); and Prentice T. Chandler, "Blinded by the White: Social Studies and Raceless Pedagogies," *Journal of Educational Thought* 43 (2009), 259–88.

261. See Marcus K. Dowling, "When Being Black and Loving Country Music's Got You Down," *Vice* (20 October 2017), http://noisey.vice.com/en_us/article/a37wae/when-being-black-and-loving-country-musics-got-you-down.

262. See Caroline Mala Corbin, "Terrorists Are Always Muslim but Never White: At the Intersection of Critical Race Theory and Propaganda," *Fordham Law Review* 86 (2017), 455–85.

263. On racial biases in death penalty sentencings (in Florida specifically and in the United States more generally), see Hans Zeisel, "Race Bias in the Administration of the Death Penalty: The Florida Experience," *Harvard Law Review* 95 (1981), 456–68; and Melynda J. Price, *At the Cross: Race, Religion, and Citizenship in the Politics of the Death Penalty* (New York: Oxford University Press, 2015).

264. Michael Dunn, jailhouse call to Rhonda Rouer, available as "Dunn Call 4" at http://www.jacksonville.com/news/2014-02-17/story/listen-state-attorneys-office-releases-michael-dunn-jailhouse-phone-calls.

265. For additional examples of (often violent, sometimes fatal) confrontations over loud music or noise disturbance, see Meghan Keneally, "Teacher Shot Dead over Loud Music at His Wife's Birthday Party," *Daily Mail* (5 June 2012), http://www.dailymail.co.uk/news/article-2155149/Man-kills-neighbor-complaining-noise-neighbors-wifes-party-says-self-defense.html; John Saor, "Japan's 'Piano Murder' Poses Key Test for Justice System," *Washington Post* (4 May 1977), http://www.washingtonpost.com/archive/politics/1977/05/04/japans-piano-murder-poses-key-test-for-justice-system/6e74e858-c95d-4cd0-b040-e2ee1200c44b/?utm_term=.af0555984a94; Lincoln Wright, "Mishawaka Man Given Max Sentence for Killing Neighbor after Loud Music Complaint," *South Bend Tribune* (22 March 2017), http://www.southbendtribune.com/news/publicsafety/mishawaka-man-given-max-sentence-for-killing-neighbor-after-loud/article_71baffdc-0f0e-11e7-b91f-8761a2348ba4.html; Peter Victor, "Neighbourhood Noise: 17 People Have Died from It," *Independent* (18 December 1994), http://www.independent.co.uk/news/uk/neighbourhood-noise-17-people-have-died-from-it-1389990.html; and Branch, "I'm a Black Doctor."

266. Jacksonville, Florida—Code of Ordinances, "Noise Control" (n.d.; last accessed 4 March 2018), http://library.municode.com/fl/jacksonville/codes/code_of_ordinances?nodeId=TITXENAF_CH368NOCO. The Council's general provisions state: "The making, creating and maintenance of excessive, unnecessary, unnatural or unusually loud noises which are prolonged, unusual and unnatural in their time,

place and use affect and are a detriment to the public health, comfort, convenience, safety, welfare and prosperity of the residents of the City."

267. On noise pollution, see Karin Bijsterveld, *Mechanical Sound: Technology, Culture, and Public Problems of Noise in the Twentieth Century* (Cambridge, MA: MIT Press, 2008).

268. Since the early 2000s, music scholars have become particularly attuned to the social, political, and moral ramifications of sound's weaponization. In this discourse, one recurring theme involves the insidiousness of such weaponization—that is, the relative ease with which people can deny sound's weaponized status (owing to the alleged immateriality, invisibility, ephemerality, and intangibility of sonic stimuli when compared to visible weapons). In the case of *People v. Dunn*, however, it becomes important to entertain the inverse: cases in which music is falsely or inaccurately accused of being offensive, incendiary, or weaponized. See, for example, Steve Goodman, *Sonic Warfare: Sound, Affect, and the Ecology of Fear* (Cambridge, MA: MIT Press, 2010); Juliette Volcler, *Extremely Loud: Sound as a Weapon*, translated by Carol Volk (New York: New Press, 2013); María Edurne Zuazu, "Loud but Non-lethal: Acoustic Stagings and State-Sponsored Violence," *Women & Music* 19 (2015), 151–59; George Prochnik, *In Pursuit of Silence: Listening for Meaning in a World of Noise* (New York: Doubleday, 2010); and Suzanne Cusick, "'You Are in a Place That Is out of the World . . .': Music in the Detention Camps of the 'Global War on Terror,'" *Journal of the Society for American Music* 2 (2008), 1–26.

269. Testimony by Leland Brunson, *People v. Dunn*, 1720; and Testimony by Tevin Thompson, *People v. Dunn*, 1672.

270. Testimony by Tevin Thompson, *People v. Dunn*, 1669, 1670.

271. Testimony by defendant, *People v. Dunn*, 2860.

272. Testimony by defendant, *People v. Dunn*, 2860.

273. Testimony by defendant, *People v. Dunn*, 2957.

274. Rouer ended up buying wine and chips, but by Dunn's own admission: "I knew she was getting wine. The chips were a surprise" (Testimony by defendant, *People v. Dunn*, 2853).

275. Testimony by Tommie Stornes, *People v. Dunn*, 1830.

276. Testimony by Tommie Stornes, *People v. Dunn*, 1831.

277. Testimony by Tommie Stornes, *People v. Dunn*, 1831.

278. During redirect, State attorney John Guy gave Stornes the chance to explain, asking, "Why did you write the song?" To which Stornes replied: "I wrote the song as a memorial to Jordan. Like if you—if you met Jordan and know Jordan, he had a big heart like this, and hopefully, you know, you can get a vibe of what type of person he was" (Testimony by Tommie Stornes, *People v. Dunn*, 1853; see also "Michael Dunn Trial—Day 2—Part 5," YouTube [7 February 2014], http://www.youtube.com/watch?v=PPA1BphzCGE, ~57:50).

279. Defense closing arguments, *People v. Dunn*, 3358.

280. "Jordan Davis 911 Calls," YouTube (24 July 2013), http://www.youtube.com/watch?v=cp_x4rvfSBk, ~7:30.

281. There have been multiple reports of police mistaking black men and women for criminals, even when these individuals were the ones who called for help in the first place. High-profile examples include Henry Louis Gates Jr. getting arrested when his neighbor called the police to investigate him (as he had been seen trying to "break into" his own house); and Charleena Lyles calling the police about a burglary, then getting shot seven times by the police when they arrived. See Robert Staples, "White Power, Black Crime, and Racial Politics," *The Black Scholar* 41 (2011), 31–41; Charles J. Ogletree, *The Presumption of Guilt: The Arrest of Henry Louis Gates, Jr. and Race, Class and Crime in America* (New York: Palgrave Macmillan, 2010); Ronnie A. Dunn, "Race and the Relevance of Citizen Complaints against the Police," *Administrative Theory & Praxis* 32 (2010), 557–77; and Phillip Atiba Goff and Kim Shayo Buchanan, "Charleena Lyles Needed Health Care. Instead, She Was Killed," *New York Times* (20 June 2016), http://nyti.ms/2sOcqks. One recent study has shown that high-profile cases of police violence in a community significantly lowers subsequent rates of police-related 911 calls; that is, when reports of police brutality break, people (especially black people) are, for the year thereafter, less likely to report crime. See Matthew Desmond, Andrew V. Papachristos, and David S. Kirk, "Police Violence and Citizen Crime Reporting in the Black Community," *American Sociological Review* 81 (2016), 857–76. On how "forensic listening" of the audio evidence surrounding Michael Brown's shooting may illuminate bystander sensitization, civilian distrust of police, and the racial biases of surveillance technology (ShotSpotter™ microphones), see Lawrence Abu Hamdan, "H[gun shot] ow c[gun shot]an I f[gun shot]orget?," *L'internationale* (12 February 2016), http://www.internationaleonline.org/research/decolonising_practices/53_h_gun_shot_ow_c_gun_shot_an_i_f_gun_shot_orget; see also Lawrence Abu Hamdan, "Aural Contract: Forensic Listening and the Reorganization of the Speaking Subject," *Cesura//Acceso* 1 (2014), 200–24. With thanks to Josh Kun for pointing me to Hamdan's work.

282. It's not clear to me why the State did not object to Strolla's line of questioning (on grounds of irrelevance or beyond the scope) with regard to Stornes's songwriting.

283. For a comparable example—Rachel Jeantel saying "Yes, sir" twenty-three times when testifying as a key witness in the trial of George Zimmerman—see Regina N. Bradley, "To Sir, with Ratchety Love: Listening to the (Dis)Respectability Politics of Rachel Jeantel," *Sounding Out!* (1 July 2013), http://soundstudiesblog.com/2013/07/01/disrespectability-politics-of-rachel-jeantel.

284. Defense closing arguments, *People v. Dunn*, 3352; and Testimony by Alexandria Molinaro, *People v. Dunn*, 2683.

285. Testimony by defendant, *People v. Dunn*, 2958.

286. Testimony by defendant, *People v. Dunn*, 2958.

287. "Lil Reese ft Lil Durk and Fredo Santana—Beef/shot by @DJKenn_AON," YouTube (5 April 2012), http://www.youtube.com/watch?v=TDh0FcJ1atA.

288. Testimony by defendant, *People v. Dunn*, 2956.

289. Testimony by defendant, *People v. Dunn*, 2964.

290. Defense closing arguments, *People v. Dunn*, 3356.

291. Defense closing arguments, *People v. Dunn*, 3356. For full video, see "Michael Dunn Trial—Day 6—Part 3 (Defense Closing Arguments)," YouTube (12 February 2014), http://www.youtube.com/watch?v=1B8Q-EoXh9M, ~19:45.

292. Defense opening statements, *People v. Dunn*, 1300, 1301.

293. Ta-Nehisi Coates, "I Am Still Called by the God I Serve to Walk This Out," *Atlantic* (25 February 2014), http://www.theatlantic.com/politics/archive/2014/02/i-am-still-called-by-the-god-i-serve-to-walk-this-out/284064.

294. Law Offices of John M. Phillips, "Jordan Davis—Jordan's Family Joins Katie Couric on Katie," YouTube (23 February 2014), http://www.youtube.com/watch?v=AtcX_qQg4D4.

295. Laura Effron, "Father of Slain Teen Jordan Davis Wants to Visit Michael Dunn in Prison," ABC News (19 February 2014), http://abcnews.go.com/US/father-slain-teen-jordan-davis-visit-michael-dunn/story?id=22588955.

296. Solotaroff, "A Most American Way to Die."

297. Solotaroff, "A Most American Way to Die."

298. Solotaroff, "A Most American Way to Die."

299. Pretrial proceedings, *People v. Dunn*, 1257–58.

300. On the multi-camera setup within the courtroom, see the production notes for *3½ Minutes, 10 Bullets*, available at http://festival-droits-de-lhomme.org/doc/2016/3_1-2_Minutes_Production_Notes_FINAL.pdf.

301. See Testimony by Ronald Davis, *People v. Dunn*. Strolla called Davis as a witness "for purposes of impeachment against Tommie [Stornes] and Tevin [Thompson]" (2628). Stornes and Thompson had both testified that, following Jordan's death, they had not discussed details of 23 November 2012 with Ron Davis. Strolla believed he could contradict the youths' claims with statements made by Ron Davis in a prior deposition.

302. See, for example, Danielle Paquette, "'This Is the Brain on Horror': The Incredible Calm of Diamond 'Lavish' Reynolds," *Washington Post* (7 July 2016), http://www.washingtonpost.com/news/wonk/wp/2016/07/07/the-incredible-calm-of-diamond-lavish-reynolds/?utm_term=.30a497dd9f7f.

303. Lydia Warren, "The Moment Mother Sobbed in Court as She Forgave White Man Who Shot Her Black Son Dead in Argument over Loud Music Blaring out of His SUV," *Daily Mail* (17 October 2014), http://www.dailymail.co.uk/news/article-2797472/white-man-shot-dead-black-teen-argument-loud-rap-music-sentenced-life-without-parole-victim-s-mother-says-forgives-him.html. Remarkably, McBath had already chosen to forgive Dunn after the *first* trial, when the hung jury failed to convict him on the first-degree murder charge; in other words, McBath had been willing to forgive Dunn long before she could receive assurance that he would face any justice for killing her son. See Ta-Nehisi Coates, "In God We Trust—But We Have Put Our Faith in Our Guns," *Atlantic* (3 February 2014), http://www.theatlantic.com/politics/archive/2014/02/in-god-we-trust-but-we-have-put-our-faith-in-our-guns/283534; and Coates, "I Am Still Called."

304. "Parents of Black Shooting Victim Close Out AACC's Black History Month Events," *Daily Campus Archive* (2 March 2015), http://dailycampusarchive.wordpress.com/

2015/03/02/parents-black-shooting-victim-close-aaccs-black-history-month-events.

305. See Shayla C. Nunnally, *Trust in Black America: Race, Discrimination, and Politics* (New York: New York University Press, 2012), 3–5; bell hooks, *Salvation: Black People and Love* (New York: William Morrow, 2001), 15; Cornel West, *Race Matters* (Boston, MA: Beacon Press, 1993), 19; Martin Luther King Jr., "Loving Your Enemies," in *Strength to Love* (Philadelphia: Fortress, 2010), 43–52; and Douglass, *My Bondage and My Freedom*, 79, 80.

306. West, *Brother West*, 232.

307. Photo of McBath obtained from Stacy M. Brown, "Film Explores Murder of Jordan Davis," *Pride Publishing Group* (3 December 2015), http://pridepublishinggroup.com/pride/2015/12/03/film-explores-murder-of-jordan-davis.

308. Stevenson, *Just Mercy*, 294, 314, emphasis added.

309. Coates, "I Am Still Called."

310. On the inextinguishability of black life even in the wake of black lives' systemic and violent negations, see Christina Sharpe, *In the Wake: On Blackness and Being* (Durham, NC: Duke University Press, 2016), 10–17; Hartman, *Scenes of Subjection*, 28–32; and "The Black Outdoors."

311. McBath's foundation is called Champion in the Making; Ron Davis's foundation is called Walk With Jordan. Both offer college scholarships for youths and in particular youths of color.

312. Lucia McBath, email and video conversation with author (24 March 2018).

313. Ron Davis, video recording for author (5 April 2018).

314. Ron Davis came to Dartmouth College to participate in a lecture and roundtable discussion about *People v. Dunn*. The event was called "His Music Was Not a Weapon: Black Noise, Breakable Skin, and the Plundered Voice of Jordan Russell Davis" (23 April 2018, Loew Auditorium in the Black Family Visual Arts Center, Hanover, NH).

315. Ron Davis, conversation with author (22 April 2018).

316. As I worked on this chapter, I frequently contemplated visiting Michael Dunn in prison. But Ron Davis convinced me that this would be a futile effort because a reporter had recently sought out Dunn and come away with no new information; Dunn has remained intent on blaming Jordan and claiming he had seen a shotgun. "We don't want to give [Dunn] a voice at all," Ron insisted (correspondence with author [25 April 2018]).

317. Warren, "Moment Mother Sobbed."

318. "Uncut: Jordan Davis' Parents React to Sentence," News 4 Jax (17 October 2014), http://www.news4jax.com/news/local/uncut-jordan-davis-parents-react-to-sentence.

Postlude

1. Kevin Powell, "Q&A: Lauryn Hill," *Rolling Stone* (17 September 1998), http://www.rollingstone.com/music/music-news/qa-lauryn-hill-241065.

2. Frederick Douglass, *Narrative of the Life of Frederick Douglass, an American Slave* (Boston, MA: Anti-Slavery Office, 1845), 6.

3. Douglass, *My Bondage and My Freedom*, 88. In this second autobiography, Douglass changed Hester's name to Esther. Christina Sharpe discerns significance in the name change, as she "locate[s] Douglass's register of a shift in the possibilities for black freedom and in his strategies and desires" (*Monstrous Intimacies: Making Post-Slavery Subjects* [Durham, NC: Duke University Press, 2010], 11).

4. Douglass, *My Bondage and My Freedom*, 88.

5. Douglass, *My Bondage and My Freedom*, 88.

6. See Jasbir Puar, *The Right to Maim: Debility, Capacity, and Disability* (Durham, NC: Duke University Press, 2017), ix–xi.

7. See Jenny Franchot, "The Punishment of Esther: Frederick Douglass and the Construction of the Feminine," in *Frederick Douglass: New Literary and Historical Essays*, edited by Eric J. Sundquist (Cambridge: Cambridge University Press, 1990), 141–65; Maurice Wallace, "Constructing the Black Masculine: Frederick Douglass, Booker T. Washington, and the Sublimits of African American Autobiography," in *Subjects and Citizens: Nation, Race, and Gender from Oroonoko to Anita Hill*, edited by Cathy N. Davidson and Michael Moon (Durham, NC: Duke University Press, 1995), 245–70; Hester Blum, "Douglass's and Melville's 'Alphabets of the Blind,'" in *Frederick Douglass and Herman Melville: Essays in Relation*, edited by Robert S. Levine and Samuel Otter (Chapel Hill: University of North Carolina Press, 2008), 257–78; and Stoever, *Sonic Color Line*, 42–48.

8. Sharpe, *Monstrous Intimacies*, 8–9.

9. Hartman, *Scenes of Subjection*, 3.

10. Hartman, *Scenes of Subjection*, 3. (An equivalent in the era of online social media would be the casual circulation of photos and videos showing the quotidian brutalization and killing of black people, sometimes with little or no warning of graphic content.)

11. Fred Moten, *In the Break: The Aesthetics of the Black Radical Tradition* (Minneapolis: University of Minnesota Press, 2003), 4, 5.

12. See Weheliye, *Habeas Viscus*, 91; Michael C. Heller, "Between Silence and Pain: Loudness and the Affective Encounter," *Sound Studies: An Interdisciplinary Journal* 1 (2015), 40–58; and Parisa Vaziri, "Blackness and the Metaethics of the Object," *Rhizomes* 29 (2016), http://doi.org/10.20415/rhiz/029.e16.

13. Moten, *In the Break*, 24.

14. "The Black Outdoors: Fred Moten & Saidiya Hartman at Duke University," YouTube (5 October 2016), http://www.youtube.com/watch?v=t_tUZ6dybrc&t=2725s, ~35:30.

15. Heller, "Between Silence and Pain," 53, emphasis removed (owing to brevity of quoted excerpt).

16. Heller, "Between Silence and Pain," 53.

17. Douglass, *My Bondage and My Freedom*, 87.

18. Theories of screams commonly appear in opera studies. See Philip Friedheim, "Wagner and the Aesthetics of the Scream," *19th-Century Music* 7 (1983), 63–70;

Berthold Hoeckner, "Elsa Screams, or the Birth of Music Drama," *Cambridge Opera Journal* 9 (1997), 97–132; and Michel Poizat, *The Angel's Cry: Beyond the Pleasure Principle in Opera* (Ithaca, NY: Cornell University Press, 1992).

19. Stefano Harney and Fred Moten, *The Undercommons: Fugitive Planning and Black Study* (New York: Minor Compositions, 2013), 20. By this, Harney and Moten mean that "we owe each other to falsify the institution," to practice collective resistance and resurgence here and now, rather than await representation from the promissory yet illusory correctives of utopian democracy, which may arrive later, if ever.

20. This brings to my mind the perceptual play of the Duck-Rabbit illusion, and the apparent impossibility of seeing both a duck and rabbit at the same time. See Ingrid Monson, "Hearing, Seeing, and Perceptual Agency," *Critical Inquiry* 34/supplement (2008), 42.

21. In an introduction to an edited volume on music after September 11, 2001, J. Martin Daughtry teases out the dialectic between the diminished and heightened significances of the musical academy: "In tense and momentous times such as these, the place of music scholarship, or even its relevance, may seem less than clear to some. At the same time, an increasing number of scholars are arguing that our current state of affairs lends a new urgency to the traditional mission of the humanities" ("Charting Courses through Terror's Wake: An Introduction," in *Music in the Post-9/11 World*, edited by Jonathan Ritter and J. Martin Daughtry [New York: Routledge, 2007], xxviii).

Works Cited

Abbate, Carolyn. *In Search of Opera*. Princeton, NJ: Princeton University Press, 2001.

Abbate, Carolyn. "Music—Drastic or Gnostic?" *Critical Inquiry* 30 (2004), 505–36.

Abbate, Carolyn. "Opera; or, the Envoicing of Women." In *Musicology and Difference: Gender and Sexuality in Music Scholarship*, edited by Ruth A. Solie, 225–58. Berkeley: University of California Press, 1993.

Abels, Caroline. "Symphony Auditions: Where Only the Strong Survive." *Pittsburgh Post-Gazette* (30 May 1999), http://old.post-gazette.com/magazine/19990530auditions1.asp.

"About Us." *International Alliance for Women in Music* (n.d.; last accessed 18 July 2018), https://iawm.org/about-us.

Adams, Cameron. "Are Y'all Ready to Hear What Britney Spears Sounds Like without AutoTuned Vocals? Sure?" *News* (9 July 2014), http://www.news.com.au/entertainment/music/are-yall-ready-to-hear-what-britney-spears-sounds-like-without-autotuned-vocals-sure/news-story/be8dc05879522bb6d4d87c11ec8c9692.

Agamben, Giorgio. *Homo Sacer: Sovereign Power and Bare Life*, translated by Daniel Heller-Roazen. Stanford, CA: Stanford University Press, 1998.

Agawu, Kofi. *Representing African Music: Postcolonial Notes, Queries, Positions*. New York: Routledge, 2003.

Agawu, Kofi. "Tonality as a Colonizing Force in Africa." In *Audible Empire: Music, Global Politics, Critique*, edited by Ronald Radano and Tejumola Olaniyan, 334–55. Durham, NC: Duke University Press, 2016.

Ahmed, Sara. *On Being Included: Racism and Diversity in Institutional Life*. Durham, NC: Duke University Press, 2012.

Ahmed, Sara. *The Promise of Happiness*. Durham, NC: Duke University Press, 2010.

Alaniz, José. *Death, Disability, and the Superhero: The Silver Age and Beyond*. Jackson: University Press of Mississippi, 2014.

Albright, Daniel. *Musicking Shakespeare: A Conflict of Theatres*. Rochester, NY: University of Rochester Press, 2007.

Alexander, Michelle. *The New Jim Crow: Mass Incarceration in the Age of Colorblindness*. New York: New Press, 2012.

"Alien NO AUTOTUNE Britney Spears FULL." YouTube (10 July 2014), http://www.youtube.com/watch?v=MUdKrtsrCBI.

"America's Got Talent 2012—Tim Poe, Singer/War Veteran." YouTube (5 June 2012), http://www.youtube.com/watch?v=hiItdgDxfMs.

"*American Idol* Contestant Jermaine Jones Booted over Criminal Charges." *Rolling Stone* (14 March 2012), http://www.rollingstone.com/music/news/american-idolcontestant-jermaine-jones-booted-over-criminal-charges-20120314.

American Musicological Society 2015 Directory. http://www.ams-net.org/administration/ethics.php (2015).

Ammer, Christine. *Unsung: A History of Women in American Music*. Portland, OR: Amadeus Press, 2001.

Anderson, Melinda D. "Why the Myth of Meritocracy Hurts Kids of Color." *Atlantic* (27 Jul7 2017), http://www.theatlantic.com/education/archive/2017/07/internalizing-the-myth-of-meritocracy/535035.

Anderson, Paul Allen. "'The Game Is the Game': Tautology and Allegory in *The Wire*." *Criticism* 52 (2010), 373–98.

Anderton, Abby. "'It Was Never a Nazi Orchestra': The American Re-education of the Berlin Philharmonic." *Music & Politics* 7 (2013), http://dx.doi.org/10.3998/mp.9460447.0007.103.

"Andrea Begley—Angel." YouTube (30 January 2014), http://www.youtube.com/watch?v=fLx0KnstmVk.

Angelou, Maya. "Human Family." In *The Complete Collected Poems of Maya Angelou*, 225. New York: Random House, 1994.

Angie the Antitheist. "Athletic Inspiration Porn Is No Excuse to Shame Me for My Disability." *Everyday Feminism* (13 May 2016), http://everydayfeminism.com/2016/05/disability-inspiration-porn.

An-Na'im, Abdullahi A. "The Legal Protection of Human Rights in Africa: How to Do More with Less." In *Human Rights: Concepts, Contests, Contingencies*, edited by Austin Sarat and Thomas R. Kearns, 89–116. Ann Arbor: University of Michigan Press, 2001.

Apolloni, Alexandra. "The Lollipop Girl's Voice: Respectability, Migration, and Millie Small's 'My Boy Lollipop.'" *Journal of Popular Music Studies* 28 (2016), 460–73.

Arnold, Gordon B. *Projecting the End of the American Dream: Hollywood's Visions of U.S. Decline.* Santa Barbara, CA: Praeger, 2013.

Arnold, Jonathan. *Sacred Music in Secular Society.* Farnham, UK: Ashgate, 2014.

Ashley, Wendy. "The Angry Black Woman: The Impact of Pejorative Stereotypes on Psychotherapy with Black Women." *Social Work in Public Health* 29 (2014), 27–34.

Associated Press. "Putin Sits Down at Piano in China, Plays Soviet Songs." *Boston Globe* (14 May 2017), http://www.bostonglobe.com/news/world/2017/05/14/putin-sits-down-piano-china-plays-soviet-songs/LYHC3zHPriZcYcNJqLKQQN/story.html.

Associated Press. "Rapper Yung Mazi, Who Survived Multiple Shootings, Dies in Another." *USA Today* (7 August 2017), http://www.usatoday.com/story/life/music/2017/08/07/rapper-yung-mazi-who-survived-multiple-shootings-dies-another/547077001.

Associated Press. "Was Media Unfair to Call Britney Spears Fat?" *Today* (10 September 2007), http://www.today.com/popculture/was-media-unfair-call-britney-spears-fat-wbna20713930.

Attwood, Feona. "Sluts and Riot Grrls: Female Identity and Sexual Agency." *Journal of Gender Studies* 16 (2007), 233–47.

Bachechi, Kimberly. "Our Icons: Ourselves. Britney Spears, Justin Timberlake, Kevin Federline, and the Construction of Whiteness in a Post-Race America." *Celebrity Studies* 6 (2015), 164–77.

Back, Les. "Voices of Hate, Sounds of Hybridity: Black Music and the Complexities of Racism." *Black Music Research Journal* 20 (2000), 127–49.

Baker, Geoffrey. *El Sistema: Orchestrating Venezuela's Youth.* New York: Oxford University Press, 2014.

Baker, Jasmine, Mark Haslett, and Scott Morgan. "Cornel West at A&M-Commerce: Transcript." KETR (7 October 2016), http://ketr.org/post/cornel-west-am-commerce-transcript.

Baldwin, James. *I Am Not Your Negro.* New York: Vintage, 2017.

Balfour, Lawrie. *Democracy's Reconstruction: Thinking Politically with W. E. B. Du Bois.* New York: Oxford University Press, 2011.

Banaji, Mahzarin R., and Anthony G. Greenwald. *Blindspot: Hidden Biases of Good People.* New York: Delacorte Press, 2013.

Barbier, Patrick. *The World of the Castrati: The History of an Extraordinary Operatic Phenomenon.* London: Souvenir Press, 1996.

Barkham, Patrick. "The Bald Truth." *Guardian* (20 February 2007), http://www. theguardian.com/world/2007/feb/20/gender.music.

Barnard, Andrew R. "In Defense of the Vienna Philharmonic: A Response to Norman Lebrecht." *ClassicalCommentator* (3 January 2015), http://www.theclassicalcommentator. com/in-defense-of-the-vienna-philharmonic-a-response-to-norman-lebrecht.

Barthes, Roland. *Image, Music, Text,* translated by Stephen Heath. London: Fontana, 1977.

Bassler, Samantha. "'But You Don't Look Sick': Dismodernism, Disability Studies and Music Therapy on Invisible Illness and the Unstable Body." *Voices: A World Forum for Music Therapy* 14 (2014), http://voices.no/index.php/voices/article/view/802/668.

Bastién, Angelica Jade. "The Case against Colorblind Casting." *Atlantic* (26 December 2015), http://www.theatlantic.com/entertainment/archive/2015/12/oscar-isaac-and-the-case-against-colorblind-casting/421668.

Becker, Judith. *Deep Listeners: Music, Emotion, and Trancing.* Bloomington: Indiana University Press, 2004.

Becker, Judith. "Music, Trancing, and the Absence of Pain." In *Pain and Its Transformations: The Interface of Biology and Culture,* edited by Sarah Coakley and Kay Kaufman Shelemay, 166–94. Cambridge, MA: Harvard University Press, 2007.

Bedi, Sonu. *Rejecting Rights.* Cambridge: Cambridge University Press, 2009.

Begley, Andrea. *I Didn't See That Coming: My Story.* London: BBC Books, 2013.

Bell, Christopher E. *American Idolatry: Celebrity, Commodity and Reality Television.* Jefferson, NC: McFarland, 2010.

Bellman, Jonathan. "All Hands." *Dial M for Musicology* (29 June 2018), http:// dialmformusicology.com/2018/06/29/06-29-18-all-hands.

Bellman, Jonathan. "Scholar Teaches Behind Bars; Is Sent to Woodshed." *Dial M for Musicology* (16 February 2016), http://dialmformusicology.com/2016/02/16/ scholar-teaches-behind-bars-is-sent-to-woodshed.

Benesch, Susan. "Inciting Genocide, Pleading Free Speech." *World Policy Journal* 21 (2004), 62–69.

Berenson, Tessa. "World-Famous Violinist Joshua Bell Performs in Union Station." *TIME* (30 September 2014), http://time.com/3450389/violinist-joshua-bell-performs-in-union-station.

Berg, Maggie, and Barbara K. Seeber. *The Slow Professor: Challenging the Culture of Speed in the Academy.* Toronto, ON: University of Toronto Press, 2016.

Berger, James. *After the End: Representations of Post-Apocalypse.* Minneapolis: University of Minnesota Press, 1999.

Berger, Karol. "The Ends of Music History, or: The Old Masters in the Supermarket of Cultures." *Journal of Musicology* 31 (2014), 186–98.

Bergeron, Katherine. "Prologue: Disciplining Music." In *Disciplining Music: Musicology and Its Others,* edited by Katherine Bergeron and Philip V. Bohlman, 1–9. Chicago: University of Chicago Press, 1992.

Bergeron, Katherine, and Philip V. Bohlman, eds. *Disciplining Music: Musicology and Its Canons.* Chicago: University of Chicago Press, 1992.

Berlant, Lauren. *Cruel Optimism*. Durham, NC: Duke University Press, 2011.

Berlant, Lauren. "Slow Death (Sovereignty, Obesity, Lateral Agency)." *Critical Inquiry* 33 (2007), 764–80.

"Bernie Sanders 'Black Lives Matter' Protester [Interview]." YouTube (11 August 2015), http://www.youtube.com/watch?v=-ajWs3z8rs0.

Bernstein, Jane, ed. *Women's Voices across Musical Worlds*. Boston: Northeastern University Press, 2004.

Bernstein, Leonard. "Something Called Terrorism," with introduction by Carol J. Oja and Mark Eden Horowitz. *American Scholar* (1 September 2008), http://theamericanscholar.org/something-called-terrorism.

Bertrand, Marianne, and Sendhil Mullainathan. "Are Emily and Greg More Employable Than Lakisha and Jamal? A Field Experiment on Labor Market Discrimination." *American Economic Review* 94 (2004), 991–1013.

Bérubé, Michael. "Afterword: If I Should Live So Long." In *Disability Studies: Enabling the Humanities*, edited by Sharon L. Snyder, Brenda Jo Brueggemann, and Rosemarie Garland-Thomson, 337–43. New York: Modern Language Association of America, 2002.

Bettcher, Talia Mae. "Evil Deceivers and Make-Believers: On Transphobic Violence and the Politics of Illusion." *Hypatia* 22 (2007), 43–65.

Beyer, Adam. "Divinity School Professor Resigns after Dispute with Colleagues about Diversity Training, Calling It a 'Waste.'" *Duke Chronicle* (9 May 2017), http://www.dukechronicle.com/article/2017/05/divinity-school-professor-resigns-after-dispute-with-colleagues-about-diversity-training-calling-it-a-waste.

Bigenho, Michelle. "Why I'm Not an Ethnomusicologist: A View from Anthropology." In *The New (Ethno)musicologies*, edited by Henry Stobart, 28–39. Lanham, MD: Scarecrow Press, 2008.

Bijsterveld, Karin. *Mechanical Sound: Technology, Culture, and Public Problems of Noise in the Twentieth Century*. Cambridge, MA: MIT Press, 2008.

"Black Juror from Michael Dunn Trial States It Wasn't about Race and He Was a Nice Guy." YouTube (24 February 2014), http://www.youtube.com/watch?v=q3UTFGI1OYc.

"Black Lives Matter Demonstration at Bernie Sanders Westlake Event Seattle (unedited)." YouTube (10 August 2015), http://www.youtube.com/watch?v=oV-ZSP0zAuI.

"The Black Outdoors: Fred Moten & Saidiya Hartman at Duke University." YouTube (5 October 2016), http://www.youtube.com/watch?v=t_tUZ6dybrc.

Blacking, John. *How Musical Is Man?* Seattle: University of Washington Press, 1973.

Blackwell, Brandon. "Witnesses Did Not Hear Cleveland Police Officer Order Tamir Rice to Show His Hands Before Shots Fired." *Cleveland.com* (13 June 2015), http://www.cleveland.com/metro/index.ssf/2015/06/witnesses_did_not_hear_clevela.html#incart_maj-story-1.

Blake, Art M. 2012. "Audible Citizenship and Audiomobility: Race, Technology, and CB Radio." In *Sound Clash: Listening to American Studies*, edited by Kara Keeling and Josh Kun, 87–109. Baltimore: Johns Hopkins University Press.

Blakeley, Kiri. "Stop with the Stupid Fat Suit Experiments, Please." *Forbes* (26 October 2011), http://www.forbes.com/sites/kiriblakeley/2011/10/26/stop-with-the-stupid-fat-suit-experiments-please.

Bloechl, Olivia, with Melanie Lowe. "Introduction: Rethinking Difference." In *Rethinking Difference in Music Scholarship*, edited by Olivia Bloechl, Melanie Lowe, and Jeffrey Kallberg, 1–52. Cambridge: Cambridge University Press, 2015.

Blum, Hester. "Douglass's and Melville's 'Alphabets of the Blind.'" In *Frederick Douglass and Herman Melville: Essays in Relation*, edited by Robert S. Levine and Samuel Otter, 257–78. Chapel Hill: University of North Carolina Press, 2008.

Board of Directors of the American Musicological Society. "Statement Opposing Executive Order Banning Immigrants and Refugees." *American Musicological Society* (1 February 2017; revised 2 February 2017), http://www.ams-net.org/AMS-condemns-executive-order.php.

Boer, J. Tom, Manuel Pastor Jr., James L. Sadd, and Lori D. Snyder. "Is There Environmental Racism? The Demographics of Hazardous Waste in Los Angeles County." *Social Science Quarterly* 78 (1997), 793–810.

Bogdan, Frank. *Freak Show: Presenting Human Oddities for Amusement and Profit*. Chicago: University of Chicago Press, 1990.

Boggs, Colleen Glenney. "American Bestiality: Sex, Animals, and the Construction of Subjectivity." *Cultural Critique* 76 (2010), 98–125.

Bonilla-Silva, Eduardo. *Racism without Racists: Color-Blind Racism and the Persistence of Racial Inequality in America*, fourth edition. Lanham, MD: Rowman & Littlefield, 2014.

Bonnette, Lakeyta M. *Pulse of the People: Political Rap Music and Black Politics*. Philadelphia: University of Pennsylvania Press, 2015.

Boren, Zachary Davies. "Bernie Sanders: Democratic Presidential Candidate Kicked off the Stage by Black Lives Matter Protesters." *Independent* (9 August 2015), http://www.independent.co.uk/news/world/americas/us-elections/bernie-sanders-democratic-presidential-candidate-kicked-off-the-stage-by-black-lives-matter-10447101.html.

Botstein, Leon. "Music, Morality, and Method." *Musical Quarterly* 81 (1997), 339–43.

Bourdieu, Pierre. *Outline of a Theory of Practice*, translated by Richard Nice. Cambridge: Cambridge University Press, 2013.

Bourke, Joanna. "Pain Sensitivity: An Unnatural History from 1800 to 1965." *Journal of Medical Humanities* 35 (2014), 301–19.

Boyd, Jean Ann. "Philip Hale, American Music Critic, Boston, 1889–1933." PhD diss., University of Texas at Austin, 1985.

Boyer, William. "Public Hearings: Sonic Encounters and Social Responsibility in the New York City Subway Systems." PhD diss., New York University, 2014.

Boyle, Susan. *The Woman I Was Born to Be: My Story*. New York: Atria Paperback, 2010.

Bradham, Bre, and Nathan Luzum. "Larry Moneta Takes 'Hiatus' from Facebook after 'Insensitive' Posts Spark Student Backlash." *Chronicle* (13 December 2018), http://www.dukechronicle.com/article/2018/12/duke-university-administrator-larry-moneta-takes-hiatus-from-facebook-after-insensitive-posts-spark-student-backlash.

Bradley, Regina N. "To Sir, with Ratchety Love: Listening to the (Dis)Respectability Politics of Rachel Jeantel." *Sounding Out!* (1 July 2013), http://soundstudiesblog.com/2013/07/01/disrespectability-politics-of-rachel-jeantel.

Bradley, Regina N. "SANDRA BLAND: #SayHerName Loud or Not at All." *Sounding Out!* (16 November 2015), http://soundstudiesblog.com/2015/11/16/sandra-bland-sayhername-loud.

Braidotti, Rosi. *The Posthuman*. Cambridge: Polity Press, 2013.

Branch, Mary. "I'm a Black Doctor. My Neighbors Called the Cops on Me for Listening to Biggie." *Washington Post* (28 May 2018), http://www.washingtonpost.com/opinions/my-white-neighbors-called-the-cops-on-me-for-listening-to-hip-hop/2018/05/28/54930d04-4fbe-11e8-af46-b1d6dc0d9bfe_story.html?utm_term=.036f53c9eb0a.

Brauer, Juliane. "How Can Music Be Torturous? Music in Nazi Concentration and Extermination Camps." *Music & Politics* 10 (2016), http://dx.doi.org/10.3998/mp.9460447.0010.103.

Brett, Philip. "Musicality, Essentialism, and the Closet." In *Queering the Pitch: The New Gay and Lesbian Musicology*, second edition, edited by Philip Brett, Elizabeth Wood, and Gary C. Thomas, 9–26. New York: Routledge, 2006.

Brison, Susan. *Aftermath: Violence and the Remaking of a Self.* Princeton, NJ: Princeton University Press, 2002.

Britan, Halbert H. "Music and Morality." *International Journal of Ethics* 15 (1904), 48–63.

"Britney a Bust." *New York Post* (10 September 2007), http://nypost.com/2007/09/10/britney-a-bust.

"Britney Inventions." *Tumblr* (24 October 2013), http://britneyinventions.tumblr.com/post/64960448604/vocal-fry-is-a-singing-technique-first-developed.

"Britney Spears—Alien (No AutoTune)." YouTube (11 July 2014), http://www.youtube.com/watch?v=BVxL2IbKldk.

"Britney Spears—Gimme More Live at MTV VMA's 2007." YouTube (28 January 2013), http://www.youtube.com/watch?v=udDlSRgyxMc.

"Britney Spears 'Primetime Interview with Diane Sawyer (Part 1)' HD." YouTube (4 September 2013), http://www.youtube.com/watch?v=qROlbBPwDG0.

Brooks, Katherine. "No, Putin's Piano Recital Doesn't Make Him Any 'Softer.'" *Huffington Post* (15 May 2017), http://www.huffingtonpost.com/entry/no-putins-piano-recital-doesnt-make-him-any-softer_us_5919b8cfe4b0031e737f3437.

Brown, Michael K., Martin Carnoy, Elliott Currie, Troy Duster, David B. Oppenheimer, Marjorie M. Shultz, and David Wellman. *Whitewashing Race: The Myth of a Color-Blind Society.* Berkeley: University of California Press, 2003.

Brown, Stacy M. "Film Explores Murder of Jordan Davis." *Pride Publishing Group* (3 December 2015), http://pridepublishinggroup.com/pride/2015/12/03/film-explores-murder-of-jordan-davis.

Brownstone, Sydney. "Bernie Sanders Adds Racial Justice Platform to Website, Says He's 'Disappointed' by Seattle Rally Interruption." *The Stranger* (9 August 2015), http://www.thestranger.com/blogs/slog/2015/08/09/22671362/bernie-sanders-adds-racial-justice-platform-to-website-says-hes-disappointed-by-seattle-rally-interruption.

Buch, Esteban. *Beethoven's Ninth: A Political History*, translated by Richard Miller. Chicago: University of Chicago Press, 2003.

Buehler, James W. "Racial/Ethnic Disparities in the Use of Lethal Force by US Police, 2010–14." *American Journal of Public Health* 107 (2017), 295–97.

Burkett, Brendan, Mike McNamee, and Wolfgang Potthast. "Shifting Boundaries in Sports Technology and Disability: Equal Rights or Unfair Advantage in the Case of Oscar Pistorius." *Disability & Society* 26 (2011), 643–54.

Burnham, Scott. *Mozart's Grace.* Princeton, NJ: Princeton University Press, 2013.

Burnham, Scott. "Theorists and 'The Music Itself.'" *Journal of Musicology* 15 (1997), 316–29.

Burns, Kris. "Press Release" (12 February 2003), available at http://www.osborne-conant.org/iawminfo.htm.

Butler, Judith. "Bodily Vulnerability, Coalitions and Street Politics." In *The State of Things*, edited by Marta Kuzma, Pablo Lafunete, and Peter Osborne, 161–98. London: Koenig Books, 2012.

Butler, Judith. *The Psychic Life of Power.* Stanford, CA: Stanford University Press, 1997.

Buzzarté, Monique. "We Need a Man for Solo Trombone: Abbie Conant's Story." *Journal of the International Alliance for Women in Music* (1996), 8–11, available at http://iawm.org/stef/articles_html/buzzarte_conant.html.

Cachia, Amanda. "Talking Blind: Disability, Access, and the Discursive Turn." *Disability Studies Quarterly* 33 (2013), http://dsq-sds.org/article/view/3758/3281.

Cain, M. Celia. "Of Pain, Passing and Longing for Music." *Disability & Society* 25 (2010), 747–51.

Calamur, Krishnadev. "The Problem with Calls for 'Resilience.'" *Atlantic* (24 March 2017), http://www.theatlantic.com/international/archive/2017/05/manchester-attack/527832.

Caldwell, Kayla. "'The Most Unattractive Moment of My Life!' Fergie Opens Up about the Now-Infamous Moment She Wet Herself Onstage." *Daily Mail* (13 November 2014), http://www.dailymail.co.uk/tvshowbiz/article-2834060/The-unattractive-moment-life-Fergie-opens-infamous-moment-wet-onstage.html.

Calvert, Dave. "'A Person with Some Sort of Learning Disability': The Aetiological Narrative and Public Construction of Susan Boyle." *Disability & Society* 29 (2014), 101–14.

Cammett, Ann. "Welfare Queen Redux: Criminalizing Black Mothers in the Age of Neoliberalism." *Southern California Interdisciplinary Law Journal* 25 (2016), 363–93.

Capehart, Jonathan. "Jazz Musician Wynton Marsalis Says Rap and Hip-Hop Are 'More Damaging Than a Statue of Robert E. Lee.'" *Washington Post* (22 May 2018), http://www.washingtonpost.com/blogs/post-partisan/wp/2018/05/22/jazz-musician-wynton-marsalis-says-rap-and-hip-hop-are-more-damaging-than-a-statue-of-robert-e-lee/?noredirect=on&utm_term=.d38aca27556e.

Capehart, Jonathan. "Playing 'Games' with Trayvon Martin's Image." *Washington Post* (6 February 2013), http://www.washingtonpost.com/blogs/post-partisan/wp/2013/02/06/playing-games-with-trayvon-martins-image/?utm_term=.60ff66326d38.

Caramanica, Jon. "Review: Mariah Carey and Her Can't-Look-Away Debut in Las Vegas." *New York Times* (7 May 2015), http://www.nytimes.com/2015/05/08/arts/music/review-mariah-carey-and-her-cant-look-away-debut-in-las-vegas.html.

"Carlos Guevara's Struggles Won't Hold Him Back." YouTube (18 September 2013), http://www.youtube.com/watch?v=3rUWDvuBOHY.

Carlson, Jen. "Erykah Badu Made $3.60 Busking in Times Square." *Gothamist* (15 October 2014), http://gothamist.com/2014/10/15/video_erykah_badu_made_360_busking.php.

Carmody, Deirdre. "*Time* Responds to Criticism over Simpson Cover." *New York Times* (25 June 1994), http://www.nytimes.com/1994/06/25/us/time-responds-to-criticism-over-simpson-cover.html.

Carpenter, Laura M. *Virginity Lost: An Intimate Portrait of First Sexual Experiences.* New York: New York University Press, 2005.

Carr, Daphne. "Sound Protocols: Street Medic Care for Sonic Energy Injury." Paper presented at CUNY's Graduate Students in Music Conference (10 March 2017).

Carr, David. "One Man's Musical Tastes as Fodder for a Flame War." *New York Times* (18 May 2006), http://www.nytimes.com/2006/05/18/arts/music/18rock.html.

Carroll, Hamilton. *Affirmative Reaction: New Formations of White Masculinity.* Durham, NC: Duke University Press, 2011.

Carroll, Rebecca. "People Who Don't 'See Race' Are Erasing Black People and Their Contributions." *Guardian* (15 February 2016), http://www.theguardian.com/

commentisfree/2016/feb/15/bill-clinton-we-are-all-mixed-race-erases-black-people?CMP=share_btn_fb.

Cartwright, Samuel A. "Diseases and Peculiarities of the Negro Race." *De Bow's Review* XI (1851), available via PBS at http://www.pbs.org/wgbh/aia/part4/4h3106t.html.

Casey, Joan A., et al. "Race/Ethnicity, Socioeconomic Status, Residential Segregation, and Spatial Variation in Noise Exposure in the Contiguous United States." *Environmental Health Perspectives* 125 (2017), http://doi.org/10.1289/EHP898.

Castilla, Emilio J., and Stephen Benard. "The Paradox of Meritocracy in Organizations." *Administrative Science Quarterly* 55 (2010), 543–76.

Castle, Terry. *The Apparitional Lesbian: Female Homosexuality and Modern Culture.* New York: Columbia University Press, 1993.

Catanese, Brandi Wilkins. *The Problem of the Color[blind]: Racial Transgression and the Politics of Black Performance.* Ann Arbor: University of Michigan Press, 2011.

"Cathy Dennis—Toxic (Demo for Britney Spears)." YouTube (10 January 2011), http://www.youtube.com/watch?v=Bhwn-7Pm9Bg.

Cavazos, John. "Civil Lawsuits against Michael Dunn Settled." News 4 Jax (4 January 2014), http://www.news4jax.com/news/florida/duval-county/civil-lawsuits-against-michael-dunn-settled.

Cellini, Adam. "Homeless Musician Finds Receptive Audience on Streets of Sarasota." *ABC News* (30 June 2015), http://www.mysuncoast.com/entertainment/news/featured/homeless-musician-finds-receptive-audience-on-streets-of-sarasota/article_ddaf749a-1f6c-11e5-9f44-03eeab4adabb.html.

Chandler, Prentice T. "Blinded by the White: Social Studies and Raceless Pedagogies." *Journal of Educational Thought* 43 (2009), 259–88.

Chang, Jeff. *We Gon' Be Alright: Notes on Race and Resegregation.* New York: Picador, 2016.

Chapman, Dale. "The 'One-Man Band' and Entrepreneurial Selfhood in Neoliberal Culture." *Popular Music* 32 (2013), 451–70.

Charlton, James I. *Nothing about Us without Us: Disability Oppression and Empowerment.* Berkeley: University of California Press, 2000.

Charlton, James. "Peripheral Everywhere." *Journal of Literary & Cultural Disability Studies* 4 (2010), 195–200.

Chasmar, Jessica. "Michael Moore Holds 'We Are All Muslim' Sign in Front of Trump Tower." *Washington Times* (17 December 2015), http://www.washingtontimes.com/news/2015/dec/17/michael-moore-holds-we-are-all-muslim-sign-in-fron.

Chęćka-Gotkowicz, Anna. "Peter Kivy's Discursive 'Weakness': The Problem of Moral Entanglement of Music." *Miscellanea Anthropologica et Sociologica* 16 (2015), 77–85.

Chen, Mel. *Animacies: Biopolitics, Racial Mattering, and Queer Affect.* Durham, NC: Duke University Press, 2012.

Chen, Tanya. "Lorde's Grammy Performance Proved Her Dancing Continues to Freak People Out." *Buzzfeed* (26 January 2014), http://www.buzzfeed.com/tanyachen/lordes-grammy-performance-proved-her-dancing-continues-to-fr?utm_term=.guvjRrvj7#.poVAZ0QAz.

Cheng, William. "Hearts for Sale: The French *Romance* and the Sexual Traffic of Musical Mimicry." *19th-Century Music* 35 (2011), 115–46.

Cheng, William. "I'm a Musician Who Can't Play Music Anymore. I Feel Like I'm Letting My Heroes Down." *Washington Post* (20 January 2016), http://www.washingtonpost.com/posteverything/wp/2016/01/20/im-a-musician-who-cant-play-music-anymore-i-feel-like-im-letting-my-heroes-down/?utm_term=.0d98d63c8576.

Cheng, William. *Just Vibrations: The Purpose of Sounding Good.* Ann Arbor: University of Michigan Press, 2016.

Cheng, William. "Pleasure's Discontents." *Journal of the American Musicological Society* 66 (2013), 840–44.

Cheng, William. *Sound Play: Video Games and the Musical Imagination.* New York: Oxford University Press, 2014.

Cheng, William. "Taking Back the Laugh: Comedic Alibis, Funny Fails." *Critical Inquiry* 43 (2017), 528–49.

Cheu, Johnson. "De-gene-erates, Replicants, and Other Aliens: (Re)defining Disability in Futuristic Film." In *Disability/Postmodernity: Embodying Disability Theory*, edited by Mairian Corker and Tom Shakespeare, 198–212. London: Continuum, 2002.

"China's Got Talent 2011 12-yr-old Mongolian Boy Singing 'Mother in the Dream.'" YouTube (6 June 2011), http://www.youtube.com/watch?v=lY7ChkI6c8A.

Choudhury, Uttara. "Amartya Sen: The Enlightened Economist." *Braingainmag.com* (2011), http://www.braingainmag.com/amartya-sen-the-enlightened-economist. htm.

Chrisman, Wendy L. "A Reflection on Inspiration: A Recuperative Call for Emotion in Disability Studies." *Journal of Literary & Cultural Disability Studies* 5 (2011), 173–84.

Chun, Wendy Hui Kyong, and Sarah Friedland. "Habits of Leaking: Of Sluts and Network Cards." *differences: A Journal of Feminist Cultural Studies* 26 (2015), 1–28.

Citron, Danielle Keats. *Hate Crimes in Cyberspace.* Cambridge, MA: Harvard University Press, 2014.

Clare, Eli. *Exile and Pride: Disability, Queerness, and Liberation.* Durham, NC: Duke University Press, 2009.

Cleveland, J. Jefferson, and William B. McClain. Excerpt from *Songs of Zion.* In *Readings in Black American Music*, second edition, edited by Eileen Southern, 298–301. New York: W. W. Norton, 1983.

Closing Arguments. *People v. Dunn. People of the State of Florida v. DUNN MICHAEL DAVID, Case No. 16-2012-CF-011572-AXXX-MA*, pages 3160–359. Available via database of Joseph Kennedy, "Law of Self-Defense" (course at UNC Chapel Hill), http://lawofselfdefense.web.unc.edu/files/2014/10/chargeconfthruStrollaclose.pdf.

CNN Wire. "Michael Dunn Found Guilty of 1st-degree Murder in Loud-Music Trial." Fox Denver (1 October 2014), http://kdvr.com/2014/10/01/michael-dunn-found-guilty-of-1st-degree-murder-in-loud-music-trial.

Coates, Ta-Nehisi. "I Am Still Called by the God I Serve to Walk This Out." *Atlantic* (25 February 2014), http://www.theatlantic.com/politics/archive/2014/02/i-am-still-called-by-the-god-i-serve-to-walk-this-out/284064.

Coates, Ta-Nehisi. "In God We Trust—But We Have Put Our Faith in Our Guns." *Atlantic* (3 February 2014), http://www.theatlantic.com/politics/archive/2014/02/in-god-we-trust-but-we-have-put-our-faith-in-our-guns/283534.

Coates, Ta-Nehisi. "To Raise, Love, and Lose a Black Child." *Atlantic* (8 October 2014), http://www.theatlantic.com/politics/archive/2014/10/to-raise-love-and-lose-a-black-child/381189.

Coates, Ta-Nehisi. *We Were Eight Years in Power.* New York: BCP Literary, 2017.

Cobb, Floyd, II, and Nicole M. Russell. "Meritocracy or Complexity: Problematizing Racial Disparities in Mathematics Assessment within the Context of Curricular Structures, Practices, and Discourse." *Journal of Education Policy* 30 (2015), 631–49.

Cobussen, Marcel, and Nanette Nielsen. *Music and Ethics.* Burlington, VT: Ashgate, 2012.

Cohen-Weisz, Susanne. *Jewish Life in Austria and Germany since 1945: Identity and Communal Reconstruction.* New York: Central European University Press, 2015.

Collier, Harry. "Vienna Philharmonic: Slow to Change Its Tune." *Good Music Guide* (2007), http://www.good-music-guide.com/forum/index.php/topic,13375.30/wap2.html.

Colomb, Gregory G. *Designs on Truth: The Poetics of the Augustan Mock-Epic.* University Park: Pennsylvania State University Press, 1992.

"Commuter Concerto Helps Writer Net Pulitzer." NPR (7 April 2008), http://www.npr.org/templates/story/story.php?storyId=89443778.

"Comprehensive Soldier Fitness: Building Resilience and Enhancing Performance." *U.S. Army Reserve* (n.d.; last accessed 16 February 2018), http://www.usar.army.mil/Featured/Resources/Comprehensive-Soldier-Fitness.

Contrera, Jessica. "Joshua Bell's Metro Encore Draws a Crowd." *Washington Post* (30 September 2014), http://www.washingtonpost.com/lifestyle/style/joshua-bells-metro-encore-draws-a-crowd/2014/09/30/c28b6c50-48d5-11e4-a046-120a8a855cca_story.html?utm_term=.4972e5b14b13.

Cook, John. "Blacklisted: Is Stephin Merritt a Racist Because He Doesn't Like Hip-Hop?" *Slate* (9 May 2006), http://www.slate.com/articles/arts/music_box/2006/05/blacklisted.html.

Cook, Nicholas. "We Are All (Ethno)musicologists Now." In *The New (Ethno)musicologies*, edited by Henry Stobart, 48–70. Lanham, MD: Scarecrow Press, 2008.

Cooley, Timothy J., and Gregory Barz. "Casting Shadows: Fieldwork Is Dead! Long Live Fieldwork!" In *Shadows in the Field: New Perspectives for Fieldwork in Ethnomusicology*, second edition, edited by Gregory Barz and Timothy J. Cooley, 3–24. New York: Oxford University Press, 2008.

Cooney, Samantha. "All the Women Who Have Accused Sen. Al Franken of Sexual Misconduct." *TIME* (6 December 2017), http://time.com/5042931/al-franken-accusers.

Cooper, Michael. "Met Opera Suspends James Levine after New Sexual Abuse Accusations." *New York Times* (3 December 2017), http://www.nytimes.com/2017/12/03/arts/music/james-levine-met-opera.html.

Corbin, Caroline Mala. "Terrorists Are Always Muslim But Never White: At the Intersection of Critical Race Theory and Propaganda." *Fordham Law Review* 86 (2017), 455–85.

Cosby, Bill, and Alvin Poussaint. *Come On, People: On the Path from Victims to Victors.* Nashville, TN: Thomas Nelson, 2007.

Cosenza, Julie. "SLOW: Crip Theory, Dyslexia and the Borderlands of Disability and Ablebodiedness." *Liminalities: A Journal of Performance Studies* 6 (2010), 1–22.

Cowell, Simon. *I Don't Mean to Be Rude, But . . . : Backstage Gossip from "American Idol" & the Secrets That Can Make You a Star.* New York: Broadway Books, 2003.

Cox, Arnie. "Embodying Music: Principles of the Mimetic Hypothesis." *Music Theory Online* 17 (2011), http://www.mtosmt.org/issues/mto.11.17.2/mto.11.17.2.cox.html.

Crawford, Richard. "On Two Traditions of Black Music Research." *Black Music Research Journal* 6 (1986), 1–9.

CTVNews.ca Staff. "Fun Police? Montreal Man Says He Was Given $149 Ticket after Singing While Driving." CTV News (22 October 2017), http://www.ctvnews.ca/canada/fun-police-montreal-man-says-he-was-given-149-ticket-after-singing-while-driving-1.3643552.

Cunha, Darlena. "Sorry, Gwyneth Paltrow, Poverty Tourism Is Gross." *TIME* (13 April 2015), http://time.com/3819349/gwyneth-paltrow-poverty-tourism.

Currie, Gregory. "Imagination and Simulation: Aesthetics Meets Cognitive Science." In *Mental Simulation: Evaluations and Applications*, edited by Martin Davies and Tony Stone, 151–69. Oxford: Blackwell Publishers, 1995.

Currie, James. "Music after All." *Journal of the American Musicological Society* 62 (2009), 145–203.

Curtis, Liane. "Rebecca Clarke and Sonata Form: Questions of Gender and Genre." *Musical Quarterly* 81 (1997), 393–429.

Curtis, Liane. "The Sexual Politics of Teaching Mozart's *Don Giovanni*." *NWSA Journal* 12 (2000), 119–42.

Cusick, Suzanne G. "Feminist Theory, Music Theory, and the Mind/Body Problem." *Perspectives of New Music* 32 (1994), 8–27.

Cusick, Suzanne G. "Musicology, Torture, Repair." *Radical Musicology* 3 (2008), http://www.radical-musicology.org.uk/2008/Cusick.htm.

Cusick, Suzanne G. "On a Lesbian Relationship with Music: A Serious Effort Not to Think Straight." In *Queering the Pitch: The New Gay and Lesbian Musicology*, second edition, edited by Philip Brett, Elizabeth Wood, and Gary C. Thomas, 67–84. New York: Routledge, 2006.

Cusick, Suzanne G. "'There Was Not One Lady Who Failed to Shed a Tear': Arianna's Lament and the Construction of Modern Womanhood." *Early Music* 22 (1994), 21–41.

Cusick, Suzanne G. "'You Are in a Place That Is out of the World . . .': Music in the Detention Camps of the 'Global War on Terror.'" *Journal of the Society for American Music* 2 (2008), 1–26.

Cutler, Jacqueline. "*America's Got Talent*: Tim Poe 'Deserves to Be Publicly Humiliated,' Says Howie Mandel." *Screener TV* (8 June 2012), http://screenertv.com/news-features/americas-got-talent-tim-poe-deserves-tobe-publicly-humiliated-says-howie-mandel.

Dahlhaus, Carl. *The Idea of Absolute Music*, translated by Roger Lustig. Chicago: University of Chicago Press, 1989.

Daily Mail Reporter. "Teen YouTube Sensation Rebecca Black under Police Protection after Receiving Death Threats." *Daily Mail* (20 April 2011), http://www.dailymail.co.uk/news/article-1378865/Rebecca-Black-police-protection-receiving-death-threats.html.

The Daily Show with Jon Stewart. Comedy Central (15 October 2015), http://www.cc.com/video-clips/4u4hqr/the-daily-show-with-jon-stewart-bill-o-reilly.

Daly, Steven. "Britney Spears, Teen Queen: Rolling Stone's 1999 Cover Story." *Rolling Stone* (15 April 1999), http://www.rollingstone.com/music/news/britney-spears-teen-queen-rolling-stones-1999-cover-story-20110329.

Darity, William A., Jr., and Patrick L. Mason. "Evidence on Discrimination in Employment: Codes of Color, Codes of Gender." *Journal of Economic Perspectives* 12 (1998), 63–90.

Daughtry, J. Martin. "Charting Courses through Terror's Wake: An Introduction." In *Music in the Post-9/11 World*, edited by Jonathan Ritter and J. Martin Daughtry, xix–xxxi. New York: Routledge, 2007.

Daughtry, J. Martin. *Listening to War: Sound, Music, Trauma, and Survival in Wartime Iraq*. New York: Oxford University Press, 2015.

David, Hans T. "The Cultural Functions of Music." *Journal of the History of Ideas* 12 (1951), 423–39.

Davidson, Justin. "How Can the Vienna Philharmonic Change without Changing?" *New York Magazine* (4 March 2014), http://nymag.com/arts/classicaldance/classical/reviews/vienna-philharmonic-2014-3.

Davies, James Q. "On Being Moved/Against Objectivity." *Representations* 132 (2015), 79–87.

Davis, Lennard. *Bending over Backwards: Disability, Dismodernism, and Other Difficult Positions.* New York: New York University Press, 1994.

Davis, Lennard. *The End of Normal: Identity in a Biocultural Era.* Ann Arbor: University of Michigan Press, 2013.

Davis, Ron. Conversation with author (22 April 2018).

Davis, Ron. Email communication with author (25 April 2018).

Davis, Ron. Video recording for author (5 April 2018).

Davis, William C. *Look Away! A History of the Confederate States of America.* New York: Free Press, 2002.

Davoudi, Simin. "Resilience: A Bridging Concept or a Dead End?" *Planning Theory & Practice* 13 (2012), 299–333.

Dawdy, Shannon Lee. *Patina: A Profane Archaeology.* Chicago: University of Chicago Press, 2016.

"The Day the Music Died: China Blacklists 120 Songs for 'Morality' Violations." *Wall Street Journal* (12 August 2015), http://blogs.wsj.com/chinarealtime/2015/08/12/the-day-the-music-died-china-blacklists-120-songs-for-morality-violations.

De Bruijne, Mark, Arjen Boin, and Michel van Eeten. "Resilience: Exploring the Concept and Its Meanings." In *Designing Resilience: Preparing for Extreme Events*, edited by Louise K. Comfort, Arjen Boin, and Chris C. Demchak, 13–32. Pittsburgh, PA: University of Pittsburgh Press, 2010.

De Man, Paul. *Blindness and Insight: Essays in the Rhetoric of Contemporary Criticism.* Minneapolis: University of Minnesota Press, 1983.

Deb, Sopan. "Trump Proposes Eliminating the Arts and Humanities Endowments." *New York Times* (15 March 2017), http://www.nytimes.com/2017/03/15/arts/nea-neh-endowments-trump.html.

Dei, George J. Sefa, Nisha Karumanchery-Luik, and Leeno Luke Karumanchery. *Playing the Race Card: Exposing White Power and Privilege.* New York: Peter Lang, 2004.

Del Novo, Matthew. *Art Music: Love, Listening, and Soulfulness.* New Brunswick, NJ: Transaction Publishers, 2013.

Delgado, Richard, and Jean Stefancic, eds. *Critical White Studies: Looking behind the Mirror.* Philadelphia: Temple University Press, 1997.

Dell'Agnese, Elena. "'Welcome to Tijuana': Popular Music on the US-Mexico Border." *Geopolitics* 20 (2015), 171–92.

Dell'Antonio, Andrew. "Introduction: Beyond Structural Listening?" In *Beyond Structural Listening? Postmodern Modes of Hearing*, edited by Andrew Dell'Antonio, 1–12. Berkeley: University of California Press, 2004.

Dell'Antonio, Andrew, and Elizabeth J. Grace. "No Musicking about Us without Us!" *Journal of the American Musicological Society* 69 (2016), 553–59.

Delott, Simon. "Britney Spears: Raw Vocals for 'Toxic' LEAKED!" *Hollywood Gossip* (9 June 2017), http://www.thehollywoodgossip.com/videos/britney-spears-leaked-raw-vocals-for-toxic-better-than-autotune.

DelReal, Jose A. "Ben Carson Calls Poverty 'A State of Mind' during Interview." *Washington Post* (24 May 2017), http://www.washingtonpost.com/news/post-politics/

wp/2017/05/24/ben-carson-calls-poverty-a-state-of-mind-during-interview/?utm_term=.687600080f74.

DeMaio, Barbara Fox. "Girls and Puberty: The Voice, It Is a-Changin'; A Discussion of Pedagogical Methods for the Training of the Voice through Puberty." In *Voicing Girlhood in Popular Music: Performance, Authority, Authenticity*, edited by Jacqueline Warwick and Allison Adrian, 99–112. New York: Routledge, 2016.

Denham, Jess. "Britney Spears Sings 'Alien' without Auto-Tune in Embarrassing Leaked Audio Clip." *Independent* (9 July 2014), http://www.independent.co.uk/arts-entertainment/music/news/britney-spears-sings-alien-without-auto-tune-in-embarrassingly-brilliant-leaked-audio-clip-9595316.html.

Dery, Mary. "Public Enemy: Confrontation." In *That's the Joint! The Hip-Hop Studies Reader*, edited by Murray Forman and Mark Anthony Neal, 407–20. New York: Routledge, 2004.

Desjarlais, Robert R. *Shelter Blues: Sanity and Selfhood among the Homeless.* Philadelphia: University of Pennsylvania Press, 1997.

Desmond, Matthew, Andrew V. Papachristos, and David S. Kirk. "Police Violence and Citizen Crime Reporting in the Black Community." *American Sociological Review* 81 (2016), 857–76.

Deveaux, Scott. *The Birth of Bebop: A Social and Musical History.* Berkeley: University of California Press, 1997.

DiAngelo, Robin. "White Fragility." *International Journal of Critical Pedagogy* 3 (2011), 54–70.

DiAngelo, Robin. *White Fragility: Why It's So Hard for White People to Talk About Racism.* Boston: Beacon Press, 2018.

Dick, Hilary Parsons. "*Una Gabacha Sinvergüenza* (A Shameless White-Trash Woman): Moral Mobility and Interdiscursivity in a Mexican Migrant Community." *American Anthropologist* 119 (2017), 223–35.

Dickinson, Kay. "'Believe'? Vocoders, Digitalised Female Identity and Camp." *Popular Music* 20 (2001), 333–47.

Dinh, James. "The Curious Case of Britney Spears's Voice: Where Did It Go?" *She Knows* (10 July 2014), http://www.sheknows.com/entertainment/articles/1043415/the-curious-case-of-britney-spears-voice-where-did-it-go.

Doane, Ashley, and Eduardo Bonilla-Silva. *White Out: The Continuing Significance of Racism.* New York: Routledge, 2003.

Dockterman, Eliana. "Listen to Britney Spears Singing 'Alien' Without Autotune." *TIME* (9 July 2014), http://time.com/2969757/britney-spears-alien-autotune.

Dolmage, Jay Timothy. *Academic Ableism: Disability and Higher Education.* Ann Arbor: University of Michigan Press, 2017.

Dolmage, Jay Timothy. "Between the Valley and the Field: Metaphor and Disability." *Prose Studies* 27 (2005), 108–19.

Dombrowski, Thomas. "Ein Thesaurus des Gedenkens." *Der Standard* (4 May 2000).

"Don Lemon to Black Lives Matter: Why Are You Yelling?" YouTube (3 September 2015), http://www.youtube.com/watch?v=q0sqaDYAW50.

"Donald Gould One Year After Being Discovered on the Streets of Downtown Sarasota." ABC 7 Sarasota (5 May 2016), http://www.youtube.com/watch?v=Qxi4AxaWnE0.

Donaldson, Elizabeth J., and Catherine Prendergast. "Disability and Emotion: 'There's No Crying in Disability Studies!'" *Journal of Literary & Cultural Disability Studies* 5 (2011), 129–35.

Donovan, Catherine, and Marianna Hester. *Domestic Violence and Sexuality: What's Love Got to Do with It?* Bristol, UK: Policy Press, 2015.

Dore, Rebecca A., Kelly M. Hoffman, Angeline S. Lillard, and Sophie Trawalter. "Children's Racial Bias in Perceptions of Others' Pain." *British Journal of Developmental Psychology* 32 (2014), 218–31.

Dorris, Jennie. "Mike Tetreault's BSO Audition." *Boston Magazine* (July 2012), http://www.bostonmagazine.com/2012/06/boston-symphony-orchestra-audition.

Douglas, Mary. *Purity and Danger: An Analysis of Concepts of Pollution and Taboo.* New York: Routledge, 1966.

Douglass, Frederick. "Happy Slaves." *North Star* (28 April 1848).

Douglass, Frederick. *My Bondage and My Freedom.* New York: Miller, Orton & Mulligan, 1855.

Douglass, Frederick. *Narrative of the Life of Frederick Douglass, an American Slave.* Boston: Anti-Slavery Office, 1845.

Dow, Dawn Marie. "Negotiating 'The Welfare Queen' and 'The Strong Black Woman': African American Middle-Class Mothers' Work and Family Perspectives." *Sociological Perspectives* 58 (2015), 36–55.

Dowling, Marcus K. "When Being Black and Loving Country Music's Got You Down." *Vice* (20 October 2017), http://noisey.vice.com/en_us/article/a37wae/when-being-black-and-loving-country-musics-got-you-down.

"Dr. Bill Cosby Speaks." *Reuters* (n.d.; last accessed 18 February 2018), http://www.rci.rutgers.edu/~schochet/101/Cosby_Speech.htm.

Du Bois, W. E. B. *The Souls of Black Folk: Essays and Sketches.* Chicago: A. C. McClurg, 1903.

Du Maurier, George. *Trilby.* New York: Harper and Brothers, 1894.

Duckworth, Angela. *Grit: The Power of Passion and Perseverance.* New York: Scribner, 2016.

Dudley, Rachel. "Toward an Understanding of the 'Medical Plantation' as a Cultural Location of Disability." *Disability Studies Quarterly* 32 (2012), http://dsq-sds.org/article/view/3248/3184.

Duff, Akeema. "Why Black People Tend to Shout." *Odyssey* (27 December 2016), http://www.theodysseyonline.com/why-black-people-tend-to-shout.

Dunn Discovery Documents. Available at http://www.scribd.com/document/198588781/Dunn-Michael-Discovery-R (2014).

Dunn, Michael. Jailhouse calls to Rhonda Rouer (2013), available at http://www.jacksonville.com/news/2014-02-17/story/listen-state-attorneys-office-releases-michael-dunn-jailhouse-phone-calls.

Dunn, Michael. Jailhouse letter to daughter (26 June 2013), available at the Law Offices of John M. Phillips, https://floridajustice.com/michael-dunns-letters-from-jail.

Dunn, Michael. Jailhouse letter to daughter (12 July 2013), available at the Law Offices of John M. Phillips, http://floridajustice.com/michael-dunns-letters-from-jail.

Dunn, Michael. Jailhouse letter to grandmother (20 February 2013), available at the Law Offices of John M. Phillips, http://floridajustice.com/michael-dunns-letters-from-jail.

Dunn, Michael. Jailhouse letter to grandmother (7 May 2013), available at the Law Offices of John M. Phillips, http://floridajustice.com/michael-dunns-letters-from-jail.

Dunn, Michael. Jailhouse letter to Michelle (20 May 2013), available at the Law Offices of John M. Phillips, http://floridajustice.com/michael-dunns-letters-from-jail.

Dunn, Michael. Jailhouse letter to Rhonda Rouer (5 December 2012), available at the Law Offices of John M. Phillips, http://floridajustice.com/michael-dunns-letters-from-jail.

Dunn, Michael. Jailhouse letter to Rhonda Rouer (2 July 2013), available at the Law Offices of John M. Phillips, http://floridajustice.com/michael-dunns-letters-from-jail.

Dunn, Michael. Jailhouse letter to Rhonda Rouer (4 July 2013), available at the Law Offices of John M. Phillips, http://floridajustice.com/michael-dunns-letters-from-jail.

Dunn, Michael. Jailhouse letter to Rhonda Rouer (23 June 2013), available at the Law Offices of John M. Phillips, http://floridajustice.com/michael-dunns-letters-from-jail.

Dunn, Michael. Jailhouse letter to sibling (2 February 2013), available at the Law Offices of John M. Phillips, http://floridajustice.com/michael-dunns-letters-from-jail.

Dunn, Ronnie A. "Race and the Relevance of Citizen Complaints against the Police." *Administrative Theory & Praxis* 32 (2010), 557–77.

Dunn, Thom. "What Is 'Vocal Fry,' and Why Doesn't Anyone Care When Men Talk Like That?" *Upworthy* (28 July 2015), http://www.upworthy.com/what-is-vocal-fry-and-why-doesnt-anyone-care-when-men-talk-like-that.

DuPree, Mary. "Beyond Music in Western Civilization: Issues in Undergraduate Music History Literacy." *College Music Symposium* 30 (1990), 100–105.

Eastman, Susan Cooper. "Florida Jury Selected for Loud Music Murder Trial." *Reuters* (6 February 2014), http://www.reuters.com/article/us-usa-florida-shooting-dunn/florida-jury-selected-for-loud-music-murder-trial-idUSBREA1516L20140206.

Eastman, Susan Cooper. "Trial Opens for Florida Man Who Killed Black Teen over Loud Music." *Reuters* (3 February 2014), http://www.reuters.com/article/us-usa-florida-shooting-dunn/trial-opens-for-florida-man-who-killed-black-teen-over-loud-music-idUSBREA121AU20140203.

Edelman, Lee. *No Future: Queer Theory and the Death Drive*. Durham, NC: Duke University Press, 2004.

Edgers, Geoff. "6 Minutes to Shine." *Boston Globe* (4 September 2005), http://archive.boston.com/news/globe/magazine/articles/2005/09/04/6_minutes_to_shine.

Edwards, Breanna. "White Woman Calls Cops on California Man Chilling in His Car Listening to Yoga CD." *The Root* (13 July 2018), http://www.theroot.com/white-woman-calls-cops-on-california-man-chilling-in-hi-1827586286.

Effron, Laura. "Father of Slain Teen Jordan Davis Wants to Visit Michael Dunn in Prison." ABC News (19 February 2014), http://abcnews.go.com/US/father-slain-teen-jordan-davis-visit-michael-dunn/story?id=22588955.

Eggenberger, Nicole. "Kim Kardashian Wears Bad Fake Teeth, Frizzy Wigs on Celebrities Undercover." *US Magazine* (19 March 2014), http://www.usmagazine.com/entertainment/news/kim-kardashian-bad-fake-teeth-frizzy-wig-celebrities-undercover-2014193.

Ehrenreich, Barbara. *Bright-Sided: How the Relentless Promotion of Positive Thinking Has Undermined America*. New York: Metropolitan Books, 2009.

Eidsheim, Nina Sun. "Marian Anderson and 'Sonic Blackness' in American Opera." *American Quarterly* 63 (2011), 641–71.

Eischeid, Susan. *The Truth about Fania Fénelon and the Women's Orchestra of Auschwitz-Birkenau*. London: Palgrave MacMillan, 2016.

Eisen, Joel B. "The Trajectory of 'Normal' after 9/11: Trauma, Recovery and Post-Traumatic Societal Adaptation." *Fordham Environmental Law Journal* 14 (2003), 499–561.

"Emmanuel Kelly, *The X Factor* 2011 Auditions." YouTube (29 August 2011), http://www.youtube.com/watch?v=W86jlvrG54o.

Engh, Barbara. "Loving It: Music and Criticism in Roland Barthes." In *Musicology and Difference: Gender and Sexuality in Music Scholarship*, edited by Ruth A. Solie, 66–79. Berkeley: University of California Press, 1993.

Esposito, Roberto. *Terms of the Political: Community, Immunity, Biopolitics*, translated by Rhiannon Noel Welch. New York: Fordham University Press, 2013.

"Exit Interview: Rion Paige—The X Factor USA." YouTube (6 December 2013), http://www.youtube.com/watch?v=-GYNAufW67A.

Fairchild, Charles. "Building the Authentic Celebrity: The 'Idol' Phenomenon in the Attention Economy." *Popular Music and Society* 30 (2007), 355–75.

Fanon, Frantz. *Black Skin, White Masks*, translated by Charles Lam Markmann. London: Pluto Press, 2008.

Farrell, Amy Erdman. *Fat Shame: Stigma and the Fat Body in American Culture*. New York: New York University Press, 2011.

Faw, Bob. "Joshua Bell." PBS (10 October 2014), http://www.pbs.org/wnet/religionandethics/2014/10/10/october-10-2014-joshua-bell/24323.

FE Online. "Russian President Vladimir Putin Shows His Soft Skills, Plays Piano as He Waits for Chinese President Xi Jinping." *Financial Express* (15 May 2017), http://www.financialexpress.com/world-news/watch-russian-president-vladimir-putin-shows-his-soft-skills-plays-piano-as-he-waits-for-chinese-president-xi-jinping/668909.

Feinberg, Scott. "Steven Spielberg Supports Diversity in Academy, 'Not 100 Percent Behind' Current Plan, Calls for Limits on Oscar Campaigning (Exclusive)." *Hollywood Reporter* (11 February 2016), http://www.hollywoodreporter.com/race/steven-spielberg-supports-diversity-academy-864310.

Feldman, Gregory. *We Are All Migrants: Political Action and the Ubiquitous Condition of Migrant-hood*. Stanford, CA: Stanford University Press, 2015.

Fénelon, Fania, with Marcelle Routier. *Sursis pour l'orchestre*, translated by Judith Landry. New York: Atheneum, 1977.

Fineberg, Joshua. *Classical Music, Why Bother? Hearing the World of Contemporary Culture through a Composer's Ears*. New York: Routledge, 2006.

Fink, Robert. "Resurrection Symphony: El Sistema as Ideology in Venezuela and Los Angeles." *Action, Criticism, and Theory for Music Education* 15 (2016), 33–56.

Fischel, Joseph. "How Calling Kevin Spacey a Pedophile Hurts the Gay Community." *Slate* (1 November 2017), http://www.slate.com/blogs/outward/2017/11/01/how_calling_kevin_spacey_a_pedophile_hurts_the_gay_community.html.

Flanagan, Robert J. *The Perilous Life of Symphony Orchestras: Artistic Triumphs and Economic Challenges*. New Haven, CT: Yale University Press, 2012.

Flett, Kathryn. "She Did It Again." *Guardian* (20 August 2005), http://www.theguardian.com/theobserver/2005/aug/21/features.review97.

Floyd Jr., Samuel A. *The Power of Black Music: Interpreting Its History from Africa to the United States*. New York: Oxford University Press, 1995.

Fogel, Matthew. "'Grey's Anatomy' Goes Colorblind." *New York Times* (8 May 2005), http://www.nytimes.com/2005/05/08/arts/television/greys-anatomy-goes-colorblind.html.

Fontoura, Maria. "Meet Niki Nakayama, One of the World's Only Female Kaiseki Chefs." *Wall Street Journal* (8 August 2014), http://www.wsj.com/articles/meet-niki-nakayama-one-of-the-worlds-only-female-kaiseki-chefs-1407509705.

Forgiarini, Matteo, Marcello Gallucci, and Angelo Maravita, "Racism and the Empathy for Pain on Our Skin." *Frontiers in Psychology* 2 (2011), 1–7.

Foucault, Michel. *Discipline and Punish: The Birth of the Prison*. New York: Random House, 1975.

Franchot, Jenny. "The Punishment of Esther: Frederick Douglass and the Construction of the Feminine." In *Frederick Douglass: New Literary and Historical Essays*, edited by Eric J. Sundquist, 141–65. Cambridge: Cambridge University Press, 1990.

Franich, Darren. "The Rise of Hate-Watching: Which TV Shows Do You Love to Despise?" *Entertainment Weekly* (16 August 2012), http://www.ew.com/article/2012/08/16/newsroom-smash-glee-hatewatch.

Frank, Robert H. "Are You Successful? If So, You've Already Won the Lottery." *New York Times* (20 May 2016), http://www.nytimes.com/2016/05/22/upshot/are-you-successful-if-so-youve-already-won-the-lottery.html?mcubz=0.

Frank, Robert H. *Success and Luck: Good Fortune and the Myth of Meritocracy*. Princeton, NJ: Princeton University Press, 2016.

Frankenberg, Ruth. "The Mirage of an Unmarked Whiteness." In *The Making and Unmaking of Whiteness*, edited by Birgit Brander Rasmussen, Eric Klinenberg, Irene J. Nexica, and Matt Wray, 72–96. Durham, NC: Duke University Press, 2001.

Fraser, Heather. "Narrating Love and Abuse in Intimate Relationships." *British Journal of Social Work* 33 (2003), 273–90.

Freud, Sigmund. *Civilization and Its Discontents*, translated by James Strachey. New York: W. W. Norton, 2010.

Friedheim, Philip. "Wagner and the Aesthetics of the Scream." *19th-Century Music* 7 (1983), 63–70.

Fukui, Hajime, and Kumiko Toyoshima. "Influence of Music on Steroid Hormones and the Relationship between Receptor Polymorphisms and Musical Ability: A Pilot Study." *Frontiers in Psychology* 4 (2013), http://www.ncbi.nlm.nih.gov/pmc/articles/PMC3848314.

Gallagher, Brianne P. "Burdens of Proof: Veteran Frauds, PTSD, Pussies, and the Spectre of the Welfare Queen." *Critical Military Studies* 2 (2016), 139–54.

Gardels, Nathan, and Mike Medavoy. *American Idol after Iraq: Competing for Hearts and Minds in the Global Media Age*. Malden, MA: Wiley-Blackwell, 2009.

Garland-Thomson, Rosemarie. "Disability Bioethics: From Theory to Practice." *Kennedy Institute of Ethics Journal* 27 (2017), 323–39.

Garland-Thomson, Rosemarie. *Extraordinary Bodies: Figuring Physical Disability in American Culture and Literature*. New York: Columbia University Press, 1997.

Garland-Thomson, Rosemarie. "Introduction: From Wonder to Error—A Genealogy of Freak Discourse in Modernity." In *Freakery: Cultural Spectacles of the Extraordinary Body*, edited by Rosemarie Garland-Thomson, 1–22. New York: New York University Press, 1996.

Garland-Thomson, Rosemarie. *Staring: How We Look*. New York: Oxford University Press, 2009.

Garrett, Charles Hiroshi. *Struggling to Define a Nation: American Music and the Twentieth Century*. Berkeley: University of California Press, 2008.

Gates Jr., Henry Louis. "Foreword." In *The Anthology of Rap*, edited by Adam Bradley and Andrew DuBois, xxii–xxviii. New Haven, CT: Yale University Press, 2010.

Gaunt, Kyra D. *The Games Black Girls Play: Learning the Ropes from Double-Dutch to Hip-Hop*. New York: New York University Press, 2006.

Geertz, Clifford. *Local Knowledge: Further Essays in Interpretive Anthropology*. New York: Basic Books, 1983.

Geller, Jay. "The Aromatics of Jewish Difference; or, Benjamin's Allegory of Aura." In *Jews and Other Differences: The New Jewish Cultural Studies*, edited by Jonathan Boyarin and Daniel Boyarin, 203–56. Minneapolis: University of Minnesota Press, 1997.

Gelt, Jessica. "Authenticity in Casting: From 'Colorblind' to 'Color Conscious,' New Rules Are Anything but Black and White." *Los Angeles Times* (13 July 2017), http://www.latimes.com/entertainment/arts/la-ca-cm-authenticity-in-casting-20170713-htmlstory.html.

George, Adrian. Email correspondence with author (2 August 2018).

Gerber, David. "The 'Careers' of People Exhibited in Freak Shows: The Problem of Volition and Valorization." In *Freakery: Cultural Spectacles of the Extraordinary Body*, edited by Rosemarie Garland Thomson, 38–54. New York: New York University Press, 1996.

Gershman, Bennett L. "Witness Coaching by Prosecutors." *Cardozo Law Review* 23 (2002), 829–63.

Gibsone, Harriet. "Raw Power: Why Mocking the Isolated Vocals of Courtney Love Is Misogynistic." *Guardian* (10 October 2014), http://www.theguardian.com/music/musicblog/2014/oct/10/raw-power-why-mocking-isolated-vocals-of-courtney-love-is-misogynistic.

Gilbert, Daniel Todd. *Stumbling on Happiness*. New York: Alfred A. Knopf, 2006.

Gilbert, Shirli. *Music in the Holocaust: Confronting Life in the Nazi Ghettos and Camps*. New York: Oxford University Press, 2005.

Gillham, Patrick F., and Gary T. Marx. "Complexity and Irony in Policing and Protesting: The World Trade Organization in Seattle." *Social Justice* 27 (2000), 212–36.

Gilroy, Paul. *Darker Than Blue: On the Moral Economies of Black Atlantic Culture*. Cambridge, MA: Belknap Press of Harvard University Press, 2010.

Girtler, Roland. "Mitgliedsaufnahme in den Noblen Bund der Wiener Philharmoniker als Mannbarkeitsritual." In *Gesellschaft und Musik: Wege zur Musiksoziologie*, edited by Wolfgang Lipp, 497–504. Berlin: Duncker & Humblot, 1992.

Gladwell, Malcolm. *Blink: The Power of Thinking without Thinking*. New York: Back Bay Books, 2005.

Glass, Nancy, Jacquelyn Campbell, Veronica Njie-Carr, and Terri-Ann Thompson. "Ending Violence against Women: Essential to Global Health and Human Rights." In *Routledge Handbook in Global Public Health*, edited by Richard Parker and Marni Sommer, 236–43. New York: Routledge, 2011.

Gleditsch, Nils Petter. "Double-Blind but More Transparent." *Journal of Peace Research* 39 (2002), 259–62.

Glenn, Cerise L., and Landra J. Cunningham. "The Power of Black Magic: The Magical Negro and White Salvation in Film." *Journal of Black Studies* 40 (2009), 135–52.

Glennie, Alasdair. "'Shy' Britain's Got Talent Contestant Alice Fredenham Accused of Faking Her Stage Fright as She's Seen Looking Confident in Low Cut Top on The Voice." *Daily Mail* (19 April 2013), http://www.dailymail.co.uk/tvshowbiz/article-2311837/Britains-Got-Talent-contestant-Alice-Fredenhamaccused-faking-stage-fright-shes-seen-looking-confident-bubbly-The-Voice.

Godfrey, Erin B., Carlos E. Santos, and Esther Burson. "For Better or Worse? System-Justifying Beliefs in Sixth-Grade Predict Trajectories of Self-Esteem and Behavior across Early Adolescence." *Child Development* 90 (2019), 180–95.

Godoy, Maria. "The Judgment of Paris: The Blind Taste Test That Decanted the World." NPR (24 May 2016), http://www.npr.org/sections/thesalt/2016/05/24/479163882/the-judgment-of-paris-the-blind-taste-test-that-decanted-the-wine-world.

Godsil, Rachel D. "Remedying Environmental Racism." *Michigan Law Review* 90 (1991), 394–427.

Godwin, Mike. "Meme, Counter-meme." *Wired* (1 October 1994), http://www.wired.com/1994/10/godwin-if-2.

Goff, Phillip Atiba, and Kim Shayo Buchanan. "Charleena Lyles Needed Health Care. Instead, She Was Killed." *New York Times* (20 June 2016), http://nyti.ms/2sOcqks.

Goffman, Erving. *The Presentation of Self in Everyday Life.* Garden City, NY: Doubleday, 1959.

Goldin, Claudia, and Cecilia Rouse. "Orchestrating Impartiality: The Impact of 'Blind' Auditions on Female Musicians." *American Economic Review* 90 (2000), 715–41.

Goldmark, Daniel. "Louisville Program Selection." *AMS Newsletter* XLV (August 2015), http://ams-net.org/newsletter/AMSNewsletter-2015-8.pdf, 25.

Gooblar, David. "Should We All Be Grading Blind?" *Chronicle Vitae* (4 November 2015), http://chroniclevitae.com/news/1186-should-we-all-be-grading-blind.

Goodman, Steve. *Sonic Warfare: Sound, Affect, and the Ecology of Fear.* Cambridge, MA: MIT Press, 2010.

Gordon, Bonnie. "In the Aftermath of Charlottesville." *Musicology Now* (8 September 2017), http://musicologynow.ams-net.org/2017/09/in-aftermath-of-charlottesville.html.

Gordon, Bonnie. "What *Don Giovanni*, an Opera about a Charismatic Rapist, Can Teach Us about Donald Trump." *Slate* (21 October 2016), http://www.slate.com/blogs/browbeat/2016/10/21/what_don_giovanni_an_opera_about_a_charismatic_rapist_can_teach_us_about.html.

Gordon, Bonnie. "What Mr. Jefferson Didn't Hear." In *Rethinking Difference in Music Scholarship*, edited by Olivia Bloechl, Melanie Lowe, and Jeffrey Kallberg, 108–32. Cambridge: Cambridge University Press, 2015.

Gorzelany-Mostak, Dana. "The Curse of 'O mio *bambino* caro': Jackie Evancho as Prodigy, Diva, and Ideal Girl." In *Voicing Girlhood in Popular Music: Performance, Authority, Authenticity*, edited by Jacqueline Warwick and Allison Adrian, 113–42. New York: Routledge, 2016.

Gorzelany-Mostak, Dana. "Hearing Jackie Evancho in the Age of Donald Trump." *American Music* 35 (2017), 467–77.

Gourlay, Kenneth A. "Towards a Humanizing Ethnomusicology." *Ethnomusicology* 26 (1982), 411–20.

Gowan, Teresa. *Hobos, Hustlers, and Backsliders: Homeless in San Francisco.* Minneapolis: University of Minnesota Press, 2010.

Gracyk, Theodore. *Listening to Popular Music: Or, How I Learned to Stop Worrying and Love Led Zeppelin.* Ann Arbor: University of Michigan Press, 2007.

Graham, Ruth. 2014. "I Don't Feel Your Pain." *Boston Globe* (15 June 2014), http://www.bostonglobe.com/ideas/2014/06/14/don-feel-your-pain/cIrKD5czM0pgZQv7PgCmxI/story.html.

Graham, Ruth. "One of *Us*." *Slate* (22 September 2016), http://www.slate.com/articles/life/the_next_20/2016/09/the_invention_of_us_weekly_s_stars_they_re_just_like_us_feature.html.

Granade, S. Andrew. *Harry Partch: Hobo Composer.* Rochester, NY: University of Rochester Press, 2014.

Green, Marcus Harrison, and James Trimarco. "Marissa Janae Johnson Changed the 2016 Presidential Election. And She's Not Finished." *Seattle News* (22

December   2015),   http://archive.seattleweekly.com/news/962375-129/
   marissa-janae-johnson-changed-the-2016.

Grigoriadis, Vanessa. "The Tragedy of Britney Spears." *Rolling Stone* (21 February
   2008),   http://www.rollingstone.com/music/news/the-tragedy-of-britney-spears-
   rolling-stones-2008-cover-story-20080221.

Grue, Jan. *Disability and Discourse Analysis*. New York: Routledge, 2015.

Guck, Marion. "Music Loving, or the Relationship with the Piece." *Music Theory Online* 2
   (1996), http://www.mtosmt.org/issues/mto.96.2.2/mto.96.2.2.guck.html.

Guck, Marion. "A Woman's (Theoretical) Work." *Perspectives of New Music* 32
   (1994), 28–43.

HaCohen, Ruth. *The Music Libel against the Jews*. New Haven, CT: Yale University Press, 2011.

Hadley, Susan, and George Yancy, eds. *Therapeutic Uses of Rap and Hip-Hop*.
   New York: Routledge, 2012.

Hadlock, Heather. *Mad Loves: Women and Music in Offenbach's* Les Contes d'Hoffmann.
   Princeton, NJ: Princeton University Press, 2000.

Halnon, Karen Bettez. *The Consumption of Inequality: Weapons of Mass Distraction*.
   New York: Palgrave Macmillan, 2013.

Halpern, Jake. "The Cop." *New Yorker* (10/17 August 2015), http://www.newyorker.com/
   magazine/2015/08/10/the-cop.

Hamdan, Lawrence Abu. "Aural Contract: Forensic Listening and the Reorganization of
   the Speaking Subject." *Cesura//Acceso* 1 (2014), 200–24.

Hamdan, Lawrence Abu. "H[gun shot]ow c[gun shot]an I f[gun shot]orget?"
   L'internationale (12 February 2016), http://www.internationaleonline.org/research/
   decolonising_practices/53_h_gun_shot_ow_c_gun_shot_an_i_f_gun_shot_orget.

Hammel, Sara. "Britney Spears: 'Kiss My A--!'" *People* (2 December 2010), http://people.
   com/celebrity/britney-spears-fights-back-kiss-my-a.

Hampson, Sarah. "No Sex Please. I'm Not Britney." *Globe and Mail* (16 July 2005), http://
   www.theglobeandmail.com/arts/no-sex-please-im-not-britney/article18241016.

Hankins, Sarah. "After Pulse: An Introduction." *Ethnomusicology Review* 20 (2016), http://
   www.ethnomusicologyreview.ucla.edu/content/after-pulse.

Hanna-Attisha, Mona. "Flint Kids: Tragic, Resilient, and Exemplary." *American Journal of
   Public Health* 107 (2017), 561–52.

Harbert, Benjamin. "I'll Keep on Living after I Die: Musical Manipulation and
   Transcendence at Louisiana State Penitentiary." *International Journal of Community
   Music* 3 (2010), 65–76.

Harbert, Benjamin. Unpublished interview with Bud Wilkerson at Louisiana State
   Penitentiary (7 November 2012).

Harney, Stefano, and Fred Moten. *The Undercommons: Fugitive Planning and Black Study*.
   New York: Minor Compositions, 2013.

Harpham, Geoffrey Galt. "Elaine Scarry and the Dream of Pain." *Salmagundi* 130–131
   (2001), 202–34.

Hart, Peter Andrew. "Bernie Sanders Shut Down by Black Lives Matter Protesters in
   Seattle." *Huffington Post* (10 August 2015), http://www.huffingtonpost.com/entry/
   bernie-sanders-black-lives-matter_us_55c68f14e4b0923c12bd197e.

Hartman, Saidiya V. *Scenes of Subjection: Terror, Slavery, and Self-Making in Nineteenth-
   Century America*. New York: Oxford University Press, 1997.

Harwood, Ronald. *The Pianist* (screenplay), final draft, 1998.

Haslanger, Sally. "Changing the Ideology and Culture of Philosophy: Not by Reason Alone." *Hypatia* 23 (2008), 210–23.

Hatherley, Owen. *The Ministry of Nostalgia*. London: Verso, 2016.

Hawkins, Stan, and John Richardson. "Remodeling Britney Spears: Matters of Intoxication and Mediation." *Popular Music and Society* 30 (2007), 605–29.

Hayes, Brian. "Computing Science: The Britney Spears Problem." *American Scientist* 96 (2008), 274–79.

Hayles, N. Katherine. *How We Became Posthuman: Virtual Bodies in Cybernetics, Literature, and Informatics*. Chicago: University of Chicago Press, 1999.

Heller, Dana. "'Calling Out around the World': The Global Appeal of Reality Dance Formats." In *Global Television Formats: Understanding Television*, edited by Tasha Oren and Sharon Shahaf, 39–55. New York: Routledge, 2012.

Heller, Michael C. "Between Silence and Pain: Loudness and the Affective Encounter." *Sound Studies: An Interdisciplinary Journal* 1 (2015), 40–58.

Hellsberg, Clemens. *Demokratie der Könige: Die Geschichte der Wiener Philharmoniker*. Zurich: Schweizer Verlagshaus, 1992.

Herman, Jan. "Taking on the Vienna Philharmonic: Composer-Activist Plays the Internet for Women's Rights." MSNBC (20 January 2000), http://www.osborne-conant.org/Taking-on.htm.

Herman, Judith. *Trauma and Recovery: The Aftermath of Violence—from Domestic Abuse to Political Terror*. New York: Basic Books, 1997.

Hetsroni, Amir, ed. *Reality Television: Merging the Global and the Local*. New York: Nova Science Publishers, 2010.

Hevey, David. "The Enfreakment of Photography." In *The Disability Studies Reader*, edited by Lennard J. Davis, 367–78. New York: Routledge, 2006.

Hickman, Matt. "Taiwan Garbage Trucks: Classical Music Accompanies Collection." *Huffington Post* (6 December 2017), http://www.huffingtonpost.com/2012/01/09/taiwan-garbage-trucks-music_n_1195020.html.

Hidalgo, Rianna, and Martha Tesema. "Silence Is Broken." *Real Change* (7 October 2015), http://realchangenews.org/2015/10/07/silence-broken.

"The Hidden Potential of Britney Spears." YouTube (3 March 2018), http://www.youtube.com/watch?v=v8xdYEO4ukw.

Hirsch, Lily E. *A Jewish Orchestra in Nazi Germany: Musical Politics and the Berlin Jewish Culture League*. Ann Arbor: University of Michigan Press, 2010.

Hirsch, Lily E. *Music in American Crime Prevention and Punishment*. Ann Arbor: University of Michigan Press, 2012.

Hirsch, Lily E. "'Playing for Change': Peace, Universality, and the Street Performer." *American Music* 28 (2010), 346–67.

Hirsch, Lisa. "Andris Nelsons, Further to Previous." *Iron Tongue of Midnight* (21 November 2017), http://irontongue.blogspot.com/2017/11/andris-nelsons-further-to-previous.html.

Hoagland, Tony. "Poor Britney Spears." *American Poetry Review* 38 (2009), 47.

Hoberman, John. *Black and Blue: The Origins and Consequences of Medical Racism*. Berkeley: University of California Press, 2012.

Hodge, Nick. "Unruly Bodies at Conference." *Disability & Society* 29 (2014), 655–58.

Hoeckner, Berthold. "Elsa Screams, or the Birth of Music Drama." *Cambridge Opera Journal* 9 (1997), 97–132.

Hoeckner, Berthold. *Programming the Absolute: Nineteenth-Century German Music and the Hermeneutics of the Moment*. Princeton, NJ: Princeton University Press, 2002.

Hoeckner, Berthold. "Wagner and the Origin of Evil." *Opera Quarterly* 23 (2007), 151–83.

Hoffman, Kelly M., Sophie Trawalter, Jordan R. Axt, and M. Norman Oliver. "Racial Bias in Pain Assessment and Treatment Recommendations, and False Beliefs about Biological Differences between Blacks and Whites." *PNAS* 113 (2016), 4296–301.

Holden, Raymond. *The Virtuoso Conductors: The Central European Tradition from Wagner to Karajan*. New Haven, CT: Yale University Press, 2005.

Holmes, Anna. "In Defense of the Badly-Behaved Britney Spears." *Jezebel* (17 August 2007), http://jezebel.com/290011/in-defense-of-the-badly-behaved-britney-spears.

Holmes, Jessica A. "Expert Listening beyond the Limits of Hearing: Music and Deafness." *Journal of the American Musicological Society* 70 (2017), 171–220.

Holmes, Nick, and Kevin Core. "Pitch Perfection? The 'Flawless' Vocal and the Rise of Auto-Tune." BBC (17 May 2013), http://www.bbc.com/news/entertainment-arts-22514705.

Holoman, D. Kern. *The Orchestra: A Very Short Introduction*. New York: Oxford University Press, 2012.

"Homeless Man Stuns Passersby by Playing Styx's 'Come Sail Away' on Street Piano." *Bored Panda* (2016), http://www.boredpanda.com/homeless-man-plays-piano-styx-come-sail-away-donald-gould-sarasota-keys.

"Homeless Piano Man Wows Internet." YouTube (1 July 2015), http://www.youtube.com/watch?v=ER0IKu86qNI.

"Homeless Veteran Plays National Anthem at NFL Game." *Wounded Times* (16 September 2015), http://www.combatptsdwoundedtimes.org/2015/09/florida-piano-playing-homeless-veteran.html.

Honisch, Stefan. "'Music . . . to Cure or Disable': Therapy for Whom?" *Voices: A World Forum for Music Therapy* 14 (2014), http://voices.no/ index.php/ voices/ article/ view/ 793/ 658.

hooks, bell. *Salvation: Black People and Love*. New York: William Morrow, 2001.

Horowitz, Joseph. *Moral Fire: Musical Portraits from America's Fin de Siècle*. Berkeley: University of California Press, 2012.

Howe, Blake, and Stephanie Jensen-Moulton. "Introduction: On the Disability Aesthetics of Music." *Journal of the American Musicological Society* 69 (2016), 525–530.

Howell, Alison. "The Demise of PTSD: From Governing through Trauma to Governing Resilience." *Alternatives: Global, Local, Political* 37 (2012), 214–26.

Howes, David. "'We Are the World' and Its Counterparts: Popular Song as Constitutional Discourse." *International Journal of Politics, Culture, and Society* 3 (1990), 315–39.

Hsu, Dennis Y., et al. "The Music of Power: Perceptual and Behavioral Consequences of Powerful Music." *Social Psychological and Personality Science* 6 (2015), 75–83.

Hubbs, Nadine. *Rednecks, Queers, and Country Music*. Berkeley: University of California Press, 2014.

Huizenga, Tom. "Charles Dutoit Facing New Sexual Assault Accusations, Royal Philharmonic Cuts Ties." NPR (11 January 2018), http://www.npr.org/sections/deceptivecadence/2018/01/11/577378738/londons-royal-philharmonic-ends-its-relationship-with-conductor-charles-dutoit.

Hung, Eric. "Performing 'Chineseness' on the Western Concert Stage: The Case of Lang Lang." *Asian Music* 40 (2009), 131–48.

Hunt, Lynn. *Inventing Human Rights: A History*. New York: W. W. Norton, 2007.

Hutcheon, Emily, and Bonnie Lashewicz. "Theorizing Resilience: Critiquing and Unbounding a Marginalizing Concept." *Disability & Society* 29 (2014), 1383–97.

"I Don't See Race." YouTube (8 April 2017), http://www.youtube.com/watch?v=5qArvBdHkJA.

Inahara, Minae. "The Rejected Voice: Towards Intersubjectivity in Speech Language Pathology." *Disability & Society* 28 (2013), 41–53.

Ioanide, Paula. *The Emotional Politics of Racism: How Feelings Trump Facts in an Era of Colorblindness.* Stanford, CA: Stanford University Press, 2015.

"Isolated Vocal Tracks—17 Voices That Marked the Last Century." *Ground Guitar* (2017), http://www.groundguitar.com/isolated-vocal-tracks-17-voices-that-marked-the-last-century.

Jackes, Francesca. "All White on the Night: Why Does the World-Famous Vienna Philharmonic Feature So Few Women and Ethnic Minorities?" *Independent* (4 March 2010), http://www.independent.co.uk/arts-entertainment/music/features/all-white-on-the-night-why-does-the-world-famous-vienna-philharmonic-feature-so-few-women-and-ethnic-1915666.html.

"Jackie Evancho on Performing at Donald Trump's Inauguration—Full Interview." YouTube (20 January 2017), http://www.youtube.com/watch?v=n7NdSL1eNrE.

Jacksonville, Florida—Code of Ordinances. "Noise Control" (n.d.; last accessed 30 March 2018), http://library.municode.com/fl/jacksonville/codes/code_of_ordinances?nodeId=TITXENAF_CH368NOCO.

Jacoby, Jeff. "Lady Justice's Blindfold." *Boston Globe* (10 May 2009), http://archive.boston.com/bostonglobe/editorial_opinion/oped/articles/2009/05/10/lady_justices_blindfold.

James, Robin M. "Deconstruction, Fetishism, and the Racial Contract: On the Politics of 'Faking It' in Music." *New Centennial Review* 7 (2007), 45–80.

James, Robin M. *Resilience & Melancholy: Pop Music, Feminism, Neoliberalism.* Alresford, UK: Zero Books, 2015.

Jarman-Ivens, Freya. *Queer Voices: Technologies, Vocalities, and the Musical Flaw.* New York: Palgrave MacMillan, 2011.

Jasen, Paul C. *Low End Theory: Bass, Bodies and the Materiality of Sonic Experience.* New York: Bloomsbury Academic, 2016.

Jayapal, Pramila. "Guest Editorial: Why Saturday's Bernie Sanders Rally Left Me Feeling Heartbroken." *The Stranger* (9 August 2015), http://www.thestranger.com/blogs/slog/2015/08/09/22671957/guest-editorial-why-saturdays-bernie-sanders-rally-left-me-feeling-heartbroken.

Jeffries, Michael P. *Thug Life: Race, Gender, and the Meaning of Hip-Hop.* Chicago: University of Chicago Press, 2011.

Jenkins, Henry. *Convergence Culture: Where Old and New Media Collide.* New York: New York University Press, 2006.

Jenkins, Henry. *The Wow Climax: Tracing the Emotional Impact of Popular Culture.* New York: New York University Press, 2007.

Jenkins, Henry, Sam Ford, and Joshua Green. *Spreadable Media: Creating Value and Meaning in a Networked Culture.* New York: New York University Press, 2013.

Jenkins, J. S. "The Lost Voice: A History of the Castrato." *Journal of Pediatric Endocrinology and Metabolism* 13 (2000), 1503–8.

Jennings, Ken. *Planet Funny: How Comedy Took Over Our Culture.* New York: Simon & Schuster, 2018.

Jensen, Robert. *The Heart of Whiteness: Confronting Race, Racism, and White Privilege.* San Francisco, CA: City Lights, 2005.

"Johns Hopkins Malpractice Study: Surgical 'Never Events' Occur At Least 4,000 Times Per Year." *Johns Hopkins Medicine* (19 December 2012), http://www.hopkinsmedicine. org/news/media/releases/johns_hopkins_malpractice_study_surgical_never_events_ occur_at_least_4000_times_per_year.

Johnsen, Sarah, Suzanne Fitzpatrick, and Beth Watts. "Homelessness and Social Control: A Typology." *Housing Studies* (2018), 1–21.

Johnson, James H. *Listening in Paris: A Cultural History*. Berkeley: University of California Press, 1996.

Johnson, Julian. *Who Needs Classical Music? Cultural Choice and Musical Value*. New York: Oxford University Press, 2002.

Johnson, Marissa Janae. "1 Year Later: BLM Protester Who Interrupted Bernie Sanders' Rally Discusses the Moment and the Movement." *The Root* (9 August 2016), http://www. theroot.com/1-year-later-blm-protester-who-interrupted-bernie-sand-1790856353.

Johnson, Scott. "Jail Calls of Michael Dunn's Conversations Released." News 4 Jax (14 February 2014), http://www.news4jax.com/news/local/jail-calls-of-michael-dunns-conversations-released_20151107153725123.

Jones, Alisha Lola. " 'We Are a Peculiar People': Meaning, Masculinity, and Competence in Gendered Gospel Performance." PhD diss., University of Chicago, 2015.

Jones, Isabel. "Britney Spears's 'Toxic' Sans Auto-Tune Will Blow Your Mind." *InStyle* (6 June 2017), http://www.instyle.com/news/britney-spears-toxic-without-auto-tune.

Jones, Jeannette DiBernardo. "Imagined Hearing: Music-Making in Deaf Culture." In *The Oxford Handbook of Music and Disability Studies*, edited by Blake Howe, Stephanie Jensen-Moulton, Neil Lerner, and Joseph Straus, 54–72. New York: Oxford University Press, 2016.

Jones, LeRoi (Amiri Baraka). *Blues People: Negro Music in White America*. New York: Harper Perennial, 2002.

Jordan, Bryant. "*Talent* Contestant's Afghan Wounds in Question." *Military* (6 June 2012), http://www.military.com/daily-news/2012/06/06/talent-contestantsafghan-wounds-in-question.html.

"Jordan Davis 911 Calls." YouTube (24 July 2013), http://www.youtube.com/watch?v=cp_x4rvfSBk.

"Jordan Davis—Jordan's Family Joins Katie Couric on Katie." YouTube (23 February 2014), http://www.youtube.com/watch?v=AtcX_qQg4D4.

"Jordan Davis—Michael Dunn Sentencing, Part 2 (Michael Dunn Speaks)." YouTube (17 October 2014), http://www.youtube.com/watch?v=J1XyyrZ3MPY.

"Joshua Bell's 'Voice of the Violin.'" NPR (11 April 2007), http://www.npr.org/templates/story/story.php?storyId=9528118.

Judge, Mark. "Britney, Auto-Tune, and Female Imperfection." *Acculturated* (12 August 2014), http://acculturated.com/britney-auto-tune-and-female-imperfection.

Judge, Monique. "Trap Music Gets 2 Baristas Fired from a Duke University Coffee Shop after School VP Complains." *The Root* (9 May 2018), http://www.theroot.com/trap-music-gets-2-baristas-fired-from-a-duke-university-182590376.

Juster, Norton. *The Phantom Tollbooth*. New York: Yearling, 1961.

Kaika, Maria. "'Don't Call Me Resilient Again!' The New Urban Agenda as Immunology . . . or . . . What Happens When Communities Refuse to Be Vaccinated with 'Smart Cities' and Indicators." *Environment & Urbanization* 29 (2017), 89–102.

Kajikawa, Loren. "Hip-Hop History in the Age of Colorblindness." *Journal of Music History Pedagogy* 5 (2014), 117–23.

Kajikawa, Loren. "The Possessive Investment in Classical Music: Confronting Legacies of White Supremacy in U.S. Schools and Departments of Music." In *Seeing Race Again: Countering Colorblindness across the Disciplines*, edited by Kimberlé Williams Crenshaw, Luke Charles Harris, Daniel Martinez HoSang, and George Lipsitz, 155–74. Berkeley: University of California Press, 2019.

Kajikawa, Loren. *Sounding Race in Rap Songs*. Berkeley: University of California Press, 2015.

Kamberelis, George, and Greg Dimitriadis. "Collectively Remembering Tupac: The Narrative Mediation of Current Events, Cultural Histories, and Social Identities." In *Afterlife as Afterimage: Understanding Posthumous Fame*, edited by Steve Jones and Joli Jensen, 143–70. New York: Peter Lang, 2005.

Kamolnick, Paul. *The Just Meritocracy: IQ, Class Mobility, and American Social Policy*. Westport, CT: Praeger, 2005.

Kapchan, Deborah. "Listening Acts: Witnessing the Pain (and Praise) of Others." In *Theorizing Sound Writing*, edited by Deborah Kapchan, 277–93. Middletown, CT: Wesleyan University Press, 2017.

Kater, Michael H. *Composers of the Nazi Era: Eight Portraits*. New York: Oxford University Press, 2000.

Kater, Michael H. "Introduction." In *Music and Nazism: Art under Tyranny, 1933–1945*, edited by Michael H. Kater and Albrecht Riethmüller, 9–14. Laaber, Germany: Laaber, 2003.

Kater, Michael H. *The Twisted Muse: Musicians and Their Music in the Third Reich*. New York: Oxford University Press, 1997.

Katz, Mark. *Capturing Sound: How Technology Has Changed Music*, revised edition. Berkeley: University of California Press, 2010.

Katz, Mark. *Groove Music: The Art and Culture of the Hip-Hop DJ*. New York: Oxford University Press, 2012.

Keating, Caitlin. "Homeless Piano Prodigy Lands Recording Contract, Asks Jimmy Fallon for a Duet: 'I Never Saw Anything Like This Ever Happening.'" *People* (17 May 2016), http://people.com/celebrity/homeless-piano-prodigy-gets-recording-contract-asks-jimmy-fallon-for-a-duet.

Kelley, Robin D. G. "Kickin' Reality, Kickin' Ballistics: Gangsta Rap and Postindustrial Los Angeles." In *Droppin' Science: Critical Essays on Rap Music and Hip Hop Culture*, edited by William Eric Perkins, 117–58. Philadelphia: Temple University Press, 1996.

Keneally, Meghan. "Teacher Shot Dead Over Loud Music at His Wife's Birthday Party." *Daily Mail* (5 June 2012), http://www.dailymail.co.uk/news/article-2155149/Man-kills-neighbor-complaining-noise-neighbors-wifes-party-says-self-defense.html.

Kennaway, James. *Bad Vibrations: The History of the Idea of Music as a Cause of Disease*. New York: Routledge, 2016.

Kennedy, Randall. *Sellout: The Politics of Racial Betrayal*. New York: Pantheon Books, 2008.

Kernodle, Tammy L. "Diggin' You Like Those Ol' Soul Records." *American Studies* 52 (2013), 181–204.

Keyes, Cheryl L. *Rap Music and Street Consciousness*. Urbana: University of Illinois Press, 2002.

Keyes, Cheryl L. "Sound, Voice, and Spirit: Teaching in the Black Music Vernacular." *Black Music Research Journal* 29 (2009), 11–24.

King, Jr., Martin Luther, *Strength to Love*. Philadelphia: Fortress, 2010.

King of the Clouds. Comment on "Alien NO AUTOTUNE Britney Spears FULL." YouTube (video uploaded on 10 July 2014; comment posted in 2016), http://www.youtube.com/watch?v=MUdKrtsrCBI.

King, Wilma. *Stolen Childhood: Slave Youth in Nineteenth-Century America.* Bloomington: Indiana University Press, 1995.

Kipnis, Laura. *Against Love: A Polemic.* New York: Vintage Books, 2003.

Kisliuk, Michelle. "(Un)doing Fieldwork: Sharing Songs, Sharing Lives." In *Shadows in the Field: New Perspectives for Fieldwork in Ethnomusicology*, second edition, edited by Gregory Barz and Timothy J. Cooley, 183–205. New York: Oxford University Press, 2008.

Kivy, Peter. *De Gustibus: Arguing about Taste and Why We Do It.* New York: Oxford University Press, 2015.

Kivy, Peter. "Musical Morality." *Revue internationale de philosophie* 4 (2008), 397–412.

Kleege, Georgina. *Sight Unseen.* New Haven, CT: Yale University Press, 1999.

Klein, Melissa. "James Levine Using 'Love' Letter to Discredit Alleged Victim." *New York Post* (16 June 2018), http://nypost.com/2018/06/16/james-levine-using-love-letter-to-discredit-alleged-victim.

Koerner, Brendan. "Where Did We Get Our Oath?" *Slate* (30 April 2004), http://www.slate.com/articles/news_and_politics/explainer/2004/04/where_did_we_get_our_oath.html.

Koestenbaum, Wayne. *The Queen's Throat: Opera, Homosexuality, and the Mystery of Desire.* New York: Poseidon Press, 1993.

Kopel, David. "Stand Your Ground Had Nothing to Do with the Dunn Verdict in Florida." *Washington Post* (17 February 2014), http://www.washingtonpost.com/news/volokh-conspiracy/wp/2014/02/17/stand-your-ground-had-nothing-to-do-with-the-dunn-verdict-in-florida/?utm_term=.b86acee547e9.

Kornhaber, Spencer. "The Reality of Those 'Real People, Not Actors' Ads." *Atlantic* (15 August 2016), http://www.theatlantic.com/entertainment/archive/2016/08/real-people-not-actors-chevrolet-olympics-ad-interview/495863.

Kosman, Joshua. "Vienna Philharmonic Must Answer for Exclusion." *SF Gate* (20 February 2011), http://www.sfgate.com/entertainment/article/Vienna-Philharmonic-must-answer-for-exclusion-2474252.php.

Kovaleski, Serge F., and Joe Coscarelli. "Is Britney Spears Ready to Stand on Her Own?" *New York Times* (4 May 2016), http://www.nytimes.com/2016/05/08/arts/music/is-britney-spears-ready-to-stand-on-her-own.html?_r=1.

Kraidy, Marwan M. *Hybridity: Or the Cultural Logic of Globalization.* Philadelphia: Temple University Press, 2005.

Kramer, Lawrence. *Why Classical Music Still Matters.* Berkeley: University of California Press, 2009.

Krauss, Melvyn. "In the #MeToo Era, the Audience Deserves a Voice." *USA Today* (18 January 2018), http://www.usatoday.com/story/opinion/2018/01/18/when-metoo-stretches-too-far-classical-music-world-audience-loses-melvyn-krauss-column/1018659001.

Krauss, Melvyn. "Running Scared at the Met." *Music Matters* (1 March 2018), http://www.musicmattersblog.net/blog/2018/3/1/running-scared-at-the-met.

Kreps, Daniel. "Kanye West: 'I'm Not a Musician. I'm an Inventor.'" *Rolling Stone* (20 April 2015), http://www.rollingstone.com/music/news/kanye-west-im-not-a-musician-im-an-inventor-20150420.

Kreps, Daniel. "Watch Disguised Adele Prank Adele Impersonators." *Rolling Stone* (21 November 2015), http://www.rollingstone.com/music/news/watch-disguised-adele-prank-adele-impersonators-20151121.

Krims, Adam. *Rap Music and the Poetics of Identity*. Cambridge: Cambridge University Press, 2000.

Kroier, Johann. "Music, Global History, and Postcoloniality." *International Review of the Aesthetics and Sociology of Music* 43 (2012), 139–86.

Kuczynski, Alex. "Traces of Terror: The Singer; 'Idol' Star Rethinks 9/11 Role." *New York Times* (7 September 2002), http://www.nytimes.com/2002/09/07/us/traces-of-terror-the-singer-idol-star-rethinks-9-11-role.html.

Kun, Josh. *Audiotopia: Music, Race, and America*. Berkeley: University of California Press, 2005.

Kun, Josh. "The Sound of Blacknuss: Rapping Master/Counternarratives of the Hip Hop Imagi-Nation." *repercussions* 3 (1994), 5–49.

Kurtzleben, Danielle. "Trump Embraces One of Russia's Favorite Propaganda Tactics—Whataboutism." NPR (17 March 2017), http://www.npr.org/2017/03/17/520435073/trump-embraces-one-of-russias-favorite-propaganda-tactics-whataboutism.

LaCom, Cindy. "Filthy Bodies, Porous Boundaries: The Politics of Shit in Disability Studies." *Disability Studies Quarterly* 27 (2007), http://dsq-sds.org/article/view/11/11.

Lamont, Michèle. *The Dignity of Working Men: Morality and the Boundaries of Race, Class, and Immigration*. Cambridge, MA: Harvard University Press, 2000.

Lamont, Michèle. *How Professors Think: Inside the Curious World of Academic Judgment*. Cambridge, MA: Harvard University Press, 2009.

Landler, Mark. "Acting on Instinct, Trump Upends His Own Foreign Policy." *New York Times* (7 April 2017), http://www.nytimes.com/2017/04/07/world/middleeast/syria-attack-trump.html?_r=0.

Langer, Lawrence. *The Holocaust and the Literary Imagination*. New Haven, CT: Yale University Press, 1975.

Larkin, Mike. "Spend It like Beckham!" *Daily Mail* (17 September 2011), http://www.dailymail.co.uk/tvshowbiz/article-2038408/David-Beckham-goes-undercover-Target-sell-aftershave-Ellen-DeGeneres.html.

Latour, Bruno. "Why Has Critique Run Out of Steam? From Matters of Fact to Matters of Concern." *Critical Inquiry* 30 (2004), 225–48.

Lau, Frederick. "'Center or Periphery?' Regional Music in Contemporary China." *International Communication of Chinese Culture* 2 (2015), 31–47.

Lazare, Sarah, and Ryan Harvey. "WikiLeaks in Baghdad." *Nation* (29 July 2010), http://www.thenation.com/article/wikileaks-baghdad.

Le Guin, Elisabeth. *Boccherini's Body: An Essay in Carnal Musicology*. Berkeley: University of California Press, 2006.

Le Guin, Elisabeth. "One Bar in Eight: Debussy and the Death of Description." In *Beyond Structural Listening? Postmodern Modes of Hearing*, edited by Andrew Dell'Antonio, 233–51. Berkeley: University of California Press, 2004.

"[LEAKED] Britney Spears—Toxic (Raw Vocals)." YouTube (6 June 2017), http://www.youtube.com/watch?v=BPzZR4CMFQ0.

Lear, Samantha. "Jordan Smith's 'The Voice' Premiere Blind Audition Was the Actual Most Shocking Ever." *Wet Paint* (22 September 2015), http://www.wetpaint.com/jordan-smith-the-voice-audition-sia-chandelier-1441618.

"Leave Britney Alone (Complete)." YouTube (11 August 2011), http://www.youtube.com/watch?v=WqSTXuJeTks.

Lebrecht, Norman. "How Many Women in the Vienna Philharmonic." *Slipped Disc* (28 November 2016), http://slippedisc.com/2016/11/how-many-women-in-the-vienna-philharmonic.

Lebrecht, Norman. *The Maestro Myth: Great Conductors in Pursuit of Power.* New York: Citadel Press, 2001.

Lebrecht, Norman. "Musicologist Went to Jail—and Got Torn to Pieces." *Slipped Disc* (18 February 2016), http://slippedisc.com/2016/02/musicologist-went-to-jail-and-got-torn-to-pieces.

Lebrecht, Norman. "Pictures at an Audition for the Vienna Philharmonic." *Slipped Disc* (30 November 2014), http://slippedisc.com/2014/11/pictures-at-an-audition-for-the-vienna-philharmonic.

Lebrecht, Norman. *Who Killed Classical Music? Maestros, Managers, and Corporate Politics.* Secaucus, NJ: Carol Pub. Group, 1997.

Lee, Barrett A., Sue Hinze Jones, and David W. Lewis. "Public Beliefs about the Causes of Homelessness." *Social Forces* 69 (1990), 253–65.

Lee, Benjamin. "We're All Africans Really." *Guardian* (11 February 2016), http://www.theguardian.com/film/2016/feb/11/meryl-streep-berlin-film-festival-diversity-were-all-africans-really.

Leeds, Jeff. "Spears's Awards Fiasco Stirs Speculation about Her Future." *New York Times* (13 September 2007), http://www.nytimes.com/2007/09/13/arts/music/13brit.html.

Leight, Elias. "Life after 'Friday': Rebecca Black's Journey Back to the Charts." *Rolling Stone* (17 April 2017), http://www.rollingstone.com/music/music-features/life-after-friday-rebecca-blacks-journey-back-to-the-charts-117179.

Lembitz, Alan, and Ted J. Clarke. "Clarifying 'Never Events' and Introducing 'Always Events.'" *Patient Safety in Surgery* 3 (2009), http://www.ncbi.nlm.nih.gov/pmc/articles/PMC2814808.

Lendino, Jamie. "The Best Audio Editing Software of 2018." *PC Mag* (12 February 2018), http://www.pcmag.com/roundup/356915/the-best-audio-editing-software.

Leonard, Mark. "Diplomacy by Other Means." *Foreign Policy* 132 (2002), 48–56.

Leppert, Richard. "Music 'Pushed to the Edge of Existence' (Adorno, Listening, and the Question of Hope)." *Cultural Critique* 60 (2005), 92–133.

Leppert, Richard. "Music, Violence, and the Stakes of Listening." In *The Oxford Handbook of the New Cultural History of Music*, edited by Jane F. Fulcher, 39–67. New York: Oxford University Press, 2011.

Levi, Erik. *Music in the Third Reich.* New York: St. Martin's Press, 1994.

Levin, Theodore, with Valentina Süzükei. *Where Rivers and Mountains Sing: Sound, Music, and Nomadism in Tuva and Beyond.* Bloomington: Indiana University Press, 2006.

Levinson, Jerrold. *Contemplating Art: Essays in Aesthetics.* New York: Oxford University Press, 2006.

Levitin, Daniel J. *The World in Six Songs: How the Musical Brain Created Human Nature.* New York: Dutton, 2008.

Levitt, Steven D. "Cheap Wine." *Freakonomics Blog* (16 July 2008), http://freakonomics.com/2008/07/16/cheap-wine.

Levitt, Steven D., and Stephen J. Dubner. *Think like a Freak.* New York: HarperCollins, 2014.

Levitz, Tamara. "The Musicological Elite." *Current Musicology* 102 (2018), 9–80.

Lewinsky, Monica. "The Price of Shame." *TED Talks* (2015). Transcript available at http://www.ted.com/talks/monica_lewinsky_the_price_of_shame/transcript?language=en.

Lewis, Lionel S. *Scaling the Ivory Tower: Merit & Its Limits in Academic Careers.* New Brunswick, NJ: Transaction Publishers, 1998.

"Lil Reese ft Lil Durk and Fredo Santana—Beef / shot by @DJKenn_AON." YouTube (5 April 2012), http://www.youtube.com/watch?v=TDh0FcJ1atA.

Lilla, Mark. "The End of Identity Liberalism." *New York Times* (18 November 2016), http://www.nytimes.com/2016/11/20/opinion/sunday/the-end-of-identity-liberalism.html.

Lipsitz, George. *How Racism Takes Place.* Philadelphia: Temple University Press, 2011.

List, George. "Concerning the Concept of the Universal and Music." *World of Music* 26 (1984), 40–49.

Little, Katie. "Donald Trump: I Am the Least Anti-Semitic Person That 'You've Ever Seen in Your Entire Life.'" *CNBC* (17 February 2017), http://www.cnbc.com/2017/02/16/donald-trump-i-am-the-least-anti-semitic-racist-person-that-youve-ever-seen.html.

Liu, Catherine. *American Idyll: Academic Antielitism as Cultural Critique.* Iowa City: University of Iowa Press, 2011.

Lockwood, Lewis. *Beethoven's Symphonies: An Artistic Vision.* New York: W. W. Norton, 2015.

Loehmann, Timothy. Statement to investigators (signed and dated 30 November 2015), available at http://i2.cdn.turner.com/cnn/2015/images/12/01/officer.loehmann.statement.pdf.

Lopez, German. "Research Says There Are Ways to Reduce Racism. Calling People Racist Isn't One of Them." *Vox* (15 November 2016), http://www.vox.com/identities/2016/11/15/13595508/racism-trump-research-study.

Lorde, Audre. "The Uses of Anger: Women Responding to Racism." In *Sister Outsider: Essays and Speeches*, 124–33. Berkeley, CA: Crossing Press, 2007.

"LORDE WITHOUT AUTOTUNE—Royals—Grammys 2014." YouTube (26 January 2014), http://www.youtube.com/watch?v=7uzR0ZoZPjU.

Lott, Eric. *Love and Theft: Black Minstrelsy and the American Working Class.* New York: Oxford University Press, 1993.

Lowe, Melanie. "Colliding Feminisms: Britney Spears, 'Tweens,' and the Politics of Reception." *Popular Music and Society* 26 (2003), 123–40.

"Luck Is the Real Key to Success?" *Fox Business* (7 May 2011), http://video.foxbusiness.com/v/3887675/?#sp=show-clips.

Lugones, María. "Playfulness, 'World' Travelling, and Loving Perception." *Hypatia* 2 (1987), 3–19.

Luong, Vivian. "Rethinking Music Loving." *Music Theory Online* 23 (2017), http://mtosmt.org/issues/mto.17.23.2/mto.17.23.2.luong.html.

Luscombe, Belinda. "Susan Boyle: Not Quite Out of Nowhere." *TIME* (23 April 2009), http://content.time.com/time/arts/article/0,8599,1893282,00.html.

Lynn, Richard. *Race Differences in Intelligence: An Evolutionary Analysis.* Augusta, GA: Washington Summit Publishers, 2006.

Ma, Bob. "A Trip into the Controversy: A Study of Slum Tourism Travel Motivations." *Penn Humanities Forum on Connections* (2010), available at http://repository.upenn.edu/cgi/viewcontent.cgi?article=1011&context=uhf_2010.

Mahon, Maureen. *Right to Rock: The Black Rock Coalition and the Cultural Politics of Race.* Durham, NC: Duke University Press, 2004.

Maler, Anabel. "Musical Expression among Deaf and Hearing Song Signers." In *The Oxford Handbook of Music and Disability Studies*, edited by Blake Howe, Stephanie Jensen-Moulton, Neil Lerner, and Joseph Straus, 73–91. New York: Oxford University Press, 2016.

Mandell, Andrea. "Adele Has 'Damaged' Vocal Cords, Cancels Final Shows." *USA Today* (30 June 2017), http://www.usatoday.com/story/life/music/2017/06/30/adele-has-damaged-vocal-cords-cancels-final-shows/103334582.

Manne, Kate. *Down Girl: The Logic of Misogyny*. New York: Oxford University Press, 2018.

Manuster. Comment on "Britney Spears—Toxic (Without Auto-Tune)—NEW VOCALS (ALTERNATE VERSION)." YouTube (video uploaded 12 July 2017; comment posted in 2017), http://www.youtube.com/watch?v=J-NrcIXz0VQ.

Marathon Productions. *"America's Got Talent,* Season 10 Release Form" (2015), http://www.americasgottalentauditions.com/wp-content/uploads/Personal-Release-Website-Fillable.pdf.

Marikar, Sheila. "Why Was Britney So Bad?" *ABC News* (10 September 2007), http://abcnews.go.com/Entertainment/story?id=3582432.

Marikar, Sheila, and Jonann Brady. "Bette Calls Britney a Wild and Woolly Slut." ABC News (8 December 2006), http://abcnews.go.com/Entertainment/story?id=2707901&page=1.

Markus, Bethania Palma. "Singing While Black: Oakland Choir Threatened with 'Nuisance' Fines after Tech Workers Enter Neighborhood." *Raw Story* (15 October 2015), http://www.rawstory.com/2015/10/singing-while-black-oakland-choir-hit-with-nuisance-fines-after-tech-workers-enter-neighborhood.

Markus, George. "Zur Forderung nach einer kritischen Aufarbeitung der Geschichte dieser Institution." *Kurier* (31 December 2012), http://kurier.at/kultur/das-neujahrskonzert-abschaffen/2.212.193.

Marquez, Xavier. "Maximizing Accountability to the Least Privileged: The Difference Principle, the Fair Value of the Political Liberties, and the Design of Democratic Institutions." *Polity* 47 (2015), 484–507.

Marshall, Jonathan. "'Blind Auditions' Putting Discrimination on Center Stage." *SF Gate* (10 February 1997), http://www.sfgate.com/business/article/Blind-Auditions-Putting-Discrimination-on-2855410.php.

Martinelli, Dario. "Introduction (to the Issue and to Zoomusicology)." *Trans: Revista transcultural de música* 12 (2008), http://www.sibetrans.com/trans/articulo/93/introduction-to-the-issue-and-to-zoomusicology.

Martinez, Theresa A. "Popular Culture as Oppositional Culture: Rap as Resistance." *Sociological Perspectives* 40 (1997), 265–86.

Massoud, Justin. "Lorde Breaks Out Some Weird Dance Moves for 'Royals' at 2014 Grammys." K945 (26 January 2014), http://k945.com/lorde-weird-dance-moves-royals-2014-grammys-video.

Masten, Ann S., and Jenifer L. Powell. "A Resilience Framework for Research, Policy, and Practice." In *Resilience and Vulnerability: Adaptation in the Context of Childhood Adversities*, edited by Suniya S. Luthar, 1–27. Cambridge: Cambridge University Press, 2003.

Matsuo, Alex. "10 Most Irritating Female Celebrity Voices." *The Richest* (13 March 2015), http://www.therichest.com/expensive-lifestyle/entertainment/10-most-irritating-celebrity-vocal-fry-offenders.

"Matt Farmer, *American Idol*'s 2013 Timothy Poe." *Guardian of Valor* (2013), http://guardianofvalor.com/matt-farmer-american-idols-2013-timothy-poe.

Matt Thompson. Comment on "Alien NO AUTOTUNE Britney Spears FULL." YouTube (video uploaded on 10 July 2014; comment posted in 2016), http://www.youtube.com/watch?v=MUdKrtsrCBI.

Matter, Bridgette. "Action News Jax Investigation Reveals Michael Dunn Is Being Held in Oregon Prison." Action News Jax (10 October 2017), http://www.actionnewsjax.com/news/local/action-news-jax-investigation-reveals-michael-dunn-is-being-held-in-oregon-prison/622728736.

Maus, Fred Everett. "Masculine Discourse in Music Theory." *Perspectives of New Music* 31 (1993), 264–93.

Mauskapf, Michael G. "Enduring Crisis, Ensuring Survival: Artistry, Economics, and the American Symphony Orchestra." PhD diss., University of Michigan, 2012.

May, Vivian M., and Beth A. Ferri. "Fixated on Ability: Questioning Ableist Metaphors in Feminist Theories of Resistance." *Prose Studies* 27 (2005), 120–40.

Maynard, John. "In VMA Comeback, Britney Makes All the Wrong Moves." *Washington Post* (10 September 2007), http://www.washingtonpost.com/wp-dyn/content/article/2007/09/09/AR2007090902135.html.

Mayrhofer, Bernadette. "Vertreibung von Wiener Philharmonikern aus dem Orchester nach 1938 und die versäumte Reintegration nach 1945." *Zeitgeschichte* 34 (2007), 72–94.

Mayrhofer, Bernadette, and Fritz Trümpi. *Orchestrierte Vertreibung: Unerwünschte Wiener Philharmoniker: Verfolgung, Ermordung und Exil.* Vienna: Mandelbaum, 2014.

McBath, Lucia. "Lucia McBath: I Chose to Forgive My Son's Murderer." *Vimeo* (2016), http://vimeo.com/152631582.

McBath, Lucia. Recorded video and email/SMS communication with author (24 March 2018).

McBride, Jessica. "Yung Mazi Dead: 5 Fast Facts You Need to Know." *Heavy* (7 August 2017), http://heavy.com/entertainment/2017/08/yung-mazi-killed-dead-shot-death-is-photos-video-suspect-young.

McClain, Amanda Scheiner. *American Ideal: How American Idol Constructs Celebrity, Collective Identity, and American Discourses.* Lanham, MD: Lexington Books, 2011.

McClendon, William H. "Black Music: Sound and Feeling for Black Liberation." *Black Scholar* 7 (1976), 20–25.

McCoy, Caroline. "Don't Attack Musicians Who Want to Perform at Trump's Inauguration." *Washington Post* (18 January 2017), http://www.washingtonpost.com/posteverything/wp/2017/01/18/dont-attack-musicians-who-want-to-perform-at-trumps-inauguration/?noredirect=on&utm_term=.7806e870c012.

McCoy, Jason. "Making Violence Ordinary: Radio, Music and the Rwandan Genocide." *African Music* 8 (2009), 85–96.

McDonald, Katrina Bell. *Embracing Sisterhood: Class, Identity, and Contemporary Black Women.* Oxford: Rowman & Littlefield, 2007.

McErlean, William M., Dennis P. Stolle, and Monica R. Brownewell Smith. "The Evolution of Witness Preparation." *Litigation* 37 (2010), 21–26.

McGinty, Doris Evans. "Black Scholars on Black Music: The Past, the Present, and the Future." *Black Music Research Journal* 13 (1993), 1–13.

McKay, George. "Skinny Blues: Karen Carpenter, Anorexia Nervosa and Popular Music." *Popular Music* 37 (2018), 1–21.

McLeod, Ken. *We Are the Champions: The Politics of Sports and Popular Music*. Burlington, VT: Ashgate, 2011.

McNamee, Stephen J., and Robert K. Miller, Jr. *The Meritocracy Myth*, second edition. Lanham, MD: Rowman & Littlefield, 2009.

McRuer, Robert. *Crip Theory: Cultural Signs of Queerness and Disability*. New York: New York University Press, 2006.

McShane, John. *Susan Boyle: Living the Dream*. London: John Blake Publishing Ltd, 2010.

McWhorter, John H. "How Hip-Hop Holds Blacks Back." *City Journal* (Summer 2003), http://www.city-journal.org/html/how-hip-hop-holds-blacks-back-12442.html.

Meeuf, Russell. "Class, Corpulence, and Neoliberal Citizenship: Melissa McCarthy on *Saturday Night Live*." *Celebrity Studies* 7 (2016), 137–53.

Mehtsun, Winta T., et al. "Surgical Never Events in the United States." *Surgery* 153 (2013), 265–72.

Meizel, Katherine. *Idolized: Music, Media, and Identity in American Idol*. Bloomington: Indiana University Press, 2011.

Melin, Julia. "Desperate Choices: Why Black Women Join the U.S. Military at Higher Rates Than Men and All Other Racial and Ethnic Groups." *New England Journal of Public Policy* 28 (2016), 14 pages.

Mendelberg, Tali. *The Race Card: Campaign Strategy, Implicit Messages, and the Norm of Equality*. Princeton, NJ: Princeton University Press, 2001.

"The Message of Music." *Vienna Philharmonic* (n.d.; last accessed 4 July 2018), http://www.wienerphilharmoniker.at/orchestra/tradition.

Meyer, Michael. "The Nazi Musicologist as Myth Maker in the Third Reich." *Journal of Contemporary History* 10 (1975), 649–65.

"Michael David Dunn—Police Interview Uncut—Part 1." YouTube (24 July 2013), http://www.youtube.com/watch?v=MWlzUHtUOyY.

"Michael Dunn Retrial—Day 2, Part 2." YouTube (26 September 2014), http://www.youtube.com/watch?v=MV4Bbi0IgdE.

"Michael Dunn Retrial—Day 5—Part 1 (Dunn Testifies)." YouTube (30 September 2014), http://www.youtube.com/watch?v=bCa2i8F_YTI.

"Michael Dunn Retrial—Day 5—Part 5 (Defense Closing Arguments)." YouTube (30 September 2014), http://www.youtube.com/watch?v=uxvBu0b66uo.

"Michael Dunn Trial—Cory Strolla—Press Conference." YouTube (13 February 2014), http://www.youtube.com/watch?v=OCJm1xvCX2s.

"Michael Dunn Trial—Day 2—Part 5." YouTube (7 February 2014), http://www.youtube.com/watch?v=PPA1BphzCGE.

"Michael Dunn Trial. Day 5. Part 6. Police Interrogation Tape Played." YouTube (11 February 2014), http://www.youtube.com/watch?v=2y8v6pRtSOQ.

"Michael Dunn Trial—Day 6—Part 2 (Prosecution Closing Arguments)." YouTube (12 February 2014), http://www.youtube.com/watch?v=B8aME1ooGlM.

"Michael Dunn Trial—Day 6—Part 3 (Defense Closing Arguments)." YouTube (12 February 2014), http://www.youtube.com/watch?v=1B8Q-EoXh9M.

"Michael Dunn Trial / Police Interrogation Tape Played." YouTube (11 February 2014), http://www.youtube.com/watch?v=2y8v6pRtSOQ.

"Michael Dunn's Neighbor Speaks to Davis Lawyer John Phillips (Highlights)." YouTube (13 February 2014), http://www.youtube.com/watch?v=aocMpoAs59o.

Michael, Melanie. "Homeless Piano Man Gets Recording Contract, Asks Jimmy Fallon for a Duet." WFLA (10 May 2016), http://wfla.com/2016/05/10/homeless-piano-man-gets-recording-contract-asks-jimmy-fallon-for-a-duet.

"Michael Moore: 'We're All Muslim, All Gay, All Trans, All Queer.'" YouTube (20 January 2017), http://www.youtube.com/watch?v=nqFhc5V-TX4.

Michaels, Walter Benn, Charles W. Mills, Linda Hirshman, and Carla Murphy. "What Is the Left without Identity Politics?" *Nation* (16 December 2016), http://www.thenation.com/article/what-is-the-left-without-identity-politics.

Midgette, Anne. "Blasting Mozart to Drive Criminals Away." *Washington Post* (20 January 2012), http://www.washingtonpost.com/lifestyle/style/blasting-mozart-to-drive-criminals-away/2011/10/11/gIQAgDqPEQ_story.html?utm_term=.194a743958e6.

Midgette, Anne. "Classical Music: Dead or Alive?" *Washington Post* (30 January 2014), http://www.washingtonpost.com/news/style/wp/2014/01/30/classical-music-dead-or-alive/?utm_term=.5eecdf059ed8.

Midgette, Anne, and Peggy McGlone. "Assaults in Dressing Rooms. Groping During Lessons. Classical Musicians Reveal a Profession Rife with Harassment." *Washington Post* (26 July 2018), http://www.washingtonpost.com/entertainment/music/assaults-in-dressing-rooms-groping-during-lessons-classical-musicians-reveal-a-profession-rife-with-harassment/2018/07/25/f47617d0-36c8-11e8-acd5-35eac230e514_story.html?tid=ss_tw&utm_term=.f8cb0b627d08.

Miller, Ben. "On Knowing and Not Knowing about James Levine." *Atavist* (7 December 2017), http://van-us.atavist.com/silence-breaking.

Miller, Claire Cain. "Is Blind Hiring the Best Hiring?" *New York Times* (25 February 2016), http://www.nytimes.com/2016/02/28/magazine/is-blind-hiring-the-best-hiring.html?_r=0&mtrref=undefined&gwh=BDB31ED44DA5DE14BFAC213B2302E19D&gwt=pay.

Miller, Karl Hagstrom. *Segregating Sound: Inventing Folk and Pop Music in the Age of Jim Crow*. Durham, NC: Duke University Press, 2010.

Miller, Patrick R. "The Emotional Citizen: Emotion as a Function of Political Sophistication." *Political Psychology* 32 (2011), 575–600.

Mills, Kelly-Ann. "Russia's President Putin Fails in Attempt to Play Piano while Waiting for Chinese Leader—and Blames 'Bad Tuning.'" *Mirror* (15 May 2017), http://www.mirror.co.uk/news/world-news/russias-president-putin-fails-attempt-10427986.

Mills, Kelly-Ann. "Russia's President Putin Fails in Attempt to Play Piano while Waiting for Chinese Leader—and Blames 'Bad Tuning.'" *Mirror* (15 May 2017), http://www.mirror.co.uk/news/world-news/russias-president-putin-fails-attempt-10427986.

Millum, Joseph, and Christine Grady. "The Ethics of Placebo-Controlled Trials: Methodological Justifications." *Contemporary Clinical Trials* 36 (2013), 510–14.

Minow, Martha. *Making All the Difference: Inclusion, Exclusion, and American Law*. Ithaca, NY: Cornell University Press, 1991.

Mitchell, David T., and Sharon L. Snyder. *The Biopolitics of Disability: Neoliberalism, Ablenationalism, and Peripheral Embodiment*. Ann Arbor: University of Michigan Press, 2015.

Mitchell, David T., and Sharon L. Snyder. *Narrative Prosthesis: Disability and the Dependencies of Discourse*. Ann Arbor: University of Michigan Press, 2000.

Mithen, Steven. *The Singing Neanderthals: The Origins of Music, Language, Mind, and Body*. Cambridge, MA: Harvard University Press, 2006.

Monson, Ingrid. "Hearing, Seeing, and Perceptual Agency." *Critical Inquiry* 34/supplement (2008), 36–58.

Monson, Ingrid. "Jazz as Political and Musical Practice." In *Musical Improvisation: Art, Education, and Society*, edited by Gabriel Solis and Bruno Nettl, 21–37. Urbana: University of Illinois Press, 2009.

Montgomery, Alice. *Susan Boyle: Dreams Can Come True*. New York: Overlook Press, 2010.

Moore, Andrea. "Neoliberalism and the Musical Entrepreneur." *Journal of the Society for American Music* 10 (2016), 33–53.

Moore, Michael. "Sign the Statement. #WeAreAllMuslim." http://michaelmoore.com/ WeAreAllMuslim.

Mora, Manolete. *Myth, Mimesis and Magic in the Music of the T'boli, Philippines*. Quezon City: Ateneo de Manila University Press, 2005.

Moreno, Joseph J. "Orpheus in Hell: Music in the Holocaust." In *Music and Manipulation: On the Social Uses and Social Control of Music*, edited by Steven Brown and Ulrik Volgsten, 264–86. New York: Berghahn Books, 2006.

Morris, David Z. "Cars with the Boom: Identity and Territory in American Postwar Automobile Sound." *Technology and Culture* 55 (2014), 326–53.

Morris, Mitchell. "On Gaily Reading Music." *repercussions* 1 (1992), 48–64.

Morris, Mitchell. *The Persistence of Sentiment: Display and Feeling in Popular Music of the 1970s*. Berkeley: University of California Press, 2013.

Morris, Mitchell. "Reading as an Opera Queen." In *Musicology and Difference: Gender and Sexuality in Music Scholarship*, edited by Ruth A. Solie, 184–200. Berkeley: University of California Press, 1993.

Morrison, Richard. "Empires Fall but the Band Plays On." *London Times* (25 March 1992).

Mosley, Imani. "MN" (19 February 2016), 4 pages.

Moten, Fred. *In the Break: The Aesthetics of the Black Radical Tradition*. Minneapolis: University of Minnesota Press, 2003.

Moyer, Justin Wm. "How Julie Andrews's Voice Was Stolen by a Medical Disaster." *Washington Post* (19 March 2015), http://www.washingtonpost.com/news/morning-mix/wp/2015/03/19/how-julie-andrewss-voice-was-stolen-by-a-medical-disaster/ ?utm_term=.672b4581a9f1.

Mundy, Rachel. *Animal Musicalities: Birds, Beasts, and Evolutionary Listening*. Middletown, CT: Wesleyan University Press, 2018.

Muñoz, José Esteban. *Cruising Utopia: The Then and There of Queer Futurity*. New York: New York University Press, 2009.

Murphy, Eliza. "Homeless Man Plays Piano So Beautifully It Might Earn Him a Job." ABC News (1 July 2015), http://abcnews.go.com/Lifestyle/homeless-man-plays-piano-beautifully-earn-job/story?id=32166650.

NAACP. "Know Your Rights: What to Do If You're Stopped by the Police," available at http://action.naacp.org/page/-/Criminal%20Justice/Racial_Profiling_Know_Your_ Rights_Supplement_6-12-12.pdf.

"National Time Out Day, June 8, 2016." *Joint Commission* (13 June 2017), http://www. jointcommission.org/national_time_out_day_2016.

"National Time Out Day." *AORN* (14 June 2017), http://www.aorn.org/timeout2017.

Nattiez, Jean-Jacques. "Under What Conditions Can One Speak of the Universality of Music?" *World of Music* 19 (1977), 92–105.

Nazaryan, Alexander. "Murdered while Black: New Documentary Slams 'Stand Your Ground.'" *Newsweek* (20 November 2015), http://www.newsweek.com/ murdered-while-black-new-documentary-slams-stand-your-ground-law-396777.

NBC's *The Voice*. "Eligibility Requirements" (2015), http://www.nbcthevoice.com/ auditions/eligibility.

NC, Marc. "Graphic Evidence of the Racism of Fox News: Racial Photoshopping." *News Corpse* (11 April 2012), http://www.newscorpse.com/ncWP/?p=6851.

Neal, Mark Anthony. *What the Music Said: Black Popular Music and Black Public Culture.* New York: Routledge, 1999.

Neale, Rick. "Michael Dunn at Sentencing: 'I Am Mortified I Took a Life." *Florida Today* (17 October 2014), http://www.floridatoday.com/story/news/crime/2014/10/17/michael-dunn-sentencing-mortified-took-life/17433269.

Nechepurenko, Ivan. "In Beijing, Vladimir Putin Plays Two Piano Tunes from His Childhood." *New York Times* (14 May 2017), http://www.nytimes.com/2017/05/14/world/europe/vladimir-putin-piano-one-belt-one-road-beijing.html.

Nelson, Linda Williamson, and Maynard T. Robison. "Which Americans Are More Equal and Why: The Linguistic Construction of Inequality in America." *Race, Gender and Class* 20 (2013), 294–306.

New York Times (@nytimes). Tweet (14 May 2017), http://twitter.com/nytimes/status/863928551111888896.

Newcomer, Colin. "Rap Music Makes Me Feel Invincible Shirt from Print Liberation." *T-Roundup* (28 January 2011), http://www.troundup.com/rap-music-makes-me-feel-invincible-shirt-from-print-liberation.

Newman, Jason. "Bruce Springsteen Cover Band Drops Out of Trump Inauguration Party." *Rolling Stone* (16 January 2017), http://www.rollingstone.com/music/news/bruce-springsteen-cover-band-drops-out-of-donald-trump-party-w461203.

"News from the AMS Board." *AMS Newsletter* (February 2017), page 12. Available at http://www.ams-net.org/newsletter/AMSNewsletter-2017-2.pdf.

"A News Quiz Made with Love." Boston Public Radio (WGBH) (17 November 2017).

Ngai, Sianne. "Merely Interesting." *Critical Inquiry* 34 (2008), 777–817.

Ngai, Sianne. "Theory of the Gimmick." *Critical Inquiry* 43 (2017), 466–505.

Niederacher, Sonja. "The Myth of Austria as Nazi Victim, the Emigrants and the Discipline of Exile Studies." *Austrian Studies* 11 (2003), 14–32.

Niemöller, Martin. "First They Came for the Socialists." *Holocaust Encyclopedia* (n.d.; last accessed 24 June 2018), http://www.ushmm.org/wlc/en/article.php?ModuleId=10007392.

"Niki Nakayama." *Chef's Table* (S1E3, 2015). Netflix Original.

Niles, Laurie. "Joshua Bell: The Man with the Violin." *Violinist* (21 January 2017), http://www.violinist.com/blog/laurie/20172/20998.

Nishime, LeiLani. *Undercover Asian: Multiracial Asian Americans in Visual Culture.* Urbana: University of Illinois Press, 2014.

Nnamdi, Kojo. "A Washington Original: Gene Weingarten" (30 December 2010), http://thekojonnamdishow.org/shows/2010-12-30/washington-original-gene-weingarten-rebroadcast.

Noda, Abi. "Why I Listen to Rap." *Abi Noda* (18 December 2013), http://abinoda.com/why-i-listen-to-rap.

Nolan, Hamilton. "Don't Piss on Your Best Friend." *Gawker* (10 August 2015), http://gawker.com/dont-piss-on-your-best-friend-1723074461.

Norden, M. F. *The Cinema of Isolation: A History of Physical Disability in the Movies.* New Brunswick, NJ: Rutgers University Press, 1994.

Nott, V. Josiah C. "Two Lectures on the Natural History of the Caucasian and Negro Races" (1844). In *The Ideology of Slavery: Proslavery Thought in the Antebellum*

South, 1830–60, edited by Drew Gilpin Faust, 206–38. Baton Rouge: Louisiana State University Press, 1981.

Nunnally, Shayla C. *Trust in Black America: Race, Discrimination, and Politics.* New York: New York University Press, 2012.

Obama, Barack. *The Audacity of Hope: Thoughts on Reclaiming the American Dream.* New York: Crown Publishers, 2006.

Ochoa Gautier, Ana María. *Aurality: Listening and Knowledge in Nineteenth-Century Colombia.* Durham, NC: Duke University Press, 2014.

Oestreich, James. "Waltzing Right Past History in Austria." *New York Times* (5 January 2014), http://www.nytimes.com/2014/01/06/arts/music/the-vienna-philharmonic-celebrates-the-new-year-twice.html?mcubz=0.

Oestreich, James. "The World According to One Musicologist." *New York Times* (15 February 2012), http://www.nytimes.com/2012/02/16/arts/music/after-the-end-of-music-history-conference-at-princeton.html.

Ogletree, Charles J. *The Presumption of Guilt: The Arrest of Henry Louis Gates, Jr. and Race, Class and Crime in America.* New York: Palgrave Macmillan, 2010.

Oliver, Kelly. *Witnessing: Beyond Recognition.* Minneapolis: University of Minnesota Press, 2001.

Oliver-Hopkins, Olivia. "'I's Got to Get Me Some Education!' Class and the Camp-Horror Nexus in *House of 1000 Corpses*." In *Sontag and the Camp Aesthetic: Advancing New Perspectives*, edited by Bruce E. Drushel and Brian M. Peters, 151–168. Lanham, MD: Lexington Books, 2017.

Olsen, Eric. "Slaves of Celebrity." *Salon* (18 September 2002), http://www.salon.com/2002/09/18/idol contract.

Oluo, Ijeoma. "Bernie Sanders, Black Lives Matter and the Racial Divide in Seattle." *Seattle Globalist* (9 August 2015), http://www.seattleglobalist.com/2015/08/09/bernie-sanders-black-lives-matter-race-divide-in-seattle/40394.

"Order Denying Defendant's Motion to Determine Confidentiality of Court Records and Motions for Protective Order Sealing Certain Court Records and Limiting the Disclosure of Discovery Materials Granting Intervenors' Motion to Set Aside Orders, to Direct Clerk Not to Seal Documents, to Unseal and Un-redact Documents, to Refrain from Further Ex Parte Communications, and Otherwise Enforce the Appellate Court Order of December 18, 2013, Granting in Part and Denying in Part Intervenor Post-Newsweek Stations Florida, Inc.'s Motion to Unseal Documents, Direct the State to Produce Documents Discussed at Ex Parte Hearing, and Direct the Clerk Not to Block Public Access to Files Absent an Order of Court." 2014. Available at http://www.scribd.com/document/202022403/Judge-Denies-Motion-to-Block-Access-to-Dunn-Documents.

Oren, Tasha, and Sharon Shahaf, eds. *Global Television Formats: Understanding Television across Borders.* New York: Routledge, 2012.

Osborne, William. "Bomb Scares and Concentration Camp Memorial Concerts" (5 April 2000), http://www.osborne-conant.org/posts/bomb.htm.

Osborne, William. "Some Notable Progress for Women, But a Blind Eye to the Exclusion of Asians" (29 December 2015), http://www.osborne-conant.org/vpo-update-2015.htm.

Osborne, William. "The Special Characteristics of the Vienna Philharmonic's Racial Ideology" (n.d.), http://www.osborne-conant.org/posts/special.htm.

Osborne, William. "Symphony Orchestras and Artist-Prophets: Cultural Isomorphism and the Allocation of Power in Music." *Leonardo Music Journal* 9 (1999), 69–75.

Osborne, William. "Why Did the Vienna Philharmonic Fire Yasuto Sugiyama?" (n.d.), http://www.osborne-conant.org/sugiyama.htm.

Osborne, William. "'You Sound like a Ladies' Orchestra': A Case History of Sexism against Abbie Conant in the Munich Philharmonic" (1994), http://www.osborne-conant.org/ladies.htm.

Oster, Andrew. "Melisma as Malady: Cavalli's *Il Giasone* (1649) and Opera's Earliest Stuttering Role." In *Sounding Off: Theorizing Disability in Music*, edited by Neil Lerner and Joseph N. Straus, 157–71. New York: Routledge, 2006.

Ostleitner, Elena. *Liebe, Lust, Last und Leid*. Vienna: Bundesministerium für Unterricht und Kunst, 1995.

Paddison, Max. "Music as Ideal: The Aesthetics of Autonomy." In *The Cambridge History of Nineteenth-Century Music*, edited by Jim Samson, 318–42. Cambridge: Cambridge University Press, 2001.

Papenfuss, Mary. "Walmart Ditches 'Bulletproof: Black Lives Matter' T-Shirt after Police Protest." *Huffington Post* (21 December 2016), http://www.huffingtonpost.com/entry/walmart-bulletproof-black-lives-matter_us_585aab22e4b0eb586484c12f.

Pappademas, Alex. "Love Letter to Auto-Tune, Final Installment." *New York Times* (12 August 2011), http://6thfloor.blogs.nytimes.com/2011/08/12/love-letter-to-auto-tune-final-installment.

Paquette, Danielle. "'This Is the Brain on Horror': The Incredible Calm of Diamond 'Lavish' Reynolds." *Washington Post* (7 July 2016), http://www.washingtonpost.com/news/wonk/wp/2016/07/07/the-incredible-calm-of-diamond-lavish-reynolds/?utm_term=.30a497dd9f7f.

"Parents of Black Shooting Victim Close Out AACC's Black History Month Events." *Daily Campus Archive* (2 March 2015), http://dailycampusarchive.wordpress.com/2015/03/02/parents-black-shooting-victim-close-aaccs-black-history-month-events.

Park, So Jeong. "Music as a Necessary Means of Moral Education: A Case Study from Reconstruction of Confucian Culture in Joseon Korea." *International Communication of Chinese Culture* 2 (2015), 123–36.

Parker, Lyndsey. "Producer William Orbit Defends Auto-Tune-Free Britney Spears Song Leak." *Yahoo* (9 July 2014), http://www.yahoo.com/music/bp/producer-william-orbit-defends-auto-tune-free-britney-spears-song-leak-211307690.html.

Paterson, Mark. "'Looking on Darkness, Which the Blind Do See': Blindness, Empathy, and Feeling Seeing." *Mosaic: An Interdisciplinary Critical Journal* 46 (2013), 159–77.

Pease, Donald E. *The New American Exceptionalism*. Minneapolis: University of Minnesota Press, 2009.

Pearl, Monica B. "The Opera Closet: Ardor, Shame, Queer Confessions." *Prose Studies* 37 (2015), 46–65.

Pecknold, Diane. "'These Stupid Little Sounds in Her Voice': Valuing and Vilifying the New Girl Voice." In *Voicing Girlhood in Popular Music: Performance, Authority, Authenticity*, edited by Jacqueline Warwick and Allison Adrian, 77–98. New York: Routledge, 2016.

Peña, Manuel. *American Mythologies: Semiological Sketches*. Burlington, VT: Ashgate, 2012.

Peraino, Judith. *Giving Voice to Love: Song and Self-Expression from the Troubadours to Guillaume de Machaut*. New York: Oxford University Press, 2011.

"Performance Questionnaire." *America's Got Talent* (2013), http://americas gottalentauditions.com/wp-content/uploads/AGT8-VTR-YES-FAQ-FINAL.pdf.

Perlez, Jane. "Vienna Philharmonic Lets Women Join in Harmony." *New York Times* (28 February 1997), http://www.nytimes.com/1997/02/28/world/vienna-philharmonic-lets-women-join-in-harmony.html?mcubz=0.

Perry, Imani. *Prophets of the Hood: Politics and Poetics in Hip Hop*. Durham, NC: Duke University Press, 2004.

Philip, Robert. *Early Recordings and Musical Style: Changing Tastes in Instrumental Performance, 1900–1950*. Cambridge: Cambridge University Press, 1992.

Philip, Robert. *Performing Music in the Age of Recording*. New Haven, CT: Yale University Press, 2014.

Philips, Chuck. "Gangsta Rap: Did Lyrics Inspire Killing of Police?" *Los Angeles Times* (17 October 1994), http://articles.latimes.com/1994-10-17/entertainment/ca-51308_1_police-officer.

Pick, Daniel. *Svengali's Web: The Alien Enchanter in Modern Culture*. New Haven, CT: Yale University Press, 2000.

Pick, Hella. *Guilty Victim: Austria from the Holocaust to Haider*. London: I. B. Tauris, 2000.

Piketty, Thomas. *Capital in the Twenty-First Century*. Cambridge, MA: Belknap Press of Harvard University Press, 2014.

Pilzer, Joshua D. *Hearts of Pine: Songs in the Lives of Three Korean Survivors of the Japanese "Comfort Women."* New York: Oxford University Press, 2012.

Pinker, Steven. *The Blank Slate: The Modern Denial of Human Nature*. New York: Viking, 2002.

Pinn, Anthony B. "Making a World with a Beat: Musical Expression's Relationship to Religious Identity and Experience." In *Noise and Spirit: The Religious and Spiritual Sensibilities of Rap Music*, edited by Anthony B. Pinn, 1–7. New York: New York University Press, 2003.

Pitchford, Jenna. "The 'Global War on Terror,' Identity, and Changing Perceptions: Iraqi Responses to America's War in Iraq." *Journal of American Studies* 45 (2011), 695–716.

Plait, Phil. "#YesAllWomen." *Slate* (27 May 2014), http://www.slate.com/blogs/bad_astronomy/2014/05/27/not_all_men_how_discussing_women_s_issues_gets_derailed.html.

"Plessy v. Ferguson, 163 U.S. 537 (1896)." Available at http://chnm.gmu.edu/courses/nclc375/harlan.html.

Poizat, Michel. *The Angel's Cry: Beyond the Pleasure Principle in Opera*. Ithaca, NY: Cornell University Press, 1992.

"Poll Finds a More Bleak View of American Dream." *New York Times* (10 December 2014), http://www.nytimes.com/interactive/2014/12/10/business/dealbook/document-poll-finds-a-more-bleak-view-of-american-dream.html.

Polzonetti, Pierpaolo. "*Don Giovanni* Goes to Prison: Teaching Opera Behind Bars." *Musica Docta: Rivista digitale di Pedagogia e Didattica della musica* 6 (2016), 99–104.

Polzonetti, Pierpaolo. "*Don Giovanni* Goes to Prison: Teaching Opera Behind Bars." *Musicology Now* (16 February 2016), http://musicologynow.ams-net.org/2016/02/don-giovanni-goes-to-prison-teaching_16.html.

Porco, Alex S. "Throw Yo' Voice Out: Disability as a Desirable Practice in Hip-Hop Vocal Performance." *Disability Studies Quarterly* 34 (2014), http://dsq-sds.org/article/view/3822/3790.

Porter, Eric. *What Is This Thing Called Jazz? African American Musicians as Artists, Critics, and Activists.* Berkeley: University of California Press, 2002.

Posner, Eric. *The Twilight of Human Rights Law.* New York: Oxford University Press, 2014.

Posselt, Julie R. *Inside Graduate Admissions: Merit, Diversity, and Faculty Gatekeeping.* Cambridge, MA: Harvard University Press, 2016.

Potter, Pamela M. "What Is 'Nazi' Music'?" *The Musical Quarterly* 88 (2005), 428–55.

Potter, Pamela M. *Art of Suppression.* Berkeley: University of California Press, 2016.

Powell, John. *Why You Love Music: From Mozart to Metallica—the Emotional Power of Beautiful Sounds.* New York: Little, Brown, and Company, 2016.

Powell, Kevin. "Q&A: Lauryn Hill." *Rolling Stone* (17 September 1998), http://www.rollingstone.com/music/music-news/qa-lauryn-hill-241065.

Power, Ian. "Why Does This Mozart Piece Make Me Cry Even Though It's Stupid and Probably Evil?" *Medium* (11 January 2019), http://medium.com/@ianpoweromg/why-does-this-mozart-piece-make-me-cry-even-though-its-stupid-and-probably-evil-80c63c60fc7f.

Powers, Ann. *Good Booty: Love and Sex, Black & White, Body and Soul in American Music.* New York: HarperCollins, 2017.

Prendergast, Catherine. "And Now, A Necessarily Pathetic Response: A Response to Susan Schweik." *American Literary History* 20 (2008), 238–44.

"President Barack Obama Victory Speech 2012: Election Remarks from Chicago Illinois." YouTube (7 November 2012), http://www.youtube.com/watch?v=ddx8t6zGWxA.

Prestholdt, Jeremy. "The Afterlives of 2Pac: Imagery and Alienation in Sierra Leone and Beyond." *Journal of African Cultural Studies* 21 (2009), 197–218.

Pre-Trial Proceedings and Opening Statements. *People v. Dunn. People of the State of Florida v. DUNN MICHAEL DAVID, Case No. 16-2012-CF-011572-AXXX-MA* (2014), pages 1250–449. Available via database of Joseph Kennedy, "Law of Self-Defense" (course at UNC Chapel Hill), http://lawofselfdefense.web.unc.edu/files/2014/10/OpeningthruGrimes.pdf.

Price, Margaret. *Mad at School: Rhetorics of Mental Disability and Academic Life.* Ann Arbor: University of Michigan Press, 2011.

Price, Melynda J. *At the Cross: Race, Religion, and Citizenship in the Politics of the Death Penalty.* New York: Oxford University Press, 2015.

Prochnik, George. *In Pursuit of Silence: Listening for Meaning in a World of Noise.* New York: Doubleday, 2010.

Prosecution Closing Arguments (Rebuttal). *People v. Dunn. People of the State of Florida v. DUNN MICHAEL DAVID, Case No. 16-2012-CF-011572-AXXX-MA* (2014), pages 3360–559. Available via database of Joseph Kennedy, "Law of Self-Defense" (course at UNC Chapel Hill), http://lawofselfdefense.web.unc.edu/files/2014/10/RebuttalandCharge.pdf.

Puar, Jasbir. *The Right to Maim: Debility, Capacity, and Disability.* Durham, NC: Duke University Press, 2017.

Puar, Jasbir. *Terrorist Assemblages: Homonationalism in Queer Times.* Durham, NC: Duke University Press, 2007.

Pulido, Laura. "Rethinking Environmental Racism: White Privilege and Urban Development in Southern California." *Annals of the Association of American Geographers* 90 (2000), 12–40.

Pulitzer Prizes (7 April 2008), http://www.pulitzer.org/winners/gene-weingarten.

Radano, Ronald. "Hot Fantasies: American Modernism and the Idea of Black Rhythm." In *Music and the Racial Imagination*, edited by Ronald Radano and Philip V. Bohlman, 459–80. Chicago: University of Chicago Press, 2000.

Radano, Ronald. "On Ownership and Value." *Black Music Research Journal* 30 (2010), 363–70.

Ramanna, Nishlyn. "Shifting Fortunes: Jazz in (Post)apartheid South Africa." *South African Music Studies* 33 (2013), 159–72.

Ramsey, Jr., Guthrie P. "The Pot Liquor Principle: Developing a Black Music Criticism in American Music Studies." *Journal of Black Studies* 35 (2004), 210–23.

Ramsey, Jr., Guthrie P. *Race Music: Black Cultures from Bebop to Hip-Hop*. Berkeley: University of California Press, 2003.

Ramsey, Jr., Guthrie P. "Who Hears Here? Black Music, Critical Bias, and the Musicological Skin Trade." *Musical Quarterly* 85 (2001), 1–52.

Rathkolb, Oliver. *Führertreu und Gottbegnadet: Künstlereliten im Dritten Reich*. Vienna: ÖBV, 1991.

Rathkolb, Oliver. *The Paradoxical Republic: Austria, 1945–2005*. New York: Berghahn Books, 2010.

Read, Alan, ed. *The Fact of Blackness: Frantz Fanon and Visual Representation*. Seattle, WA: Bay Press, 1996.

"Rebecca Black—The 'Friday' Follow-Up." *TMZ* (1 April 2011), http://www.tmz.com/2011/04/01/rebecca-black-kids-choice-awards-nickelodeon-reporter-ryan-seacrest-productions.

Redmond, Sean. "Pieces of Me: Celebrity Confessional Carnality." *Social Semiotics* 18 (2008), 149–61.

Redmond, Shana. *Anthem: Social Movements and the Sound of Solidarity in the African Diaspora*. New York: New York University Press, 2013.

Reeves, Marcus. *Somebody Scream! Rap Music's Rise to Prominence in the Aftershocks of Black Power*. New York: Farrar, Strauss & Giroux, 2009.

Reeves, Richard V. *Dream Hoarders: How the American Upper Middle Class Is Leaving Everyone Else in the Dust, Why That Is a Problem, and What to Do about It*. Washington, DC: Brookings Institution Press, 2017.

Rehding, Alexander. *Beethoven's Symphony No. 9*. New York: Oxford University Press, 2018.

Reich, Nancy B. "Rebecca Clarke: An Uncommon Woman." In *A Rebecca Clarke Reader*, edited by Liane Curtis, 10–18. Bloomington: Indiana University Press, 2004.

Reily, Suzel A., and Katherine Brucher. *The Routledge Companion to the Study of Local Musicking*. New York: Routledge, 2018.

Renee, Mia. "The Curious Case of Britney Spears' 'Baby Voice.'" *Miareneecole.com* (2016), http://miareneecole.com/2016/10/11/the-curious-case-of-britney-spears-baby-voice.

Resnikoff, Paul. "Vladimir Putin Plays Piano Like a 3rd Grader." *Digital Music News* (15 May 2017), http://www.digitalmusicnews.com/2017/05/15/vladimir-putin-plays-piano-china.

"Resources for Unconscious Bias Training." *American Musicological Society* (2017), http://www.ams-net.org/committees/cre/unconsciousbias.php.

"Retta—Classical Music." *Comedy Central: Premium Blend* (S2E12, 22 February 2000), http://www.cc.com/video-clips/p3901a/premium-blend-classical-music.

Reynolds, Rory. "Susan Boyle Audience Member Blasts BGT Producers for Hate Campaign." *Deadline* (8 November 2009), http://www.deadlinenews.co.uk/2009/11/08/11258-2113.

Rice, Curt. "How Blind Auditions Help Orchestras to Eliminate Gender Bias." *Guardian* (14 October 2013), http://www.theguardian.com/women-in-leadership/2013/oct/14/blind-auditions-orchestras-gender-bias.

Rich, Katey. "Watch Lin-Manuel Miranda's Emotional Tony Awards Acceptance Sonnet." *Vanity Fair* (12 June 2016), http://www.vanityfair.com/culture/2016/06/lin-manuel-miranda-tony-speech.

Riley, Erin. "Naomi Wolf Misses the Point about 'Vocal Fry.' It's Just an Excuse Not to Listen to Women." *Guardian* (27 July 2015), http://www.theguardian.com/commentisfree/2015/jul/28/naomi-wolf-misses-the-point-about-vocal-fry-its-just-an-excuse-not-to-listen-to-women.

Riley, Matthew. "Civilizing the Savage: Johann Georg Sulzer and the 'Aesthetic Force' of Music." *Journal of the Royal Music Association* 127 (2002), 1–22.

Riley, Ralph. *Why Black People Tend to Shout: Cold Facts and Wry Views from a Black Man's World.* New York: Penguin Books, 1991.

Rivers, W. H. R., and H. N. Webber. "The Action of Caffeine on the Capacity for Muscular Work." *Journal of Physiology* 36 (1907), 33–47.

Roberson, Justin. "25 Rap Songs That Make Us Want to Punch Someone in the Face." *Complex* (8 May 2013), http://www.complex.com/music/2013/05/25-rap-songs-that-make-us-want-to-punch-someone-in-the-face.

Robin, William. "Classical Music Isn't Dead." *New Yorker* (29 January 2014), http://www.newyorker.com/culture/culture-desk/the-fat-lady-is-still-singing.

Robinson, Phoebe. *You Can't Touch My Hair and Other Things I Still Have to Explain.* New York: Random House, 2016.

Roegle, Heinz. "Notes on 26 Years as Official Nonentity (Interview with Anna Lelkes)," transcribed by Jan Herman and translated from German by Mike Wiessner. *Los Angeles Times* (5 March 1997), http://articles.latimes.com/1997-03-05/news/mn-35044_1_vienna-philharmonic-orchestra.

Ronson, Jon. *So You've Been Publicly Shamed.* New York: Riverhead Books, 2015.

Rose, Tricia. *The Hip Hop Wars: What We Talk about When We Talk about Hip Hop—and Why It Matters.* New York: Basic Books, 2008.

Rose, Tricia. *Black Noise: Rap Music and Black Culture in Contemporary America.* Middletown, CT: Wesleyan University Press, 1994.

Rosen, Charles. *Critical Entertainments: Music Old and New.* Cambridge, MA: Harvard University Press, 2000.

Rosenberg, Alyssa. "Why Terrorists Attack Concert Halls." *Chicago Tribune* (24 May 2017), http://www.chicagotribune.com/news/opinion/commentary/ct-manchester-concert-terrorist-attacks-20170524-story.html.

Rosenberg, Noah A., Jonathan K. Pritchard, James L. Weber, Howard M. Cann, Kenneth K. Kidd, Lev A. Zhivotovsky, and Marcus W. Feldman. "Genetic Structure of Human Populations." *Science* 298 (2002), 2381–85.

Rosenberger, Robert. "How Cities Use Design to Drive Homeless People Away." *Atlantic* (19 June 2014), http://www.theatlantic.com/business/archive/2014/06/how-cities-use-design-to-drive-homeless-people-away/373067.

Ross, Alex. "Metropolitan Lives." *New Yorker* (5 November 2001), http://www.newyorker.com/magazine/2001/11/05/metropolitan-lives.

Ross, Alex (@alexrossmusic). Tweet (4 December 2017), http://twitter.com/alexrossmusic/status/937701099976327173?lang=en.

Rousso, Harilyn. *Don't Call Me Inspirational: A Disabled Feminist Talks Back.* Philadelphia: Temple University Press, 2013.

Roy, Jessica. "Erasing Stephen Hawking's Disability Erases an Important Part of Who He Was." *Los Angeles Times* (16 March 2018), http://www.latimes.com/science/sciencenow/la-sci-sn-stephen-hawking-disability-rights-20180316-story.html.

Rupp, Leila J. "Everyone's Queer." *OAH Magazine of History* 20 (2006), 8–11.

Rushfield, Richard. *American Idol: The Untold Story.* New York: Hyperion, 2011.

Ryan, Erin Gloria. "Donald Trump's Lackeys Blame Women and Blacks for How He Talks about Women." *Daily Beast* (11 October 2016), http://www.thedailybeast.com/donald-trumps-lackeys-blame-women-and-blacks-for-how-he-talks-about-women.

Ryland, Amber. "Britney Spears: Overwhelmingly the Worst Interview of the Year in Chicago—'It Was a Struggle For Her to Form a Sentence.'" *Radar Online* (23 December 2013), http://radaronline.com/exclusives/2013/12/britney-spears-worst-interview-of-year-chicago.

S., Danielle. "I Used to Be a Respectable Negro, But Then I Woke Up." *Mamademics* (1 May 2015), http://mamademics.com/i-used-to-be-a-respectable-negro-but-then-i-woke-up.

Samuel, Lawrence R. *The American Dream: A Cultural History.* Syracuse, NY: Syracuse University Press, 2012.

Samuels, David. "Shooting Britney." *Atlantic* (April 2008), http://www.theatlantic.com/magazine/archive/2008/04/shooting-britney/306735.

Sandberg, Sheryl. *Lean In: Women, Work, and the Will to Lead.* New York: Alfred A. Knopf, 2013.

Sanders, Bernie. "On the Issues" (n.d.; last accessed 16 February 2018), http://berniesanders.com/issues.

Sanders, Katie. "A Real Photo of Trayvon Martin? Chain Email Makes False Claim." *Politifact* (17 July 2012), http://www.politifact.com/florida/statements/2012/jul/17/chain-email/real-photo-trayvon-martin-chain-email-says-so.

Santella, Anna-Lise P. "Modeling Music: Early Organizational Structures of American Women's Orchestras." In *American Orchestras in the Nineteenth Century*, edited by John Spitzer, 53–77. Chicago: University of Chicago Press, 2012.

Saor, John. "Japan's 'Piano Murder' Poses Key Test for Justice System." *Washington Post* (4 May 1977), http://www.washingtonpost.com/archive/politics/1977/05/04/japans-piano-murder-poses-key-test-for-justice-system/6e74e858-c95d-4cd0-b040-e2ee1200c44b/?utm_term=.af0555984a94.

"Sarasota Homeless Man Plays National Anthem at NFL Game." YouTube (15 September 2015), http://www.youtube.com/watch?v=Oasd_AStets.

"Sarasota Keys Return to Downtown." *Arts and Cultural Alliance* (18 January 2016), http://www.sarasotaarts.org/community/sarasotakeys.

Sarat, Austin, and Thomas R. Kearns. "The Unsettled Status of Human Rights: An Introduction." In *Human Rights: Concepts, Contests, Contingencies*, edited by Austin Sarat and Thomas R. Kearns, 1–24. Ann Arbor: University of Michigan Press, 2001.

Scarry, Elaine. "Beauty and the Scholar's Duty to Justice." *Profession* (2000), 21–31.

Scarry, Elaine. *On Beauty and Being Just.* Princeton, NJ: Princeton University Press, 1999.

Scheinman, Ted. "The Mythical Virtues of Non-Violent Resistance." *Pacific Standard* (28 July 2015), http://psmag.com/news/sandra-bland-and-the-myth-of-black-obedience.

Scheper-Hughes, Nancy. "A Talent for Life: Reflections on Human Vulnerability and Resilience." *Ethnos: Journal of Anthropology* 73 (2008), 25–56.

Scherzinger, Martin. "Notes on a Postcolonial Musicology: Kofi Agawu and the Critique of Cultural Difference." *Current Musicology* 75 (2003), 223–50.

Schmidt, James. "'Not These Sounds': Beethoven at Mauthausen." *Philosophy and Literature* 29 (2005), 146–63.

Schofield, Katherine Butler. "Reviving the Golden Age Again: 'Classicization,' Hindustani Music, and the Mughals." *Ethnomusicology* 54 (2010), 484–517.

Schoon, Ingrid. *Risk and Resilience: Adaptations in Changing Times.* Cambridge: Cambridge University Press, 2006.

Schor, Naomi. "Blindness as Metaphor." *differences: A Journal of Feminist Cultural Studies* 11 (1999), 76–105.

Schrift, Melissa. "The Angola Prison Rodeo: Inmate Cowboys and Institutional Tourism." *Ethnology* 43 (2004), 331–44.

Schwartz, Marie Jenkins. *Birthing a Slave: Motherhood and Medicine in the Antebellum South.* Cambridge, MA: Harvard University Press, 2006.

Schwarz, Hillel. "Inner and Outer Sancta: Earplugs and Hospitals." In *The Oxford Handbook of Sound Studies*, edited by Trevor Pinch and Karin Bijsterveld, 273–97. New York: Oxford University Press, 2012.

Schweik, Susan. "Begging the Question: Disability, Mendicancy, Speech and the Law." *Narrative* 15 (2007), 58–70.

Schweik, Susan. *The Ugly Laws: Disability in Public.* New York: New York University Press, 2010.

Scott, Eugene. "Six Times President Trump Said He Is the Least Racist Person." *Washington Post* (17 January 2018), http://www.washingtonpost.com/news/the-fix/wp/2018/01/17/six-times-president-trump-said-he-is-the-least-racist-person/?noredirect=on&utm_term=.418705398b11.

Sedgwick, Eve Kosofsky. "Paranoid Reading and Reparative Reading, or, You're So Paranoid, You Probably Think This Essay Is about You." In *Touching Feeling: Affect, Pedagogy, Performativity*, 123–51. Durham, NC: Duke University Press, 2003.

Seeger, Anthony. "Theories Forged in the Crucible of Action: The Joys, Dangers, and Potentials of Advocacy and Fieldwork." In *Shadows in the Field: New Perspectives for Fieldwork in Ethnomusicology*, second edition, edited by Gregory Barz and Timothy J. Cooley, 271–88. New York: Oxford University Press, 2008.

Segato, R. L. "The Color-Blind Subject of Myth; or, Where to Find Africa in the Nation." *Annual Review of Anthropology* 27 (1998), 129–51.

Sen, Amartya. "Merit and Justice." In *Meritocracy and Economic Inequality*, edited by Kenneth Joseph Arrow, Samuel Bowles, and Steven N. Durlauf, 5–16. Princeton, NJ: Princeton University Press, 2000.

Sen, Amartya. *Poverty and Famines: An Essay on Entitlement and Deprivation.* Oxford: Clarendon Press, 1981.

Senna, Irene, Angelo Maravita, Nadia Bolognini, and Cesare V. Parise. "The Marble-Hand Illusion." *PLOS ONE* 9 (2014), http://doi.org/10.1371/journal.pone.0091688.

Shadle, Douglas W. *Orchestrating the Nation: The Nineteenth-Century American Symphonic Enterprise.* New York: Oxford University Press, 2016.

Shakespeare, Tom. *The Sexual Politics of Disability: Untold Desires.* London: Cassell, 1996.

Shanahan, Mark. "BSO's Andris Nelsons Says Sexual Harassment Isn't a Problem in Classical Music." *Boston Globe* (20 November 2017), http://www.bostonglobe.com/lifestyle/names/2017/11/20/bso-andris-nelsons-says-sexual-harassment-isn-problem-classical-music/RS4BiGKOcT4nLUWP9szsGP/story.html.

Shank, Barry. *The Political Force of Musical Beauty.* Durham, NC: Duke University Press, 2014.

Sharot, Tali, Christoph W. Korn, and Raymond J. Dolan. "How Unrealistic Optimism Is Maintained in the Face of Reality." *Nature Neuroscience* 14 (2011), 1475–79.

Sharpe, Christina. *In the Wake: On Blackness and Being.* Durham, NC: Duke University Press, 2016.

Sharpe, Christina. *Monstrous Intimacies: Making Post-Slavery Subjects.* Durham, NC: Duke University Press, 2010.

Shaver-Gleason, Linda. "Is Music a Universal Language?" *Not Another Music History Cliché!* (4 January 2018), http://notanothermusichistorycliche.blogspot.com/2018/01/is-music-universal-language.html.

Shaver-Gleason, Linda. "The Morality of Musical Men: From Victorian Propriety to the Era of #MeToo." Lecture delivered at Utah State University (26 January 2018), http://hcommons.org/deposits/objects/hc:18044/datastreams/CONTENT/content.

Sheffield, Rob. "Britney Spears' 'Blackout': A Salute to Her Misunderstood Punk Masterpiece." *Rolling Stone* (30 October 2017), http://www.rollingstone.com/music/news/rob-sheffield-on-britney-spears-blackout-punk-masterpiece-w510038.

Sheinbaum, John J. *Good Music: What It Is and Who Gets to Decide.* Chicago: University of Chicago Press, 2019.

Shelemay, Kay Kaufman. "The Impact and Ethics of Musical Scholarship." In *Rethinking Music,* edited by Nicholas Cook and Mark Everist, 531–44. New York: Oxford University Press, 1999.

Shelemay, Kay Kaufman. *A Song of Longing: An Ethiopian Journey.* Urbana: University of Illinois Press, 1991.

Shildrick, Margrit. *Leaky Bodies and Boundaries: Feminism, Postmodernism, and (Bio) ethics.* New York: Routledge, 1997.

Shirakawa, Sam H. *The Devil's Music Master: The Controversial Life and Career of Wilhelm Furtwängler.* New York: Oxford University Press, 1992.

Showler, Suzannah. "*The Voice* from Above." *Slate* (14 December 2015), http://www.slate.com/articles/arts/culturebox/2015/12/god_religion_and_jordan_smith_on_the_voice.html.

Shreffler, Anne C., Boris von Haken, and Christopher Browning. "Musicology, Biography, and National Socialism: The Case of Hans Heinrich Eggebrecht." *German Studies Review* 35 (2012), 289–318.

Shusterman, Richard. *Pragmatist Aesthetics: Living Beauty, Rethinking Art.* Oxford: Blackwell, 1992.

Siebers, Tobin. *Disability Aesthetics.* Ann Arbor: University of Michigan Press, 2010.

Siebers, Tobin. *Disability Theory.* Ann Arbor: University of Michigan Press, 2008.

Sieczkowski, Cavan. "You Have to Listen to Britney Spears Singing 'Toxic' without Auto-Tune." *Huffington Post* (7 June 2017), http://www.huffingtonpost.com/entry/britney-spears-toxic-no-auto-tune_us_59381280e4b01fc18d3f69d0.

Silver, Marc. *3½ Minutes, 10 Bullets.* HBO Documentary Films (2015).

Silver, Sonya. "Autotune. Simple Irony, Really." *Gearslutz* (11 January 2010), http://www.gearslutz.com/board/the-moan-zone/455796-autotune-simple-irony-really.html.

Silverman, Stephen M. "Britney Spears Says She Was at 'Rock Bottom' in Rehab." *People* (29 May 2007), http://people.com/celebrity/britney-spears-says-she-was-at-rock-bottom-in-rehab.

Silverstein, Jason. "I Don't Feel Your Pain." *Slate* (27 June 2013), http://www.slate.com/articles/health_and_science/science/2013/06/racial_empathy_gap_people_don_t_perceive_pain_in_other_races.html

"Simone Young to Conduct Vienna Philharmonic." *Sydney Morning Herald* (9 November 2005), http://www.smh.com.au/entertainment/art-and-design/simone-young-to-conduct-vienna-philharmonic-20051109-gdmeqv.html.

Singal, Jesse. "Why Americans Ignore the Role of Luck in Everything." *New York Magazine* (12 May 2016), http://nymag.com/scienceofus/2016/05/why-americans-ignore-the-role-of-luck-in-everything.html.

Skaggs, Steven, and Carl R. Hausman. "Toward a New Elitism." *Journal of Aesthetic Education* 46 (2012), 83–106.

Sklar, Howard. "'What the Hell Happened to Maggie?': Stereotype, Sympathy, and Disability in Toni Morrison's 'Recitatif.'" *Journal of Literary & Cultural Disability Studies* 5 (2011), 137–54.

Skyring, Kerry. "The Vienna Philharmonic Reveals Its Nazi Past." *Deutsche Welle* (12 March 2013), http://p.dw.com/p/17vWV.

Slater, Tom. "The Resilience of Neoliberal Urbanism." *Open Democracy* (28 January 2014), http://www.opendemocracy.net/opensecurity/tom-slater/resilience-of-neoliberal-urbanism.

Slut Machine. "Who's Crazier: Britney Spears or the Rest of Us for Giving a Shit?" *Jezebel* (4 January 2008), http://jezebel.com/340504/whos-crazier-britney-spears-or-the-rest-of-us-for-giving-a-shit.

Small, Christopher. *Musicking: The Meanings of Performing and Listening.* Hanover, NH: Wesleyan University Press, 1998.

Smart, Mary Ann, ed. *Siren Songs: Representations of Gender and Sexuality in Opera.* Princeton, NJ: Princeton University Press, 2000.

Smit, Christopher R. *The Exile of Britney Spears: A Tale of 21st-Century Consumption.* Chicago: Intellect, 2011.

Smith, David Livingstone. *Less Than Human: Why We Demean, Enslave, and Exterminate Others.* New York: St. Martin's Press, 2011.

Smith, Mark M. *How Race Is Made: Slavery, Segregation, and the Senses.* Chapel Hill: University of North Carolina Press, 2006.

Smith, Mark M. *Listening to Nineteenth-Century America.* Chapel Hill: University of North Carolina Press, 2001.

Smith, Robert Courtney. "'Don't Let the Illegals Vote!': The Myths of Illegal Latino Voters and Voter Fraud in Contested Local Immigrant Integration." *Russell Sage Foundation Journal of the Social Sciences* 3 (2017), 148–75.

Smith, Steve. "Agony of TV Teenager Filmed Sneering during Susan Boyle's Debut." *Daily Record* (22 November 2009), http://www.dailyrecord.co.uk/news/real-life/exclusive-agony-of-tv-teenager-filmed-1042797.

Snediker, Michael. *Queer Optimism: Lyric Personhood and Other Felicitous Persuasions.* Minneapolis: University of Minnesota Press, 2009.

Snyder, Sharon L., and David T. Mitchell. "Introduction: Ablenationalism and the Geo-Politics of Disability." *Journal of Literary & Cultural Disability Studies* 4 (2010), 113–25.

"Social Responsibility of the Vienna Philharmonic." *Vienna Philharmonic* (n.d.; last accessed 4 July 2018), http://www.wienerphilharmoniker.at/orchestra/social- responsibility.

Solie, Ruth, ed. *Musicology and Difference: Gender and Sexuality in Music Scholarship.* Berkeley: University of California Press, 1993.

Solotaroff, Paul. "A Most American Way to Die." *Rolling Stone* (25 April 2013), http://www.rollingstone.com/culture/news/jordan-davis-stand-your-grounds-latest-victim-20130425.

Solove, Daniel J. *The Future of Reputation: Gossip, Rumor, and Privacy on the Internet*. New Haven, CT: Yale University Press, 2007.

Sontag, Susan. *AIDS and Its Metaphors*. New York: Farrar, Straus and Giroux, 1989.

Sontag, Susan. *Illness as Metaphor*. New York: Farrar, Straus and Giroux, 1978.

Southern, Eileen, and Josephine Wright. *Images: Iconography of Music in African-American Culture, 1770s–1920s*. New York: Garland, 2000.

Southern, Eileen. *The Music of Black Americans: A History*, third edition. New York: W. W. Norton, 1997.

Spears, Lynne. *Through the Storm: A Real Story of Fame and Family in a Tabloid World*. Nashville, TN: Thomas Nelson, 2008.

Special Issue. "Universals/Le Problème des Universaux." *World of Music* 19 (1977).

Spigel, Lynn. "Entertainment Wars: Television Culture after 9/11." *American Quarterly* 56 (2004), 235–70.

Stahl, Jeremy. "Cleveland Police Union Boss Says Awful Thing about Tamir Rice Again." *Slate* (25 April 2016), http://www.slate.com/blogs/the_slatest/2016/04/25/steve_loomis_says_awful_thing_about_tamir_rice_again.html.

Stahl, Matthew Wheelock. "A Moment Like This: *American Idol* and Narratives of Meritocracy." In *Bad Music: The Music We Love to Hate*, edited by Christopher Washburne and Maiken Derno, 212–32. New York: Routledge, 2004.

Stainova, Yana. "Musical Slums: Playing for Your Life in Venezuela's El Sistema." *ReVista: Harvard Review of Latin America* (2016), http://revista.drclas.harvard.edu/book/musical-slums.

Stanton, Burke. "Musicking in the Borders: Toward Decolonizing Methodologies." *Philosophy of Music Education Review* 26 (2018), 4–23.

Staples, Robert. "The Myth of the Black Matriarchy." *The Black Scholar* 1 (1970), 8–16.

Staples, Robert. "White Power, Black Crime, and Racial Politics." *The Black Scholar* 41 (2011), 31–41.

State of Missouri v. Darren Wilson. Grand Jury Volume IV (10 September 2014), available at http://www.documentcloud.org/documents/1370494-grand-jury-volume-4.html.

State of Missouri v. Darren Wilson. Grand Jury Volume V (16 September 2014), available at http://www.documentcloud.org/documents/1370494-grand-jury-volume-5.html.

Steele, Claude M. *Whistling Vivaldi: How Stereotypes Affect Us and What We Can Do*. New York: W. W. Norton, 2010.

Steinberg, Michael, and Larry Rothe. *For the Love of Music: Invitations to Listening*. New York: Oxford University Press, 2006.

Sterne, Jonathan. *The Audible Past: Cultural Origins of Sound Reproduction*. Durham, NC: Duke University Press, 2003.

Sterne, Jonathan. "Sounds Like the Mall of America: Programmed Music and the Architectonics of Commercial Spaces." *Ethnomusicology* 41 (1997), 22–50.

Stevenson, Bryan. *Just Mercy: A Story of Justice and Redemption*. New York: Spiegel & Grau, 2014.

Stewart, Jane Bowyer. "Behind the Curtain: Auditioning for the NSO." *National Symphony Orchestra* (4 July 2016), http://nsomusicians.org/blog/2016/7/4/behind-the-curtain.

Stimeling, Travis. *Cosmic Cowboys and New Hicks: The Countercultural Sounds of Austin's Progressive Country Music Scene*. New York: Oxford University Press, 2011.

"Sting Busked to Improve Confidence." *Irish Examiner* (1 May 2005), http://www.irishexaminer.com/breakingnews/entertainment/sting-busked-to-improve-confidence-200567.html.

Stinson, Kathy, and Dušan Petričić. *The Man with the Violin*. Toronto, ON: Annick Press, 2013.

Stoever, Jennifer Lynn. *The Sonic Color Line: Race and the Cultural Politics of Listening*. New York: New York University Press, 2016.

Storycorps. "Not Sorry: The Woman Who Interrupted Bernie Sanders in Seattle." KUOW (29 February 2016), http://kuow.org/post/not-sorry-woman-who-interrupted-bernie-sanders-seattle.

Strainchamps, Edmond, and Maria Rika Maniates, with Christopher Hatch. *Music and Civilization: Essays in Honor of Paul Henry Lang*. New York: W. W. Norton, 1984.

Stras, Laurie. "'The Organ of the Soul': Voice, Damage, and Affect." In *Sounding Off: Theorizing Disability in Music*, edited by Neil Lerner and Joseph N. Straus, 173–84. New York: Routledge, 2006.

Stras, Laurie. "Voice of the Beehive: Vocal Technique at the Turn of the 1960s." In *She's So Fine: Reflections on Whiteness, Femininity, Adolescence and Class in 1960s Music*, edited by Laurie Stras, 33–55. Burlington, VT: Ashgate, 2010.

Strasser, Otto (I). *Und dafür wird man noch bezahlt: Mein Leben mit den Wiener Philharmonikern*. Munich: Deutscher Taschenbuch Verlag, 1978.

Strasser, Otto (II). *Hitler and I*. Translated by Gwenda David and Eric Mosbacher. Boston: Houghton Mifflin, 1940.

Straus, Joseph. "Idiots Savants, Retarded Savants, Talented Aments, Mono-Savants, Autistic Savants, Just Plain Savants, People with Savant Syndrome, and Autistic People Who Are Good at Things: A View from Disability Studies." *Disability Studies Quarterly* 34 (2014), http://dsq-sds.org/article/view/3407/3640.

"Stuart Varney Net Worth." *The Richest* (retrieved 28 June 2017), http://www.therichest.com/celebnetworth/celeb/journalist/stuart-varney-net-worth.

Stuckey, Torri. "'What about Black-on-Black Crime?' What about Pink Polka Dotted Unicorns?" *Huffington Post* (6 December 2017), http://www.huffingtonpost.com/torri-stuckey/what-about-blackonblack-c_b_10905534.html.

Sturgeon, Jonathan. "Is Magnetic Fields' Stephin Merritt a Racist Troll, Literary Celebrittante, or Both?" *Flavorwire* (31 March 2015), http://flavorwire.com/511904/is-stephin-merritt-a-racist-troll-literary-celebrittante-or-both.

Subotnik, Rose Rosengard. "Afterword: Toward the Next Paradigm of Musical Scholarship." In *Beyond Structural Listening? Postmodern Modes of Hearing*, edited by Andrew Dell'Antonio, 279–302. Berkeley: University of California Press, 2004.

Sue, Derald Wing. "The Invisible Whiteness of Being: Whiteness, White Supremacy, White Privilege, and Racism." In *Addressing Racism: Facilitating Cultural Competence in Mental Health and Educational Settings*, edited by Madonna G. Constantine and Derald Wing Sue, 15–30. Hoboken, NJ: Wiley & Sons, 2006.

Sue, Derald Wing. *Race Talk and the Conspiracy of Silence: Understanding and Facilitating Difficult Dialogues on Race*. Hoboken, NJ: John Wiley & Sons, 2015.

Sue, Derald Wing, et al. "Racial Microaggressions in Everyday Life." *American Psychologist* 62 (2007), 271–86.

Summers, Nick. "Fox News Coverage of the Trayvon Martin Case Criticized." *Daily Beast* (21 March 2012), http://www.thedailybeast.com/fox-news-coverage-of-the-trayvon-martin-case-criticized.

Sun, Cecilia. "Brian Eno, the Influential 'Non-Musician,' at 66." *OUP Blog* (15 May 2014), http://blog.oup.com/2014/05/brian-eno-influential-non-musician.

Supičič, Ivan. "Aesthetics of Music—Particularity and Universality." *World of Music* 25 (1983), 16–25.

Supičič, Ivo. *Music in Society: A Guide to the Sociology of Music.* Stuyvesant, NY: Pendragon Press, 1987.

"Susan Boyle—Britain's Got Talent 2009 Episode 1—Saturday 11th April." YouTube (11 April 2009), http://www.youtube.com/watch?v=RxPZh4AnWyk.

Sutton, Craig. "Why Are Low-Income High Achievers So Underrepresented at Elite Schools?" *Washington Post* (18 December 2015), http://www.washingtonpost.com/opinions/closing-the-income-gap-at-elite-colleges/2015/12/18/90f91054-a057-11e5-a3c5-c77f2cc5a43c_story.html?utm_term=.b35f9beddcaf.

Svonkin, Craig. "Manishevitz and Sake, the Kaddish and Sutras: Allen Ginsberg's Spiritual Self-Othering." *College Literature* 37 (2010), 166–93.

Swayne, Steve. "Music Is Power: Michael Dunn, Jordan Davis, and How We Respond When People Turn Up the Volume." *Pacific Standard* (5 March 2014), http://psmag.com/social-justice/music-power-volume-sound-michael-dunn-jordan-davis-75929.

Sweeney, Gael. "The King of White Trash Culture: Elvis Presley and the Aesthetics of Excess." In *White Trash: Race and Class in America*, edited by Matt Wray and Annalee Newitz, 249–66. New York: Routledge, 1997.

Szpilman, Władysław. *The Pianist: The Extraordinary Story of One Man's Survival in Warsaw, 1939–1945*, translated by Anthea Bell. New York: Picador, 1999.

Taber, George M. *Judgment of Paris.* New York: Scribner, 2005.

"Tamir Rice's Death: A Lawful Tragedy." CNN (28 December 2015), http://www.cnn.com/2015/12/28/opinions/holloway-tamir-rice-case/index.html.

Tan, Kenneth Paul. "Meritocracy and Elitism in a Global City: Ideological Shifts in Singapore." *International Political Science Review* 29 (2008), 7–27.

Tanaka, Alisa. "Dear Scott Hamilton: A Bad Attitude Is Not the Only Disability." *The Mighty* (27 June 2016), http://themighty.com/2016/06/dear-scott-hamilton-a-bad-attitude-is-not-the-only-disability.

Taruskin, Richard. "Agents and Causes and Ends, Oh My." *Journal of Musicology* 31 (2014), 272–93.

Taruskin, Richard. *The Danger of Music and Other Anti-Utopian Essays.* Berkeley: University of California Press, 2009.

Taruskin, Richard. "Is There a Baby in the Bathwater? (Part II)." *Archiv für Musikwissenschaft* 63 (2006), 309–27.

Taruskin, Richard. "The Musical Mystique." *New Republic* (22 October 2007), http://newrepublic.com/article/64350/books-the-musical-mystique.

Taruskin, Richard. *The Oxford History of Western Music*, vol. 1. New York: Oxford University Press, 2005.

Tate, Greg, ed. *Everything but the Burden: What White People Are Taking from Black Culture.* New York: Broadway Books, 2003.

Taylor Best. Comment on "Alien NO AUTOTUNE Britney Spears FULL." YouTube (video uploaded on 10 July 2014; comment posted in 2016), http://www.youtube.com/watch?v=MUdKrtsrCBI.

Taylor, Diane. "Homeless People Demand M&S Apology over Deterrent Alarm." *Guardian* (26 July 2017), http://www.theguardian.com/society/2017/jul/26/homeless-people-demand-ms-apology-over-deterrent-alarm.

Taylor, Sunny. "The Right Not to Work: Power and Disability." *Monthly Review* 55 (2004), http://monthlyreview.org/2004/03/01/the-right-not-to-work-power-and-disability.

"Teen YouTube Sensation Rebecca Black under Police Protection after Receiving Death Threats." *Daily Mail* (20 April 2011), http://www.dailymail.co.uk/news/article-1378865/Rebecca-Black-police-protection-receiving-death-threats.html.

Teitelbaum, Benjamin R. *Lions of the North: Sounds of the New Nordic Radical Nationalism.* New York: Oxford University Press, 2017.

Testimony by Alexandria Molinaro. *People v. Dunn. People of the State of Florida v. DUNN MICHAEL DAVID, Case No. 16-2012-CF-011572-AXXX-MA* (2014), pages 2676–85. Available via database of Joseph Kennedy, "Law of Self-Defense" (course at UNC Chapel Hill), http://lawofselfdefense.web.unc.edu/files/2014/10/Alexandria-Molinaro.pdf.

Testimony by Beverly Berry. *People v. Dunn. People of the State of Florida v. DUNN MICHAEL DAVID, Case No. 16-2012-CF-011572-AXXX-MA* (2014), pages 2574–85. Available via database of Joseph Kennedy, "Law of Self-Defense" (course at UNC Chapel Hill), http://lawofselfdefense.web.unc.edu/files/2014/10/Beverly-Berry.pdf.

Testimony by Defendant (Michael Dunn). *People of the State of Florida v. DUNN MICHAEL DAVID, Case No. 16-2012-CF-011572-AXXX-MA* (2014), pages 2834–3026. Available via database of Joseph Kennedy, "Law of Self-Defense" (course at UNC Chapel Hill), http://lawofselfdefense.web.unc.edu/files/2014/10/Defendant.pdf.

Testimony by Frank Thompson. *People v. Dunn. People of the State of Florida v. DUNN MICHAEL DAVID, Case No. 16-2012-CF-011572-AXXX-MA* (2014), pages 2586–89. Available via database of Joseph Kennedy, "Law of Self-Defense" (course at UNC Chapel Hill), http://lawofselfdefense.web.unc.edu/files/2014/10/Frank-Thompson.pdf.

Testimony by Leland Brunson. *People v. Dunn. People of the State of Florida v. DUNN MICHAEL DAVID, Case No. 16-2012-CF-011572-AXXX-MA* (2014), pages 1708–73. Available via database of Joseph Kennedy, "Law of Self-Defense" (course at UNC Chapel Hill), http://lawofselfdefense.web.unc.edu/files/2014/10/Leland-Brunson.pdf.

Testimony by Randy Berry. *People v. Dunn. People of the State of Florida v. DUNN MICHAEL DAVID, Case No. 16-2012-CF-011572-AXXX-MA* (2014), pages 2566–74. Available via database of Joseph Kennedy, "Law of Self-Defense" (course at UNC Chapel Hill), http://lawofselfdefense.web.unc.edu/files/2014/10/Randy-Berry.pdf.

Testimony by Rhonda Rouer (Rebuttal). *People v. Dunn. People of the State of Florida v. DUNN MICHAEL DAVID, Case No. 16-2012-CF-011572-AXXX-MA* (2014), pages 3059–3065. Available via database of Joseph Kennedy, "Law of Self-Defense" (course at UNC Chapel Hill), http://lawofselfdefense.web.unc.edu/files/2014/10/Rhonda-Rouer-rebuttal.pdf.

Testimony by Ronald Davis. *People v. Dunn. People of the State of Florida v. DUNN MICHAEL DAVID, Case No. 16-2012-CF-011572-AXXX-MA* (2014), pages 2625–43. Available via database of Joseph Kennedy, "Law of Self-Defense" (course at UNC Chapel Hill), http://lawofselfdefense.web.unc.edu/files/2014/10/Ronald-Davis.pdf.

Testimony by Shawn Atkins. *People of the State of Florida v. DUNN MICHAEL DAVID, Case No. 16-2012-CF-011572-AXXX-MA* (2014), pages 1404–46. Available via database of Joseph Kennedy, "Law of Self-Defense" (course at UNC Chapel Hill), http://lawofselfdefense.web.unc.edu/files/2014/10/Shawn-Atkins.pdf.

Testimony by Steven Smith. *People of the State of Florida v. DUNN MICHAEL DAVID, Case No. 16-2012-CF-011572-AXXX-MA* (2014), pages 1326–72. Available via database of Joseph Kennedy, "Law of Self-Defense" (course at UNC Chapel Hill), http://lawofselfdefense.web.unc.edu/files/2014/10/Steven-Smith.pdf.

Testimony by Tevin Thompson. *People v. Dunn. People of the State of Florida v. DUNN MICHAEL DAVID, Case No. 16-2012-CF-011572-AXXX-MA* (2014), pages 1623–704. Available via database of Joseph Kennedy, "Law of Self-Defense" (course at UNC Chapel Hill), http://lawofselfdefense.web.unc.edu/files/2014/10/Tevin-Thompson.pdf.

Testimony by Tommie Stornes. *People v. Dunn. People of the State of Florida v. DUNN MICHAEL DAVID, Case No. 16-2012-CF-011572-AXXX-MA* (2014), pages 1785–853. Available via database of Joseph Kennedy, "Law of Self-Defense" (course at UNC Chapel Hill), http://lawofselfdefense.web.unc.edu/files/2014/10/Tommie-Stornes.pdf.

"Texts of the Oaths of Office for Supreme Court Justices." *Supreme Court* (Version 2014.2), http://www.supremecourt.gov/about/oath/textoftheoathsofoffice2009.aspx.

Thaler, Linda Kaplan, and Robin Koval. *Grit to Great: How Perseverance, Passion, and Pluck Take You from Ordinary to Extraordinary.* New York: Crown Business, 2015.

Thiagarajan, Kamala. "Donald Trump Jr. Is Impressed by the 'Smile on a Face' of India's Poor." NPR (21 February 2018), http://www.npr.org/sections/goatsandsoda/2018/02/21/587604741/donald-trump-jr-is-impressed-by-the-smile-on-a-face-of-indias-poor.

Thompson, Desire. "Rest in Peace: Today Would Have Been Jordan Davis' 21st Birthday." *Vibe* (16 February 2016), http://www.vibe.com/2016/02/jordan-davis-twenty-first-birthday.

Thompson, Marie. *Beyond Unwanted Sound: Noise, Affect and Aesthetic Moralism.* New York: Bloomsbury Academic, 2017.

Thurman, Kira. "Singing the Civilized Mission in the Land of Bach, Beethoven, and Brahms: The Fisk Jubilee Singers in Nineteenth-Century Germany." *Journal of World History* 27 (2016), 443–71.

Tochka, Nicholas. "To 'Enlighten and Beautify': Western Music and the Modern Project of Personhood in Albania, c. 1906–24." *Ethnomusicology* 59 (2015), 398–420.

Todd A. "This Will Be Our Reply to Violence." *Medium* (8 July 2016), http://medium.com/hey-todd-a/this-will-be-our-reply-to-violence-223e12fc9910.

Tolentino, Jia. "Jackie Evancho, Trump's Inauguration, and the Politics of Childhood." *New Yorker* (19 January 2017), http://www.newyorker.com/culture/jia-tolentino/jackie-evancho-and-the-politics-of-childhood.

Tomlinson, Gary. "Evolutionary Studies in the Humanities: The Case of Music." *Critical Inquiry* 39 (2013), 647–75.

Tomlinson, Gary. *A Million Years of Music: The Emergence of Human Modernity.* New York: Zone Books, 2015.

Tommasini, Anthony. "Critic's Notebook: Glorious, Yes, but Resisting Today's World; Vienna Philharmonic Returns, Virtually a Male Bastion." *New York Times* (15 March 1999), http://www.nytimes.com/1999/03/15/arts/critic-s-notebook-glorious-yes-but-resisting-today-s-world-vienna-philharmonic.html?mcubz=0.

Tommasini, Anthony. "Trump Is Wrong If He Thinks Symphonies Are Superior." *New York Times* (30 July 2017), http://www.nytimes.com/2017/07/30/arts/music/trump-classical-music.html.

Tough, Paul. *How Children Succeed: Grit, Curiosity, and the Hidden Power of Character.* New York: Houghton Mifflin Harcourt, 2012.

Trainor, Charles. "Fielding and the Morality of Music." *Neophilologus* 97 (2013), 775–83.

Travis Jr., Raphael. *The Healing Power of Hip Hop.* Santa Barbara, CA: ABC-CLIO, 2016.

"Travis Pratt." YouTube (14 June 2013), http://www.youtube.com/watch?v=CEaMaEb6HIo.

Trawalter, Sophie, Kelly M. Hoffman, and Adam Waytz. "Racial Bias in Perceptions of Others' Pain." *PLOS ONE* 7 (2012), http://doi.org/10.1371/journal.pone.0048546.

Treffert, Darold A. *Islands of Genius: The Bountiful Mind of the Autistic, Acquired, and Sudden Savant.* Philadelphia: Jessica Kingsley, 2010.

Trelawny, Petroc. "The New Year Tradition with a Dark History." BBC (1 January 2015), http://www.bbc.com/news/magazine-30536313.

Tremain, Shelley L. *Foucault and Feminist Philosophy of Disability.* Ann Arbor: University of Michigan Press, 2017.

Trump, Ivanka. *Women Who Work: Rewriting the Rules for Success.* New York: Portfolio, 2017.

Trümpi, Fritz. *The Political Orchestra: The Vienna and Berlin Philharmonics during the Third Reich,* translated by Kenneth Kronenberg. Chicago: University of Chicago Press, 2016.

Trümpi, Fritz. "The Vienna Philharmonic's Nazi Past: Lifting the Veil of Deliberate Ignorance." *Guardian* (16 March 2013), http://www.theguardian.com/commentisfree/2013/mar/16/vienna-philharmonic-nazi-past.

Tsioulcas, Anastasia. "Putin Plays the Piano, with Perhaps Unintentional Undertones." NPR (15 May 2017), http://www.npr.org/sections/thetwo-way/2017/05/15/528451430/putin-plays-the-piano-with-perhaps-unintentional-undertones.

Tsioulcas, Anastasia. "Why Was a Prominent Muslim Musician Gunned Down in Pakistan?" NPR (26 June 2016), http://www.npr.org/2016/06/26/483231557/why-was-a-prominent-muslim-musician-gunned-down-in-pakistan.

"Tyra Banks Experiences Obesity through Fat Suit." ABC (4 November 2005), http://abcnews.go.com/GMA/BeautySecrets/story?id=1280787.

Uffeviking. "Vienna Philharmonic: Slow to Change Its Tune." *Good Music Guide* (2007), http://www.good-music-guide.com/forum/index.php/topic,13375.15/wap2.html.

"Uncut: Jordan Davis' Parents React to Sentence." News 4 Jax (17 October 2014), http://www.news4jax.com/news/local/uncut-jordan-davis-parents-react-to-sentence.

"Understanding Unconscious Bias." YouTube (17 November 2015), http://www.youtube.com/watch?v=dVp9Z5k0dEE.

United Nations Educational, Scientific and Cultural Organization. "What Do We Mean by 'Youth'?" (n.d.; last accessed 3 March 2018), http://www.unesco.org/new/en/social-and-human-sciences/themes/youth/youth-definition.

Usner, Eric Martin. "'The Condition of Mozart': Mozart Year 2006 and the New Vienna." *Ethnomusicology Forum* 20 (2011), 413–42.

Vanhoenacker, Mark. "Requiem: Classical Music in America Is Dead." *Slate* (21 January 2014), http://www.slate.com/articles/arts/culturebox/2014/01/classical_music_sales_decline_is_classical_on_death_s_door.html.

Vaziri, Parisa. "Blackness and the Metaethics of the Object." *Rhizomes* 29 (2016), http://doi.org/10.20415/rhiz/029.e16.

Verchick, Robert R.M. "Same-Sex and the City." *Urban Lawyer* 37 (2005), 191–99.

Victor, Peter. "Neighbourhood Noise: 17 People Have Died from It." *Independent* (18 December 1994), http://www.independent.co.uk/news/uk/neighbourhood-noise-17-people-have-died-from-it-1389990.html.

Vienna Philharmonic/Wiener Philharmoniker, photo (1) by Jun Keller (uploaded 28 November 2014), Facebook, http://www.facebook.com/ViennaPhilharmonic/

photos/a.761606443917167.1073741880.320213934723089/761608477250297/
?type=3&theater.

Vienna Philharmonic/Wiener Philharmoniker, photo (2) by Jun Keller (uploaded 28 November 2014), Facebook, http://www.facebook.com/ViennaPhilharmonic/ photos/a.761606443917167.1073741880.320213934723089/761608477250297/ ?type=3&theater.

"The Vienna Philharmonic." *Vienna Philharmonic* (n.d.; last accessed 15 July 2018), http://www.wienerphilharmoniker.at/orchestra/tradition.

"The Vienna Philharmonic under National Socialism (1938–1945)." *Vienna Philharmonic* (n.d.; last accessed 15 July 2018), http://www.wienerphilharmoniker.at/orchestra/history/national-socialism.

Vincent, Alice. "A Decade Later: How Britney Moved on from Her Year of Hell." *Telegraph* (16 February 2017), http://www.telegraph.co.uk/music/artists/miming-through-the-heartbreak-the-story-behind-britney-spearss-t.

"Violinist Joshua Bell Talks Viral Video Fame, New Album and Shares Exclusive Playlist." *Music Times* (26 June 2016), http://www.musictimes.com/articles/71382/20160626/ joshua-bell-violinist-viral-video-new-album-exclusive-playlist-subway.htm.

"Vladimir Putin Doing Manly Things." CBS (n.d.; last accessed 8 March 2018), http://www.cbsnews.com/pictures/vladimir-putin-doing-manly-things.

"The Voice 2015 Blind Audition—Jordan Smith: 'Chandelier.'" YouTube (21 September 2015), http://www.youtube.com/watch?v=vHR4oOIcVZo.

Volcler, Juliette. *Extremely Loud: Sound as a Weapon*, translated by Carol Volk. New York: New Press, 2013.

Wade, Bonnie C. *Composing Japanese Musical Modernity.* Chicago: University of Chicago Press, 2014.

Wade, Lisa. "The Racial Empathy Gap." *Pacific Standard* (26 September 2013), http:// psmag.com/social-justice/racial-empathy-gap-race-black-white-psychology-66993.

Wade, Stephen. *The Beautiful Music All around Us: Field Recordings and the American Experience.* Urbana: University of Illinois Press, 2012.

Wald, Gayle. "How Svengali Lost His Jewish Accent." *Sounding Out!* (26 September 2011), http://soundstudiesblog.com/author/gaylewald1.

Wallace, Maurice. "Constructing the Black Masculine: Frederick Douglass, Booker T. Washington, and the Sublimits of African American Autobiography." In *Subjects and Citizens: Nation, Race, and Gender from Oroonoko to Anita Hill*, edited by Cathy N. Davidson and Michael Moon, 245–70. Durham, NC: Duke University Press, 1995.

Wallace, Michael. "Heat Pump Up the Volume, Rout Mavs." *ESPN* (30 March 2012), http://www.espn.com/nba/dailydime/_/page/dime-120329/daily-dime.

Wallace-Wells, Benjamin. "Is the Alt-Right for Real?" *New Yorker* (5 May 2016), http:// www.newyorker.com/news/benjamin-wallace-wells/is-the-alt-right-for-real.

Waller, Chris. "'Darker Than the Dungeon': Music, Ambivalence, and the Carceral Subject." *International Journal for the Semiotics of Law* 31 (2018), 275–99.

Walls, Jeannette. "Oops, Spears Switched Religions Again." *Today* (18 January 2006), http:// www.today.com/popculture/oops-spears-switched-religions-again-wbna10696063.

Walton, Benjamin. "Quirk Shame." *Representations* 132 (2015), 121–29.

Walton, Kendall L. "Projectivism, Empathy, and Musical Tension." *Philosophical Topics* 26 (1999), 407–40.

Wan, Catherine Y., et al. "The Therapeutic Effects of Singing in Neurological Disorders." *Music Perception* 27 (2010), 287–95.

Wang, Amy B. "'Nevertheless, She Persisted' Becomes New Battle Cry after McConnell Silences Elizabeth Warren." *Washington Post* (8 February 2017), http://www.washingtonpost.com/news/the-fix/wp/2017/02/08/nevertheless-she-persisted-becomes-new-battle-cry-after-mcconnell-silences-elizabeth-warren/?utm_term=.8e6548e4f252.

Wang, Grace. *Soundtracks of Asian America: Navigating Race through Musical Performance.* Durham, NC: Duke University Press, 2015.

Warren, Lydia. "The Moment Mother Sobbed in Court as She Forgave White Man Who Shot Her Black Son Dead in Argument over Loud Music Blaring out of His SUV." *Daily Mail* (17 October 2014), http://www.dailymail.co.uk/news/article-2797472/white-man-shot-dead-black-teen-argument-loud-rap-music-sentenced-life-without-parole-victim-s-mother-says-forgives-him.html.

Warwick, Jacqueline, and Allison Adrian. "Introduction." In *Voicing Girlhood in Popular Music: Performance, Authority, Authenticity*, edited by Jacqueline Warwick and Allison Adrian, 1–11. New York: Routledge, 2016.

Warwick, Jacqueline. *Girl Groups, Girl Culture: Popular Music and Identity in the 1960s.* New York: Routledge, 2007.

"Watch Heart-Stopping Moment Homeless 'Piano Man' Performs National Anthem at Football Game." *Inside Edition* (15 September 2015), http://www.insideedition.com/headlines/11920-watch-heart-stopping-moment-homeless-piano-man-performs-national-anthem-at-football-game.

Watermeyer, Brian. "Claiming Loss in Disability." *Disability & Society* 24 (2009), 91–102.

Wax, Amy, and Larry Alexander. "Paying the Price for Breakdown of the Country's Bourgeois Culture." *Philadelphia Inquirer* (9 August 2017), http://www.philly.com/philly/opinion/commentary/paying-the-price-for-breakdown-of-the-countrys-bourgeois-culture-20170809.html.

Waytz, Adam, Kelly Marie Hoffman, and Sophie Trawalter. "A Superhumanization Bias in Whites' Perceptions of Blacks." *Social Psychological and Personality Science* 6 (2015), 352–59.

Weaver, Hilary. "Jennifer Aniston Says She Can't Escape Baby-Bump-Rumor Photos." *Vanity Fair* (30 November 2016), http://www.vanityfair.com/style/2016/11/jennifer-aniston-says-she-cant-escape-baby-bump-rumor-photos.

Weber, Brenda R. "Stark Raving Fat: Celebrity, Cellulite, and the Sliding Scale of Sanity." *Feminism & Psychology* 22 (2012), 344–59.

Weber, Lindsey, and Dan McQuade. "Chris Pine Cries through 'Glory' on Behalf of Us All." *Vulture* (23 February 2015), http://www.vulture.com/2015/02/chris-pine-cries-through-glory-for-us-all.html.

Weber, Sandra. "Boxed-In by My School Uniform." *Counterpoints* 220 (2004), 61–65.

Wegman, Rob C. "Historical Musicology: Is It Still Possible?" In *The Cultural Study of Music: A Critical Introduction*, edited by Martin Clayton, Trevor Herbert, and Richard Middleton, 40–48. New York: Routledge, 2012.

Weheliye, Alexander G. *Habeas Viscus: Racializing Assemblages, Biopolitics, and Black Feminist Theories of the Human.* Durham, NC: Duke University Press, 2014.

Weingarten, Gene. "Pearls before Breakfast: Can One of the Nation's Great Musicians Cut through the Fog of a D.C. Rush Hour? Let's Find Out." *Washington Post* (8 April 2007), http://www.washingtonpost.com/lifestyle/magazine/pearls-before-breakfast-can-one-of-the-nations-great-musicians-cut-through-the-fog-of-a-dc-rush-hour-lets-find-out/2014/09/23/8a6d46da-4331-11e4-b47c-f5889e061e5f_story.html.

Weingarten, Gene. "Setting the Record Straight on the Joshua Bell Experiment." *Washington Post* (14 October 2014), http://www.washingtonpost.com/news/style/wp/2014/10/14/gene-weingarten-setting-the-record-straight-on-the-joshua-bell-experiment/?utm_term=.167728785d98.

Weingarten, Gene. "Too Busy to Stop and Hear the Music." *Post Magazine* (9 April 2007), http://www.washingtonpost.com/wp-dyn/content/discussion/2007/04/06/DI2007040601228.html.

Weinstein, Deena. "Rock Critics Need Bad Music." In *Bad Music: The Music We Love to Hate*, edited by Christopher J. Washburne and Maiken Derno, 294–310. New York: Routledge, 2004.

Weitzman, Steven. "Mimic Jews and Jewish Mimics in Antiquity: A Non-Girardian Approach to Mimetic Rivalry." *Journal of the American Academy of Religion* 77 (2009), 922–40.

Wendell, Susan. *The Rejected Body: Feminist Philosophical Reflections on Disability.* New York: Routledge, 1996.

West, Cornel. "Clinton vs. Sanders, Statecraft vs. Soulcraft." *Boston Globe* (18 February 2016), http://www.bostonglobe.com/2016/02/18/clinton-sanders-statecraft-soulcraft/eLUEdch57hR0dbmaysaJhO/story.html.

West, Cornel. "Intellectual Vocation and Political Struggle in the Trump Moment." YouTube (17 May 2017), http://www.youtube.com/watch?v=zwddUhgPpew&feature=youtu.be.

West, Cornel. *Race Matters*. Boston: Beacon Press, 1993.

West, Lindsey M., Roxanne A. Donovan, and Amanda R. Daniel. "The Price of Strength: Black College Women's Perspectives on the Strong Black Woman Stereotype." *Women & Therapy* 39 (2016), 390–412.

Whaley, Natalege. "What's Happening in the Jordan Davis Case?" BET (17 October 2014), http://www.bet.com/news/national/photos/2014/02/what-s-happening-in-jordan-davis-case.html.

White, Emily. *Fast Girls: Teenage Tribes and the Myth of the Slut*. New York: Scribner, 2002.

White, Michael. "The Nazi Musicians Who Changed Their Tune." *Telegraph* (11 March 2013), http://www.telegraph.co.uk/culture/music/classicalmusic/9922592/The-Nazi-musicians-who-changed-their-tune.html.

White, Shane, and Graham J. White. *The Sounds of Slavery: Discovering African American History through Songs, Sermons, and Speech*. Boston: Beacon Press, 2005.

Whiteman, Bobbie. "'Can a Sistah Get One Fan?' Brandy Goes Incognito as She Belts Out a Song in a New York Subway Car . . . and Everyone Ignores Her." *Daily Mail* (14 July 2015), http://www.dailymail.co.uk/tvshowbiz/article-3161312/Brandy-goes-incognito-belts-song-New-York-subway-car-ignores-her.html.

Whitworth, Dan. "'Worst Song Ever' Gets 29m Views after Going Viral." BBC (21 March 2011), http://www.bbc.co.uk/newsbeat/article/12784330/worst-song-ever-gets-29m-views-after-going-viral.

Whyte, Kyle Powys, Evan Selinger, and Kevin Outterson. "Poverty Tourism and the Problem of Consent." *Journal of Global Ethics* 7 (2011), 337–48.

Wieseltier, Leon. "Against Identity." *New Republic* (27 November 1994), http://newrepublic.com/article/92857/against-identity.

Will, Richard. "*Don Giovanni* and the Resilience of Rape Culture." *Journal of the American Musicological Society* 71 (2018), 218–22.

Williams, David R., and Selina A. Mohammed. "Racism and Health I: Pathways and Scientific Evidence." *American Behavioral Scientist* 57 (2013), http://www.ncbi.nlm.nih.gov/pubmed/24347666.

Williams, Jean Calterone. "The Politics of Homelessness: Shelter Now and Political Protest." *Political Research Quarterly* 58 (2005), 497–509.

Williams, Joseph. "Busking in Musical Thought: Value, Affect, and Becoming." *Journal of Musicological Research* 35 (2016), 142–55.

Williams, Linda. "Film Bodies: Gender, Genre, and Excess." *Film Quarterly* 44 (1991), 2–13.

Williams, Ted, with Bret Witter. *A Golden Voice: How Faith, Hard Work, and Humility Brought Me from the Streets to Salvation.* New York: Gotham Books, 2012.

Williamson, Milly. "Female Celebrities and the Media: The Gendered Denigration of the 'Ordinary' Celebrity." *Celebrity Studies* 1 (2010), 118–20.

"Willie Jones 2." YouTube (22 June 2015), http://www.youtube.com/watch?v=jdwnHkNj1fM.

Willman, Chris. "Fergie Sexes Up National Anthem at NBA All-Star Game and America Isn't Having It." *Variety* (18 February 2018), http://variety.com/2018/music/news/fergie-nba-all-star-game-national-anthem-1202704177.

Wilson, John Paul, Nicholas O. Rule, and Kurt Hugenberg. "Racial Bias in Judgments of Physical Size and Formidability: From Size to Threat." *Journal of Personality and Social Psychology* 113 (2017), 59–80.

Wise, Tim. *Between Barack and a Hard Place: Racism and White Denial in the Age of Obama.* San Francisco: City Light Books, 2009.

Wise, Tim. *Colorblind: The Rise of Post-Racial Politics and the Retreat from Racial Equity.* San Francisco: City Lights Books, 2010.

Wlodarski, Amy Lynn. *Musical Witness and Holocaust Representation.* Cambridge: Cambridge University Press, 2015.

Wolf, Naomi. "Young Women, Give Up the Vocal Fry and Reclaim Your Strong Female Voice." *Guardian* (24 July 2015), http://www.theguardian.com/commentisfree/2015/jul/24/vocal-fry-strong-female-voice.

Wong, Deborah. *Speak It Louder: Asian Americans Making Music.* New York: Routledge, 2004.

Wood, Gaby. "Patti Smith: 'I'm Not a Musician, People's Concept of Me Is So Off the Mark.'" *Telegraph* (3 October 2015), http://www.telegraph.co.uk/music/artists/patti-smith-interview-not-a-musician.

Wortham, Jenna. "When Everyone Can Be 'Queer,' Is Anyone?" *New York Times* (12 July 2016), http://www.nytimes.com/2016/07/17/magazine/when-everyone-can-be-queer-is-anyone.html.

Wray, Matt. *Not Quite White: White Trash and the Boundaries of Whiteness.* Durham, NC: Duke University Press, 2006.

Wray, Matt, and Annalee Newitz, eds. *White Trash: Race and Class in America.* New York: Routledge, 1997.

Wright, Lincoln. "Mishawaka Man Given Max Sentence for Killing Neighbor after Loud Music Complaint." *South Bend Tribune* (22 March 2017), http://www.southbendtribune.com/news/publicsafety/mishawaka-man-given-max-sentence-for-killing-neighbor-after-loud/article_71baffdc-0f0e-11e7-b91f-8761a2348ba4.html.

Wright, Robert. "'I'd Sell You Suicide': Pop Music and Moral Panic in the Age of Marilyn Manson." *Popular Music* 19 (2000), 365–85.

Wyatt, Jean. "Patricia Hill Collins's *Black Sexual Politics* and the Genealogy of the Strong Black Woman." *Studies in Gender and Sexuality* 9 (2008), 52–67.

"X-Factor Ukraine Aida Nikolaichuk." YouTube (15 July 2012), http://www.youtube.com/watch?v=TPoWDDFRmgg.

Yablo, Stephen. *Aboutness*. Princeton, NJ: Princeton University Press, 2014.

Yang, Mina. "East Meets West in the Concert Hall: Asians and Classical Music in the Century of Imperialism, Post-Colonialism, and Multiculturalism." *Asian Music* 38 (2007), 1–30.

Yang, Mina. *Planet Beethoven: Classical Music at the Turn of the Millennium*. Middletown, CT: Wesleyan University Press, 2014.

Yglesias, Matthew. "Sweet Sorrow." *Slate* (9 August 2013), http://www.slate.com/articles/business/rivalries/2013/08/pepsi_paradox_why_people_prefer_coke_even_though_pepsi_wins_in_taste_tests.html.

Yoshihara, Mari. *Musicians from a Different Shore: Asians and Asian Americans in Classical Music*. Philadelphia: Temple University Press, 2007.

Young, Michael. "Down with Meritocracy." *Guardian* (28 June 2011), http://www.theguardian.com/politics/2001/jun/29/comment.

Young, Michael. *The Rise of the Meritocracy, 1870–2033: An Essay on Education and Equality*. London: Thames and Hudson, 1958.

Young, Stella. "There Is No X-Factor in Patronising Judgement." ABC Australia (20 September 2011), http://www.abc.net.au/rampup/articles/2011/09/20/3321673.htm.

Young, Stella. "We're Not Here for Your Inspiration." ABC Australia (2 July 2012), http://www.abc.net.au/news/2012-07-03/young-inspiration-porn/4107006.

Yúdice, George. "We Are Not the World." *Social Text* 31/32 (1992), 202–16.

Zeisel, Hans. "Race Bias in the Administration of the Death Penalty: The Florida Experience." *Harvard Law Review* 95 (1981), 456–68.

Zimmerman, Jess. "Not All Men: A Brief History of Every Dude's Favorite Argument." *TIME* (28 April 2014), http://time.com/79357/not-all-men-a-brief-history-of-every-dudes-favorite-argument.

Zimring, Carl A. *Clean and White: A History of Environmental Racism in the United States*. New York: New York University Press, 2015.

Zola, Irving Kenneth. "Self, Identity and the Naming Question: Reflections on the Language of Disability." *Social Science and Medicine* 36 (1993), 167–73.

Zoladz, Lindsay. "Leaving Britney Alone." *The Ringer* (30 August 2016), http://theringer.com/britney-spears-glory-album-vmas-42701dddac4c#.7g4wyj60r.

Zon, Bennett. "Disorienting Race: Humanizing the Musical Savage and the Rise of British Ethnomusicology." *Nineteenth-Century Music Review* 3 (2006), 25–43.

Zuazu, María Edurne. "Loud but Non-lethal: Acoustic Stagings and State-Sponsored Violence." *Women & Music* 19 (2015), 151–59.

Zwaan, Koos, and Joost de Bruin, eds. *Adapting Idols: Authenticity, Identity and Performance in a Global Television Format*. Burlington, VT: Ashgate, 2012.

Zwölftöner [Sebastian Smallshaw]. "Philharmonic Archives and the Austrian Art of Remembering." *Von heute auf morgen* (3 January 2013), http://vonheuteaufmorgen.blogspot.com/2013/01/philharmonic-archives-and-austrian-art.html#more.

Index

For the benefit of digital users, indexed terms that span two pages (e.g., 52–53) may, on occasion, appear on only one of those pages.

Figures are indicated by *f* following the page number